1989

SYRIA AND THE FRENCH MANDATE

PRINCETON STUDIES ON THE NEAR EAST

PHILIP S. KHOURY

SYRIA AND THE FRENCH MANDATE

The Politics of Arab Nationalism

1920-1945

Princeton University Press

Library of Congress Cataloging in Publication Data will be
found on the last printed page of this book

ISBN 0-691-05486-X

This book has been composed in Linotron Aldus

Clothbound editions of Princeton University Press books
are printed on acid-free paper, and binding materials
are chosen for strength and durability

Printed in the United States of America
by Princeton University Press,
Princeton, New Jersey

for

MARY CHRISTINA WILSON

CONTENTS

LIST OF ILLUSTRATIONS AND MAPS

ILLUSTRATIONS

MAPS

LIST OF TABLES

FOREWORD

Philip Khoury's book makes a major contribution to our knowledge of an important but neglected subject. During the last twenty years a number of significant works have been published on the history of Syria during the last period of Ottoman rule, among them Ernest Dawn's essays collected in *From Ottomanism to Arabism*, Linda Schatkowski Schilcher's *Families in Politics*, and Dr. Khoury's own previous book, *Urban Notables and Arab Nationalism*. There have also been some good studies of the political history of Syria since it became independent; Patrick Seale's *The Struggle for Syria* is outstanding among them. Little interest, however, has been shown in the period during which France ruled Syria under Mandate from the League of Nations, apart from S. H. Longrigg's *Syria and Lebanon under French Mandate*.

The reasons for this neglect are not difficult to find. The essential archival sources were not available until recently. As Dr. Khoury points out, relevant documents in France and Syria were not open to public use until the 1970s. Moreover, Syrian historians have tended to show greater interest in earlier periods of history, when the great cities of their country played a more important role as centers of trade, culture, and power: French historians for their part could find little to attract them in an episode of their imperial history that could not, like that of the British in India, be regarded as one of fulfillment and voluntary transfer of power. It is only in the last few years that a change has begun to take place. A recent book, *La Syrie d'aujourd'hui*, edited by André Raymond, shows what important work is now being done by French scholars, and a number of valuable memoirs have been published by Syrians who played a part in the political life of the time.

Dr. Khoury has made full use of the sources that are now available. His bibliography shows how wide his inquiries have been: into Syrian, French, British, and American archives, collections of private papers, and a great variety of printed sources. He has also interviewed some forty Syrians and others who shed light upon the story he narrates. He gives the reader full information, but—more important—he also provides a key to understanding it.

His main theme is the fate of a local ruling elite who, both individually and as a group, found their lives cut in two by the disappearance of the Ottoman Empire. As Dr. Khoury showed in his previous book, by the end of the nineteenth century there had emerged, in Damascus and the other large Syrian cities, a more or less unified group of powerful families, deriving wealth and social position from ownership of land, having access to the Ottoman government, and able to maintain a "delicate balance between central authority and provincial influence." To an increasing extent they were educated in Ottoman schools and held office in the administration or army, and, being for the most part Sunni Muslims, they could regard themselves as forming part, even if a subordinate part, of the ruling institution. For a brief moment after the withdrawal of Ottoman forces in 1918, they could hope to become the rulers of a new Syrian state, but after the French occupation of Damascus they found themselves subjects of a foreign government with which it would be difficult to reestablish the "delicate balance."

After a failure in the years 1936–39, when an accommodation reached with the French broke down, partly because of their own administrative failures but mainly because of opposition in France, the new circumstances created by the Second World War made it possible for the Syrian elite to achieve more than they could have hoped for previously, the total withdrawal of French forces and complete independence unfettered by a treaty of alliance. Their triumph was short-lived, however, for their control of Syrian political life was already being challenged. New political ideas—of radical nationalism, social reform, and Islamic reassertion—were becoming important and provided the channels through which other social groups could pursue their interests: the growing middle class of the cities, teachers and students, and the army officers, many of them of rural origin and destined in the end to destroy the basis of the social power of the old elite, their control of the land. The space of Syrian politics also changed, as the center of economic and social life moved from the old cities to the new quarters that had grown up around them.

Philip Khoury's book is important in more than one way: it is a lively narrative history, a contribution to our understanding of the fate of Arab nationalism in the country in which it was born, and a study in political sociology. It will take its place as one of the small number of indispensable works on the history of the Middle East in the twentieth century.

Albert Hourani

PREFACE

This study is the sequel to my first book, *Urban Notables and Arab Nationalism. The Politics of Damascus 1860–1920* (Cambridge University Press, 1983). That work explored the birth of Arab nationalism within the social fabric of Damascus. In particular, it explained how Ottoman reformation and agrarian commercialization acted together in the nineteenth century to produce a fairly cohesive and stable social class of landowners and bureaucrats. Out of this class emerged the elite which shaped the new ideology of Arab nationalism. It is this elite and its use of Arab nationalism within the spectrum of Syrian political, social, and economic relationships that is the subject of the present book.

This book investigates in detail the development of Arab nationalism in Syria during the French Mandate, considering in particular the political needs of the elite which led the nationalist movement. In a sense it is the story of a certain continuity of political form and of political need. The form was the "politics of notables," so aptly described by Albert Hourani, whereby a local elite mediated between a distant overlord, whether Istanbul or Paris, and local society. The need of this elite was to maintain a unique position of power within local society. Yet, within this continuity the seeds of change germinated, for the story of Arab nationalism in Syria is not simply the story of struggle against the overweening French overlord, it is also the story of conflict between bourgeois and radical nationalism.

In my view, the interwar years are a period of transition between two political cultures. The old framework of urban notable politics which I described in my first book remained in place as Syria approached independence in 1945, but the cracks in the framework had become clearly visible by the late 1930s. By independence, nascent radical forces had begun to challenge the old political leadership. This challenge, emerging at the same time that independence had broken the old framework of the politics of notables, eventually brought about the demise of the veteran nationalist elite.

Although I concentrate on the Syrian nationalist elite and its struggle for power in the interwar period, no elite can or should be discussed in isolation from the society and political culture which produce it and which it, in turn, tries to shape or lead to its own advantage. Hence, I have included a significant portion of material on other groups and classes within Syrian society insofar as they touch on the elite's ability to maintain its position through the use of the ideology of Arab nationalism. I also, for obvious reasons, discuss French attitudes and policy toward Syria.

I owe a debt of gratitude to those scholars who have written about Syria during the interwar period such as Albert Hourani and Stephen H. Longrigg. But, they are few. Indeed, it is surprising that while Palestine under Mandate has been written about exhaustively and Iraq, if not exhaustively at least penetratingly, Syria has yet to receive anywhere near such attention. It is surprising, for Syria was the cradle of Arab nationalism. It was to Syria that nationalists throughout the Arab world looked for guidance and moral support during the Mandate period, and it was out of Syria that emerged the most systematic, far-reaching, and lasting ideological expression of Arab nationalism, the radical Arabism of the Baʿth Party.

In part, this reticence on the topic of Syria can be laid at the door of the two major protagonists, the Syrians and the French, who have failed to address the interwar period satisfactorily. Syrian historians have written voluminously on the subject, but not, with rare exception, analytically. Some have displayed too great an emotional involvement in the subject. French historians have almost completely ignored the period which they regard as a blemish on their imperial past because French rule produced little that was beneficial either to France or to Syria. But this noticeable neglect of Syria has also been due to archival restrictions: only since 1975 has it been possible to have full access to Mandate materials in the Syrian state archives in Damascus, while the archives of the French Ministries of Foreign Affairs and Defense for the entire Mandate period have been open to scholars only since 1979.

This study is offered in an attempt to remedy that neglect. It is primarily narrative in form because national independence movements are, by their very nature, heroic movements, and therefore lend themselves particularly well to narrative history. My intention, however, has been to weave the narrative around several interlocking themes while maintaining some sense of chronological sequence. These major themes are four: First, the process by which a society, ordered primarily according to relations of personal interdependence, begins to undergo changes that permit the birth of conscious competitive social classes. Second, how this process transforms habitual political mechanisms; specifically, how in Syria the locus of urban politics shifts from ancient institutions and spaces, such as mosques and quarters, to new ones, such as secondary schools, political parties, and modern places of business. Third, how the veteran nationalist elite adjusts to the new and wider base of political life in order to remain at the summit of interwar politics alongside the French. Fourth, how the power and influence of the elite are gradually eroded by those lower down the social scale who have developed new, more vigorous, and more complex ideologies that address not only independence *per se*, but the broader, related issues of social change and economic development.

To address these questions and others, I have drawn on a variety of source materials. Apart from the archival sources in Damascus and Paris, I have depended on the unpublished papers of Syrian politicians in Damascus, Beirut, and Oxford; British and American consular archives in London and Washington; a wide range of Arabic political memoirs and histories; political pamphlets, newspapers, and magazines from Syria, Lebanon, France, Italy, and Britain; and extensive interviews and conversations with Syrian, Lebanese, Palestinian, French, and British officials and leaders of the interwar period.

ACKNOWLEDGMENTS

In researching and writing this study, I have been generously supported by several fellowships. These include a Harvard Travelling Fellowship in 1975–76, a Fulbright-Hays Doctoral Dissertation Fellowship in 1976–77, a Social Science Research Council Postdoctoral Fellowship and an Old Dominion Fellowship from the Massachusetts Institute of Technology, both in 1983–84. I have also received additional research funds from several other M.I.T. sources, including the Aga Khan Program for Islamic Architecture, the Class of 1922 Career Development Professorship, and the I. Austin Kelly, III Fund. I am deeply indebted to these institutions for their beneficence.

I should also mention that my research and writing were greatly facilitated by the following institutions: the Center for Middle Eastern Studies of Harvard University where I completed my doctoral dissertation, which is the basis of this book, and where I revised that dissertation as a Postdoctoral Fellow in 1983–84; the History Faculty at M.I.T. which extended itself far beyond normal boundaries to help me see this book through to completion; St. Antony's College in the University of Oxford, where I launched my research and where I was fortunate to be an Associate in 1974–75 and 1976–77; the Jafet Library of the American University of Beirut; and the *Institut Français d'Etudes Arabes* in Damascus. It goes without saying that this study would have never advanced far were it not for the access I was given to the various government and private archives I consulted in Syria, Lebanon, France, England, and the United States. I should mention in particular the Center for Historical Documents (*Markaz al-wathā'iq al-tārīkhiyya*) in Damascus; the archives of the *Ministère des Affaires Etrangères* and *Centre de Hautes Etudes Administratives sur l'Afrique et l'Asie Modernes* in Paris and the *Ministère de la Défense* in Vincennes; the Foreign Office and Colonial Office archives of the Public Record Office in London; the National Archives of the United States in Washington; and the private papers collections at the Middle East Centre of St. Antony's College in Oxford and the Institute for Palestine Studies in Beirut.

Versions of three chapters have previously been published elsewhere. Chapter 9 appeared as "Factionalism among Syrian Nationalists during the French Mandate" in the *International Journal of Middle East Studies,* November 1981, and Chapter 11 appeared in the November 1984 issue of the same journal as "Syrian Urban Politics in Transition: The Quarters of Damascus during the French Mandate." Chapter 21 was published in July 1985 as "Divided Loyalties? Syria and the Question of Palestine, 1919–1939" in *Middle Eastern Studies.* I am grateful to the editors and publishers who gave me permission to reprint these chapters in modified form.

Many teachers, colleagues, friends, and family members have guided me over the years and, in one way or another, contributed to the making of this book. Permit me to mention the Warden and Fellows of St. Antony's College, Oxford, Roger Owen, Derek Hopwood, Salma Mardam, Aziz al-Azmeh, Abdul-Karim Rafeq, Jean-Paul Pascual, Regina Heinecke, Thierry Bianquis, Khayriyya al-Qasimiyya, Dominique Chevallier, André Raymond, Ramez G. Tomeh, George and Rose Tomeh, Hanna Batatu, Qustantin Zurayq, Edmond Rabbath, Wajih Fanous, Rashid Hamid, Samir Khalaf, Yusuf Ibish, Muhsin Mahdi, the late A. J. Meyer, Dennis Skiotis, Pauline Maier, Richard M. Douglas, Bruce Mazlish, Robert I. Rotberg, Peter H. Smith, William L. Porter, Peter Perdue, Melinda Glidden, Kathleen Bielawski, Salma M. Jurdak, Yousef and Salwa Nawas, George S. Khoury, Angela Jurdak Khoury, and the late Shukry E. Khoury.

I especially wish to thank Salma Mardam for providing me with several of the photographs of Syrian political leaders which appear in the book. Other photographs appear with the permission of Colonel J. A. Aylmer, Literary Executor of the Papers of Sir Edward Spears, and Gillian Grant, Archivist at the Middle East Centre, Oxford.

I owe a special debt of gratitude to William L. Cleveland and Charles Issawi who read my manuscript for Princeton University Press and who offered invaluable comments and criticisms. I am also deeply grateful to my editor, Margaret Case, who contributed her great skill and knowledge to the making of this book. My copyeditor, Ann E. Hirst, saved me from more technical inconsistencies and infelicities of style than I care to mention.

My greatest debt, however, is to two very dear friends. Albert Hourani put me on to my subject, guided me by the hand through the sources, spent countless days and nights reading and re-reading the manuscript in its many versions, and presented me with the most detailed, precise suggestions for its improvement. But, more importantly, through his lectures and seminars and in our tutorials and frequent informal gatherings at Harvard and in Oxford, he imparted to me his "vision of history"—a framework of analysis and ideas which the discerning reader will discover in somewhat adulterated form in the pages to follow. Like so many other members of his tribe, I can say that I owe to him the better part of my intellectual formation—my understanding of the process of history and of Middle Eastern society and politics.

Mary Christina Wilson has been my other source of inspiration. She helped me turn a cumbersome, rather inelegantly written manuscript into a book of which I can be proud. She also sharpened my ideas about the larger Arab political process, of which Syria is part. And she did this and much more while fully engaged in her own research and teaching. She has been my loyal companion throughout the years, the individual who has given me the greatest happiness and affection, and it is but a very small token of my appreciation and love that I dedicate this book to her.

Cambridge, Massachusetts   *P.S.K.*
June 1985

NOTE ON TRANSCRIPTION

Ayns and *hamzas* are the only diacritics included in the transcription of Arabic technical terms and personal names in the text and notes. Otherwise commonly accepted English forms are used, especially for Arabic place names. A more complete transcription of technical terms and personal names can be found in the Glossary and the appropriate Tables and in Arabic sources in the Appendix and Bibliography.

LIST OF SPECIAL ABBREVIATIONS

AIR	Air Ministry, London
CHEAM	Centre de Hautes Etudes Administratives sur l'Afrique et l'Asie Modernes, Paris
CO	Colonial Office, London
CZA	Central Zionist Archives, Jerusalem
FO	Foreign Office, London
IPS	Institute for Palestine Studies, Beirut
MAE	Ministère des Affaires Etrangères, Paris
MD	Ministère de la Défense, Vincennes
MWT	Markaz al-wathā'iq al-tārīkhiyya, Damascus
PMC	Permanent Mandates Commission, Geneva
PRO	Public Record Office, London
USNA	National Archives of the United States, Washington

SYRIA AND THE FRENCH MANDATE

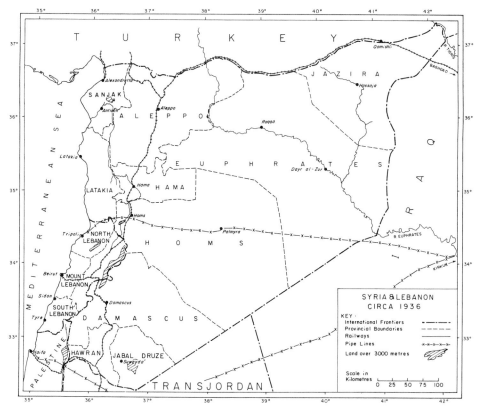

Syria and Lebanon during the French Mandate, circa 1936

INTRODUCTION

"IN AN ERA of upheaval, it is continuity and stability that need explanation."[1] The end of 400 years of Ottoman rule, the vast destruction of world war, the imposition of European, of Christian rule, the sting of a thousand injuries, and the discovery, out of these injuries, of the common bond of Arab nationalism were all momentous events in the lives of the men and women of the Middle East. By 1920 the familiar outlines of Middle Eastern life appeared to have dissolved. Alien governments imposed from distant capitals set up in *sérails* and government houses. New mores, both social and political, and foreign languages restricted local comprehension and participation. The fabric of daily life was stretched taut. Riots and revolts broke out across the Middle East. And yet, for all the outward appearance of cataclysmic upheaval and for all the inward sense of grievance and rage, there was no sharp break in the political life of Syria, in the forms and aims of political action, or in the actors themselves during the French Mandate.

In the first generation after the collapse of the Ottoman Empire, the major political movements in Syria were led by members of urban upper class families and former officials of the Sultan who brought a certain style of political action and a common way of looking at the world to the new political circumstances. Indeed, there was a remarkable degree of continuity in the exercise of local political power in Syria which was not disrupted by the dissolution of the Ottoman Empire. For the most part, men important in local affairs under the Ottomans were the same men, or their sons, who wielded political influence under the French. Political leaders organized their personal support systems in interwar Syria as they had in Ottoman Syria. In Ottoman times, political power was based in the city and then extended from there to the settled countryside and eventually into the semi-nomadic tribal areas. Under the French, political power likewise emanated from the city. Moreover, the methods urban leaders used to acquire political power and their aims remained consistent. Whatever the projected scope of power and whoever the political overlord, the basic building block of political influence in Syria was the same: urban leadership.

Within the city, the political and social influence of local leaders was

---

[1] Charles S. Maier, *Recasting Bourgeois Europe. Stabilization in France, Germany, and Italy in the Decade after World War I* (Princeton, 1975), p. 3.

rooted in some cases in ancient status as descendants of the Prophet (ash-raf), leaders of religious orders, and jurists and educators; in other cases, it grew from military or commercial position.[2] In the last decades of Ottoman rule, landowning and office-holding augmented and gradually supplanted older bases of influence. The marriage bed, financial arrangements, and the acquisition of Ottoman cultural trappings including fluency in Turkish knit together the urban upper class of the Arab provinces.

But urban political position was not simply a passive status based on birth, wealth, and style. Urban politics was a delicate balancing act: local leaders could neither appear to oppose the interests of the government because they risked being deprived of their access to the ruler, nor could they jeopardize the interests of their local clientele because they risked losing their independent influence and thus their usefulness to the ruler. It was usual for local leaders to defend the social and political order by supporting the government. But there were occasions when they led movements against the government by mobilizing those popular forces from which they derived their independent influence. Such occasions arose when a particularly strong government sought to dissolve the partnership or when a weak government could no longer maintain the stability which ensured the prosperity of the local urban leadership. Rarely, however, did urban leaders aim to overthrow the system of rule. Rather, their intention was to restore the delicate balance between government and society. Although in the last decades of the nineteenth century the Syrian provinces enjoyed comparative stability and tranquility which local urban leaders wholeheartedly supported in their capacity as officials of the Ottoman state, by the First World War the delicate balance between central authority and provincial influence had been sufficiently upset by changes in Istanbul to warrant a re-assessment of the partnership with the Ottoman government.

The advent of French rule in Syria did not fundamentally change the behavior patterns of urban leaders or the fundamental character of political life. But there was a significant difference in the nature of the new imperial authority: it was illegitimate and thus was unstable. France was not recognized to be a legitimate overlord, as the Sultan-Caliph of the Ottoman Empire had been. The Ottoman Empire had behind it four centuries of rule and the very important component of a common religious tradition.[3] France had the dubious, even in Western eyes, legitimization conferred by the weak and imperfectly conceived Mandate system. Be-

---

[2] The following section is based on my *Urban Notables and Arab Nationalism. The Politics of Damascus 1860–1920* (Cambridge, 1983), pp. 1–52.

[3] Albert Hourani, "Revolution in the Arab Middle East," in P. J. Vatikiotis (ed.), *Revolution in the Middle East and Other Case Studies* (London, 1972), pp. 70–71.

cause France had historically tried to establish and strengthen her position in the Levant by posing as the protector of Christians, she was doubly distrusted by the Muslim majority of the region. In part because she was illegitimate and in part because of certain exogenous factors—the international and moral restrictions of the Mandate system and the fragility of France's postwar economic and political order—her position in Syria was inherently unstable, much more so than the Ottoman position had ever been.

Contributing to this instability were specific French policies in Syria which inflamed traditional sectarian conflict by distinctly favoring religious minorities and by promoting a series of administratively isolated minority enclaves. The French threatened the Muslim majority by seizing control of their institutions and debasing the symbols of their culture. France was also unwilling to promote any recognizable financial and economic interests, other than her own and those of her principal minority clients. French monetary policies had disastrous financial repercussions on Syria. The devastation wrought by World War I, the debilitating reorientation forced on the Syrian economy by the partition of geographical Syria and the creation of distinct and separate mandatory regimes, and the continued erosion of Syrian industry by the spread of the European economy helped to create and maintain a situation of widespread unemployment and high inflation, all of which added to the political instability inherent in the Mandate situation.

In such circumstances, Syria's urban leadership was obliged to create a new balance of power between itself and the French. The French, like the Ottomans before them, had to govern in association with elements from the urban upper classes. But, given the intrinsic illegitimacy of France's position in Syria and her penchant for dictatorial policy without regard for the position and interests of the local elite, urban leaders became opposition forces—the spokesmen of the people in the halls of power—rather than the agents of a foreign ruler. To gain recognition from this strong-minded regime, they would not only have to mobilize the active forces of society on a more regular basis, but they would also have to seek broader political alliances than before. Hence, they required not only a shared dedication of purpose, but an ideology to express this new solidarity and drive. Nationalism provided the kind of ideological cohesion and emotional appeal urban leaders needed to be politically effective between the wars.

The rise of nationalism in the early twentieth century initially reflected broad changes in Arab society, especially within the urban upper class of Syria: the rising number of Syrians attending professional schools in Istanbul, increased exposure to European ideas, the accelerated pace of

Ottomanization, and, after the rise of the Young Turks in 1908, growing Turkish insensitivity to local Syrian needs. All of these changes encouraged "more frequent inter-Arab contacts," "the emergence of pan-Arab clubs and societies," and a "greater interest in Arab history" and culture. Above all, "the pull of a common language" and "ethnic origin" gave the new loyalty to the nation greater attraction, enabling it to grow at the expense of other loyalties to religion, family, tribe, and region.[4] But it was the collapse of Ottoman authority at the end of World War I and with it the demise of the ideology of Ottomanism, of an Ottoman nation of Turks and Arabs, and the imposition of French rule in 1920, that allowed nationalism to emerge as the dominant political ideology in Syria.

In the hands of members of the urban upper class, nationalism never acquired revolutionary content; rather, it was fashioned to restore a balance of power between government and society which had been upset by the French occupation. Nationalism could be directed against the French without harming the local status quo. With its romanticized vision of the Arab past, nationalism appealed to the hearts and minds of a broad section of the population—both to traditional merchants, artisans, and popular religious leaders and to newly educated youth, the growing professional class, and an incipient modern working class. It was an attractive and compelling ideology, more so, for example, than Islam which had lost much of its power owing to the spread of secularism. Nationalism capitalized on Islam's political misfortunes by absorbing the still important component of religious solidarity into its ideological formation and expression. Yet it was cast in a secular idiom, which was best suited to counter the force of sectarianism, which French policies exacerbated, and it blended comfortably with the behavior and style of the urban leadership who, for the most part, had been trained in secular professional schools and nurtured in the secular environment of Young Turk politics, and who had grown accustomed to working together in secret Arab societies and for the brief period of Amir Faysal's Arab Kingdom after World War I.

For all its appeal, interwar nationalism was contradictory and poorly articulated. Perhaps the most visible tension was between nationalism's highest aim, the achievement of pan-Arab unity and independence, and its tendency toward provincialism. The division of the Arab provinces of the Ottoman Empire into separate administrative units under British and French authority and the further separation of Syria from Lebanon frac-

[4] Hanna Batatu, *The Old Social Classes and the Revolutionary Movements of Iraq* (Princeton, 1978), p. 23. Batatu examines the impact of these same changes on Iraqi society in the early twentieth century.

tured Arab nationalist forces and strength. The Syrian leadership came to concentrate its efforts on securing Syrian independence before all else. In this way, nationalism acquired a rather narrow focus.

THE SCALE OF POLITICS

Within the newly created Syrian state, the scale of the nationalist movement was virtually restricted to the domain of urban politics during the Mandate. If it is possible to speak of a code of behavior to which political actors in Syria generally adhered, then one of its major tenets was that the use of the countryside as a political weapon was to be discouraged. Indeed, it was only during the early years of the French Mandate that nationalist leaders carried their resistance into the countryside and then only because the French were in temporary control of their political bases in the towns. Why was this code adopted and enforced by Syrian urban leaders? One reason is that it was more difficult to organize the countryside and peasant society for resistance to French rule because of the comparatively low level of political consciousness of the peasantry. An equally important reason was the deep-seated fear that if rural society were encouraged to mount resistance to the French then agrarian productive forces would suffer, thereby jeopardizing the financial interests of the urban absentee landowning class from which the nationalist leadership was drawn.

But to explain how urban leadership kept rural forces in check during the political upheavals of the interwar period, we must briefly examine the relations of power between town and countryside in Syria. One of the primary consequences of the European commerical and financial penetration of Syria in the nineteenth century was a more decisive shift in the balance of power between town and countryside in the direction of the town, and a considerable expansion of the town's authority into the countryside. The widespread decline of Syria's native handicraft industries, which brought urban productive forces to a near standstill, and the gradual introduction of capitalist agriculture made the towns increasingly conscious of the need to intensify their exploitation of the countryside for enrichment. The agricultural areas around the city, which had always been one of several vital functions sustaining urban life, were now saddled with the burden of keeping the city economically viable. The desire to tie the countryside more securely to the towns was given added impetus particularly in grain-producing regions, which was reflected in the growing demand for cash crops for urban consumption and for export. This desire was particularly keen in the interior Syrian towns which had experienced a relative loss of commercial importance as coastal towns enjoyed a new era of prosperity owing to their vital role in the revived Mediterranean trade with Europe.[5]

In tandem with these developments, a reinvigorated Ottoman state, in need of more taxes to support its vast reform efforts and to impose stability in its central Islamic lands, expanded the frontiers of settlement in Syria. Military force and financial inducements in the form of land grants and special tax concessions gradually turned tribal chiefs into landlords and their tribesmen into cultivators.[6] Agrarian commercialization encouraged urban groups, particularly merchants already in possession of tax farms, to expand their landholdings by the manipulation of land laws and by usury, and when the opportunity arose in the 1860s, by legalizing the process of land accumulation in the form of private property rights.[7]

Landownership in Syria was to a very large degree an urban-engineered process. Land became more and more concentrated in the hands of urban dwellers as the countryside was drawn more rigidly into the orbit of the city. Small peasant proprietorship was significantly reduced as large and middle-sized estates and intensively cultivated plantations owned by a powerful group of townspeople were more formally organized around the metropolis.[8]

Big landowners were usually permanent residents of cities, though

[5] See Dominique Chevallier, "Un exemple de résistance technique de l'artisinat syrien aux 19e et 20e siècles. Les tissus ikatés d'Alep et de Damas," *Syria*, 39 (1962), pp. 300–24; Chevallier, "A Damas. Production et société à la fin du 19e siècle," *Annales*, 19 (1964), pp. 966–72; Jacques Weulersse, "La primauté des cités dans l'économie syrienne (Etude des relations entre villes et campagnes dans le Nord-Syrie avec exemples choisis à Antioch, Hama, et Lattaquié)," *C. R. Congrès International de Géographie* (Amsterdam, 1938), pp. 233–39. Also see Roger Owen, *The Middle East in the World Economy, 1800–1914* (London, 1981).

[6] See Philip S. Khoury, "The Tribal Shaykh, French Tribal Policy, and the Nationalist Movement in Syria between Two World Wars," *Middle Eastern Studies*, 18 (April 1982), pp. 180–93.

[7] R. Montagne, "Le pouvoir des chefs et les élites en Orient," CHEAM, no. 17 (12 May 1938), pp. 3–4. Also see ʿAbdullah Hanna, *al-Qadiyya al-ziraʿiyya wa al-harakat al-fallahiyya fi suriyya wa lubnan, vol. 1, 1820–1920* (Beirut, 1975). Peter Sluglett and Marion Farouk-Sluglett, "The Application of the 1858 Land Code in Greater Syria: Some Preliminary Observations," in Tarif Khalidi (ed.), *Land Tenure and Social Transformation in the Middle East* (Beirut, 1984), pp. 409–21.

[8] On the process of large-scale accumulation of land in Syria by region see, for Aleppo: Charles Pavie, *Etat d'Alep. Renseignements agricoles* (Aleppo, 1924), pp. 105, 113–14, 118, and Abdul-Rahman Hamidé, *La région d'Alep. Etude de géographie rurale* (Paris, 1959); for Hama: [J. Gaulmier], "Note sur la propriété foncière dans la Syrie centrale," *L'Asie Française*, no. 309 (April 1933), 130–37; for Homs: P. Berthelot, "Notes sur la mise en valeur de la région du ʿCazaʾ d'Homs," CHEAM, no. 249 (Feb. 1938), and A. Naaman, "Précisions sur la structure agraire dans la région de Homs-Hama (Syrie)," *Bulletin de l'Association de Géographes Français*, 208–09 (March–April 1950), pp. 53–59; for Jazira, where many Aleppines also owned land: Roupen Boghossian, *La Haute-Djézireh* (Aleppo, 1952), pp. 122–40.

many also maintained estate homes or farm cottages for social purposes. There also existed a more diffuse group of rural landowning notables in each province whose ties with the provincial capital were maintained through the closest regional market center. But, because rural landowners were scattered and tended to be completely preoccupied with organizing the exploitation of their individual estates, they found it more difficult to strike up the type of political alliances which were commonplace among absentee landowners in the city.[9]

With so many big landowners residing in the city and depending on agents to administer the system of agricultural production and rent collection, it is not surprising that proprietors came to regard their peasants and not the land on which they toiled as the domain of exploitation. Absentee landowners were neither farmers nor agricultural entrepreneurs but town dwellers, preoccupied with urban life. They viewed the countryside as little more than a source of steady income and social prestige, not as a place in which to work or to risk capital. They showed little interest in putting their profits back into land development schemes.[10] Landowners found that the practice of usury, which required only small capital outlays, served their immediate financial interests better than reinvesting in the land. It not only increased their percentage of the rent, but it also strengthened their hold over cultivators by keeping them permanently dependent.[11]

As the Syrian town expanded control over its agricultural hinterland, rural society grew more dependent on the urban families who owned large portions of the surrounding countryside. In a sense, towns had become "parasites" living off the exploitation of the countryside and giving little in return. Rural society certainly regarded the city as a "foreign"

[9] Conversation with ʿAli ʿAbd al-Karim al-Dandashi (Damascus, 21 October 1975). The Danadashi clan was the biggest landowning family of Tall Kalakh, between Homs and Tripoli.

[10] During the interwar years, several big landowning families in Damascus, Homs, and Hama had sons who were trained in agricultural sciences in Europe (at Cirencester Agricultural College in England and at Grenoble and Montpellier in France). Although they were normally assigned to look after the family estates, few showed interest in land development and most preferred to leave the actual management to an agent (*wakil*) whose primary task was to collect rents. Information was found in George Faris, *Man huwa fi suriyya 1949* (Damascus, 1950), and FO 371/2142, vol. 20849, 6 May 1937. In 1930, a member of one big landowning family (the ʿAjlanis) in the Damascus region was brought to trial for having a tractor which was being used on a neighbor's estate destroyed. The defendant claimed that the tractor threatened his system of land exploitation because some of his sharecroppers had become curious about the uses of the tractor and had begun to ask if one could be bought for use on the ʿAjlani estate. MWT, *Registre des jugements du Tribunal de l^{ere} Instance Correctionnelle, 1931 et 1932*, pp. 22–25.

[11] Saʿid B. Himadeh, *The Monetary and Banking System in Syria* (Beirut, 1935), pp. 255–56.

creation bent on exploitation, as a devious outsider which offered little in exchange for labor and surplus except land appropriation and usury. But towns could never have engineered such a thorough and consistent exploitation of their hinterland had the absentee landowning class not had direct access to and even control of the various institutional components of government and the judiciary.[12] It had such access during the late Ottoman period, but the advent of a French regime with French institutions and an interest in creating a clientele in the countryside as a counterweight to hostile urban politicians threatened to alter urban–rural relations.

The scale of the independence movement was not simply restricted to the towns, but in fact to only four towns: Damascus, Homs, Hama, and Aleppo. They were the only permanent centers of nationalist activity during the Mandate. In other towns and districts, especially those containing the compact minorities—Alawites and Druzes—the movement operated on an intermittent basis. But, although in territorial terms the movement was limited, in demographic terms it was extensive, especially given that it concentrated on the mobilization of urban forces. If the four towns received most of the nationalist leadership's attention, they well deserved it; they were the four most populated areas in Syria. What these cities and the regions under their influence represented to Syria in demographic terms enabled the nationalist leadership to legitimize its claim to represent the will of the Syrian people.

During the Mandate, Aleppo was slightly larger than Damascus and both towns dwarfed Homs and Hama, which themselves were roughly the same size. Aleppo and Damascus were each larger than the combined populations of Homs, Hama, and the next five largest towns in Syria: Antioch, Dayr al-Zur, Latakia, Alexandretta, and Idlib (see Table I-1). Together, Aleppo and Damascus held 60 percent of Syria's total urban population; with the addition of Homs and Hama, nearly 80 percent of Syria's urban population was represented.

In those Syrian provinces where a rough demographic balance existed between rural and urban society, the nationalist movement thrived. Ob-

---

[12] This is one of the central arguments made in my *Urban Notables*. In Damascus, the great urban families who controlled the land system in the province—the ʿAzm, ʿAbid, Yusuf, Mardam-Beg, Quwwatli, Barudi, ʿAjlani, Ghazzi, Hasibi, Kaylani, and Jazaʾiri families—produced a high percentage of its administrators, judges, and financiers. In Aleppo, Hama, and Homs, a similar situation existed. Among the big landowning families of Aleppo and its province were the Jabiri, Kayyali, Qudsi, Rifaʿi, Mudarris, Marʿashli, Ibrahim Pasha, Kikhya (Ketkhuda), Nayyal, and Hananu families. In Hama, four families—the ʿAzm, Kaylani, Barazi, and Tayfur—monopolized power in the town and district. In Homs, the big landowning families included the Atasi, Jundi, Raslan, Suwaydan, Durubi, and Sibaʿi.

TABLE I-1
Population of Important Cities and Towns in Syria
During the French Mandate

City or town	1932	1936	1943
Aleppo	232,000	254,696	319,867
Damascus	216,000	238,480	286,310
Homs	65,000	68,981	100,042
Hama	50,000	50,313	71,391
Antioch	30,000	34,716	—
Dayr al-Zur	30,000	33,716	61,139
Latakia	24,000	—	36,687
Alexandretta	16,000	18,097	—
Idlib	13,000	14,527	18,719
Qamishli	—	—	18,188
Duma	12,000	11,830	17,863
Bab	7,000	10,707	15,148
Dir'a	8,000	—	10,737
Salimiyya	6,000	10,378	13,368
Nabk	—	—	10,681
Suwayda'	6,000	—	8,000
Hassaja	—	—	7,835
Tartus	—	5,000	—

SOURCES: Robert Widmer, "Population," in S. B. Himadeh (ed.), *Economic Organization of Syria* (Beirut, 1936); Emile Fauquenot, "L'état civil en Syrie en relation avec les questions de nationalité et de statut personnel des communautés religieuses," CHEAM, no. 50, n.d.; *Recueil de Statistiques de la Syrie et du Liban, 1942–43.*

versely, in regions where the size of the urban population was relatively insignificant, nationalist activity was limited. Damascus housed 48 percent of the population of its *muhafaza* (governorate); Aleppo, 37 percent (see Table I-2). By contrast, Suwayda' contained 10 percent of the Jabal Druze and Latakia 8 percent of its *muhafaza*. Furthermore, the Latakia province and Jabal Druze contained Syria's two largest compact minorities respectively and both were farming communities. Rural minority communities were the least susceptible to the forces of nationalism, a reality the French sought to maintain.

Of greater importance than demography in defining the scale of the nationalist movement was the relative uniformity and sophistication of urban political culture in the four towns. To start with, the characteristics of the local upper classes in these towns were strikingly similar. In each, this class was composed of a socially integrated network of families whose material resource base was built on large-scale landownership. In late Otto-

TABLE 1-2

Breakdown of Urban and Rural Population in Syria by *Muhafaza* (1943)

Muhafaza	*Pop. of capital city*	*% of total pop.*	*Total urban pop.*	*% of total pop.*	*Total rural pop.*	*% of total pop.*	*Total pop. of muhafaza*
Aleppo	320,167 (Aleppo)	37.0	354,034[a]	40.5	516,105	59.5	870,139
Damascus	286,310 (Damascus)	47.5	314,854[b]	52.0	289,035	48.0	603,889
Homs	100,042 (Homs)	47.0	100,042[c]	47.0	112,382	53.0	212,424
Hama	71,391 (Hama)	45.5	84,759[d]	54.0	72,699	46.0	157,458
Hawran	10,737 (Dir'a)	9.5	10,737[e]	9.5	102,105	90.5	112,842
Euphrates	61,139 (Dayr al-Zur)	27.0	61,139[f]	27.0	163,884	73.0	225,023
Jazira	18,188 (Qamishli)	12.5	25,933[g]	18.0	120,048	82.0	146,001
Jabal Druze	8,000 (Suwayda')	10.0	8,000[h]	10.0	72,128	90.0	80,128
Latakia	36,687 (Latakia)	8.0	41,687[i]	9.0	410,820	91.0	452,507
GRAND TOTAL	912,661	32.0	1,001,205	35.0	1,859,820	65.0	2,860,411[j]

SOURCES: For population by *muhafaza*, see A. H. Hourani, *Syria and Lebanon* (London, 1946), p. 385. For population of towns and cities, see *Recueil de Statistiques de la Syrie et du Liban, 1942–43.*

[a] Aleppo, Idlib, Bab
[b] Damascus, Duma, Nabk
[c] Homs
[d] Hama, Salimiyya
[e] Dir'a
[f] Dayr al-Zur
[g] Qamishli, Hassaja
[h] Suwayda'
[i] Latakia, Tartus
[j] This figure does not include nomadic and semi-nomadic populations, estimated in 1943 at 300,000–400,000.

man times, this class furnished the high-ranking bureaucrats and top local politicians as well as many cultural and religious leaders. Members of
this class had gone to Istanbul for a modern secular education, had served
in the provincial administration, and were among the first to promote the
idea of a separate Arab nation on the eve of World War I.

Although ethnically the great families were of mixed stock—Arab,
Turkish, and Kurdish—they were all Arabic-speaking (many also spoke
Turkish) and Sunni Muslim. The bonds of a common language and religion were strong enough to mitigate the potential for ethnic conflict
within the class. Its qualities—its nature, style, and political behavior—
underscored a high level of social and cultural homogeneity which helped
to reinforce its class solidarity. A relatively high degree of social and religious uniformity and cohesion in urban society itself allowed the urban
upper class to pose successfully as a "natural" leadership.[13] In a sense, its
domination of urban society was "legitimized" because a high proportion
of the population in each town—a population that, despite the dramatic
changes of the era, was still very much attached to its traditional religious
beliefs, cultural practices, and customs—identified the defenders of faith
and the guardians of culture as well as the providers of vital goods and
services with the local upper class. In brief, a cohesive Sunni Muslim upper class in the four towns not only patronized but also represented a predominantly Sunni Muslim populace, providing it with its cultural and religious leaders who embodied and articulated its beliefs and enforced its
code of moral behavior. This permitted the birth of the nationalist movement within a relatively unified and integrated political culture.

The individual power of the elite families stemmed from relations of
personal dependence which cut vertically through the social strata of their
respective towns and surrounding countryside, just as it had during the
Ottoman period. These relations, from the top down, were built on the
premise that both urban leader and client provided a service valued by the
other. Political benefits normally favored the leader. Clients usually did
not act independently in the political arena but instead depended on their
patrons to solve their political problems for them. Patrons bound clients
to themselves by distributing benefits downwards which generally discouraged clients from organizing themselves in any meaningful horizon-
tally-bound interest groups. Even trade unions, which might have been
expected to approximate horizontal or class-based organizations, were
often personal support systems integrated into the patronage network of
a great urban family.

---

[13] Albert Hourani adopts the term "natural" in "Ottoman Reform and the Politics of Notables," in William R. Polk and Richard L. Chambers (eds.), *Beginnings of Modernization
in the Middle East* (Chicago, 1968), pp. 41–68.

Only at the uppermost level of politics were horizontal alliances regularly formed—among urban leaders themselves—in order to strengthen their position vis-à-vis the state and to protect themselves better against pressures from further down the social scale. The need for a pulling together of forces was at no time more necessary than during the Mandate period. It helped that urban leaders were homogeneous in the sense of belonging to a particular class and not severely divided along ethnic, religious, linguistic, or other categorical lines. But, because they were relatively secure in their exclusive position at the summit of politics, they felt little obligation to maintain closed ranks and to clarify common interests on crucial political issues. Consequently, alliances among the urban leaders were rarely stable; indeed, intense factionalism and shifting alliances characterized the summit of political life in Syria.

Although urban leaders from the four largest towns were cut from the same social fabric and defined their interests in a similar fashion, there was no natural reason for them to link up in a common political front until the early twentieth century, when historical forces created both an opportunity and a need for collaboration.

It is true that by virtue of their language, religion, and customs the bulk of the inhabitants of Syria possessed common bonds and also formed part of a wider unit, the Arab people. However, certain Syrians were differentiated from one another and from their neighbors in their outlook and perhaps also in their interests. For instance, although the majority of Syrians during the Mandate era were Muslim, a significant minority of them were heterodox Muslims, and there were also many Christians. Of the total population of that part of geographical Syria which came under French control after World War I (corresponding to the modern Syrian republic), 69 percent were Sunni Muslims and 16 percent were heterodox Muslims (Alawites, Druzes, Isma'ilis). As for the 14 percent of the population who were Christians, some were Catholics or Uniates (that is, members of churches which recognize Papal supremacy but preserve certain special traditions), while others belonged to other rites, in particular the Greek Orthodox rite. There were also several thousand Arabized Jews in the large towns. (For a population breakdown by religion, see Tables I-3 and I-4.) This multiplicity of sects gave rise in Syria to a fierce sectarianism which was exacerbated by the Ottoman system of granting a certain degree of self-government to each recognized religious community or *millet* and by the intervention of the Western powers during the nineteenth century.

Syria also had other socio-economic and cultural differences which contributed to the reinforcement of local loyalties and to internal conflict. Some of them were inseparable from the religious divisions. The moun-

TABLE I-3

Percentage Distribution of Syria's Religious and Ethnic Minorities by *Muhafaza* (1945)[a]

Muhafazat (Governorates)	Alawites	Druzes	Isma'ilis/ Shi'ites	Greek Orthodox Christians	Other Christians	Armenian Orthodox/ Catholics	Jews/ Yazidis	Sunnis
Euphrates	0.4			0.1	0.8	1.1		98.0
Hawran	0.7	2.5		2.6	4.4	0.1		92.5
Damascus	0.3	0.2	0.1	3.9	4.7	3.2	2.2	82.7
Aleppo	0.1		1.0	1.1	4.3	8.9	1.8	82.4
Jazira			0.2	0.2	22.4	6.8	2.4	67.9
Homs	10.4		1.3	9.4	11.2	1.4		66.3
Hama	9.5		13.2	11.0	1.3	0.4		64.6
Latakia	62.1		1.8	12.8	3.1	1.3		18.9
Jabal Druze		87.6		5.7	4.2	0.7		1.8
TOTAL	11.5[b]	3.0[c]	1.5[d]	4.7[e]	5.2[f]	4.2[g]	1.2[h]	68.7[i]

SOURCES: Gabriel Baer, *Population and Society in the Arab East* (London, 1964), p. 109; Republic of Syria, Ministry of National Economy, Department of Statistics, *Statistical Abstract of Syria* (Damascus, 1952), p. 20.

[a] Total population of Syria in 1945 was 2,949,819.
[b] Alawites numbered 335,454.
[c] Druzes numbered 89,796.
[d] Isma'ilis and other Shi'ites numbered 42,757.
[e] Orthodox Christians numbered 140,832.
[f] Other Christians (Syrian Orthodox/Catholic, Greek Catholic, "Latin," Maronites, Chaldeans, Protestants, Nestorians) numbered 152,769.
[g] Armenian Orthodox/Catholics numbered 121,310 (Armenian Orthodox, 104,331).
[h] Jews numbered 30,309; Yazidis numbered 2,858; total was 33,167.
[i] Sunnis numbered 2,033,734.

Urban Kurds were predominantly Sunni Muslim and assimilated culturally and linguistically into Arab society; however, 8.5 percent of the total population of Syria in 1945 were Kurdish speakers, mainly semi-nomadic Kurdish tribes of the Euphrates and Jazira regions. In 1945 Turkish was used as a first language by 3 percent of the Syrian population.

TABLE I-4
Populations of Damascus and Aleppo by Religious Community

	1935		1943	
	Damascus	Aleppo	Damascus	Aleppo
Sunnis	186,726	155,558	227,674[b]	196,745[c]
Alawites	—	—	40	480
Shi'ites	166	—	167	5
Isma'ilis	—	—	9	3
Druzes	287	—	493	16
Yazidis	—	—	6	1
Jews	4,179?	10,094	13,007	13,361
Greek Orthodox	5,162?	2,579	10,217	5,984
Greek Catholic	5,098	10,190	9,806	11,846
Syrian Orthodox	1,431	4,557	899	5,393
Syrian Catholic	1,447	5,183	2,076	6,009
Armenian Orthodox	5,682	49,563	16,785	59,850
Armenian Catholic	1,517	6,843	2,062	8,777
"Latins"[a]	101	1,868	423	2,713
Maronites	265	3,185	936	3,636
Chaldeans	102	1,888	188	2,202
Nestorians	—	—	—	—
Protestants	860	2,045	857	2,846
Unknown	—	—	665	—
TOTAL	213,023	253,553	286,310	319,867

SOURCES: For 1935: Emile Fauquenot, "Les institutions gouvernementales de la Syrie,"
    CHEAM, no. 201 (17 June 1937).
    For 1943: Emile Fauquenot, "L'état civil en Syrie en relation avec les questions
    de nationalité et de statut personnel des communautés religieuses," CHEAM,
    no. 50, n.d.
[a] "Latins" are Roman Catholics of the Latin rite.
[b] Sunnis represented 79.5 percent of the total population of Damascus.
[c] Sunnis represented 61.5 percent of the total population of Aleppo.

tains and hill districts harbored the compact minorities: Druzes southeast
of Damascus and Alawites in the northwest. Sparsely settled areas such
as the Jazira in the far northeast contained significant communities of
Christians and Kurds. The First World War forced large numbers of Armenian Christians to take refuge from Turkish oppression in Syria, es-

pecially in Aleppo. There were also local differences not based on religion: for example, those between Damascus and Aleppo, which were two different provincial capitals with different political traditions and different economic orientations, and between the coastal areas which face the Mediterranean and the interior which faces the desert.

Beyond these religious and social divisions were others which are characteristic of the entire Middle East: the division between townspeople, peasants, and nomads and, by the interwar period, the differences in the degree of contact with the West by individuals, communities, districts, and generations as a result of Western missionary activity and the expansion of the Western economy into the region.[14]

As a consequence, there was a low degree of political integration in Syria when the French arrived. Political cooperation between her most important towns, Aleppo and Damascus, was not extensive. Although under the Ottomans both towns were capitals of neighboring provinces, administered through identical sets of institutions, and connected by road and eventually by rail, their political and economic orientations took quite different directions. Damascus was a large provincial market center for its more immediate vegetable orchards and fruit gardens and for the Hawran and the Biqaʿ. It maintained strong trading links with northern Palestine and was firmly tied to Beirut, its main outlet to the Mediterranean, by the mid-nineteeth century. It also carried on a brisk trade with the Hijaz by virtue of its important role as the eastern gathering point for the pilgrimage. Its previously lucrative trade with Baghdad across the Syrian desert waned after the opening of the Suez Canal.

Aleppo was regarded as Ottoman Syria's leading commercial center; however, its preoccupation was with regions to its north and east. It served as the chief market center for northern Syria, northwestern Iraq, and southeastern Anatolia, and lay along the great northern trade route from Iran and further East. The port of Alexandretta was Aleppo's outlet to the Mediterranean world.

The political horizons of Damascus and Aleppo reflected their different economic orientation and their geographical location. The bonds between them were loose and tenuous. They even employed different sets of weights and measurements and different currencies, and they showed a relatively wide variation in the price of the same commodity, suggesting different marketing conditions in each. Moreover, because both towns were of vital importance to the Ottoman Empire, Damascus for its politi-

---

[14] FO 371/8310, vol. 27319. "Syria and Lebanon," report by A. H. Hourani, 5 Dec. 1941, p. 2.

cal and cultural influence and Aleppo for its strategic economic role, each answered directly to Istanbul rather than to one another.

Homs and Hama were always less important entities, with small town mentalities, even by Syrian standards. Unlike Aleppo or Damascus, they were never great entrepôts for international trade nor centers of traditional learning, nor anywhere near as cosmopolitan. Their roles were a function of their size and thus were restricted to servicing and exploiting their agricultural hinterlands and to serving as exchange centers for the tribes of central Syria. The Ottoman provincial re-organization of Syria in the 1860s placed both Homs and Hama more firmly under the administrative jurisidiction of Damascus. Consequently, both became increasingly prone to political influences emanating from Damascus. However, of the two, Hama, though it was further from Damascus, had stronger ties with its provincial capital, if only because by the eighteenth century two of Hama's most powerful families had influential branches in Damascus.[15] The coastal outlet for Homs was Tripoli to which it was more closely tied than to Damascus, while Hama depended on the port of Latakia and to a lesser extent Tripoli. Both towns, which are near one another, were in the habit of political squabbling owing to an ancient but persistent conflict over the allocation of water resources from the Orontes River.[16]

What sparked the development of closer political ties between the four largest towns was an externally induced crisis. Although the upper classes were not free of internal political factionalism, after consolidating their social and political hold within the towns of Syria in the late nineteenth century, they enjoyed several decades of political stability and comparative economic security. The Young Turk Revolt of 1908 brought an end to this era. The Young Turks' renewed emphasis on centralization and Turkification of the Arab provinces sufficiently threatened the interests of a significant number of the Syrian political elite to elicit a violent reaction. To legitimize their opposition to the Young Turks, factions within the elite tapped a number of new intellectual currents which had developed in reaction to or in defense of the forces of modernization and secularization that had penetrated Syria and other parts of the Empire in the course of the nineteenth century. These currents were a mixture of traditional Islamic and modern secularist elements. At their core lay an emphasis on the primacy of the Arabs, their great cultural influence upon Islam, and their language, from which an ideological weapon, Arabism,

---

[15] The 'Azm and Kaylani families.

[16] J. Gaulmier, "Note sur une épisode poétique de la rivalité séculaire entre Homs et Hama," *Bulletin d'Etudes Orientales*, 2 (1932), pp. 83–90.

was fashioned. Using Arabism, disaffected members of the urban elite could both justify and advance their opposition movement.[17]

In its early stages of development, the ideology of Arabism brought together disaffected leaders from Syrian towns in order to widen the base of their opposition to Turkish policies and to redress the balance of power. Some leaders formed literary societies which emphasized Arabic culture and called for political decentralization, while others met at the Ottoman Parliament in Istanbul where they pressed for greater administrative autonomy in the provinces. Younger elements formed clandestine organizations which were more radical in their aims and pressed for Arab independence on the eve of World War I. It was at this time that urban leaders in Syria first began to discover how much they had in common; and it was then that some began to reject their Ottoman identity for a Syrian-Arab one.

Although the framework of political collaboration between Syrian towns was under construction by the First World War, it was not until the collapse of the Ottoman Empire and its replacement by an Arab state (1918–20) based on the principles of Arab national unity and independence that it becomes possible to speak of an articulated desire and need for these towns to link up politically. During the brief existence of Faysal's Kingdom of Syria, the radius of its authority did not really extend beyond the four towns.[18]

The important point is that nationalism would not have spread so quickly had these towns not had a unified and cohesive local upper class which came to regard the national idea as a viable and useful substitute for "Ottomanism," an ideology which after 1918 no longer served its interests. The receptivity of the four towns to nationalism, although it varied in intensity and timing,[19] was the result of a political culture that was very much this urban leadership's own creation and which it willingly embodied and represented. Nationalism reflected a conflict within the local upper class and, as long as it remained a vehicle of elements from this class, it was not regarded as a destructive force but rather as the best available weapon to defend its interests.

If the espousal of Arabism was the first stage in the development of political links between the four towns, and Faysal's Arab Kingdom was the second stage, it was the imposition of French rule in Syria in 1920 which accelerated this process and, as a consequence, more clearly defined the scale of nationalist politics in interwar Syria. The official partition of ge-

[17] I have detailed this argument in my *Urban Notables*, Chapter 3.

[18] *Ibid.*, Chapter 4.

[19] The urban leadership in Aleppo adopted nationalism later than did the Damascus leadership; and, after the collapse of Ottoman rule, Aleppo lived in a politically inferior position to Damascus. The reasons for this are examined in Chapter 4.

ographical Syria into separately administered Mandates under French and British authority isolated a truncated Syria surrounded by new, artificial and hostile frontiers and customs barriers which obstructed the free passage of goods and peoples. The placement of Syria and Lebanon under French Mandate alone and Syria's administrative separation from Lebanon eventually brought the four towns under a single administrative set-up.

Periodization

This study will examine the evolution of the independence movement by tracing political developments in Syria during the French Mandate through four phases. In these phases certain factors remained constant, in particular the French government's determination to safeguard its own essential interests and France's friendly attitude to the minorities. Other factors, however, changed, most notably the relationship between the French and the nationalist leadership.

The first phase lasted until 1927 and was marked by a head-on confrontation between the French and the nationalist leadership. After toppling Faysal's Arab government in Damascus, the French constructed an administrative system which separated Lebanon from Syria and then divided Syria into separate units along ethno-religious and regional lines. The French centralized power in their own hands and adopted measures which caused serious discontent throughout much of the country. Nationalists transformed a local uprising in the Jabal Druze in 1925 into a revolt of national proportions which lasted for two years but which ultimately was crushed. The Great Revolt was itself a watershed because it created the opportunity for a more stable balance of power between government and society, something both the nationalist leadership and the French desired.

In the second phase which lasted until 1936, the French realized the need to make some concession to the desire for self-government in Syria. A constitution was promulgated and a parliament elected. Meanwhile, the failure of the Great Revolt convinced the nationalist leadership to drop armed confrontation as a strategy for winning French recognition. Instead, it adopted an evolutionary approach to the nationalist goals of unity and independence. This more delicate strategy reflected the urban leadership's preference for an ideology which aimed at restoring a balance between foreign rule and local leadership which had been operative in late Ottoman times. Armed struggle and revolutionary upheaval were never again regarded as serious alternatives during the interwar years. The National Bloc, an alliance formed of nationalists in the four towns, became the most important political organization of the Mandate era; it would steer the course of the nationalist movement until independence was finally achieved at the end of World War II. This second phase ended in a sense in 1933 when the radical wing of the National Bloc found unacceptable the terms of the treaty which the French had negotiated with a ministry which included moderate nationalists.

In 1936, the revival of measured confrontational tactics in the form of a General Strike, together with events in Egypt and Ethiopia, caused the French government to recognize the necessity of coming to an agreement with the nationalists. A Syrian delegation composed mainly of National Bloc leaders went to Paris to negotiate another treaty. At first discussions did not go smoothly, but when the left-wing Popular Front came to power in June, negotiations reached a relatively swift and satisfactory conclusion. The terms of the treaty were hammered out and it was agreed it would not come into force for three years. These years were to serve as a transitional period in which the National Bloc was permitted to govern and to share power with the French High Commission.

But this transitional period was not allowed to run its course. In France, the quick decline of the Popular Front brought into power some who had never believed in the policy of 1936. And, many who had believed in it changed their opinion, either because the international situation made it important that French authority should not be weakened in Syria and Lebanon, or else because events in Syria convinced them of the country's unreadiness for self-government. Similarly, the nationalists came to doubt the sincerity of French intentions, above all because the French ceded the district of Alexandretta to Turkey, but also because it became clear that the French Parliament would not ratify the treaty of 1936, even after the nationalist government granted additional concessions to France. Meanwhile, the government's strength declined as suspicious minority communities, quietly encouraged by French agents, caused frequent disturbances, and radical nationalists attacked it on the grounds that it had compromised Syria's integrity and future as a politically independent state. This third phase ended with the resignation of the National Bloc government in early 1939 and the placement once again of the compact minorities under separate administrations. The nationalists had not advanced their demands for unity and independence much beyond the stage they had reached in the mid-1920s.

The final phase covered the years of the Second World War and culminated in Syrian independence in 1945. Although in Syria there was a certain sympathy with the Allied cause there was clearly no great enthusiasm. Memories of the misery and starvation experienced during World War I were still fresh. Moreover, the broken promises of the last war, the Alexandretta debacle, and the unratified treaty of 1936 made Syrians from all walks of life wary of French intentions. However, the Allied invasion in June 1941 introduced direct British influence into Syria and the possibility of re-establishing a more equitable balance of power between foreign rule and local leadership. Denied access to the French who still preferred to prop up discredited Syrian notables in government, the National Bloc sought British support for its return to power. Owing to a perceptible difference in her policy toward Arab nationalism, Britain encouraged the nationalist movement while she applied subtle pressure on the more rigid but weakened French High Commission. As a consequence, a nationalist government supported by a newly elected nationalist Parliament returned to office in 1943, and remained there after France withdrew from the Levant at the end of the war. The nationalist leadership had secured Syria's independence in the manner which it preferred, by patient negotiation and measured pressure, not by revolutionary means which might upset the local status quo.

Challenges from Within

Although this study emphasizes the remarkable degree of continuity in the character of political life in Syria under Ottoman and French rule, it also has to account for why the interwar years were an important pivotal period for political life in Syria. Many new features were introduced into politics which had their origins in the changes that had swept Syria since the second half of the nineteenth century—in administration and law, in commerce, industry, and agriculture, in the movement of goods, peoples, and ideas, and, above all, in her relations with Europe. Such changes encouraged the development of new, more broadly-based, and better-organized movements of protest and resistance than previously known in Syria.

In the interwar period, rapid population growth, an inflated cost of living, the collapse of traditional industries, and a changing intellectual climate produced tensions and dislocations in urban society which eventually required more sophisticated responses than a narrowly focused nationalism provided. Before the end of the Mandate, the character and instruments of urban politics had changed sufficiently to pose a challenge to the old behavior, style, and aims of the urban political leadership. By the late 1930s patronage had become a fairly sophisticated and complex operation and was no longer able to keep pace with demographic growth in the towns. Increasing numbers of people sought support and services outside the old framework of patronage. They looked to and drew their strength from new social and cultural institutions such as secondary schools, universities, and youth organizations. Similarly, the locus of political life gradually shifted outside the old residential quarters and central marketplace to newer, modern districts where these new institutions were located.

There, modern ideological parties headed by a rising generation posed a challenge to the old political order and to the National Bloc's monopoly of the nationalist idea. Its leaders belonged to emerging professional classes and organizations, were educated either in the West or locally, and found the Ottoman political legacy alien. Although willing to accept the bourgeois liberal idioms of nationalism as expressed by the National Bloc—constitutionalism, parliamentary forms, and personal freedoms—they emphasized major economic and social reforms, something the old leadership had ignored. Furthermore, unlike the nationalist leadership which had resigned itself to working within the political and administrative framework established by the French Mandate—that of a truncated Syria, separated from Lebanon and from the other Arab neighbors—this ascendant generation adopted pan-Arabism and a more revolutionary strategy for achieving independence and unity.

The National Bloc leadership, however, was schooled in the tactics of survival and met the challenge posed by the rising elites. Indeed, the National Bloc ushered Syria toward her independence and was in control of government when the French finally evacuated the country. But, already by the late 1930s it was clear that the political expertise of the veteran nationalists had lost much of its vitality. New ideological organizations were preparing for the dramatic changes Syria would experience soon after independence. It was independence in 1945 rather than the destruction of the Ottoman order in 1918 that finally broke the mold of the "the politics of notables" characteristic of both the Ottoman and Mandate periods. For with independence, the median position of notables, between distant ruler and local society, suddenly disappeared. The notables themselves became the government and their actions were subject to a new set of rules.

THE FRENCH IN SYRIA

CHAPTER ONE

PRELUDE TO MANDATE

In 1920, France received the Mandate for Syria and Lebanon in recognition of the "special" position she had established for herself in these territories before World War I. This is especially remarkable since after the war her military and political position was inferior to Britain's, the composition of her interests in Syria and Lebanon were, to say the least, grossly uneven, and only a small number of Frenchmen, representing a rather narrow range of interests in France, were actively committed to adding this region to the French Empire. France's claim to such a position rested on three pillars: moral, political, and economic. Although the foundations of each pillar were laid well before the twentieth century, it was only in the years immediately preceding the Great War that these pillars were significantly reinforced. Even then, each pillar contained structural flaws which were to bring instability to French rule after 1920.

THE THREE PILLARS

French moral influence stemmed from her religious protectorate, which dated from the seventeenth century and spanned the entire Middle East. After 1900, France not only deepened her religious and cultural interests but also narrowed their focus to Syria and Lebanon. Apart from a network of Catholic schools and other religious institutions supported by an array of missionary societies and the French government, French moral influence was disseminated through a growing system of lay education.[1]

Use of a religious protectorate to establish a sphere of influence caused serious problems for French policy. Most glaring was that France's educational and other missionary activities appealed only to Syria's Uniate communities, especially the Maronites who were concentrated in Mount Lebanon and Beirut. French commitment to a Catholic protectorate automatically raised cultural and political barriers between Frenchmen directly involved in Syrian affairs—whether missionaries, traders, or officials of the Quai d'Orsay—and the Muslim majority. In support of France's focus, a rather simplistic, if not biased, understanding of the nature of social relations and interaction in Syria was developed. To the

---

[1] See William I. Shorrock, *French Imperialism in the Middle East* (Madison, 1976), pp. 63–64; J. P. Spagnolo, "French Influence in Syria prior to World War I: The Functional Weakness of Imperialism," *Middle East Journal*, 23 (1969), p. 60.

French, Syria contained a variety of religious and ethnic communities generally at odds with the Muslim majority to which they were bound by little more than common language, geography, and superficial political history. Given the skew of French moral influence, Frenchmen preferred to emphasize social and cultural differences among Syrians and to interpret these as the product of endemic sectarian conflict. In so doing, Frenchmen overlooked or discounted certain socio-economic and cultural affinities which encouraged members of different religious communities to undertake collective political action.[2] This facile interpretation of the nature of Syrian society in terms of sectarian conflict also incorporated the French notion of "progress" which, in the Syrian situation, pitted a numerically weak but socially and culturally superior Christian minority, with an unquenchable thirst for European knowledge and values, against a large community of fanatical, narrow-minded, and intellectually underdeveloped Muslims bent on obstructing progress in all areas of Syrian life. The French proclivity to interpret all unrest in terms of sectarian ties and conflicts precluded a proper understanding of collective Arab aims and common political action on the eve of the First World War.[3]

The French government expanded its political influence in the early twentieth century by developing ties with ascendant political movements in the region. The way it did so reflected French misconceptions and biases about the nature of Syria and the rather narrow range of French influence there. In particular, the French sought influence with two political movements, one Lebanese and the other Syrian-Arab. Both were reformist and increasingly nationalistic. The Lebanese movement, led by Maronites and purely Christian in membership, called for greater political autonomy from the Ottoman Turks for the special district of Mount Lebanon, known as the *mutasarrifiyya*. After the Young Turk Revolution of 1908 and growing Ottoman efforts to tie the Empire's provinces

[2] Spagnolo, "French Influence," p. 57; Fritz Steppat, "The Penetration of Secular Socio-Political Concepts in the Nineteenth Century," paper presented to the Second International Congress on the History of *Bilad al-Sham* (Damascus, 27 Nov.–3 Dec. 1978). A translation of this paper has since appeared in Proceedings of *Al-Mu'tamar al-dawli al-thani li-tarikh bilad al-sham* (Damascus, 1980), vol. 2, pp. 601–16.

[3] Spagnolo, "French Influence," p. 61. French appreciation of Arab Muslim society in Syria owes much to the scholarship and literature of French orientalists and even more to French colonial studies of North African society which developed in the second half of the nineteenth century. An illuminating introduction to both influences can be found in Edmund Burke III, "The Sociology of Islam: The French Tradition," in Malcolm H. Kerr (ed.), *Islamic Studies: A Tradition and Its Problems* (Malibu, 1980), pp. 73–88. Also see Marwan R. Buheiry, "Colonial Scholarship and Muslim Revivalism in 1900," *Arab Studies Quarterly*, 4 (1982), pp. 1-16.

more tightly to Istanbul, the Lebanese movement adopted ideas of political separatism and territorial expansion under French protection.[4] The Syrian-Arab movement was composed of Muslims and Christians, although its effective leadership was Muslim. It also agitated for greater administrative decentralization in the Syrian provinces.[5] Not surprisingly, the Quai d'Orsay showed much greater sympathy and understanding for the aspirations of the Lebanese. The French government became closely involved with the Lebanese reform movement from the beginning of the century; it only began to take serious notice of Syrian political aspirations in 1912.

In that year, France decided to deepen her political influence in the key centers of political activity—Damascus and Beirut—by making official contact with and offering cautious support to the disaffected leadership of the Syrian-Arab reform movement. At the same time, French officials advised radical elements against any separation from the Ottoman Empire. By so doing, the Quai d'Orsay hoped to obstruct the efforts of other European Powers, especially Britain, to secure a political foothold in Syria through an alliance with the reform movement and to prevent the type of political upheavals that could internationalize the Syrian political question and threaten France's claim to exclusive influence in the whole region.[6]

Although leaders of the Syrian reform movement distrusted French intentions, owing in large part to the religious thrust of French moral influence, they nevertheless concluded that only the European Powers were capable of persuading the Ottoman government of the importance of administrative decentralization. Political leaders in Damascus and Beirut never concealed their worries about French ambitions in Syria, but they hoped that France might use her good offices to assist them in wresting concessions from Istanbul. An appeal to European assistance did not guarantee that it would be forthcoming, however.[7]

Syrian activists held an Arab Congress in Paris in June 1913. It adopted a reform program which the French government backed in Istanbul. Despite French advocacy, the Ottoman government refused to accept the fundamental principles of decentralization enumerated in the Congress program and Syrian sentiment moved toward separatism.[8] In the meantime, the French government entered into complicated and lengthy ne-

[4] See Shorrock, *French Imperialism*, pp. 83–113.

[5] See Philip S. Khoury, *Urban Notables*, Chapter 3.

[6] Shorrock, *French Imperialism*, pp. 87–89.

[7] See Rashid I. Khalidi, *British Policy Towards Syria and Palestine, 1906–1914* (London, 1980).

[8] Shorrock, *French Imperialism*, pp. 89, 96–98.

gotiations with the Porte regarding a large French loan to Istanbul in return for exclusive railroad concessions in Syria. Syrian nationalist leaders, who had been led to believe by the French Consul in Damascus that one of the conditions of the loan was the establishment of a suitable Syrian reform program, had their hopes dashed when a final agreement was signed in April 1914. The Empire got its loan and France her railroad concessions as well as formal guarantees for her religious establishments in Syria, but there was no mention of a Syrian reform program.[9]

Whether the French government had actually misled the Syrian reform movement leadership is a moot point: the Syrians thought they had done so. From their perspective, France had abandoned the reform program in order to satisfy her own economic interests as well as those of her Christian clients. In the four months before the war broke out, the sentiments of the Syrian reformers became increasingly separatist in orientation and blatantly anti-French. A massive propaganda campaign was waged in Damascus, Aleppo, and Beirut against French influence in Syria. France was accused of abandoning the Syrian-Arab reform movement for an exclusive sphere of economic influence in Syria.

The French decision to withdraw support from the reform program was in line with France's imperialist logic. Viable and secure economic interests in Syria gave her the international recognition needed to finalize her claim to an exclusive position there. In the process, however, France failed to gauge the depth of national sentiment in Syria. Although she had helped to guarantee her claim to Syria, she hampered her ability to win popularity and political influence among the vast majority of Syrians.[10]

The third pillar of French influence in Syria was economic. France was at the vanguard of European efforts to absorb the Ottoman Empire into the world market, even though her total investment in the Empire was less than 40 percent of what she had invested in Russia and only equal to her investments in Egypt. Nevertheless, between 1890 and 1914 France was by far the largest investor in the Ottoman Empire.[11] On the eve of World War I, her investments were more than double that of her nearest rival, Germany. Britain's investments, which ranked third, were minuscule by comparison.[12] In 1913, French capitalists controlled 63 percent of

---

[9] *Ibid.*, pp. 97–99; Spagnolo, "French Influence," pp. 61–62.

[10] Shorrock, *French Imperialism*, pp. 99–101.

[11] The most exhaustive treatment of French interests in the Ottoman Empire since the late nineteeth century is Jacques Thobie, *Intérêts et impérialisme français dans l'empire ottoman: 1895–1914* (Paris, 1977).

[12] "L'importance des intérêts français dans l'empire ottoman," in *L'Asie Française* (1920), pp. 179–83; Jean Ducruet, *Les capitaux européens au Proche-Orient* (Paris, 1964), p. 6.

the Ottoman Public Debt. They, along with their British counterparts, owned and directed the Imperial Ottoman Bank which "controlled the tobacco monopoly, several utilities, railway and industrial issues, and other business ramifications."[13]

By 1900, French financial investments in Syria were firmly established, although the value of French trade with Syria was less than the value of trade of France's European rivals in the region, a gap she sought to narrow.[14] The Imperial Ottoman Bank, which issued the Ottoman currency and often served as an agent of the Quai d'Orsay, had active branches in Damascus, Aleppo, Homs, and Tripoli. The Beirut branch of the Crédit Lyonnais was a key link between the silk industry of Mount Lebanon and silk factories in Lyons.[15] In the transportation sector, French investors constructed the first paved road connecting Beirut with Damascus in 1857, and a French-owned company monopolized transport along the road. In the 1890s, French companies also constructed the port of Beirut and a railroad line connecting Beirut with Damascus and the Hawran.[16]

The bulk of European investments in Syrian industries were also French. Financiers were primarily concerned with providing home industries with processed raw materials. The growing demand of Lyons and Marseilles silk factories for spun silk after the mid-nineteenth century, owing in large part to the destruction of French sericulture by disease, encouraged French banks and individual capitalists to finance new sericulture ventures and the construction of silk-spinning factories. By the early twentieth century, French capital financed the majority of Lebanese factories.[17] The Régie de Tabac, a French-owned company established in 1883, completely replaced the Ottoman government in determining the mode of tobacco production in the Empire and collecting taxes on the crop and customs duties on all imports and exports of tobacco products by 1904. The Régie was one result of a "series of arrangements made by the Ottoman government with its European creditors in the wake of its bank-

---

[13] E.G. Mears (ed.), Modern Turkey (New York, 1924), p. 357; Z. Y. Hershlag, Introduction to the Modern Economic History of the Middle East (Leiden, 1964), p. 65; Shorrock, French Imperialism, p. 138.

[14] See Thobie, Intérêts et impérialisme.

[15] M. Abdul-Kader al-Nayal, "Industry and Dependency with Special Reference to Syria: 1920–1957," M.A. Dissertation (Institute of Social Studies, The Hague, 1974), p. 42.

[16] Ibid., p. 40.

[17] Ibid., p. 53; Dominique Chevallier, "Lyon et la Syrie en 1919. Les bases d'une intervention," Revue Historique, 224 (Oct.-Dec. 1960), pp. 275–300; Paul Saba, "The Creation of the Lebanese Economy—Economic Growth in the Nineteenth and Early Twentieth Centuries," in Roger Owen (ed.), Essays on the Crisis in Lebanon (London, 1976), pp. 18–21. Also see Michel Seurat, "Le rôle du Lyon dans l'installation du Mandat français en Syrie: intérêts économiques et culturels, luttes d'opinion (1915–1925)," Bulletin d'Etudes Orientales, 31 (1979), pp. 131–64.

ruptcy" in the mid-1870s. It appeared at a time when tobacco growing in Syria was undergoing a major revival, which led the Régie to construct tobacco-processing factories in Damascus and Aleppo.[18] By 1914, French companies not only owned all but one of the railroads that crisscrossed Syria (the exception being the Muslim-owned Hijaz Railway), but French capital had also been put into public utilities in Beirut, Damascus, and Aleppo.

This type of expansion based on capital export and trade reflected a particular stage of Western capitalist development and manifested itself in intensified European competition for spheres of economic influence after 1870. It also had uneven effects on the development of the Syrian economy, as it did in so many other primary-producing regions of the world. The most noticeable feature of this lopsided development was that the Syrian coast and Mount Lebanon received far more attention from French capitalism than did the Syrian interior, even though the heavy concentration of French capital in railway lines and roads helped to bridge the geographical division between coast and interior created by two mountain ranges and thereby provided an outlet to the sea for agricultural produce and other raw materials from Syria's interior plains.[19] The uneven effects of French investment on the Syrian economy correlated almost perfectly with the uneven effects of French moral and political influence.

France's financial investments in the region, like her religious and political investments, were concentrated in Beirut and Mount Lebanon where her strongest moral and political links were to the Christians. Thus, whereas the Syrian coast and interior became more economically interdependent, France's relationship favored the coast, and particularly Beirut, with its inextricable link to the French economy. The easy accessibility of the coastal strip and Mount Lebanon to France allowed the Christians of Beirut and the *mutasarrifiyya* to reap the lion's share of economic and political benefits created by the overall French involvement in Syria. By 1914, the effects of this unbalanced French expansion were already visible in the divergent political aspirations of Lebanese Maronites and other Catholics and Syria's Muslim majority. Nevertheless, by 1914, France had established her claim to an exclusive option on Syria in the event of the collapse of the Ottoman Empire. The war struck the long-awaited death blow to the Empire and France's claim was delivered in 1920, in the package of a Mandate for Syria and Lebanon.

---

[18] Saba, "The Creation," p. 17; Badr al-Din al-Siba'i, *Adwa' 'ala al-rasmal al-ajnabi fi suriyya 1850–1958* (Damascus, 1968), p. 44.
[19] Al-Nayal, "Industry," p. 44.

Delivery of the French Claim

In a recent study, Christopher M. Andrew and A. S. Kanya-Forstner convincingly argue that France owes her last stage of imperial expansion, along the southern and eastern shores of the Mediterranean in the early twentieth century, to a small but dedicated group of officials, politicians, businessmen, scholars, and missionaries who were known as the *parti colonial*.[20] This group managed to expand the frontiers of the French Empire in spite of a lack of enthusiasm amongst the French public at large.

The colonial party was not a modern political party but several dozen pressure groups with overlapping memberships and aims. As far as its members can be categorized, they tended to be right of center politically, to belong to the bourgeoisie, and to be republicans. Few were on the extreme Left and extreme Right. Some were principally motivated by a *mission civilisatrice* and the idea of a "Greater France" while others

> had been turned by their careers into professional defenders of the national interest, anxious to defend that interest against the conflicting claims of other powers in those areas of the globe for which they bore responsibility.[21]

To make a case for imperial expansion, the colonial party relied more on appeals to "national prestige" than to economic gain, even in those territories where French businessmen were actively engaged.[22] In the early twentieth century, Morocco drew most of the colonial party's attention. The colonial party showed little interest in Syria until France established the Moroccan Protectorate in 1912. But, as war approached it became increasingly concerned about the break-up of the Ottoman Empire and pushed the government to stake out a firm claim to Syria.[23] The dominant feeling among French colonialists was that Syria should remain part of the Ottoman Empire, with the understanding among European powers that the territory was an exclusive sphere of French influence.

The war gave the colonial party's appeal for expansion greater resonance, owing to the feeling that France ought to get something out of the war. It also gave the Syrian question much greater urgency, with the break-up of the Ottoman Empire. However, British forces were in control of allied military operations in the Middle East and appeared to threaten French interests in Syria. The colonial party's definition of Syria included

[20] *The Climax of French Imperial Expansion 1914–1924* (Stanford, 1981). Also see Jan Karl Tannenbaum, "France and the Arab Middle East, 1914–1920, *Transactions of the American Philosophical Society*, 68 (October 1978).

[21] Andrew and Kanya-Forstner, *The Climax*, p. 27.

[22] Andrew and Kanya-Forstner, "The French Colonial Party and French Colonial War Aims, 1914–1918," *The Historical Journal*, 17 (1974), p. 106.

[23] Andrew and Kanya-Forstner, *The Climax*, Chapter 1.

Lebanon and Palestine—*la Syrie intégrale*—a definition the British (and a number of Frenchmen) had difficulty accepting.[24]

French governments had great difficulty evolving and carrying out imperial policy. Third Republic cabinets were often weak and preoccupied with domestic issues and the nation lacked interest in empire. Imperial policy formulation and implementation were dominated by a small number of colonialists in the Ministries of Foreign Affairs and Colonies, who received encouragement from like-minded politicians in parliament and members of the French business community with interests abroad. Together these forces charted the course of French imperial expansion in its last stage.

At the Quai d'Orsay, which was responsible for French foreign affairs, a handful of officials and diplomats were involved in French policy in Syria before and during the war. Nearly all these men belonged to the principal pressure group concerned with French interests in the Middle East, the Comité de l'Asie Française. Among them were Philippe Berthelot, Robert de Caix, and François Georges-Picot. During and after the war, they received the support of a number of prominent French politicians in parliament and in government who were deeply interested in extending France's Empire into the eastern Mediterranean, including Pierre-Etienne Flandin, Georges Leygues, and Stephen Pichon. The colonial party did not achieve all that it wanted in Syria but it was remarkably successful. Despite its small numbers and its narrow interests, it succeeded in committing the French government to expanding the Empire after the war.[25]

France's sphere of influence was recognized during the war by the Anglo-French partition plan known as the Sykes–Picot Agreement. But owing to the exigencies of war, British rather than French influence was paramount in Syria by 1918. And Britain supported Faysal's nationalist Arab regime which was openly hostile to France.

Britain and France had agreed in 1916 to set up an Arab state in part of Syria, but France's interpretation of the Sykes–Picot Agreement remained consistent with her prewar aims: the Arab state fell within a clearly defined French sphere of influence. When Arab nationalists called for an independent Syria, the French reaction was predictable: they accused Britain of trying to deprive them of Syria and their share of the Ottoman Empire as formally delineated in the Sykes–Picot Agreement.[26]

There was considerable truth in the French accusation. After the war,

[24] *Ibid.*, p. 44.
[25] *Ibid.*, pp. 44–47.
[26] Elie Kedourie, *England and the Middle East* (London, 1956), pp. 132–33.

Britain faced the problem of having to reconcile conflicting promises made to the Arabs about future independence in the Husayn–McMahon Correspondence of 1915–16, and to the French in the Sykes–Picot Agreement. Complicating matters was the Balfour Declaration of November 1917 in which the British government announced its support for a homeland in Palestine for the Jews. Indeed, the British, in spite of their preponderant strength in the Middle East at the end of the war, found themselves in a quandary: how to choose between the French and Faysal and at the same time to satisfy Britain's own ambitions in the Arab East, which by 1918 included exclusive control over Palestine and the Mosul region of Iraq with its great promise of oil. Both ambitions contradicted the Sykes–Picot Agreement. From the British perspective, the pledges made to the Arabs and to the French during the war were open to reinterpretation at the end of the war. Albert Hourani remarked sixty years later that

> such agreements were made in a hurry and under stress, and for an immediate purpose: not to decide what should happen once the War was ended, but to achieve the minimum of agreement without which campaigns could not be fought in common. In a difficult negotiation, when there is an urgent need to reach an agreement, it is natural and legitimate to try to devise a formula which can be interpreted in more than one way, and to leave the question of which interpretation should prevail to be decided by the balance of strength when the war was over.[27]

In 1918, Lloyd George and his political advisers found unrealistic the French position that the solution to the Eastern Question lay exclusively in the Sykes–Picot Agreement. That agreement no longer corresponded to the postwar balance of power. Britain was the preponderant military power in the Arab East, France had only a token force in Syria, Russia had abandoned her claims to a share of the Ottoman inheritance, and the Arabs were demanding their due. From the British government's perspective, France was out of touch with new realities in the Middle East. Of these new realities, nationalism was the most important.

Complicating matters was Faysal ibn al-Husayn's precarious Arab regime in Syria, which the British had helped to install and to support militarily and financially after the occupation. Damascus became a magnet for nationalist elements from Iraq, the Hijaz, Palestine, and elsewhere in Syria. While Faysal tried to build an acceptable administrative framework amidst insurmountable political and economic divisions in the country,

[27] Albert Hourani, "The Arab Awakening Forty Years After," in Hourani, The Emergence of the Modern Middle East (London, 1981), p. 210.

he sought ways of buttressing his diplomatic position in Europe. Eventually, he became completely absorbed in negotiations there in an effort to ensure that the British continued to support his government's independence in the face of French ambitions.[28]

Although British statesmen found themselves at the war's end in a stronger bargaining position vis-à-vis France, both in Europe and in the Arab East, they could not afford to obstruct French designs on Syria for fear of losing French support in Europe. The establishment of a lasting solution to the political situation in Europe had to take precedence over any such solution in the Arab territories. Furthermore, Britain, her eye on Iraq, could not easily deny a similar French interest in Syria. Yet, it took nearly a year of bitter negotiations between David Lloyd George and Georges Clemenceau before the British government showed any willingness to relinquish some of its influence in the region.[29]

To soften the British position on Syria, Clemenceau consented in late 1918 to forfeit to Britain Mosul, which lay in the French zone as delineated in 1916, and France's part in what was to have been an internationally-supervised Palestine. The colonial party viewed Clemenceau's bargain as a great sacrifice of the French national interest, but it was powerless to oppose him. He was the strongest Prime Minister of the Third Republic and he had usurped the Quai d'Orsay's power in major foreign policy decisions. He was not especially interested in Syria and, more importantly, he recognized France's glaringly weak physical presence in the region. Some members of the colonial party, notably Robert de Caix at the Foreign Affairs ministry, grudgingly accepted Clemenceau's compromise, especially with regard to Palestine where de Caix foresaw endless troubles for the British, and focused their sights on those areas of geographical Syria where French moral, political, and economic interests were strongest. On this issue, their aims and Clemenceau's corresponded: in order to secure a French occupation of Damascus and Aleppo, the British first had to be persuaded to leave the Syrian interior and to allow the French to deal exclusively with Faysal's Arab regime.

During the first half of 1919, Lloyd George tried to induce Clemenceau to include Amir Faysal and the United States in negotiations. By September it was apparent that Clemenceau would not budge and American involvement would not go beyond sending out a Commission of Inquiry (King–Crane Commission) to investigate the political aspirations of the Syrian people. But as Andrew and Kanya-Forstner have suggested, the British Prime Minister's decision to give in to French demands had much

[28] For an evaluation of Faysal's Arab government, see Khoury, *Urban Notables*, Chapter 4.

[29] Kedourie, *England*, Chapter 5.

less to do with the activities of the colonial party in France than it did with a reassessment of British imperial defense strategy.

In 1919 British lines of imperial communication were threatened at virtually every point. A Muslim insurrection had broken out in the Punjab and a nationalist revolt in Egypt. Mustafa Kemal was beginning to organize Turkish national resistance against the Allies; there was unrest in Afghanistan, and there would shortly be full-scale rebellion in Mesopotamia. Britain no longer had the military strength to cope with all these crises simultaneously, confronted as she was by a still more serious crisis in Ireland and by the domestic clamour for accelerated demobilization.[30]

On September 15, Lloyd George revealed a plan based on the underlying principles of the Sykes–Picot Agreement, whereby Britain would immediately hand over to France military command in Cilicia, followed by its garrisons in western Syria. In the four towns of the Syrian interior which formed the backbone of the Arab state, he proposed that British troops transfer their garrisons to Faysal. Although Clemenceau's original demand that French troops be permitted to occupy both Lebanon and Syria had been reduced to the occupation of Lebanon alone, Britain at long last had been removed as a buffer between France and Faysal.[31]

Once Britain had withdrawn from Syria, Faysal had no choice but to negotiate exclusively with the French to maintain his government in Damascus. On a visit to London in October 1919, he was told at Whitehall that he must go to Paris alone and try to reach a "friendly agreement" with Clemenceau, for in all probability this would be his last opportunity for salvation. From the end of October until the new year, innumerable difficulties clouded the Paris discussions as Faysal sought an "honorable," face-saving solution. In early January, an agreement was reached which "recognized Syria's right to self-government and guaranteed its independence and territorial integrity" in return for Faysal's agreement to accept foreign assistance "exclusively from France."

France would handle Syria's foreign relations; French counsellors would help to organize all the civil and military administrations, including the treasury, police and army; France would have priority over all foreign powers in the award of economic concessions.[32]

[30] Andrew and Kanya-Forstner, *The Climax*, pp. 170–72, 200.

[31] Jukka Nevakivi, *Britain, France and the Arab Middle East, 1914–1920* (London, 1969), pp. 172–96; Kedourie, *England*, pp. 165–66.

[32] Andrew and Kanya-Forstner, *The Climax*, p. 204. For the text, see *Documents on British Foreign Policy, 1919–1939* (eds. E.L. Woodward and R. Butler). 1st series, IV (London, 1952), pp. 625–27.

Although this agreement was "honorable," given Faysal's weak bargaining position, it proved unacceptable both to his ultra-nationalist supporters back home and to the new government that replaced Clemenceau's later that month.

All along, the small but vocal colonial party had been calling for the military occupation of Syria and its unification under French rule. One of the most effective organizations pushing this line was the Lyons Chamber of Commerce which, like the Comité de l'Asie Française and other societies, had encouraged the French government before the war to establish economic and political footholds to demarcate Syria as an exclusive French preserve. Since October 1918, the Lyons Chamber—supported by the Council of the University of Lyons and the Rector of the University of St. Joseph in Beirut (a Jesuit institution with strong links to Lyons)— had campaigned intensely to prevent the Clemenceau government from forfeiting France's right to control the Syrian interior. Politicians and businessmen—mostly silk merchants, university officials, and Jesuits— formed a Comité lyonnais des intérêts français en Syrie which was primarily concerned with safeguarding the financial and educational investments of Lyons, most of which were concentrated in Beirut and Mount Lebanon. Although its principal motives for annexation were economic and moral, the Comité lyonnais couched its argument in a familiar nationalist idiom in the hope of attracting the attention of the French public. To protect French interests and to stem the rising tide of British influence in Syria, the interior had to be placed under direct French control. To check the spread of nationalism to French North Africa, the activities of the nationalist movement—centered in Damascus—had to be curtailed. To continue the advancement of French civilization in the Muslim world, French religious and cultural establishments had to take a more avid interest in Syria's Muslim population. In short, the Comité lyonnais argued that without a formal French presence in the Syrian interior France could never round off her Mediterranean policy, which was so vital to the preservation of a large chunk of her colonial empire.[33]

As long as Clemenceau directed Middle Eastern policy, the colonial party was insecure. Nonetheless, there were occasional moments when it felt that its ambitions might one day be realized. The removal of the British factor in the overall diplomatic equation in the fall of 1919 was a great relief. So was Clemenceau's appointment of Henri Gouraud in early October as High Commissioner of the French Republic in Syria and Commander of the Army of the Levant.[34] The choice of Gouraud, a respected

---

[33] Chevallier, "Lyon," pp. 305–11; also see Seurat, "Le rôle de Lyon."
[34] Chevallier, "Lyon," p. 312; Edmund Burke III, "A Comparative View of French Native Policy in Morocco and Syria, 1912–1925," *Middle Eastern Studies*, 9 (May 1973), p. 177.

general, close collaborator of Maréchal Lyautey in Morocco, and a devout Catholic, pleased all elements in the colonial party. Gouraud openly advocated a French military presence in the Syrian interior, he defended the French religious protectorate in Syria, and, above all, he promised to promote French, and specifically Lyons, commerce in Syria.[35] From the start, he used his new post in Beirut to facilitate the flow of French products to Syria. He shared the imperialist logic that French policy-makers had begun to apply to Syria just before the war, and he was convinced that the surest way to buttress French political influence was to trigger the development of stronger French commercial relations in the region. This would, in addition, reduce French economic dependence on Britain and America.[36] To help chart the course toward Damascus, Gouraud chose as his Secretary-General and chief political strategist, Robert de Caix.[37]

For the colonial party, the most encouraging sign of France's commitment to uphold her claim to Syria came when Clemenceau lost his bid in January 1920 for the French presidency and resigned as premier. The new prime minister, Alexandre Millerand, was a staunch nationalist regarding imperial issues and French policy vis-à-vis Britain, in spite of his socialist past. Moreover, he appointed Philippe Berthelot as secretary-general at the Quai d'Orsay.[38] Thus colonial fever had succeeded in infecting government, parliament, and a significant section of the French public by 1920, although it never reached epidemic proportions.

From the end of February till mid-April 1920, Millerand and Lloyd George, with the aid of Berthelot and Curzon, laid the groundwork for the decisions that were sanctioned by the Conference of San Remo. That it took a seemingly endless amount of time for the French and British governments to agree on mutually acceptable terms for the division of oil shares (France finally received a 23.75 percent share of Mosul oil) and for the revision of territorial boundaries, indicated a "hardening of the French attitude"[39] in the Middle East. France's attitude to Amir Faysal was even more rigid. Whereas Faysal had been able to negotiate directly with Clemenceau, Millerand, supported by Berthelot, purposely blocked all channels to a Franco-Syrian understanding. Even if Faysal could have

---

[35] Chevallier, "Lyon," pp. 312–13; also see *La Syrie et le Liban sous l'occupation et le Mandat français 1919–1927* (Paris, n.d.), p. 29.

[36] MAE, Syrie–Liban 1918–29. Gouraud to Millerand, 5 June 1920, vol. 47A, p. 17. Also see Général H.J.E. Gouraud, *La France en Syrie* (Corbeil, 1922).

[37] Andrew and Kanya-Forstner, *The Climax*, p. 202.

[38] Nevakivi, *Britain, France*, pp. 232–33, 237; *Journal Officiel* (28 March 1920), p. 267; FO 371/2541, vol. 5034. Derby to Curzon, 29 March 1920; Chevallier, "Lyon," pp. 315–16; Andrew and Kanya-Forstner, *The Climax*, p. 213.

[39] Nevakivi, *Britain, France*, p. 244.

convinced his suspicious nationalist supporters to moderate their opposition to the terms of his agreement with Clemenceau (although this seemed unlikely, for after his return to Damascus he became a captive of the extremist factions around him), the French government was never really prepared to accept any nationalist government in Damascus. With de Caix and Berthelot in charge, the Millerand government's strategy was designed to force Faysal into the arms of his extremist supporters and to resist the French. France would then have a suitable pretext for occupying Syria. This occurred more than a month before San Remo when the nationalist-dominated Syrian Congress in Damascus declared Syria an independent constitutional monarchy and Faysal King.

The Conference at San Remo in April 1920 "legalized the situation that had existed since the fulfillment of the agreement of September 1919, and transformed the demarcation lines between the British and the French occupation zones into political boundaries for future Mandates."[40] France was finally authorized by European consensus to take steps in the direction of Damascus. Preparations were made for the full-scale occupation of Syria at the earliest possible date. Not long after San Remo, Millerand and his political advisers, in conjunction with General Gouraud and de Caix, reached a final decision on the fate of the Arab government: it would be dismantled.

There were several immediate reasons underlying the French decision. In reaction to the San Remo decisions, King Faysal's government in Damascus became ardently anti-French. It increased its support to rebel bands composed of tribesmen and "military irregulars" which, since the end of 1919, had been harassing Christian areas in Lebanon known to be sympathetic to the French.[41] Meanwhile, throughout the region the economic situation was rapidly deteriorating. Business was practically at a standstill on the coast and in the interior. Emigration had reached alarming proportions, thousands having left the region during the previous four months.[42] The monetary system—based on the Egyptian pound which the British had imposed during the war—was neither favorable to French trade nor to the maintenance of an expensive army of occupation. In May, the French introduced a Syrian currency, issued by the French-owned *Banque de Syrie* and tied it to the franc. But merchants in Lebanon and Syria refused to adopt this new money and the Damascus government refused to accept the Syrian paper currency as "official exchange," issuing its own *dinar* instead.[43]

[40] *Ibid.*, p. 251.
[41] USNA, Syria. 800d. Beirut Consul to Bristol, 26 May 1920.
[42] *Ibid.*
[43] *Correspondance d'Orient* (30 May 1920), pp. 457, 505; Nevakivi, *Britain, France*, pp. 253–54.

Other problems testing French nerves included persistent attacks along the Aleppo–Rayak Railway, hindering the movement of French troops in northern Syria, and material assistance funnelled to rebel forces in northern Syria by Mustafa Kemal's Turkish nationalist movement.[44] Equally alarming was a noticeable decline in the level of French prestige among Christians in Lebanon, particularly among certain influential political and business leaders in Beirut who, in response to the deteriorating situation, came to believe that the French were prepared to sacrifice the interests of Lebanon for their own colonial ambitions. Many Christians were also angry that France had not fulfilled her promise to protect them against Muslim harassment.[45] Toward the end of May, several prominent Christian members of the Administrative Council of Beirut publicly advocated the complete independence of Lebanon and an economic union with Syria on the grounds that the region's division into two separate zones would be the economic and commercial ruin of both.[46]

French officials on the scene were alarmed. The prospects of Christians in Lebanon coming to terms with and falling under the influence of Damascus could only be prevented by unseating Faysal's government. The timing of the French decision to occupy Damascus was clearly based on Lebanese considerations. In the third week of July, General Gouraud gave Faysal an "ultimatum" that he must demobilize his army, recognize the French Mandate, and dismiss his extremist supporters or else he would be removed from Damascus. Even though Faysal reluctantly accepted the ultimatum, the French Army was already advancing. By July 25, Damascus had fallen into French hands and Faysal had to leave Syria for good. Although the idea of *la Syrie intégrale* was scrapped along the way, and although the vast majority of inhabitants of the region opposed the French coming, France had realized her claim to Syria.

FRANCE'S ASSUMPTION OF RULE in Syria may have eased the pain of a severely damaged national ego and obstructed what French policy-makers construed to be a devious plan to place the entire Arab East under British tutelage. But France also had other motives for seizing Syria that were not concerned with ephemeral morale-boosting or the stimulation of defensive reflexes each time Britain coughed. These concerned her special economic, political, and ecclesiastical interests in Syria, most of which had been articulated before the war. In 1920, France still had the largest

[44] Amin Sa'id, *al-Thawra al-'arabiyya al-kubra* (Cairo, 1934), vol. 2, p. 116.

[45] FO 371/6487, vol. 5120. Wratislaw (Beirut) to FO, 25 May 1920; USNA, Syria. 800d. Beirut Consul to Bristol, 26 May 1920, p. 2 and 890d.01/1, de Biller to Secretary of State, 29 March 1920.

[46] FO 371/6487, vol. 5120. Wratislaw to FO, 25 May 1920.

financial investments in Syria, with the preponderance of her capital concentrated in the banking, public utilities, and transportation sectors, and
in silk and tobacco production. French religious and educational investments were also considerable.

In addition to her consolidated prewar interests, France had additional
motives for occupying Syria which surfaced after 1914. These included
specific long-term strategic goals connected with the French position in
North Africa and new economic prospects in petroleum and cotton development.[47] After consolidating her North African Empire in 1912, France
became a serious competitor of Britain in the quest for strategic domination of the Mediterranean. French strategists had come to regard the
Mediterranean as the major "axis" of the French defense network, in
which North Africa was the cornerstone.[48] Together, Tunisia, Algeria,
and Morocco were the most populous French possessions. Nearly 75 percent of French Empire trade was with North Africa, 55 percent of this
trade with Algeria alone. Moreover, French investments in and trade
with North Africa expanded after the war. To guarantee the security of
this significant chunk of empire, France stationed one-quarter of her
standing military forces there.[49] What was missing, however, was a secure outpost in the eastern Mediterranean. The development of several
harbors on the Syrian coast as terminals for oil pipelines from northern
Iraq, as commercial outlets for Aleppo and central Syria, and for overland
trade from Iraq and Iran would round out her overall Mediterranean policy.[50]

But France's growing strategic interest in the Syrian coast during and
after the war was only the tip of the iceberg. French strategists believed
that without a stronghold in the interior, the French position from Alexandretta along the Syrian littoral to Tyre, where she had established a
military presence in 1919, would be continually threatened by the Arab
nationalist movement centered in Damascus and imbued with a mixture
of secular pan-Arab ideas and pan-Islamic zeal. By this time, the movement had advanced beyond the embryonic stage to be the dominant polit-

[47] *Journal Officiel*, Briand (28 March 1920), p. 67; FO 371/2541, File 5043. Derby to Curzon, 29 March 1920; E. Achard, "Etudes sur la Syrie et la Cilicie: Le coton en Cilicie et en
Syrie," *L'Asie Française (Documents économiques, politiques et scientifiques)*, no. 3 (June
1922), pp. 19–62 and 4 (July–Aug. 1922), pp. 65–113.

[48] On French strategy see Stephen H. Roberts, *A History of French Colonial Policy 1870–
1925* (London, 1929), p. 591. Among others, Flandin argued for the Mediterranean as the
axis. See *Journal Officiel*, Deputés, 6 April 1921.

[49] Elizabeth Monroe, *The Mediterranean in Politics* (London, 1938), p. 71; Jacques de
Monicault, *Le port de Beyrouth et l'économie des pays du Levant sous le mandat français*
(Paris, 1936), p. 102; Andrew and Kanya-Forstner, *The Climax*, p. 248.

[50] MD, 7N 4186, Dossier 6. Weygand to MAE, 10 Nov. 1924; Roberts, *A History*, pp.
591–92.

ical and ideological force in geographical Syria. To French policy-makers, Arab nationalism now threatened not only French financial and religious investments along the Syrian coast and in Mount Lebanon but, more importantly, French North Africa. To check the spread of nationalism, France had to establish hegemony over Damascus. Britain was already well-ensconced in Jerusalem and Cairo and only Damascus could serve French purposes adequately both in the Middle East and North Africa. It was revered as a cultural center of Islam and was the chief rallying point of eastern pilgrims bound for the Holy Cities.[51] Control of Damascus would increase France's prestige in her largely Muslim empire and thus its occupation became a strong factor in French imperial thinking.

Besides the strategic interest of Syria for French empire-builders, there were French financial and commercial interests, both established and potential. Of Syrian raw materials, silk[52] and cotton were of most interest to the French economy in 1920. Although cotton production in the Syrian interior had been close to nil for some time, French capitalists touted northern Syria as a potential French cotton plantation.[53] They were keen to develop new sources of cheap cotton so as to reduce French demand for United States imports, which now filled over 75 percent of French cotton demand.[54] This attitude was part of a growing postwar appeal-cum-"illusion" created above all by businessmen and politicians in the colonial party that the surest and quickest way to turn around a ravaged, war-weary economy was to develop the French Empire.[55] It was at this moment, when the colonial movement in France was enjoying its greatest popularity in years, that the fate of Syria was decided.

[51] MD, 16N 3201, Dossier 1, no. 97. *Note* of the Général Supérieur of the Jesuit Mission in Syria, 27 Oct. 1918; *ibid.*, 7N 4186, Dossier 10. "La France en Syrie vis-à-vis de l'Angleterre et de l'Italie (1927);" Monroe, *The Mediterranean*, p. 89; Burke, "A Comparative View," p. 176.

[52] Silk cocoon production had prospered in Mount Lebanon in the nineteeth century; but during the wartime famine, it had given way to food cultivation. After the war, Lyons' silk factories again encouraged production. But fashions had changed and rayon had been discovered. The French retarded Lebanon's economic development by encouraging a product that was no longer profitable while, if left to itself, Mount Lebanon would have continued its fruit and grain cultivation developed during wartime. See Chevallier, "Lyon," pp. 275–320 and Saba, "The Creation."

[53] Albert Khuri, "Agriculture," in Sa'id B. Himadeh (ed.), *Economic Organization of Syria* (Beirut, 1936), p. 79. In the Middle Ages Syria had been one of the world's important cotton producers.

[54] MAE, Syrie–Liban 1918–29. "Wilhelm Report," 19 Nov. 1923, vol. 339, p. 119. In 1921, the French colonies supplied less than one percent of cotton imported by mainland France.

[55] Andrew and Kanya-Forstner, *The Climax*, pp. 212, 226.

CHAPTER TWO

DISCORDANT RULE

A SMALL BUT TENACIOUS group of Frenchmen in government, politics, and business, whose influence over imperial issues was far out of proportion to its size, capitalized on the "defensive patriotism" wrought by World War I to commit France to the military occupation of Syria in 1920. But, seizing Syria by force was one thing; governing the country was quite another. The French spent an unhappy, unrewarding, and turmoil-filled quarter century in Syria because, unlike elsewhere in the French Empire, they were unable to devise an adequate formula for governing the country.

Why did France fail to come up with a consistent and effective policy in Syria? In part, France's failure was inherent in the very nature of her presence in Syria, based on an unbalanced composition of cultural, political, and economic interests. There were also the international restrictions imposed by that new, peculiar form of imperial control, the Mandate system. And, there was the growing force of nationalism which was more developed in Syria than anywhere else in the French Empire. There were reasons not essentially connected with Syria: the economic fragility of postwar France and the nature of French political life between the wars, in particular the weakness of shaky coalition governments and the corresponding strength of political lobbies like the colonial party. Above all, there was North Africa. Not only was every act of policy in Syria judged by its likely repercussions in North Africa, but the categories in terms of which the French understood Syria were drawn from their experience in North Africa.

BARRIERS TO AN IMPERIAL POLICY

The first and most obvious obstacle hindering the development of an imperial policy was the Mandate system itself. As a concession to postwar international consciousness embodied in Woodrow Wilson's "fourteen points" and in the League of Nations, the theory of Mandate[1] was devel-

---

[1] Several studies on the theoretical underpinnings of the Mandate system and its development were written in the 1920s and 1930s. One of the most outstanding from the point of view of international organization is Quincy Wright, *Mandates under the League of Nations* (Chicago, 1930). In addition, a plethora of studies from a juridicial perspective were published in France in this period on the application of the Mandate system to Syria and Lebanon. Among these are, O. Djabry, *La Syrie sous le régime du mandat* (Toulouse,

oped to dress up outright colonial expansion. The ultimate object of a
Mandate was to invest the mandatory power with the legal and moral
duty to lead backward nations to a higher level of civilization, whose
flower was independence and democracy. The mandatory power was to
exercise this duty in a spirit of disinterested goodwill toward the backward, not in the service of self-interest. However, there was a paradox
inherent in the application of the Mandate idea. Whereas both France and
Britain claimed their Mandates on the strength of their special interests,
they were nevertheless expected to carry out a mandatory role oblivious
to these interests.[2] Thus, from the beginning, mandatory policy was
schizophrenic: partially determined by the legal and moral conception of
Mandate and partially by self-interest. France was largely unsuccessful in
carrying out policies in either category.

A Mandate was neither a colony nor a protectorate, neither an Algeria
nor a Morocco. By definition it was "transitory."[3] It was to lead, eventually, to self-government. The realization that French rule in Syria was
finite detracted from Syria's initial attractiveness; Syria came to be regarded as a burden, even a source of embarrassment, a territory French
officials and investors eventually preferred to neglect.[4]

1934); A. Joffre, *Le mandat de la France sur la Syrie et le Grand-Liban* (Lyon, 1924); J. M.
Jones, *La fin du Mandat français en Syrie et au Liban* (Paris, 1939); Nadir Kuzbari, *La question de la cessation du Mandat français sur la Syrie* (Paris, 1937); J. Lapierre, *Le Mandat
français en Syrie* (Paris, 1937); P. LaMazière, *Partant pour la Syrie* (Paris, 1926);
R. O'Zoux, *Les états du Levant sous Mandat français* (Paris, 1931); E. Rabbath, *L'évolution politique de la Syrie sous mandat* (Paris, 1928). Several of the aforementioned studies
were dissertations written by Syrians at French universities.

[2] A complete text of "The Mandate for Syria and Lebanon, 24 July 1922" can be found in
Hourani, *Syria and Lebanon*, pp. 308–14. Among the most important Articles that required
France to ignore her special interests were 1, 4, and 11.

[3] For an "official" interpretation of how the French conceived of Mandate, Robert de Caix
is worth quoting: "The Mandate is a provisional system designed to enable populations
which, politically speaking, are still minors to educate themselves so as to arrive one day at
full self-government. . . . It is necessary . . . that the mandatory Power should be in a position not only to give advice but also to correct the working of the native governments and
even to make up for their deficiencies. I say 'make up for their deficiencies,' for one of the
most frequent situations which may have to be faced in these countries is that the governments do not fulfill their essential duties within a reasonable period of time." PMC, *Minutes*, 8/6/503, 19 Feb. 1926.

[4] Thirty years after the termination of the Mandate, French historians still seem to be
embarrassed! There are few critical, detailed examinations of France's Mandate policy and
experience in Syria and Lebanon. A former French adviser to the Syrian Ministry of Public
Instruction during the Mandate claims that critical studies have not been written by French
scholars because they find it extremely difficult to say anything important about something
so haphazardly devised and inconsistent as French Mandate policy in Syria. He also asserted
that French historians have hidden behind the fact that the archives of the Ministère des
Affaires Etrangères in Paris have until recently been closed for the Mandate period. Con-

There were also insurmountable economic and financial barriers in France itself which made her presence in the Levant all the more awkward and insecure. The material and psychological costs of World War I had been great. The war had decimated France's male population and had destroyed or absorbed a large share of her fixed capital. The inflationary methods used to finance the war and the ensuing period of reconstruction increased France's long-term debt and created a continuous crisis of monetary instability. The French nation emerged from the war not only with a "defeatist" mentality but with a "restrictionist" one as well. The view that it was necessary to "hang on to what had been acquired but not to take risks in order to secure a larger but uncertain return on the future"[5] dominated. Syria was not a resource-rich area and given France's postwar economic plight, the amount of capital required to develop Syria and to buttress the French presence there was simply not available. In time, even those colonialist groups who in 1920–21 linked the reconstruction of the French economy with the development of the empire began to see the light. At most, the French would have to be highly selective in their choice of investments. Self-interest dictated that the little capital available for Syria should be concentrated on extracting the few available raw materials demanded by the vanguard sectors of the French economy or on supporting enterprises with guaranteed returns, like public utilities.

Political conflicts and divisions in France also placed constraints on investment in Syria. The interwar years were plagued by fierce ideological struggles between political parties and coalitions on the Right and Left; between generals and politicians, colonialists and anti-colonialists, clericalists and anti-clericalists. Between 1920 and 1940, the office of Premier changed hands no less than 33 times and was filled by 19 different men. At the Quai d'Orsay, responsible for French Mandates, 14 different men became Foreign Minister. French policy in Syria could not but be affected by the frequent political shifts in Paris. Not surprisingly, it lacked rhythm and continuity.

French political conflicts determined, among other things, the annual budget of the High Commission. Even before the French had pacified Syria, there were pressures to reduce French responsibilities in the country. The extreme Left wanted a complete evacuation.[6] More moderate anti-clerical and "restrictionist" parties maintained that France's special

---

versation with Jean Gaulmier (Paris, 7 March 1977). Gaulmier was one of the most sensitive and astute observers of Syrian society and politics in the early 1930s.

[5] On the massive human and material losses suffered by France during World War I, see Tom Kemp, *The French Economy 1913–39. The History of a Decline* (London, 1972), pp. 14, 59, 60–61, 66–82, 165–66; M. Huber, *La population de la France pendant la guerre* (Paris, 1931).

[6] Roberts, *French Colonial Policy*, p. 593; *L'Humanité* (26 July 1920); FO 371/11619, File 645. Hardinge (Paris) to Curzon, 21 Oct. 1920.

interests in Syria—on which she based her claim to be there in the first place—were too paltry to warrant the large expenditures that colonial groups and the High Commissioner were lobbying for in 1920–21. Although a complete withdrawal was out of the question, owing to French commitments in Syria and France's wider Muslim policy, moderates did not hesitate to attack the Millerand government for committing the French nation to expensive and profitless schemes in Syria.[7]

Nonetheless, the French government stood firm in its conviction that French interests in Syria went beyond moral obligations to a backward people; of vital importance was the preservation and expansion of current strategic and economic investments. But radical differences of opinion were bound to take their toll. The government, unable to persuade the French Senate that it actually had an imperial policy in Syria, had to accept gradual but successive reductions in financial credits for Syria.[8]

Between the two world wars, France concentrated her strategic and military energy in the western Mediterranean and buttressed her position in North Africa. She failed, however, to round-out her overall Mediterranean policy. True, she expanded her financial and cultural investments in the Levant, developed important air and wireless communications with the Far East, and protected the Tripoli terminus of the oil pipeline from Kirkuk in Iraq, which supplied over 40 percent of French oil needs by the mid-1930s. But she never built a naval base east of Tunisia.[9] French strategists came to dismiss the eastern Mediterranean as relatively unimportant for French security needs. Instead, they were preoccupied after World War I with the "threat" of a German *revanche*. Hence, the focus of French strategy was on strengthening French defensive capabilities on the Maginot Line and in the western Mediterranean. This new strategic calculation was based on one crucial factor—Britain. A French naval stronghold in the eastern Mediterranean was not vital, so long as Britain, with her overwhelming naval strength in the eastern Mediterranean, remained a staunch ally.[10] This shift in strategic priorities first became apparent in 1921, when France ceded Cilicia to Turkey.[11]

JUST AS THE SYRIAN littoral proved to be a strategic superfluity, so too did Syria prove to be an economic disappointment. Even before World War I,

[7] Roberts, *French Colonial Policy*, p. 593; *Le Temps* (26 July 1920).

[8] FO 371/3622, vol. 7845. Hardinge (Paris) to FO, 4 April 1922.

[9] Monroe, *The Mediterranean*, pp. 75–76.

[10] *Ibid.*, pp. 75-76, 79. By 1937, France had invested approximately 26 billion francs in Egypt.

[11] Interestingly, the major opponents of this strategic school of thought were headed by General Maxime Weygand who was the second High Commissioner in Syria and Lebanon (1923–24). *Ibid.*, p. 76; MD, 7N 4186, Dossier 6. Weygand to MAE, 10 Nov. 1924.

France ranked behind Britain, Austria, and Egypt in exports to Syria and second only to Egypt, although well ahead of Britain in imports from Syria.[12] Because Syria in late Ottoman times produced only humble surpluses for export, mainly raw materials, the comparatively self-sufficient French economy looked more to Syria as a market for manufactured goods than as a source of raw materials.[13] This pattern became even clearer after France received her Mandate.

Between the wars, the French capitalized on their physical presence in Syria and Lebanon to become the biggest overall trader in these territories, just nudging out Britain. But even so, in 1933, midway through the Mandate, France had only a 14 percent share of Syria's foreign trade. She only took a 7.5 percent share of Syria's total exports and ranked a distant second to Palestine which absorbed 21 percent. And whereas she now ranked first in total exports to Syria, her share of the market was only 17 percent,[14] a share that dropped after 1933, owing in large part to the significant increase in the import of Japanese goods into Syria.[15]

French trade with Syria in the interwar period grew more slowly than

[12] E. Weakley, "Report on the Conditions and Prospects of British Trade in Syria," Great Britain, *Accounts and Papers*. 1911. LXXXVII, in Charles Issawi (ed.), *The Economic History of the Middle East 1800–1914* (Chicago, 1966), pp. 278–79. The rankings are for the year 1908.

[13] Mohammad Thomé, *Le rôle du crédit dans le développement économique de la Syrie* (Madrid, 1953); Norman Burns and Allen D. Edwards, "Foreign Trade," in Saʿid B. Himadeh (ed.), *Economic Organization of Syria* (Beirut, 1936), pp. 229–30.

[14] These percentages have been calculated using Syria's foreign trade statistics found in: Haut-Commissariat de la République Française en Syrie et au Liban, *Statistique générale du commerce extérieur des Etats du Levant sous Mandat français, 1931–1933* (Beirut, 1934); Burns and Edwards, "Foreign Trade," pp. 231–54. It must be added that servicing a large army of occupation helped to inflate French import percentages, although eventually the French army did make efforts to purchase goods on the local market. Moreover, it was only during the depression years that France finally overtook Britain once and for all as the leading exporter to Syria. Before 1930 their rankings changed regularly. See *Bulletin Economique Trimestriel (Syrie-Liban)*. First Quarter (1927); FO 371/3427, vol. 12306. Hole to Department of Overseas Trade, 10 July 1927. By comparison, Britain's share of Iraq's total imports was significantly higher than France's share of Syria's total imports. Britain's share between 1925 and 1932 was 31.5 percent, while between 1933 and 1939 it was 29.0 percent. See Hanna Batatu, *The Old Social Classes and the Revolutionary Movements of Iraq* (Princeton, 1978), p. 270.

[15] For example, Japan, in 1933–34, showed a gain in value of her total trade with Syria of 19 percent, enough of an increase to displace Britain as Syria's second leading trading partner after France. Japan's share of Syria's total imports rose from 7 to 11.5 percent while Britain's rose from 10 to 11 percent at this time. On the other hand, the French share dropped in the same period from 17 to 16 percent of total Syrian imports. FO 371/4188, vol. 19023. Harvard to FO, 21 June 1935. On the issue of the so-called Japanese "dumping" in Syria in the 1930s, see Hiroshi Shimizu, "The Mandatory Power and Japan's Trade Expansion into Syria in the Inter-war Period," *Middle Eastern Studies*, 21 (April 1985), pp. 152–171.

French trade with the rest of the Empire.[16] Moreover, although France was the biggest overall trader with Syria and manipulated Mandate regulations to favor French transactions over others, the total value of this trade was minuscule, both in relative and absolute terms. When compared with French North Africa or, for that matter, with French Indochina, Syria looked like a commercial backwater. For example, the value of French exports to Morocco was four times greater than it was to Syria, while the value of French imports from Morocco was 18 times greater than it was from Syria (see Table 2-1).[17]

On the eve of World War I, France was the largest single investor in Syria, although her commerical relations with the Levant were not as extensive as were Britain's. It is estimated that by 1914 the French had invested some 200 million francs in the region, mainly in public utilities, railroads, and silk and tobacco production.[18] In the interwar period, they invested an additional one billion francs, monopolizing investment

TABLE 2-1
France's Commerce with Her Empire, 1933

Territory	French exports (in millions of francs)	French imports (in millions of francs)	Terms of Trade
Algeria	3,305	3,858	0.9
Tunisia	665	450	1.5
Morocco	584	465	1.3
Indochina	443	582	0.8
A.O.F.	215	376	0.6
Madagascar	221	261	0.8
Syria/Lebanon	152	26	5.8
Other Colonies and African Mandates	404	702	0.6

SOURCE: Jacques de Monicault, *Le port de Beyrouth et l'économie des pays du Levant sous le mandat français* (Paris, 1936), p. 102.

[16] De Monicault, *Le port de Beyrouth,* p. 102.

[17] *Ibid.*; Royal Institute of International Affairs, *The French Colonial Empire.* Information Department Papers, no. 25 (London, 1940), pp. 18, 39–40; John P. Halstead, *Rebirth of a Nation. The Origins and Rise of Moroccan Nationalism, 1912–1944* (Cambridge, Mass., 1967), p. 94.

[18] Badr al-Din al-Siba'i, *Adwa' 'ala al-rasmal al-ajnabi fi suriyya 1850–1958* (Damascus, 1968), pp. 35–36; Howard M. Sachar, *Europe Leaves the Middle East, 1936-1954* (New York, 1972), p. 7.

there.[19] Three-quarters of this new investment was placed in the banking sector, whose main function was to finance French exports and imports; another fifth was placed in public utilities such as electricity and tramways.[20] But, one billion francs was a drop in the bucket when compared to French investment in North Africa, where they placed most of their capital, or even in Egypt, where, by 1937, 17 billion francs had been invested in the Suez Canal Company alone.[21] Moreover, to protect a few valuable interests in Syria and Lebanon, like air and wireless communications and oil,[22] France plowed more than four billion francs into unproductive military expenditure by 1939. In financial terms, Syria was clearly more of a liability than an asset to France.[23]

One possible French venture, the expansion of cotton production, was projected onto Syria after France gave up her claim to Cilicia in 1921, in return for the cessation of Turkish activities in northern Syria. Nevertheless, the Union Economique de Syrie, an association of 75 French banks, joint-stock companies, and chambers of commerce dedicated to the "defense and development of the agricultural, commercial and industrial interests" of France in Syria, financed a feasibility study which concluded in 1922 that the plains of northern Syria and the Territory of the Alawites contained 300,000 hectares of irrigated land on which cotton could be cultivated.[24] The *Union's* report unambiguously stated that the extension of

[19] Al-Siba'i, *Adwa'*, p. 148; Adnan Farra, *L'industrialisation en Syrie* (Geneva, 1950); al-Nayal, "Industry," p. 75.

[20] Farra, *L'industrialisation*; al-Nayal, "Industry," Table 7, p. 148. Two percent of French capital was placed in ports and customs warehouses; 1.5 percent in railroads; 3 percent in diverse holdings such as a radio station, hotels, asphalt and petroleum companies.

[21] Andrew and Kanya-Forstner write that "between 1914 and 1940 the amount of French capital invested in the Empire, the bulk of it in North Africa, increased fourfold, and the Empire's share of total French foreign investment grew from 9 percent to perhaps 45 percent." *The Climax*, p. 248. They base this on information provided in J. Marseille, "L'investissement français dans l'Empire colonial: l'enquête du gouvernement de Vichy (1943)," *Revue Historique*, 122 (1974), pp. 409–32. Apart from French capital, the only other significant amounts of foreign capital invested in Syria before World War II were British (Iraq Petroleum Company) and Italian (Banco di Roma). Al-Nayal, "Industry," pp. 75–76. The most important French enterprise constructed in Syria before 1928 was a large flour mill in the Maydan quarter of Damascus (Société Meunière du Levant) at a cost of 7 million francs. Its capital was 5 million francs. MAE, Syrie–Liban 1918–29. Lucien Baumann to Jouvenel, 21 Nov. 1925, vol. 394, pp. 79–81.

[22] J. Henry-Haye and Pierre Viénot, *Les relations de la France et de la Syrie* (Paris, 1939), p. 22.

[23] Actually, by 1936 the Mandate had cost France 4.843 billion francs of which 4.3 billion went to military expenditure and 543 million to civil expenditure. There are no accurate figures for how much of the civil expenditure went into capital goods, though it is unlikely that it could have been a very high percentage. As for private investment from France, by 1939, 1.1 billion had been invested in Syria and Lebanon. Hourani, *Syria and Lebanon*, p. 155; A. Farra, *L'industrialisation*.

[24] MAE, Syrie–Liban 1918–29. Gouraud to Poincaré, 29 June 1922, vol. 339, pp. 10–11;

cotton production in these regions would serve the interests of French industry and would also contribute to the revival of the stagnant Syrian economy.[25]

The following year, the High Commission conducted two studies which supported the conclusions of the Union Economique de Syrie and suggested programs of scientific research into cotton production for export. The development of the ʿAmq plain, which contained nearly 60,000 hectares, was to be the starting point.[26] The High Commission suggested that since this land was largely state-owned, it could be sold at the dirt-cheap price of 30 francs per hectare to a French concessionary company. As for local landowners, they would not hesitate to let a French company develop their lands if the price was right. Furthermore, Armenian refugees from Cilicia with previous experience in cotton cultivation would be a valuable labor source.[27] Citing these different reports, High Commissioner Weygand urged the Poincaré government to promote French investment in Syrian cotton. Otherwise, Weygand argued, cotton development would fall into the hands of the British, the Italians, or the Americans who, under the Mandate Charter, were equally entitled to concessions in Syria.[28] Meanwhile, Weygand sent an emissary to France to drum up support in banking and industrial circles.[29] There, Auguste Terrier, head of the Union Economique de Syrie, was already acting as the High Commissioner's unofficial lobby at the Quai d'Orsay. Terrier was a French capitalist, a longtime member of the Comité de l'Asie Française, and intimately associated with the Lyons-Marseilles group of businessmen involved in Syria.[30]

The initial response to Weygand's campaign was positive. By 1924, French capital had begun to penetrate the Syrian cotton sector, especially in the Aleppo province. By the end of the following year cotton produc-

FO 371/9566, vol. 7848. Palmer (Damascus) to FO, 23 Aug. 1922. The Union's members included the *Banque de Syrie*, the *Crédit Foncier d'Algérie et de Tunisie*, the *Banque Française de Syrie*, the *Compagnie des Messageries Maritimes*, the *Compagnie Générale des Colonies*, the *Société du Chemin de Fer de Damas-Hamah & Prolongements*, the *Crédit Foncier de Syrie*, the *Compagnie Française du Levant*, the *Consortium Franco-Syrien*, the *Banque Impériale Ottomane*, the *Société Cotonnière d'Adana*, the *Société Française de Sériculture*, the *Compagnie d'Entreprises de Cilicie*, the *Société Anonyme Ottomane des Tramways Libannais*, and the *Association des Commerçants et Industriels du Levant*. This land was located in the plains of ʿAkkar, Ghab, and ʿAmq.

25 FO 371/9566, vol. 7848. Palmer (Damascus) to FO, 23 Aug. 1922.
26 MAE, Syrie–Liban 1918–29. "Achard Report," 9 June 1923; "Wilhelm Report," 19 Nov. 1923, vol. 339, pp. 63–68, 92–119.
27 *Ibid.*
28 MAE, Syrie–Liban 1918–29. Weygand to Poincaré, 3 Dec. 1923, vol. 339, pp. 83–84.
29 *Ibid.*
30 MAE, Syrie–Liban 1918–29. Gouraud to Poincaré, 29 June 1922, vol. 339, pp. 10–11; FO 371/9566, vol. 7848. Palmer (Damascus) to FO, 23 Aug. 1922.

tion in Syria had increased by 25 percent.[31] But for the next few years, both cotton production and the area under cotton cultivation were reduced significantly; indeed, it was not until the late 1930s that Syrian production advanced beyond the 1925 level of 3,100 tons.[32] The great future of cotton production after the loss of Cilicia was never fulfilled. Reasons for this failure included inefficiency in the High Commission's organization of local production and the world depression of the early 1930s, which hurt Syria's processed raw materials, particularly cotton and silk because they were "distinct" market products which tended to suffer with the fall in world market prices.[33] Even though cotton (but not silk) production recovered after the depression and reached new heights by World War II, French demand for cotton (like silk) had already begun to decline, owing to the growth of the French synthetics industry. Although Syrian cotton production increased after 1935, the French share of Syrian cotton exports actually decreased.[34] Cotton may have helped to whet France's appetite for Syria, but long before the French abandoned Syria that appetite had been satisfied.

EXTERNAL STRUCTURAL BARRIERS were not the only factors which prevented France from developing a balanced policy in Syria. The very conception of her task and the policy devised to fit it were predicated on a historic misreading of the country, its social composition, and the customs and values of its people. The French continued mistakenly to assume that they had a strong grasp on Syrian reality when in fact their understanding of the nature, aims, and aspirations of Syrian society remained grossly defective. In particular, France underestimated and misinterpreted Arab nationalism.

[31] *International Cotton Bulletin*, 17 (April 1939), p. 304; Sir Alexander Gibb and Partners, *Economic Development of Syria* (London, 1947), p. 24. The Aleppo province, which contained 84 percent of Syria's cultivated lands for cotton production, produced 73 percent of Syria's total cotton production. See FO 371/451, vol. 10850. Beirut Consul to FO, 9 Jan. 1925.

[32] Izzat Traboulsi, *L'agriculture syrienne entre les deux guerres* (Beirut, 1948), p. 156; Khuri, "Agriculture," pp. 79, 83; *International Cotton Bulletin*, 17 (April 1939), p. 304; MAE, *Rapport à la Société des Nations sur la situation de la Syrie et du Liban, 1931–1933*.

[33] MAE, Syrie–Liban 1918–29. High Commissioner's "Report," May 1929, vol. 340, pp. 184–94; Khuri, "Agriculture," p. 80; Great Britain: Department of Overseas Trade, *Report on Economic and Commercial Conditions in Syria and Lebanon (June 1936)*, G. T. Havard (London, 1936), p. 18.

[34] The great depression hit French textile industries hard between 1929 and 1932. In all, French exports of textiles fell by nearly 80 percent in this period; cotton exports fell by 65 percent. In Syria, raw cotton production fell by 82 percent in the same period. Kemp, *French Economy*, pp. 92–93; George Hakim, "Industry," in Sa'id B. Himadeh (ed.), *Economic Organization of Syria* (Beirut, 1936), p. 143.

The French attitude toward Arab nationalism during the Mandate was based on an unsophisticated perception the French had been nurturing over the past one hundred years, itself derived from the strikingly uneven composition of French interests in the region.

First, there was the belief that Arab nationalism at its core was Muslim fanaticism bent on obstructing the spread of Western civilization and progress in the East, whose animating force was France. Underlying this belief was a view of Syrian society as a crazy quilt of religious and ethnic communities, a "mosaic of races and religions." This emphasis on minorities allowed the French to develop ideal types for each community, often framed in terms of an ability to wage war, or loyalty, intelligence, and discipline, or the absence of these qualities. The French did not conceal their preference for Christians above Muslims and for the mountain minorities (Maronites, Alawites, Druzes, and Turcomans) above the majority Sunni Arabs of the coast, desert, and cities. Coastal peoples and townsmen were, in comparison with mountain communities, physically mediocre, less intelligent, fanatic, and untrustworthy.[35] Unlike the British, whose political strategy was to cultivate the Sunni Muslim establishment in the towns, the French preferred to fall back on their influence with certain minorities. Naturally, their abandonment of the Syrian nationalist movement in 1914 did not endear them to Muslim political forces in the interior towns or, for that matter, in Beirut.

Another view of Arab nationalism stemmed from French Anglophobia. The French postulated that Britain encouraged, if not inspired, Arab nationalism and helped to translate it into a political movement in order to weaken French influence in the Arab East and eventually to drive the French out of the region altogether. In the French view, Britain surrounded Syria with Hashemite thrones, pushed a Hashemite for the Caliphate, and promoted Zionist expansion, all to curtail and threaten French influence. Anglophobia was particularly virulent during the first seven years of the French Mandate, but was then latent until the Second World War. That British activities in the Middle East stimulated French Anglophobia in the early twenties and again during World War II is certain. And not surprisingly, these were the same periods when the colonial party in France exercised its greatest influence over its government's foreign policy.

The third and perhaps most alarming French view of Arab nationalism pictured it as an infectious disease spreading to North Africa and menacing French rule in this most valuable part of the empire. The small but vocal combination of business groups, politicians, and foreign office offi-

[35] MD, 7N 4192. "Manuel Colonial, 1923–1925"; *ibid.*, 7N 4181. A. Dreik to Maréchal d'Esperry, 22 Nov. 1930.

cials pushing for a strong French presence in Syria found this last view
the easiest to propagate with the French public.

There was at least one reflective French view[36] of Arab nationalism
which gained currency in the 1930s: Albert Hourani has called it "enlightened imperialism."[37] Some left-of-center parties posited that the
ideology of Arab nationalism was destined to triumph in Syria and in
other Arab territories under foreign rule and that therefore France ought
to accommodate it under a benevolent Mandate regime. In this way, it
could be contained and its form and direction could be specified. Idealists
aimed to render nationalism sympathetic to France while skeptics felt the
best that could be achieved would be to render it benign. One variant of
this enlightened approach emphasized the need to promote an independent Syrian national identity which would reduce the threat to French interests of a larger Arab national identity. French High Commissioner
Maxime Weygand, among others, hoped "to create a Syrian nationalism
which would radiate around" that which is "historic, religious" and
[around] "Damascus." He believed that such a Syrian national identity
would weaken the force of Arab nationalism and would resemble developments in Egypt and Turkey, both of which were asserting their own
national identities.[38]

Unfortunately, Weygand seems to have developed his ideas on the eve
of his departure from Syria in late 1924. French policy-makers in general
continued to regard nationalism as more harmful than useful. It was little
more than a combat weapon to be wielded against France. The dominant
view of Arab nationalism as Muslim fanaticism manipulated from behind
the scenes by the British and capable of infecting the Muslim populations
in French North Africa prevailed. This was translated into a policy of direct confrontation with Arab nationalism; if Arab nationalism could be
isolated and disarmed then it could be completely ignored.[39]

In Syria, the French response to Arab nationalism was doomed to fail.

[36] Another view of course was that held by the extreme Left, and particularly the French
Communist Party, which suggested that bourgeois nationalist movements in Asia struggling against colonialism should be cautiously supported. This fit communist stage theory
of a bourgeois democratic revolution on the road to socialism. See Alec Gordon, "The Theory of the 'Progressive' National Bourgeoisie," *Journal of Contemporary Asia*, 3 (1973), pp.
192–203.

[37] Hourani, *Syria and Lebanon*, p. 168.

[38] MD, 7N 4186, Dossier 6. Weygand to MAE, 10 Nov. 1924. A similar approach was
suggested in *ibid.*, 7N 4186, Dossier 4. Service des Renseignements, "Les dangers présents
de l'Islam," Beirut, 25 Sept. 1921.

[39] Anon., "Etude sur les possibilités actuelles de la politique syrienne." Unpublished secret French report, found in the ʿAdil al-ʿAzma Papers [Syria], File 3/101. 1 Nov. 1937, pp.
11–13. Institute for Palestine Studies, Beirut; MD, 7N 4184, Dossier 2. "*Questions de
Syrie*, Etat major de l'Armée," 2ᵉ Bureau. 22 Feb. 1922 and 4 March 1922.

Despite the rather poor ideological articulation of Arab nationalism (which certainly contributed to France's underestimation), it represented something attractive, almost seductive, to an increasingly wide segment of Syrian society; more so than the French either realized or were willing to acknowledge. Because they grossly underestimated its appeal, ironically they ended up fostering, rather than retarding, the nationalist movement.

THE MOROCCAN FORMULA

Because of the uncertainty and ambiguity of the Mandate idea and because the League of Nations did not formalize the Mandate system until 1922, the French preferred to look to their past experiences in colonial administration for a formula with which to rule their most recent acquisition. Only one experience seemed applicable to Syria: French native policy in Morocco.

Morocco was the last predominantly Arab Muslim territory to fall within the orbit of French colonization before the First World War. In 1912, France negotiated a treaty of protectorate which placed Morocco under an internationally recognized French administration; in the process she consolidated her North African Empire. The advent of the Moroccan Protectorate marked, in practical terms, the triumph of a new and more progressive theory of colonial rule, *association*, at the expense of the old Eurocentric theory of *assimilation*. Rule by association meant the sharing of functions between European and native and, at least in theory, the development of colonial policy mainly along native lines.[40] Under assimilation, Europeans ruled directly and the development of policy was strictly along European lines.[41] It so happened that many Frenchmen first sent out to administer France's Mandate for Syria and Lebanon had previously served in Morocco. Because their experience in "Islam's westernmost outpost" had generally been satisfactory, if not rewarding, it was not surprising that they applied what they had learned in Morocco to the Syrian situation.[42]

The system developed for administering the Arab Muslim population

[40] For a critique of this theory, see Roberts, *French Colonial Policy*, pp. 110–23, and Raymond F. Betts, *Assimilation and Association in French Colonial Theory, 1890–1914* (New York, 1961).

[41] Simply put, *assimilation* means the "assimilation of the natives to French citizens, assimilation of a colonial economic organization to that of France, and . . . assimilation of political organization to that of a French *département*." According to Roberts, by 1905, the failure of *assimilation* as a theory and as a "means of actual administration" was already perceptible. But only with the Moroccan Protectorate was an adequate substitute implemented, i.e., administration by *association*. *French Colonial Policy*, pp. 27–29.

[42] A penetrating analysis of the influence of French native policy in Morocco on policy in Syria during the early Mandate can be found in Burke, "A Comparative View," pp. 175–86.

of Morocco was very much identified with one man, General (later Maréchal) Louis-Hubert Lyautey (1854–1934), the most revered and influential French colonial administrator of all time.[43]

Lyautey described the system he developed for governing Morocco

> as the economic and moral penetration of a people, not by subjection
> to our forces or even to our liberties, but by a close association, in
> which we administer them in peace by their own organs of govern-
> ment and according to their own customs and laws.[44]

This system put a premium on the "subtle exploitation of the strengths
and weaknesses" of native society, respect for local religion, customs, and
law,[45] rule through native institutions, and economic (though not necessarily industrial) development.[46] It achieved considerable success in Morocco, particularly during World War I when France could not afford, financially or militarily, to reinforce her position there.[47] Considering
French financial constraints and manpower shortages after the war, indirect colonial rule seemed to be a ready-made formula for administering
France's new outpost in the eastern Mediterranean.

The Lyautey system rested on a handpicked elite corps of French native
affairs officers with knowledge of Arabic and/or Berber, and of the Islamic
religion, culture, and customs. These officers were, in theory, equipped
to recognize and exploit the political, social, and ethnic divisions in Morocco and to pacify large areas of the country without resorting to force.
The French predicated their Moroccan policy on a subtle wooing of potentially cooperative elements from among the traditional urban and tribal
elites. Material benefits were the bait. These allies could then be used
against hostile and uncompromising leaders and groups. The colonial
army was to be employed as a coercive force only when other methods of
persuasion had failed; its ubiquity, however, was a constant reminder
that cooperation with the French was better than resistance.[48]

The establishment of the French Mandate in Syria was contingent
upon weakening Arab nationalism, as was the maintenance of French rule
in North Africa. French experience in Morocco offered three specific
strategies which, if skillfully applied, could help to mollify widespread

[43] Lyautey's previous colonial posts were, for the most part, in Muslim-inhabited territories. Roberts, *French Colonial Policy*, pp. 558–59.

[44] Lyautey, Introduction to "Rapport général sur la situation du Protectorat du Maroc au
31 juillet 1914" (1916), cited by Roberts, *French Colonial Policy*, p. 566.

[45] Burke, "A Comparative View," p. 176.

[46] *Association*, in theory and in practice, showed a strong tendency toward orienting colonies as producers of manufactured goods for export. See J. L. de Lanessan, *La Tunisie*, 2nd
ed. (Paris, 1917), pp. 182–84.

[47] Burke, "A Comparative View," p. 176.

[48] *Ibid.*, p. 177.

antagonism to the occupation of Syria and to buttress French rule in the country, all at the expense of the nationalist movement. These strategies were the exploitation of minority differences through the establishment of autonomously administered zones in Syria; the pitting of rural areas against nationalist centers; and the use of malleable elements from the traditional Syrian political elite to help govern.[49]

TERRITORIAL PARTITION

The official partition of geographical Syria in 1920 into separately administered Mandates under French and British supervision isolated a truncated Syria and surrounded it by artificial boundaries and customs barriers which obstructed the free passage of goods and people. The people of Aleppo were cut off from their natural hinterland in Turkey and Iraq while Damascenes had to cross a policed border into Palestine. But the carving up of geographical Syria was only the first stage of the partition process. Once the French seized their share of the pie, they immediately sought to divide it into even smaller pieces in order to isolate and contain the Arab nationalist movement.

To begin with, Greater Lebanon—the Maronite dream—was finally realized. At the end of August 1920, the French decreed the new state of Lebanon. It comprised, in addition to the largely Christian mountain, the predominantly Muslim coastal cities of Tripoli, Sidon, and Tyre and their administrative hinterlands, the capital Beirut, with a population nearly evenly mixed between Christians and Muslims, and the fertile, largely Muslim-inhabited Biqaʿ Valley. Most of Lebanon's newly acquired "citizens" did not want to be part of a Maronite-dominated Lebanon and agitated for union with the rest of Syria. Although the inclusion of these areas was perhaps necessary to make a territorially and economically viable unit, it hardly contributed to political viability. The creation of Greater Lebanon did more than pass the reins of government to a minority ruling group; it also perpetuated Maronite dependency on French support to remain in power.

The Lebanese spent most of their time under French tutelage in sectarian bargaining for political power in government institutions. Because the French were partial to the Maronites and other Uniates, other sects naturally formed an anti-French, anti-Maronite alliance. Yet, the French did not want to exclude the Muslims from participating in the Lebanese government. After all, the separate existence of Lebanon depended on Lebanese Muslim acceptance. By the mid-1930s, Lebanese Muslim leaders were willing to take part in the political haggling designed to lay down

[49] *Ibid.*, p. 182.

the rules of confessional office-holding in the country. Although their rhetoric still focused on a Lebanese union with Syria, Muslim politicians had come to appreciate that, whereas they might be of first-rate importance in Lebanon, in a greater Syria they would at best be second-rate next to political leaders from Damascus and Aleppo. So these politicians, true to the traditions of the urban notability, rallied mass support by advocating union with Syria, but used this support as a tool to gain political leverage within the Lebanese arena.[50] Concurrently, the burgeoning Muslim and Christian mercantile bourgeoisie in Beirut was won over to the idea of Greater Lebanon to protect its economic interests.[51] But France's favoritism toward Greater Lebanon exacerbated the anti-French sentiments of the Syrian nationalist movement.

In the rest of Syria, France followed a policy of divide and rule, atomizing the territory along regional and ethnic lines. In emphasizing communal differences and aspirations, the French claimed to be bowing to political reality and popular desire. However, their interpretation of political reality conveniently fit their desire to weaken pan-Syrian sentiment and Arab nationalism, and to strengthen French rule by courting potentially Francophile minorities.

During the Mandate years, the French put Syria through several legal and territorial permutations in a bid to keep the country from uniting politically. They created the two separate states of Damascus and Aleppo in 1920 out of the two former Ottoman provinces. Both were ruled by a local governor supported by French advisers (*conseillers*). Within the Aleppo state, the Sanjak of Alexandretta, with its significant Turkish population, enjoyed a largely autonomous administration. The still sparsely-settled northeastern region around Dayr al-Zur was nominally in Aleppo's orbit. The Damascus state included the districts of Homs and Hama. In 1922, the Jabal Druze was proclaimed a separate unit under French protection, with its own governor and elected congress. The mountain districts behind Latakia, with their large Alawite population, became a special administrative regime under heavy French protection and was proclaimed a state. Meanwhile, the desert tribes of Syria, particularly those of the remote northeast, were placed under the military authority

[50] On the attitude of Lebanese Muslims to the idea of an independent Lebanon and the relationship between Lebanon and Syria during the Mandate see Najla Wadih Atiyah, "The Attitude of the Lebanese Sunnis Towards the State of Lebanon," Ph.D. Dissertation (University of London, 1973). For the Mandate period, see pp. 38–178.

[51] See Atiyah, "The Attitude of the Lebanese Sunnis," pp. 80–104; Michael Johnson, "Confessionalism and Individualism in Lebanon: A Critique of Leonard Binder (ed.), *Politics in Lebanon*, John Wiley: New York, 1966," *Review of Middle Eastern Studies*, 1 (1975), pp. 83–84; also see Chapter 23.

of the French Contrôle Bédouin. Later, in 1922, a Syrian Federation, including the Aleppo, Damascus, and Alawite states, was proclaimed. It was dissolved at the end of 1924 and replaced by a Syrian state comprising the states of Aleppo and Damascus and a separate (from Aleppo) Sanjak of Alexandretta. The Alawite state, however, was excluded from the new arrangement.[52] It was not until 1936 that the Alawite state (also known as the Territory of the Alawites) and the Jabal Druze were formally incorporated into Syria. But in 1939, with the scuttling of the Franco-Syrian Treaty and the fall of the nationalist government, these two districts were once again separated from Syria; they were reunited with the Syrian state under wartime pressures in 1942. In 1939, after two long years of haggling, France breached her mandatory duty to respect the territorial integrity of the state in trust by ceding the Sanjak of Alexandretta to Turkey in a bid for Turkish neutrality in the event of war.

Despite the variety of administration in Syria's outlying areas, as of 1925 Damascus, Homs, Hama, and Aleppo were consistently under one administration. France was forced to unite Damascus and Aleppo for two reasons: nationalist pressure and expense. The Sanjak of Alexandretta, the Territory of the Alawites, and the Jabal Druze were kept in varying degrees of administrative isolation and political insulation from these nationalist centers for the better part of France's tenure in Syria. French policy was clear: if the Mandate authority could not break the back of the nationalist movement, the next best alternative was to contain it in its heartland.

This strategy helped to define the scale of the nationalist movement; for much of the Mandate era, the French managed to hinder the movement from infecting the minority-inhabited areas. At the same time, many of the forces which galvanized Damascus, Aleppo, Hama, and Homs into a nationalist front in opposition to French rule in Syria were absent in the peripheral regions. Consequently, the Syrian nationalist movement encountered great difficulties in expanding the base of its activities beyond the four nationalist centers.

Whereas some of Syria's religious and ethnic minorities—the various Christian sects, Jews, Armenians and Kurds—were (and still are) widely dispersed and did not enjoy a geographical base which could give rise to political importance, others, namely the Alawites and Druzes, were compact regional minorities with considerable political importance in Syria.[53] Under the Ottomans, their religious differences, cultural and political backwardness, and physical isolation kept these two minorities out of the

[52] *Arrêté*, no. 1459*bis*, 28 June 1922; *Arrêté*, no. 2980, 5 Dec. 1924; *Arrêté*, no. 2979, 5 Dec. 1924.
[53] See Table I-3.

mainstream of political culture. Between the wars, the French authorities spared no efforts to promote and exploit this separatism.

In the end, however, the Alawite and Druze communities were not viable as national entities, even with French support. From the early years of the Mandate, local fifth columns such as the Sunni landowning class in Latakia and the young, professionally trained Druze contenders for power, aligned with the ascendant Syrian nationalist movement to upset French strategy so that by the end of the Mandate the French had to permit the incorporation of the compact-minority areas into the larger Syrian state. But minority consciousness—reinforced by a combination of factors including geography, religious differences, communal isolation, and regional separatism—had a damaging impact on Syrian political life long after the Mandate. It severely hindered the emergence and crystallization of a Syrian political community with a unified national and territorial identity.

Countryside against Town

The second major strategy adopted by the French in Syria was to isolate the nationalist movement by pitting rural areas against the more politically conscious and hostile urban nationalist centers. The focus of such a strategy was to change the rules of landownership which was the basis of the urban political leadership's wealth and power.

Immediately after the occupation, France sought to break the traditional relations of dependence between the urban absentee landowning class and the Syrian peasantry. The High Commission's motives seem to have been a mixture of traditional French idealism and political opportunism. On the one hand, the French, with so many of their own countrymen still attached to the soil, saw in an independent free-holding peasantry the embodiment of the ideals of freedom and independence which were so highly prized and defended by the French nation. The French "breathed more easily in a simple village society than in the more complex and hostile towns" of Syria.[54] On the other hand, the promotion of widespread peasant proprietorship in Syria and the development of capi-

---

[54] See D. W. Brogan, *The Development of Modern France (1870–1939)* (London, 1940). As late as 1914, 44 percent of France's population was involved in agricultural pursuits, and, roughly half of the farm population could be considered independent farmers as opposed to farm or wage laborers. The number of Frenchmen involved in agriculture outnumbered those involved in industry until the Second World War. In contrast, by 1850 only a quarter of Britain's male work force was engaged in agriculture. Also see Gordon Wright, *France in Modern Times* (London, 1962), p. 360; David S. Landes, *The Unbound Prometheus. Technological Change and Industrial Development in Western Europe from 1750 to the Present* (Cambridge, 1969), pp. 187–88.

talist relations in agriculture would weaken the system of latifundia on which the upper classes of the big towns (from which the nationalist leadership was drawn) depended for self-preservation. For the French, the logical starting point was to transform economic relations in the countryside close to nationalist centers to give peasants greater social and economic security.[55]

The first steps taken by the French High Commission in line with its "pro-peasant strategy" was to establish a cadastral survey. A Régie du Cadastre was instituted early in the Mandate under the control of the High Commission, but paid for by the various states in proportion to the works effected in each. Its tasks were several. First, it had to regularize the land registry system which had been left in a chaotic state by the Turks who either destroyed or carried back with them to Istanbul the land registers of Damascus and Aleppo in 1918. Even before the final collapse of Ottoman administration in Syria, officials of the *defterkhane* (land registry) had begun to predate land titles and sell them to the highest bidders. When the registers were removed, it became very difficult to check the validity of titles. Only influential families were able to safeguard their property rights. Furthermore, many such had taken advantage of their government connections and vast political and economic insecurity to defraud small proprietors of their heritable rights. The First World War itself caused a considerable turnover in land. The war created a situation of severe primary commodity shortages, which speculation and profiteering intensified. The prices of foodstuffs skyrocketed during and after the war, forcing many small proprietors and village communities to borrow cash from merchant-moneylenders, who were often big landowners, to purchase staples. Inability to repay these loans then led to foreclosures. Whole villages throughout Syria were annexed to the estates of big landowners and semi-independent village communities were transformed overnight into dependent sharecropping communities.[56]

Secondly, the Régie du Cadastre sought to break up the unproductive *musha'* tenure, which was the most common feature of the Syrian land system, and which prevailed alongside large privately-owned estates in extensively cultivated grain belts. This system placed severe limitations

[55] Evidence suggesting that French land policy was directed against large landowners because a large share of the nationalist elite belonged to this class can be found in the French archival sources. For example, see MAE, Syrie–Liban 1918–29. "De Reffye Note," Jouvenel to P.M., 29 June 1926, vol. 199, p. 58.

[56] PMC, *Minutes*, 5/14/333, 31 Oct. 1924. Robert de Caix, pp. 108–9; MAE, Syrie–Liban 1918–29. "Note" of Crédit Foncier d'Algérie et de Tunisie to High Commissioner, 24 June 1921, vol. 72, pp. 156–58; Cadastre des Etats, *Notice sur le Démembrement des Mouchaa* (Pamphlet published by Haut-Commissariat de la France en Syrie et au Liban) (1935), pp. 3–5.

on the formation of small private holdings and thus on agricultural de-velopment. *Musha'* lands were difficult to exploit since farmers were re-quired to follow a traditional rotation system. The village community ad-ministered the land system on the basis of a periodic redistribution of plots among its individual members and paid the land tithe on a corporate rather than on an individual basis. Rotation rendered irrigation and drainage difficult. Consequently, *musha'* lands were often denied the capital or credits necessary for proper development. This provided an op-portunity for absentee landowners with access to the judicial system to extend usury into the countryside to incorporate villages into their es-tates. As a consequence, even before the arrival of the French, traditional village society was already in the process of being gradually transformed into communities of sharecroppers which paid a high percentage (from 40 to 60 percent) of the annual yield as a rent to big landowners.[57] The French wanted to hasten the disintegration of the *musha'* system but not in such a way as to allow big landowners to become the principal benefi-ciaries of this development.

The French had no intention of destroying the social landscape of the countryside; rather, they wanted to reshape it by stressing the family in-stead of the communal village organization or tribe as the prime socio-economic unit. This strategy hinged on the imposition of a new taxation system. The existing system was full of gross inequalities. Whereas vil-lages owned by big landlords often paid only minimal taxes or were ex-onerated from them altogether, either because of their owner's influence in local administration or because many owners were tax farmers who re-fused to collect taxes on their own domains, under the *musha'* system corporately-owned lands were susceptible to heavy tax burdens. The same was true of small privately-owned peasant holdings. The new and more equitable taxation system could only be applied to lands which the cadastral survey covered and where property rights were clearly estab-lished. Thus, it was imperative that the High Commission extend land reforms as widely and as quickly as possible.[58]

The French land surveys were first conducted in the fertile coastal plains of Lebanon and Latakia, in the Biqa', in the Ghuta oasis around Damascus, in the plains of the Orontes River in central Syria, and in the districts around Aleppo and Antioch. These were followed by a survey of Crown Lands extending from Salimiyya to the southeastern fringes of Aleppo. Finally, the zones designated for cotton development projects in

---

[57] MAE, Syrie–Liban 1918–29. "Note" of Crédit Foncier d'Algérie et de Tunisie to High Commissioner, 24 June 1921, vol. 72, pp. 157–58; Cadastre des Etats, *Notice sur le Dé-membrement des Mouchaa*, pp. 3–5.

[58] Jacques Weulersse, *Paysans de Syrie et du Proche-Orient* (Paris, 1946), pp. 194–95; Cadastre des Etats, *Notice*, p. 5.

the ʿAmq depression and the Ghab plain were surveyed. In 1926, a law reinforcing the compulsory registration of all immovable property was implemented. Provisions were also made for dividing up state domains among small peasant proprietors to ensure the continued cultivation of former *musha*ʿ lands by one and the same family. The aim was to improve crop rotation and cultivation methods. Between 1926 and 1931, 181,000 hectares of Crown Lands cultivated under *musha*ʿ tenure, comprising 182 villages, were redistributed to 6,000 peasant families. In 1930, a new *Code de la Propriété* was enacted which attempted to reinforce compulsory registration and to dissolve most of the distinctions between different forms of land ownership in Syria.[59]

The work of the Régie du Cadastre did not function smoothly, however. The costs of undertaking such a vast survey in such a poor and underdeveloped country were high, and the lack of trained surveyors made the task all the more difficult. More importantly, owing to widespread political instability in the opening years of the Mandate culminating in the Great Revolt of 1925–27, work on the survey was suspended for several years. It was not resumed until the late 1920s. In 1934, it was again suspended owing to the lack of funds. By 1938, the cadastral survey covered only a little more than 25 percent of arable Syrian land. The new tax system was in force on 85 percent of this surveyed land.[60]

Undoubtedly, the French presence brought a greater measure of physical security to the Syrian peasantry. The efforts of French native affairs officers in the Services Spéciaux de l'Armée du Levant and the Contrôle Bédouin to speed up the process of tribal sedentarization by installing tribesmen as agricultural laborers on the margins of recently cultivated zones made raiding less common during the early Mandate. In Syria's outlying regions, such as in some areas of the Alawite territory, the French also improved the peasantry's lot by legally and, when necessary, physically defending its property rights against big landowners.[61]

French efforts, however, to weaken the urban landowning class were largely unsuccessful. In the first place, the transitory nature of the Mandate impeded the flow of French capital necessary to carry out land reforms. Despite the pressures of the High Commission and a few private

[59] Weulersse, *Paysans*, pp. 188, 195; Z. Y. Hershlag, *Introduction to the Modern Economic History of the Middle East* (Leiden, 1964), p. 249; al-Sibaʿi, *Adwaʾ*, p. 136.

[60] Weulersse, *Paysans*, p. 186.

[61] See Philip S. Khoury, "The Tribal Shaykh, French Tribal Policy, and the Nationalist Movement in Syria between Two World Wars," *Middle Eastern Studies*, 18 (April 1982), pp. 180–93 and Weulersse, *Paysans*, pp. 180, 196. For instance, the French-controlled administration in the Alawite territory in 1929 defended small Alawite proprietors by expropriating some lands of certain Sunni urban absentee landowners of Hama. In 1922, the French had detached a number of Alawite villages from the Hama district and attached them to the Alawite territory. MAE, Syrie–Liban 1918–29. Feb. 1922, vol. 109, p. 48.

banks and interest groups with investments in Syria, the French government did not undertake costly land reforms or make long-term investments in Syria. Furthermore, the postwar French emphasis on economic
restrictionism was reinforced, in the case of Syria, by widespread political
instability, especially during the first decade of French rule.[62] Political instability also discouraged big landowners from investing in land development.

But there were still other obstacles which hampered French efforts to
transform agrarian relations in Syria. The illiterate and conservative
peasantry, especially in the extensively cultivated grain belts of central
Syria and the Hawran, was clearly suspicious of French intentions, which
were regarded as attempts to disrupt a traditional way of life. The result
was that the new class of small proprietors created by the reforms was
vulnerable to further exploitation by a remarkably tenacious class of big
urban and rural landowners solely interested in preserving and expanding
its privileged position and material resource base in the countryside. This
class maintained its grip on rural society by expropriating the recently established holdings of small proprietors through the untramelled manipulation of usurious capital as quickly as the French were able to register
and distribute lands to the peasantry.[63] Furthermore, big landowners had
considerable leeway for maneuver in the countryside because French capitalized agricultural credit banks, which had applied considerable pressure
on the High Commission to institute widespread land reforms during the
early Mandate, refused to lend money to small proprietors or village
communities.[64] Only big landowners were able to borrow money from
these banks which they then re-lent to their sharecroppers or to small
proprietors at a much higher interest rate.[65]

[62] Ibid., "Note" of the Crédit Foncier d'Algérie et de Tunisie to High Commissioner, 24
June 1921, vol. 72, pp. 152–54; Weulersse, Paysans, pp. 176, 196.

[63] Weulersse, Paysans, pp. 196–97.

[64] Agricultural credit banks could only function within the framework of private landownership. And only these banks could operate on a good profit margin in Syria. MAE,
Syrie–Liban 1918–29. "Note" of Crédit Foncier d'Algérie et de Tunisie, 24 June 1921, vol.
72, pp. 152–54.

[65] A big landowner could borrow from agricultural credit banks like the Crédit Foncier
d'Algérie et de Tunisie at a standard 6–9 percent per annum, up to 70 percent against the
value of his real estate. However, when the big landowner lent money to a sharecropper
who had no collateral, the interest rate depended on the availability of credit in the particular
region as well as on the success of the particular annual harvest. Generally, it averaged from
20 to 25 percent per annum to sharecroppers although it could soar to 100 percent. For small
proprietors who could offer their land as collateral, the average interest rate on a loan was
between 9 and 20 percent, though it, too, could soar in times of bad harvest. See Himadeh,
The Monetary and Banking System in Syria, pp. 258–60; Abdullah F. Azmeh, L'évolution
de la banque commerciale dans le cadre économique de la Syrie (1920–1957) (Lausanne,
1961), p. 59; al-Sibaʿi, Adwaʾ, p. 232.

The impact of this process became clearer over time. The breakdown of the *musha'* system did not lead to a significant growth of a small land-owning class in Syria. On the contrary, the failure of the High Commission to transform the land system and agrarian productive forces actually stimulated land accumulation in the hands of fewer owners. In regions where village communal holdings were transformed into a series of small independent family holdings, the survival of the small proprietor was precarious. Many were quickly transformed into sharecroppers, or fled their lands as they were annexed by powerful moneylending landowners.[66] For example, in the Aleppo province the number of small privately-owned holdings (less than ten hectares) decreased as a percentage of the total number of privately-owned holdings in the province from 33 to 16 percent between 1924 and 1944. During the same period, the number of medium-sized holdings (10 to 100 hectares) increased from 22 to 39 percent and the number of large holdings (over 100 hectares) increased from 24 to 45 percent.[67] These figures suggest that land was being concentrated in the hands of middle-sized and big landowners. Similarly, in the Homs district in the late 1930s, 55 percent of all privately-owned lands belonged to big landowners; and of the 114 villages in the Hama district in 1933, 92 were completely owned by four families. In both Homs and Hama, the number of owners cultivating their own lands declined under the Mandate.[68]

There was one other obstacle hindering French efforts to isolate the Syrian countryside from the cities. Given the various restraints on the French, the Mandate system was based on *indirect* colonial rule. Without the resources to govern directly or to train local administrative cadres, the High Commission relied on local intermediaries with past administrative experience and, preferably, with their own independent influence. Only one social class in Syria provided such intermediaries: the absentee land-owning class of the interior towns that had served the Ottoman state as an aristocracy of service. To tamper with the material (landowning) base

---

[66] Usury by big landowners in the Syrian interior was very common. They exploited the peasantry by advancing loans in difficult times, when no agricultural bank would, at exorbitant interest rates. Since local industry in the countryside was usually minor or non-existent, the peasant had difficulty leaving the land. Indeed, even the cities offered few opportunities. Instead, the peasant was often forced to become a sharecropper. If he was already a sharecropper and unable to pay back his debt on time, the interest simply accumulated, increasing the landlord's grip over his sharecropper. See [Gaulmier], "Note sur la propriété foncière dans la Syrie centrale," *L'Asie Française*, no. 309 (April 1933), pp. 130–37.

[67] Pavie, *Etat d'Alep*, pp. 59, 118; Gibb and Partners, *Economic Development*, p. 120.

[68] P. Berthelot, "Note sur la mise en valeur de la région du 'Caza' de Homs," CHEAM, no. 249 (Feb. 1938), pp. 21–23. [Gaulmier], "Note sur la propriété," pp. 131–33; M. Anwar Naaman, "Précisions sur la structure agraire dans la région de Homs-Hama (Syrie)," *Bulletin de l'Association de Géographes Français* (March–April 1950), p. 58.

of this class therefore presented the French with a delicate problem.[69] The web of social and financial relationships which bound this class together made it exceedingly difficult to isolate its nationalist members from those elements willing to cooperate with the High Commission. This obstacle, when combined with the slow diffusion of structural changes in the Syrian land system, preserved the material and political bases of the landowning class and insulated it fairly well from challenges further down the Syrian social scale during the Mandate era.[70] In the end, France was left with the sole possibility of playing rural-based landowners and tribal shaykhs against city notables and these notables against one another. Setting the peasantry against their masters was out of the question. It was only after independence that the Syrian countryside posed a serious political challenge to the towns.

ELITE AGAINST ELITE

The third principal strategy adopted from the Lyautey experience in Morocco was the attempt to govern through cooperative elements within the traditional political elite. Direct rule had long been obsolete in many French colonies. The international restrictions imposed on France by the Mandate system, the relatively high level of elite political consciousness and organization found in Syria, and the inability or unwillingness of the French to muster the requisite human and material resources to govern the country along European lines dictated that French administration in Syria would evolve along native lines. But, without a significant group of influential local collaborators in the nationalist centers of the interior to help promote French respectability and carry out French policy, France was doomed to an eternity of maladministration and, therefore, insecurity in Syria.

[69] Georges Catroux (who in the early 1920s was the French Delegate to Damascus) wrote that landowners aligned with the Mandate as soon as it became apparent that their material interests were not to be touched. This was particularly so in the case of the big landowners of Hama and Homs who started off as nationalists but, on realizing that the Mandate was not a "democratic" system that would "distribute their lands," began to cooperate with the French authorities. Catroux wrote: "I was of the conviction that it was necessary to reassure them" of this fact. "This was the best way to win their support. The demands were agreed upon and guarantees were given that would reassure their personal conservative dignity. These landlords contributed to the success of Mandate policy; since they controlled public opinion in the countryside, we were able to register a large and important gain. Homs and Hama were no longer fortresses of the nationalist doctrine." Although landowners in these districts were not at the vanguard of the nationalist movement, their cooperation with the French took the form of silence rather than active participation in colonial administration. Général Catroux, *Deux missions en Moyen-Orient, 1919–1922* (Paris, 1958), p. x.

[70] Weulersse, *Paysans*, p. 196.

The French did find two small groups of sympathizers in the over-whelmingly hostile nationalist towns. One was the Uniate communities in Damascus[71] and Aleppo.[72] These communities partially overlapped with the predominantly Christian comprador bourgeoisie who, for nearly a century, had been tied to French (and other European) commercial interests and who had received French political protection. The other contained members of the Muslim urban notability, who had been part of the higher Ottoman administration in the Syrian provinces before its collapse in 1918. Because the towns of the Syrian interior were inhabited by an Arab Muslim majority,[73] it was the Muslim political elite, members of the landowning-bureaucratic class, which the French High Commission had to cultivate in order to develop an effective native policy in Syria.

For deep-seated, though not necessarily politically sound, reasons some members of the traditional urban elite were willing to go against the mounting tide of Syrian nationalism, even at the expense of sacrificing their own credibility and independent influence in local society. Politicians and bureaucrats who chose to cooperate with the French immediately after occupation were often those members of the urban absentee landowning and bureaucratic class who had systematically expanded and consolidated their political and financial interests under the Ottoman administrative umbrella. They had clung tightly, if not confidently, to the Ottoman state, despite the emergence of Arab nationalist ideology after 1908, which was articulated by a growing number of disenfranchised politicians and intellectuals from their own class and even from their own families. On behalf of the Ottoman state and through the political appa-

[71] The Catholic and Uniate population of Damascus in 1928 was only 4.3 percent (8,504) of the town's total population of 198,427. In 1935 it was 4 percent (8,428) of a population of 213,026. In 1943 it was 5.4 percent (15,303) of a population of 286,000. The percentage of Christians in the total population of Damascus in 1928, 1935 and 1943 was respectively 8.5, 10, and 15.5. These figures include Armenian Catholics and Orthodox. Jews in 1928, 1935, and 1943 were respectively, 3.1, 2.0 and 4.5 percent of the town's population. MWT, al-Intidab al-faransi. 79/942/513. Mutasarrif of Damascus to Lieutenant Roland, 6 March 1928; Emile Fauquenot, "Les institutions gouvernementales de la Syrie," CHEAM, no. 201 (17 June 1937); "L'état civil," CHEAM, no. 50, n.d.

[72] The Catholic and Uniate population in Aleppo in 1935 was 10.75 percent (27,269) of a total population of 253,553. In 1943, it was 10.3 percent. The total Christian population of Aleppo in 1935 and 1943 was respectively 34.6 and 34.1 percent. However, Armenians (the majority of whom were Orthodox) were in 1935 and 1943 respectively 22.2 and 21.4 percent. Most Armenians were recent settlers in Aleppo after the Turkish massacres in southern and eastern Anatolia during and after World War I. In Aleppo, Jews in 1935 and 1943 were respectively 4.0 and 4.3 percent of the population. Ibid.

[73] In Damascus, Sunni Muslims in 1935 and 1943 were respectively 89 percent and 80 percent of the total population. In Aleppo, in 1935 and 1943, they were respectively 61 and 61.5 percent of the population. MWT, al-Intidab al-faransi. 79/942/513; Fauquenot, "Les institutions"; "L'état civil."

ratus which it provided, senior Ottoman-Arab officials competed successfully with their new Arab nationalist rivals. But, in 1918 when the Ottoman umbrella was closed for good, these functionaries were summarily
dismissed from public office and consigned to the margins of political life
by Arab nationalists.

Under Amir Faysal's Arab nationalist regime, many prominent urban
notables and ex-Ottoman functionaries found few opportunities to regain
their seats of power. The nationalist elite running the Arab state disliked
and distrusted them; consequently, every effort was made to keep them
out of government. Such strong antipathies were mutual. Many notables
who had been forced to the political sidelines sought support from French
political officers while waiting for the downfall of the young militant nationalists. But Faysal did not appoint a cabinet of non-nationalist notables
until the French had reached the doorstep of Damascus in late July 1920.
And it was this cabinet which had the ignominious duty of surrendering
Syria to France.

It can be argued that the old guard of urban notables had already been
discredited by its nationalist rivals before the French invaded Syria. Their
refusal to cooperate willingly with the nationalist movement undercut
their position of independent influence in Damascus, Aleppo, and elsewhere; this position had already begun to show signs of erosion during
the First World War when notables cooperated with the Turkish authorities in suppressing Syrian activists sympathetic to the Arab Revolt. This
section of the traditional urban elite was clearly identified with an oppres-
sive regime and thus won a reputation for selfishly bolstering its personal
interests at the expense of the general welfare. But, whereas the notability easily justified its role as a provincial aristocracy of service in the Ottoman Empire, cooperation with a European authority in Syria posed
some difficulty.[74] The Ottoman government was, after all, Muslim and
had the prestige and legitimacy of 400 years of rule behind it.

The choice to cooperate with the French was not easy, but it was fairly
convenient. The primary justification was that Syria, after the great economic hardships suffered during the war and the psychological and political vacuum created by the collapse of four centuries of Ottoman rule,
desperately needed a strong external force to re-establish stability in the
country. By working with the French, these notables felt that more could
be achieved for Syria.[75] Behind this rationale, however, were several defensive perceptions. First, notables who had staked their government careers and power on the continuation of the system of Empire, and who,
after harmonizing their interests with those of the Ottoman state pros-

[74] Conversation with Nadim Demichkie (London, 25 June 1975).
[75] Conversation with Yusuf al-Hakim (Damascus, 21 Feb. 1976).

pered under its protection, realized that the only way they could resume
their traditional place as an aristocracy of service was to sue for peace and
tranquility at any cost, even if this meant collaborating with a power
which had played a conspicuous role in bringing about the Empire's demise.[76] Secondly, these notables, although they belonged to the same local upper class families that produced their Arab nationalist rivals, were
generally powerless to compete with the nationalist leadership for influence in Syrian society. Vast sections of the Syrian population already recognized the nationalist leadership as the one fraction of the local upper
class that was committed to defend its traditional values and beliefs
against the onslaught of an aggressive foreign ruler. However, the enforced dispersion of the nationalist leadership by the French in 1920 allowed non-nationalist notables to present themselves as the only qualified local leadership with the education, training, and stature to take over
the high administrative functions left open by the sudden departure of
their nationalist rivals.[77]

The French strategy of isolating and exploiting the divisions and conflicts within the Syrian political elite was all the easier since the political
arena in 1920 was still very small. The French realized that while the political elite was a fairly cohesive socio-economic class, it was politically
factionalized; personal interests more than shared ideology conditioned
its members' loyalties. They discerned that competitive and often unstable coalitions of families mediated the upper level of politics in the towns.
Although these families were interested in preserving the material bases
of their power, they felt confident enough to compete with one another
because they were relatively free of class pressures from below. The
French were interested in creating and widening rivalries and then supporting the cooperative factions against the intransigent ones.[78]

On balance, however, the French strategy of exploiting the weaknesses
and divisions within the Syrian political elite by attracting potential collaborators to the colonial administration and then playing them off
against their nationalist rivals never worked smoothly. After the nationalist defeat in 1920, it took some time for the dispersed and exiled nationalist leadership to return to the political scene and to display its strength
and popular support in Damascus and Aleppo. In the interim, the French
grew somewhat complacent; they continued to underestimate the depth
of nationalist sentiment in Syria, at least in the strategic urban strongholds in the interior. And although a number of old guard notables took
advantage of the nationalist leadership's absence to develop relations with

[76] Conversation with Hasan al-Hakim (Damascus, 21 March 1976)
[77] Conversation with Farid Zayn al-Din (Damascus, 18 Oct. 1975).
[78] Conversation with Qustantin Zurayq (Beirut, 10 Jan. 1976).

the French authorities, many jeopardized their credibility with their personal followings by touching base with a conquering power that was foreign, non-Muslim, and exploitative.

In the early Mandate years, financial problems in France and an expensive administrative set-up in Syria restricted the availability of French benefits which could attract and retain an effective core of local collaborators. Indeed, these benefits were barely sufficient to satisfy cooperative senior officials let alone to persuade the personal followings of nationalist leaders to switch their allegiance to notables in the colonial administration. Although the High Commission agreed to expand local administration, at great financial cost both to France and to Syria, to accommodate willing collaborators and to co-opt dissidents, there were still not enough top jobs to go around. Thus collaborators were shuffled in and out of office with alarming frequency in order to distribute the benefits of office to as many as possible. Native government during the Mandate was characterized by a high turnover of politicians and bureaucrats at the ministerial level.[79]

The rapid circulation of non-nationalist notables in and out of government indicated that they possessed insufficient independent influence to enforce their permanence. But their failure to build up strong personal followings outside government circles was not simply because they had few resources at their command; it was also because their close identification with and dependence on a much hated colonial authority made them easy targets for the personal recriminations of the nationalist opposition with its pervasive independent influence in the towns. In the name of Syrian national independence and territorial integrity, nationalists regularly mobilized the urban masses to demonstrate or strike against the French. These attacks had two related purposes. They were not only against the flagrant reality of foreign occupation, but they were also designed to discredit high-ranking collaborators. Eventually, the French were forced to acknowledge their strategy of ruling through disrespected and distrusted members of the traditional Syrian political elite had failed.

---

[79] Between the first appointment of a native Council of Directors by the French in 1920 (September) and the formation of the first completely nationalist Cabinet of Ministers in December 1936, Syria had 16 different Councils of Directors and Cabinets. Of the 38 individuals who were directors and/or ministers in this period, only five were recognized nationalists. Twenty-four were from Damascus (63 percent of the total number), 11 from Aleppo, 2 from Hama, and 1 from Homs. In this period, there were 93 available directors' or ministers' slots. Damascenes filled 62 of these slots or 67 percent of the total. See Hasan al-Hakim, *Mudhakkirati* (Beirut, 1966), vol. 2, pp. 154–71.

CHAPTER THREE

IMPLEMENTATION

SYRIA WAS NOT a settler-state, unlike Morocco, which between the wars contained a sizeable French residential community of more than 7,000 functionaries and 130,000 *colons*.[1] Besides the 350-member staff of the High Commission and the approximately 1,000 French officers of the Armée du Levant, there was only a small, compact, and semi-permanent residential community of French merchants, educators, and missionaries in Syria.[2] Most French (and other European) residents in the Levant states were concentrated in Beirut. In Damascus and Aleppo, which contained minute French communities, French interests and attention were overwhelmingly devoted to local Christian minorities, with whom the French were most involved and felt most comfortable.

Relations between French officials and local collaborators were neither cordial nor informal.[3] Fraternization was largely restricted to official social functions. In government, the French had little respect for Syrian officials and regularly disparaged their competence and honesty. French staff officers generally held a low opinion of Arab Muslims, Kurds, and Druzes. Christians, particularly Maronites, were regarded as more "intelligent and open-minded." As one French official put it, "they think in French."[4] Although many French officials in Syria were committed anticlericalists, they nevertheless felt more at ease with the Christian minor-

---

[1] This figure is for 1928. MAE, Syrie–Liban 1918–29. 30 Oct. 1928, vol. 205, pp. 106–8.

[2] There were 23,422 foreign nationals in Syria and Lebanon in 1933, 3,807 of whom were French. Most foreign nationals were Syrian emigrants who had returned from abroad, and most of these were residents of Beirut. See Robert Widmer, "Population," in S. B. Himadeh (ed.), *Economic Organization of Syria* (Beirut, 1936), pp. 21–22.

[3] See "La politique du Mandat français—Irak et Syrie," *L'Asie Française*, no. 257 (Feb. 1928), p. 65.

[4] An extreme example of French officialdom's attitude to Syrian officials was General (formerly Colonel) Robert Collet (b. 1891), who lived in Syria 22 years where he was best known as Chief Political Officer and Commander of the Circassian Regiment. Collet was very familiar with Syria, but after years of living with Muslims he still only had respect for Christians. Glubb Pasha, the British commander of the Arab Legion in Transjordan, observed that even "his right hand orderly, though dressed like a Circassian in full national costume, turned out to be an Armenian." FO 371/182, vol. 31465. Glubb Note on Visit to Syria, 27/28 November 1941. On the French attitude to different Syrian minorities, see MD, 7N 4192. "Manuel Colonial, 1923–1925"; *ibid.*, 7N 4181. A. Derik to Maréchal d'Esperry, 22 Nov. 1930.

ity which attempted, if only superficially, to adopt French manners and customs.[5]

The attitude of high-ranking Syrian functionaries toward the High Commission staff, though concealed, was also disrespectful. They were normally fluent in French—a necessity when so few French officials spoke Arabic—but only a handful admitted to being comfortable in a French cultural milieu. Only the very cream of Damascus and Aleppo society made efforts to bridge the social and cultural gap between Frenchmen and Syrians. In the late 1920s, some Francophile notables in Damascus founded a Franco-Syrian social club in conjunction with the French Delegate and the British Consul. The club was located in the modern district of al-Shuhada' on fashionable Salhiyya street. Bridge parties and dinner-dances were its main events. Although the club founders regarded it as an important vehicle for improving Franco-Syrian relations, its membership never numbered more than one hundred, including the wives of French and Syrian officials. Its exclusive character, restricted to the cooperative upper crust of Damascus society, irked nationalists and their supporters, while conservative religious leaders frowned upon its rather risqué activities.[6]

EXECUTORS

The French administrative program in Syria resembled what France had applied with fair success in Morocco.[7] But although the "same sets of services and organs of control"[8] were applied in Syria and Morocco, the French in Syria were unable to live up to the Lyautey ideal. They may have intended to seek a compromise between force and consent, but they discovered a more ideologically sophisticated and politically organized society in Syria than they had in Morocco. Most Syrians did not desire French control, and many openly resisted it. Thus, behind the facade of native figureheads, the French governed Syria directly and avoided, as best they could, any relaxation of authority which was likely to hasten the political education of Syrians.[9]

While the preponderance of middle and low-ranking functionaries were sent directly from France, at the top of the French administrative

[5] *Ibid.* In contrast, there was a certain personal ease about British dealings with Iraqis and Palestinians (but not Egyptians) which was missing in French dealings with Syrians.

[6] Khalid al-'Azm, *Mudhakkirat Khalid al-'Azm* (Beirut, 1973), vol. 1, p. 165.

[7] FO 371/311, vol. 10159. Smart (Beirut) to FO, 15 Dec. 1923.

[8] Burke, "A Comparative View," p. 183.

[9] The Acting British Consul in Beirut observed that "[Syrian] officials have thus none of the responsibilities which train men to use political and administrative power effectively." FO 371/311, vol. 10159. Smart to FO, 15 Dec. 1923.

hierarchy the Moroccan connection was pervasive. The appointment of General Henri Gouraud as High Commissioner in 1919 was indicative of this trend. Gouraud had previously served in Mauritania and, from 1911 to 1917, in Morocco where he was promoted to the rank of General, the youngest Frenchman to hold this rank at the time. It was also in Morocco that he became Lyautey's chief understudy, and briefly his replacement as Resident-General. From Morocco, Gouraud gained the reputation of a distinguished colonial administrator; he had pacified Fez but had nonetheless won the respect of its local population. A hero of the First World War, he was an obvious candidate for the post of High Commissioner in the Levant. He was a popular military figure and a close disciple of Lyautey at a time when the French government was groping for both a strongman and a suitable formula to apply to the complex situation in Syria. Gouraud was also a devout Catholic which, it was believed, would sit well with the Christian population in Lebanon.[10]

Several other French military officers with prior experience in Morocco and elsewhere in North Africa were either personally recruited by Gouraud or directly transferred by the French government to Syria. General de Lamothe, an ardent Catholic who had served under Gouraud in Marrakech, was the first French Delegate to Aleppo.[11] His task was to pacify northern Syria and hold the line against Mustafa Kemal's Turkish army. In the Alawite territory, which was in open revolt against the French between 1919 and 1921, two French officers who had been in the Moroccan service, Colonel Niéger and his successor, General Billotte, were appointed as Delegates.[12] In 1922, Billotte replaced the unpopular de Lamothe as Delegate in Aleppo. Later, he became Chief of Staff of the Armée du Levant.[13] Colonel (later General) Georges Catroux was the first Delegate to Damascus, where he distinguished himself as an expert on Bedouin and Druze affairs. A product of the Morocco service, Catroux fit the Lyautey mold more closely than any French official in Syria.[14]

Although it was largely senior military officers drawn from the French colonial service in Morocco who determined the nature and direction of French administration during the early Mandate, there was also an influential group of civilians in Gouraud's administration with a Moroccan connection. Robert de Caix, one of the leading French officials in the colo-

[10] Burke, "A Comparative View," pp. 178–79.

[11] *Ibid.*, p. 179; FO 371/11762, vol. 10165. Hough (Aleppo) to FO, 22 Dec. 1924.

[12] See Niéger, "Choix de documents sur le Territoire des Alaouites," pp. 1–69.

[13] Longrigg, *Syria*, p. 125; FO 371/11762, vol. 10165. Hough to FO, 22 Dec. 1924; FO 371/5074, vol. 11516. Crewe (Paris) to FO, 30 Aug. 1926.

[14] USNA, Syria. 890d.01/58. Damascus Consul to Secretary of State, 15 March 1922. For Catroux's experiences in Syria see his memoirs: Général Catroux, *Deux Missions en Moyen-Orient, 1919–1922* (Paris, 1958).

nial party and the architect of French native policy in Syria, was Gouraud's Secretary-General and the highest-ranking civilian in the French
administration until his departure in 1924. His administrative formulas
were colored by his deep admiration for Lyautey's policies in Morocco.
He even chose as his aide-de-camp Pierre Lyautey, the Maréchal's
nephew.[15]

In time, however, the Moroccan strain in French officialdom in Syria
became diluted. By the early 1930s, the senior staff at the High Commission consisted more of French agents with a colonial background in the
Far East than of those with a Moroccan background. The appointment of
each new High Commissioner brought with it a turnover in senior French
staff and, in the early years of the Mandate, High Commissioners came
and went in rapid succession. The aides and advisers a High Commissioner brought to Syria had often served with him in other regions of the
French Empire or back in France.[16] Under Gouraud, the senior French
staff was invariably drawn from the French colonial service in Morocco or
elsewhere in North Africa. But, under Henri Ponsot (1926–1933) and
Damien de Martel (1933–1938), both of whom had served as diplomats in
the Far East, the staff was recruited from French Indochina, Bangkok, or
Tokyo.[17] Similarly, whereas the first three High Commissioners—Gouraud, Weygand, and Sarrail—were all generals and packed the senior staff
with military men, their successors were civilians and preferred civilian
to military advisers. High Commissoners also came to Syria with different kinds of professional experience and different political proclivities
and, within an established framework, approached the governing of Syria
differently. Gouraud was the favorite of colonial interest groups while
Sarrail, an ardent anti-clericalist and Freemason, was popular with the
French Left. Gouraud was also popular with Christians in Syria and Lebanon; Sarrail was not. Among the civilian High Commissioners, Henry
de Jouvenel was a journalist and liberal politician and Martel was of an
aristocratic family and an ambassador. Ponsot and Gabriel Puaux, a Protestant, were both foreign service officers. Throughout the Mandate, personal jealousies between old and new French recruits to Syria were common. Often when a High Commissioner resigned or was recalled some of
his closest aides stayed on in the service of the Mandate. Old loyalties
were difficult to change and when a new High Commissioner arrived with
his own recruits those officials still on the scene could make life difficult

[15] Burke, "A Comparative View," pp. 179, 185 fn.
[16] Conversation with Sir Geoffrey Furlonge (London, 26 March 1975); FO 371/6954, vol.
11516. Crewe to Chamberlain, 30 Aug. 1926.
[17] See FO 371/2124, vol. 20849. "Personalities," 6 May 1937; FO 371/5398. "Personalities," 26 Aug. 1936.

for the new regime.[18] There was another persistent problem which affected the flow of High Commission directives. Whereas military High
Commissioners were simultaneously chiefs of the Armée du Levant,
their civilian successors were not and at times conflicts arose between the
High Commissioner and the military over solutions to thorny political
problems. Civilians were normally more flexible and preferred non-violent means of persuasion, while their military counterparts were prone to
using armed force.[19]

The calibre of French officials in Syria varied. Some were well trained
in the language, religion, and culture of the territory; others were sound
administrators but with little or no emotional interest in Syrian social and
political conditions. Many, however, were unqualified for the tasks they
were assigned. Outstanding colonial officials were rarely seconded to
Syria.

Although anti-French sentiment among Syrians stemmed from several sources, one of the main sources was the incompetence of French
functionaries themselves. Syrians were not alone in recognizing this fact.
Robert de Caix bemoaned the absence of competent French officials and
regularly complained to the Quai d'Orsay about the general ineptitude of
low- and middle-level functionaries in Syria.[20] But even the harshest
Syrian or French criticisms of the quality of French military and civilian
personnel[21] could not alter the reality that few Frenchmen with the
proper training and experience were keen on serving in Syria. The prevalent view of Syria in French colonial circles was that it was the most difficult place for a career-minded administrator to make a name for himself.
In the opening years of the Mandate, several up-and-coming French officials were forced to leave Syria prematurely with tarnished records. The
peculiarities of the Mandate system, the economic constraints on French
investment, and the intensity of organized Syrian political opposition
made Syria a most difficult place to work.

Hence, the incompetence of French officials in Syria was not owing to
their "misfortune of not succeeding in the metropolis," as Raymond

[18] Fuad K. Mufarrij, "Syria and Lebanon under the French Mandate," M.A. Dissertation
(American University of Beirut, 1935), p. 213, citing author's personal interview with the
French Consul-General in Beirut in 1935, M. Delenda.

[19] *Ibid.*, p. 214.

[20] FO 371/630, vol. 6453. Fontana (Beirut) to FO.

[21] General Gamelin, Commander of the Armée du Levant during the Great Revolt of
1925, wrote that both high- and low-ranking French officers were "actually mediocre" and
"they have a poor reputation. Among the metropolitan troops, a great number of officers
sent to the Levant do not possess the general knowledge nor the special aptitude necessary
to utilize immediately when commanding units and columns." MD, 7N 4181. Gamelin
(Beirut) to Ministère de la Guerre, 10 Feb. 1926 and 29 May 1926.

Poincaré suggested about the great bulk of French officials.[22] Rather, it was owing to their unfamiliarity with and preconditioned bias toward the political and socio-economic conditions in the territory. As one contemporary Frenchman observed,

> it is in the French colonies that the major part of our Syrian administrative force—civilian as well as military—receives their education. It thus comes to pass that they tend to deal with an evolved and civilized country as Syria which has its highly political and social-intellectual "elite" as if they were dealing with the Atlas tribes or the Blacks in the Sudan.[23]

The French assumed that they understood the Levant when in fact they did not. French officials assigned to Syria were rarely familiar with conditions in the country before setting foot there. Instead, they were forced to rely on previous experiences and training in other French colonies where conditions were often strikingly different.

It was only in the late 1930s that Frenchmen began to produce detailed studies and to disseminate information and ideas on a wide scale about the social and economic realities of the country they had been governing for nearly two decades.[24] With the victory of the Leftist Popular Front in 1936, a specialized institution, the Centre de Hautes Etudes d'Administration Musulmane, was established in Paris to provide additional training for some of the government functionaries serving in French North Africa and in Syria and Lebanon. The CHEAM gave functionaries an opportunity to compare their experiences and mutual concerns, and provided recruits to the French colonial and Mandate services with a better understanding of the political and socio-economic realities found in the Muslim areas. But its contribution to improving French policy in Syria came much too late.[25]

[22] *Revue des Deux Mondes* (15 Oct. 1921).

[23] Rousseau de Beauplan, *Où va la Syrie?* (Paris, 1929), cited in Mufarrij, "Syria and Lebanon."

[24] Pierre Rondot, "L'expérience du Mandat français en Syrie et au Liban (1918–1945)," *Revue Générale de Droit International Publique*, 3–4 (1948), p. 390. Among the most important studies conducted by French officials and scholars in Syria were: A. de Boucheman, *Une petite cité caravanière: Suhné* (Damascus, 1939); and Jacques Weulersse, *Le pays des Alaouites* (Tours, 1940).

[25] The CHEAM program has been described in a study of French Colonial Services as follows: "Government officials who had been in public service for six or more years, at least four of them in Islamic areas overseas, were eligible to compete for entrance to the Center. The competition consisted of two stages: first, the writing of an essay [*mémoire*] on some political, social, or economic aspect of the area in which they served and second, an oral examination in an African or Asian language. At the Center a series of seminars was offered dealing with contemporary problems, fundamentals of sociology, ethnology, economics, applied psychology, and the civilizations, religions and ideologies of Africa (after 1946) and

With the exception of a handful of gifted and innovative French administrators, most officials in Syria plodded along their bureaucratic path with little imagination or initiative. Some proved to be notoriously corrupt and paid heavy penalties for their dishonesty.[26] At best, the proclivity of French officialdom in the Levant was to apply stopgap measures learned elsewhere, instead of dealing constructively with the problems before them.[27]

Instruments of Execution

French administration was an oversized and expensive bureaucratic ship. At its helm was the High Commissioner for Syria and Lebanon who was directly responsible to the French Ministry of Foreign Affairs. His headquarters were at the Grand Sérail in Beirut. He issued decrees (*arrêtés*) and had final veto power. He did not have to consult the Syrian public before taking a decision and he rarely depended on directives from Paris. His reports to the Quai d'Orsay were neither regular nor detailed.[28]

Directly under the High Commissioner's control was the Secretary-General who, in the early years of the Mandate, had broad responsibility for the development and application of French policy in Syria. So too were the Services Spéciaux, an information bureau with "specialized branches dealing with Intelligence, the press, propaganda, and the Sûreté Générale."[29] French native affairs officers, mainly drawn from the colonial service, belonged to the Special Services. They were found in every

---

Asia. After attending the Center for three months, its members had to present another *mémoire*, again dealing with some aspect of the area in which they served, and had to pass examinations in the following fields: general problems of the Islamic world, the French colonies in general, the foreign empires, and an African or Asian language. Upon finishing those requirements, the students were awarded a *brevet*." "The name of the Center was changed to *Centre de hautes études administratives sur l'Afrique et l'Asie modernes*." See William B. Cohen, *Rulers of Empire: The French Colonial Service in Africa* (Stanford, 1971), p. 147. Among those French officials in the 1930s who contributed *mémoires en stage* at the CHEAM were: Emile Fauquenot (Adviser to the Syrian Ministry of Interior in 1936 and later Delegate at Aleppo); Jean Gaulmier (Adviser to the Ministry of Finance in the Syrian state), and Robert Montagne (Assistant Delegate in the Syrian state, and later Director of the Institut Français d'Etudes Arabes de Damas and of the CHEAM).

[26] Some French financial advisers were renowned for turning their posts into profitable ventures. For example, the French Adviser on Finances in Beirut was dismissed in June 1923 when irregularities were discovered during a spot inspection. A few months earlier the Financial Adviser in Damascus committed suicide on the very morning he would have had to produce his books for inspection. FO 371/7689, vol. 9056. Damascus Consul to FO, 10 July 1923.

[27] USNA, Syria. 890.d.01/58. Damascus Consul to Secretary of State, 15 March 1923.

[28] The archives of the Ministère des Affaires Etrangères indicate that the High Commissioner submitted reports only on an occasional basis.

[29] Longrigg, *Syria*, p. 115.

district and practically, if not formally, exercised much influence over local administration and political life. The most important branch was the
Service des Renseignements, or intelligence service, which was modelled
on Lyautey's crack corps of intelligence officers in Morocco. It was the
cornerstone of French administration in Syria, serving as the link between the civilian regime and the military. There were less than one
hundred officers in the Service des Renseignements; many were trained
in the Arabic language and were familiar with the dominant religion, culture, and customs of the country. The Service des Renseignements did
not just report on "Levantine political intrigue," but made a methodical
inventory of the social and political forces in Syria and Lebanon and, with
this information, manipulated the levers of command in the entire region.[30]

There was also a number of governmental departments located in Beirut—public security, education, public works, antiquities, and Bedouin
affairs—which French officials staffed at the upper echelons. Departments that dealt with matters of interest to both Syria and Lebanon and
therefore could not be wholly controlled by regional governments were
under the immediate jurisdiction of the High Commission. These were
called the Common Interests (Intérêts Communs) and included customs,
the postal and telegraph services, and control of concessionary companies.

Outside of the Special Services and the Common Interests, there were
two main categories of French officials operating in the different Syrian
states. The first consisted of officials directly appointed by the High Commissioner and paid from his budget. These included the Delegates (Délé-
gués) to each state and the staff of advisers (conseillers) attached to the
states' various administrative departments, such as finance, education,
and public works. The Delegate had veto power over the local governor
and French advisers had the same power over local directors. Furthermore, whenever a complex or controversial problem arose, the Delegate
referred it to the High Commissioner, thus giving the French the final decision on all important matters of state. In each qada' (district) or sanjak,
an identical situation was reproduced: an Assistant Delegate (Délégué-
Adjoint), rather than the local mutasarrif (district commissioner), was
the final authority.[31]

The second category was more ambiguous. It was comprised of French
officials whom local governments hired directly under contract and who
were paid out of local state budgets. These officials were also attached to

[30] MAE, Syrie–Liban 1918–29. 28 Dec. 1928, vol. 115, p. 141. In 1928, the Service des
Renseignements was staffed by 71 officers.
[31] PMC, Minutes, 8/3/494, 17 Feb. 1926. Statement of Robert de Caix, p. 15.

local directors or ministers and hence mainly duplicated the functions of French-appointed advisers.[32] In 1921, the total number of French advisers in Syria was 500, although the French reduced their number to around 300 by 1926, with the High Commissioner appointing over 60 percent of them.[33]

The French created a number of states in Syria. Each had its own administration reproducing at the regional level the same departmental structures found at the center. French administration was thus elaborate and expensive. But through it the High Commission controlled nearly all areas of administration, discouraging, if not prohibiting, local initiative.

THE MAINSTAY OF THE MANDATE defense and public security system was the Armée du Levant. It included Foreign Legion battalions, a few artillery batteries, and an engineer and aviation corps sent directly from France. However, French colonies supplied the bulk of men in French uniform: North Africans, Madagascans, and Sengalese, commanded by French officers.[34] For the Syrian people, the day-to-day reality of living in the shadow of a brutal army of occupation was even harsher and more humiliating since its rank and file was composed of other colonized peoples regarded by Syrians as culturally inferior. While Frenchmen in uniform maintained a low profile in the towns, Black Africans and Moroccan Arabs were called upon to maintain order.

The size of the Armée du Levant was at first enormous. At the end of 1921 it stood at 70,000 men. However, as of January 1921, the French Senate had already begun to vote significant reductions in war credits for Syria and Lebanon which led to a dramatic reduction in the strength of the army. By the end of 1924, the army had been trimmed to 15,000.[35] Only during the Great Revolt of 1925–27, and again during World War II, was the size of the army increased beyond this figure.

In the beginning, the French government defrayed almost the entire

[32] *Ibid.* De Caix claimed that these "indirect agents" were "prone to playing in local intrigues."

[33] See Fuad K. Mufarrij, "Syria and Lebanon under French Mandate," M.A. Dissertation (American University of Beirut, 1935), p. 217; Saffiuddin Joarder, "The Early Phase of the French Mandatory Administration in Syria; with special reference to the Uprising, 1925–1927," Ph.D. Dissertation (Harvard University, 1968).

[34] Longrigg, *Syria,* p. 137. On the Foreign Legion, see John Harvey, *With the Foreign Legion in Syria* (London, 1928).

[35] FO 371/11908, vol. 7845. Military Attaché (Paris) to Ambassador (Paris), 27 Oct. 1922; FO 371/6232, vol. 9055. Paris Ambassador to FO, 13 June 1923. For distribution of the army in 1922, see FO 371/13091, vol. 7850. Paris Embassy to FO, 20 Nov. 1922.

cost of the Armée du Levant.[36] But after the Great Revolt, the High Commission shifted much of the financial burden of defense and public security onto the Syrian people. Whereas in 1926, the states under Mandate contributed only 4 percent or 10 million francs to the budget of the Troupes du Levant, in 1927 they were forced to contribute 24 percent, or 93 million francs.[37] What this share represented in real terms is staggering. On the average, each state after 1926 was required to pay roughly one-third of its total annual receipts, mainly drawn from its share in the Common Interests, for defense and public security. By World War II, France had invested in Syria and Lebanon some 5 billion francs, of which 4 billion had been spent on defense. With so much capital tied up in this sector, very little was left for productive investment.[38]

In addition to the regular troops of the Armée du Levant, the French also established a Syrian Legion (Troupes Spéciales) recruited almost exclusively from the local population, which became the embryo of a national army. By 1924, the Legion included some 6,500 men commanded by 137 French and 48 native officers. The Great Revolt forced an expansion of the Legion's ranks. By the mid-1930s, its strength had more than doubled to 14,000 troops and 378 officers, 201 of whom were Syrians and Lebanese.[39]

The native officer corps of the Syrian Legion was largely trained at the Military Academy founded in November 1920 in Damascus and transferred in 1932 to Homs. Entrance to the Academy was by examination, although the personal intercession of a prominent Syrian politician or a high-ranking French officer sometimes sufficed. Once admitted, recruits underwent a fairly rigorous training program under the supervision of French instructors.[40]

The urban, absentee landowning aristocracy in Syria had no firm military tradition. Notable families in the late Ottoman period looked down on the army as a poor career choice and used connections and money to secure military exemptions for their sons. During the Mandate era, their view of the army changed from disdain to hatred. Their failure to position

---

[36] See MAE, *Rapport à la Société des Nations sur la situation de la Syrie et du Liban, 1922–1923*, p. 55; *Journal Officiel.* Sénat, 1 Jan. 1922, 26 Oct. 1922.

[37] Raymond O'Zoux, *Les états du Levant sous Mandat français* (Paris, 1931), pp. 214–15; *Rapport à la Société des Nations, 1924*, p. 17.

[38] Hershlag, *Introduction to the Modern Economic History*, p. 241.

[39] *Rapport à la Société des Nations, 1924*, p. 14. Michael H. Van Dusen, "Intra- and Inter-Generational Conflict in the Syrian Army," Ph.D. Dissertation (The Johns Hopkins University, 1971).

[40] MWT, *al-Qism al-khass*, Fakhri al-Barudi Papers. Lieutenant-Colonel Bourget to Barudi, 26 Aug. 1937. For the training programs offered at the academy, see Troupes du Levant, Ecole militaire de Damas, "Programme des conditions d'admission à l'école en 1928 et règlement général." Unpublished pamphlet, n.d.

themselves squarely in the military institution enabled other classes and communities to control the Syrian Army after independence and to contribute eventually to the demise of the old ruling class. And even though some farsighted nationalist leaders encouraged talented young men imbued with the ideals of national patriotism to pursue military careers, the sons of "good families" who entered the Academy were rarely from the most influential or wealthiest branches, a phenomenon which also had dire consequences for these families and the nationalist leadership after independence.[41]

French efforts to prevent the army from having an institutionalized political role also contributed to the poor civil-military relations in mandated Syria.[42] Here, the French were remarkably successful. Their distinct preference for officers from the religious and ethnic minorities and from the countryside certainly helped to isolate the army from the independence movement. Minorities and rural Sunni Arabs were thought to be less susceptible to Arab nationalist influences and therefore the French encouraged them to enter the Academy and promoted them in the military hierarchy. Many of the officers who graduated from the Academy were Christian Arabs, Armenians, Alawites, Circassians, Druzes, and Sunni Arabs from rural districts.[43] Similarly, the rank and file of the Syrian Legion had a significant minority component. There were infantry batallions and cavalry squadrons composed exclusively of Alawites, Kurds, Circassians, Armenians, Isma'ilis, and Druzes.[44] The Syrian Gendarmerie, which policed the countryside and competed with the Syrian Legion, had an even stronger minority component.[45] Under French patronage, the compact minorities and other poor rural elements used the military as a vehicle for social advancement. After independence and the

[41] Patrick Seale, *The Struggle for Syria. A Study of Post-War Arab Politics, 1945–1958* (London, 1965), Chapter 18; *Revue des Troupes du Levant*, 4 (Oct. 1936), pp. 145–47; Conversation with Hani al-Hindi (Beirut, 28 Aug. 1975).

[42] See Van Dusen, "Syrian Army," pp. 166, 181–86.

[43] The Circassians of Syria numbered (by French estimates) 60,000 during the Mandate and lived mainly in the Damascus and Aleppo regions. After they fled the Caucasus to Turkey, the Ottoman state tried to settle them between rival or warring communities or populations, and armed them. One of the most important regions of settlement was in al-Qunaytra where a colony of 13 villages containing between 12,000 and 15,000 Circassians was established, strategically placed between Jabal Druze and Mt. Hermon in order to keep the Druzes and Bedouin tribes in the area apart. Circassian troops were loyal both to the Ottoman state and to the French. During the Mandate they were used to suppress the Great Revolt of 1925. See MAE, Syrie–Liban 1918–29. Captain Collet, "Note sur les Tcherkess," vol. 237, pp. 137–38; *Revue des Troupes du Levant*, 2 (April 1926), pp. 45–58.

[44] See Hanna Batatu, "Some Observations on the Social Roots of Syria's Ruling Military Group and the Causes for its Dominance," *Middle East Journal*, 35 (Summer 1981), pp. 342–43.

[45] Van Dusen, "Syrian Army," p. 44.

establishment of a greatly expanded national army, Druzes and Alawites found the military an eminently suitable vehicle for reaching political power.[46]

Aspects of Administrative Alienation

One of the more contentious aspects of French administration in Syria and Lebanon was the preservation of a judicial system which allowed cases involving foreign nationals to be tried before special courts, despite Article 5 of the Mandate which stated that

> the privileges and immunities of foreigners, including the benefits of consular jurisdiction and protection as formerly enjoyed by capitulation or usage in the Ottoman Empire, shall not be applicable.[47]

Until July 1923, when the High Commissioner decided to reorganize the "jurisdiction of foreign cases," the cost of maintaining such a system had been borne by the budget of the High Commissioner. But, with annual credit reductions by an increasingly parsimonious French Parliament, it became necessary to pass the cost on to the state governments in order to preserve foreign privileges. By the late 1920s, the Syrian state was contributing nearly 6 percent of its annual current expenditures to its Justice Department and an additional 5 percent to its Interior Department.[48]

Basically, the new judicial reforms permitted any foreign national involved in a commercial or civil dispute to have his case tried in a court presided over by a French judge. In addition, if he or any other party so requested, the majority of judges were to be Frenchmen. French clerks were also attached to the Tribunals of the First Instance and Courts of Appeal and Annulment. French judges, who were paid from state budgets, were named by the President of the Syrian Federation (in Lebanon by the Governor), but only with the approval of the High Commissioner. Finally, these judges were granted the right to inspect the native civil court system.[49]

The promulgation of this new judicial regulation was met by heavy criticism in the Syrian and Lebanese press and by well-orchestrated strikes in 1925 and 1926, organized by the nationalist Union of Lawyers

[46] See Nikolaos van Dam, "Sectarian and Regional Factionalism in the Syrian Political Elite," *Middle East Journal*, 32 (Spring 1978), pp. 201–10.

[47] See Hourani, *Syria and Lebanon*, p. 310.

[48] Calculated from Himadeh, *Economic Organization of Syria*, Appendix X, F, p. 434.

[49] After 1928, Mixed Courts were restricted to parties from "ex-capitulatory powers" and to the Japanese. Longrigg, *Syria*, p. 263; Joarder, "The Early Phase," p. 102; PMC, *Minutes*, 5/19/333, De Caix Testimony, 31 Oct. 1924, p. 105.

in Damascus.[50] Two grievances were registered. The first focused not so much on the re-establishment of the Mixed Courts, nor on the general body of French legal reform which native legal experts regarded as an important step toward the rationalization and unification of the Syrian legal system,[51] but rather on the powers of inspection granted to French judges, which gave them enormous influence over Syrian judges.[52] No judicial reform brought out more explicitly the degree of power the French authorities had over the local population. The other grievance focused on the contradiction between what the French claimed to be the establishment of a greatly improved judicial system and the stark reality of life in a garrison state in which the French arrested and jailed or exiled scores of their political opponents, using specially constituted military tribunals headed by Frenchmen.[53]

In fact, the main features of the judicial system in Syria and Lebanon underwent little substantive change during the Mandate. With the exception of some French efforts to reorganize and streamline procedural matters in the *nizamiyya* (general courts for civil, commercial, and criminal cases), the only excessive French interference concerned affairs of personal status, which traditionally were reserved for the *'ulama'* and the religious leaders of the minorities. French attempts to redefine these rights were specifically intended to demote Syria's Sunni Muslim majority to the status of one sect among many and were met by fierce opposition from the Muslim religious establishment. In practice, local Muslim judges consistently refrained from applying French revisions of personal status law.[54]

The French also interfered in the administration of *awqaf* (charitable endowments), another important domain of the Muslim establishment. In the chaotic final years of Ottoman rule and during Faysal's short interlude in Syria, the administration of Muslim charitable endowments had fallen into disarray. At the executive level, the Controller-General, who had been appointed by and responsible to the "Supreme Muslim Council for the inspection of *awqaf*," was now to be appointed by and directly responsible to the High Commissioner. In addition, the High Commissioner was at liberty to veto all Council decisions not pertaining to Muslim law.[55]

[50] Joarder, "The Early Phase," p. 106.
[51] Edmond Rabbath, *L'évolution politique de la Syrie sous Mandat* (Paris, 1928), p. 187, cited by Joarder, "The Early Phase," p. 106.
[52] O'Zoux, *Les états du Levant*, pp. 109–22.
[53] See *Arrêté*, no. 4/s, 10 Jan 1925.
[54] See *al-Ayyam*, no. 1877 (16 June 1939); Hourani, *Syria and Lebanon*, pp. 225–26.
[55] *Arrêté*, no. 753, 2 March 1921; O'Zoux, *Les états du Levant*, pp. 143–44; Longrigg, *Syria*, p. 137. The kernel of Muslim institutions was the *qada'* or *caza* which contained all

Above all, the massive corruption that had plagued *awqaf* administration was significantly reduced. This also led to greater French control. The reforms instituted by Gouraud and his successors eventually led to greater administrative and financial systematization in what was certainly one of the most complex and far-reaching institutions in Syria. However, the High Commission's decision to seize ultimate control over *awqaf* galvanized Muslim opposition. On the surface, protests focused on the issue of non-Muslim interference in a purely Muslim institution. Underneath lay the *ʿulama's* fear that forces of secularization and modernization were progressively undermining their position in Syrian society. An estimated 5,000 Muslim religious leaders stood to lose the material base of their influence—the profits from charitable endowments.[56] Joining the religious establishment in its opposition was the secularized nationalist leadership, which was looking for as many issues as it could find to rally the Syrian masses against French rule.[57]

No incident of tampering with *awqaf* caused a bigger outcry and protest in Syria than the transfer of the Syrian section of the Muslim-owned Hijaz Railway to a French railroad company in 1924. The completion in 1908 of the Hijaz line between Damascus and Medina had been a great source of pride for Syrian Muslims. It was the only railway in Syria not built and owned by Europeans and, among other things, was intended to compete with the European lines. For the duration of the Mandate, the Hijaz Railway issue was a focal point of Muslim opposition to French rule.[58]

The primary motivation behind French efforts to alter the law of personal status and to supervise the administration of charitable endow-

---

the organs of Muslim legal affairs, the *qadi*, *mufti*, and the administration of *awqaf*. PMC, *Minutes*, 5/14/333. "De Caix Testimony," 31 Oct. 1924, p. 106.

[56] Longrigg provides the figure of 5,000 mosque and connected staff. Beneficiaries of charitable endowments numbered nearly 80,000. In 1934, approximately 4,000 *waqfs* existed whose value was estimated to be 500 million francs. About 20 percent of these were directly administered by *awqaf* authorities. *Syria*, p. 264 fn.

[57] For example, in 1935 religious and nationalist leaders accused the Municipality of Aleppo of expropriating *awqaf* lands whenever it saw a profit to be made. By expropriating lands for a road, building, park, etc., their price tended to rise quickly, allowing the Municipality to sell the lands for homes or industrial workshops at a healthy profit. Muslim leaders claimed that these *awqaf* protected thousands of poor Aleppine residents against famine. *Alif ba'*, no. 4295, (20 April 1935); no. 4320, (21 May 1935); *al-Jihad* (Aleppo), no. 198, (1 May 1935); *al-Mudhik al-mubki*, no. 268, (21 Sept. 1935); no. 290, (23 May 1936); no. 293, (20 June 1936).

[58] *Arrêté*, no. 1954, 21 May 1923; *Arrêté*, no. 2044bis, 19 July 1923; Joseph Thureau, "Les chemins de fer en Syrie et en Palestine," *Revue Politique et Parlementaire*, 9 (1918); *Arrêtés*, nos. 2355, 2356, 2357, 22 Feb. 1924; FO 684/6, vol. 2879. Hole (Damascus) to FO, 18 Jan. 1932; FO 371/2661, vol. 10161. Damascus Consul to FO, 4 March 1924; FO 371/8131, vol. 10161. Damascus Consul to FO, 11 March 1924.

ments in Syria was to weaken the country's Muslim majority by upsetting the legal and religious status quo in which Sunni doctrine was clearly dominant. Thus, it was not simply a matter of the French promoting the equality of all religious communities; they feared that if religious shaykhs in alignment with urban nationalist leaders were permitted to organize the mass of Muslims outside the authority of the Mandate government, then the Muslim majority would become an extremely dangerous political weapon.[59]

FRENCH FINANCIAL POLICIES

French financial policies in Syria inevitably were framed with an eye to economic realities in Paris. During a period of severe retrenchment and wild monetary fluctuations at home, French pacification of Syria had cost over one billion francs.[60] Consequently, a niggardly and "suspicious"[61] French Parliament had begun to trim government credits for Syria, forcing the High Commission to transfer an increasingly greater share of the cost of civil administration onto the backs of the local governments. At the same time, however, France's financial policies had two longer-term goals: to perpetuate her political domination over Syria and, whenever possible, to promote her economic interests there. Toward these goals, France assumed control of the Syrian monetary system—a decisive step in reshaping the Syrian economy into a dependency of the French economy.

In 1918, Britain had introduced the Egyptian pound as the unit of exchange in the area, replacing the Turkish pound.[62] Once the French took charge in Syria, they replaced the Egyptian pound with a new paper note, the Syrian-Lebanese pound, directly pegged to the French franc at a fixed ratio of £S 1 to 20 francs. By creating monetary parity between the metropolis and the colony, the French government aimed to pay for its expensive army of occupation in the new local currency and to use the Egyptian pound (redeemable in pounds sterling) to help cover external expenditure.[63]

In 1920, the French government granted the exclusive right to issue the

[59] MAE, Syrie–Liban 1918–29. "Gennardi Note," vol. 274, Feb. 1928.

[60] Most of the cost went to pacifying the Alawite territory, the Antioch region, and the districts around Aleppo. MAE, *Rapport à la Société des Nations, 1922-1923*, p. 55.

[61] FO 371/3622, vol. 7845. Hardinge (Paris) to FO, 4 April 1922.

[62] PMC, *Minutes*, 8/14/518, 25 Feb. 1926, p. 108; Himadeh, "Monetary and Banking System," in *Economic Organization of Syria* (Beirut, 1936), p. 263.

[63] PMC, *Minutes*, 8/14/518, 25 Feb. 1926. "Statement of Robert de Caix," p. 111; al-Nayal, "Industry," p. 53; Thomé, *Le rôle du crédit*, pp. 76–78; Himadeh, "Monetary and Banking System," p. 264.

Syrian currency to a private French bank, the Banque de Syrie; in 1924 this right was renewed for another fifteen years by a convention signed between the Bank (now called the Banque de Syrie et du Grand Liban [BSL]) and largely handpicked representative councils in Lebanon and Syria. The convention also confirmed the BSL as the sole deposit holder of the local governments under Mandate.[64]

From the outset, Syrian merchants were highly suspicious of the new currency. They feared, for example, that it was backed by an insufficient amount of gold and that gold was being drained from the Syrian economy. They also distrusted the other functions of the BSL, because its management was in the hands of a board of directors, composed primarily of Frenchmen residing in Paris.[65] Despite the High Commissioner's law that the only legal monetary unit of exchange for salaries, taxes, and internal and foreign expenditures was the Syrian paper note, in the interior towns the Turkish gold pound remained the preferred unit in private transactions. Merchants set their prices and kept their accounts in gold pounds.[66]

It so happened that immediately after introducing the new currency, France entered a six-year period of severe monetary instability, in which the exchange value of the franc depreciated. The parity system meant that the Syrian paper currency was tied to the fate of the franc. Even when the Syrian economy was stable, the fluctuations of the franc could and did create panics.[67] Between 1920 and 1926, "the franc fell to half its value vis-à-vis the U.S. dollar and to one-third its value in relation to the pound sterling."[68] Over the following ten years, the franc actually appreciated by one-third, only to plummet to less than half its value against the dollar and the pound sterling between 1936 and 1939. Nevertheless, the French, when interrogated by the Permanent Mandates Commission in 1926, defended Syrian bank issues as being more beneficial than detri-

[64] FO 371/12006, vol. 9057. Beirut Consul to FO, 19 Dec. 1923. Himadeh, "Monetary and Banking System" pp. 265–66; Edmund Y. Asfour, *Syria: Development and Monetary Policy* (Cambridge, Mass., 1959), p. 45; *al-Mufid*, no. 45 (11 March 1924).

[65] Himadeh, "Monetary and Banking System," p. 277; 4 of the 16 Directors were Syrian and Lebanese. Stockholders had little say in the decisions the BSL took. The BSL was governed by French banking laws and statutes. PMC, *Minutes*, 8/14/518, 25 Feb. 1926, p. 108.

[66] Himadeh, "Monetary and Banking System," p. 268. The Syrian-Lebanese paper note came into widespread usage only on the Lebanese coast, mainly in Beirut. In the Syrian interior even commercial advertisements in newspapers and magazines listed prices in Turkish gold pounds. PMC, *Minutes*, 8/14/518, 25 Feb. 1926, p. 108.

[67] For example, in early 1924, when the franc began to fall rapidly, a local panic occurred as people desperately tried to unload their Syrian paper notes in return for Turkish gold pounds. Great Britain: Department of Overseas Trade, *Report on the Trade, Industry and Finances of Syria. May 1925*, by H.E. Satow (London, 1925), p. 7.

[68] Himadeh, "Monetary and Banking System," p. 266; Asfour, *Syria*, pp. 46–47. In 1926, the franc returned to a gold standard and was stabilized by the government of Raymond Poincaré. Also see Kemp, *French Economy*, pp. 73–82.

mental because they encouraged French spending in Syria. They also claimed that since they could not prevent commercial transactions in gold, only salaried officials, both Syrian and French, suffered from the franc fluctuations.[69] But, with thousands of urban dwellers—many belonging to the most educated and politically-conscious strata in the country—employed in local Mandate administration, antagonism toward the French, owing to their monetary policy, was considerable. The middle-level bureaucrat could not help but feel resentment as his monthly salary lost more and more of its purchasing power.

Although parity between the franc and the Syrian pound may have encouraged trade and investment, as France claimed, other BSL practices did not. In the first place, the BSL was not a proper central bank; it did not "hold the cash reserves of other banks in the country, nor did it effect a suitable contraction and expansion of credit in the public interest."[70] Its lending policy was, to say the least, conservative, based on a low-risk philosophy. During inflationary periods it raised the discount rate but during periods of contraction it did not sufficiently lower it. It kept a high ratio of deposits in the Bank of France and its investment of reserves was mostly in French securities. As a consequence, local businesses were denied the opportunity of easy credit which otherwise might have stimulated economic activity in Syria.[71] Merchants and small industrialists regarded the BSL as a selfish, profit-hungry concern bent on retarding the economic development of their country.[72]

In the realm of public finance, the High Commission's primary goal was to have Syria and Lebanon pay for themselves.[73] Public finances dur-

---

[69] Robert de Caix's testimony as the French official assigned to defend the French position before the League of Nations. PMC, *Minutes*, 8/14/518, 25 Feb. 1926, pp. 113–15, 120. Taxes were also collected in Syrian pounds.

[70] Himadeh, "Monetary and Banking System," p. 282.

[71] *Ibid.*, p. 284; Hershlag, *Introduction*, p. 239.

[72] Among the many accusations Syrian businessmen levelled at the French during the Mandate was that from the start of occupation the French secretly began to smuggle gold out of Syria to France. Robert de Caix denied this accusation before the Permanent Mandates Commission in 1926, claiming that the gold taken as indemnities or fines from the towns had been re-spent in Syria. Furthermore, since salaries and taxes were paid in paper notes such operations prevented a great amount of gold from passing through the treasury of the BSL and on to France. PMC, *Minutes*, 8/15/522, 26 Feb. 1926, p. 120. In fact, Syrians exported gold in large quantities to France, the U.S., Iraq, and Palestine. The profits to be made by selling Turkish gold on the Baghdad or Palestine markets were certainly worth the risk. Smugglers, bankers, and merchants engaged in this activity in the early years of the Mandate, so much so that estimates of the total stock of gold in Syria in 1923 were 20 to 40 percent of what they had been in 1919. FO 371/2514, vol. 10160. Aleppo Consul to Department of Overseas Trade, 6 March 1923.

[73] Between 1918 and 1930, the expenditures of the High Commission in Syria and Lebanon totaled FFr 459,262,315. Between 1922 and 1930, annual expenditures hovered be-

ing the Mandate were grouped into four separate budgets: the budgets of
the High Commission, the state government, the Common Interests, and
what were called auxiliary budgets. If taken together, these four budgets
accounted for all current expenditures for public security, administration
and justice, economic and developmental purposes, and social and cultural
services.[74] Annual expenditures for defense and public security were
greater than all other expenditures put together. Even if French contributions were ignored, the state governments paid an average of 32 percent of their total expenditures on public security.[75] Since the High Commission wanted local governments to maintain balanced budgets at all
times, and borrowing was therefore discouraged, the amount of revenues
for productive expenditures and investments was further constricted.

By the end of 1923, the various state governments began to generate
surpluses, unaided by French supplementary grants,[76] and for the duration of the Mandate each state continued periodically to register budgetary surpluses, a fact touted by the French long after their departure from
Syria and Lebanon.[77] Syrians and Lebanese of all classes, however, saw
no reason to thank the High Commission for its extreme tightfistedness.
The flow of public revenues was in the direction of French, not Syrian,
priorities. Public expenditure on defense, public security, administration,
and justice were as strikingly high as expenditures for economic development and social services were low.[78]

State budget revenues were drawn from four different sources: the
Common Interests, direct taxes, excise duties, and non-tax revenues. In
the Syrian state, the Common Interests and direct taxes contributed the

---

tween FFr 15 and 21 million. For a breakdown of these expenditures by state and by category
(such as public works, education, etc.), see MD, 7N 4190, Dossier 2. MAE to Ministry of
Finance, 30 June 1931; MAE, Syrie–Liban 1930–40, vol. 481, pp. 181–211.

[74] O'Zoux, Les états du Levant, p. 151; George Hakim, "Fiscal System," in S. B. Himadeh (ed.), Economic Organization of Syria (Beirut, 1936), p. 387.

[75] Calculated for the six-year period, 1927–1932, from Table XXVIII in Hakim, "Fiscal
System," p. 388, and from Appendix X, H., of Himadeh (ed.), Economic Organization of
Syria, p. 436.

[76] MAE, Rapport à la Société des Nations, 1922–1923, p. 55; PMC, Minutes, 8/5/5000,
18 Feb. 1926, p. 41; al-Muqtabas (20 Jan. 1922). The budgetary surplus for all the mandated territories was 20 million francs in 1923 and 60 million in 1924. For the State of Syria
(including the Sanjak of Alexandretta) between 1925 and 1927 it was respectively 28 million
francs, 33.5 million francs and 69.5 million francs. O'Zoux, Les états du Levant, p. 153.

[77] Conversation with Jean Gaulmier (Paris, 23 June 1976).

[78] Between 1928 and 1933, Syrian state expenditures averaged as follows: Defense and
Public Security (32 percent); Administration and Justice (29 percent); Economic Development (23 percent); Social Services (10 percent); Extraordinary Expenditures (7 percent).
The Common Interests supplied 25 percent and the Local State budget supplied 75 percent
of these expenditures. This information is based on data found in MAE, Rapport à la Société
des Nations, 1928–33.

biggest shares, approximately 37 percent each per annum, while excise duties and non-tax revenues each provided shares of 13 percent.[79]

The High Commission directly administered the budget of the Common Interests, the bulk of whose revenues (95 percent annually) came from customs receipts. Since the states under French Mandate lived within a single customs zone it was difficult to distribute equitably revenues from the Common Interests among the different state budgets. It was also difficult to establish ratios for state budget contributions to the Customs and the Cadastral Survey administrations, and to the Ottoman Public Debt. Because the states were unable to reach an agreement among themselves (Lebanon demanded a 70 percent share of customs receipts owing to her higher standard of living and hence to her greater consumption of imports, whereas Syria demanded a 70 percent share on demographic and territorial grounds), the High Commission imposed its own terms in the Customs Union Accord of 1930. Receipts were to be distributed on a quota basis, the coefficient being calculated on estimates of consumption of imported products. Although much contested by both parties, the Accord granted Syria (including the Alawite territory and the Jabal Druze) a 53 percent share and Lebanon a 47 percent share.[80]

The Benefits of France's Special Position

In the early years of the Mandate, the French treated Syria as an imperial possession to be exploited in the "old colonial manner." Their economic policies promoted French economic interests, and, in the process, perpetuated their political domination. From the first days of occupation, the High Commission used all its power to promote the expansion of French commercial and financial activity in Syria at the expense of breaking the Mandate charter which stipulated an "open door" and the equality of opportunity for all member states of the League of Nations. Indeed, the High Commission favored French products and its own nationals when handing out concessions. To get around Mandate restrictions, it invoked a clause which stipulated that no obstacle should be placed in the way of the mandatory in developing the natural resources of the country and that any organization under "its control" could be used to aid this devel-

[79] *Ibid.*; Widmer, "Population," p. 5; *Ibid.*, Appendixes X, A., X, D., pp. 427, 430–31.

[80] FO 371/2093, vol. 16974. MacKereth to Simon, 31 March 1933. The Customs Union was terminated in 1950. Also see Hakim, "Fiscal System," pp. 335–37; Hershlag, *Introduction*, p. 260. Syrians complained that their population was three times the size of Lebanon's and that it consumed 74 percent of all imported goods into the French mandated territories. FO 371/4998, vol. 9053. Damascus Consul to FO, 28 April 1923.

opment.[81] In other words, the High Commission could hand out concessions to whomever it pleased. French traders and financiers clearly had an
edge in Syria and Lebanon and the High Commission kept it that way by
providing exclusive French facilities, such as the French Commercial Office in Beirut, with monthly subsidies.[82]

During the early years of the Mandate, when governments tended to
be puppets of the High Commission, the most significant concessions distributed were practically all public concessions awarded to companies
"wholly or mainly French in ownership." The concessions granted to
French concerns which caused most local resentment were the public utilities. In Aleppo, after protracted negotiations, a French group received
the electricity and tramways concession in 1924. The Crédit Foncier d'Algérie et de Tunisie floated the capital issue, the Société Française d'Entreprises received the construction contract, and the Electricity and Tramway Company of Damascus—a Franco-Belgian concern which had been
established before World War I—managed the enterprise. The concessionaire demanded a guaranteed revenue of eight percent of the invested
capital. At first, the Aleppo Municipality agreed to the project, but, after
more details became known, it balked and negotiated under the "banner"
of opposition to "capitalist exploitation." The French group used the argument that it was impossible to undertake such a project in an unknown
place like Aleppo unless its interests were guaranteed by something fairly
solid. Although the residents of Aleppo and their municipal council continued to oppose the concession, the Aleppo state council, dominated by
moderate and pro-French deputies from the town's outlying districts, approved it. During the Mandate, the electricity and tramway concession
was the focus of protest and boycotts, despite its provision of much-
needed electricity and public transportation. Aleppines had every reason
to be concerned since electricity prices rose frequently in the 1930s and
net profits annually averaged nearly 10 percent of the initial capital out-
lay for construction of powerhouses and reservoirs.[83]

The High Commission's preferential treatment of French traders and
investors angered and frustrated the indigenous population and annoyed
France's European and American competitors. For example, with the increased demand for motor vehicles in Syria in the thirties, the French
auto industry encountered greater competition from the United States.
To weaken the American position, the High Commission decided to

[81] By Article 11 of the *Mandate for Syria and Lebanon, 24 July 1922*. See MAE, Syrie–
Liban 1918–29. "Note on Article 11 of I. Wilhelm," 13 Jan. 1924, vol. 319.

[82] *Ibid.*, Gouraud to Briand, 11 Aug. 1921, vol. 47A, pp. 141–42.

[83] FO 371/9206, vol. 10167. Aleppo Consul to Department of Overseas Trade, 4 Oct.
1924; *al-Ayyam*, no. 578 (22 Aug. 1934); Charles Godard, *Alep. Essai de géographie urbaine et d'économie politique et sociale* (Aleppo, 1938), pp. 55–56, 65, 66.

charge customs duties on automobiles by weight and not price. This drove the retail price of the heavier American automobile up, making it prohibitive except to the very wealthy.[84]

The High Commission also served French commercial interests by manipulating markets. On several occasions, the High Commission secretly spread rumors of short harvests, which enabled it to ban grain exports from Syria. Grain prices dropped rapidly, enabling French agents to buy up large quantities cheaply. Shortly thereafter, the High Commission would announce that the rumors were false and re-open the borders for export, permitting French agents to make quick and substantial profits. Some of the most vehemently anti-French Syrians during the Mandate were the local grain merchants of Damascus.[85]

French customs policy contributed a large share of state revenues and facilitated the penetration of French machine-made goods into Syria, helping to kill off many local handicrafts and to retard the growth of modern industry. Of course, there were other contributing factors favoring foreign imports, such as population shifts and growth, changes in modes of living and taste structure, and the demand created by a large French army of occupation. Nevertheless, Syrian industry was not given adequate protection by the High Commission.

It was not until 1924 that the old Ottoman tariff schedule of 11 percent on almost all imports was raised to 15 percent. Two years later it was raised to 25 percent for members of the League of Nations and to 50 percent for non-members. Although the demise of many traditional industries began before World War I, under the devastating impact of European competition French customs policy in Syria helped to accelerate the decline, eventually causing, during the world depression, the final extinction of several important industries. The depression also caused the curtailment of emigrants' remittances, a severe fall in the price of agricultural products, the reduction in the purchasing power of those classes (the peasantry and the urban lower-middle class) which demanded locally-made goods, a drop in the price of foreign manufactures, and the growth of economic nationalism, which meant the heightening of tariff barriers in the neighboring countries to which Syrian crafts were normally exported. These factors combined to intensify competition in Syria's internal markets, making the survival of traditional industries ever more difficult.

The most serious effect of this decline was the growth of unemployment in the towns, especially among handloom weavers and silk spinners. To add to this problem, Damascus and Aleppo also faced an influx of

---

[84] Conversation with Husni Sawwaf (Beirut, 25 Aug. 1975).
[85] Ibid.

migrants, fleeing the difficult conditions in the countryside.[86] By 1937, the total number of workers and artisans employed in traditional industries had dropped by nearly one-half, to 171,000 from 310,000 in 1913 (see Table 3-1). Furthermore, the number of workers in the few modern industries which sprang up under the protection of higher tariffs had only reached 33,000 by 1937, reflecting the inability of modern industry to absorb the mass of urban unemployed, which in 1932 was reported to be as high as 77,000.

By the mid-1930s, the High Commission faced a growing wave of economically motivated anti-French unrest in the form of demonstrations and strikes against insufficient protection from foreign goods and especially Japanese "dumping," which severely impaired the local cloth industry. In this period, boycotts against French-made goods and French-owned concessions were also frequent.

Although it would be a mistake to downplay what the French did to build Syria's infrastructure during the Mandate, nevertheless French policies hindered economic development in Syria before the Second World War. French banking and monetary practices, the excessive share of the Syrian budget which went to unproductive defense expenditures, the High Commission's preferential treatment of its own nationals, the high

TABLE 3-1
Syrian Workers in Traditional and Modern Industries, 1913 and 1937

	1913 Traditional Industry	1937 Traditional Industry	1937 Modern Industry	1937 Total
Total number of workers/artisans	309,535	170,778	33,149	203,927
Men	142,934	90,065	24,007	114,072
Women	131,651	58,431	6,379	64,810
Children	34,940	22,300	2,763	25,063
In factory	101,605	89,063	33,149	122,212
At home	207,920	81,710	—	81,710
Day Wages	62,294	54,739	17,710	72,449
Piece Work	247,231	116,039	15,439	131,478

SOURCE: Elisabeth Longuenesse, "La classe ouvrière en Syrie. Une classe en formation," 3ème cycle Dissertation (Ecole des Hautes Etudes en Sciences Sociales, Paris, 1977), p. 36.

[86] Hakim, "Industry," pp. 123–29.

prices and fees charged by French-owned or operated electricity and railroad companies, the burdens of old debts such as the Syrian share of the Ottoman Public Debt which by 1934 had bled Syrian resources to the tune of 153.5 million francs,[87] the inadequate protection provided by the French-run customs administration which, incidentally, was rife with corruption, and the heavy tax burden placed on the commercial bourgeoisie by a more efficient tax system were some of the more obvious obstacles to local development. These combined with widespread political instability in the early Mandate and the world depression to deny Syria the capital accumulation required to stimulate and sustain industrial growth.

FRENCH POLICIES from the start provoked a series of uprisings in Syria which culminated in the Great Revolt of 1925–27, the longest and most powerful rebellion in the Arab East in the decade of the 1920s. Among the many grievances fueling these uprisings, some stood out more than others. There was strong opposition to those French policies which fostered and exacerbated traditional sectarian conflicts in the country, demonstrated a distinct favoritism toward the religious minorities, promoted a series of administratively isolated minority enclaves, tampered with the internal affairs of Syria's various communities, and humiliated and emasculated the Muslim majority by seizing control of their institutions while debasing the symbols of their pride. Other grounds for provocation concerned France's inability or unwillingness to promote any recognizable financial and economic interests other than her own. French monetary policy, which tied a new Syrian paper currency to a continuously depreciating French franc, appeared to be melting away a considerable portion of Syria's national wealth. Meanwhile, the debilitating re-orientation forced on the Syrian economy by the partition of geographic Syria in the aftermath of World War I, and the continued erosion of Syrian industry by the spread of the European economy, helped to create and maintain a situation of widespread unemployment and to accelerate inflation in the country. On the one hand, the French supported a tightfisted fiscal policy in areas such as education, agricultural development, public works, and industry; on the other, they spent profusely on the repressive arms of the state—the army and the police, on unwieldly and overlapping state administrations, and on such useless propaganda as the display of democratic institutions which were in fact completely under French control.

On the political level, French policies were specifically tailored to weaken and isolate the forces of nationalism. During the early years of

[87] Al-Siba'i, Adwa', p. 145.

French occupation, nationalist leaders were regularly frustrated in their efforts to assert an effective claim to adequate consideration from the ruling system in Syria. Despite their high degree of independent influence, especially among the politically conscious and active populations in the towns of the Syrian interior, and their recognition as "natural" leaders of urban society, nationalists were completely ignored by the French High Commission which refused to appoint them to the top government posts they so coveted and felt they deserved.

Although the French reinforced the narrow parameters of political life known in Syria in Ottoman times, by confining the summit of politics to interactions between themselves, as replacements for the Turks, and the urban notables who formed the backbone of the absentee landowning class, they still managed to deny the nationalist fraction of this class an effective resource base in government. In fact, the High Commission widened the scope for intra-class conflict which had been the moving force behind the rise of nationalism in Syria in the last years of the Ottoman Empire, by rewarding with government posts those elements who had been rendered politically marginal by their nationalist rivals during the Faysal interlude in Syria and who, with the arrival of the French, found a golden opportunity to re-establish their power and influence by hanging onto the coattails of the High Commission.

French Mandate policy therefore not only sparked outright revolt; it also obliged a large fraction of the Syrian political elite to participate in the popular resistance movement to French rule. But the elite's objectives were not so much to overthrow French rule as they were to shift the local balance of power such that mutual recognition and cooperation between the French and the nationalist elite might then be possible. The nationalist movement was led, after all, by a fundamentally accommodating class of absentee landowners who rebelled in order to re-establish the basis upon which the politics of urban notables could once again thrive. Ironically, the survival of the Syrian political elite and the maintenance of French rule for a quarter century was linked ultimately to France's unwillingness or inability to break the back of the landowning class from which the local political leadership was drawn or to promote, through the creation of a colonial economy, the formation of new social classes and political forces which could pose a more effective challenge to the traditional leadership and, ultimately, to French hegemony.

PART II

INITIAL CONFRONTATIONS, 1920–1924

CHAPTER FOUR

PATTERNS OF EARLY RESISTANCE

THE DIFFUSION OF a new, national feeling in Syria before World War I was the product of several factors: the stepped-up pace of Ottoman centralization, the growing Turkish insensitivity to local Arab needs, and increased exposure to European modes of thought. Nationalism became an ideological instrument for some individuals from two urban groups, the Christian commercial bourgeoisie and the absentee landowners and bureaucrats. Although nationalism was clearly a rising star before the war, it was the French occupation of the Syrian interior in 1920 that ensured the dominance of the new ideology. Direct European control made nationalism the most relevant and topical political idea of the interwar era.

OCCUPATION AND PACIFICATION

The French occupation of the Syrian interior in July 1920 was met with resistance in some regions and acquiescence in others. Where there was armed resistance, it was incapable of halting the French. Yusuf al-ʿAzma, Amir Faysal's Minister of War, led what remained of the poorly disciplined Sharifian Army and a large group of irregulars from the popular quarters of Damascus against the French invasionary force. In a desperate attempt to check the invasion, ʿAzma's motley army entered into battle with the French on July 24, at Khan Maysalun. In a few short hours the Arab forces were soundly defeated. On the following day, the French Army occupied Damascus, meeting little resistance from the demoralized population.[1]

Among the dead at Maysalun lay General ʿAzma. Only 36 years old, he was henceforth immortalized by Syrians as the supreme national martyr. An ex-Ottoman officer who had studied military science in Istanbul and Germany, he had risen to the post of Chief of Staff of the First Ottoman Army in Istanbul before defecting to the Sharifian cause in 1916.

---

[1] Approximately 150 Arabs were killed and another 1,500 were wounded at Maysalun. The French claim to have lost 42 men, with another 152 wounded and 14 missing. The size of the Arab forces has been estimated at anywhere from 4,000 troops (including volunteers) to one division. The French invasionary force was composed mainly of Algerians and Senegalese. For various accounts of the Battle of Maysalun, see Satiʿ al-Husri, *Yawm Maysalun* (Beirut, 1947), p. 343 *passim*; MD, 7N 4192. "L'effort militaire français au Levant," 1 nov. 1919–18 août 1921, 3ᵉ Bureau; *Le livre d'or des troupes du Levant, 1918–1936* (n.pl., n.d.); Longrigg, *Syria*, p. 158.

Despite his extreme Francophobia, he was among the first to warn Faysal in those last days of the Arab Kingdom that resistance would be suicidal. Just a month before Maysalun, he had toured northern Syria to recruit more troops and to make contact with the embryonic Turkish nationalist movement in Cilicia. But, he felt undercurrents of resistance to conscription, particularly in the town of Aleppo. Although discouraged, ʿAzma managed to reinforce his army in preparation for the inevitable French invasion. A gifted military man and a dedicated nationalist, ʿAzma knew his task well. Regardless of the sacrifice, a gesture of defiance had to be made.[2]

Actually, French columns, penetrating from the northwest, had occupied Aleppo two days before Damascus fell. When word of General Gouraud's "ultimatum" to Faysal reached Aleppo on July 15, tribesmen living on its outskirts began moving into the city-center. Five days later French planes circled Aleppo, dropping leaflets carrying Gouraud's proclamation that local residents must submit to French occupation. On the 21st, when it was confirmed that Faysal had accepted the "ultimatum," Bedouin and townspeople went on the rampage, looting and destroying shops, bringing commerce to a dead halt. On July 23, the French Army occupied Aleppo and by the 25th as many as 18,000 French troops were stationed in and around the city. Meanwhile, 9,000 troops under the command of General Goybet took control of Damascus and its vicinity. Gouraud imposed an idemnity of £E 200,000 (10 million francs) on Syria; residents of the nationalist towns were made to foot a large part of the bill.[3]

The French Army had little trouble subduing Syria's towns. Martial law was declared and resisters were quickly rounded up and jailed without trial. Much of the Syrian nationalist leadership in Damascus had already fled across the borders into Transjordan and Palestine. From there, many moved on to Cairo and a life of political exile. The only cordial welcome extended to the French was from those urban notables who had been pushed aside by nationalist forces during the previous two years.

In Damascus, the High Commission staff allowed the moderate government of ʿAla al-Din al-Durubi, which Faysal had appointed just before his departure, to remain in office. It included some of the bitterest enemies of the Syrian nationalist movement, notables like ʿAbd al-Rahman al-Yusuf and Badiʿ Muʾayyad al-ʿAzm. It did not last long, how-

---

[2] Adham al-Jundi, *Tarikh al-thawrat al-suriyya* (Damascus, 1960), p. 168; USNA, Syria. 800. Jackson to Bristol, 14 June 1920.

[3] Amin Saʿid, *al-Thawra al-ʿarabiyya al-kubra* (Cairo, 1934), vol. 3, p. 215; USNA, Syria. 890d.00/34. Jackson to Bristol, 21 July 1920; *ibid.*, 890d.00/35. Jackson to Bristol, 30 July 1920; *ibid.*, 890d.00/48. Young (Damascus) to Bristol, 12 Aug. 1920. At first, the war tax "was levied on certain rich notables, then distributed more equitably." FO 371/3808, vol. 6453. Palmer to Curzon, 10 March 1921.

ever, for Durubi and Yusuf were ambushed and killed during a tour of the Hawran on August 20. Their assailants managed to escape, but the French levied a heavy idemnity on the local Druze community.[4]

In Aleppo, the French Army had few problems. The mayor of the municipality greeted the High Commissioner's representative, General de Lamothe, with an invitation to a sumptuous banquet in his honor that members of the consular corps and 150 local notables attended. None of the town's nationalist leadership were present, however; many had fled into the surrounding countryside or across the Turkish frontier in search of support from Kemalist forces.[5]

Before occupation, local government in Aleppo had been largely in the hands of Iraqi officers and Damascenes, appointees of Amir Faysal. When the French arrived those senior officials who did not resign were summarily dismissed by General de Lamothe. In their place, he appointed a group of cooperative bureaucrats and notables to head the government of the newly proclaimed Aleppo state. For governor (wali), Lamothe chose an old and feeble man of 75 years, Kamil Pasha al-Qudsi. From one of the great landed and religious families of Aleppo, Qudsi was a retired Ottoman colonel who, for twenty years, had headed Sultan Abdülhamid's secret service in the town. He had been an opponent of Faysal's nationalist supporters and, to Lamothe, seemed a perfect choice. What Lamothe neglected to gauge was Qudsi's influence in Aleppo, which was virtually nil.[6]

ALAWITE RESISTANCE

But it was not the interior towns—the centers of nationalist activity—which posed a serious challenge to the French in the first year of their occupation. Rather, it was the countryside. Two regions provided sustained resistance to pacification: the Alawite mountain and the northwestern districts of the Aleppo state.

The French had taken effective possession of the northern coastal strip of Syria nearly two years before they occupied the interior. After the last Turkish officials withdrew from the port of Latakia in October 1918, Sunni Muslim notables in the town formed a provisional government and proclaimed their allegiance to the nationalist government in Damascus. The authority of the Latakia government, however, did not stretch beyond the town's walls because the mountain range behind Latakia,

[4] Hasan al-Hakim, *Mudhakkirati* (Beirut, 1966), vol. 2, p. 153; USNA, Syria. 800. Young to Bristol, 23 Sept. 1920. Also see 'Abd al-Latif al-Yunis, *Thawrat al-Shaykh Salih al-'Ali* (Damascus, n.d.), p. 55.

[5] USNA, Syria. 890d.00/35. Jackson to Bristol, 30 July 1920.

[6] FO 371/11569, vol. 5040. Fontana (Beirut) to Curzon, 1 Sept. 1920; USNA, Syria. 890d.00/93. Aleppo Consulate to Secretary of State, 9 Nov. 1921.

known as the Jabal Ansariyya, was in a state of complete anarchy, filled with roving bands of Alawite rebels who held the territory "at their mercy."

In early November, the first French military detachment reached Latakia by sea from Tripoli. Its commander dismissed the nationalist provisional government and proclaimed France's sovereignty over the whole territory. But after he studied the situation in the mountain he realized that only force could ensure French sovereignty.[7]

When word reached the mountain that the French had occupied the coastal area and were moving into the interior, an Alawite tribal chieftain and venerated religious leader in the district of Tartus summoned twelve of the leading notables of the region to his retreat in al-Shaykh Badr to discuss a plan for unified resistance.[8] Shaykh Salih al-ʿAli, a 35-year-old landowner with a reputation for courage and fair-play built on his earlier resistance to Ottoman interference in his district, easily convinced the notables to contribute their respective fighting forces to the guerilla army he was organizing.[9] Shaykh Salih was not motivated by Arab nationalist sentiments emanating from Damascus; on the contrary, he was interested only in protecting the Alawite districts from all external interference. Nevertheless, he believed that Damascus nationalists were less threatening to Alawite autonomy than were the French. He willingly accepted material assistance from Faysal's government and, in turn, declared his solidarity with the Arab nationalist movement.

The catalyst for the Alawite revolt was a conflict which French authorities tried to arbitrate between Ismaʿilis and Alawites in the county of al-Qadmus, just north of Shaykh Salih's home. Previously, French agents had tried to negotiate with the Alawite chiefs in the region, including Shaykh Salih, but they had been rebuffed. This time Shaykh Salih's partisans drove French garrisons near al-Shaykh Badr out of the area. By July his guerilla bands were in control of much of the mountain. Shaykh Salih owed much of his success to external events. Early in the summer of 1919, the Dandashi clan, whose chiefs supported Amir Faysal, seized Tall Kalakh, southeast of Shaykh Salih's fief, forcing French troops there to withdraw southwards in the direction of Tripoli. Meanwhile, further north in the Antioch region Turkish irregulars (chetehs), armed and financed by the Kemalist movement which was fighting the French for control of Cilicia, marched toward Latakia. Although a small French garrison stationed some twenty miles northeast of the port halted their advance,

---

[7] Jacques Weulersse, Le pays des Alaouites (Tours, 1940), p. 118. Latakia was the headquarters of the Sanjak of Latakia.

[8] Al-Yunis, Thawrat, p. 105; al-Jundi, Tarikh, p. 31. Al-Shaykh Badr was in the district (qadaʾ) of Tartus, in the eastern part of the mountain. See Weulersse, Le pays, map, p. 25.

[9] Al-Yunis, Thawrat, pp. 67–74. Shaykh Salih was no upstart, having inherited from his father Shaykh ʿAli Sulayman the leadership of the Tartus district.

Turkish bands had managed to distract the French army long enough to divert it from its original aim of pacifying the central part of the Alawite mountain.[10] For the next twelve months, until July 1920, the French made no military headway in the mountain.

By the summer of 1920, France was gearing up to occupy all of Syria. Gouraud concluded an armistice with Mustafa Kemal at the end of May. On June 12, he requested a truce with Shaykh Salih. One week earlier, however, General Yusuf al-ʿAzma had visited Shaykh Salih to encourage his continued resistance. ʿAzma was on his way back to Damascus after his disappointing recruitment tour in northern Syria and he knew full well that Gouraud wanted to secure his Turkish and Alawite fronts before marching on Aleppo and Damascus. Although French liaison officers in the Alawite territory had bought off several of Shaykh Salih's rivals and even a few partisans, continued material aid from Damascus, from Kemalist forces, and from the most influential Sunni landowning families in Latakia, the Haruns and Shraytihs, who had their own private militias, encouraged Shaykh Salih to continue his revolt.[11]

The balance of power in the Alawite mountain did not begin to shift in favor of the French until the occupation of Damascus. The demise of the nationalist government slowed the progress of the Alawite revolt by cutting off one source of military assistance. This setback, however, was temporarily alleviated by a new revolt in the districts between Antioch and Aleppo, which spread after the French occupied Aleppo. It opened up a second major front in Syria which not only helped to relieve some of the pressure on Shaykh Salih's guerilla army, but also offered it material aid and much needed moral support.[12]

It was not until the Turkish nationalists and the French gradually came to an arrangement over Cilicia in March 1921 that the fate of the Alawite revolt took an irreversible turn for the worse.[13] Following a series of suc-

---

[10] Al-Yunis, *Thawrat*, p. 107; al-Jundi, *Tarikh*, p. 31. For the official French account of the Alawite revolt, see MD, 7N 4192. "L'effort militaire français au Levant," 3ᵉ Bureau; ibid., 7N 4186, Dossiers 1,2; also see Weulersse, *Le pays*, p. 118; conversation with ʿAli ʿAbd al-Karim al-Dandashi (Damascus, 9 March 1976); Yusuf al-Hakim, *Suriyya wa al-ʿahd al-Faysali* (Beirut, 1966), p. 93.

[11] Al-Jundi, *Tarikh*, pp. 38–39; USNA, Syria. 800. Jackson to Bristol, 14 June 1920; MAE, Syrie–Liban 1918–29. vol. 427B. *Bulletin de Service des Renseignements*, 47 (20 Oct.–10 June 1922), pp. 6–7; al-Jundi, *Tarikh*, pp. 26–28. The head of the landowning Harun family at the time was ʿAziz Agha (1868–1933), the chief liaison of Amir Faysal with Shaykh Salih as well as the latter's main fund-raiser.

[12] Weulersse, *Le pays*, p. 119; al-Yunis, *Thawrat*, pp. 187–188. It seems that Shaykh Salih first contacted Ibrahim Hananu on 10 Feb. 1921 about securing military assistance, which Hananu sent him. Both leaders signed a joint petition to the League of Nations in early 1921 calling for the freedom and independence of Syria in accordance with the League's charter and President Wilson's "14 points." Translations of this petition are found in FO 371/4942, vol. 6454, and USNA, Syria. 890d.00/76, 13 May 1921.

[13] Mustafa Kemal had agreed to an armistice of twenty days with the French; it was nul-

cessful Alawite raids on French posts in the winter and early spring of
1921, three French columns encircled the Alawite mountain, from Latakia and Baniyas on the west and from Hama on the east. Engagements
over the next two months gave France the military edge, although not
without heavy casualties. By the end of summer, the French had established their authority over much of the mountain. By November, Turkish
aid had again been cut off owing to the Franklin-Bouillon Agreement of
October 20 which brought Franco-Turkish hostilities to an end and a
French military withdrawal, and the Alawite rebels surrendered after
more than two years of resistance. Eventually Shaykh Salih was pardoned. Until his death in 1926, he lived in the Alawite mountain in relative seclusion, only occasionally becoming involved in local politics.[14] In
the nationalist towns of the Syrian interior, he was honored as a great
freedom fighter who had struggled heroically for the territorial integrity
and independence of the Syrian nation. In his own region, however, his
followers honored him not as a nationalist but as the defender of Alawite
independence from foreign hegemony. With the failure of his revolt, the
High Commission began to implement its policy of isolating the Territory of the Alawites from nationalist forces in the Syrian interior.[15]

Syrian historiography has ascribed nationalist motivations to all the
revolts against the French during the early Mandate. Although some uprisings were nationalist in flavor, those like the Alawite movement which
involved compact minorities were more often inspired by local considerations or, at least, non-ideological ones. What gave Shaykh Salih's anti-
French rebellion a different coloration from previous Alawite uprisings
against Ottoman interference was that for the first time Alawites found a
need and an opportunity to coordinate their activities with other resistance activities in Syria in a common struggle against foreign rule. Shaykh
Salih's movement was in contact both with Damascus and the growing
resistance in the Aleppo province. Political movements in Syria were acquiring new, more complex organizational forms, even if their fundamental aims were old and familiar.

HANANU'S REVOLT

Aleppo, like Damascus, expressed its anti-French sentiments long before
occupation. The movement of the Aleppine political elite into the main-

---

lified on May 30 by renewed fighting. MD, 7N 4186. "L'effort militaire français au Levant,"
Dossier 1; Longrigg, *Syria*, p. 118.

  [14] Weulersse, *Le pays*, p. 119; MAE, Syrie–Liban 1918–29. vol. 427B, pp. 6–7. Longrigg,
Syria, pp. 121–22; FO 371/7847, vol. 7801, 28 June 1922; MD, 7N 4184, Dossier 2. Gouraud to Ministère de la Guerre, 3 June 1922; Edmond Rabbath, *Courte Histoire du Mandat
en Syrie et au Liban*, section 1, p. 45.

  [15] For example, see al-Jundi, *Tarikh*.

stream of Syrian-Arab nationalist politics, however, was slower and more deliberate. The contribution of Aleppines to the rise of Arabism in Syria before the First World War was slight, as was the role of Aleppines in the Arab Revolt of 1916.[16] It was not until 1918, when the Aleppo province joined Faysal's Arab state, that a split within the Aleppine political elite along nationalist and non-nationalist lines occurred.

There are several reasons for Aleppo's slower comingling in the stream of Arab nationalism. While Damascus had a fairly homogeneous Arab Muslim population, Aleppo was far more ethnically and religiously heterogeneous. Aleppo was not as important a seat of Islamic learning as was Damascus nor was it a gathering point for the pilgrimage. Perhaps most important, its natural hinterland was culturally more Turkish than Arab.

Like the Damascene political elite, the Aleppine elite had served the Ottoman state as an "aristocracy of service." But, it had absorbed even more of the Ottoman-Turkish trappings of language, culture, and style than the Damascus elite. In Damascus, Turkish came to be spoken politely alongside Arabic in aristocratic homes only in the latter half of the nineteenth century; in Aleppo, Turkish had been commonly spoken since the Ottoman conquest of northern Syria in the sixteenth century. Because of Aleppo's geographical proximity to Anatolia and its links to Istanbul, a high proportion of the Aleppine notability possessed a partly Turkish lineage (there was also a high incidence of Kurdish stock). Marriages with Turkish and Turco-Circassian families were not only normal, but preferred.[17]

Aleppo's social and cultural ties to Turkey were largely the product of its age-old economic orientation toward its north. Anatolia was its major market and greatest source of raw materials and foodstuffs, and Aleppo's livelihood and prosperity depended on free commercial access to Anatolia. Consequently the Aleppine political elite, although interested in greater political autonomy for the Aleppo province at the time of the Arab Revolt, maintained a stronger attachment to Istanbul and to Ottoman temporal authority than did the Damascus elite.[18]

The Arab Revolt was regretted in some Aleppine political circles. Even Aleppines who had joined the revolt did not expect or want it to go as far

[16] C. Ernest Dawn, "The Rise of Arabism in Syria," *From Ottomanism to Arabism* (Urbana, 1973), p. 174. Their marginality has been deduced from a careful study of key biographical dictionaries. See Faris, *Man huwa 1949*; Adham al-Jundi, *Shuhada' al-harb al-'alamiyya al-kubra* (Damascus, 1960); al-Jundi, *Tarikh*.

[17] Conversation with Edmond Rabbath (Beirut, 3 Sept. 1975). According to Rabbath, Istanbul was renowned in Aleppo for its beautiful women and second, there was great prestige attributed to marrying a Turk. The Jabiri family frequently married Turks.

[18] *La Syrie* (31 Jan. 1925). Quoted in FO 371/966, vol. 10850. Aleppo Consul to FO, 5 Feb. 1925.

as it did;[19] it had broken the ranks of Islamic unity, it had helped to bring about the collapse of the Ottoman Empire, and it had separated Aleppo from its Turkish hinterland.

The reluctance of Aleppine notables to jump on the nationalist bandwagon was compounded by resentment at the predominance of Damascus during the Faysal era. Under Ottoman rule Aleppo had been the administrative capital of its own province and of equal stature with Damascus. Under the Sharifian government it found itself subordinate to the new national capital. Although some Aleppine politicians held sway with Faysal and in the nationalist organizations in Damascus, back home in Aleppo the highest authorities were Iraqis and Damascenes.[20] The unequal relationship between the towns engendered doubt and jealousy among Aleppo's political elite and contributed to a certain weakness of national sentiment in and around Aleppo.

Nonetheless, it was a mistake to assume, as many French officials did at the time, that Aleppo was likely to remain politically quiescent. The partition of northern Syria which created commercial barriers between Aleppo and its natural Turkish hinterland not only helped to spark Aleppo's resistance to French rule, it obliged Aleppines to take a greater interest in matters "Syrian" and gradually even to assume a new Syrian identity.[21] In competition with Damascus, Aleppo did not go over to the French. Rather, it vigorously resisted occupation in order that its voice be heard in the new political climate.

As the French Army moved into northern Syria, Aleppine political leaders, who felt it was imperative to organize resistance, turned to the Turkish nationalist movement for support. Some did so with the long-range goal of reuniting their territory with Turkey. Others, and they

---

[19] No less an observer of Syrian affairs than the renowned French orientalist, Louis Massignon, was "confounded" by what he referred to, in a 1920 report to the Quai d'Orsay, as a "switch" after World War I to a pro-Turkish sentiment founded on grounds of Islamic unity by many of the same leaders who had revolted against the Turks during the war. He said that this was especially true of leaders from Aleppo, Homs, and Damascus. Other French officials observed that in the 1920s Syria was literally divided between a pro-Turkish sympathy in the north and Arab nationalism in the south. Still others noted that the "majority of Muslims" desired the unity of Syria. MAE, Syrie–Liban 1918–29. Nov. 1920, vol. 35, pp. 138, 234.

[20] One of Faysal's closest advisers and confidants, however, was the Aleppine Ihsan al-Jabiri, who served as the Amir's Chamberlain and head of his *diwan* (inner council). In 1920, he was elected mayor of the city of Aleppo. During Faysal's reign, the civilian governor of the Aleppo province was an Iraqi, Naji Suwaydi; the Chief of Police was a Damascene, Nabih al-'Azma. USNA, Syria. 890d.01/2. Aleppo Consul to Secretary of State, 13 March 1920; FO 371/11569, vol. 5040. Fontana to Curzon, 1 Sept. 1920.

[21] MD, 20N 1089. "Armée du Levant, Syrie et Liban, Rapport mensuel," no. 1 (June 1921), p. xi; also see the impressions of the British and Italian Consuls in FO 371/12162, vol. 9053. Aleppo Consul to FO, 9 Nov. 1923.

seem to have been in the majority, aligned themselves with Kemalist forces when it became obvious that the French had paralyzed Arab nationalist forces in Damascus. But whether the Turks were approached openly or with caution, the overwhelming sentiment in Aleppo in July 1920 was distinctly pro-Turkish and anti-French.

In fact, the northern Syrian resistance movement was far more influenced by the Turkish nationalist movement than it was by the Arab nationalist movement. The Turks were simultaneously fighting the French for control of a large area of northern Syria, which formed a semicircle stretching westwards from the district of ʿUrfa through Maʿrash down to the Mediterranean coast and the districts of Antioch and Alexandretta.[22] Within the semicircle the northern Syrian revolt originated and an alliance developed with the Kemalist movement.

The central figure of this resistance to the French was a former Ottoman bureaucrat of Kurdish extraction, Ibrahim Hananu. Born in 1869 in Kafr Takharim, a fertile olive-growing area in the Harim district west of Aleppo, Hananu was the son of a wealthy rural notable. On completing his secondary education in Aleppo, he defied his father's wish that he remain on the land by going to Istanbul for further education. He spent seven years earning two diplomas at the prestigious *Mülkiye* (the principal school of public administration) and a law degree. Afterwards, he returned to Aleppo, where he served in several government departments for a few years until he chose to retire prematurely to assume the management of his estates. When the Arab Revolt broke out, Hananu joined Faysal's Arab Army as an officer. He entered Aleppo with the Allies in 1918. Having embraced the nationalist cause, he joined the secret nationalist society *al-Fatat* and, in the summer of 1919, he was elected as Harim's representative to the Syrian Congress in Damascus.[23]

The Congress, however, was not to Hananu's taste. A man of action who rarely minced his words, he found the smoke-filled congressional chamber a place where nationalist politicians glorified the Arab Revolt and harangued the French and one another, but did little else. He realized that the only way to defend northern Syria was to mobilize popular forces in Aleppo and he left the Congress after its first session.

Back in Aleppo, Hananu recruited young men into his own League of National Defense. With the support of several prominent merchants, religious leaders, and members of the liberal professions, the League collected 2,000 gold pounds and 1,700 rifles for the 680 recruits being trained

[22] See "Map of Syrian Wilayats and Sanjaks in 1910," in Eugen Wirth, *Syrien. Eine Geographische Landeskunde* (Darmstadt, 1971), p. 30.

[23] Al-Jundi, *Tarikh*, p. 116; Khayr al-Din al-Zirikli, *al-Aʿlam; qamus tarajim li-ashhar al-rijal wa al-nisaʾ min al-ʿarab wa al-mustaʿribin wa al-mustashriqin* (Cairo, 1954–1957), vol. 1, p. 35; Yusuf al-Hakim, *Suriyya wa al-ʿahd al-Faysali* (Beirut, 1966), p. 92.

by Hananu and his aides. Alongside the League of National Defense, a political organ emerged to propagate the idea of Syrian national unity. Known as the Arab Club of Aleppo, its founders included Hananu, Najib Baqi Zadih, a prosperous merchant, and ʿAbd al-Rahman al-Kayyali, an American-trained physician from an aristocratic family. The club president was one of Aleppo's leading religious figures, Shaykh Masʿud al-Kawakibi.[24]

The political coloring of these two organizations was a blend of Aleppine regionalism and Arab nationalism. Under the influence of Ibrahim Hananu and other leaders of a similar political persuasion, Aleppo's Muslim elite gradually assumed an Arab national identity. The decisive watershed in its conversion was not, however, the Arab Revolt of 1916, but what has come to be known in Syrian nationalist historiography as the "Hananu revolt."[25]

The Hananu revolt was not an urban revolt. It broke out in the autumn of 1919 in the countryside surrounding Aleppo, ten months before the French occupied the city. When France did occupy Aleppo in July 1920, French military superiority quieted most urban agitation and drove much of the nationalist leadership into the safer confines of the rebellious countryside. Townspeople surreptitiously provided material aid to Hananu partisans operating in the districts west of the town; but, the form of their own resistance was, perforce, passive.

Like the Alawite rebellion, Hananu's revolt depended on aid from Turkish nationalists. The Turkish nationalist movement under Mustafa Kemal's command, which was simultaneously battling the French Army of the Levant for control of Cilicia and southern Anatolia,[26] contributed men, money, and arms in large quantities to Hananu's forces. The Turks also supported a wide network of political committees and organizations in northern Syria for the dissemination of pro-Turkish and anti-French propaganda.[27] Interspersed with this was a measure of Bolshevik propaganda—mainly in leaflet form—calling for the Syrian people to overthrow their French colonizers. Such propaganda aroused the worst fears of the French (as well as of the British). Pro-Hashemite factions in Amman, Baghdad, and Cairo, with ties to nationalist groups in Damascus,

[24] Al-Jundi, Tarikh, p. 62; USNA, Syria. 890d.01/2. Consul to Secretary of State, 13 March 1920.

[25] See Jamil Ibrahim Pasha, Nidal al-ahrar fi sabil al-istiqlal (Aleppo, 1959). Detailed accounts of the Hananu revolt can be found in al-Jundi, Tarikh, pp. 61–148; Munir al-Rayyis, al-Kitab al-dhahabi lil-thawrat al-wataniyya fi al-mashriq al-ʿarabi. al-Thawra al-suriyya al-kubra (Beirut, 1969), pp. 116–41.

[26] Al-Jundi, Tarikh, pp. 64, 71, 72–73, 130; FO 371/2142, vol. 20849. 6 May 1937.

[27] MAE, Syrie–Liban 1918–29. Report of Capitaine de Vaud, vol. 208, pp. 145–52; FO 371/9657, vol. 6455. Damascus to FO, 9 Aug. 1921.

were also alarmed and sent strong warnings to the people of northern Syria about Turco-Bolshevik designs on their territory.[28] Ibrahim Hananu and his closest aides, some of whom were Turkish army officers, were not about to bite the hand that fed them. Although there existed a degree of mutual suspicion between Aleppine nationalists and Kemalists, both parties recognized that they were fighting a common enemy.[29] On the popular level, the Syrian masses applauded and supported the Turkish independence struggle, and religious solidarity with the Turks, at least in northern Syria, was especially strong.[30]

Several individuals supporting the Hananu revolt were regular emissaries to Mustafa Kemal in 1920 and 1921. Probably the most influential liaison was provided by an absentee landowner of Aleppo, Jamil Ibrahim Pasha, who had studied in the Military College in Istanbul, joined the Committee of Union and Progress, fought in the Balkan Wars, and supported the unity of the Ottoman Empire until the conclusion of the First World War. Toward the end of summer 1920, Ibrahim Pasha (who, like Hananu, was an Arabized Kurd) visited Mustafa Kemal at his ʿAyntab headquarters to finalize plans for a joint military campaign against the French. According to Ibrahim Pasha, a firm agreement was reached soon afterwards. By December, a Turkish-financed anti-French propaganda campaign was underway inside Aleppo.[31]

In occupied Aleppo, economic and social distress galvanized anti-French sentiment. The stagnation of commerce, owing to the disruption of trade routes between the town and its natural hinterland and the recent influx of Armenian refugees from Turkey, contributed to rising unemployment. Hoarding and profiteering, especially of flour whose price had

[28] Some Bolshevik circulars printed in Arabic and signed by Lenin were addressed and distributed to the Aleppo population, advising it to adopt communism as a means to fight the French and thereby to save the East for the Muslim peoples. See USNA, Syria. 890d.00/ 58. Vice-Consul (Aleppo) to Bristol, 13 Dec. 1920; MD, 7N 4184, Dossier 2bis, 1922; FO 371/535, vol. 6453, 1 April 1921.

[29] Aleppine nationalists were mainly interested in securing Turkish assistance for their revolt against the French. Some feared the possibility of a Turkish occupation of Aleppo. They could not forget that Mustafa Kemal led the Turkish Army in retreat from Syria when the Allies entered Aleppo in October 1918. These same nationalists had aided the Allies at the time. USNA, Syria. 890d.00/44, 890d.00/145. Allen to Beirut Consul, 20, 29 Sept. 1922.

[30] One example of continued popular support for the Turks occurred in 1922, when demonstrations in Aleppo broke out in favor of a Turkish victory over the British-supported Greeks. The local population looked upon this war as a great victory for Islam over Christianity. But, by then Arab nationalists and the better educated Muslims of Aleppo were hostile to the Turks because of their recent settlement and treaty with France which helped to end the Hananu revolt. USNA, Syria. 890d.00/145. Allen to Beirut Consul, 29 Sept. 1922.

[31] Faris, *Man huwa 1949*, pp. 9–10; Ibrahim Pasha, *Nidal*, pp. 30–31; USNA, Syria. 890d.00/60. Aleppo Consul to Istanbul, 20 Dec. 1920.

soared, led to food riots; famine was even reported in some quarters. Under martial law, the High Commission curtailed the freedoms of speech, association, and travel.[32] As a consequence, Aleppo willingly supplied the Hananu revolt with men, money, and arms. Quarter bosses recruited fighters into rebel bands, and contributions flowed in from Aleppo's landowners and merchants.[33]

But, with much of Aleppo's nationalist leadership either in exile or in jail, and with 5,000 French (mainly Senegalese) troops stationed in the town and another 15,000 in its vicinity,[34] a sustained urban revolt never materialized. Instead, Muslim residents in the town's poorer quarters took out their frustrations on those least able to defend themselves, the Christian minorities (approximately 35 percent of the city's population), who were traditionally, though not always correctly, identified with European interests. Incidents of violence against Christians abounded in Aleppo and Christians were even prevented from residing in the large southeastern suburb, Bab al-Nayrab, Aleppo's equivalent of the popular quarter of al-Maydan in Damascus.[35]

The Hananu revolt also received some encouragement from Amir ʿAbdullah in Transjordan, after his arrival there in early 1921. The major go-between was a Bedouin chief of Dayr al-Zur, Ramadan Pasha Shallash; he was an ex-Ottoman army officer, close to ʿAbdullah, and a declared supporter of Hananu.[36] The assistance that ʿAbdullah supplied, although small, was particularly provoking, for the French feared that his personal ambitions in Syria were part of a British plot to ease them out of the country. The Hananu revolt spread rapidly after the occupation of Aleppo. From the low figure of 800 men in the summer of 1920, its ranks swelled to a reported 5,000 by the time rebel bands resumed their offensive in November. Hananu's bands included Aleppine volunteers and conscripts, villagers, and Bedouins. Turkish officers, supplied by Mustafa

---

[32] FO 371/6049, vol. 6454. Aleppo Consul to Curzon, 14 May 1921; USNA, Syria. 890d.00/93. Aleppo Consul to Secretary of State, 9 Nov. 1921; USNA, Syria. 890d.00/58. Aleppo Consul to Bristol, 13 Dec. 1920.

[33] Ibrahim Pasha, *Nidal*, p. 6.

[34] USNA, Syria. 890d.00/72. Aleppo Consul to Bristol, 12 April 1921.

[35] USNA, Syria. 890d.00/58. Aleppo Consul to Bristol, 12 Dec. 1920. The heterogeneous Bab al-Nayrab was the largest quarter of Aleppo in the early 1920s, with a population of 12,000. It housed peasants from the rural districts around Aleppo and semi-sedentarized tribes from the Euphrates Valley. MAE, Syrie–Liban 1918–29. vol. 33, pp. 119–20; Abdul-Rahman Hamidé, *La ville d'Alep* (Paris, 1959), pp. 25–26.

[36] MD, 20N 1089. *Bulletin de Renseignements*, 206, 23 June 1921. Ramadan Shallash was a member of the Al Bu Saraya Tribe of Dayr al-Zur. He was a graduate of the Military School for Bedouin Chiefs in Istanbul. In 1916, he fought in the Sharifian Army at Medina. In 1920, he led a band of tribesmen against the French. See *Oriente Moderno*, 6 (1926), pp. 93–94.

Kemal, led some bands. But, although Hananu was in command of the largest bands in the districts between Antioch and Aleppo, his authority did not extend to a number of smaller bands of Turkish irregulars operating in the area, or to the small Syrian bands organized specifically for pillaging and looting that had become a common feature of the Aleppine countryside in this period.[37]

Although the Hananu forces were poorly equipped, possessing only two cannons and twelve machine guns, in addition to small arms and ammunition supplied by the Turks, they were able to take advantage of the rugged and, to the French, unfamiliar terrain. A particularly effective tactic was to conduct night operations using a reflector system (which the French believed the British had supplied). By the end of November 1920, the districts and towns from Harim to Jisr al-Shaghur were in the hands of Hananu partisans. The important town of Idlib to the north of Aleppo and Ma'arrat al-Nu'man to the south appeared to be next on the rebel agenda. Meanwhile, with the collapse in September 1920 of the Franco-Turkish armistice that had cut off Turkish aid to rebels since May, revolt in the districts between Antioch and Latakia had been rekindled, led by Kemalist officers and Turkish irregulars around Antioch and by Shaykh Salih al-'Ali in the Alawite mountain.[38] The repeated destruction of railroad and telegraph lines connecting Aleppo with Alexandretta and Beirut placed the whole of northwestern Syria in danger of a rebel takeover.

General de Lamothe at Aleppo began casting about for reinforcements. By early December, he had managed to scrape together two columns— one at Hammam (north of Harim) and the other at Idlib. After several attacks and counterattacks, rebel positions from Harim to Jisr al-Shaghur fell to the Hamman column. Syrian rebels and Turkish troops made one last major effort to retake these positions during Christmas week and a reversal actually seemed possible until another French relief column entered to turn the tide.[39] The military campaigns of December 1920 were a decisive setback for the Hananu revolt.

Retreating Syrian forces took refuge in the rugged Jabal al-Zawiya, south of Idlib, where Ibrahim Hananu and other rebel leaders organized them into several small detachments. France and Turkey reached agreement over Cilicia and Turkish assistance gradually dried up. Hananu desperately employed local bandits to extract money and provisions from the

---

[37] USNA, Syria. 890d.00/58, 890d.00/72. Aleppo Consul to Bristol, 13 Dec. 1920, 12 April 1921.

[38] USNA, Syria. 890d.00/58. 13 Dec. 1920; al-Jundi, *Tarikh*, p. 75; Longrigg, *Syria*, p. 121.

[39] For details of the battles fought during November and December, see al-Jundi, *Tarikh*, pp. 75–81; Longrigg, *Syria*, p. 121.

inhabitants of Jabal al-Zawiya and neighboring districts. His only source of arms was now in Hama and Maʿarrat al-Nuʿman. Rebel operations continued through the winter and spring of 1921. But Syrian forces, now contained in Jabal al-Zawiya, suffered one defeat after another, and their leadership disintegrated. Hananu fled Syria in July, taking refuge with exiled Syrian nationalists in Transjordan. But in mid-August, British intelligence officers arrested him during a trip to Jerusalem and, in accordance with a previous agreement with France, extradited him to Syria.[40]

Hananu spent six months in prison in Aleppo. Finally, in March 1922 he got his day in court. In a dramatic courtroom defense, his young Aleppine Christian lawyer, Fathallah al-Saqqal, argued that his client was a national hero, not a criminal. When Hananu took the stand, he denounced all aspects of France's "illegal occupation of Syria." He also claimed that the military operations had been entirely in the hands of the Ankara government of Mustafa Kemal.[41] After a three-day trial, he was surprisingly acquitted of organizing rebel bands, acts of brigandage, murder, and the destruction of railroads and public works. There seems little doubt, however, that the verdict would have been different had Franco-Turkish relations not improved since the signing of the Franklin-Bouillon Agreement in October 1921, and had Hananu not become a legend in his own time.[42]

The Hananu revolt, like the revolt of Shaykh Salih al-ʿAli, failed because of the withdrawal of Turkish military assistance.[43] Scattered bands of Hananu partisans continued their resistance into the fall of 1921, but did not possess the matériel to sustain a revolt. Turkish nationalists, after a show of force, were able to secure by negotiation the withdrawal of French garrisons from Cilicia, and from the districts of ʿAyntab, Rum Qalʿa, Maʿrash, and ʿUrfa, which had been part of the Aleppo *vilayet*. Nationalists in Syria, however, failed to muster sufficient force to dislodge France's stubborn hold or to get France to adopt a more accommodating posture.[44]

[40] Al-Jundi, *Tarikh*, pp. 90, 95–100; MD, 20N 1089. *Bulletin de Renseignements*, 177, 14 May 1921, p. 4; FO 371/1102, vol. 6456. Satow to FO, 24 Sept. 1921.

[41] See the memoirs of Fathallah al-Saqqal, *Dhikrayati fi al-muhama fi misr wa suriyya* (Aleppo, 1958); al-Jundi, *Tarikh*, p. 113.

[42] For a detailed account of the Hananu trial, see al-Jundi, *Tarikh*, pp. 101–12.

[43] The French reported that after the settlement of the "Northern Gates" or Cilicia (which included Killis and ʿAyntab), the Turks sent political agents into northern Syria disguised as merchants to encourage the population to give in to the French and accept the benefits they had to offer. FO 371/6038, vol 6454. Citing French "Secret Intelligence Report," 25 May 1921.

[44] Longrigg, *Syria*, p. 119; MAE, Syrie–Liban 1918–29. "La Propagande," 19 April 1923, vol. 208.

URBAN PACIFICATION

The Franco-Turkish *rapprochement* increased security in the Sanjak of Alexandretta, from which goods and passengers began to reach Aleppo with greater regularity. But Aleppo's commerce with southern Anatolia remained frozen. There was a certain degree of cooperation between Turkish and French border patrols in the north, but brigandage was still widespread. Although the Turks tried to suppress the flow of contraband across the undelimited frontier with Syria, a flow which had intensified owing to the prohibitive tariffs levied on Syrian goods by the Ankara government, they continued to aid small rebel bands operating against the French in these areas, which contained mixed and mutually antagonistic populations of Kurds, Arabs, and Turks.[45] Meanwhile, they pressed their claim to the Sanjak of Alexandretta by encouraging Turkish rebels there to maintain a constant level of tension and unrest.

The reduction of Turkish aid after the Franklin-Bouillon Agreement had soured Syrian-Turkish relations. The nationalist leadership in the North felt betrayed. Defeated and helpless, nationalists angrily watched as the Turks, with French cognizance, annexed northern districts of the former Ottoman province of Aleppo, from 'Urfa to Ma'rash.[46] The French also did little to thwart Turkish activities in the Sanjak of Alexandretta, claimed by Turkey, but which, by the Franklin-Bouillon Agreement, remained attached to Syria under a French-manipulated "special regime."[47] Merchants and nationalist leaders in Aleppo feared that the Sanjak's autonomy would make it vulnerable to Turkish control, cutting Aleppo off from the Mediterranean. With Aleppo already suffering from its loss of trade with Turkey, the additional loss of the Alexandretta connection would have been an economic disaster.[48]

Although some Aleppine nationalists still hoped that continued Turkish penetration and harassment would weaken the French grip on the

[45] FO 371/11182, vol. 6456. Beirut Consul to FO, 5 Oct. 1921. FO 371/3468, vol. 7846. Aleppo Consul to FO, 15 March 1922; FO 371/7801, vol. 7847. Translation of "Secret French Report on the Situation in Syria and Cilicia," 28 June 1922; Hourani, *Syria and Lebanon*, p. 58; FO 371/11883, vol. 7848, 18 Oct. 1922.

[46] See MAE, Syrie–Liban 1918–29. "La propagande," 19 April 1923, vol. 208; USNA, Syria. 890d.00/145. Aleppo Consul to Secretary of State, 29 Sept. 1922.

[47] MD, 7N 4183, Dossier 3. Wegand (Aley) to MAE, 4 Aug. 1923; FO 371/8309, vol. 6455. Admiralty to FO, 18 July 1922.

[48] To quote from one newspaper of Aleppo: "The Sanjak of Alexandretta is the mouth of Aleppo, its economic life and its most active member. . . . The poor revenues of this Sanjak and its great dependence upon the export of agricultural produce and of the articles produced by industries in the State of Aleppo prevent it from separating itself from its body, Aleppo, to which it is connected by the above mentioned ties." *Tarikat al-suri* (Aleppo) (19 Dec. 1923), quoted in FO 371/895, vol. 10159. Aleppo Consul to FO, 27 Dec. 1923; FO 371/8309, vol. 6455. Admiralty to FO, 18 July 1921.

North and that commercial relations with Turkey would resume, their
growing disillusionment with the Kemalists warranted a re-orientation of
their political strategy. Following the collapse of the Hananu revolt,
Aleppo nationalists shifted their political direction. They finally embraced wholeheartedly the idea of a unified Syrian struggle for national
independence, and began to strengthen their ties with Damascus.

French efforts to organize a civilian administration in Aleppo had begun at the end of October 1920 when General Gouraud issued a decree on
the "temporary organization" of the Aleppo state. First, a French officer
delegated by the High Commissioner was to be directly responsible for
the operation of local government and several technical advisers were to
accompany the Delegate to oversee all political and administrative matters. Secondly, the Delegate was to approve all decisions of the local government before their implementation, and all native officials had to submit their decisions to French advisers for approval before they reached the
Delegate. Thirdly, the High Commissioner, in consultation with the Delegate, would appoint a local governor.[49]
Those Syrians selected by the French to serve as window dressing were
anti-nationalist and often pro-French. This became perfectly clear when
Gouraud, after his proclamation, approved a Council of Directors for
Aleppo. Four undistinguished and, in some cases, incompetent Aleppines
with proven French leanings were selected to complement Governor Kamil al-Qudsi, who showed no discretion in office by appointing sixty
members of his own family to various posts in the bureaucracy.[50]
French authorities quickly noticed the alignment of Aleppine and
Damascene nationalists. The French Delegate to the Aleppo state, while
still fearful of the Turkish threat in the North, became increasingly concerned with Arab nationalist activities in the area, which he firmly believed to be financed by British agents.[51] With the reduction of hostilities
between France and Turkey, he began to move against local nationalist
leaders and their supporters, utilizing martial law to jail or exile them.[52]
Meanwhile, he improved relations with those ex-Ottoman administrators who demonstrated a willingness to collaborate with his staff by offering them high posts in the local bureaucracy.[53]

[49] FO 371/485, vol. 6453, 29 Oct. 1920; FO 371/ 11569, vol. 5040. Fontana to Curzon, 1
Sept. 1920.
[50] USNA, Syria. 890d.00/93. Aleppo Consul to Secretary of State, 9 Nov. 1921. See also
FO 371/14691, vol. 5041. Fontana to FO, 30 Oct. 1920; FO 371/3468, vol. 846. Aleppo
Consul to FO, 15 March 1922.
[51] FO 371/6332, vol. 9053. Smart to FO, 31 May 1923.
[52] FO 371/5764, vol. 7847. Aleppo Consul to FO, 22 May 1923.
[53] USNA, Syria. 890d.00/144. Aleppo Consul to Beirut Consul, 20 Sept. 1922.

Many such bureaucrats were at heart Turcophiles, largely owing to economic considerations.[54] They were unsympathetic to Arab nationalism, for during the Faysal era they had been shunted aside in favor of nationalists, from Damascus and elsewhere. They were therefore a suitable choice for office, desiring only to recreate the type of political and economic stability that would enable them to resume their traditional role in society, that of an "aristocracy of service."

Although the collaborationist faction in Aleppo had no self-appointed or elected head, it did have a spokesman, Shakir Ni'mat al-Sha'bani. The middle-aged and well-heeled Sha'bani was an ex-colonel who had spent many years in Europe, mainly in France, as a representative of the Ottoman government. Perfectly at ease in a French milieu, he had long been an avowed Francophile. As an elected deputy from Aleppo to the Ottoman Parliament in 1916, he vehemently opposed the Arab Revolt and Hashemite claims to Syria.[55] In 1919, when the political direction of Faysal's government became clear, Sha'bani formed his own political organization, the Democratic Party of Aleppo. The Party appealed mainly to former Ottoman senior officials ignored by the nationalist regime in Damascus. Before the French occupation, it took a cautious political line: instead of openly proclaiming its allegiance to France, it maintained secret contacts with French liaison officers in the region in anticipation of the occupation. Once the French seized Aleppo, the Democratic Party chose to cooperate with the new Mandate administration. But Sha'bani, a clever political operator in the classic Ottoman tradition, did not ignore Aleppine nationalist leaders, whom he encouraged to compromise with the French in order to save Aleppo and northern Syria from further political and economic disintegration.[56] His aim was to become the most influential politician in the region, but his efforts were in vain. Prominent Aleppine nationalist families like the Ibrahim Pashas and the Jabiris, who were long-time rivals of the Sha'banis, rejected Shakir Ni'mat's concessionary posture.[57] They denounced him and other urban notables, who had cooperated with the High Commission from the first days of occupation, as traitors, driving them deeper into the French embrace.

For those traditional leaders who were still sitting on the fence hedging their political bets or, who, as British officials reported, were "for sale," the ranks of local administration were opened wide.[58] The result was a torrential rush for posts. Notables took the high offices and filled those further down the ladder with their relatives and clients. By 1922, the

[54] FO 371/6332, vol. 9053. Smart to FO, 31 May 1923.
[55] *Oriente Moderno*, 6 (1926), p. 283.
[56] Ibrahim Pasha, *Nidal*, pp. 13–16.
[57] *Ibid.*, p. 16.
[58] See FO 371/2142, vol. 20849, 6 May 1937.

Aleppo bureaucracy had become more unwieldy and inefficient than it had been in the last years of Turkish rule. French political officers were delighted to see so many potential troublemakers off Aleppo's streets and in government and maintained that the additional financial costs were worthwhile. Tightfisted French financial advisers, however, were aghast. To pay so many new salaries for so little productivity required a bigger budget.[59] With the steady erosion of credits from Paris, the money would have to come from customs revenues and increased local taxation.[60] The already impoverished Aleppine citizenry would not accept such increases silently; in 1922, there were regular reports of government tax collectors having their fingers cut off on the job, and rich landowners being forced to pay, at gunpoint, the taxes of their tenants.[61]

In the first years of the Mandate, the French rather successfully controlled who entered local government in Aleppo, excluding most nationalists. But it was the nationalists who had the support of the vast majority of the population. Although the nationalist movement in the North was incapable of mounting any effective resistance after Hananu's revolt was crushed, France's narrow base among the traditional political elite and her utter exclusion of nationalists from government could, in the future, spell trouble.

THE PACIFICATION OF the Damascus region was not nearly as difficult as the pacification of the North. One need only compare the extent of French military presence in both areas. In 1921, 10 infantry battalions, 6 cavalry squadrons, and 8 batteries were deployed in the Aleppo state, whereas in the Damascus state there were only 5 infantry battalions, 3 cavalry squadrons and 3 batteries.[62] France's war with Turkey certainly had much to do with this imbalance. But, France was also able to concentrate her army in northern Syria, where her position was most threatened, because there was no major uprising in the region of Damascus.

[59] MAE, Syrie–Liban 1918–29. "Report of General Billotte," 19 Nov. 1926, vol. 200, p. 268.

[60] For example, the *tamattu* tax. In Ottoman times, it was usually a proportional (though occasionally a fixed) tax based on "rough indices of income which varied between 2 and 10 percent of annual income" and which normally was applied to merchants and manufacturers; it was levied in a wider and more arbitrary manner during the early Mandate. FO 371/9250, vol. 7848. Morgan to FO, 28 Aug. 1922; S. Shamiyeh, "The Taxation System of Syria," M.A. Dissertation (American University of Beirut, 1945), p. 39; Sa'id B. Himadeh (ed.), *Economic Organization of Palestine* (Beirut, 1936).

[61] See FO 371/2142, vol. 20849. Aleppo Consul to FO, 8 Aug. 1922.

[62] As of 1 January 1922, there were a total of 70,000 regular French troops in Syria and Lebanon. By November 1, the number had been reduced to 25,000. FO 371/13019, vol. 7850. Paris Embassy to FO, 20 Nov. 1922.

Why was the South quiescent? In the first place, Damascus nationalists did not get the external assistance that Aleppine nationalists received from the Turks. Mustafa Kemal's nationalist army, already battling the British-backed Greeks on its western flank, had enough difficulties holding ground against the French in southern Anatolia and Cilicia. Moreover, Turkish territorial interests in Syria did not extend beyond the districts of Antioch and Alexandretta. And, as much as the Turks would have welcomed a diversionary revolt in the Damascus region, their relations with nationalists there had long been problematic. Nor could nationalists in Damascus count on substantial material support from their Arab brethren. ʿAbdullah did not reach Amman until March 1921. His new base was closest to Damascus, and he had personal ambitions in Syria, but he had promised the British not to attack the French there. Although he was in contact with nationalists in Damascus and with key tribal shaykhs nearby, giving them some cash and arms, his poverty and Britain's restraining hand prevented him from extending his influence as much as he would have liked.[63] As for Faysal, he had no base to speak of until the summer of 1921 when the British set him up as King of Iraq. By this time, the French had already broken the back of the revolt in the North. Meanwhile, the embryonic Palestinian-Arab national movement was preoccupied with the British and Zionists and could offer Damascus nationalists nothing more substantial than a refuge.

Conditions in Damascus itself were also unsuitable for a sustained uprising. On the eve of occupation many local nationalists fled the town. But whereas Aleppine nationalists were able to take refuge on their lands or with Hananu forces and their Turkish allies, Damascene nationalists, whose lands were often too close to the town for comfort, went to Transjordan, Palestine, or Egypt to escape the French dragnet. For the absent nationalists there was only one political activity, waging an irritating propaganda campaign against the French. In Damascus itself, there was no nationalist organization to rally the demoralized population against the French.

The early successes of French policy helped keep a lid on internal disturbances in the Damascus region. Following the pattern devised by the High Commission for governing the Aleppo state, General Gouraud established in November 1920 a Damascus state. He appointed a native governor and Council of Directors. As in Aleppo, they were the charges of the French Delegate, through his advisers and members of the Service des Renseignements assigned to the state. The French exercised "all leg-

[63] See Mary C. Wilson, *King Abdullah of Jordan: A Political Biography* (Cambridge University Press, forthcoming).

islative, financial and administrative control above the levels of mere formality or routine."[64]

Haqqi al-ʿAzm was appointed the first governor of the Damascus state. He was a former Ottoman official who had turned Arab nationalist after losing a Young Turk-rigged parliamentary election in 1912. He then moved to Cairo for several years where he and his cousin, Rafiq, ran the proto-nationalist Ottoman Party of Administrative Decentralization. During the first years of the war, he remained actively engaged in nationalist activities and pursued contacts with British political officers. In Cairo, he also married the ex-wife of a prominent member of the Egyptian royal family who brought into marriage 700 acres of rich cotton land in the Delta which yielded a handsome annual revenue of £E 6,000,[65] certainly enough to support Haqqi Bey's political career. By 1917, Haqqi al-ʿAzm had grown distant from the Arab nationalist movement, now controlled by the Hashemites, and he shifted his allegiance to the French.[66] On returning to liberated Damascus in 1918, he made efforts to straighten out his problems with the Hashemites in order to land a post in the new Arab government. But he was unable to do so owing to his Francophile stigma and a personal quarrel with Faysal.[67] The frustrated ʿAzm then tried to form his own anti-monarchical party but with no success. Although eminently connected to the Damascene aristocracy, he could not muster much support from the disenfranchised bloc of non-nationalist notables who remembered his earlier nationalist proclivities. Labeled a turncoat by all political factions, only the French willingly extended their hand to him.

The French frequently entrusted high government posts to men who had little administrative experience. They regarded such experience as of secondary importance, despite their often repeated complaint that there was a scarcity of trained bureaucrats in Syria. What was most important was that a governor buckle under to the authority of the French Delegate and his advisers. If obsequious and cooperative, then the native official could get away with all manner of inefficiency and worse. He could, for

[64] Longrigg, *Syria*, p. 126.

[65] MAE, Syria–Liban 1918–29. Nov. 1920, vol. 235, pp. 134–35; Ahmad Qudama, *Maʿalim wa aʿlam fi bilad al-ʿarab* (Damascus, 1965), vol. 1, pp. 111–12; USNA, Syria. 890d.01/47. Damascus Consul to Secretary of State, 1 March 1924; conversation with Wajiha al-Yusuf [Ibish] (Beirut, 29 Aug. 1975); FO 371/2142, vol. 20849, 6 May 1937; Faris, *Man huwa 1949*, p. 302.

[66] The French claimed that ʿAzm was their first big conversion among Syrian nationalists. MAE, Syria–Liban 1918–29. Nov. 1920, vol. 235, pp. 134–35.

[67] In 1919, ʿAzm attacked Hashemite rule in Syria as the "conquest of barbarism over civilization," and as "dangerous as Zionism to the Arabs." *Al-Qibla*, no. 264 (13 March 1919). Also see USNA, Syria. 890d.00/47. Damascus Consul to Secretary of State, 7 Sept. 1921; *al-Mudhik al-mubki*, no. 6 (1929), p. 5.

example, devote his time to ceremonial functions, money-making schemes, or political intrigue.

Haqqi al-ʿAzm indulged in all three. He was a stickler for ceremonial pomp. For instance, he was anxious to have all ranking local officials appear in brocade on ceremonial occasions. His idea was to have different uniforms and gold lace for each class of government official. At one cabinet meeting, he even brought in his personal tailor to fit his colleagues. When Muhammad Kurd ʿAli, then Education Director, refused to be fitted, ʿAzm reported him to the French Delegate. Kurd ʿAli claims to have threatened to resign and the issue was dropped.[68]

Holding public office also had its financial rewards, the opportunity to secure investment information in advance of the public for one. During ʿAzm's term as governor, a French consortium composed of several large banks became interested in developing a valuable tract of land comprising 40,000 dunams (approximately 10,000 acres) in the Duma district. This property, formerly Ottoman Crown Land belonging to the late Sultan Abdülhamid, was now government owned. It had been left uncultivated since 1918, and was reported to be rich in minerals. When ʿAzm learned of the consortium's interest, he secretly formed a private company with three of his ʿAzm cousins to cultivate the property. By placing it under the plow, the ʿAzms could claim its title deed. Word of their enterprise eventually leaked out to some other notables and, to silence them, they were taken on as partners. When local newspapers learned of the scheme, the ʿAzms bribed their editors to keep silent. Although they were unable to raise the capital required to develop the property profitably, they nevertheless cultivated it sufficiently to secure its deed. Then, they sold the property to the French group, managing to recoup their investment and even to turn a tidy profit, all at the public's expense.[69]

Political intrigue was rampant during the early Mandate. Haqqi al-ʿAzm began his governorship with few friends or clients. In a few short months, however, he had made peace with several of his rivals in government, while he curried favor with French officials. On one hand, he adeptly positioned himself between his colleagues and the French staff, keeping individual directors from developing too close a relationship with the French.[70] On the other hand, Haqqi developed a small but precious clientele, by handing out jobs right and left. While his ʿAzm and Muʾayyad relatives had largely ignored him before he became governor, once in office they flocked to him for posts. He needed their support and

---

[68] See Muhammad Kurd ʿAli, al-Mudhakkirat (Damascus, 1948–51), vol. 2, p. 110; FO 371/3851, vol. 7846. Damascus Consul to FO, 11 April 1922.

[69] FO 371/7683, vol. 7847. Palmer to FO, 21 July 1922; Kurd ʿAli, al-Mudhakkirat, vol. 2, p. 121; conversation with Zafir al-Qasimi (Beirut, 26 July 1975).

[70] Kurd ʿAli, al-Mudhakkirat, vol. 2, p. 108.

they needed salaries. Soon, the governor's palace and the municipality were filled with his cousins and nephews, their friends, and clients. In this way, he broadened his political base. The ʿAzms were, after all, the most influential family in Damascus and the unpopular High Commission needed their support and acquiescence. At the same time, however, the ʿAzm government became a public scandal.[71]

The ʿAzm government lasted 19 months, until 27 June 1922.[72] In this period, it served the French as a rubber stamp. But although it was obliged to adopt, follow, and defend High Commission policies, or be dismissed, it was not particularly pleased with its precarious situation; it was ultimately dependent on a foreign power when popular opinion was clearly antagonistic to that power. ʿAzm and his colleagues realized that the disgruntled Damascus public would not accept for long governmental proclamations rationalizing the status quo. This public firmly rejected the French assertion that "the conditions of chaos and harshness Syria was forced to bear during World War I and under Faysal" warranted France's intervention to restore order.

The ʿAzm government tried to secure a greater measure of authority from the French Delegate in order to satisfy some more "reasonable" local demands. In this way, it hoped to gain greater legitimacy and, at the same time, to mollify its nationalist opponents who accused it of betraying the Syrian nation. But the High Commissioner was completely inflexible on the question of sharing any authority, however petty, during the first two years of occupation.[73]

BEGINNINGS OF URBAN RESISTANCE

The absence of sustained popular resistance in Damascus in the early months of the French occupation was largely owing to the absence of the town's natural leadership. With so many nationalists in exile or in prison, the local populace had no leadership to organize it and to express its deep anger and frustration.

For the first 20 months of occupation, the general pattern of protest in Damascus included submitting petitions and occasionally closing the

[71] Ibid., p. 109; al-Mudhik al-mubki, no. 207 (March 1934), p. 6. In 1922, when Haqqi was governor of the Damascus state, Sami Bey al-ʿAzm was his chief adviser in the Palace; Badiʿ Muʾayyad al-ʿAzm was Director General of Justice; Wathiq al-Muʾayyad was Director of the Census Bureau; and Safuh al-Muʾayyad was the Director of Prisons. E. and G. Gédéon (eds.), L'Indicateur Libano-syrienne (Beirut, 1923).

[72] Haqqi al-ʿAzm remained governor of the Damascus state until January 1923, when he was forced to resign. ʿAta al-Ayyubi, a moderately pro-French notable, replaced ʿAzm. FO 371/1036, vol. 9054. Damascus Consul to FO, 16 Jan. 1923.

[73] MAE, Syrie–Liban 1918–29. "Rapport sur la propagande francophobe dans l'état de Damas," vol. 190, p. 120.

city's great bazaars, but little else. Each time the High Commissioner issued a decree or took a decision which the local population regarded unfavorably, his Delegate in Damascus could expect to find several signed complaints on his desk the following morning. Hundreds of petitions were received only to be disregarded. Few demands were ever satisfied. The British and American Consuls also regularly received petitions. But neither was in a position to do anything. The French were deeply distrustful of the British Consul whom they suspected of trying to undermine their position on orders from London. The American Consul was without influence, except when Damascenes were in need of immigration visas to the United States. The closing of the central marketplace, usually in protest over some decree which complicated an already chaotic economic situation or over the arrest of a political leader, rarely lasted more than a day; otherwise, the French authorities threatened shopowners with heavy fines or more arrests.

With the French pacification of Syria nearly complete by the fall of 1921, General Gouraud felt confident enough to grant an amnesty to many nationalist exiles, most of whom were from Damascus. Many exiles returned immediately and again the Damascus population had a leadership to which it could turn. Once resettled in Damascus, these political leaders, who had built heroic reputations for themselves during the Faysal era and later in jail or exile, formed a nationalist society, the first since occupation. But because martial law denied Syrians the right of organized political association, the Iron Hand Society (*Jam'iyyat al-qabda al-hadidiyya*), as it was called, had to operate discreetly.[74] Unable to confront the French directly, its leaders devoted most of their time to discrediting the ʿAzm government and to re-establishing contacts with merchants, quarter bosses, and high school and university students. Meanwhile, the Iron Hand awaited the right occasion to display publicly its strength and popularity.

The guiding inspiration behind the Iron Hand Society was ʿAbd al-Rahman Shahbandar, the most influential and controversial nationalist leader of the early Mandate. Shahbandar was born in Damascus in 1880, the son of a relatively prosperous merchant.[75] As a child, he had shown

---

[74] Also known as *al-Hizb al-hadidi* or the *Parti de Fer*. FO 371/1611, vol. 7845. Palmer to FO, 20 Jan. 1922; FO 371/6457, vol. 13496. Damascus Consul to FO, 23 Nov. 1921.

[75] Shahbandar was known as the "Zaghlul of Syria" (Zaghlul was the leader of the Egyptian nationalist movement) and the "Father of Liberty." MD, 7N 4185. "Renseignement" of 30 Nov. 1923; Also see Muhammad Adib Taqi al-Din al-Husni, *Muntakhabat al-tawarikh li-dimashq* (Damascus, 1928), vol. 2, p. 901. Although his family did not belong to the local upper class, Shahbandar was married to the sister of Nazih Muʾayyad al-ʿAzm, whose family did. Shahbandar derived income from his wife's lands and inherited some property from his grandmother. MWT, *al-Qism al-khass*, Nazih Muʾayyad al-ʿAzm Papers. Shahbandar (Paris) to al-Muʾayyad, no. 51, 27 Dec. 1923.

such intellectual capacity that his father sent him to Beirut to complete his secondary education at the preparatory division of the American-run Syrian Protestant College (after 1920, known as the American University of Beirut), a rather unusual decision for a Damascene Muslim at the time. Taking his diploma in 1901, he returned to Damascus where he came into contact with a reformist circle of theologians and students, presided over by Shaykh Tahir al-Jaza'iri, which was critical of Turkish policies in the Arab provinces. Already somewhat of a "free thinker," Shahbandar penned at this time a controversial essay on law and personal behavior, in which he implicitly suggested that the Ottoman presence in the Syrian provinces was beginning to resemble one of "occupation." This essay and a spurious accusation that he had sent secret correspondence of Sultan Abdülhamid to the Cairo newspaper *al-Muqattam* put him in bad odor with the local Turkish authorities who had him referred to the courts. Only his young age saved him from imprisonment.[76]

After his scrape with the law, Shahbandar decided to pursue a medical career and returned to Beirut to study at the Syrian Protestant College. A brilliant student of anatomy and chemistry, he also engaged in the political controversies of the day as a student leader on campus. In particular, he stirred up protest among his Muslim classmates against the College ruling that all students, regardless of religious persuasion, attend daily prayer service in the campus chapel. In what has come down in the annals of the College as a landmark decision, he managed to have the ruling annulled.[77]

When Shahbandar graduated from the College in 1906 at the top of his class, he was nominated to a post on the Faculty of Medicine.[78] After teaching for two years, he returned to Damascus where he set up a private practice and began to involve himself in local politics. Still only 26, his rather progressive education predisposed him to the ideas of Arab reformers and Turkish liberals. When the Young Turk Revolt of 1908 broke out, he enthusiastically supported the young Turkish officers and their allies in Damascus. But, when it became clear that the Unionist reform program aimed to "Turkify" the Syrian provinces, he switched his allegiance to a group of Syrian deputies in the Ottoman Parliament who supported greater political and administrative autonomy in the provinces. With that step, Shahbandar joined a select but growing group of educated

[76] Hasan al-Hakim, "Mujaz tarjama hayat al-za'im al-khalid al-maghfur lahu al-duktur 'Abd al-Rahman al-Shahbandar." Unpublished biographical sketch, p. 1; Virginia Vacca, "Notizie Biografiche su uomini politici ministri e deputati siriani," *Oriente Moderno*, 17 (October 1937), pp. 473–74.

[77] FO 684/7/1, vol. 2257.

[78] Hasan al-Hakim, "Mujaz tarjama," p. 2; Vacca, "Notizie," p. 474; The American University of Beirut, *Directory of Alumni 1870–1952* (Beirut, 1953), p. 42.

liberals in Damascus and other Syrian towns who, by 1914, were more or less resigned to promoting the secession of the Arab provinces from the Ottoman Empire.[79]

Shahbandar remained in Damascus when the war broke out, unlike some of his Arabist colleagues who took refuge in Cairo. Carefully watched by the Turkish governor, Jamal Pasha, he maintained a low profile. In 1916, shortly after Turkish authorities hanged a number of Syrian leaders for conspiring with the European powers against the Ottoman state, the Turks began to hound known dissidents. Later that year Shahbandar left Damascus for safer parts. Soon, he surfaced in Cairo and joined his nationalist colleagues in their propaganda work in support of the Arab Revolt. In Cairo, he also developed close contacts with British officials of the Arab Bureau, including its Director, the noted Oxford archaeologist, David Hogarth.[80] This British connection later caused him additional difficulties with the French.

On returning to Damascus in early 1919, Shahbandar took an active part in nationalist politics. He was one of the few prewar nationalists to play a major political role under Amir Faysal. His first duty on behalf of the Hashemite ruler was to prepare key personalities, political parties, and interest groups to receive the United States Commission of Inquiry (King–Crane Commission), due to arrive in Syria that summer. During the American delegation's visit he also served as the interpreter for Charles Crane, one of the Commission's co-chairmen. The two became very friendly. In addition, Shahbandar served as Faysal's chief liaison with the British in Syria, especially during the Amir's frequent absences from the country.[81] Finally, in May 1920, when the recently crowned King Faysal appointed a radicalized nationalist government, Shahbandar became the Minister of Foreign Affairs.[82] But he barely had time to try out his new job. Six weeks later the French overturned the Faysal regime and, like so many other nationalists whom the French sentenced to death, Shahbandar fled to Egypt.

[79] Vacca, "Notizie," p. 474.
[80] FO 684/7/1, vol. 2257; Vacca, "Notizie," pp. 474–75; Hogarth, in a letter to the Foreign Office dated 22 June 1924, wrote that Shahbandar was a "Syrian Patriot," an "honourable and cultivated man," and a "very loyal admirer of ourselves," i.e., the British. It seems that Shahbandar rendered much service to the British during the war. FO 371/5774, vol. 10164. Shahbandar was one of seven nationalists who on 11 June 1917 met Sir Mark Sykes in Cairo and received from him a British pledge (known as the Declaration to the Seven) which supposedly contained "assurances" that the Arab provinces of the prewar period and the Arab provinces liberated by the military actions of their inhabitants during the war would become completely independent. T. E. Lawrence in The Times (11 Sept. 1919), p. 11.
[81] Vacca, "Notizie," pp. 474–75; al-Hakim, "Mujaz tarjama," p. 3; FO 371/2043, vol. 10164, 19 Sept. 1923.
[82] Hasan al-Hakim, Mudhakkirati, vol. 2, p. 151.

In Cairo, once again he joined several other Syrian nationalist exiles and émigrés in forming a loosely-knit organization, the Syrian–Palestine Congress, which disseminated nationalist propaganda both in the Arab territories now under European rule and at the League of Nations in Geneva.[83] But with the announcement of the first French amnesty in the summer of 1921, Shahbandar gave up these activities to return to Damascus.

The occasion chosen by Shahbandar and the Iron Hand Society to mount a serious challenge to France's right to be in Syria was the second visit of Charles Crane to Damascus on 5 April 1922.[84] Crane's first visit to Syria had been in 1919, when he served as co-chairman of the U.S. Commission of Inquiry. The Commission had discovered, after extensive investigation, that a majority of Syrians vehemently rejected the idea of a French Mandate or any other form of French presence in Syria. Although the Commission's final report (submitted to the President of the United States) noted this sentiment and the desire of the Syrian political elite for complete independence, it was disregarded in Washington and among the peacemakers at Versailles.[85] Crane, however, had left Syria with a special fondness and sympathy for its inhabitants and particularly for members of its educated elite, among them ʿAbd al-Rahman Shahbandar.

The French authorities—always suspicious of prominent visitors to Syria—kept especially close tabs on Crane during his stay.[86] In Damascus, he was the guest of his friend, Dr. Shahbandar, who escorted him from one meeting to the next with notables, religious leaders, intellectuals, merchants, and newspaper editors, who presented him with the hard, if occasionally exaggerated, facts of life under French rule. Crane was told again and again that the Syrian people wanted full independence immediately; that less-developed countries like the Philippines were about to receive independence while Syria might be stuck with the French forever. They complained about the economy, choked by the artificial frontiers with Palestine, Iraq, and Turkey. They offered, as an example, the once flourishing textile trade with Palestine which had nearly stopped because of customs restrictions, forcing Palestine to import cloth from Egypt. Merchants and landowners grumbled about the various taxes, which were four to ten times higher than before the war and which

[83] On the Syrian–Palestine Congress, see Chapter 9.
[84] USNA, Syria. 890d.000/100. Telegram to Secretary of State, 13 April 1922.
[85] George Antonius, *The Arab Awakening. The Story of the Arab National Movement* (London, 1938), pp. 295–98. Antonius's fascinating and controversial book might never have been written had he not received the generous support of Charles Crane, to whom the book is dedicated. Also see Harry N. Howard, *The King–Crane Commission* (Beirut, 1963).
[86] MD, 7N 4184, Dossier 2. Telegrams of 8 April 1922 (*Armée*) and 13 April 1922 (de Caix).

mainly supported the French military or paid the salaries and expenses of High Commission officials. They expressed a growing fear that France was only interested in promoting industries that were beneficial to her own economy and that Syria's gold and other securities were being smuggled out of the country to Paris. They cited massive unemployment in Damascus and Aleppo where over 25 percent of the male labor force was out of work, while the French preferred to hire refugees, like the Armenians, for various public works. Last, but not least, the delegations Crane met complained that the French treated the Syrian people contemptuously, showing utter disregard for their culture and heritage, their customs and habits.[87]

After a hectic schedule of meetings, Crane addressed a large gathering at the home of a leading notable on the day of his departure. Once again, Dr. Shahbandar served as his interpreter, turning his rather unprovocative speech into a masterpiece of anti-French vituperation. The aroused audience responded with a cry for demonstrations. Meanwhile, at the Quwwatli café—since the turn of the century one of the most popular watering-holes of young intellectuals and politicians—a meeting had been underway since morning to prepare for such activities.[88]

Crane's presence had afforded the leaders of the Iron Hand Society protection from French security forces. But his departure placed them in jeopardy. Striking swiftly, the French arrested Dr. Shahbandar first. On his person, they found a check for the sum of $1,000 made out to him by Charles Crane which they immediately claimed was earmarked for subversive activities against the Mandate.[89] The arrest of four other Iron Hand leaders followed.[90]

These arrests were the catalyst for a violent city-wide protest. The following day, April 8, 8,000 people gathered at the Umayyad Mosque for Friday prayers. Afterwards, nationalist spokesmen delivered inflammatory speeches attacking French policy. The decision to demonstrate was unanimous. On leaving the Mosque the crowd, which had swelled to over

[87] USNA, Syria. 890d.00/120; FO 371/4442, vol. 7846, 8 April 1922.

[88] Hasan al-Hakim, *Mudhakkirati*, vol. 1, p. 71; FO 371/4203, vol. 7846. Damascus Consul to FO, 8 April 1922.

[89] Crane was a philanthropist. He told the U.S. Consul that the check was for medical services, interpretation, and services still to be rendered by Shahbandar for Crane's upcoming visit to Arabia. USNA, Syria. 890d.00/120.

[90] Including Hasan al-Hakim. Hakim (b. 1886) had studied at the *Mülkiye* in Istanbul and had previously served King Faysal as his Director of Posts and Telegraphs. He came from a prominent family of the upper Maydan quarter who derived its wealth from *awqaf* in the Hawran. With the French occupation he escaped to Cairo, and then worked for a short while for Amir ʿAbdullah in Transjordan as his Director-General of Finance. He was amnestied in 1921. His association with Dr. Shahbandar never wavered. Al-Hakim, *Mudhakkirati*, vol. 1, pp. 68–71; conversation with al-Hakim (Damascus, 12 March 1976); al-Jundi, *Tarikh*, pp. 182–83; Faris, *Man huwa 1949*, pp. 121–22.

10,000, marched through the main bazaar, Suq al-Hamidiyya, whose prosperous merchants had voluntarily closed their shops, to the Citadel near the opening of the marketplace, where the arrested leaders were being held. At the head of the procession were nationalists, religious leaders, and merchants. The rank and file included students—demonstrating for the first time since occupation[91]—quarter bosses with their neighborhood gangs, and even members of the Naqshabandi *sufi* order.[92] But the protestors, who were armed only with sticks, slingshots, and knives, were no match for French security, which had deployed around the Citadel the local gendarmerie, Moroccan *spahis*, some French troops, and several armored cars and tanks.[93] On the first day of confrontation, 46 Damascenes were arrested and many more were injured.

After one day of relative calm, demonstrations broke out again and a pattern was set that would be repeated often during the Mandate. Departing from the Umayyad Mosque, the traditional center of all protest in Damascus, marchers advanced through Suq al-Hamidiyya, its shops closed, to the Citadel, only to be driven back and dispersed. On April 11, leaders added a slight variation to the pattern. At the front of the long procession, they placed 40 women, including the wives of Shahbandar and other imprisoned nationalists. Holding petitions and tearing their faces with their nails, the women ululated at an unbearably high pitch, bringing the thousands of men behind them to an explosive roar. Commanders were hesitant to take action with women standing in the front lines. But, as the demonstrators moved closer and the familiar chants of "we will buy our independence with our blood" grew louder, the French decided to take the offensive. This time they displayed more brutality than previously. Three Syrians were left dead and many others, including several women, were injured.[94] Another 35 persons were arrested and imprisoned alongside their comrades in the Citadel.

After another day of demonstrations, order was temporarily restored in the city. Only a handful of armed men remained inside the Umayyad Mosque, which was guarded by a French tank. However, despite French threats of heavy fines, all shops and factories throughout the town remained closed for another 15 days as Damascus awaited the decision of the military tribunal on the fate of Dr. Shahbandar and his comrades.[95]

[91] Khalid al-ʿAzm, *Mudhakkirat Khalid al-ʿAzm* (Beirut, 1973), vol. 1, pp. 142–43.

[92] Al-Hakim, *Mudhakkirati*, vol. 1, pp. 40, 77–79.

[93] FO 371/4442, vol. 7846. Damascus Consul to FO, 12 April 1922. The *spahis* were cavalrymen in towns and in the countryside of Syria.

[94] Al-Hakim, *Mudhakkirati*, vol. 1, pp. 79–82; FO 371/3932, 4442, vol. 7846. Damascus Consul to FO, 11 and 12 April 1922.

[95] FO 371/4803, vol. 7846. 22 April 1922; FO 371/4442, vol. 7846. 12 April 1922; FO 371/4803, vol. 7846. 22 April 1922.

The trials were brief. Several lawyers, including Faris al-Khuri, organized Shahbandar's defense. A graduate of the Syrian Protestant College, Khuri was the most respected trial lawyer in Damascus.[96] However, his defense speech, in which he eloquently expressed the grievances of the Syrian nation against French rule, was to no avail. As the ringleader, Dr. Shahbandar received 20 years. Other leaders received lighter sentences, ranging from 5 to 15 years. To prevent the imprisonment of the nationalists from becoming a major issue on which their supporters could focus their hostilities, Shahbandar and the others were interned on Arwad Island, off the coast of Tartus.[97]

The demonstrations that came in the wake of the Crane visit to Damascus enabled the nationalist leadership of the Iron Hand to establish its credentials. It had demonstrated an ability to mobilize vast sections of the local population for violent civil disobedience and it had closed down a city of 175,000 inhabitants for nearly three weeks. In addition, the April events had triggered political unrest in Homs, Hama, and Aleppo, where branches of the Iron Hand had also been established,[98] and significant anti-French propaganda campaigns in Palestine and Egypt. At the League of Nations, the unofficial but permanent delegation of the Syrian-Palestine Congress registered a strong protest on behalf of the Syrian people. The French authorities, after two years of relative quiet in Syria's urban centers, were now unhappily cognizant of what could be expected.

The Aleppo equivalent of the Iron Hand, and an outgrowth of that society, was the Red Hand led by Saʿdallah al-Jabiri. Born in 1893 into one of the wealthiest and most prestigious landowning families in Aleppo, Saʿdallah studied law in Istanbul. Unlike most Aleppine nationalists, he was an advocate of Arab nationalism before the First World War, while still in his teens. During the war, he was conscripted by the Turks and he fought in the Caucasus. He returned to Syria in 1919, and was elected a deputy to the Syrian Congress from his town. With the French occupa-

[96] Faris al-Khuri, a Protestant, was born in what is today southern Lebanon in 1877. He received his primary studies at the American School in Sidon and his B.A. from the Syrian Protestant College in 1897, where he taught for a few years. For a short while he served as the Dragoman of the British Consulate in Damascus. But when the Ottoman Constitution was reimposed after the Young Turk Revolt of 1908, he practiced law and later was elected as a Christian deputy to the Ottoman Parliament in Istanbul. When World War I broke out the Turks accused him of complicity with the Syrian nationalists and sent him before a military tribunal at Aley (Lebanon), where he was acquitted. In 1917, Talaʿt Pasha appointed him to the *majlis shura* (consultative council) of the Syrian Province.

[97] See al-Hakim, *Mudhakkirati*, vol. 1, pp. 87–100.

[98] A branch of the Iron Hand Society was also formed in Salimiyya, a town near Homs which was largely populated by Ismaʿilis. MAE, Syrie–Liban 1918–29. "Rapport sur la propagande francophobe dans l'état de Damas," July–Dec. 1922, vol. 190, p. 116.

tion he fled to Egypt, returning in early 1921 to assist the Hananu revolt. His nationalist activities landed him in prison in Safita for six months.[99]

The Red Hand's activities, which the French suspected were British-financed, took three directions: discrediting collaborators, petitioning the French Delegate, and encouraging an underground Islamic fundamentalist movement.[100] But the activities of the Red Hand did not achieve the explosive finale of the Iron Hand in Damascus.

The imprisonment of Dr. Shahbandar and his comrades did not stop the Iron Hand Society from continuing its agitation. However, by reinforcing security forces in Damascus, the French reduced the Iron Hand's activities to underground agitation and propaganda work.[101] On May 9, French detectives, relying on information provided by local informants, raided the Iron Hand's secret headquarters in Damascus, arresting 17 members on the premises. Among them were Jamil Mardam and Nazih Mu'ayyad al-'Azm, Dr. Shahbandar's brother-in-law.[102] More Iron Hand members were arrested on April 13, and when some of the town's leading notables in government tried to intervene on their behalf, the French Delegate forced 50 of them to resign their posts on the Council of Directors and the Administrative Council.[103] A week later, five of the Iron Hand "conspirators" were sentenced to prison terms, ranging from 1 to 15 years, while 15 other partisans were expelled from the country.[104] As an organization, the Iron Hand had been destroyed. Effective resistance to French rule took another three years to manifest itself.

[99] Al-Jundi, *Tarikh*, pp. 132–33; *Oriente Moderno*, 17 (1937), p. 33. Other members of the Red Hand included the leading nationalist notables in Aleppo: Ibrahim Hananu, Jamil and Hasan Fu'ad Ibrahim Pasha, 'Abd al-Rahman al-Kayyali, Najib Baqi Zadih, Hajj Fatih al-Mar'ashli, Fu'ad al-Mudarris, As'ad al-Kawakibi, and 'Abd al-Hamid and Tahir al-Jabiri. The French believed that the British supported the Red Hand because it was interested in re-establishing the Caliphate and making it dependent on them. Najib Baqi Zadih was reported to be the distributor of British funds to the Red Hand (also known as the Committee of Unionists or *al-Wahiddin*). MAE, Syrie–Liban 1918–29. 13 Sept. 1923, vol. 208, pp. 159–66; MD, 7N 4185, 1923.

[100] FO 371/10962, vol. 784. Aleppo Consul to FO, 22 Sept. 1922; MAE, Syrie–Liban 1918–29. 22 March 1923, vol. 191, p. 77; FO 371/6332, vol. 9053. Smart to FO, 31 May 1923.

[101] MAE, Syrie–Liban 1918–29. "Rapport sur la propagande francophobe," vol. 190, p. 134. The Iron Hand Society was supported by Amir Shakib Arslan, who, with Ihsan al-Jabiri, headed the unofficial Syrian delegation at the League of Nations. The French believed that the Society was "monarchist," with strong Hashemite tendencies. *Ibid.*, p. 123.

[102] FO 371/5285, vol. 7847. Damascus Consul to FO, 10 May 1922.

[103] *Ibid.*

[104] FO 371/7864, vol. 7847. Damascus Consul to FO, 21 May 1922; FO 371/5854, vol. 7847. Damascus Consul to FO, 29 May 1922. Among those exiled was Jamil Mardam.

CHAPTER FIVE

TINKERING WITH
THE POLITICAL SYSTEM

THE POLITICAL DISTURBANCES in the spring of 1922 convinced France that it was time to experiment with new forms of administrative organization. In June, General Gouraud created a Federal Council consisting of fifteen appointees from the Administrative Councils of the three states of Damascus, Aleppo, and the Alawite territory. Although he made no provisions for the future integration of Lebanon and the Jabal Druze,[1] most of Syria was to be unified under one administrative umbrella.

Council meetings were to alternate each year between Aleppo and Damascus. There would be a President elected by the Federal Council but each state retained its local governor.[2] The transition to Syrian unity was to be gradual: Federal Council members were to retain their seats for four years.[3]

At its first meeting in late July 1922, the Federal Council elected the Antioch resistance leader, Subhi Barakat, as President. Barakat was no longer the Francophobe of 1919. He had moved his political operations to Aleppo where he proved to be a satisfactory candidate for French patronage. A native Turkish speaker who was incapable of uttering more than a few consecutive words of grammatically correct Arabic, he was neither a committed nationalist[4] nor a Damascene, which augured well for a High Commission that sought to prevent Damascus from exercising too much influence over the Council. He was a clever intriguer who, for more than two years, kept Aleppine nationalists out of the Council.

Although the establishment of the Federal Council coincided with a decline in political unrest in Syria, it immediately became a bone of contention within the country and especially between Damascus and Aleppo. In the first place, nationalists were uninterested in supporting a council that contained only a very small number of their ilk. Membership on the Ad-

---

[1] Longrigg, *Syria*, p. 129.

[2] FO 371/6856, vol. 7847. Damascus Consul to FO, 26 June 1922.

[3] *Ibid.*; FO 371/7624, vol. 7847. Beirut Consul to FO, 1 July 1922; USNA, Syria. 890d.032/2. Damascus Consul to Secretary of State, 1 Jan. 1924.

[4] After Barakat and his fighters were forced to surrender to the French in June 1920, the French promised him lucrative offers to collaborate. In fact, he tried to convince Hananu partisans in 1920-21 to surrender as the continuation of the northern Syrian revolt was doomed to failure. Al-Jundi, *Tarikh*, pp. 67, 70–71.

ministrative Council of each state had been limited since the occupation to either Francophile notables or political neutrals. Moreover, the partisans of the many nationalist leaders still in jail or in exile were not prepared to cooperate with the High Commission until their leaders were pardoned. Secondly, both Aleppo and Damascus were angered by the equal representation given the Alawite state, with its small, culturally and economically underdeveloped population.[5] Thirdly, many non-nationalist Aleppine merchants and landowners, Muslim and Christian, did not want to join the Federation, preferring that Aleppo remain autonomous under the High Commission's Delegate. The selection of Aleppo as the first seat of the Federal Council had induced them to participate. But when the High Commissioner decided to move the Council permanently to Damascus in April 1923, Aleppines felt that they had been tricked and their town's interests sacrificed. They claimed that Aleppo was economically more vital to the development of Syria than Damascus—a claim not without foundation—and that revenues from the town's regularly balanced budget would be used to reduce the budgetary deficit in the Damascus state and to aid the grossly underdeveloped Alawite territory.[6]

The federalization of certain state services (Finances, Justice, Public Works, State Domains and Land Registry, Awqaf, the Gendarmerie, Higher Education, and Posts and Telegraphs) under Directorates supervised by French advisers did not work in Aleppo's favor.[7] For instance, the town was required to subscribe money for the Syrian University in Damascus, several hundred kilometers away. While young Damascenes could more conveniently study law or medicine there, qualified Aleppine youth were often denied the same opportunity, owing to travel and housing costs. Aleppines also complained that the designation of Damascus as the permanent seat of the Federal Council meant that Damascenes were given the most and the choicest bureaucratic posts. Government employees were also better paid in Damascus than in Aleppo.[8]

WITHIN THE FRAMEWORK of the tri-state Federation, no provisions existed for the development of elective institutions. General Gouraud was not

[5] FO 371/7624, vol. 7847. Beirut Consul to FO, 1 July 1922.

[6] The British Consul in Aleppo reported that Aleppo was "marked for the role of milch cow of the Syrian Federation." FO 371/3500, vol. 9053. Smart to FO, 5 April 1923. *Al-Muqtabas* (20 Jan. 1922), cited in FO 371/1614, vol. 7845. Damascus Consul to FO, 29 Jan. 1922.

[7] FO 371/530/531, vol. 9053. Damascus Consul to FO, 12 Jan. 1923; Longrigg, *Syria*, p. 129.

[8] *La Syrie* (Beirut, 25 Dec. 1923). Also see FO 371/6416, vol. 10160. Aleppo Consul to FO, 15 July 1924. FO 371/8075, vol. 9053. Aleppo Consul to FO, 23 July 1923.

prepared to apply "democratic" innovations in Syria. Not only did he lack confidence in the governing abilities of the Syrian people, but he also feared that vehemently anti-French nationalist politicians, if given the opportunity to participate in the political system, would legitimize their position as the only viable leadership in Syria.[9] However, Gouraud's successor was more flexible and had a wider vision. General Maxime Weygand was a staff officer of considerable repute and, although a staunch clericalist like Gouraud, he was willing to experiment with slightly more progressive administrative procedures which Robert de Caix, who continued as Secretary-General, had proposed. In June 1923, Weygand permitted the first general elections since the Faysal era. Each state was to elect its own Representative Council.[10]

Weygand decided to maintain the Ottoman two-tier electoral system. Voting was restricted to propertied adult (25 +) males. In the first stage, the primaries, districts in each state picked a group of electors from among quarter bosses, urban and rural notables, and the leaders of religious sects, on the average of 1 per 100 persons. This was based on an undependable preliminary census taken by the High Commission. The electors, in turn, selected the deputies, on the average of 1 per 6,000 voters, who would constitute the Representative Council in each state. Those deputies elected in the second round chose from among themselves five members who would represent the state on the Federal Council.[11]

The French enforced this electoral procedure because it served their interests better than did direct elections. They calculated, as the Turks had earlier, that the smaller group of electors to emerge from the primaries could be more easily divided and manipulated than the whole electoral population. Moreover, to ensure that city-based nationalists did not make significant gains, the High Commission used its weighted census to guarantee that rural districts selected a disproportionate number of electors in the primaries. Isolated rural districts were far less politicized than the interior towns; for the most part they were outside of the mainstream of nationalist political activity. Widespread illiteracy and traditionally rigid relations of personal dependence with big landowners allowed the French to control the Syrian peasantry more easily. Elections were often *pro*

[9] Général Catroux, *Deux missions en Moyen-Orient, 1919–1922* (Paris, 1958), pp. 119–21.

[10] See Philip C. F. Bankwitz, *Maxime Weygand and Civil–Military Relations in Modern France* (Cambridge, Mass., 1967); Longrigg, *Syria*, p. 128.

[11] FO 371/11009, vol. 9053. Palmer (Damascus) to FO, 29 Oct. 1923. Candidates had to meet a six-month residency requirement in order to stand for election. PMC, *Minutes*, 3/11/514, 23 Feb. 1926, pp. 81–82.

forma. In many cases, rural notables were not even elected, but rather were the handpicked nominees of French officials.[12]

The reaction in the towns to two-stage elections was mixed. Candidates who preferred the traditional system were often those who had to worry about financing their own campaigns, or who had insufficient government or personal resources and connections to offer a large clientele the services that could assure allegiance. Distributing largesse among 60 electors was far less costly than among 6,000 voters. More often than not, the Ottoman system favored candidates who had access to the High Commission rather than those who had a vast popular following in the cities. Nationalist politicians, who had strong popular backing and thus whose financial burdens were not so severe, were opposed to the two-tier electoral law. They felt that direct elections would guarantee landslide nationalist victories, while the two-stage system would allow French pressure and intrigue to intervene in favor of their non-nationalist rivals.[13]

In Damascus, four political groupings with little organization or ideology emerged after the announcement of elections. Two were government "parties"; the other two constituted the opposition. The most influential government faction was headed by Haqqi al-ʿAzm and his cousin, Badiʿ Muʾayyad al-ʿAzm. It was composed of several notables who had acquiesced to French rule from the first hour of occupation. Since nationalists had virtually discredited all its adherents, the ʿAzm group was heavily dependent on the French.[14] The second government faction was led by Rida Pasha al-Rikabi, formerly the Military Governor and Chief of the Council of State under Faysal.[15] A political chameleon whom the French had assessed in 1920 as vehemently anti-French, Rikabi took up residence in Transjordan after Faysal was ousted from Syria.[16] One of several Syrian exiles to serve Amir ʿAbdullah, he became his Chief Adviser in March 1922. In this period, he also managed to iron out many of his differences

---

[12] Conversation with ʿAli al-Dandashi (Damascus, 21 Oct. 1975).

[13] *Ibid.*

[14] MAE, Syrie–Liban 1918–29. "Rapport sur les élections du Conseil Représentatif de l'Etat de Damas," Jan. 1923–May 1924, vol. 191, pp. 191–94; Henri Froidevaux, "Les élections aux Conseils Représentatifs des états sous Mandat," *L'Asie Française* (Jan. 1924), p. 9.

[15] *Ibid.*

[16] Capt. C. D. Brunton, "Who's Who in Damascus, 1919." Brunton Papers, Middle East Centre, St. Antony's College, Oxford; FO 371/117, vol. 6454. Palmer to FO, 27 April 1921. Rikabi had a long career under the Ottomans. He was first a lieutenant in the Ottoman Army in Istanbul, then, in succession, *qaʾimmaqam* of Jerusalem, Governor of Medina, Deputy to the Governor of Basra, Mayor of Damascus, General in the Ottoman Army. *Al-Mudhik al-mubki,* no. 247 (23 March 1935).

with the French, making him suspect in the eyes of British officials in Amman. After a quarrel with H. St. John Philby, the Chief British Representative in Amman, Rikabi returned to Damascus and, with French blessing, put himself up as a candidate for council elections.[17] Despised by nationalists for his unscrupulousness and feared by the ʿAzm faction because of his challenge to its political ambitions, Rikabi ran a close second to the latter for French sponsorship. His following consisted of other retired military officers, bureaucrats, and independents who were more often indifferent rather than hostile to the Mandate. However, the 63-year-old Rikabi made certain that his allies posed as collaborators in hopes of receiving the French backing necessary to secure his share of seats on the Representative Council.[18]

Of the two opposition groups, only one planned to take part in the elections. The French labeled this group "extremist," but it was merely composed of young men, impatient to play a role in government, and of older notables who were hesitant to cooperate with the French under current conditions. It called for the unification of Syria and an amnesty for all political prisoners and exiles, but not for the immediate cessation of the French Mandate.[19] It was headed by Fawzi al-Ghazzi, a 33-year-old nationalist lawyer from a landowning-scholarly family, and Wathiq Muʾayyad al-ʿAzm, the 38-year-old cousin of Haqqi and Badiʿ, and the son of the nationalist martyr, Shafiq Muʾayyad al-ʿAzm, whom the Turks had hanged in 1916. Wathiq's opposition to his cousins in the pro-French faction was personal and seems to have dated from the incidents of 1916.[20]

The second opposition group in Damascus comprised the Arab nationalist partisans of Dr. Shahbandar and other jailed leaders of the Iron Hand

[17] FO 371/2142/630, vol. 20849, 6 May 1937. Rikabi would return to Transjordan and again serve ʿAbdullah.

[18] MAE, Syrie–Liban 1918–29. "Rapport sur les élections," vol. 191, pp. 191–94; Froidevaux, "Les élections," p. 9. When Rikabi returned to Damascus at the beginning of April 1923, he was threatened by Amir Saʿid al-Jazaʾiri and his family who accused him of responsibility for the murder in 1918 of Saʿid's brother, ʿAbd al-Qadir, when the Jazaʾiris led their followers against the Allies and the Sharifian Army during the occupation of Damascus. Rikabi was at the time Military Governor of Damascus. Amir Saʿid would not consider a reconciliation, though his stubbornness was as much a protest over the reduction of his family's subsidy by the French (who were now on better terms with Rikabi) as it was over the murder of his late brother. FO 371/3939, vol. 9054. Damascus Consul to FO, 2 April 1923.

[19] MAE, Syrie–Liban 1918–29. "Rapport sur les élections," vol. 191, pp. 191–94; Froidevaux, "Les élections," p.9.

[20] FO 371/2142, vol. 20849, 6 May 1937; conversation with Zafir al-Qasimi (Beirut, 26 July 1975). FO 371/11009, vol. 9053. Palmer to FO, 29 October 1933; Faris, *Man huwa 1949*, pp. 137–38.

Society. It stood for the complete independence of Syria and the immediate departure of the French. Although it was far and away the most influential faction in Damascus, much of its leadership was still in prison or in exile. Rather than participate in the elections, it tried to disrupt them.[21] Since the elections had been arranged to exclude nationalist candidates as far as possible, nationalists called for a country-wide boycott.[22] On October 19, practically all Muslim-owned establishments in Damascus, except for food stores and restaurants, shut their doors in protest against the Mandate's electoral policy. Three days later Christian- and Jewish-owned establishments followed suit. Inspired by the Iron Hand Society and the Syrian–Palestine Congress in Cairo, and enforced by quarter bosses and leaders of the various religious communities, the eleven-day shutdown was a graphic protest against French ideas of "free" elections.[23]

The boycott proved quite successful not only in Damascus but also in other nationalist strongholds. In the primaries, only 25 percent of the registered voters (49,000) in Damascus cast their ballots. In Aleppo, Hama, and Homs the figure was higher, 49 percent, although unremarkable considering that this was the first election held under French rule. French observers commented that townspeople were simply not interested in sacrificing their daily wages to turn out for an election.[24] In rural districts, which were more firmly under French control, and where elections were rarely contested, voter turnout was very high. In some Aleppo districts, 99 percent of those registered cast their ballots, obviously with French inducements, while in the Alawite state 77 percent of the voters turned out to vote for electors whom French officials had already assured of victory.[25]

Fraud in the primaries caused many notables to withdraw as candidates in the second round and to join the ongoing boycott.[26] Electors were to select their Council deputies on October 26, but the French suddenly postponed the elections in order to take some steam out of the boycott and to have more time to make deals with electors.[27] Then on October 29, the second round was held without prior warning. Besides leaving electoral boxes unguarded, the French secretly summoned secondary electors from villages around the towns at midnight to vote for French-sponsored candidates. Not surprisingly, the ʿAzm list won in Damascus, taking most of

[21] MAE, Syrie–Liban 1918–29. "Rapport sur les élections," vol. 191, pp. 191–94.
[22] FO 371/11009, vol. 9053. Palmer to FO, 29 Oct. 1923; FO 371/11014, vol. 9053. Damascus Consul to FO, 31 Oct. 1923.
[23] USNA, Syria. 890d. 01/165. Damascus Consul to Secretary of State, 27 Oct. 1923.
[24] MAE, Syrie–Liban 1918–29. "Rapport sur les élections," vol. 191, p. 212.
[25] Ibid.
[26] FO 371/11014, vol. 9053, 31 Oct. 1923.
[27] USNA, Syria. 890d. 01/165. Damascus Consul to Secretary of State, 27 Oct. 1923.

the town's 11 seats.[28] In the Aleppo state, which included the autonomous Sanjak of Alexandretta, the Barakat list took the greatest number
of seats, 16 out of 19 in the capital alone. Meanwhile, in the Alawite state,
10 of 12 seats went to pro-French candidates.[29]

Once the Council elections were over, the newly elected councilmen
were not yet home free.[30] In Damascus, the nationalist opposition pressured the recently elected to resign. Two deputies received special attention. ʿAbd al-Hamid al-ʿAttar, at one time a respected religious figure,
suffered a beating in his own home. Then, on the Friday following the
election, when he proceeded to lead evening prayers at the Great Mosque
as usual, he looked over his shoulder only to discover that the faithful had
left him for another *imam*.[31] Rushdi al-Sukkari, one of the wealthiest
provisions merchants in Damascus, faced a city-wide boycott of his
goods.[32] All deputies received threatening letters ornamented with pictures of a bullet and a dagger. But only one heeded the threats and resigned.[33]

The election for President of the new Federal Council pitted Badiʿ
Muʾayyad al-ʿAzm against Subhi Barakat. Barakat, the incumbent, had
the obvious edge owing to his personal strength in Aleppo and because he
was still identified in some political circles as an opponent of the French.
After the second round, Muʾayyad al-ʿAzm gained the support of Rida
Pasha al-Rikabi and two influential members of the Damascus Representative Council. But their backing was insufficient. The ʿAzm family had
generated too much criticism in Damascus, owing to its unabashed collaboration with the French, especially during the elections. Despite the High
Commission's preference for Muʾayyad al-ʿAzm, Barakat was easily re-
elected President. As a consolation, the French assured Muʾayyad al-
ʿAzm of the Presidency of the Damascus Representative Council.[34]

[28] Rikabi's failure to secure French support in the elections led to his alleged remark that
"France will have to pay in blood for her treatment of me! I shall not forget." Philby Papers.
"Stepping Stones Across the Jordan," pp. 260–61, unpublished manuscript of H. St. John
Philby, Middle East Centre, St. Antony's College, Oxford.

[29] Froidevaux, "Les élections," pp. 12–13; FO 371/1109, vol. 9053. Palmer to FO, 29 Oct.
1923; USNA, Syria. 890d.00/176. 10 Nov. 1923; FO 371/10964, vol. 9053. Aleppo Consul
to FO, 27 Oct. 1923.

[30] USNA, Syria. 890d. 01/170. Damascus Consul to Secretary of State, 28 Nov. 1923.

[31] FO 371/11020, vol. 9053. Damascus Consul to FO, 3 Nov. 1923.

[32] Sukkari's business house was in the provisions center of Damascus, known as Suq al-
Bzuriyya. MWT, *Registre civil* (Damascus, June 1926–Feb. 1928).

[33] FO 371/11243, vol. 9053, 6 Nov. 1923; FO 371/12012, vol. 9053, 20 Dec. 1923.

[34] FO 371/11014, vol. 9053. Damascus Consul to FO, 31 Oct. 1923. FO 371/11243, vol.
9053. Damascus Consul to FO, 6 Nov. 1923.

THE REPRESENTATIVE COUNCILS were not a very good introduction to parliamentary life. Most of the deputies were beholden to the French for
their election. In fact, if they represented anyone's interests, they represented those of their European patrons and of the big landowning class.
The Councils were also completely devoid of power. They were unable,
for example, to legislate any laws without first securing the High Commission's authorization, and they were answerable not to the Syrian public, but to the French.[35]

Although the new deputies may not have been nationalists,[36] the
Councils nevertheless served as forums to air critical views of French policy. The Aleppo Council was especially critical of French policy in the
Sanjak of Alexandretta. The debate over this issue eventually led to the
demise of federalism. Aleppines in general feared that the Sanjak's "autonomous" status would in time lead to its union with Turkey. In the recent federal elections, the Sanjak returned five deputies, four of whom
were Turks from Antioch and the other an Alawite from Alexandretta.
All were nominees of the French Assistant Delegate in Antioch, M. Pruneaud, and opponents of Subhi Barakat. More importantly, the four
Turkish deputies favored the Sanjak's union with Turkey.[37]

Pruneaud's actions led to heated debates in the Aleppo Council on the
future of Alexandretta, something the High Commission had wanted to
avoid. The Council became a nationalist mouthpiece on the issue of the
Sanjak's status, even though it included few nationalist deputies.[38] Meanwhile, the nationalist press in Aleppo circulated rumors that the autonomy of the Sanjak was part of a secret clause in the Franklin–Bouillon
Agreement that allowed for the cession of the entire territory to Turkey
in the near future. These rumors were given credibility by Ankara-in-
spired disturbances around Antioch, which the French Army appeared
unable to halt.[39]

As a reaction to the heightened tensions between the High Commission and the native government in Aleppo, Mustafa Barmada, the Gov-

[35] USNA, Syria. 890d./176. Aleppo Consul to Secretary of State, 10 Nov. 1923; FO 371/
11049, vol. 9053. Beirut Consul to FO, 31 Oct. 1923. For example, there was much debate
in the Aleppo Representative Council over whether Turkish could be used as a second official
language in Council meetings. Finally, to please Subhi Barakat who was not fluent in Arabic, Turkish was accepted. Aleppine nationalists were furious. In protest, local newspapers
printed Barakat's speech in the exact Arabic that he spoke to show readers the incorrectness
of the language used and its purely Turkish construction. FO 371/895, vol. 10159. Aleppo
Consul to FO, 27 Dec. 1923.

[36] Longrigg, *Syria*, p. 129.

[37] FO 371/896, vol. 10160. Aleppo Consul to FO, 28 Dec. 1923.

[38] *Ibid*.

[39] USNA, Syria. 890d.00/177. Aleppo Consul to Secretary of State, 19 Nov. 1923.

ernor of the Aleppo state, resigned on 5 January 1924.[40] In an effort to placate the local population after the Franklin–Bouillon Agreement, the French had originally chosen him to replace the unpopular Kamil al-Qudsi as Governor. But Barmada, an Istanbul-trained legal expert and moderate nationalist, never got along well with his French patrons. Throughout his eight months in office he obstructed the implementation of French policies.[41] His resignation—reportedly because he could not accept the French plan to replace gold as the monetary exchange with paper currency—was untimely for the High Commission.[42] In Aleppo and elsewhere, the French policy of selecting docile elements from among the "native" governing classes in the Syrian towns, through whom the High Commission could exercise control of administration, was hardly successful.

By now there was growing dissatisfaction in Aleppo with French policy and a perceptible change in the attitude of many influential Aleppines—Christians and Muslims—who, to date, had not opposed the French.[43] Unstable political conditions and frontier difficulties in northern Syria had severely reduced Aleppo's historically lucrative trade with Turkey. The commercial bourgeoisie, which contained a high proportion of Christians, found it increasingly difficult to maintain its standard of living. The High Commission had also failed to work out a favorable customs agreement with Turkey. And though Aleppine textiles were slowly beginning to be redistributed in Anatolia, while considerable quantities of wool, pistachios, and fruits were reaching the Aleppo market, the bulk of trade was limited to local needs. Its volume was also insufficient to keep many local industries alive. In addition, the influx of approximately 40,000 Armenian refugees into Aleppo aggravated the depressed economy. The Aleppo Chamber of Commerce lobbied on behalf of the town's commercial classes but the French turned a deaf ear. Urban landlords protested new rent laws which favored the lessee. Government employees threatened to strike unless salaries were raised to compensate for the massive depreciation of the Syrian pound. And everyone tried to resist the imposition of stiffer taxes which followed the termination of the Capitulations.[44]

---

[40] USNA, Syria. 890d.00/189. Aleppo Consul to Secretary of State, 31 Jan. 1921.

[41] Najm al-Din al-Ghazzi, al-Kawakib al-sa'ira bi-a'yan al-mi'a al-'ashira (Beirut, 1945), vol. 1, pp. 496–97; Faris, Man huwa 1949, p. 63; FO 371/4327, vol. 9056. Aleppo Consul to FO, 7 April 1923. Barmada was installed as Governor in April 1923.

[42] USNA, Syria. 890d.01/189. Aleppo Consul to Secretary of State, 31 Jan. 1924.

[43] Ibid.; FO 371/1548, vol. 10164. Aleppo Consul to FO, 25 Jan. 1924. Christians constituted 34 percent of the Aleppo town population. 21 percent of these were Armenians. Emile Fauquenot, "L'état civil en Syrie en relation avec les questions de nationalités et de statut personnel des communautés religieuses," CHEAM, no. 50.

[44] USNA, Syria. 890d.01/177. Aleppo Consul to Secretary of State, 19 Nov. 1923.

Then, on 12 January 1924, *Alif ba'*, the semi-official daily newspaper of Damascus, reported that the Sanjak of Alexandretta would soon be annexed to the Alawite state and administered separately from Aleppo and Damascus.[45] Four days later the Syrian Federal Council, meeting in special session, took two important decisions. It voted to reject a Banque de Syrie proposal that renewed its privilege of issuing bank notes without gold coverage, claiming that the Syrian nation was unanimously opposed to it. And, it declared a Syrian Union, in effect voting itself out of existence.[46]

Thus the federalist system collapsed 18 months after its introduction, placing General Weygand and his staff in a quandary. Although they could not reverse the process toward unification, they were hesitant to concede the union that their Syrian critics demanded.

From Federalism to Union

Almost from the creation of the separate states, their maintenance with identical sets of institutions had been a financial catastrophe. Since mid-1922, the High Commission had to trim individual state budgets, the number of French advisers, and the size of each state administration. As Paris regularly reduced the amount of credits for Syria and Lebanon, the High Commission had to make drastic budgetary cuts. The first to suffer from this policy were middle-level bureaucrats who lost their jobs.[47] Many had been politically neutral, but once out of office they joined the ranks of the anti-French opposition.

But the budget was still in the red. Regular tax increases only alienated greater numbers of Syrians, who were already suffering from rampant inflation.[48] State budgets drew nearly half their revenues from customs receipts and other income collected from the various branches of the

---

[45] *Alif ba'* (12 Jan. 1924).

[46] FO 371/1298, vol. 10160. Damascus Consul to FO, 21 Jan. 1924.

[47] FO 371/4327, vol. 9056. Aleppo Consul to FO, 7 April 1923. By the end of 1922, de Caix claimed to have dismissed some 2,000 petty officials, gendarmes, etc., through the new Federation. FO 371/867, vol. 9053, 10 Jan. 1923.

[48] J. Grellet, "Mémoire sur la fiscalité municipale en Syrie," CHEAM, no. 331, n.d., pp. 1–9. S. Shamiyeh, "The Taxation System of Syria," M.A. Dissertation (American University of Beirut, 1945), pp. 45–46. FO 337/7767, vol. 6459. "Tableau of Chief Municipal Taxes at present in town and district of Damascus," 8 June 1921. A comparative study of prices of prime necessities for family consumption showed a 72 percent increase between February 1924 and February 1925. In the first place, Aleppo's cost of living rose quickly because of poor harvests, owing to frost in winter and drought in summer which ruined fruits and then wheat and barley crops. In Aleppo the lack of wheat stocks was exacerbated by Turkey's unwillingness to export wheat across its high tariff borders to Aleppo. MAE, Syrie–Liban 1918–29. *Bulletin de Renseignements*, 1–14 Feb. 1925, vol. 427B, p. 2.

Common Interests. Yet each state had to contribute roughly 50 percent of its total annual receipts to the unproductive defense and security sector.[49] Together, the three Syrian states received only 53 percent of the annual revenues collected by the Common Interests, although their total population was more than twice that of Lebanon, which received the remaining 47 percent.[50]

Exacerbating economic grievances, the French franc plummeted to half its value during the opening months of 1924.[51] Since the Syrian pound was tied to the franc, the "franc crisis" led to the depreciation of the pound, and to massive speculation. Government salaries and other official transactions continued to be paid in Syrian paper notes issued by the Banque de Syrie, but no immediate compensation was made for the sudden devaluation. Instead, taxes were increased.[52]

Syria's financial and economic difficulties obliged the High Commission to search for a new administrative formula for the country. The dilemma was how best to keep the compact minorities isolated from the influences of Arab nationalism while relieving the immense financial burdens created by the administrative redundancies of the multi-state system.[53] For a solution, the High Commissioner looked to Robert de Caix, the architect of the federal system in question.

Just before de Caix left Syria in February 1924 to become France's new Delegate to the Permanent Mandates Commission in Geneva, he reluctantly submitted a proposal to General Weygand, outlining the third administrative and territorial permutation of Syria. His plan relied heavily on secret reports submitted by two French officials in close touch with Syrian affairs: M. Schoeffler, the Delegate in Damascus, and Major Tommy Martin, of the Service des Renseignements.[54] Schoeffler reported that the majority of Syrians aspired to union and that the present administrative and political divisions had cost the French the support and affection of the Syrian public. He bluntly stated, "that we cannot afford to be less liberal than our [British] rivals in Iraq." He proposed that Damascus be made the capital of a united Syria but that Aleppo and the Alawite territory be made distinct districts within the union and be given small autonomous budgets to cover local expenses. After admitting that Alawite

[49] Z. Y. Hershlag, Introduction, p. 241; MAE, Rapport à la Société des Nations sur la situation de la Syrie et du Liban, 1922–1923, p. 55.

[50] PMC, Minutes, 8/14/518, 25 Feb. 1926, p. 108.

[51] Tom Kemp, The French Economy, pp. 76–77; Mohammad Thomé, Le rôle du crédit, pp. 76–78.

[52] PMC, Minutes, 8/14/518, 25 Feb. 1926, pp. 113–14.

[53] PMC, Minutes, 8/10/512, 23 Feb. 1926, p. 26.

[54] Extracts of these reports were secretly received by the American Consul in Beirut and transmitted to Washington. USNA, Syria. 890d.01/215. Beirut Consul to Secretary of State, 31 Jan. 1925.

separatism was largely a French creation, he said, "we cannot by means of
our millions [of francs] give the prosperity which would reduce to silence
the voice of national sentiment. The granting of more and more extended
liberties is the ransom of our impoverishment."[55]

Major Martin also believed that the unity of Syria was an absolute necessity. The French

> policy of granting autonomy to minority areas in Syria ignored that
> Christians and Muslims are all Syrians, of one language. We cut in
> their eyes the figure of a retrograde people in our willingness to di-
> vide them by rites and religions.

But Martin's conception of Syrian unity excluded Greater Lebanon and
the Alawite state. He also disagreed with Schoeffler over the choice of a
permanent capital. He preferred Homs because Damascus was too "Ara-
bophile" and Aleppo, too "Turcophile." Finally, he wanted to see the
mandated states function as a *Zollverein*, with a postal and customs union
and no barriers between the Druze, Alawite and Lebanese states.[56]

On June 26 the High Commissioner announced France's plan for a Syrian Union. The governments of Aleppo and Damascus were, at long last,
to be fused into a unitary state, thereby formally dissolving the Syrian
Federation. But the Alawite state resumed its separate existence while the
Jabal Druze remained independent. The Sanjak of Alexandretta joined
the new Syrian state, but was independent of Aleppo. The Representative
Councils in Damascus and Aleppo were merged into one. Damascus was
named the permanent capital of Syria.[57]

The French wished to create a permanent cleavage between the coastal
states and the predominantly Sunni Muslim interior, whose affection, as
one high-ranking Mandate official remarked at the time, "they could
never hope to regain." With a Christian-dominated Lebanon and an anti-
Sunni Alawite state placed tightly in their orbit, the French would be in
possession of a coastal rampart into which they could retire, if need be,
with a fair prospect of safety.[58]

Public reaction to Weygand's administrative re-organization was negative. Dissatisfaction with the new truncated version of Syria was not the
only grievance of the nationalist opposition.[59] The proscribed character of
the Syrian state was, itself, equally alarming. Apart from the unification
of Aleppo and Damascus, little else had changed. The President of Syria
was to be elected by the unified Representative Council but, as always,

[55] *Ibid.*
[56] *Ibid.*
[57] FO 371/6118, vol. 10160. Damascus Consul to FO, 4 July 1924.
[58] Comment of M. de Reffye. See FO 371/6118, vol. 10160. Smart to FO, 4 July 1924.
[59] *Al-Muqtabas*, no. 4149 (14 Dec. 1924).

candidates were subject to the High Commissioner's approval. A cabinet of five Ministers, upgraded from Directors in name only, was to be appointed by the President, but again only with the High Commissioner's approval. The President was empowered to nominate all senior officials but only in concurrence with the High Commissioner and his Delegates. French advisers remained attached to each ministry. The Representative Council continued to be devoid of real powers. In theory, the Council could draft legislation but could not hope to see it enacted without the countersignatures of the President and the High Commissioner. Even then, "the High Commissioner continued to issue, often without prior consultation, the bulk of new legislation."[60]

General Weygand did not remain in Beirut long enough to see his Syrian Union scheme implemented. He was recalled in November and departed for Paris in early December, eventually to assume the less glamorous post of Director of the Centre des Hautes Etudes Militaires. His dismissal, though sudden, was predictable. The new, left-wing anti-clerical government in Paris, breaking with tradition, sought to assert its "progressive" views not only in mainland France, but abroad in the colonies. Despite Weygand's popularity at home and his respect as a judicious administrator in the mandated territories, he did not fit into the plans of the new Prime Minister, M. Herriot. Weygand was a creature of the Right, a conservative clericalist who represented political opinions antithetical to those of the Cartel des Gauches. Indeed, the only thing he and his successor had in common was that both were generals.

ON 2 JANUARY 1925, Maurice Sarrail, just a year shy of seventy, a hero of the Marne, the favorite General of the French Left, and possibly the most controversial military man in France, landed in Beirut to assume the post of High Commissioner.[61] An impatient and authoritarian personality, Sarrail wanted to make it clear from the very beginning that his arrival meant a break with the past.

On his first day in Beirut, Sarrail dismissed the French Governor of Lebanon, a clericalist who had only recently been appointed by General Weygand. This led to a conflict with the local Representative Council in

[60] Longrigg, *Syria*, p. 131. See *Arrêtés*, nos. 2979, 2989, 2904 of 5 Dec. 1924, decreeing Syrian unity. *Recueil des Actes administratifs du Haut-Commissariat de la République Française en Syrie et au Liban* (Beirut, 1924); FO 371/11711, vol. 10160. Aleppo Consul to FO, 15 Dec. 1924.

[61] Sarrail, who was born in 1856, was eleven years older than his two predecessors, Gouraud and Weygand. On his career, see Jan Karl Tannenbaum, *General Maurice Sarrail: the French Army and Left Wing Politics* (Chapel Hill, 1974).

Beirut over whether a Lebanese (Sarrail's preference) or a Frenchman
(the Christian faction in the Council's choice) should fill the vacancy. The
result was the dissolution of the Council and the appointment of an anti-
clericalist French Governor with full legislative powers.[62] Then, in a confusing gesture of liberalism, the new High Commissioner decreed an end
to subsidies to pro-French newspapers and the reinstatement of several
newspapers that had previously been banned. Other papers that continued to criticize French policies, however, were suppressed. Even more
baffling was his decree terminating the system of martial law, which had
been in effect since occupation. Although state governments were now
charged with the responsibility of keeping order, the French Army still
had the authority to intervene without their permission in case of disturbances.[63]

There was nothing confusing about General Sarrail's other early demonstration of change. Making a complete break with protocol, he boycotted the "Latin" religious ceremony customarily held to honor each new
representative of France as the "Protector" of the Catholic population in
the "Orient." At first the Herriot government, consistent with its anti-
clerical character, fully supported Sarrail's snub as a personal choice and
not an official act. However, outcries in Beirut, Rome, the French press
and Parliament eventually forced Herriot to send a formal apology to the
Apostolic Delegate in Lebanon. But Sarrail was not moved. He even aggravated the situation by waiting two months to return the visit which
the Maronite Patriarch had paid him in early January.[64]

Although Lebanese Christians were incensed by the actions of their
new "Protector," Lebanese Muslims were not. They were pleased by Sarrail's anti-clerical stance which seemed to promise religious impartiality
and they expected a greater share in government as a result. This was particularly true of Sunni Muslim bureaucrats and politicians, many of
whom were, like the new High Commissioner, Freemasons.[65]

Nationalist and religious leaders in Syria also welcomed, if somewhat
more hesitantly, the appearance of General Sarrail. His initial efforts to
court Syrian leaders encouraged a nationalist delegation from Damascus,
Homs, and Hama to travel to Beirut to present their demands. His willingness to receive nationalists seemed to indicate a change in French policy.

But his meeting with the nationalist delegation was disappointing. Nationalist arguments in favor of unity and independence made no impact,

[62] For details, see Gustave Gautherot, *Le Général Sarrail. Haut-Commissaire en Syrie
(Janvier 1925)*. Pamphlet (Paris, 1925), pp. 6, 10–15.

[63] *Ibid.*, pp. 16–20; Longrigg, *Syria*, p. 149.

[64] FO 371/476, vol. 10850. Crewe (Paris) to FO, 27 Jan. 1925; Longrigg, *Syria*, pp. 149–
50; Gautherot, *Général Sarrail*, pp. 7–8, 31–36.

[65] FO 371/11423, vol. 10165. Beirut Consul to FO, 8 Dec. 1924.

although, when the delegation complained continually about Subhi Barakat and the unfairness of the federal elections, Sarrail promised that in October 1925 new elections would be held. Hinting that some further political liberalization was forthcoming, he added that the various factions should take steps to make the true voice of the nation heard; first and foremost they should unify their "parties."[66] The delegation left Beirut feeling rather ambivalent about the new High Commissioner. While he was clearly more willing than his predecessors to listen to nationalist demands and had shown greater even-handedness in Lebanon, he had done his best to skirt the issue of Syrian unity and independence.

The misgivings of Syrian nationalists were not allayed by Sarrail's first visit to Damascus on February 4. At a reception for local dignitaries at the High Commissioner's Residency, an incident occurred in connection with a delegation of lawyers headed by Faris al-Khuri. At the time of the reinstitution of the Mixed Courts in 1924, the nationalist Lawyers' Union of Damascus had agreed to hold an annual 14-day strike as a protest against the Mixed Court's infringement of Syria's national sovereignty. Sarrail's visit happened to coincide with the appointed day of the strike. When Khuri and his colleagues entered the reception hall, Sarrail left the room, refusing to return until they had departed. On the following day matters got worse. Nationalists planned a large demonstration to be held in the street leading to the Residency. When Sarrail learned of this, he immediately sent out troops to forestall the demonstration. Equally irritating to the nationalists was the High Commissioner's excessive praise of Subhi Barakat.[67]

With no immediate prospect for a radical shift in French policy, Damascus nationalists decided to seize the one concession Sarrail had offered them: the right to organize a legal political party in preparation for the October elections.

THE PEOPLE'S PARTY

The prime mover behind the establishment of the first legal nationalist political party was ʿAbd al-Rahman Shahbandar. In the spring of 1922 he had been sentenced to 20 years in prison by a special military tribunal for his role in the violent disturbances that followed Charles Crane's visit to Damascus. After spending 17 months on Arwad Island, General Weygand exiled him. Shahbandar proceeded immediately to Paris and then to

[66] FO 684/32/115. Smart to FO, 21 Jan. 1925. The Aleppine nationalist leader, ʿAbd al-Rahman al-Kayyali, has suggested that General Sarrail encouraged the formation of a party like the Radical Party in France headed by Herriot and Painlevé, to which he was linked. ʿAbd al-Rahman al-Kayyali, al-Jihad al-siyasi (Aleppo, 1946), pp. 69–70.

[67] FO 371/1101, vol. 10850. Smart to FO, 12 Feb. 1925; Gautherot, Général Sarrail, pp. 26–27.

London, where some British Conservative Party members invited him to attend a session at Westminster. This caused an outcry from the Quai d'Orsay which had always suspected him of being a British agent. After London, Shahbandar paid a brief visit to the United States where he met with his good friend Charles Crane. In the nine months that he was abroad, he devoted most of his time to publicizing the cause of Syrian independence on behalf of the Syrian–Palestine Congress.[68] In the early summer of 1924, the French finally allowed him to return to Syria, in all likelihood a gesture of good will on the part of the Cartel des Gauches, which had recently come to power in France.

Although the official inauguration of the nationalist People's Party (Hizb al-sha'b) was not until June 1925, it began to take shape in Damascus at the end of January as an unstructured pressure group and propaganda arm of the Syrian independence movement.[69] Its first major activity focused on the new, unified Representative Assembly of the Syrian state. Coaxed by the Party leadership to emphasize the discrepancies and ambiguities in the decree which unified Aleppo and Damascus, the Assembly complained to President Barakat that the decree did not safeguard the independence of the Syrian nation. Representatives wanted to know why Article II, which explicitly affirmed that the Syrian head of state had to be elected by an absolute majority of the Assembly, was contradicted by Article XII, which gave the High Commissioner the right to annul or confirm the election and thereby abrogated the Assembly's executive right.[70] Although Barakat could not provide a convincing answer, Sarrail made some effort to allay nationalist fears by publishing an open letter, in which he emphasized that the cabinet should be responsible to the Assembly and that this important modification would be enshrined in the Syrian Organic Law being prepared for submission to the Permanent Mandates Commission at Geneva. A pessimistic People's Party immediately began to collect funds to send nationalist delegates to Europe to plead for the right of the Syrian people to have an effective voice in drafting the Organic Law.[71]

The second major activity of the People's Party came on April 8 during

---

[68] *Oriente Moderno*, 17 (1937), p. 32; FO 371/2043, vol. 10164.

[69] On the foundation and growth of the People's Party, see 'Abd al-Rahman Shahbandar, *al-Thawra al-suriyya al-wataniyya. Mudhakkirat 'Abd al-Rahman Shahbandar* (Damascus, 1933), p. 126; *La Syrie* (1 Sept. 1925); Hisham Nashabi, "The Political Parties in Syria 1918–1933, M.A. Dissertation (American University of Beirut, 1952), p. 95; Muhammad Harb Farzat, *al-Hayah al-hizbiyya fi suriyya bayn 1920–1955* (Damascus, 1955), p. 103; MAE, *Rapport à la Société des Nations sur la situation de la Syrie et du Liban 1925*, pp. 9–10; MD, 7N 4186, Dossier 7. "Renseignement," no. 605, 16–23 May 1925.

[70] FO 371/1939, vol. 10850. Damascus Consul to FO, 18 March 1925; FO 371/2109, vol. 10850. Damascus Consul to FO, 25 March 1925.

[71] *Al-Muqtabas*, no. 4241 (31 March 1925).

a brief visit by Lord Balfour, whose signature graced the 1917 British Declaration favoring a national home for Jews in Palestine. Many critical articles had appeared in the Damascus press during Balfour's March visit to Palestine. Now huge demonstrations in the town were organized against him. Some 10,000 protestors, including hundreds of high school students, gathered at the Umayyad Mosque. While police and gendarmes tried to break up the crowds, Balfour made a hurried exodus to Beirut, escorted by French troops and airplanes. Twenty-six casualties were reported and fears of a reprisal against the town's ancient Jewish community provoked the French to tighten security in Damascus. The American Consul, however, suggested that French authorities did not do all they could to prevent the riots, in order to remind Britain and the Permanent Mandates Commission that there was considerable anti-British feeling among the Arabs too.[72]

During the winter and spring, the People's Party gradually expanded its ranks and consolidated its organization under the leadership of Dr. Shahbandar and the Central Committee. By June, some 1,000 persons in Damascus had joined the Party.[73] Although there were no membership qualifications, most members were from the educated elite of the town: absentee landowners, lawyers, engineers, doctors, teachers, and journalists.[74] In addition, several influential Muslim merchants, some of whom sat on the Municipal Council, also belonged. Syrian government officials were not permitted to join, but there was passive support for the party in some administrative circles.[75]

Because the People's Party did not charge membership dues, its finances consisted completely of contributions from members, especially landowners and merchants, and from professional associations such as the Lawyers' Union. Funds also came from the Syrian–Palestine Congress in Cairo and Syrian emigrants in the Americas, with whom Party leaders were in contact. Funds covered such costs as the rent of the Party office located in the Hijaz Railway Station and propaganda work includ-

[72] USNA, Syria. 800d.00/191. Damascus Consulate to Secretary of State, 19 April 1925; Muhi al-Din al-Safarjalani, *Tarikh al-thawra al-suriyya* (Damascus, 1961), pp. 121–23.

[73] The Party claimed that its membership lists included 350 influential leaders in Damascus. *Oriente Moderno*, 5 (1925), p. 462.

[74] Secondary school students were not official members. Since the April demonstrations against Balfour, in which students had a large role, a decree had been passed which stated that any student who participated in any political activities or in demonstrations, or who wrote any political manifesto, would automatically be expelled from school. See MWT, *al-Intidab al-faransi; qadaya mukhtalifa*, 7/1109/1093. Subhi Barakat to Minister of Interior, 23 April 1925, citing *Arrêté*, no. 70, 15 April 1925.

[75] Général Andréa, *La revolte druze et l'insurrection de Damas, 1925–1926* (Paris, 1937), p. 78; Nashabi, "The Political Parties," pp. 91–92.

ing financial assistance to the leading nationalist newspaper in Damascus, *al-Mufid*.[76] Party officials, all of whom were financially comfortable, did not receive salaries. The Party budget was humble.[77]

The official opening of the People's Party took place on June 5 at the Damascus Opera House. Well over 1,000 people crowded into the auditorium to hear their leaders express, freely and legally for the first time since the Syrian Congress of 1920, "the will of the Syrian people." The Party's Vice-President, Faris al-Khuri, began the ceremony (*hafla*) by calling for a constitutional government supporting national sovereignty. Regarded as the major link between the nationalists and the Christian minority in Damascus, Khuri emphasized that in an independent Syria there would be no religious or class distinctions and the economy would no longer be controlled by foreigners.

Khuri then introduced his close friend and fellow Syrian Protestant College alumnus, ʿAbd al-Rahman Shahbandar. There was no more renowned orator in the whole country and certainly no more popular figure with the Damascus public. In his address, which brought the audience to its feet, Dr. Shahbandar likened the People's Party to the Committee of Union and Progress that had made the revolt in Istanbul in 1908. "It was an instrument of liberation which would shatter the despotic rule Syria was now forced to live under." He added, however, that his Party was not just interested in the unity of natural Syria; it also aimed to keep the whole Arab nation united and independent. For Shahbandar, the Party had a progressive role to play in the development of the Arab nation and, as he bluntly stated, "if I believe that Communism does not suit the Eastern instinct, I do believe however, that a reasonable degree of socialism is not incompatible with Eastern ideals."[78] After some concluding remarks and a recital of nationalist poetry, the ceremony ended. As the crowd filed out of the Opera House, another 100 people joined the Party.[79]

Besides Shahbandar and Khuri, the Party leadership included ten other prominent Damascus residents, all of whom had previously been active in the Arab nationalist movement. Three were wealthy merchants: Lutfi al-Haffar, ʿAbd al-Majid Tabbakh, and Abuʾl Khayr al-Mawqiʿ. Three were lawyers: Fawzi al-Ghazzi, Ihsan al-Sharif, and Saʿid Haydar, a member of the prominent Shiʿi landowning family of Baʿlabakk. Two were absentee landowners: Jamil Mardam and Tawfiq Shamiyya, an American-

---

[76] *Al-Mufid* was founded in 1924 by the Haydars, a prominent Shiʿi landowning-bureaucratic family of Baʿlabakk. Al-Jundi, *Tarikh*, pp. 183–84; *A Post-War Bibliography of the Near Eastern Mandates* (Beirut, 1933), pp. 43–51.

[77] Nashabi, "The Political Parties," p. 100; Farzat, *al-Hayah al-hizbiyya*, p. 102.

[78] *Haflat iftitah hizb al-shaʿb*. Pamphlet (Damascus, 1925). Also see, Nashabi, "The Political Parties," pp. 92–95.

[79] Farzat, *al-Hayah al- hizbiyya*, p. 103.

educated Orthodox Christian. Finally, there were Adib al-Safadi, a political journalist from a family that had produced several high-ranking administrators during late Ottoman times, and Hasan al-Hakim, an ex-functionary from the Maydan quarter who had gone to prison with Shahbandar and Haydar in 1922.[80]

The public regarded all Party leaders as dedicated nationalists—men who had been imprisoned or exiled on account of their political beliefs and activities. Shahbandar, Khuri, Ghazzi, Mardam, and Sharif were among the most articulate members of the Syrian intelligentsia and were recognized as the natural spokesmen for and interpreters of the aspirations of Syrian society. Of the twelve members on the Party's Central Committee, five had been educated at Western universities, and another three at Ottoman professional schools in Istanbul.[81]

In spite of its popular support, the People's Party was essentially an elitist organization. Whether absentee landowner, merchant, or intellectual, each leader was the representative of his class or interest group and the exponent of its grievances against the French. Each possessed, in varying degrees, sufficient independent influence to contribute a personal support system to the Party cause. And each perceived the Party as the

[80] See *Oriente Moderno*, 5 (1925), p. 462; Amin Sa'id, *al-Thawra al-'arabiyya al-kubra* (Cairo, 1934), vol. 3, p. 292; Farzat, *al-Hayah al-hizbiyya*, p. 101. On al-Haffar, a wealthy textiles merchant, see Chapter 10; Faris, *Man huwa 1949*, pp. 118–19; Lutfi al-Haffar, *Dhikrayat* (Damascus, 1954), vol. 1, p. 14; Virginia Vacca, "Notizie," pp. 483–84. Ishan al-Sharif was born in 1893 into a religious family of Damascus. He was the second Syrian to receive a Doctorate in Law from France (Paris) and was Fawzi al-Ghazzi's law partner. FO 371/5398, vol. 20067, "Records of the Leading Personalities in Syria and the Lebanon," 26 Aug. 1936. Sa'id Haydar was born in 1890 in Ba'labakk into a wealthy landowning-bureaucratic family. He studied law in Istanbul and taught it at the Faculty of Law in Damascus during the Faysal era. He was also elected at this time to the Syrian Congress from Ba'labakk. With the French occupation he fled to Egypt but was amnestied in 1921. He returned to Damascus to practice law. In 1922 he was jailed with Shahbandar and Hasan al-Hakim at Arwad Island for his activities in the disturbances following the Crane visit to Damascus. In 1924 he helped his brother Yusuf resume publication of the nationalist newspaper, *al-Mufid* (in Damascus), which the French had closed down shortly after the occupation. Ahmad Qudama, *Ma'alim wa a'lam fi bilad al-'arab* (Damascus, 1965), vol. 1, p. 355; al-Jundi, *Tarikh*, pp. 183–184. Tawfiq Shamiyya was born in 1885 in Damascus and educated at the Syrian Protestant College. His father, Jubran, owned with his brothers 60,000 dunams (15,000 acres) of land in Qalamun and in the Ba'labakk region which they had begun to purchase in the late nineteenth century. The Shamiyyas were one of the two biggest Christian landowning families of Damascus. The Shamiyya home in Bab Tuma was one of the most exquisite in Damascus; it is where the German Kaiser Wilhelm stayed in 1899 on his visit to Damascus. During the Faysal era, Tawfiq was a member of the Amir's political bureau. Conversation with Tawfiq's son, Jubran Shamiyya (Beirut, 29 July 1975); FO 371/5398, vol. 20067, 26 Aug. 1926.

[81] One pro-French Damascus newspaper erroneously criticized the People's Party leadership by remarking that men like Shahbandar, Khuri, and Shamiyya spoke better English than Arabic. *Al-Zaman* cited with no date in FO 684/32/146. Smart to FO, 12 August 1925.

symbol of his own power. The Party had no organized cadres, just personal followings loyal to individual leaders. Its leaders never intended that political forces should be mobilized on a permanent basis but rather intermittently, in conformity with the traditional politics of urban notables. Their goal was to discredit their Syrian rivals in government, the collaborating notables, not to overturn the social hierarchy.

The Party's program clearly supported the interests of its leadership. It was far more sober than the fiery rhetoric of Party leaders might lead one to suspect. Article I called for the realization of Syrian national sovereignty and unity within Syria's natural boundaries (Greater Syria); personal freedom in all its forms; the education of the people toward a social, democratic, and civil polity; the protection of Syria's national industries; the fuller development and exploitation of her natural resources; and the unification of the educational system, including compulsory and universal elementary education. Article II stated that the Party endeavored to realize these principles by "legal means," an indication that its program was to serve as the nationalist platform in the upcoming elections in October.[82]

Perhaps what distinguished the People's Party leadership most clearly from other political factions in Syria was its strong secular orientation. It assiduously avoided reference to religion in its program and public pronouncements, except to emphasize that all religious communities supported the unity and independence of Syria and that individual liberties would be guaranteed in an independent Syria. The Muslim religious establishment in Syria supported the People's Party, although no religious leader belonged to its Central Committee. The absence of religious leaders from the nationalist leadership, despite their undoubted sympathy with nationalist goals, had historical roots. Even before the rise of Arabism, political influence and social prestige had passed from the religious establishment to those who owned large amounts of lands, who had acquired an Ottoman professional education, including the Turkish language (in addition to Arabic), who wore the fez and the frock coat, and who had key posts in the modern secular wing of Ottoman administration. Although the foundation of Arab nationalism was a mixture of religious and secular sentiments, religious leaders stressed religious solidarity primarily in hopes of regaining their traditional positions of

---

[82] *Haflat iftitah hizb al-sha'b*. Pamphlet (Damascus, 1925); also see MD, 7N 4186, Dossier 7. "Renseignement," no. 605, 16–23 May 1925; FO 684/32/711. Smart to FO, 16 June 1925; USNA, Syria. 890d.00/214, 14 Sept. 1925. Syrian unity did not include a small Lebanon. Other points in the Party program included the end of Mixed Courts; the end of all French control over administration, including *awqaf* and especially the Hijaz Railway; the unification of the monetary system on the gold standard; and the annulment of the *Banque de Syrie* Convention.

leadership among Arab Muslims in the face of increasing secularization and governmental control over Muslim institutions. With the exception of a few religious scholars whose influence on intellectual life in Syria cannot be ignored, religious figures played a secondary role in the birth of Arab nationalism.

This trend continued during the Mandate as the influence of religious leaders was further eroded. French policy aimed at curtailing what remained of the independent influence of the religious establishment and, in the important arena of diplomatic relations, religious leaders deferred to modern, educated politicians who were much better qualified to argue the Syrian case in an idiom intelligible to the French. Although religious figures willingly used their positions in the mosques and religious schools to rally the urban masses against the French, they usually took direct political action at the behest of the nationalist leadership. The Muslim religious establishment became but one of several intermediaries between the nationalist leadership and the Syrian public.

This is not to suggest that the religious establishment agreed in all matters with the nationalist elite. Culturally and, to a growing extent, socially, the two groups came from different worlds. Politically they were not always in harmony. But both shared the common feeling of having been denied their place in society by the French. In the case of the nationalists, the French denied them legitimate political power. From the perspective of Muslim religious leaders, the High Commission upset the legal and religious status quo in Syria on which they based their claim to independent influence among the masses. By denying the religious establishment final authority over the administration of charitable endowments and adjudication in matters of personal status, the French also attacked the material sources of that authority.

ONE OTHER POLITICAL PARTY was established during this brief period of political liberalization. This party, the Syrian Union Party (Hizb al-wahda al-suriyya), was secretly sponsored by the High Commission to offset the growing influence of Dr. Shahbandar's organization. In an effort to be consistent with the times, it aped the People's Party by calling for the unity of Syria, national sovereignty, economic revival, reduction of taxes, improvement of the conditions of the working class, and harmony and freedom of all religious communities in the country.[83] But the Union Party's true character was revealed by its leadership: its president was none other than Subhi Barakat, the President of the Syrian state, and other

[83] *Alif ba'* (14 May 1925); MD, 7N 4186. "Renseignement," no. 611, 13 May 1925.

members included prominent bureaucrats and journalists in collaboration with the French.[84]

The Union Party's official newspaper, *al-Zaman*, accused the leaders of the People's Party of political opportunism and of espousing democratic ideals when in reality they favored the supremacy of Islam at the expense of other religions. It criticized them for their conception of a large Arab State without questioning how Syrians, Lebanese, and Palestinians, with their well-developed intellects and sophisticated urbane backgrounds, could be expected to live under one roof with primitive tribes of the Iraqi desert and the Hijaz. It accused the People's Party of really aiming for a Hashemite-dominated Islamic state behind a smoke screen of lofty ideals and democratic slogans. Instead, the Union Party suggested that until the people were properly educated to feel that they belonged to a nation rather than different religious communities, the best possible solution was to cooperate with their foreign tutors.[85]

As the October elections drew closer, the bickering between these two Damascus-based parties continued apace. In the meantime, serious trouble was brewing elsewhere in Syria.

[84] See FO 371/4348, vol. 6483. Palmer (Damascus) to FO, 23 March 1921; FO 371/4968, vol. 6454. Palmer to FO, 30 March 1921; *al-Muqtabas*, no. 4295, 5 June 1925; Farzat, *al-Hayah al-hizbiyya*, p. 105.

[85] *Al-Zaman*, cited with no date in FO 684/32/1246. Smart to FO, 12 Aug. 1925; *La Syrie* (1 Sept. 1925).

PART III

THE GREAT REVOLT, 1925–1927

CHAPTER SIX

ORIGINS: THE DRUZE CONNECTION

ON 18 JULY 1925, Druze highlanders opened fire on a French airplane cir-
cling the Jabal Druze. Two days later, the Druze leader Sultan al-Atrash
and a group of his armed horsemen attacked and occupied Salkhad, the
second town of the Jabal. On July 21, Sultan Pasha's band ambushed 166
Algerian and Syrian troops under the command of Captain Normand
who had been dispatched to rescue some stranded airmen. Less than half
the Normand column survived the assault. That same evening Sultan al-
Atrash's forces laid siege to Suwayda', the capital of the Jabal Druze and
the central point of French administration there.[1]

The initial success of the Druze rebels aroused intense eagerness and
enthusiasm in Sultan al-Atrash's camp. In the last week of July, Druzes
from all over the Jabal rushed to his side, transforming his small band
into an army of between 8,000 and 10,000 men, in a region whose total
population was only 50,000. In the neighboring Hawran, parts of which
had been at the mercy of the Jabal for generations, panic spread among its
mixed population of Christian, Muslim, and Druze peasants who feared
reprisals if they did not heed Sultan Pasha's call to arms. Some peasants
fled to safer areas in the Hawran or into Palestine. Others, mainly Christians, sought refuge in Damascus, bringing tales of massacre and pillage.
Druze rebels burnt at least five Christian villages.[2]

At the end of July, a French relief column of 3,000 troops under the
command of General Roger Michaud set out from Izra' to break the seige
of Suwayda' twenty miles away. On August 2, just seven miles shy of its
destination, Druze horsemen led by Sultan al-Atrash surprised and
routed the French column. French casualties were heavy: 14 killed, 385
wounded, and 432 missing. The French commander of a company of
Madagascans who had panicked and fled, committed suicide. Even General Michaud left the scene prematurely. The Druze rebels had also cap-

---

[1] Munir al-Rayyis, al-Kitab al-dhahabi lil-thawrat al-wataniyya fi al-mashriq al-ʿarabi. al-Thawra al-suriyya al-kubra. (Beirut, 1969), pp. 165–67; Andréa, La révolte druze,
pp. 52–53.

[2] One report claimed that by the end of July 1925, there were 8,000 to 10,000 Druze rebels. Another estimated that Sultan al-Atrash commanded 15,000–20,000 armed men. See
FO 371/4475, vol. 10850. Smart to FO, 27 July 1925. Elizabeth P. MacCallum, The Nationalist Crusade in Syria (New York, 1928), p. 118. FO 371/4475, vol. 10850. Colonial Office
to FO, 28 July 1925; FO 371/4739, vol. 10850. Smart to FO, 29 July 1925.

tured 2,000 rifles,[3] and it began to look as though the Druze uprising might spread to the rest of Syria.[4]

THE IMMEDIATE PROVOCATION for the revolt had been the arrest of three Druze chiefs on July 11. However, discontent in the Jabal Druze had been on the rise for the preceding two years, ever since the appointment of Captain Carbillet as the top French official in the area in 1923. But lest blame for the massive Syria-wide revolt that was to follow be laid unfairly on the shoulders of one man, it must again be emphasized that the cause of Druze, as of Syrian discontent lay in France's persistence in applying methods learned in North Africa to the very different Syrian situation.[5]

French strategy for governing the Jabal Druze was a microcosm of the general imperial strategy for Syria. In Syria at large, French strategy focused on setting rural areas against the nationalist towns, on isolating Syria's compact regional minorities from the mainstream of Syrian-Arab political culture, and on playing elite against elite. This grand design, a derivative of French imperial strategy in Morocco, seemed ideally suited to the Jabal Druze.[6] The Druzes inhabited a remote, inaccessible mountainous agricultural area. They constituted a compact minority; ninety percent of the Jabal's population were Druze with religious and social customs sufficiently distinct from those of the Sunni Muslim Arabs of the plains and towns.[7] And local authority in the Jabal was divided between rival clans, prone to intense factionalism.

The formula adopted by the French for governing the Jabal Druze concentrated on the development of a special and direct relationship with the

[3] FO 371/5576, vol. 10851. Crewe (Paris) to Chamberlain, 15 Sept. 1925; al-Rayyis, *al-Kitab al-dhahabi*, pp. 167-69; MacCallum, *Crusade*, p. 119; Tannenbaum, *Sarrail*, pp. 202–3; Zafir al-Qasimi, *Watha'iq jadida min al-thawra al-suriyya al-kubra* (Damascus, 1965), pp. 119–26.

[4] Tannenbaum, *Sarrail*, p. 201, citing "Les Affaires de Syrie," Fonds Painlevé, Box 42, File: *Syrie* (Notes Carbillet), pp. 34–35, located in the Archives Nationales, Paris.

[5] The French made their first diplomatic inroads in the Jabal Druze in the late nineteenth century. Before the 1880s, Britain was the only European power with influence among Druzes, largely because she had protected their community in Mount Lebanon in the aftermath of the 1858–60 civil war. But continued British support of the Ottoman state led some Druzes to seek French support. The French seized the opportunity but chose to develop ties with the ʿAmr clan, the major rival of the Atrash clan. David Buchanan McDowall, "The Druze Revolt, 1925–27, and its Background in the Late Ottoman Period," B.Litt. Dissertation (University of Oxford, 1972), pp. 153–68. Attempts to keep foreigners out of the affairs of the Jabal Druze were reinforced after the British Consul in Damascus, Sir Richard Burton, became involved in intrigues in the Jabal in 1869–71. MAE, Syrie–Liban 1918–29. Carbillet, "La paix avec les Druses," 10 Feb. 1926, vol. 197, p. 2.

[6] Burke, "A Comparative View," pp. 175–86.

[7] Gabriel Baer, *Population and Society in the Arab East* (London, 1964), p. 109.

Druzes that would recognize local customs and at the same time circumvent Damascus. The first French High Commissioner, General Gouraud, chose a trusted aide, Colonel Georges Catroux, who like Gouraud was a veteran of Morocco, to reach an accord with the Druze community.[8] In November 1920, Catroux initiated negotiations with the ruling clans of the Jabal which led to a Franco-Druze Treaty in March 1921. Its terms stated that the Jabal Druze was to form a special administrative unit distinct from the Damascus state[9] with an elected native governor and a representative council (*majlis*). Administration was to be under Druze control. In return, the Druzes had to recognize the French Mandate and accept the usual array of French advisers and the garrisoning of French troops at Suwayda'.

The first governor to preside over this new arrangement was Salim al-Atrash, the paramount chief of the Druze community.[10] Whereas Salim Pasha had been one of the first Druze chiefs to recognize Amir Faysal's authority in 1918, and had been recognized by Faysal as governor (*mutasarrif*) of the Jabal Druze, with the French occupation he felt he had to strike a balance between Druze aspirations and French needs. His elevation from a position in the Druze power structure of *primus inter pares* to that of governor of a separate Druze state, however, gained Salim al-Atrash little more than verbal recognition from other Druze leaders.[11] For Atrash chieftains, the French-imposed system of constitutional office-holding threatened to erode the tradition of familial hierarchy that had characterized the structure of power in the Jabal since the eighteenth century. It enabled those Druze chiefs who managed to gain control of the new political institutions to isolate their rivals more effectively than before since traditional channels to political office and benefits were now blocked. A *majlis* of Druze notables created by the French served as a counterweight to the governorship, and French influence with its members was a check on the Atrash clan. Furthermore, the French could veto the selection of an Atrash governor, if they found him undesirable.[12]

There was bound to be deep resentment in certain Druze quarters against the new administrative system which sanctioned foreign intervention in the Jabal. Violent altercations between Druzes and the French followed the March 1921 treaty.

The first significant Druze uprising against French rule started in July

[8] McDowall, "The Druze Revolt," pp. 220–26.

[9] In 1922, the French proclaimed the Jabal Druze a separate unit under French protection. Also see MacCallum, *Crusade*, p. 105.

[10] The Atrash established themselves as the paramount clan after 1869 (replacing the Hamdani). See McDowall, "The Druze Revolt," pp. xxviii, 40.

[11] In fact, Salim's loudest critics were his own relatives, particularly 'Abd al-Ghaffar and Sultan al-Atrash. FO 371/6384, vol. 7847. Damascus Consul to FO, 8 June 1922.

[12] MacCallum, *Crusade*, p. 106.

1922. Its catalyst was the arrest in the Jabal Druze of a certain Adham Khanjar, a Lebanese, whom French authorities accused of belonging to a rebel band that had tried to assassinate General Gouraud 13 months earlier. Khanjar's interrogation revealed that he had been on his way to visit Sultan al-Atrash, the Druze chieftain most feared by the French. When Sultan Pasha learned of Khanjar's arrest, he immediately requested the senior French official in Suwayda', Commandant Trenga, to place the prisoner in his custody, as Druze custom dictated this minimal hospitality. When Trenga did not reply, Sultan al-Atrash went to Suwayda' to deal with the matter personally. There, he learned that the French were transferring Khanjar to Damascus. He quickly organized a recovery party and attacked the armored convoy escorting the prisoner. The French responded by sending troops to destroy Sultan al-Atrash's home. The first French raid failed but a second succeeded at the end of August. Intent on teaching Sultan Pasha an unforgettable lesson, the French not only plundered his home but afterwards sent planes to bomb it.

Sultan al-Atrash had been looking for an opportunity to rally Druzes against French interference in the Jabal and the Khanjar incident in the summer of 1922 created the opportunity. For nearly a year, Druze rebels waged guerilla warfare throughout the Jabal. Sultan Pasha, however, was forced to seek refuge across the border in Transjordan at the end of the summer. Under pressure from the French, the British agreed to oust him from Transjordan in April 1923. Soon afterwards, he surrendered to the French who, not wanting to prolong the rebellion, reached a truce with him.[13]

During this first major Druze uprising against the French, Sultan al-Atrash was in contact with and received the backing of nationalists in Damascus and Amman, contrary to French hopes that cultural differences could prevent these links from being made. But the precarious situation of nationalists at the time prevented them from offering Atrash much more than moral support. Nevertheless, he proclaimed his revolt in the name of Syrian independence and the Jabal's reunification with Damascus. Despite his limited formal education, he was familiar with the nationalist creed, as were his closest Druze allies. He was opposed to any form of French mandatory rule in Syria and considered himself a nationalist.

Even before Sultan al-Atrash's surrender, Salim Pasha had retired as governor of the Jabal Druze, leaving Commandant Trenga, the highest-ranking French official at the time, temporarily in charge of his functions. One important reason for Salim's resignation was that he had suffered an appreciable loss of influence among Atrash chieftains and with the *majlis*.

---

[13] Al-Jundi, *Tarikh*, pp. 184–85; MacCallum, *Crusade*, pp. 108–9; al-Qasimi, *Watha'iq*, pp. 175–77.

Throughout his governorship, Salim al-Atrash had quarrelled with Sultan Pasha as well as with 'Abd al-Ghaffar al-Atrash, the most influential member of the *majlis* and the major stumbling block to French administrative reform in the Jabal Druze. Salim Pasha's subsequent death in mid-September 1923 led to a fierce struggle within the Atrash clan over political succession. The clan's failure to agree on a candidate for governor led the *majlis* to go outside not only the Atrash clan but the entire Druze community, and to appoint Trenga's replacement in the Jabal Druze, Captain Gabriel Carbillet, as temporary governor. Then, as Atrash rivalries were played out, a frustrated *majlis*, manipulated by Carbillet, broke with Druze political tradition altogether and confirmed him as governor.[14]

Until the arrival of Captain Carbillet, the French strategy of isolating the Jabal Druze from Damascus and of creating a direct and special relationship with the Druze leadership had worked fairly well. Indeed, the French had allowed the Druzes a large degree of autonomy over local administrative matters. Commandant Trenga had shown flexibility in a very difficult situation and had also managed to initiate reforms and development projects of benefit to the Druze community. He established a regular budget and a Druze gendarmerie; he built roads for automotive traffic; and he began reconstructing the dilapidated irrigation system around Suwayda'. Organized political opposition to the French, although never insignificant, had yet to reach alarming proportions. For the time being, Sultan al-Atrash's movement had been successfully checked.

Captain Carbillet came to the Jabal Druze with previous experience as a native affairs officer in French West Africa. A young, energetic innovator, he proved to be an indefatigable but impatient modernizer. He suddenly altered the delicate relationships Catroux and then Trenga had worked so hard to cultivate by choosing to administer the Jabal Druze directly, and with a distinct flavor of personal demagoguery. His aim was to destroy the Jabal's ancient feudal system which he considered retrograde.[15]

In the spirit of the Lyautey tradition of French rule in Morocco, Car-

[14] FO 371/5762, vol. 7847. Damascus Consul to FO, 22 May 1922; FO 371/6384, vol. 7847. Damascus Consul to FO, 8 June 1922. 'Abd al-Ghaffar came from the most important branch of the Atrash clan, the Joub Isma'il; however, he did not come from the same sub-branch as Salim Pasha, Nasib Bey and Sultan Pasha. 'Abd al-Ghaffar was thought to be close to the British and thus was held in great suspicion by the French. MAE, Syrie–Liban 1918–29. "La paix avec les Druses," 10 Feb. 1926, vol. 197, pp. 13–15; Capitaine G. Carbillet, *Au Djébel Druse* (Paris, 1929), pp. 103–7; FO 371/9868, vol. 9054. Palmer (Damascus) to FO, 18 Sept. 1923. One Syrian historian claims that Carbillet coerced the *majlis* into nominating him Governor of the Jabal. See Hani Abi-Rashid, *Jabal al-Duruz* (Beirut, 1961), pp. 190–92.

[15] MAE, Syrie–Liban 1918–29. "Enquête de M. Daclin: Djébel Druse," Part i, 7 Sept. 1926, vol. 234, pp. 51–52; MacCallum, *Crusade*, p. 106.

billet developed an efficient economic administration with few troops and trained native officials to carry out his plans.[16] In 20 months he completed Trenga's highway projects and added another 125 roadmiles for motor vehicles. He paved the streets of Suwayda' and built over 100 miles of irrigation ditches. He also rationalized the Jabal's judicial system and established a Court of Appeals at Suwayda'. He increased the number of schools and improved the public sanitation system. However, Carbillet, the tireless reformer, the man whose love of the Jabal Druze was "second only to his love for France,"[17] imperfectly fit Maréchal Lyautey's model of the elite French native affairs officer. Although he belonged to the elite Service des Renseignements, spoke Arabic, and was familiar with Druze religious and social practices, his method of rule was not at all subtle. Rather, it was the antithesis of rule along native lines (association) that Lyautey had favored, for Carbillet completely refused to operate within the framework of Druze political tradition.[18]

Carbillet's most ambitious project was to free the Druze peasantry from its historic economic insecurity by transforming the Druze feudal system. Communal property was still prevalent in the agricultural areas of the Jabal, although a peasant revolt in 1889–90 had established property rights for Druze peasants in some districts. Common lands were redistributed on a triennial basis but the Druze notability normally received the most productive third of the lands of the previous rotation, which peasants generally farmed in addition to their own two-thirds share. Carbillet—consistent with the early idealism of French agrarian policy in Syria whose central idea was to create a nation of small peasant proprietors at the expense of the big landowning classes—eagerly offered Druze peasants individual ownership rights on lands planted with grapevines.[19]

Although some peasants became owners of small plots, the overall im-

[16] See Roberts, *French Colonial Policy*; Burke, "A Comparative View," pp. 175–86; MAE, Syrie-Liban 1918–29. "Enquête de M. Daclin," 7 Sept. 1926, vol. 234, p. 52.

[17] MacCallum, *Crusade*, p. 112.

[18] MAE, Syrie–Liban 1918–29. "Enquête de M. Daclin," pp. 53–55. The Beirut-based Liaison Officer of the British Air Ministry, who knew Carbillet quite well, described the French Captain as a "rugged looking individual with a long, unkempt beard" who "after so many years isolated in the wilds of the Jebel Druze country . . . has become almost a Druze himself." FO 371/4810, vol. 10835. Air Ministry to FO, 13 Aug. 1925. Yet, Carbillet was "totally incapable of understanding the native psychology, harsh and overbearing to his inferiors and heedless of local sentiment and prejudice." FO 371/5576, vol. 10851. Crewe (Paris) to Chamberlain, 15 Sept. 1925.

[19] MacCallum, *Crusade*, pp. 112–13; Joyce Laverty Miller, "The Syrian Revolt of 1925," *International Journal of Middle East Studies*, 8 (1977), p. 552, citing *Oriente Moderno*, 4 (1924), p. 38; MAE, *Rapport à la Société des Nations sur la situation de la Syrie et du Liban*, 1925, pp. 13–19. According to MacCallum, in 1924 one million vines were planted on land that had been "cleared of stones and enclosed by low stone walls to designate the boundaries of the vineyards." *Crusade*, p. 111.

pact of Carbillet's land reform was slight. The conservative, suspicious Druze peasantry—still dominated by and dependent on the great Druze clans—did not take advantage of his offer because it threatened a traditional way of life and because they were discouraged from doing so by their Druze lords. In fact, suspicion turned to alienation when Carbillet resorted to forced peasant labor, in lieu of taxation, to complete his various public works projects, particularly the road network, in record-breaking time. Peasants did not appreciate "the advantage of roads" designed for "wheeled vehicles they did not possess."[20]

Carbillet adopted tactics in his game of divide and rule which pitted class against class, that is, French-backed peasants against their Druze lords. Yet, he failed to secure the peasantry's support and, as a result, he reduced the potential of his other option: to exploit the divisions and antagonisms at the summit of the Druze power structure within the paramount Atrash clan and between it and its rivals on the *majlis*. Although Carbillet's attempt to destroy the power structure led to a diminution of the political authority and privileges of the Atrash chieftains, it eventually fanned Atrash discontent with his regime into another and far more serious Druze revolt.[21]

Disenchantment with Captain Carbillet's reforms and autocratic administrative methods spread rapidly in the Jabal. He received a series of death threats in December 1923, and Atrash chiefs prepared a full-scale revolt against the French for April 1924. French Intelligence, however, caught wind of it beforehand and successfully defused it. Nevertheless, by the end of 1924 Druze opposition to Carbillet was in evidence in all quarters, and the campaign against him began to build up steam. Peasants distrusted his land reforms and resisted his forced labor policy. Local functionaries were outraged by his direct one-man rule which bypassed them. Rubbing salt in their wounds, Carbillet enforced a strict surveillance of administrative practices to prevent functionaries from manipulating their offices for personal benefit. Most important was the intensely hostile reaction of the great Druze clans, particularly the Atrash. Carbillet's land reforms and his personal rule were undermining their material base in land and the traditional system of political bargaining and decision-making.[22]

[20] MAE, *Rapport à la Société des Nations*, 1925, pp. 16–19; MacCallum, *Crusade*, p. 113.

[21] MAE, Syrie–Liban 1918–29. "Enquête de M. Daclin," pp. 55–56.

[22] FO 371/5527, vol. 10160. Damascus Consul to FO, 16 June 1925; Tannenbaum, *Sarrail*, p. 199; MAE, Syrie–Liban 1918–29. "Enquête de M. Daclin," 7 Sept. 1926, vol. 234, pp. 187–88. It should be mentioned that by Syrian standards, the major Druze clans which dominated Druze society, economy, and politics were not big landowners. But in the eyes of Druze peasants, they were perceived as big landowners. One scholar has recently suggested that the largest landowners in the Jabal Druze were actually rich peasants, most of

In the spring of 1925, the Atrash clan—temporarily laying aside its personal differences—sent a delegation to Beirut to complain about Carbillet to High Commissioner Sarrail. These Atrash chiefs demanded that a Druze be made governor, as promised by the Franco-Druze Treaty of 1921. Although Sarrail categorically refused to dismiss Carbillet, he instructed him to take a leave of absence in mid-May.[23] In the interim, the High Commission appointed Captain Antoine Raynaud, who had been stationed in the Jabal Druze for some time, as provisional governor. Apparently more in touch with the dynamics of Druze politics than Carbillet, Raynaud struck up cordial relations with Sultan al-Atrash at the expense of the *majlis,* which was mainly composed of lesser Druze dignitaries who had been Carbillet's only support in the Jabal. Perfectly aware of the seething dissatisfaction with Carbillet's rule, Raynaud reported to Sarrail at the beginning of June that a revolt was likely. He also suggested that one way to avoid such a disturbance would be to undertake a full-scale investigation of Druze allegations against the vacationing Carbillet.[24]

Raynaud's alarming report on the deteriorating situation in the Jabal Druze annoyed Sarrail who suspected that Raynaud's criticisms of Carbillet's rule were motivated by personal ambition. Raynaud's close relationship with Sultan al-Atrash and the fact that the Druze separatist faction on the *majlis* had already re-elected Carbillet governor for another term the previous February convinced the High Commissioner to recall Raynaud at once.[25]

His replacement was Major Tommy Martin of the Service des Renseignements. After Martin reported a sudden increase in the number of violent incidents in the Jabal, Sarrail had a change of heart and instructed him to investigate the accusations against Carbillet. On July 11, Martin transmitted to Beirut his first impressions of the causes of trouble in the

---

whom lived in villages nearby their lands. In this sense, they must be differentiated from the absentee landowning classes in the principal nationalist towns of Syria. James A. Reilly, "A Peasant War in Syria: The Jabal Druze Revolt of 1925–1927." Unpublished paper (Georgetown University, 1984), p. 10. On this subject, see also ʿAbdullah Hanna, *al-Qadiyya al-ziraʿiyya wa al-harakat al-fallahiyya fi suriyya wa lubnan (1920–1945)* (Beirut, 1978), vol. 2, pp. 44–48.

[23] MacCallum, *Crusade,* p. 114.

[24] Miller, "The Syrian Revolt," p. 552; Tannenbaum, *Sarrail,* p. 200; MAE, Syrie–Liban 1918–29. "Enquête de M. Daclin," p. 57.

[25] There is strong evidence of intrigue on the part of Raynaud. See Tannenbaum, *Sarrail,* p. 202. Carbillet certainly thought so, accusing Raynaud of intriguing with the French Assistant Delegate to the State of Damascus. FO 371/4810, vol. 10835. Air Ministry to FO, 3 Aug. 1925; MacCallum, *Crusade,* p. 116; Miller, "The Syrian Revolt," p. 552. By this time, the Atrash leadership was willing to settle for Raynaud as Governor, but definitely not Carbillet. FO 371/4005, vol. 10850. Damascus Consul to FO, 23 June 1925.

Jabal. He confirmed Raynaud's earlier warning that the Atrash clan was preparing a major revolt. Evidence abounded that Sultan al-Atrash—backed by the united Atrash clan and joined by the influential ʿIzz al-Din al-Halabis,[26] a powerful clan of the northern Jabal thought to be the most cosmopolitan and educated of the Druze clans with the strongest ties to nationalists in Damascus—was rallying Druze bureaucrats and peasants. But Tommy Martin's observations either went unnoticed or they were purposely ignored by the High Commissioner who had clearly begun to show the signs of crankiness and impatience of his 70 years.[27] Sarrail had already decided to take a tough stand against the Atrash leadership.

On the same day that Martin sent off his report, three Atrash chiefs arrived in Damascus at the High Commission's invitation to discuss their grievances. Instead, they were arrested at their hotel and deported to Palmyra. Sultan al-Atrash had also been invited but he had anticipated French tactics and stayed away.[28]

General Sarrail's arrest of the Atrash chiefs was the catalyst for the massive Druze uprising a week later. Sultan al-Atrash, knowing that he was a marked man, preferred resistance to certain imprisonment. He also knew that he could tap the anti-French sentiments that had been brewing in the Jabal Druze for the past few years. Although the arrest of his relatives prompted the once divided Atrash clan to close ranks around its now undisputed strongman, such a movement had been underway since 1923, when Captain Carbillet first tried to reduce Atrash primacy by playing the lesser dignitaries of the *majlis* against the clan and by attacking the material base of its power through land reform. With his clan reunited and local rivals hamstrung by the absence of their French patron, Sultan Pasha faced little internal resistance to his call for a general revolt.[29] He could count on support from disaffected bureaucrats who had suffered a significant loss of influence and income under Carbillet's one-man rule;

[26] Muhammad ʿIzz al-Din al-Halabi (b. 1889) was one of the most important Druze leaders of the revolt, and well connected in Damascus political circles. He had been active in Druze politics and military activities for some time. Educated at the military college in Istanbul, he led a party of guerillas in the Jabal Druze and Ghuta (gardens of Damascus). During the Faysal era in Damascus, he was a member of the nationalist Arab Club (*Nadi al-ʿarabi*) and the Istiqlal Party (*Hizb al-istiqlal al-ʿarabi*) and fought against the French invading forces at Khan Maysalun in July 1920. Faris, *Man huwa 1949*, pp. 129–30.

[27] MAE, Syrie–Liban 1918–29. "Rapport" of Tommy Martin, 11 July 1925, vol. 234, p. 102; Tannenbaum, *Sarrail*, p. 200.

[28] FO 371/4810, vol. 10835. Air Ministry to FO, 13 Aug. 1925; Saffiuddin Joarder, "The Syrian Nationalist Uprising (1925–1927) and Henri de Jouvenel," *Muslim World*, 66 (July 1977), p. 187.

[29] Although there was no visible resistance to revolt in the Jabal, it seems that at first Druze religious leaders and "several tribal factions refused to join the rebellion." Tannenbaum, *Sarrail*, p. 202.

from a group of young, educated Druzes with pronounced Syrian nationalist sympathies who saw the revolt as an opportunity to challenge the
authority of the traditional Druze elite; and from the alienated peasantry
whose lot had not perceptibly improved after the French governor's attack on the feudal privileges of the Jabal's big landowning clans.

The Damascus Connection

The nationalist People's Party was not planning a major revolt at the time
of the Druze uprising at the end of July 1925. It was neither sufficiently
organized for such an undertaking nor was its leadership attracted to the
idea of armed struggle against the French. Furthermore, Damascus was
well fortified by the French as were other nationalist towns. The effects,
however, of a paralyzing economic depression and renewed signs of
French inflexibility on the political front clearly suggested to the nationalist leadership that it should increase pressure on the French. This leadership had to make it clear once and for all that it not only enjoyed wide
public support in towns like Damascus but that it also commanded the allegiance of those districts in Syria, like the Jabal Druze, which the French
intended to keep administratively isolated from the nationalist heartland.
Thus, the outbreak of rebellion in the Jabal Druze created a new opportunity for the nationalist leadership to press its case.

Contacts between Damascus and the Jabal, which was only 75 miles
southeast of the Syrian capital, were manifold. Despite the insular and
defensive attitude of the Druze community, with its esoteric religious beliefs,[30] feudal social structure, physical isolation, and long history of
armed resistance to external interference in the Jabal's affairs,[31] by World
War I the Jabal had been irretrievably lured into the orbit of Damascus.[32]

[30] On the Druze religion, which was a splinter of Islam from the eleventh century, see
Antoine Issac Silvestre de Sacy, *Exposé de la religion des Druzes* (Paris, 1838), and M.G.S.
Hodgson, "Duruz," *Encyclopedia of Islam*, new ed., vol. 2, pp. 631–34.

[31] Whenever the Druze community felt that the Ottoman state was impinging on its autonomy, the usual impulse was to revolt. Between 1899 and 1910, when Ottoman efforts to
impose direct control over the Jabal were strongest, the Druze mounted six armed insurrections. See Commandant Hassler, "Les insurrections druses avant la guerre de 1914–1918,"
L'Asie Française, no. 239 (March 1926), pp. 143–47; Shakeeb Salih, "The British–Druze
Connection and the Druze Rising of 1896 in the Hawran," *Middle Eastern Studies*, 13 (May
1977), pp. 251–57. These revolts were against increased taxation and conscription, and
against efforts to halt the expansion of Druze influence in the Hawran grain belt.

[32] McDowall, "The Druze Revolt," p. 181. McDowall suggests, quite convincingly, that
in times of political upheaval, minorities like the Druzes seldom connected themselves to
one of the main protagonists; rather they tried their best to play Turk off Arab and *vice
versa*. Also see al-Jundi, *Tarikh*, p. 233; Dhuqan Qarqut, *Tatawwur al-haraka al-wataniyya fi suriyya, 1920–1939* (Beirut, 1975), p. 62; Hassler, "Les insurrections druses," pp.
143–47. In 1910, hostilities between Druzes and the Bani Miqdad tribe of the Hawran

Under the pressure of agrarian commercialization and modern transportation, the Jabal Druze had opened up to the outside world. Merchants and moneylenders of the Maydan quarter, where the grain trade was organized, were frequent visitors to the Hawran and the Jabal, whose cereal crops they financed. Similarly, Druze notables paid periodic visits to Damascus where they came into contact with its Ottomanized elite. Some spent the winter months in homes they owned or rented there. On the political level, the Atrash clan maintained formal links with nationalists through the Druze Agency, a consular-like office which the separate Druze state maintained in Damascus in the early 1920s.[33]

Among Damascene nationalists, Nasib al-Bakri was clearly the most respected by Druze leaders and the most involved in Druze politics. He belonged to an aristocratic landowning family that claimed descent from the Prophet. He was the second of five sons of ʿAta al-Bakri, who had been an influential member of the Damascus Municipal and District Councils from the 1890s until his death in 1914. Nasib was a graduate of the elite preparatory school of Damascus, Maktab ʿAnbar, which had produced many first generation Arab nationalists.

The Bakris had lost their high offices after the Young Turk Revolt of 1908, because of their close links to Sultan Abdülhamid II. They were also close to the branch of the Hashemites headed by Sharif Husayn in Mecca, whom Nasib's father had first met in Istanbul before Husayn had assumed his post in Mecca. In 1909, when Sharif Husayn's son ʿAbdullah and his brother Sharif Nasir visited Damascus, they stayed at the Bakri home. Later in 1915, when Amir Faysal visited Syria, he stayed at the Bakri's country home in the Ghuta. By this time, Nasib al-Bakri and two of his brothers, Fawzi and Sami, had joined the secret nationalist society al-Fatat, of which Nasib was Secretary. Nasib introduced Faysal to the party and he reportedly became a member.[34]

Nasib al-Bakri rushed to the Hijaz to offer his services to Sharif Husayn when the Arab Revolt was proclaimed in 1916. His assignment was to return to Syria to organize a rebellion against the Turks in the Jabal Druze and the Hawran. In the Jabal, he found a party of Druze chieftains

---

brought in the Turkish Army. Traditionally, the Druze were in a protector–client relationship with the peasantry of the Hawran but, after 1900, peasants could no longer rely on Druzes for protection against the Bedouin and were forced to turn to Damascus and the Ottoman military for protection. See McDowall, ''The Druze Revolt,'' p. 127.

[33] FO 371/6457, vol. 13512. Damascus Consul to FO, 17 Nov. 1921; FO 371/5762, vol. 7847. Damascus Consul to FO, 22 May 1922.

[34] Muhammad Adib Taqi al-Din al-Husni, *Kitab muntakhabat al-tawarikh li-dimashq* (Damascus, 1928), vol. 2, pp. 819–22; *Salname: Suriye vilayeti*, 1312 A.H./1894–95 A.D., pp. 77–78; MD, 7N 2141. Akaba, 20 June 1918. See Index to Zafir al-Qasimi's *Maktab ʿanbar* (Beirut, 1967); also see Faris, *Man huwa 1949*, p. 67; MWT, *al-Qism al-khass*, Nasib al-Bakri Papers, ''Biography of ʿAta b. Nasib al-Bakri.''

headed by Sultan al-Atrash willing to revolt against Ottoman rule. Nasib al-Bakri and Sultan Pasha led 500 Druze horseman into the Hawran to occupy and control its main arteries in anticipation of the Allied invasion from the South.[35]

Nasib al-Bakri's close relationship with Amir Faysal landed him the post of *chef de cabinet* in Faysal's government in Damascus in 1918. Not surprisingly, Faysal also chose Bakri to be his special emissary to the Jabal Druze to promote its unification with Damascus. His personal relationship with Sultan al-Atrash made him the logical choice for this delicate task. After the French occupation of Damascus in 1920, Nasib al-Bakri and his brothers maintained a conspicuously low profile, that is, until the summer of 1925, when he became the chief liaison of the People's Party with his former comrades-in-arms in the Jabal Druze.[36]

When news of the collapse and defeat of the Michaud column in early August reached Damascus, nationalist leaders began to meet secretly, moving from one home to the next, to plan a course of action. The meetings were attended by members of the People's Party, local bosses (*qabadayat*) from the quarters of ʿAmara, Suq Saruja, Shaghur, and the Maydan, and political leaders from Hama. Although excited by the news from the Jabal, they were also apprehensive. For nationalist leaders in Damascus and other towns like Hama to encourage a full-scale uprising without guarantees that external support would be available was militarily and politically suicidal. These towns were still relatively well-fortified by French garrisons and a gendarmerie; and the popular forces that the People's Party hoped to rally were not even equipped with small firearms. The Druze leadership's willingness to bring its revolt to the gates of Damascus, however, was just the assurance the People's Party needed to drop its preparations for upcoming elections and to intensify its pressures on the French in the nationalist towns. Envoys from the Jabal Druze supplied information about the military situation there and Nasib al-Bakri met regularly with ʿAbd al-Ghaffar al-Atrash, the Suwaydaʾ notable who was in Damascus to work out a joint plan for escalating the revolt.[37]

The first nationalist delegation to confer directly with Sultan al-Atrash

[35] *Oriente Moderno,* 5 (1925), pp. 462–63.

[36] *Ibid.,* pp. 466–67. al-Qasimi, *Wathaʾiq,* pp. 205–7.

[37] MWT, *al-Qism al-khass,* Nazih Muʿayyad al-ʿAzm Papers. "Notes on the Outbreak of the Revolt," no. 203, 1925; FO 371/5039, vol. 10851. Damascus Consul to FO, 2 Aug. 1925; FO 371/4730, vol. 10850. Liaison Officer (Beirut) to FO, 10 Aug. 1925; Nashabi, "The Political Parties," p. 102. Hasan al-Hakim, "Mujaz tarjama"; FO 684/2/55/158. Smart to FO, 30 Jan. 1925. Conversations with Hasan al-Hakim (Damascus, 21 March 1976) and Sabri Farid al-Bidaywi (Damascus, 17 July 1977), both of whom were veterans of the Great Revolt.

after he launched his uprising arrived in the Jabal Druze on August 19, just a month into the rebellion. It was headed by Nasib al-Bakri and included Shaykh Muhammad al-Ashmar, a popular religious leader from the Maydan quarter, and Yahya al-Hayati, the representative of a group of ex-Ottoman army officers who had served Amir Faysal and wished to contribute their talents to the revolt. The Damascus delegation and Sultan Pasha exchanged solemn oaths that the two parties would cooperate closely to drive the French out of Syria. The delegation promised the Druze leader that the people of Damascus were prepared to revolt if they received signs of encouragement from his rebel forces. Some nationalist leaders were skeptical about the revolt's prospects but Sultan al-Atrash remained extremely optimistic. So far his forces had not suffered a single set-back and armed tribesmen had just arrived from Transjordan to augment his forces.[38] Three days later at a secret meeting at the Ghuta villa of Jamil Mardam, a prominent young nationalist, Nasib al-Bakri reported the results of his discussions with Sultan al-Atrash to Dr. Shahbandar, the People's Party President. Shahbander decided to urge Atrash to make a surprise advance on Damascus in order to take advantage of the temporary absence of French troops tied down in the Jabal Druze and the Hawran. On August 24, rumors circulated in Damascus that Sultan Pasha's army of Druzes and Bedouins was approaching. Panic spread as bazaar merchants started to move goods from their shops to their residences, and quarter bosses organized voluntary neighborhood guards. An uprising, however, never materialized: Sultan al-Atrash's rebel army was stopped five miles southeast of Damascus by three squadrons of Moroccan *spahis* supported by the French airforce.[39] Afterwards, the French Delegate in Damascus initiated a house-to-house search for all suspected nationalist leaders. Many were apprehended and jailed without trial on Arwad Island, some for the second time since the French occupation. French troops

[38] Qarqut, *Tatawwur*, p. 218. Actually Nasib al-Bakri's nephew, As'ad b. Fawzi, had been in the Jabal Druze with Sultan al-Atrash since 3 August 1925. See al-Qasimi, *Watha'iq*, p. 233; FO 371/5039, vol. 10851. Damascus Consul to FO, 12 Aug. 1925; FO 371/5571, vol. 10851. Crewe (Paris) to Chamberlain, 15 Sept. 1925; Amir 'Abdullah's chief adviser, the Syrian 'Ali Rida al-Rikabi, allegedly funneled £ 5,000 sterling to Sultan al-Atrash for the organization of the rebellion. There is no evidence to suggest that 'Abdullah approved of this support. Later some Syrian leaders would accuse him of turning his back on their revolt. See Philby's "Stepping Stones in Jordan: 1922-24." Manuscript in H. St. John Philby Papers, Middle East Centre, St. Antony's College, Oxford, pp. 260-61.

[39] Conversation with Hasan al-Hakim (Damascus, 21 March 1976). MAE, Syrie–Liban 1918–29. 4 Sept. 1925, vol. 193, pp. 56; al-Jundi, *Tarikh*, pp. 195, 336-37; MAE, Syrie–Liban 1918–29. 1 Sept.–9 Oct. 1925, vol. 193, pp. 99–102; FO 371/5273, vol. 10851. Damascus Consul to FO, 25 Aug. 1925; FO 371/5576, vol. 10851. Crewe to Chamberlain, 15 Sept. 1925; FO 371/5252, vol. 10851. Smart to Department of Overseas Trade, 21 Aug. 1925; al-Rayyis, *al-Kitab al-dhahabi*, pp. 190–92.

also began to inhibit movement in the town with barbed wire, creating more panic.[40]

The most important nationalist leaders, including Dr. Shahbandar and the Bakri family, managed to escape the French dragnet. They took refuge in the one area in southern Syria still relatively safe, the Jabal Druze.[41] Damascus was once again stripped of its most important leaders and spokesmen. Meanwhile, French security dismantled what was left of the People's Party. Barred from Damascus, the People's Party and the Druze leadership set up a nationalist provisional government in the Jabal Druze on September 9, with the stated goals of Syrian unity and independence from the Mediterranean coast to the depths of the Syrian interior. Nowhere in their program for action was there a call to pan-Islamism or to revolution against the French on the grounds of religion.[42] Uprisings first in Hama and then in Damascus in the following month ignited rebellion throughout Syrian territory. By the end of October large areas of Syria were in full revolt. It was not a revolt consisting of several isolated local uprisings, but rather one whose component parts were intimately linked. Contrary to French hopes, a broad nationalist front had been forged and with considerable ease.

ALTHOUGH THE DRUZES revolted against French efforts to upset the traditional power structure in the Jabal Druze, it is no coincidence that the leaders of the uprising had political and social ties to Damascus. In fact, Druze rebel leaders were familiar with and sympathetic to the nationalist creed of Syrian unity preached by the nationalist elite in the capital; several considered themselves Syrian nationalists. They were attracted to a new system of secular ideas radiating from Damascus and they also found nationalism a convenient instrument to counter French intervention and, in particular, the growing influence of the rival branch of the Druze elite, patronized by the French and predisposed to a separate Druze existence under French protection.

Druze rebel leaders were eager to disseminate their rebellion as widely as possible. They fully realized that their movement had a greater chance of success if its scope could be widened and therefore proclaimed it in the name of Syrian unity and independence from French rule. Thus, in the larger scheme of the Syrian independence struggle, Druze rebel chiefs

[40] FO 371/5273, vol. 10851. Damascus to FO, 25 Aug. 1925.

[41] *Ibid.*; MacCallum, *Crusade*, p. 124. Other nationalist leaders who took refuge in the Jabal Druze included Nazih Mu'ayyad al-'Azm, Hasan al-Hakim, Jamil Mardam, and Sa'id Haydar.

[42] MD, 7N 4171. 2ᵉ Bureau, 15 May 1926.

were by no means passive actors taking their cues from nationalist leaders in Damascus.[43]

This last point needs emphasis for two important reasons. First, it suggests that to understand the extent of the Druze contribution to the Great Revolt, it is necessary to place the Druze uprising more squarely in the context of Syrian political life. Secondly, it suggests that the contribution of the Syrian nationalist leadership in Damascus and other nationalist centers to the Great Revolt also needs reassessment. Because historians fail to see the Druze uprising as directly linked to the general development of nationalism in Syria, they misrepresent the actual objectives of the nationalist leadership and misclassify the Great Revolt. Their tendency is to exaggerate the contribution of the nationalist People's Party in Damascus. Indeed, one historian goes so far as to define the aims of the nationalist leadership in Damascus as "revolutionary"—"the establishment of an independent, federated Syrian state molded on a Western model," while those of the Druze rebel leaders were "counterrevolutionary"—"the retention of power and prestige in their own hands."[44]

It is more satisfactory to view the Great Revolt and its component parts, like the entire Mandate era itself, as belonging to a transitional stage in the political evolution of the Arab East.[45] Movements of protest and resistance in the interwar period should be seen as moving between the traditional and the modern, but at an uneven pace and with an uneven rhythm, not unlike the way the economy and society were evolving at this time. Because such movements reveal a complex mixture of traditional and modern features, they cannot easily be classified as either traditional or modern. Those elements or aspects of interwar movements that have generally been viewed as traditional or even retrograde were something more evolved, while those generally thought to have been modern or even revolutionary tended to be something less.

In the case of the Great Revolt, its leaders clung to an older set of political objectives. Neither Damascene nor Druze leaders can be said to have adopted a revolutionary framework of ideas and objectives. They did not seek to overturn the French-controlled system of rule; rather, they sought something less, the modification of the existing system and the relaxation of French control. Their real objective was to shift the balance of power between themselves and the French back in their own direction

---

[43] The impression that the Syrian nationalist leadership in Damascus convinced Sultan al-Atrash and the Druze rebel leadership to extend their rebellion is misleading. Miller's "The Syrian Revolt," creates this impression; see pp. 558–59.

[44] *Ibid.*, p. 561.

[45] Although Miller seems to imply that the Great Revolt may be seen as a transitional stage in the development of political movements in Syria, she fails to see the Druze uprising in this light and thus misrepresents the character of the overall revolt. *Ibid.*, pp. 546–47.

so as to restore their traditional influence over local politics—an influence which the French had undercut both in the nationalist towns and in the Jabal Druze.[46]

But even if their objectives were not particularly revolutionary, they nevertheless had to employ new, more sophisticated methods to achieve them. The growth and spread of nationalism itself forged broader political alliances than previously known in Syria. Moreover, the disruptive effects of French rule, which by its very nature was perceived as illegitimate,[47] required new, more highly developed mechanisms for resisting the French. Political movements of protest and resistance tended to be more intense and of longer duration, and they no longer remained localized affairs but assumed national proportions. They now embraced new patterns of political organization linked to a new system of secular ideas, and operated on a much larger territorial scale than ever before.

The Great Revolt was a signal event in the history of modern Syria, and in the Arab world at large, for it revealed new broadly-based alliances linking together different elites like the Druzes and Damascenes, both urban and rural forces, and different social classes and religious communities. Even though France eventually crushed the revolt and kept the Jabal Druze administratively autonomous from the Syrian state for another decade, the Druze rebel leadership remained actively involved in nationalist politics and committed to a "successful assimilation of the Druzes into a Syrian-Arab political community."[48]

The Great Revolt of 1925–27 was a major watershed in the history of modern Syria and in the national independence struggle against the French. In terms of its style, intensity, duration, scale, and methods, it compared favorably with other resistance movements beginning to leave their mark on the countries of the Arab East after World War I, in particular the Egyptian Revolution of 1919, and later the Rebellion of 1936–

---

[46] Syrian nationalists participated in the revolt somewhat reluctantly, after making no progress on the diplomatic front for five years with the intransigent French. The point is that they did not perceive their participation as some revolutionary activity but rather as the most expedient way of convincing the French to recognize them politically and to accept at least some of their demands. Many nationalist leaders in Damascus had no interest whatsoever in a prolonged rebellion that might engulf the countryside around the Syrian capital and possibly jeopardize their most important material interests in the form of landownership and rents. There seems little doubt that revolutionary activity was not their favorite strategy; although they were not inexperienced, they were uncomfortable with such activity. Limited and targeted urban political protests such as demonstrations and strikes were the preferred tactics, not full-scale rebellion.

[47] See Hourani, "Revolution in the Arab Middle East," pp. 65–72.

[48] See Itamar Rabinovich, "The Compact Minorities and the Syrian State, 1918–1945," *Journal of Contemporary History*, 14 (1979), pp. 701–2.

39 in Palestine.[49] The Great Revolt was popular insofar as its active participants were drawn from nearly all walks of life in Syria—urban and rural, Muslim and Christian, rich and poor. Its leadership formulated its aims and appeal in the new nationalist idiom of the times. And the revolt itself let this new sentiment of nationalism spread faster, wider, and deeper than ever before, enabling it to become the dominant organizing principle of Syrian political life during the Mandate. Moreover, the Great Revolt sought and won attention and support from parallel independence movements in the Arab countries, from the Muslim world at large, and from Syrian émigré communities in the West. Its sheer size and scale ensured it of international headlines, especially in France, where it had a damaging impact on domestic politics and contributed to a serious change in French perceptions about how best to govern Syria.[50]

The Great Revolt is fascinating for several reasons, but perhaps most strikingly because it did not break out first in Syria's nationalist towns, but in the remote Jabal Druze among a compact religious minority with no apparent attachment to the nationalist sentiments radiating from towns like Damascus. Nonetheless, the leaders of the Druze rebellion did not perceive it as an isolated phenomenon, nor did they intend to restrict it to parochial concerns. A closer look reveals these leaders to have been sympathetic to Arab nationalism and in direct and regular contact with nationalist circles in Damascus.

The Druze leadership's objectives may have been old and familiar—the retention or restoration of its power in the Jabal—but the tactics they adopted were clearly new. Druze leaders had a wider vision of political realities than historians have previously acknowledged. They actively sought alliances beyond the Jabal that cut across regional, class, and religious lines and that, in the process, helped to give political movements in Syria greater breadth and force.

[49] On the 1919 revolution in Egypt, see Jacques Berque, *Egypt: Imperialism and Revolution* (New York, 1972), part III, and Marius Deeb, "The 1919 Popular Uprising: A Genesis of Nationalism," *Canadian Review of Studies in Nationalism* 1 (Fall 1973), pp. 105–19. On the 1936–39 revolt in Palestine, see Y. Porath, *The Palestine Arab National Movement 1929–1939* (London, 1977), Chapter 9; Tom Bowden, "The Politics of the Arab Rebellion in Palestine 1936–1939," *Middle Eastern Studies*, 11 (1975), pp. 147–74; Ghassan Kanafani, *The 1936–39 Rebellion in Palestine* (Committee for Democratic Palestine, n.d.).

[50] See my "Factionalism among Syrian Nationalists during the French Mandate," *International Journal of Middle East Studies*, 13 (November 1981), p. 453; Tannenbaum, *Sarrail*; Hourani, "Revolution in the Arab Middle East," pp. 69–72; Burke, "A Comparative View," pp. 173–86.

CHAPTER SEVEN

FROM LOCAL TO NATIONAL REVOLT

THERE WERE FORCES beyond the control of either Frenchmen or Syrians that contributed to the growth of the Great Revolt. For example, the weather. It so happened that the Great Revolt coincided with one of the most severe droughts in recent years, which caused a disastrous wheat harvest in the Hawran, the breadbasket of Damascus. In fact, the summer desiccation was the culmination of what had been an especially bizarre winter and spring throughout Syria. February and March 1925 had been two of the coldest months in memory and an unusually late frost at the beginning of April caused widespread damage to the gardens around Damascus whose fruits were among the capital's leading exports.[1]

The losses suffered by the tribes and villagers, owing to the severe winter and subsequent drought, were heavy. Whole villages were abandoned in the Hawran as springs and wells dried up. The penetration of Bedouin into the cultivated zones to the south and east of Damascus was deeper than in previous winters, owing to their desperate situation. Cultivators hurt by bad weather suffered additional losses because of increased tribal raiding and the encroachment of tribal herds. Crop production around Hama and Homs, although not subject to the climatic crisis in the south, was well below average owing to an insect pest which destroyed a large proportion of the cereal crop.[2]

The worsening economic conditions in the Hawran and around Damascus led to widespread disorder and brigandage fanned on one side by the appearance of Druze rebels in these areas and on the other by the sight of French troops sweeping through the region in full marching order. Throughout August and most of September, however, the French were unable to halt the unrest south of Damascus as Bedouin, peasants, deserters from the Syrian Legion, and unemployed artisans from large villages conducted daring raids near the Syrian capital. Often the villages in whose vicinity these bands operated assisted in the attacks on French gar-

---

[1] FO 371/5252, vol. 10851. Smart to Department of Overseas Trade, 17 Aug. 1925; USNA, Syria. 890d.00/284. Antoine Coudsi to Damascus Consulate, 28 Oct. 1925. Apricot trees suffered considerable damage. Apricots in their dried form and in dry paste were the leading fruit export of Damascus. The Aleppo region suffered from the same bad weather throughout 1924 and during the winter of 1924–25, damaging fruits, barley and wheat crops. MAE, Syrie–Liban 1918–29. *Bulletin de Renseignements*, 7–14 (Feb. 1925), vol. 427B, p. 2.

[2] FO 371/5252, vol. 10851. Smart to Department of Overseas Trade, 17 Aug. 1925.

risons. French reprisals took the form of burning and plundering cooperative villages, which only provided new recruits for the rebels.[3]

In the towns of the Syrian interior, which had never willingly accepted the French Mandate, popular discontent swelled under the impact of the enervating economic depression. Prices of foodstuffs and other necessities soared. Unemployment reached a new high, driving many artisans, casual laborers, and recently settled families on the outskirts of Damascus back to their ancestral villages and often into the roving bands of rebels and bandits that had become a common feature of the Syrian countryside.[4]

Merchants and moneylenders in Damascus were troubled by the poor harvests. It was estimated that they had advanced in 1925 £T 200,000 to cultivators in the Hawran and the Jabal Druze on their crops, and they feared that a peace imposed by French bayonets would cause the total ruination of the already meager harvest, and the loss of their advances at a time when commerce was stagnant. They therefore pressed for a negotiated peace. Bazaar moneylenders and banks began to restrict credit, aggravating the commercial depression. The Chamber of Commerce frantically assembled in mid-August to figure out how merchants could cut their losses. The French had already granted a moratorium on the payment of taxes and some merchants, realizing that the chances of collecting their debts were slim, suggested that the Chamber also call for a moratorium on loan repayments. This was met by considerable opposition led by the biggest grain dealers of the Maydan quarter who felt that such a measure would be disastrous to their future credit ratings with bankers. Meanwhile, rumors of impending bankruptcies spread, causing a financial panic.[5]

Apart from the specific economic crisis of 1925, French economic policies in general created a background for revolt. France was unable or unwilling to promote financial and economic interests in Syria, other than her own. French monetary policy, which tied the new Syrian paper currency to the continuously depreciating French franc, appeared to be melting away a considerable portion of Syria's national wealth. The sudden reorientation forced on the Syrian economy by the partition of geo-

[3] *Ibid.*; FO 371/7297, vol. 10852, Damascus Consul to FO.

[4] For instance, in Aleppo the French estimated that the price of goods of primary necessity rose 72 percent between February 1924 and February 1925. MAE, Syrie–Liban 1918–29. *Bulletin de Renseignements*, 7–14 Feb. 1925, vol. 427B, p. 2. FO 371/5252, vol. 10851. Smart to Department of Overseas Trade, 17 Aug. 1925; MAE, Syrie–Liban 1918–29. 10 Sept. 1925, vol. 193, p. 65.

[5] USNA, Syria. 890d.00/284. Coudsi to Damascus Consulate, 28 Oct. 1928; MAE, Syrie–Liban 1918–29. Henry de Jouvenel to Foreign Minister, 9 Jan. 1926, vol. 214. FO 371/5252, vol. 10851. Smart to Department of Overseas Trade, 17 Aug. 1925.

graphic Syria after World War I and the continued erosion of Syrian industry in the face of European competition helped to create and maintain high unemployment and inflation. The French supported a tightfisted fiscal policy in areas such as education, agricultural development, public works, and industry, yet they spent profusely on the army and police, and on unwieldly and overlapping state administrations.[6] Finally, in the political sphere there was the French bias toward the minorities and the callousness with which they dealt with the Muslim community and Muslim institutions, not to mention French unwillingness to accord the political leadership of the national independence movement the recognition and access it felt it deserved. Although the revolt was by no means inevitable, preconditions for such an event were clearly in place by 1925.

During the summer of that year, the French did not so much fear the challenge of Druze rebels and the nationalist People's Party as they did their own demoralization. French troops walked around Damascus openly blaming General Sarrail for the series of defeats since late July. They wondered if French reinforcements were ever going to arrive. French officials were also depressed and there was virtually no rapport between the High Commissioner and his staff.[7] Meanwhile, back in Paris, Frenchmen levelled all sorts of accusations against Sarrail.

French reinforcements finally reached Beirut in late August. Most were sent on to Damascus where General Gamelin, Michaud's replacement as Chief of Staff, immediately deployed 10,000 troops in the rebellious districts between the Jabal Druze and Damascus. He kept an equal number in and around Damascus and the other nationalist towns. Until the third week of September, the Armée du Levant, which included the 6,500-man Syrian Legion composed mainly of Circassian and Kurdish recruits, was unable to stop the forays of Druze and Bedouin rebels in the Hawran.[8] Brigandage continued unabated as rebels pillaged and burnt to the ground village after village. Then, on September 24, Gamelin tried to lift the two-month siege of Suwayda', where a French garrison still held out. He captured the Druze capital thanks to the daring of the French Foreign Legion, but in the assault many Syrian troops deserted to the rebel forces. A shortage of provisions eventually forced the French to retire from the town, but not before destroying large sections of it.[9] With Druze

    [6] See Chapters 2 and 3.

    [7] FO 371/5450, vol. 10851. Damascus Consul to FO, 29 Aug. 1925; FO 371/4810, vol. 10835. Air Ministry to FO, 13 Aug. 1925.

    [8] FO 371/5576, vol. 10851. Crewe to Chamberlain, 15 Sept. 1925.

    [9] MacCallum, *Crusade*, p. 126; al-Rayyis, *al-Kitab al-dhahabi*, pp. 232–36; al-Jundi, *Tarikh*, pp. 198–99.

forces back in control of Suwayda' and in the Jabal at large, there was now a military stalemate. Attention shifted to central Syria where a new front had opened up at Hama.

HAMA IN REVOLT

Hama, the fourth largest town in Syria, was generally regarded as the most religiously conservative and outwardly anti-French town in the country. On 4 October 1925, a rebellious captain in the Syrian Legion, Fawzi al-Qawuqji, led a mixed force of dissident Legionnaires and several hundred armed Bedouin from the Mawali tribe of Ma'arrat al-Nu'man and its environs against French installations there. Government buildings housing French and native officials were the primary targets, including the Sérail, the Régie de Tabac, the office of Ottoman Public Debt, and the Directorate of the Awqaf. In two days, the Qawuqji band razed much of Hama's central district, and with the willing cooperation of local residents, who disarmed the local police force.[10]

The assault surprised the town's small French garrison. Reinforcements, rushed from Aleppo and Damascus, attacked Hama from the ground and the air with impunity. French airplanes bombed its commercial district, completely destroying two bazaars and over 115 shops. Senegalese troops were particularly ruthless, burning to the ground the residences of many local notables and occupying others. By the time Fawzi al-Qawuqji and his band, which had grown to 1,000 fighters, took flight on October 7, 344 persons had been killed, mostly unarmed civilians, among them 65 women and children. Damage was estimated at between £T 150,000 and 200,000 gold.[11]

Of Turcoman origin, Fawzi al-Qawuqji was born in 1887 in Tripoli. A junior officer in the Ottoman Army, he joined the Arab Revolt in 1916. Although he fought the French invasion of 1920, he accepted a French offer of a post in the newly established Syrian Legion. He was made a commander of a cavalry company composed of Isma'ilis from Salimiyya and Circassians stationed near Hama. At the time, Qawuqji's French superior

[10] FO 684/2/87. Smart to FO, 10 Oct. 1925; *Alif ba'* (10 Oct. 1925); Widmer, "Population," pp. 8–9. Hama's population in 1925 was between 50,000 and 60,000. For Hama's history, see FO 371/6099, vol. 9054. Damascus Consul to FO, 25 May 1923; D. Sourdel, "Hamat," *Encyclopaedia of Islam,* new ed., vol. 3, pp. 120–21; Foreign Office, *Handbook: Syria* (London, 1920), pp. 82–83, 121, 124; Eugen Wirth, *Syrien. Eine Geographische Landeskunde* (Darmstadt, 1971), Map, p. 340; Karl Baedeker, *Palestine and Syria,* 4th ed. (Leipzig, 1906), pp. 368–69.

[11] MAE, Syrie–Liban 1918–29. "Rapport d'enquête du Col. Raynal," 25 July 1926, vol. 236, pp. 6–30; FO 684/2/87. Smart to FO, 10 Oct. 1925; USNA, Syria. 890d.00/284, 28 Oct. 1925.

fomented unrest in the district by indiscreetly spying on village chiefs, religious shaykhs, and the nationalist *mutasarrif* of Hama. Qawuqji, himself, was always made to feel inferior in his dealings with French officers.[12]

Although Qawuqji's attack caught the French by surprise,[13] he had begun to plan it in July, using his position in the Syrian Legion to secure French maps giving the locations of military installations throughout Syria. These he distributed to nationalist agitators in Hama and elsewhere.[14] He was in communication with Sultan al-Atrash and wanted to synchronize his attack with activities in the Jabal Druze and the Hawran.[15] He and some other native officers were also in contact with a religious organization, Hizb Allah (The Party of God), which disaffected religious leaders of Hama had founded. Through the Hizb Allah, the officers became familiar with local nationalists who maintained a loose affiliation with the People's Party in Damascus. In early August, when Dr. Shahbandar and other People's Party leaders conferred secretly in Damascus with Druze emissaries about the possibility of turning the rebellion in the Jabal into a Syrian-wide revolt, some Hama nationalists close to Qawuqji were present.[16]

But, what enabled Qawuqji to make headway in his plan were the guarantees of support from nationalist forces inside Hama. The town's absentee landowning aristocracy was particularly interested in driving the French out of its district and, if possible, out of Syria altogether. French land reforms were specially designed to break the domination of the four great landowning families of the town: the Barazi, Kaylani, ʿAzm, and Tayfur. Members of these families provided much of Hama's predominantly nationalist political leadership.[17] They steered the mobs straight to

[12] *Mudhakkirat Fawzi al-Qawuqji, 1914–1932*, vol. 1 (ed. Dr. Khayriyya al-Qasimiyya) (Beirut, 1975), pp. 11–72, 73–74; al-Jundi, *Tarikh*, p. 553; Jean Gaulmier, "Notes sur le mouvement syndicaliste à Hama," *Revue des Etudes Islamiques*, 6 (1932), pp. 99–100.

[13] Hama's *mutasarrif*, Faydi al-Atasi, knew in advance about the attack but was reluctant to notify the French authorities out of fear for his personal safety. See Qudama, *Maʿalim*, pp. 9–10; MAE, Syrie–Liban 1918–29, vol. 242, pp. 125–26.

[14] MAE, Syrie–Liban 1918–29. "Rapport d'enquête du Col. Raynal," 25 July 1926, vol. 236, pp. 23–25.

[15] al-Rayyis, *al-Kitab al-dhahabi*, pp. 255–56; FO 684/2/55/158. Smart to FO, 30 Jan. 1925.

[16] al-Rayyis, *al-Kitab al-dhahabi*, pp. 82–84. On Hama's role in the Syrian independence struggle, see ʿUthman al-Haddad, Hasan al-Qattan, ʿAbd al-Hasib al-Shaykh Saʿid, *Thawrat hamat ʿala al-tughyan al-faransi* (Hama, 1945). For the early Mandate period, see Ihsan al-Hindi, *Kifah al-shaʿb al-ʿarabi al-suri, 1908–1948* (Damascus, 1962), pp. 89–102; MWT, *al-Qism al-khass*, Nazih Muʾayyad al-ʿAzm Papers, no. 203, 1925.

[17] [Gaulmier], "Note sur la propriété foncière dans la Syrie centrale," *L'Asie Française*, no. 309 (April 1933), pp. 131–33.

the Sérail, which housed the French High Commission staff, the Registre du Cadastre, and the Bureau of Taxation. The Sérail was completely destroyed and its archives burnt.[18] In return, more than half of the buildings destroyed by French bombing in the commercial district were owned by the four notable families and leased to bazaar merchants.[19]

Other leaders in Hama, either from the poorer branches of the great landowning families or from the middle stratum, also played an important role in the uprising. They were mainly young intellectuals and professionals belonging to one or the other of Hama's two Masonic Lodges and they rallied like-minded individuals as well as secondary and elementary school students.[20] Meanwhile, the popular classes in Hama were also eager to manifest their growing dissatisfaction with life under the French, if only because of staggering inflation and vast unemployment during the past year.

Qawuqji did not begin to mobilize the Mawali tribe until he had received a green light from nationalist leaders in Hama. The Mawali, like the peasantry of the region, had suffered from the poor harvests and general depression which plagued much of Syria in the fall of 1925. They also had sincere grievances with the French Contrôle Bédouin which, in its attempt to pacify the margins of cultivated zones, had interfered in the Mawali's bitter and longstanding rivalry with the Hadidiyin tribe.[21]

Although the Hama uprising was nipped in the bud before it could spread, it sent shock waves rippling through Syria's other nationalist centers. It also prefigured a pattern of revolt which was later repeated in other Syrian towns. This was a pattern of cooperation between elements outside town walls and nationalists within. The spark for urban revolts consistently came from outside, while groundwork laid within ensured that the spark would ignite a conflagration.

---

[18] MAE, Syrie–Liban 1918–29, vol. 242, pp. 125–26; *ibid.*, "Rapport d'enquête du Col. Raynal," 25 July 1926, vol. 236, pp. 4, 23–26.

[19] Of the 108 shops burnt by the French aerial bombardment of Hama's suqs, 63 were owned by the 4 families. MAE, Syrie–Liban 1918–29. "Rapport d'enquête du Col. Raynal," 25 July 1926, vol. 236, p. 9.

[20] Al-Jundi, *Tarikh*, p. 257; MAE, Syrie–Liban 1918–29. "Rapport d'enquête du Col. Raynal," 25 July 1926, vol. 236, p. 9.

[21] Haut-Commissariat de la République Française: Direction du Service des Renseignements du Levant, *Les tribus nomades et semi-nomades des états du Levant placés sous Mandat Français* (Beirut, 1930), pp. 75–79; also see A. de Boucheman, "Note sur la rivalité de deux tribus moutonnières de Syrie: Les 'Mawali' et les 'Hadidiyin'," *Revue des Etudes Islamiques*, 8 (1934), pp. 9–58; *Oriente Moderno*, 5 (1925), p. 524. On French tribal policy, see my "The Tribal Shaykh, French Tribal Policy, and the Nationalist Movement in Syria between Two World Wars," *Middle Eastern Studies*, 18 (April 1982), pp. 180–93.

Damascus in Revolt

From late September, there was a marked increase in the amount of rebel activity around Damascus, mainly in the dense orchards to its east and south. As in Hama, it was this agitation coming from outside the town walls which eventually ignited rebellion within. Although the August attempt to spark a revolt in Damascus had failed, as soon as the People's Party leadership reached the safety of the Jabal Druze afterwards, plans were set afoot to ignite another.

Among the Damascenes who moved to the Jabal at this time was the 64-year-old Hasan al-Kharrat, formerly a guard in the gardens of his native Shaghur and later the chief nightwatchman of the quarter. When the nationalists and Sultan Pasha agreed to engineer a Syria-wide rebellion, he was given the task of preparing Damascus for revolt. Kharrat was to notify the Jabal Druze when he thought Damascus was prepared to accept and assist infiltrators.[22] Toward the end of September those organized by Kharrat—twenty quarter bosses, among them Abu ʿAbdu Dib al-Shaykh of ʿAmara, and their armed retainers—launched a guerilla war against the French Army stationed in the gardens to the east and south of the capital.[23]

At about the same time, members of the nationalist People's Party still in Damascus took advantage of the religious celebration commemorating the Prophet's birthday to stage a large political demonstration against French rule. Ten days of preparation went into the event, which popular religious leaders and quarter bosses supported and which entailed, among other things, the traditional custom of stringing rugs from the entrance of Suq al-Tawil (The Street Called Straight) to Maktab ʿAnbar in the Kharab quarter and over to Suq al-Hamidiyya and the Umayyad Mosque. This time, however, instead of attaching the usual pious phrases to the rugs, pictures of nationalist leaders and nationalist slogans were substituted. On the anniversary, the whole town shut down as tens of thousands of Damascenes gathered in Bab al-Jabiyya to begin a long procession along the trail blazed by the hanging rugs. A special detour was made to the ancient Jewish and Christian quarters where members of the town's religious minorities joined in the final lap to the Great Mosque.[24] En route the celebrants, marching in platoons by quarter, chanted violent denunciations of the French expressed in religious terms.

---

[22] MAE, Syrie–Liban 1918–29. 20 Sept. 1926, vol. 237, p. 160; al-Jundi, *Tarikh*, pp. 354–55; Qudama, *Maʿalim*, pp. 369–70; al-Qasimi, *Watha'iq*, pp. 182–86.

[23] MAE, Syrie–Liban 1918–29. 20 Sept. 1926, vol. 237, p. 160.

[24] See J. Lecerf and R. Tresse, "Les ʿarada de Damas," *Bulletin d'Etudes Orientales*, 7–8 (1937–1938), pp. 240–41, 261; al-Qasimi, *Watha'iq*, pp. 63–65; conversation with Hasan (Abu ʿAli) al-Kilawi (Damascus, 15 May 1976).

An individual from each quarter chosen for his memory and booming voice led the chanting. Normally, his comrades carried him on their shoulders and after he chanted a line or two of verse, the marchers from his quarter responded in refrain.[25] On reaching the Umayyad Mosque, various nationalist orators harangued the crowds with praises for the Arab nation, the Syrian people, and their leader, Dr. Shahbandar. As the demonstration broke up, French troops arrested several quarter leaders, including two chiefs from the militantly anti-French Shaghur.

Daily, the atmosphere in Damascus grew more tense and French residents in the town began to depart for the safer confines of Beirut. Two weeks after the Prophet's birthday, the French Army stepped up its campaign to stamp out brigandage and highway murders, which had become a regular feature of the Damascus countryside. Circassian troops were dispatched to destroy villages reportedly harboring bandits east of the city. The troops returned with 115 prisoners and 24 corpses. They dumped the dead Syrians in Marjé Square in the center of town, and the prisoners—tied together by ropes—were made to march around them. As an added insult, the Circassians threw a dead dog into the center of the ring. The French rejected claims that the dead and captured were innocent peasants who only happened to live in the areas where bandits were operating. Later in the day, Circassian and French troops were seen selling booty stolen from the villagers to residents of the Christian quarter.[26]

Although this humiliating episode was obviously intended as a warning to the Damascus populace, it had an entirely opposite effect. On October 15, Circassian soldiers again launched an attack in the Ghuta, pillaging and burning two more villages. One of them, Jarmana, was the fief of Nasib al-Bakri and was entirely inhabited by Druzes.[27] That evening a curfew was imposed on Damascus, restricting all movement after 8:00. But the town did not accept these repressive measures passively. Two days later, the corpses of 12 Circassians still dressed in their French uniforms were discovered lying just outside Bab al-Sharqi.[28]

---

[25] Normally, at celebrations like the Prophet's birthday each quarter would send its strongmen and youth to pay visits to other quarters and engage in competitive sloganeering, each praising their own youth and strength. The individual selected to chant on behalf of the quarter was known as the *shaykh al-shabab*. The competition for this hallowed title was usually fierce as were fights between the quarters, though less so under the Mandate when a need for unity against the French was overpowering. The Maydan and Shaghur quarters had the reputation of being the most militant quarters in Damascus. Lecerf and Tresse, "Les 'arada," pp. 241–42, 244–45.

[26] Al-Qasimi, *Watha'iq*, p. 74; USNA, Syria. 890d.00/273. Beirut Consul to Secretary of State, 9 Nov. 1925; *ibid.*, 890d.00/279. Damascus Consul to Secretary of State, 23 Oct. 1925.

[27] MAE, Syrie-Liban 1918-29. "Rapport d'enquête de Damas," 28 Sept. 1926, vol. 237, pp. 97–98.

[28] *Ibid.*; *The Times* (27 Oct. 1925).

It was in this charged atmosphere that Kharrat signalled Damascus's readiness for revolt. Nasib al-Bakri and Sultan al-Atrash had instructed him to await an 800-man Druze cavalry unit before turning toward Damascus. After some delay, which momentarily made Kharrat fear a betrayal, only 200 horsemen armed with rifles and grenades appeared on October 17 at the appointed place, a farm a few miles southeast of Damascus owned by the Yusuf family. A third band led by Ramadan Pasha Shallash, a tribal chieftain of Dayr al-Zur who had recently arrived from Hama where he had fought the French alongside Fawzi al-Qawuqji,[29] was also to have joined Kharrat and Bakri, but it was late. To avoid another delay, the two bands set out for the town.

Before dawn, on October 18, a band of 40 men commanded by Hasan al-Kharrat penetrated the Shaghur quarter from the east, quietly murdering a number of Moroccan soldiers who were sleeping off an evening at one of the quarter's infamous brothels. The rebels moved stealthily through Shaghur, setting fire to its police station and a Jewish-owned boutique.[30] A little later in the day a second band of 200 Druze insurgents, many of whom came from the recently razed Bakri village of Jarmana, invaded the Maydan. Local grain merchants, headed by the Sukkar family, ensured it smooth access.[31] Commanded by Nasib al-Bakri himself, several Maydani *aghawat*, and the Kilawi brothers of Bab al-Jabiyya, the rebels began by murdering some Armenians in a refugee camp, ostensibly for their participation in the looting and burning of Ghuta villages.[32] As both bands edged toward the commercial center of Damascus, they picked up along the way scores of local partisans. At the center they were joined by the Shallash band, composed of Druzes and Bedouin.

The Kharrat and Shallash bands set their sights on the ʿAzm Palace, the splendid home of the eighteenth-century governors of Damascus which the French had purchased for their Institut d'Art et d'Archéologie Musulman. Recently, one wing of the palace had been converted into a *pied à terre* for the High Commissioner during his periodic visits to the capital. The rebels had been informed that General Sarrail himself was in residence. Actually, he had travelled early that morning, before word of the invasion had spread, to the Hawran. That afternoon rebels occupied

---

[29] MAE, Syrie–Liban 1918–29. 20 Sept. 1926, vol. 237, p. 163.

[30] MAE, Syrie–Liban 1918–29. "Testimony of Fakhri b. Hasan al-Kharrat," vol. 237, pp. 160–62; *The Times* (27 Oct. 1925); USNA, Syria. 890d.00/280. U.S. Consul to Secretary of State, 26 Oct. 1925; FO 371/6884, vol. 10851. Smart to Chamberlain, 25 Oct. 1925; *Oriente Moderno*, 5 (1925), p. 594.

[31] MAE, Syrie–Liban 1918–29. "Testimony of Fakhri b. Hasan al-Kharrat," vol. 237, pp. 161–63; al-Jundi, *Tarikh*, pp. 537–39; Hasan (Abu ʿAli) al-Kilawi, *Thawrat ʿamma 1925. Al-Faransiyyin fi suriyya.* Unpublished memoir of the author's role in the October uprising in Damascus, pp. 1–2.

[32] Al-Kilawi, *Thawrat ʿamma 1925*, pp. 2–5.

the ʿAzm Palace, and when the High Commissioner was not found they burnt his quarters and looted or destroyed many of the palace's archaeological treasures, beautiful marble fittings, and mosaic work.[33]

Earlier, at midday, the French sent tanks through the city and its bazaars. Mobs erected barricades to slow their pace, making them easier targets for snipers. As reports circulated that the local police and many gendarmes had peacefully surrendered to the rebels and that a large Druze army was approaching Damascus, French reinforcements joined the Army stationed in the northern suburbs. The alarmed French command had already begun to construct barricades across Damascus, separating the northern districts from the rebel-infiltrated southern quarters. By sunset, the bulk of the French Army was stationed along positions north of the old city, covering the government buildings, the Hijaz Railway Station, and the Citadel. Then, at 6 p.m., without warning the European residents scattered throughout the old city, the French used artillery and airplanes to shell the southern area of Damascus. The bombardment continued intermittently throughout the night, though at first the shells used were blanks. The next morning, again without warning, all troops were withdrawn from the old city, including the Christian quarter, to the northern line. From 10 o'clock until noon the following day, the bombing continued mercilessly, this time with high explosive shells striking in all quarters from the central bazaars down to the middle of the Maydan.[34]

The plea for a cease-fire by some prominent Damascus notables, including Amir Saʿid al-Jazaʾiri, brought the shelling to a halt. As rebels began to leave Damascus or hid in the denser popular quarters, General Gamelin met with notables on Tuesday afternoon. He demanded that Damascus pay an indemnity of £T 100,000 and surrender 3,000 rifles by October 24; otherwise, shelling would be renewed. He also made the notables responsible for preventing rebel bands from entering the city.[35] But, when it became apparent to Gamelin and the French Delegate that the notables were unable to meet the stiff French terms, which nationalists in the town and elsewhere vehemently rejected, they ordered Subhi Barakat's government to raise the money. This relieved the notables, who generally despised Barakat for his seeming indifference to the destruction caused by French shelling.[36]

[33] FO 371/6884, vol. 10851. Smart to Chamberlain, 20 Oct. 1925; *The Times*, 27 Oct. 1925; USNA, Syria. 890d.00/280. 26 Oct. 1925.

[34] *The Times* (27 Oct. 1925); MacCallum, *Crusade*, p. 133; USNA, Syria. 890d.00/280, 26 Oct. 1925; al-Rayyis, *al-Kitab al-dhahabi*, pp. 282–92; MAE, Syrie–Liban 1918–29. Telegram from Armée Française du Levant, 3 Nov. 1925.

[35] MAE, Syrie–Liban 1918–29. "Rapport de Gamelin," 6 Dec. 1925–9 Feb. 1926, vol. 196, pp. 146–50; USNA, Syria. 890d.00/280. Damascus Consul to Secretary of State, 19 Oct. 1925; FO 371/6884, vol. 10851. Smart to Chamberlain, 25 Oct. 1925.

[36] Kurd ʿAli, *al-Mudhakkirat*, vol. 2, p. 328.

As to the resumption of the shelling, when the French recovered from their panic they recognized the immense destruction they had inflicted. They faced, moreover, the possibility of considerable foreign claims against them, and general international condemnation for the inhuman treatment of a civilian population.[37]

The death toll after two days of shelling was high. The French Communist newspaper, L'Humanité, circulated figures provided by the Damascus Municipality of 1,416 killed, including 336 women and children.[38] The official French version placed the number of "civilian casualties" at 150.[39] The first estimate was probably much closer to the mark, especially when the intensity of the shelling, its range, and the amount of physical destruction it caused are compared with the results of the shelling of Hama. Damascus had four times the population of Hama, the area bombed in Damascus was much greater than that bombed in Hama, and the shelling went on for twice as long. Significantly, the official French estimate of Hama's death toll was one-quarter of the Damascus Municipality's estimate for Damascus.

The French blamed the vast destruction of Damascus as much on rebel looting and pillaging as they did on their own shelling. The evidence, however, clearly indicts the French. French bombs and artillery ruined much of the area between the two great commercial arteries, Suq al-Hamidiyya and Suq Midhat Pasha. The latter bazaar, including the main food market of the town, al-Bzuriyya, sustained the greatest damage. Its corrugated roof was blown off at the center causing the collapse of nearly 100 yards of its eastern section.[40] The Times correspondent observed that "in both bazaars shop after shop was destroyed either by tank machine-gun, which riddled the iron shutters as they dashed through, or by shell or by fire."[41] French estimates, which for obvious reasons were lower than Syrian or other European estimates, placed the number of shops entirely burnt and pillaged in the bazaars at 220, an estimated loss of £T 500,000 (fifty million francs). In the residential districts of Shaghur (including the Jewish quarter), Madinat al-Shahm, al-Kharab, and Bab al-Jabiyya, 150 homes were either partially or completely burnt by the shelling and looting was extensive. In al-Qanawat, Bab al-Srija, al-Suwayqa, and the Lower Maydan, 98 houses were damaged by the bombardment. The stately homes of well-known families opposed to the French, such as the Quwwatli, Bakri, and Rikabi Palaces, were also com-

[37] Ibid.

[38] L'Humanité (17 Nov. 1925), cited in MacCallum, Crusade, p. 136.

[39] Ibid.

[40] The Times (27 Oct. 1925); MAE, Syrie–Liban 1918–29. 4 Nov. 1925–5 Dec. 1925, vol. 195, pp. 1–3; USNA, Syria. 890d.00/173, 24 Oct. 1925.

[41] The Times (27 Oct. 1925).

pletely destroyed.[42] The Quwwatli residence in Shaghur was one of the showplaces of Damascus; like the ʿAzm Palace, which shells had also damaged, it was a "gem of Arabesque art."[43] Amazingly, the Great Mosque at the eastern end of Suq al-Hamidiyya escaped untouched, but the beautiful green and blue tiled Mosque of Sinan Pasha on the edge of Bab al-Jabiyya was not so fortunate. A shell made an enormous hole in its dome and some of its mosaic windows were destroyed.[44] The French estimated the total damage to buildings and merchandise at £T 1,000,000 (100 million francs).[45] Whatever the estimate, the real losses were staggering.

The Christian quarter of Bab Tuma, which also housed a significant European community, panicked when French troops suddenly withdrew from the quarter on October 19. As shells fell, a frantic crowd of 3,000 Armenian and Syrian Christians invaded the British hospital grounds on the quarter's outskirts. Meanwhile, Amir Saʿid al-Jazaʾiri, probably in a bid for French attention and support for his own personal ambitions, reenacted his grandfather's 1860 role by going in to Bab Tuma with his armed retainers to protect its defenseless residents from rebels and bandits. Praise for his chivalry came from several different directions: from the angry British who had not been warned of the withdrawal and bombing; from local Christians thankful for his protection; and from nationalist leaders who were relieved to know that the Christian population had not been molested by nationalist forces. Nevertheless, the paranoid French even arrested him and his cousin Tahir, a moderate nationalist, owing to their activities during the revolt.[46]

International criticism of French shelling focused on the destruction of architectural and archaeological treasures, rather than on human suffering and loss of life. The British and American consuls criticized the French for over-reacting rather than questioning the right of a mandatory regime to use such murderous force. By their reckoning, the disturbances in Damascus were not as serious as the French made out. They believed that the level of coordination among rebel bands and between them and their supporters in Damascus was low. But they belittled the depth and breadth of opposition to French rule in Syria and the ability of the

[42] MAE, Syrie–Liban 1918–29. 4 Nov. 1925–5 Dec. 1925, vol. 195, pp. 1–3. There was also significant damage in the ʿAmara quarter and some as well in Suq Saruja.

[43] The Times (27 Oct. 1925).

[44] Ibid.

[45] MAE, Syrie–Liban, 1918–29. 4 Nov.–5 Dec. 1925, vol. 195, p. 3; FO 371/6884, vol. 10851, 25 Oct. 1925.

[46] Ibid. Jazaʾiri's "heroic" role in the events of 1925 in Damascus was not so much a humanitarian gesture as it was an attempt to please the British in the hopes that they would respond in the future with political favors. FO 371/7298, vol. 10852. Damascus Consul to FO, 9 Nov. 1925.

nationalist movement to organize and direct that opposition in a rational manner. When the bands invaded Damascus, they did so in synchronization. They do not seem to have aimed at making a serious assault on French positions in the town, for which they were ill-equipped, but rather in sparking a general revolt which would force the French Army to withdraw to the north, away from the city. If the rebels had one specific target, it was the ʿAzm Palace, where General Sarrail was believed to be. Their penetration, first through Shaghur and the lower Maydan, was well calculated since they were the easiest approaches to the city center, their density provided ample cover, and in them Kharrat and Bakri could count on widespread support.[47]

AFTER THE BOMBARDMENT, the center of resistance to the French shifted back to the Ghuta. However, forays into the Maydan quarter continued and the number of Damascenes operating near the town increased significantly. In general, rebel spirits remained high, although this was not true of the weary populace inside Damascus which had borne the brunt of French pacification. Indeed, panic spread quickly in Damascus each time a large raiding party was reported to be approaching the town. On October 26, a Druze band under the command of Zayd al-Atrash, Sultan Pasha's 20-year-old brother, neared Damascus only to be diverted at the last moment by a group of Maydani notables who begged the Druze chieftain not to enter the town for fear of renewed shelling.[48]

By early November, anarchy reigned in the eastern garden districts of Damascus. French expeditionary forces, consisting of Foreign Legionnaires, Moroccan *spahis*, and Circassian irregulars, continued their plunder of villages, often owned by wealthy notables in the capital. The spectacle of troops returning to Damascus "laden" with booty only added to the demoralization of the populace. The rebels, nevertheless, managed to hold their own. Each French assault on Ghuta villages added to the number of homeless peasants, many of whom joined rebel bands.[49]

North of the Ghuta and all along the eastern anti-Lebanon mountain range as far north as Nabk, rebel bands were in control. Meanwhile, in the Wadi al-ʿAjam district on the slopes of Mount Hermon, Zayd al-Atrash organized Druze villagers for an assault on southern Lebanon. In

[47] In some parts of Shaghur and the Lower Maydan, the density per hectare was as high as 800 persons. Only Bab Tuma and Halbuni had higher densities, of up to 1,000–1,200 persons per hectare. See René Danger, "L'urbanisme en Syrie: la ville de Damas," *Urbanisme* (revue mensuelle) (1937), p. 136.

[48] Al-Jundi, *Tarikh*, p. 235; FO 371/7250, vol. 10852. Smart to Chamberlain, 10 Nov. 1925.

[49] FO 371/7099, vol. 10852. Smart to Chamberlain, 2 Nov. 1925.

Damascus, the French military reinforced their positions in the northern suburbs and merchants once again carted their goods back to their homes for safekeeping—only days after they had returned them to their stores.[50]

On November 9, Zayd al-Atrash's band captured Hasbaya on the western slopes of Mount Hermon. The following day it also seized the Maronite village of Kawkaba, where a massacre took place.[51] Eleven days later, the Druze invaded Rashaya. The spread of the revolt into Lebanon and rumors of Christian massacres not only sent shivers throughout the southern districts but also alarmed French authorities, who feared a general Druze and Shi'i uprising might transform a basically anti-French struggle into a civil war.[52] Moreover, the coast would be threatened if the Beirut–Damascus railway were cut.[53] But, Hasbaya and Rashaya were the farthest outposts of the rebellion. After considerable preparation, the French shelled Hasbaya from the air, recapturing the town on December 5. Although rebel operations continued inside Lebanon, the country had been cleared of the largest rebel bands.[54]

ONE OF THE CASUALTIES of the Damascus events was General Sarrail. The military set-backs in Syria and criticism in the rightist press embarrassed the French cabinet. The anti-Sarrail campaign gained momentum from a series of articles in L'Echo de Paris published between September 29 and October 6. Dissaffected French officers in Syria had provided indisputable evidence that Sarrail had received solid intelligence reports which indicated that a revolt in the Jabal Druze was probable, but that he ignored them. He also seems to have dismissed a third report by the late Major Aujac, just ten days before the Druze assault on the Michaud column, that the Madagascan troops under his command were unsuitable for combat.[55] Premier Painlevé was clearly disturbed by these revelations.[56]

The French Left, while seemingly uninterested in criticizing the gen-

[50] Ibid.

[51] Al-Jundi, Tarikh, p. 235; al-Rayyis, al-Kitab al-dhahabi, pp. 299–309; FO 371/7291, vol. 10852. Mayers (Beirut) to Chamberlain, 15 Nov. 1925.

[52] FO 371/7921, vol. 10852. Mayers to Chamberlain, 15 Nov. 1925.

[53] FO 371/7099, vol. 10852. Smart to Chamberlain, 2 Nov. 1925; Joarder, "The Syrian Nationalist Uprising," p. 192.

[54] FO 371/7921, vol. 10853. Beirut to FO, 6 Dec. 1925.

[55] L'Echo de Paris (29, 30 Sept., and 1, 2, 4, 6 Oct. 1925), cited in Tannenbaum, Sarrail, pp. 204–5. For Sarrail's rebuttal of the charges in these articles, which he made before leaving Beirut, see MD, 7N 4187, Dossier 1. On General Michaud's indictment and his defense, see ibid., 7N 4187, Dossier 2. Rapport du Général Duport," 21 July–3 Aug. 1925.

[56] FO 371/4692, vol. 10851. Crewe to Chamberlain, 9 Aug. 1925; FO 371/5576, vol. 10851. Crewe to Chamberlain, 15 Sept. 1925.

eral ineptitude of French policy, vigorously, indeed recklessly, defended
Sarrail against the incessant attacks of the Right. They asked why General Lyautey, a Loyalist and a man of the Right, was not equally subject
to severe criticism, since he was directly responsible for the French failure
to quell the rebellion of 'Abd al-Krim in Morocco. These mounting attacks and counterattacks created a dilemma. On the one hand, any attempt to remove Sarrail would infuriate the Radicals and the Republican
Socialists. Painlevé's government was already under fire for having uti-
lized the Right to counterbalance the defection of Socialists over the Morocco crisis and Finance Bill. Somehow Painlevé had to avoid being
pushed too far to the Right.[57]

One way for Painlevé to clear the path for Sarrail's recall and to still
hold on to his Radical and Republican Socialist support was to deflate
Lyautey's prestigious bubble in Morocco, something the Left demanded.
So Painlevé stripped Lyautey of his military functions on August 18,
which paved the way for Lyautey's resignation the following month.
This freed Painlevé to recall Sarrail, whom he had already deprived of his
military command.[58] Spurring Painlevé on was his Foreign Minister
Aristide Briand, who had the thankless task of answering the accusations
of European governments that the bombardment of Damascus had been
unneccessary.

On October 30, Sarrail was summoned home. He reached Paris two
weeks later to find himself at the center of an acrimonious debate between
the French Right and Left.[59] His recall demonstrates the considerable influence that events in Syria had on internal French politics.

A CIVILIAN HIGH COMMISSIONER

Breaking with tradition, Painlevé appointed a civilian to succeed General
Sarrail. He was Henry de Jouvenel, a 60-year-old liberal politician and
journalist who had begun his career just after the turn of the century as
private secretary to several cabinet ministers. Jouvenel then joined the
staff of the Paris daily, Le Matin, eventually becoming its editor. In 1921,
he was elected Senator from Corrèze, joining the Groupe de la Gauche
Démocratique. Between March and May 1924 he served as Minister of

---

[57] FO 371/5576, vol. 10851. Crewe to Chamberlain, 15 Sept. 1925; Tannenbaum, Sarrail, p. 205. The Left actually blamed Lyautey's failure in the Rif for the outbreak of revolt
in Syria. FO 371/5576, vol. 10851. Crewe to Chamberlain, 15 Sept. 1925. There was hardly
any mention in the rightist or leftist press about how much the Syrian Revolt had cost the
French Treasury, which was already severely strained by the unexpected demands of the
Moroccan situation.
[58] Tannenbaum, Sarrail, p. 208.
[59] Ibid., pp. 208–9.

Public Instruction in the cabinet of Raymond Poincaré and on several occasions he represented France at the League of Nations. Most recently, he had been Assistant Delegate to the League of Nations Assembly. Because of the respect he enjoyed at the League, the Painlevé government hoped that his appointment would raise France's drooping prestige in the international community. In France, Jouvenel commanded the support of politicians as different as Herriot and Poincaré.[60]

Even before Jouvenel had been named High Commissioner, a new French Delegate, M. de Reffye, had already set out for Damascus. He came up with a program to control the political situation tailored to complement French military operations which, at the time, concentrated on refortifying and isolating Damascus from the Jabal Druze. His plan pinpointed the People's Party as France's major enemy. To check its activities, Reffye suggested several strategies. The French should cooperate more closely with sympathetic Damascus notables and get them to suggest names of like-minded individuals who might be willing to participate in government. Certain key moderate nationalists who were "correct with the High Commission" should be prevented from making common cause with the People's Party. Subhi Barakat and his cronies should be dismissed once the French had shaped a more satisfactory governmental clique. Subsidies to moderate nationalist newspapers should be increased while monthly grants of up to 6,000 francs should be extended to more radical newspapers like al-Mufid and al-Muqtabas in order to dilute their nationalist fervor. Reffye also wanted to tie the interests of religious leaders to the French administration; he proposed trimming the number of obsolete functionaries in the Awqaf administration while strengthening relations with ranking members of the religious establishment. He also proposed that the French try to attract a few members of the People's Party to their side while expanding their surveillance network in the towns, particularly in the cafés and other popular nationalist gathering spots. Finally, since Damascus was the ideological and political locus of opposition, Reffye felt that the High Commission must renew its efforts to contain the revolt to the capital. One way would be to return administrative and financial autonomy to Aleppo so as to remove it from the Damascus orbit.[61]

When Jouvenel arrived in Beirut in early December (after an unsuccessful meeting in Cairo with exiled Syrian leaders), he immediately announced his intentions with the words "peace to those who wish peace and war for those who wish war." He advised that he would consolidate

[60] Henry de Jouvenel was born in 1865 in Paris. See FO 371/6954, vol. 10852. Crewe to Chamberlain, 10 Nov. 1925. At one time he was also married to the French writer Colette.

[61] MAE, Syrie–Liban 1918–29. "Rapport de M. de Reffye," 3 Nov. 1925, vol. 194, pp. 257, 259–61, 264–66, 274.

the territorial status quo ante and disarm the insurrectionists. On December 5, he proclaimed the right of the Lebanese people to vote for a constitution and affirmed that the French Mandate for Syria and Lebanon would not be relinquished.[62] He then began to implement Reffye's political blueprint.

Jouvenel pursued a policy of political decentralization designed to isolate Damascus from other districts in revolt and from regions which were still relatively tranquil. He dispatched a delegation to the Jabal Druze, headed by a prominent Lebanese Druze chieftain, Amin Arslan, to work out peace proposals. But, Sultan al-Atrash rebuffed the Arslan mission; he refused to dissociate himself from the nationalist movement and issued his own proposals, which were totally unacceptable to the French. At the end of December, Jouvenel made one last half-hearted attempt to get the Druze to lay down their arms in return for the right to create their own constitution and choose their own leaders and government.[63] He wanted to convey the impression to the League of Nations and to those French critics who continued to accuse France of misconduct in governing Syria that he had done all he could to secure a lasting peace. Then, if France had to resort again to excessively repressive measures, blame could be put on the insurgents' uncompromising attitude.[64]

Subhi Barakat resigned as President of the Syrian state on December 21,[65] forcing Jouvenel to look to other notables to form a new government. The next day the High Commissioner summoned a delegation of Damascus patricians to Beirut to discuss the matter. But the terms these dignitaries proposed—the formation of a national provisional government, free elections, a constitution based on the principles of national sovereignty, the unity of Syria excluding pre-1920 Lebanon, and a general amnesty—were unacceptable. Even so-called moderates could not ignore the popularity of the People's Party or the depth of nationalist sentiment.[66] As soon as Jouvenel saw that discussions were not progressing,

[62] *Ibid.*, pp. 16–19; *al-Ahrar* (Cairo) (1 December 1925), cited in USNA, Syria. 890d.00/349; FO 684/76-1649. Mayers (Beirut) to FO, 6 Dec. 1925.

[63] MD, 7N 4186, Dossier 8. "Historique de la Mission de M. Henry de Jouvenel en Syrie et au Liban," Dec. 1925–July 1926; Rabbath, *Courte Histoire*, p. 20.

[64] FO 371/416, vol. 11505. Smart to Chamberlain, 4 Jan. 1926; Rabbath, *Courte Histoire*, p. 23. The Druze *majlis* presented unacceptable demands: recognition of Syrian independence, Syrian unity (excluding pre-1920 Lebanon), a Franco-Syrian Treaty guaranteeing French interests without prejudicing national sovereignty, the withdrawal of the French Army to the coast, a Constituent Assembly, and a general amnesty.

[65] MAE, Syrie–Liban 1918–29. "Les Négociations qui suivirent le bombardement de Damas," vol. 197, pp. 26–34. According to Kurd ʿAli, Subhi Barakat boasted that ". . . he had never slept so soundly as when Damascus was being bombarded in October 1925." He even brought dancing girls to his home and celebrated his wedding while Damascus was burning.

[66] Rabbath, *Courte Histoire*, p. 26.

he left his Beirut representative, M. Mélia,[67] in charge and rushed to Aleppo in a move intended to undercut the bargaining position of Damascus. His strategy was to hold elections for a Constituent Assembly, but only in districts which the French had not placed under martial law, that is, everywhere but Damascus, the Hawran, and the Jabal Druze. Jouvenel believed that the "unreasonable attitude" prevailing in these districts did not warrant such a "reward."[68]

DEVELOPMENTS IN THE NORTH

Since the outbreak of the revolt, Aleppo was unusually tense as restless Bedouin on the town's outskirts threatened to invade. In part, the unsettled atmosphere was a product of organized tribal raiding in Aleppo's environs, led by the Mawali. But the underlying cause was the economic depression of 1925, whose impact had been felt earlier in Aleppo than elsewhere. Drought had stricken the region nearly a year before it visited the South, and Aleppo's traditional commercial outlets in Turkey remained blocked. The Turks had recently added a 50 percent *ad valorem* surtax on all goods imported through Syria.[69] Commercial stagnation led to severe credit restrictions on merchants, while the price of staples climbed. This deterioration gave added weight to nationalist accusations that the French were ruining the country. Not only had the High Commission failed to grant greater political freedom to Aleppines, it had also neglected to regenerate the local economy. Jouvenel's announcement that elections would be held did nothing to reverse this trend, for past experience had taught that French electioneering methods were less than democratic. Furthermore, French aims were clear: the holding of elections was an attempt to isolate and alienate Aleppo from Damascus and

[67] FO 371/459, vol. 11505. Smart to Chamberlain, 11 Jan. 1926. Jean Mélia was a former *chef de cabinet* of the Governor-General of Algeria and an expert on Eastern affairs; like Jouvenel, he was also a man of letters.

[68] *Ibid.*, pp. 26–27; FO 371/866, vol. 11505. Mayers to Chamberlain, 25 Jan. 1926.

[69] The British Consul reported at the time that trade in Aleppo "couldn't be worse. . . . Political troubles in the south gave no direct repercussions in the Aleppo area [but] they have created a general uneasiness unfavorable to business. Political troubles in eastern Turkey have been the reason for the refusal of all facilities of travel between there and Aleppo. . . . No doubt Turks influenced by a desire to kill the trade of Aleppo were motivated by economic and political considerations. Nothing could have fitted in better with Turkish aims as business between Aleppo and its markets was always done by personal visits of traders and by its nature can hardly be done in any other way. There has been a general tendency of the more enterprising commercial bosses to switch more and more to produce export business and for the import business to establish branch houses in Mersina. Aleppo is and will remain the normal distributing centre for eastern Turkey but the resumption of normal trade channels is too remote a prospect at present to be idly awaited." FO 371/839, vol. 11517. Hough (Aleppo) to Board of Trade, 18 Feb. 1926.

hence to handicap the nationalist movement, both morally and politically.

During the first few days of the new year, the organization of a city-wide boycott of elections got underway. Declarations, manifestos, and signed petitions began to appear all over Aleppo.[70] Boycott organizers met secretly in the homes of quarter bosses, and nationalist leaders visited candidates to persuade them not to run on pro-French lists. A score of candidates buckled under to nationalist pressure, but thoroughly discredited collaborators like Subhi Barakat, who had recently returned to Aleppo to stand as a candidate (and to become the agent of an international oil company), and Shakir Ni'mat al-Sha'bani, a perennial opponent of the nationalists, were not as easily scared off.[71]

Unlike the election boycott of 1923, this boycott was a resounding success. Following the suggestion of Jamil Ibrahim Pasha, whose direct links to Aleppo's popular quarters were stronger than any other political leader's, high school students were stationed at ballot boxes to discourage residents from voting.[72] Only 23 percent (as opposed to 40 percent in 1923) of Aleppo's registered voters participated in the first degree elections, and these were mainly from the Armenian and Syrian Catholic communities. As in 1923, however, in the ten rural districts of the Aleppo province, where the High Commission had a relatively free hand in manipulating the electoral process, a staggering 81 percent of the voters cast their ballots.[73]

Although Aleppo's commercial bourgeoisie, largely Christian in make-up, was generally in favor of greater administrative and financial autonomy for the province, many businessmen did not dare oppose the boycott. In fact, the local Christian leadership refused to call its communities to the polls "en masse." The Muslim landowning class, although torn on the internal political level by its jealousy of Damascene political supremacy, was unwilling to jeopardize the chances of complete Syrian unity by going along with Jouvenel's scheme. For the French, the nationalists' show of strength in Aleppo was distressing. In retaliation, the boycott leaders, 43 in all, including eight Jabiris and five Kayyalis, were arrested.[74]

On January 10, a crowd of 1,500 persons gathered at the Great Mosque in Aleppo and shops throughout the Muslim quarters closed to protest

---

[70] See USNA, Syria. 890d.00/332. Aleppo Consul to Secretary of State, 7 Jan. 1926.

[71] Ibrahim Pasha, *Nidal*, pp. 33–35.

[72] *Ibid.*, pp. 35–36.

[73] MAE, Syrie–Liban 1918–29. "Reffye Telegram," 6 Dec. 1925–9 Feb. 1926, 10 Feb. 1926, vol. 196, pp. 266–67; FO 371/641, vol. 11515. Hough (Aleppo) to Chamberlain, 15 Jan. 1926.

[74] FO 371/603, vol. 11505. Hough to Chamberlain, 13 Jan. 1926.

the arrests. A procession headed by Aleppo's mufti, a relative of the arrested Dr. Kayyali, made its way to the Sérail. There, the aged governor of the province, Mariʿ Pasha al-Mallah, came out to address the angry crowds, claiming he had nothing to do with the arrests, even though his signature had been on the warrants. In the middle of his speech, demonstrators began to stone him and he just managed to escape, thanks to the assistance of Moroccan troops. That evening he submitted his resignation; not only were the accusations levelled against him by the Aleppine public damaging, but his son was among those arrested.[75]

After this incident, the crowds in the courtyard of the Sérail were harangued by nationalists, including Saʿdallah al-Jabiri, who had been arrested and who spoke from his prison window overlooking the courtyard. The nervous French military command, which had stationed additional troops and tanks around the courtyard, prepared to deal with the hostile situation in its typically excessive manner. When the crowd tried to help a number of prisoners to make an escape, a company of mounted troops with bared sabres charged the unarmed mob, which turned in flight only to face a burst of machine-gun fire from the nearby Citadel. In a few minutes, the whole area was empty; everyone in the town center took refuge behind closed doors as Moroccan *spahis*, supported by tanks, patrolled the major boulevards.[76] This demonstration marked a high point in Aleppo's resistance. It was also the most violent clash yet; French machine gunners killed 15 people and seriously wounded another 60.[77]

The second degree elections in Aleppo were conducted without incident between January 21 and 23, under the protection of French reinforcements. In any case, the nationalists had made their point: few, if any, of the 250 electors were known personalities, except in the case of certain Christian electors, many of whom were Armenians. For the Sunni majority, the pickings were slim as most candidates had withdrawn their names from the electoral list after the disturbances that followed the first degree elections. Besides the three minority deputies (an Orthodox Christian, a Greek Catholic, and a Jew), four Muslims were elected to the National Constituent Assembly: Ghalib Ibrahim Pasha, a Francophile who since 1918 had been President of the Aleppo Municipality; Rashid al-Mudarris, the scion of a great landowning family with strong Turkish connections; Shakir Niʿmat al-Shaʿbani, and, of course, the incumbent, Subhi Barakat. In general, the policy of the victors, as far as a policy can be ascribed

[75] USNA, Syria. 890d.00/339. Aleppo to Secretary to State, 11 Jan. 1926; FO 371/602, vol. 11515. Hough to Chamberlain, 13 Jan. 1926.

[76] USNA, Syria. 890d.00/352. Aleppo Consul to Secretary of State, 11 Jan. 1926; FO 371/480, vol. 11515. Hough to Chamberlain, 11 Jan. 1926; Ibrahim Pasha, *Nidal*, p. 54.

[77] USNA, Syria. 890d.00/352. Aleppo Consul to Secretary of State, 11 Jan. 1926.

to them, was for greater decentralization but not for complete autonomy, as the French had wished.[78]

To the High Commission's relief, elections in the Alawite state and the Sanjak of Alexandretta proceeded according to plan. In the Alawite state, 77 percent of the registered voters cast their ballots without incident. There had been some worry that Shaykh Salih al-'Ali, the Alawite rebel leader, might disrupt the balloting, but he died on the eve of the elections. On February 2, the Representative Council of the Alawites proclaimed "its firm desire to maintain the independence of the State and the consolidation of its relations with other states under French Mandate," namely Lebanon and Syria.[79] Obviously, the nationalist movement had made little headway in this heavily protected region.

In the Sanjak of Alexandretta, with its significant Turkish population, 75 percent of the registered voters turned out, eventually electing six deputies to the National Constituent Assembly. Their first demand was that the Sanjak be detached from the Syrian state. Later, on March 19, five of the deputies proclaimed the independence of the Sanjak, something the French authorities were unprepared to recognize.[80] Again the nationalist movement had failed to make political advances in this region.

The story in Hama and Homs was radically different. These towns, which were major seats of opposition to French rule, completely boycotted the elections. No candidate dared stand in either town. There was little the French could do but arrest and deport to Arwad Island the boycott's ringleaders, among them Hashim al-Atasi, Prime Minister under Amir Faysal in 1920 and the most influential politician in Homs, and Mazhar Raslan, also a Homsi, who only recently had returned to Syria from Transjordan, where he had held several posts, including that of Chief Adviser to Amir 'Abdullah. Meanwhile, military posts were established around Hama and Homs to combat rebel bands still operating in the region.[81]

BEARING DOWN ON DAMASCUS

While the first degree elections were underway in northern and central Syria, the High Commission continued its search for someone to form a new national government. Jouvenel felt that the choice would have to be a Damascene to assuage local notables in the capital who had been passed

[78] USNA, Syria. 890d.00/352. Aleppo Consul to Secretary of State, 28 Jan. 1926; FO 371/905, vol. 11515. Hough to FO, 26 Jan. 1926.

[79] Rabbath, *Courte Histoire*, p. 21.

[80] MAE, Syrie–Liban 1918–29. 10 Feb. 1926, vol. 196, pp. 266–67; Rabbath, *Courte Histoire*, p. 21.

[81] FO 371/926, vol. 11505. Smart to Chamberlain.

over for highest office. This was particularly important, given the locus of the revolt.

For some time, the French Delegate in Beirut had been cultivating one potential candidate who seemed both qualified and willing, Shaykh Muhammad Taj al-Din al-Hasani. Born in 1885 in Damascus, Taj was the son of Shaykh Badr al-Din al-Hasani, the most revered and popular religious scholar in Syria, a pious divine respected by Syrians and foreigners alike.[82] Even the moderate Shaykh Taj, however, had to be cautious. With a nationalist revolt raging in the Damascus region, he certainly could not offer himself to the High Commission on a silver platter; he had to demonstrate a certain measure of independent influence in Damascus, as well as commitment to the cause of Syrian unity and independence in order to be able to position himself between the High Commission and the revolt leadership, no mean feat in such turbulent times. His terms of cooperation had to be framed in such a way as to attract the French and at the same time to acknowledge the nationalist movement's minimalist demands. In January, he proposed that the Biqaʿ be rejoined to Syria; the populations in the districts of Tripoli, Sidon, and Tyre decide by plebiscite whether they wanted to be part of Syria; Franco-Syrian relations be regulated by a treaty; Syria be eventually admitted to the League of Nations; and a general amnesty be granted. The High Commissioner generally approved of Taj's proposals, especially the idea of a treaty favorable to France. However, Taj's attitude toward Syrian unity was vague and hence troublesome. Jouvenel was not prepared to change the autonomous or independent status of the Druzes and Alawites and he could only allow minor rectifications of the Syrian-Lebanese frontier, not the major shifts Taj called for. The High Commissioner's counterproposals were too inflexible and negotiations broke down.[83]

Unable to find either a pro-French notable willing to risk his reputation and possibly his life, or a moderate nationalist with acceptable conditions for cooperation, Jouvenel reimposed direct French rule on Syria. On February 9, he charged his special envoy, Pierre Alype, with the administration of the Syrian state. The facade of indirect rule, which the French had clumsily erected in Syria in 1920, had finally collapsed.[84]

It can be argued, as some observers did, that until this time the High

[82] Shaykh Badr al-Din al-Hasani (1851–1935) was the son of Yusuf al-Maghrabi (denoting his North African ancestry) and a woman from the old and respected religious family of Kuzbari in Damascus. He studied with Shaykh Abu'l-Khayr al-Khatib, the late nineteenth-century preacher, and between 1900 and 1916 resided in Mecca. *Oriente Moderno*, 15 (1935), p. 382.

[83] MD, 7N 4186, Dossier 8. "Historique de la Mission de M. Henry de Jouvenel"; Rabbath, *Courte Histoire*, p. 29.

[84] Rabbath, *Courte Histoire*, pp. 29–30.

Commissioner had been "honestly animated by the democratic ideals to which he held allegiance."[85] His administration was certainly a refreshing break with that of his predecessor's. Whereas General Sarrail's circle resembled a "sergeant's mess," Jouvenel's entourage was reminiscent of a "pre-revolutionary salon." Indeed, his closest aides were civilians; like Jouvenel, some were men of letters.[86] Yet, since his main mission in Syria was to save France's prestige, he could not be perfectly true to his ideals. At best, he hoped to strike a balance between force and compromise by sealing all pockets of armed resistance, while he encouraged all local forces to unite behind a reasonable set of demands. But, to Jouvenel's dismay, the French moral and political position in Syria continued to deteriorate. France's inability to maintain order in Damascus in spite of a large military force of 10,000 troops, the failure to secure native cooperation, the growing economic misery in the towns and countryside (for which France was blamed), and the excessive destruction caused by French military operations increased popular discontent and widened the gulf between France and her Syrian subjects.[87]

The appointment of M. Alype cleared the way for the French military to launch a massive offensive to break the back of the Syrian revolt. Damascus, itself, was to be given primary attention. By the end of November 1925, the town was again under martial law and a 6 p.m. curfew.[88] Yet, rebel bands still operated quite unencumbered in the Maydan and Shaghur quarters, and they continued to attack French positions in the northern suburbs.[89]

One of Jouvenel's first actions on arriving in Beirut at the beginning of December had been to appoint General Charles Andréa as Commander-in-Chief of French troops in the Damascus region.[90] Andréa's first assignment was to develop a security plan for Damascus. Three years earlier an expansion and beautification plan had been submitted to the Municipal Council which called for boulevards to connect the center of the town with its extremities, and new quarters to relieve the congestion of the overpopulated town center. The plan had been scrapped at that time owing to inadequate financial resources.[91] Now, in late 1925, Andréa hoped to revive and modify it to suit French security needs. On the advice of the French Corps of Army Engineers, he proposed the construction of a belt-

[85] FO 371/1209, vol. 11515. Mayers to FO, 7 Feb. 1926.
[86] FO 371/631, vol. 11505. Mayers to Chamberlain, 17 Jan. 1926.
[87] FO 371/973, vol. 11505. Smart to Chamberlain, 24 Jan. 1926.
[88] MacCallum, *Crusade*, p. 145.
[89] FO 371/1298, vol. 11505. Smart to Chamberlain, 15 Feb. 1926; FO 371/973, vol. 11505. Smart to Chamberlain, 31 Jan. 1926.
[90] FO 371/7796, vol. 10853. Smart to FO, 9 Dec. 1925.
[91] Andréa, *La révolte druze*, p. 82.

way around Damascus which would enclose most of the town except for the Muhajirin quarter to the north and parts of the Maydan to the south. On the west, the beltway would also incorporate some villages where rebels were operating. The "inner edge" of the beltway was to be laced with barbed wire and fourteen garrison posts. In addition, two roads—one stretching from the Hijaz Station southwards through the Maydan, and the other from the Baramké Station westwards into the Ghuta—and southwards to the Maydan Station—were to be built.[92]

The labor required to complete the project was readily available. The economic depression, aggravated by revolt, had created a large pool of unemployed laborers. Construction began with a force of 1,500 laborers in the second week of December. By early February 1926, Damascus was completely encircled by a barbed-wire boulevard dotted with machine-gun posts.[93]

But these expensive precautionary measures were not a deterrent to rebels, who were still able to cut through and even carry away the barbed wire "entanglement." Nor did mines and other sophisticated devices prevent their passage through the barricades. Meanwhile, since late January a spate of kidnappings of Syrians associated with the French, including the son-in-law of the President of the Municipality, highlighted the dangers Damascenes faced from both sides.[94]

Rebel bands had little difficulty moving in and out of the long narrow southern arm of the city, flanked by gardens on both sides. After the destructive bombardment of the Maydan in October, its populace did not receive any substantial French protection. The military command adopted a policy of willful neglect. It stayed in the northern suburbs, occasionally making fruitless forays into the town's eastern gardens. Consequently, by the end of January the Maydan was completely controlled by nationalist rebel bands.[95]

In an attempt to check these bands, Circassian and Armenian irregulars, supported by tanks and armored cars, marched through the southernmost checkpoint of the new security belt into the Maydan and advanced the whole length of the quarter's main thoroughfare and back, shelling houses on both sides along the way. As rebels returned French fire from side streets and rooftops, the irregulars broke into houses and set several on fire. On the following day, a number of homes were razed to cut a swathe through the northern part of the Maydan; barbed wire

[92] Ibid., map, p. 85; MacCallum, Crusade, pp. 149–50.

[93] Andréa, La révolte druze, p. 86.

[94] FO 371/1298, vol. 11505. Smart to Chamberlain, 15 Feb. 1926; FO 371/973, vol. 11505. Smart to Chamberlain, 31 Jan. 1926.

[95] Al-Jundi, Tarikh, p. 367; FO 371/1589, vol. 11505. Smart to Chamberlain, 23 Feb. 1926.

barricades were then erected, leaving the greater part of the quarter outside these defenses.[96]

The ruthless violence of the poorly disciplined Circassian and Armenian conscripts far exceeded what even the French had intended.[97] Houses
were looted and there were reports of old people and children being mu-
tilated and women being violated. In the popular outcry which followed,
reprisals against the Armenians were called for. Threats against the
Christian quarter also circulated. Fortunately, Shaykh Badr al-Din al-
Hasani and other influential Muslims interceded at the request of Christian leaders to avert a Christian bloodbath. But, there is little doubt that
the weather, which took a spell for the worse just as tensions had reached
their peak, and the dismissal of dozens of irregular troops and the return
of captured booty to its rightful owners, helped to temper confessional
conflict.[98]

UNTIL THE SPRING OF 1926, French military strategy in Syria seemed designed to crush the revolt "by the maximum use of every mechanical
contrivance" available but "with the minimum use of French soldiers."
The French preferred to rely on poorly trained irregulars, recruited
largely from among the Circassian, Kurdish, and Armenian minorities.
Rather than take the military offensive, the French preferred to let the
rebels exhaust themselves.[99]

In pursuing this defensive strategy in the countryside, the French
could count on the complicity of many, though not all, of the big rural

[96] Al-Jundi, Tarikh, p. 367; FO 371/1638, vol. 11505. Smart to Chamberlain, 25 Feb.
1926.

[97] MWT, al-Thawra al-suriyya, 4/4820. General Andréa to Mutasarrif (Damascus), 4
March 1926.

[98] Ibid. Much blame was laid on the French-appointed Chief of Police at the time of invasion of the Maydan, a certain Armenian, M. Béjean. Actually, growing Muslim resentment
toward Armenians, who had come as refugees from Turkey under French assistance and
who now served in the Syrian Legion, had been observed in the Damascus region for a cou-
ple of years. Although they were refugees, they were better craftsmen than the locals. They
were also willing to receive lower wages. The role of Armenians in the suppression of the
revolt in Damascus only contributed to the alienation of the Muslim population from the
minorities and the French. One of the biggest French errors was to use local residents from
Syria's minority communities as frontline troops against the Syrian populace. See FO 371/
236, vol. 11517. Smart to FO, 30 Dec. 1925. This problem was even more acute in Aleppo
where Armenians accounted for approximately 18 percent of the population. In Damascus
they were only 7 percent. Fauquenot, "L'état civil."

[99] French attempts to recruit irregulars from the Kurdish quarter of Damascus (Hayy al-
Akrad) began after the October bombardment of the city. Negotiations were conducted with
two of the most prominent Kurdish notables of the town, Husayn Ibish and 'Umar Agha
Shimdin. FO 371/623, vol. 10852. Smart to FO.

landlords and village heads (*mukhtars*), whom they had cultivated ever since occupation. But although big rural landlords and *mukhtars* seemed to be nothing more than pawns in the French game of divide and rule, in fact, they willingly collaborated with political agents of the Service des Renseignements because their economic and political interests so dictated. Both recognized a real need to suppress the revolt before it upset their bases of power in the countryside. In this sense, their interests and those of their French rulers converged.

Yet, despite the contribution made by landlords and *mukhtars* to suppressing the revolt, the several rebel bands operating in the Ghuta and northwestern districts of Damascus, while numbering not more than 1,000 armed fighters at any one time, used the human and physical geography advantageously. Rebels were able to move freely in the region between Damascus and Nabk and further north around Homs, assisted by scores of villages which supplied both cover and refuge as well as reinforcements.

Rebel bands around Damascus also relied on revenues from their own taxation system. In most districts under rebel control, the practice was to levy a tax of one-third of the agricultural harvest. If certain villages or *mukhtars* were suspected of having cooperated with the French, stiffer assessments were made. Actually, villagers do not seem to have found this system any more ruthless than the one imposed on them by their landlords, who often doubled as government tax collectors. In the irrigated gardens around Damascus, especially to the east of the city where the fighting was heaviest, some pro-French landlords reluctantly contributed their share of taxes to the rebels rather than lose all their revenues. The High Commission estimated that the apricot harvest alone may have netted the rebel leaders as much as £E 300,000 in 1926. In the unirrigated vegetable and grain producing lands of the Zabadani and Duma districts which suffered from drought, rebels often confiscated outright the small harvests in the first half of 1926. Big landowners like the ʿAjlanis, Quwwatlis, Mardams, and Dalatis then demanded that the French grant a moratorium on land taxes for the year.[100]

---

[100] On the other hand, the French taxed villages, town quarters, and entire towns if they found evidence of complicty with rebels. For example, both Duma and Damascus were taxed on a town-wide basis, while in Damascus both the ʿUqayba and the Maydan quarters were taxed individually for assisting bands. The village of Jawbar in the Ghuta was also fined £T 1,000 gold for the complicity of its *mukhtar* and council of elders. See MWT, *al-Thawra al-suriyya.* Mutasarrif of Damascus to Commandant Traquet, 53/4840, 19 April 1927. In Homs, when two of the more notorious rebel-cum-bandits of the revolt were finally apprehended in early 1929, the quarter in which they were hiding was fined £T 900 gold and the entire town had to pay an additional £T 1,500 gold. The French treated town quarters as basically autonomous within the city and thus they could legitimately be singled out. MAE,

Neither the death of Hasan al-Kharrat in late 1925, nor the surrender of Ramadan Shallash in January 1926, nor the High Commission's concerted effort to force the submission of other rebel leaders like the Bakris by confiscating their properties were regarded as major setbacks. On the contrary, Ghuta rebel forces maintained their *esprit de corps* by staying in direct communication with one another and with Dr. Shahbandar and Sultan al-Atrash in the Jabal Druze. It is also known that the bands benefited from the expertise of several retired ex-Sharifian army officers both on the battlefield and in Damascus.[101]

After the French assault on the Maydan quarter in February, several Damascus notables tried to convince rebel leaders to negotiate a peace settlement with the High Commission. Most of the notables were either big landowners in the districts of the fiercest fighting or merchants whose livelihoods depended on a regular supply of agricultural produce or livestock to Damascus. Attending secret discussions in the Ghuta at the end of the month were rebel leaders from the 13 bands operating in the districts between Homs and Damascus. Among them were 'Abd al-Qadir Agha Sukkar of the Maydan, whose band had been the major rebel fighting force in Bab Musalla and which was now active in the Duma area; Abu 'Abdu Dib al-Shaykh of 'Amara, who had succeeded Hasan al-Kharrat in the eastern Ghuta; Sa'id 'Akkash, whose band held positions northwest of Damascus from Duma to Zabadani; and Juma' Susaq, who commanded the largest of the bands, some 400 armed men operating between Nabk and Homs. To the dismay of the notables, the results of the

---

Syrie–Liban 1918–29. 20 March 1929, vol. 206, pp. 12–14, 23; FO 371/2598, vol. 13802. Hole to Chamberlain, 24 April 1929; al-Jundi, *Tarikh*, p. 275.

[101] MWT, *al-Thawra al-suriyya*, 1/4788. Qa'immaqam of Duma to Mutasarrif of Damascus, 17 Oct. 1925; *ibid.*, 4/4791, Minister of Interior to Mutasarrif of Damascus, 28 Oct. 1925; *ibid.*, 3/4790 Qa'immaqam of Duma to Mutasarrif of Damascus, 26 Oct. 1925; *ibid.*, 9/4796. Qa'immaqam of Duma to Mutasarrif of Damascus, 2 Nov. 1925; *ibid.*, 11/4798, Minister of Interior to Mutasarrif of Damascus, 12 Nov. 1925; MAE, Syrie–Liban 1918–29. *Bulletin de Services des Renseignements*, 169 (7–9 Aug. 1926), vol. 430. FO 371/972, vol. 11505. Smart to Chamberlain, 29 Jan. 1926. The people of Damascus gave Kharrat the title of *pasha*; he was immortalized as one of the great heroes of the revolt. His son, Fakhri, was captured, tried by a Mixed Court, and hanged in early February 1926. On what happened to the Bakri family, see MWT, *al-Qism al-khass*, Nasib al-Bakri Papers, nos. 1–25. On Hayati, see al-Jundi, *Tarikh*, p. 585. Col. Catroux claimed that on occupation in 1920 he found 700 to 800 officers of Faysal's Arab Army still in Damascus. He had many arrested. See MAE, Syrie–Liban 1918–29. Catroux to Daclin, vol. 242, pp. 192–93. Among those ex-Sharifian officers who were instrumental to the Great Revolt were General Yahya al-Hayati, a German-trained ex-Ottoman officer who planned strategy from secret headquarters in the Ghuta (see al-Jundi, *Tarikh*, p. 585), and Col. Ahmad al-Lahham, who had been part of Faysal's General Staff and, at the time of the revolt, was a member of the Damascus Municipal Council. See Faris, *Man huwa 1949*, p. 389. Also see MWT, *al-Qism al-khass*, Nasib al-Bakri Papers, no. 26. Sultan al-Atrash to al-Bakri, 1926.

parley were negative: rebel leaders claimed that they had no authority to negotiate with the French as this power was vested solely in the revolutionary provisional government in the Jabal Druze, headed by Sultan Pasha al-Atrash and Dr. Shahbandar.[102]

A month later, the French launched their first military offensive since October. Sweeping operations to the east and west of Mount Hermon and between Homs and Nabk resulted in the recapture of large stretches of countryside which the rebels had controlled for the previous five months. Then, the French removed all their costly outposts in the Ghuta in preparation for an artillery and air barrage on villages suspected of harboring rebels. For the first time since the Ghuta had joined the revolt, rebels lurking there were forced to move either southward into the Jabal Druze or northward into the anti-Lebanon. Although the French achieved their aim of driving rebels scattered in various parts of Syria into one corner of the country where they could eventually be rounded up, parts of the Ghuta and southern Lebanon remained under rebel control. In retrospect, it seems that General Andréa's offensive was merely a preliminary maneuver designed to clear the way for one massive final drive.[103]

The Ghuta campaign prompted the political and military leadership of the revolt to consolidate forces under a "National Revolutionary Committee of the Ghuta." Its first president was Mustafa Wasfi al-Samman, a 38-year-old ex-Ottoman officer from the ʿAmara quarter and an early member of the nationalist secret society, al-ʿAhd. Other members of the committee included Nasib al-Bakri and Nazih Muʾayyad al-ʿAzm.[104]

While the Ghuta shelling was underway, General Andréa launched an assault on Suwaydaʾ, which had been in Atrash hands since September 1925. On April 25, French forces recaptured the Druze capital. But, apart from Suwaydaʾ and certain areas in the northern part of the Jabal where the pro-French ʿAmr clan presided, Sultan al-Atrash's guerillas were still in control.[105]

---

[102] MAE, Syrie–Liban 1918–29. 25 Jan. 1922, vol. 38, p. 78. al-Kilawi, *Thawrat*, pp. 5–6; *Oriente Moderno*, 5 (1925), pp. 594, 597; MAE, Syrie–Liban 1918–29. *Bulletin de Services des Renseignements*, no. 48, 9–10 Feb. 1926, vol. 428; *Ibid.*, no. 64, 4–5 March 1926, vol. 429; *ibid.*, no. 66, vol. 429.

[103] FO 371/459, vol. 11505. Smart to Chamberlain, 11 Jan. 1926. Also see FO 2933, vol. 11506. Smart to FO, 27 April 1926; MacCallum, *Crusade*, pp. 154–55.

[104] MAE, Syrie–Liban 1918–29. *Bulletin de Services des Renseignements*, nos. 128–29, 5–8 June 1926, vol. 430. Conversation with Sabri Farid al-Bidaywi (Damascus, 9 July 1977); al-Jundi, *Tarikh*, pp. 558–59; C. Ernest Dawn, "The Rise of Arabism in Syria," *From Ottomanism to Arabism* (Urbana, 1973), p. 175.

[105] Six thousand armed Druzes led the resistance in Suwaydaʾ. The assault took the French six hours to complete; approximately 1,000 Druzes were killed, while the French lost 89 men and another 310 were wounded. MD, 7N 4186, Dossier 8. "Historique de la Mission de M. Henry de Jouvenel." In late April 1926, the French estimated the size of the entire

The third prong of the French Army's spring offensive pointed at the Maydan quarter, last visited in February. The Circassian and Armenian assault had virtually emptied the southernmost suburb, known as the Maydan fawqani (upper Maydan) of its population, leaving it an open field for rebels trying to infiltrate the areas of the city enclosed by barbed-wire entanglements and which now incorporated the lower Maydan.[106] The quarter itself was the grain entrepôt of Damascus, owing to its proximity to the Hawran. It also contained the city's largest flour mills. It provided the rebel bands in the Ghuta with much of their military leadership, their access to the city, and a refuge when needed. It had also provided relentless resistance to French forces since October.

General Gamelin claimed that the second major assault on the Maydan was planned as early as the third week of April and was part of the overall spring offensive. The plan called for the surprise encirclement and penetration of the quarter under artillery and air cover. A major target was a large house in the southern section of the quarter from which rebels coordinated operations.[107] The attack finally came on May 7; in less than 12 hours the French Army struck with more intensity than it had either in October or in February. The number of houses and shops destroyed during the aerial bombardment or as a result of incendiaries was estimated at well over 1,000. The death toll was equally staggering, between 600 and 1,000. The vast majority of casualties were unarmed civilians, including a large number of women and children; only 50 rebels were reported killed in the attack.[108] Afterwards, the troops indulged in pillaging and looting and then paraded their spoils through the streets in the city center, in many cases displaying them to the survivors of the raid who "in a stream of cowed and wretched humanity moved into other parts of Damascus (where they could find temporary shelter) bearing the few objects which they had been able to save." The French assault made of a formerly busy quarter of 30,000 people a virtually deserted ruin. By May 17, calm had at long last been restored to Damascus. For the first time in months, the minarets of Damascus were lit up.[109]

Druze army at 15,000 men, of good fighting caliber. The infantry was composed of Druzes and the cavalry largely of Arab Bedouin. Its commanders were ex-Ottoman army officers headed by Colonel As'ad Bey. MD, 7N 4171. 2ᵉ Bureau (28 April 1926). Also see Mac-Callum, *Crusade*, pp. 154–55.

[106] MAE, Syrie–Liban 1918–29. "Rapport du Général Gamelin," 19 May 1926, vol. 198, pp. 231–34.

[107] *Ibid.*

[108] *The Times* (2 June 1926) estimated that the bombardment destroyed 1,200 houses and 400 shops, and killed 1,000 people; it estimated damages at about £700,000 sterling. *The Daily Express* (20 May 1926) claimed that 600 people had been killed. The French claimed only 200 homes were destroyed. MAE, Syrie–Liban 1918–29. 19 May 1926, vol. 198, pp. 231–34.

[109] MD, 7N 4186. "Historique de la Mission de M. Henry de Jouvenel"; FO 371/3243,

The overcrowding in Damascus as a result of the exodus from the Maydan was aggravated by refugees from ruined villages in the Ghuta and
from destroyed or abandoned Christian villages in the Hawran and Wadi
al-ʿAjam. The French were unwilling to alleviate this distress; indeed,
they relied upon the growing state of misery, which they attributed to the
rebellion, to force the rebels and their supporters into submission.[110]

AT THE SAME TIME that the French bombarded the Ghuta and moved on
Suwaydaʾ, Henry de Jouvenel decided to piece together a native ministry,
after nearly three months of direct French rule under Pierre Alype's provisional government. His choice to form a cabinet was not a Damascene
but an outsider, a tall, strikingly handsome and well-mannered 46-year-
old Circassian aristocrat of Beirut, the Damad Ahmad Nami. He was the
grandson of an *aide de camp* of Ibrahim Pasha, who had settled in Beirut
after the Egyptian withdrawal from Syria in 1840. His father had been
President of the Beirut Municipality. Ahmad Nami also happened to be
the son-in-law of Sultan Abdülhamid (thus the title *Damad* which he
chose to retain after his divorce). He was a wealthy landlord educated at
the military college in Istanbul and in Paris, where he had become a Freemason. Although in French and local aristocratic circles his reputation
reached far and wide, he was not especially popular with the Damascus
notability. Only the French seem to have shown any political interest in
him. As early as 1921, General Gouraud reported to the Quai d'Orsay
that the Damad had been an active partisan of the French throughout
their struggle with Faysal, despite his opposition to the idea of a separate
Lebanon. He headed a group of Beirut notables linked by their Masonic
ties to *le Grand Orient de France* and by their interest in achieving Syrian
unity under French patronage. According to Gouraud, the Damad also
nurtured at this time the hope of becoming the sovereign of a united Syrian principality.[111]

Ahmad Nami's first act on being appointed Prime Minister on April 27
was to publish in the local press the text of an agreement with the High

---

vol. 11506. Vaughan-Russell to Chamberlain, 15 May 1926; FO 371/3878, vol. 11507.
Vaughan-Russell to Chamberlain, 7 June 1926.

[110] MD, 7N 4186. "Historique de la Mission de M. Henry de Jouvenel"; FO 371/3758,
vol. 11507. Damascus Consul to FO, 9 June 1926.

[111] MAE, Syrie–Liban 1918–29. "Gouraud Telegram," 6 Oct. 1921, vol. 37, pp. 102–3;
FO 371/2032, vol. 11516. Vaughan-Russell to Chamberlain, 27 April 1926; Rabbath,
Courte Histoire, pp. 30–31; The Damad's grandfather, Amir Mahmud, had emigrated to
Egypt after the Russians conquered the Caucasus and was on the first cultural mission sent
by Muhammad ʿAli to France in 1826. Later, he was governor of the Sanjak of Tripoli
whose capital was Beirut. The Damad's father, Ibrahim Fakhri, held a number of high posts,
including the governorship of Nablus in 1885. See MAE, Gabriel Puaux Papers, Carton 33,
Dossier S-8, 1926 Note.

Commissioner which called for the conclusion of a 30-year Franco-Syrian treaty and the right for Syrians to vote for their own constitution. It conveniently avoided the thorny question of Syrian unity.[112] The declaration allowed him to form a cabinet which, surprisingly, included three declared nationalists, all members of the outlawed People's Party: Faris al-Khuri (Education), Lutfi al-Haffar (Public Works), and Husni al-Barazi (Interior), a 33-year-old Istanbul-educated lawyer from one of the great landed families of Hama, and a member of the nationalist Orontes Masonic lodge, which had played such an active role in the Hama uprising of October. The new cabinet was the most balanced one yet, and it immediately generated optimism in some political circles. Its formation, however, came just a few days before the savage French assault on the Maydan.[113]

With the Maydan still smouldering from the previous week's shelling, on May 15 Ahmad Nami issued a ten-point program, an embellished version of his April declaration. It repeated the call for a constitution and a 30-year treaty, and now demanded Syrian unity, a unified judicial system, a national army, the gradual evacuation of French troops, membership in the League of Nations, the reform of the Syrian monetary system, a general amnesty, and a no-fault clause for Damascus.[114] It was a remarkable document, given the political and military situation in May, but its implementation hinged on Jouvenel's ability to get his government's approval.

What actually transpired in the 30 days after the Damad published his program is not entirely clear. The three nationalist ministers had joined his government with certain reservations. Although Jouvenel publicly announced his approval of the program, no important reforms were forthcoming. It appears likely that Khuri and Haffar (though not necessarily Barazi, who remained an unknown political quantity, despite his nationalistic pronouncements) had joined the government on the basis of the deteriorating military situation in the Ghuta and elsewhere. Khuri, with his links to the minorities, and Haffar, with his intimate connections to the inner city and its commercial classes, occupied realistic vantage points from which to gauge the overall situation in the country. During the preceding two months, both had become convinced that if the revolt continued it was likely to lead to a humiliating defeat for the rebels and

[112] Rabbath, *Courte Histoire*, pp. 31–32.
[113] FO 371/3038, vol. 11516. Vaughan-Russell to Chamberlain, 6 May 1926; FO 226/ 233/31. Spears to Eden, 28 April 1942; Faris, *Man huwa 1949*, p. 58. Barazi was the son of Sulayman Agha al-Barazi. His family were Arabized Kurds. Conversation with Yusuf al-Hakim (Damascus, 21 Feb. 1976). Sha'bani was a long-time friend of the Damad from their days together in Istanbul. *Oriente Moderno*, 6 (1926), p. 283.
[114] Rabbath, *Courte Histoire*, pp. 32–33.

ultimately to disaster for the independence movement. As thousands of French reinforcements poured into Syria, the two ministers felt a pressing need to cut nationalist losses if the terms of a settlement and the future of Syria could be assured. Moreover, their agreement to join the Nami government had the backing of other nationalist leaders.

Jouvenel found Ahmad Nami's program quite acceptable on paper (even the issue of Syrian unity was worded to remain vague, which allowed him to grant "Greater Lebanon" a constitution on May 24) because it was first and foremost designed to remove the *raison d'être* of the Syrian insurrectionists. But Paris reacted negatively. Paris found Jouvenel's approach too conciliatory at a time when the military balance in Syria had clearly begun to shift in France's favor. Meanwhile, the internal political situation in Syria had failed to advance, causing relations between the new government in Damascus and Jouvenel to sour. The nationalists were angry with the new Lebanese Constitution, which had a French imprimatur, and which, by reaffirming the annexations, left no room for debate or reinterpretation.[115]

To confuse matters, the French military command, which had never been pleased with the appointment of a civilian as High Commissioner, especially one of such a liberal persuasion, declared in early June that the Ghuta was a "war zone." Neither the Damascus government nor, it seems, Jouvenel himself, was consulted.[116] Although discouraged, Jouvenel had no choice but to support the military's declaration. After all, a rebellion was still raging, one whose impact on French political life had already been significant. His predecessor, Sarrail, had found himself at the center of a painful controversy between Right and Left, and although it had died down significantly after April, it could be reopened at any moment, something Jouvenel, a long-time member of the fourth estate, purposely wanted to avoid.[117]

There were still other factors prodding Jouvenel to support the military in Syria. One was that ʿAbd al-Krim's rebel forces in Morocco had suffered an irreversible set-back which now put additional pressure on the High Commission to put the Syrian revolt on the same course. Another was the Permanent Mandates Commission's final report on Syria, which was full of praise for France's role as a mandatory power. At an earlier

---

[115] MacCallum, *Crusade*, pp. 190–92.

[116] Rabbath, *Courte Histoire*, p. 35.

[117] By the late spring of 1926, Syria had nearly ceased to be a topic of debate in the French Parliament or a subject for newspaper articles apart from an occasional notice in the press reporting some successful military action against the rebels. Jouvenel was not a great cause for commotion or conflict. Unlike his predecessor, Sarrail, he was neither a sworn enemy of the Right nor the idol of the Socialists, neither a Freemason nor an anti-clericalist. FO 371/5013, vol. 11516. Crewe (Paris) to Chamberlain, 27 Aug. 1926.

session in Rome, the Commission had criticized France, occasionally in undiplomatic language, for her harsh policy. The French representative, Robert de Caix, an old Syrian hand, had been put on the defensive by a barrage of provocative questions. He had denied, to the disbelief of most Commission members, any French responsibility for the events in Syria, blaming instead a small group of fanatics and other nationalists, notably the Syrian–Palestine Congress in Cairo, which he intimated was in the pay of certain foreign powers. In part, the PMC's dressing down of the Quai d'Orsay was attributable to a successful Syrian campaign supported by a flood of petitions from Syrian solidarity committees all over the world, and detailed reports, sometimes from high Syrian functionaries. But the June report clearly whitewashed French policy, providing Jouvenel—a great believer in the importance of the League as an international political barometer—considerable relief.[118] The French military command, whose image at home and abroad had been tarnished by the PMC's earlier criticisms, was now free to pursue even more savage reprisals in Syria.

Jouvenel's last move was to get his client, Ahmad Nami, to draft a declaration to the rebels which called on them to disarm and to have confidence in the fairness of the Mandate authorities. Implicit in the declaration, however, was the acceptance of sole responsibility for the continuation of hostilities by the nationalists. It was Ahmad Nami's duty to get his cabinet to sign the declaration, which the three nationalist ministers categorically refused to do. On the same day (June 11) that all this transpired, Khuri, Haffar, and Barazi were arrested on charges of having close connections with rebel forces and the Syrian–Palestine Congress in Cairo. They soon joined many of their nationalist colleagues in the jails of Hassaja in the remote Euphrates region.[119]

In the wake of the arrests, Ahmad Nami formed a new cabinet of moderates from Damascus and Aleppo.[120] The dissolution of the more radical cabinet was a clear indication that the French were determined "to ride roughshod over the country" and to gain a complete surrender at any price. With no nationalist in the cabinet to defend the rights and aspirations of the insurgents, the French Army could go about its business of extinguishing the revolt, studiously ignoring the existence of any na-

[118] PMC, *Minutes*, Eighth and Ninth Sessions, 1926; Rabbath, *Courte Histoire*, pp. 36–38.

[119] Rabbath, *Courte Histoire*, p. 35; FO 371/4080, vol. 11507. Air Minister to FO, 17 June 1926. MAE, Syrie–Liban 1918–29. Jouvenel to Premier, 29 June 1926, vol. 199, pp. 66–68.

[120] Faris, *Man huwa 1949*, pp. 305–6; FO 371/3150, vol. 11516. Damascus Consul to FO, 14 June 1926.

tional and patriotic feelings among the rebels—feelings that had intensified over the past several months.[121]

By mid-June, French artillery had resumed shelling the Ghuta and military operations were stepped up in the Jabal Druze and southern Lebanon. Toward the end of the month, Jouvenel, who was in Paris for consultations, requested the sanction of his government to crack down on the rebellion, "to remove this thorn in the side of France." He called for more arms and ammunition to stamp it out, a request which he knew had already been fulfilled.[122]

THE LAST OFFENSIVE

On July 18, after considerable preparation, the French launched their biggest and, as it turned out, their last real offensive in the Ghuta. The sweeping operations of four columns composed of 5,000 troops, supported by tanks, armored cars, field artillery, and airplanes, encountered some resistance and the number of rebels actually swelled, owing to the severity of French repression. But, in the process, the French inflicted heavy casualties; an estimate of the number killed in the three days of heaviest fighting was 1,500, of which 400 were reportedly rebels. The French claimed to have lost 49 men and an additional 98 wounded, although more reliable estimates put the figure at 200 French troops killed. The Ghuta drive continued for another six days, during which the French adopted another tactic: the blocking of water channels that irrigated a large part of the garden system around Damascus in an effort to force the rebels into submission. By now, the French regarded all residents of the Ghuta as guerillas.[123]

The intensive bombardment and clearing operations of late July gravely demoralized the nationalists. The sack of the Ghuta deprived them of their source of supply. Many of the rebel rank and file threw away their arms and ran for their lives, some back to Damascus with the new wave of refugees from the war-devastated zones. Some well-found rumors that rebel leaders were at long last willing to come to the peace table circulated in Damascus and abroad. But the French military command, relishing its victory and intransigent in its belief that the rebels were nothing more than professional brigands, would settle for nothing less than unconditional surrender.[124]

[121] FO 371/3150, vol. 11516. Damascus Consul to FO, 14 June 1926.

[122] MAE, Syrie–Liban 1918–29. Jouvenel to Premier, 29 June 1926, vol. 199, pp. 70–73.

[123] FO 371/4684, vol. 11507. Air Minister to FO, 22 July 1926; FO 371/4743, vol. 11507. Vaughan-Russell to Chamberlain, 2 Aug. 1926; MacCallum, Crusade, pp. 155–75.

[124] FO 371/5167, vol. 11507. Hole to Damascus, 19 Aug. 1926; FO 371/ 5188, vol. 11507. Hole to Damascus, 26 Aug. 1926.

While the Ghuta campaign was in progress, Jouvenel made several public statements from Paris that suggested a peace settlement was close at hand. In private, he had informed a Palestinian notable visiting Paris at the beginning of July that his government was willing to agree to reasonable terms for Syria. This encouraged a prominent delegation from the Syrian–Palestine Congress to journey to Paris for discussions in early August. But, after several days, negotiations collapsed.[125] The government of M. Poincaré, which had taken office on July 24 in the midst of a severe economic and political crisis surrounding the French franc, was not prepared to make the compromises Jouvenel had in mind. The government of National Union was a clear break with the Cartel des Gauches of Messrs. Herriot and Painlevé. Unlike his predecessors, Poincaré had the confidence and support of the big bourgeoisie and middle classes in France and particularly of the nation's biggest financial interests, as he set out to stabilize the franc.[126] The rapid progress Poincaré made in this direction, coupled with the optimistic news from the Rif and Damascus, encouraged him to press for a military victory in Syria before dealing with the nationalists.

Jouvenel vocally disagreed with this strategy and resigned as High Commissioner. He believed that the successful July offensive in the Ghuta was sufficient to effect a lasting peace. His departure ended a short career which had been fertile in promise but barren in reality. In the six months he served in the Levant, he never really came to grips with the crux of the political problem in Syria, which lay in Damascus, a town in which he always felt uncomfortable. His rather clumsy attempt to split nationalist ranks, by isolating the Druze rebel leadership from the Damascus rebel leadership and by isolating Aleppo, revealed his lack of comprehension that the Syrian revolt was steered by nationalists who, despite their want of a diplomatic presence and a precise program, were committed to the idea of Syrian unity. He had tried to approach the complex problem of Damascus by giving support to the Damad's program, but he neither had the force nor the will to implement it. The Quai d'Orsay, under pressure from French alarmists on the Right, who conveniently resurrected the name of Maurice Sarrail, judged Jouvenel's attempts to bring about a settlement as too compromising. In the end, Jouvenel had been caught between Paris intrigues and his own unwillingness to effect long-term compromises with Syrian nationalists.[127]

[125] E. Jung. L'Islam et l'Asie devant l'impérialisme (Paris, 1927), pp. 85–87; Rabbath, Courte Histoire, pp. 42–43.

[126] Kemp, French Economy, pp. 79–82.

[127] Despite his efforts to split nationalist ranks, Jouvenel proposed at least twice (on 21 Dec. 1925 and 10 Jan. 1926) the idea of France concluding treaties with Syria and Lebanon.

NOWHERE IN SYRIA did the revolt suddenly come to an end. Despite French efforts to convey the impression that all was over and that calm had been completely restored,[128] disturbances continued near Aleppo, in the Hama–Homs region, in and around Damascus, in the Hawran and the Jabal Druze, and on the western slopes of Mount Hermon. At a nationalist conference held in late August at al-Azraq on the Transjordan frontier, Damascene and Druze rebel leaders renewed their pledges of the previous August to prosecute the revolt until victory. Inspired by Dr. Shahbandar and Sultan al-Atrash, rebel bands commanded by Fawzi al-Qawuqji, Shaykh Muhammad al-Ashmar, and Saʿid ʿAkkash, reappeared in the Ghuta and even briefly penetrated Damascus in late August.[129]

But, although rebel chiefs still displayed a degree of internal cohesion, by September a lack of funds and ammunition hindered further efforts to weld several rebel bands into a coherent fighting force. Rebel tactics had to be reformulated. Their strategy now concentrated on maintaining a constant level of tension throughout Syria which, though more annoying than actually threatening to the French military, still required the French to spend large sums of money on an army of irregulars or mercenaries. The hope was that the Paris government would eventually be forced to seek a negotiated peace on terms more favorable to the nationalists.[130]

By the end of November 1926, hostilities had been almost suspended and the revolt teetered on collapse. The French military command in Syria had at their disposal 50,000 troops, some of whom were fresh from victory in Morocco; this was nearly four times the number when the revolt began 16 months earlier.[131] The French, however, had to wait until the long winter months had passed before undertaking their final mopping-up campaign.

Only two regions still sustained rebel activity in the spring of 1927: Hama, where Fawzi al-Qawuqji in command of a rebel force of 200 men continued to carry on guerilla warfare, and the Jabal Druze and al-Laja, a treacherous 400 square miles of rocky terrain on the edge of the Jabal

---

MD, 7N 4186, Dossier 8. "Historique de la Mission de M. Henry de Jouvenel"; *ibid.*, 7N 4171. 2ᵉ Bureau, Section de Renseignements, 7 Jan. 1926.

[128] FO 371/5317, vol. 11507. Hole to Chamberlain, 3 Sept. 1926.

[129] FO 371/5188, vol. 11507. Hole to Chamberlain, 26 Aug. 1926; *ibid.*, 5509, vol. 11508. Hole to Chamberlain, 15 Sept. 1926. French military authorities tried to get Qawuqji to negotiate on August 31, but he refused, claiming that negotiations could be discussed only with Shahbandar and Sultan al-Atrash. See FO 371/5110, vol. 11507. Hole to Chamberlain, 2 Sept. 1926.

[130] FO 371/5317, vol. 11507. Hole to Chamberlain, 3 Sept. 1926.

[131] In June 1925, France had 14,000 troops stationed in Syria and Lebanon.

which had served from time immemorial as a refuge for rebels and bandits alike.[132]

On April 22, French troops invaded Hama in search of Qawuqji, who was reported to be hiding in the residential quarter of the town's fiercely anti-French landowning class. When the rebel chief could not be found, the French shelled the quarter, in yet another bid to intimidate the landowners into halting their assistance to rebel forces. By the end of the month, the French had dispersed Qawuqji's band and forced its leader to seek refuge in Iraq.[133]

For Druze rebels, al-Azraq in Transjordan had become the major depot and base for their operations against the French. A refugee camp had been built there and was beginning to assume an air of permanence. A flour mill had been constructed and Druze laborers were engaged in a recently developed salt-panning industry, which began to yield profits. It was near al-Azraq that Sultan al-Atrash had his headquarters. The French accused the British of facilitating the revolt by allowing Transjordan to become a base for guerilla actions against the Mandate and they accused 'Abdullah of not preventing tribes from 'Ajlun and other border areas from participating in the Syrian revolt and harboring rebels.[134]

Actually, British authorities in Amman and elsewhere conducted a widespread surveillance of Syrian nationalist leaders and their activities, though not from the revolt's inception. Finally, in April 1927, after threatening for some time to eject Sultan al-Atrash from Transjordan, British troops raided the Druze leader's camp, forcing him to move his headquarters across the frontier into Syria. This led to a brief crescendo in rebel operations in the Jabal Druze and the Ghuta. However, by June, with most of the important Druze rebel leaders having already surrendered to the French authorities, Sultan Pasha and several hundred of his armed fighters had to take refuge once again in Transjordan and, in the Druze chieftain's case, eventually further south in Arabia.[135] After two long years, the French had finally extinguished the Great Syrian Revolt.

[132] FO 371/2111, vol. 12303. Hole to Chamberlain, 27 April 1927; MacCallum, *Crusade*, pp. 170–72. Al-Laja had been bombarded in October 1926 by French airplanes and for ten consecutive days in March 1927, which finally drove the rebels out of their hiding places.

[133] *Ibid.*; al-Jundi, *Tarikh*, p. 553.

[134] FO 371/556, vol. 12302. Colonial Office to FO, 1 Feb. 1927; FO 371/569, vol. 12302. Report of E. R. Stratford (second in command of Transjordan police), 10 Jan. 1927.

[135] FO 371/2111, vol. 12303, 27 April 1927.

CHAPTER EIGHT

CLASS AND NATIONALISM

THE GREAT REVOLT was a popular and widespread anti-imperialist uprising with a pronounced nationalist orientation. It was popular insofar as
its active participants were drawn from nearly all walks of life in Syria—
from the urban absentee landowning class, the commercial bourgeoisie
and traditional artisanal classes in the towns, the middle class intelligentsia including Western-educated professionals, and members of the Muslim religious establishment, the peasantry, and even some Bedouin
tribes.[1] In territorial terms, although the revolt erupted in the remote Jabal Druze, it quickly spread, engulfing the Hawran, the region between
Damascus and Aleppo, and even southern Lebanon. The revolt had the
moral and material support of the Syrian people in the interior, particularly in the large towns and their immediate surroundings where French
rule was so deeply felt. As for the revolt's anti-imperialist character, from
its inception it focused on the French presence in Syria, which, by its very
existence, deflected the class, religious, and urban–rural conflicts at the
heart of Syrian society.

Yet, despite the undoubted popular, anti-imperialist, and nationalist
character of the Great Revolt, there were certain classes and communities
which either did not join the revolt or sided with the French. For example,
the revolt did not involve the Alawite territory, which remained well in-

---

[1] Considerable evidence can be marshalled to illustrate multi-class and multi-strata participation in the Great Revolt. The best sources are the uncatalogued Criminal Court Registers for the period, which are housed at the Center for Historical Documentation (MWT)
in Damascus. These registers list the date of charge, arrest (when it took place), place of
residence of the accused, profession, etc. Among those nationalist leaders and prominent
men in society charged (but not necessarily apprehended, brought to trial, etc.) with political subversion, murder, theft, treason, etc., were Nasib al-Bakri, Hasan al-Kharrat, 'Adil
Arslan, Sami al-Bakri, Mazhar al-Bakri, Sultan al-Atrash, Yahya al-Hayati, Jamil Mardam,
Rushdi al-Bakri, 'Abd al-Qadir Sukkar, Fakhri al-Barudi, Fawzi al-Bakri, Nazih al-
Mu'ayyad, Fawzi al-Qawuqji, Mustafa al-'Azm, Sa'id Haydar, Hasan al-Hakim, Shukri al-
Quwwatli, 'Umar 'Abdu Dib al-Shaykh, 'Abd al-Rahman Shahbandar, Fawzi al-Ghazzi,
Faris al-Khuri, Ihsan al-Sharif, Shaykh Kamil al-Qassab, Najib Rayyis, Husni al-Barazi,
and Lutfi al-Haffar. MWT, *Registre des plaintes I*, 1925–1926; *ibid.*, Cour de Justice, *Juge
d'instruction* (Jan. 1926–Jan. 1927). Also see al-Safarjalani, *Tarikh al-thawra*, pp. 556–640;
Hasan al-Hakim, *Mudhakkirati*, vol. 1, pp. 400–402; MWT, *al-Qism al-khass*, Nazih
Mu'ayyad al-'Azm Papers, no. 147, Cairo, 1926; MAE, Syrie–Liban 1918–29, vol. 210, p.
270; FO 371/2933, vol. 11509. Vaughan-Russell to Chamberlain, 1 April 1926.

sulated under French protection, or the Sanjak of Alexandretta, with its vocal Turkish minority. Certain ethnic minorities actually cooperated with the French in suppressing the revolt. The Circassians, with their strong tradition of military service developed in late Ottoman times, were easily recruited into the Syrian Legion.[2] Armenian refugees recently arrived from Turkey were also enlisted. Much disliked in the towns where they competed with local artisans and other workers for jobs in a depressed economy, the Armenians were dependent on French protection and became a client community of the state. Even some tribes, such as the Rwala of southern Syria which nursed an old enmity with the Druzes, cooperated with the French Army in a few operations in the Jabal Druze. But cash inducements were the tribe's main incentive and French officials expressed grave concern that some tribes might revolt if their chiefs were not granted cash subsidies to ensure their quiescence.[3]

Two other groups, the non-nationalist wing of the absentee landowning-bureaucratic class and the Syrian Christian minorities, stood aloof from the revolt. But, if they did not go out of their way to assist the nationalists neither did they throw their considerable weight behind the French. The Syrian Christian minorities in the towns adopted a wait-and-see attitude in an effort to prevent the revolt from spreading to their quarters. Some prominent city-based landowners preferred to perform the traditional function of serving as intermediaries between local society and the state. Often, they tried to negotiate a settlement favorable to rebel forces, especially after the tide of the revolt began to shift in the spring of 1926.[4] The timing of their activity, however, made their motives suspect. It betrayed an increasingly familiar pattern of urban notable behavior: whenever nationalist forces showed signs of weakness, one faction or another of conservative notables tried to capitalize on the situation by putting itself forward to the High Commission as the most reasonable candidate to form a new government.

---

[2] MAE, Syrie–Liban 1918–29. Capitaine Collet, "Note sur les Tcherkess," vol. 237, pp. 137–38.

[3] A. de Boucheman, "Les Bédouins en Syrie," CHEAM, no. 126 (23 April 1937), p. 7; MAE, Syrie–Liban 1918–29. Reffye to Prime Minister, 11 Aug. 1926, vol. 199, p. 174. The French became quite concerned about the ability of the People's Party to excite Bedouin tribes to revolt, especially during the late winter of 1926 as spring approached and transhumant movements were about to be resumed. Reffye had asked at the time for a special grant from the French government of 800,000 francs (£S 40,000) to be paid to a certain number of tribal chiefs during the spring to ensure the quiescence of their tribes. MAE, Syrie–Liban 1918–29. 10 Feb.–31 March 1926, vol. 197, pp. 4–5.

[4] Among these landowners and bureaucrats were Rushdi al-Safadi, 'Ata al-Ayyubi, Shamsi al-Malki, Ahmad al-Hasibi, 'Umar Agha Shamdin, Anwar al-Bakri, Iklil al-Mu'ayyad, 'Umar al-'Abid, and Sa'id al-Jaza'iri. See *Oriente Moderno*, 6 (1926), p. 436.

THREE CLASSES WERE especially instrumental in keeping the revolt alive
after it spread across Syria in the autumn of 1925: the Muslim commercial bourgeoisie, the absentee landowning class, and the peasantry. The
role played by each in the revolt was varied and rarely entirely consistent,
owing to divisions within each class. The causes of these divisions were
sometimes simple, a matter of geography for example, and sometimes
complex. Above all, it was still difficult to draw sharp lines of political division between the owners of agricultural land and real estate, merchants,
manufacturers, and even bankers and moneylenders, because their interests remained interwoven by family ties and because the same individuals
or family often filled slots in different branches of the economy.

MERCHANTS

In the towns, the commercial bourgeoisie formed two wings. One comprised the comprador bourgeoisie, those merchant-moneylenders who in
the course of the nineteenth century emerged as local agents of European
trading houses. The European economic impact on Syria contributed to
the rise of a new class which served first as an intermediary for the fun-
neling of European manufactured goods into the country and eventually
as a major conduit in the absorption of the Syrian economy into Europe's.
The religious minorities, mostly Christians and a sprinkling of Jews with
whom the Europeans felt most comfortable, were preponderant in the
comprador bourgeoisie. The religious protection that Christians sought
and received from the European powers and the education afforded them
by missionaries specially prepared them to serve as agents of European
commercial and political interests.

By the mid-nineteenth century, Muslim merchants, artisans, and
peasants increasingly identified local Christians with hostile and damaging European interests. Not only were Christian merchants more easily
able to purchase Syrian raw materials with cash advances from European
traders, they facilitated the flow of European manufactures into the Syrian market which brought about the destruction of many local handicrafts. The 1860 massacre of Christians in Damascus was in part a product
of deep Muslim resentment toward the growth in power and economic
influence of this class, with its strong European connection.

The incidents of 1860 ushered in a new era of security for Syria's religious minorities, owing largely to increased European pressures on the
Ottoman state to guarantee their protection. Local Christian merchants
in Damascus and Aleppo, many with European consular protection, established themselves as the local bankers for Muslim merchants and a
rapidly emerging group of absentee landowners. However, the political

and administrative chaos Syria faced during and after World War I created grave economic difficulties for all but a handful of ruthless profiteers
in Syria. A significant proportion, though by no means all, of the comprador bourgeoisie suffered heavy losses as trade with Europe dried up
during the war and landowners and peasants frequently defaulted on
loans from merchants. Consequently, the French occupation was greeted
with a deep sense of relief. For the compradors, it brought greater hope of
political stability and economic and physical security. Only one other
group in Syrian society felt a similar sense of relief: the ex-Ottoman
functionaries who had suffered a significant loss of influence at the hands
of Amir Faysal and his nationalist supporters after the war.

The French occupation enabled the comprador class to renew and refor-
tify its mediating role between French commercial interests and the Syrian economy. It had little reason to support the Great Revolt which jeopardized its material interests. Indeed, with trade disrupted and so much
capital lent out to landlords, small industrialists, and peasants, it longed
for a quick and decisive French victory, which would introduce a period of
welcome stability. However, despite the threat to its economic interests,
the comprador class adopted a neutral pose because of its large minority
component. It maintained a certain distance from its French patron in order to avoid creating grounds for a violent anti-Christian backlash from
the local Muslim population. Memories of the 1860 massacres remained
vivid.[5]

The second major component of the Syrian commercial bourgeoisie included Muslim merchants with strong ties to the absentee landowning
class and who, like the landowners, had little or no access to foreign capital. In late Ottoman times, this group could roughly be broken down into
two overlapping segments. The first included the local distributors and
exporters of indigenous manufactures such as soap, textiles, and leather
goods to the neighboring provinces of the Empire. These merchants,
whether commission agents or manufacturers, had survived the economic upheaval of the nineteenth century by continuing to find markets
for their comparatively low-quality goods in traditional sectors of the
Syrian and Anatolian market. The other segment included merchants
who specialized mainly in the domestic and regional trade of cash crops
such as wheat and fruits, and in livestock. Many engaged in moneylending and some were also involved in the re-export of European goods to
neighboring areas of the Empire. Both segments were intimately connected with the urban absentee landowning class through financial deal-

    [5] See Mohammad Saʿid Kalla, "The Role of Foreign Trade in the Economic Development
of Syria, 1831–1914," Ph.D. Dissertation (American University, Washington, D.C., 1969),
p. 122; al-Nayal, "Industry," pp. 36–38.

ings, such as the provision of loans and seed, the marketing and processing of crops, and increasingly through marriage. In fact, many grain and
livestock merchants eventually acquired lands outright through the manipulation of usurious capital in wheat and fruit producing regions such
as the Hawran and the Ghuta.

As the nineteenth century unfolded, the Muslim commercial
bourgeoisie and the absentee landowning class grew more financially interdependent, particularly after the establishment of private landownership rights and the formation of large estates in the second half of the century. But, despite the ongoing process of financial interpenetration, both
classes by the turn of the century could still be distinguished from one
another. Social differentiation was less a matter of material wealth than
it was of profession and social prestige, of education, culture, and politics.
While absentee landowners sent their sons to Istanbul for an Ottoman
professional education in preparation for high administrative posts in the
Empire, rich Muslim merchants continued to give their sons a basic Islamic education and then practical training in their business houses. This
was especially true of the big grain and livestock merchants of Damascus.
Whereas the sons of landowners filled bureaucratic positions and dominated local and regional political life, the sons of the commercial
bourgeoisie had neither the proper education and skills nor the time to
combine business and upper level politics beyond seats on local Municipal
Councils.

Despite the social and political gulf between Muslim landowners and
merchants, economic links eventually evolved into a growing political interdependence in the early twentieth century. The nationalist wing of the
landowning-bureaucratic class took shape on the eve of the First World
War, in response to the intensification of Young Turk centralization and
Turkification policies, and because qualified elements from this class were
increasingly unable to compete for places in the Ottoman administrative
structure. Similarly, Muslim merchants in the Syrian towns displayed
growing resentment at these same policies, and at others, such as Turkish
economic compromises with the European powers. Suddenly, merchants
were obliged to listen to commercial court proceedings in Turkish, to deal
with government functionaries in Turkish, and even to make their sons
study the language in school. Meanwhile, European interests continued
to expand and deepen in Syria, strengthening the grip of the minority-
dominated comprador class at the expense of the Muslim mercantile
groups. It was at this time that prominent Muslim merchants began to
identify their political interests with those of the emerging Arab nationalist movement.

The events which followed the Allied victory gave this identification
added strength. The carving up of the Ottoman Empire's eastern prov-

inces along artificial and often arbitrary lines severely eroded the position of the Muslim commercial bourgeoisie as distributors of goods to neighboring regions, notably to Palestine, Iraq, and Turkey. The opposition of Muslim merchants to the new geopolitical formations grew, as traditional trade patterns and markets disappeared and local industries collapsed. For many merchants and artisans, the standard of living declined. When the French introduced a new paper currency tied to the unstable French franc and new banking regulations which placed tight restrictions on credits for the development of new enterprises, tensions blossomed into open conflict. Merchants and landowners were forced into a greater dependence on native banks which, though more lax in matters of debt repayment, charged much higher interest rates and did not possess the capital resources to extend credit on a large enough scale to finance, for example, industrial development. Meanwhile, Mandate customs policy clearly favored French and other European imports at the expense of local manufacturing. This not only strengthened European economic control in Syria but it also buttressed the comprador class, with its strong links to European trading houses, while Muslim merchants struggled to hold on in increasingly adverse circumstances.

The Muslim segment of the commercial bourgeoisie had few reservations about adopting an anti-imperialist stance. And, with the idea of Arab nationalism in the ascendance, merchants found a ready-made ideological weapon at their disposal. Although the commercial bourgeoisie had yet to encounter threatening class pressures from below in the form of independent workers' or peasant organizations, the ideology of nationalism created a cushion should such pressures one day materialize. On the one hand, it provided the Muslim bourgeoisie, which had suffered severe losses of economic and political power at the hands of France and her local allies, with a vehicle to regain its influence. On the other, the nationalist movement could be used to divert the attention of workers and peasants from their daily conflicts and struggles with the commercial bourgeoisie and landowning classes.[6]

Thus, the Muslim segment of the commercial bourgeoisie, as it grew more intertwined with the landowning class, saw a real need and a good opportunity to contribute its support to the nationalist movement. But, big city merchants played mainly support roles and only occasionally filled leadership slots, because of the nature of their base and because the landowning class, in collaboration with a rapidly increasing number of middle-class professionals, monopolized the leadership of the Syrian nationalist movement.

    [6] Conversations with Hani al-Hindi (Beirut, 28 Aug. 1975) and Zafir al-Qasimi (Beirut, 24 July 1975); al-Nayyal, "Industry," pp. 36–38; Hourani, *Syria and Lebanon*, p. 92.

When the Syrian revolt erupted in July 1925, the big grain and live-stock merchants in the Maydan and Shaghur quarters were the first to come out fully in support of it. Even though revolt threatened to jeopardize the wheat harvest in the Hawran which these merchants had financed and which was already expected to be meager owing to the long summer drought, once the People's Party linked up with the Druze rebels and the revolt spread into the Damascus region, grain merchants realized that the harvest and consequently their investment were irredeemable. Furthermore, the early victories scored by the rebels generated much optimism in Damascus and elsewhere; it was hoped that the French, after realizing that the uprising was not a passing phenomenon, would pack up and go home. Since French policies, particularly in the area of taxation and tariffs, were clearly inimical to the interests of the predominantly Muslim commercial bourgeoisie, any effort to help speed up a French evacuation was deemed patriotic.[7] The wealthy grain merchants of Damascus not only contributed money, arms, and men to the revolt, but they also formed their own bands, which fought in Damascus and in the gardens around it.

Further inside Damascus, the affluent shopowners and provisions merchants of the great bazaars—al-Hamidiyya, al-Bzuriyya, and Midhat Pasha—shut their doors in opposition to the French as rebel bands neared Damascus; however, they were hesitant to participate actively for fear of French reprisals. But, once rebel bands penetrated the old city and the French responded by launching a very destructive artillery and aerial bombardment of the bazaars, shopowners, big merchants, and artisans actively supported the revolt. Two weeks earlier in Hama the same phe-

[7] Grain merchants and other provisions merchants perceived French fiscal policy as greatly detrimental to their commercial and financial interests. For instance, when the French decided to increase customs duties from 11 to 15 percent *ad valorem* as of 1 May 1924 for member states of the League of Nations plus the United States, and from 11 to 30 percent for the general tariff, certain exceptions to the general increase were granted. There was no augmentation of the duty on livestock, cereals, flour, rice, coffee, sugar, preserves, butter, milk, cheese, mineral waters, timber, and chemical fertilizers. The French were obviously interested in avoiding another rise in the cost of living which at the time was abnormally high, particularly as the franc's value was plummeting. However, these increases did not help to protect big grain and livestock merchants who happened soon thereafter to contribute heavily to the revolt. See FO 371/1421, vol. 10164. Beirut Consulate to Department of Overseas Trade, 28 April 1924; FO 371/4031, vol. 10164; FO 371/4312, vol. 10164. But this increase and the one which followed in 1926, which raised the average customs duty on imports to Syria from 15 to 25 percent *ad valorem* for League members, also did not stimulate the production of raw materials (because the same exceptions were effected); rather they raised state revenues, which helped to make up the losses caused by the big devaluation and the Great Revolt. MAE, Syrie–Liban 1918–29. Reffye to High Commissioner, 12 Feb. 1927, vol. 341, p. 147.

nomenon had occurred. French military assaults on these two cities only helped to increase the revolt's momentum.[8]

When the French eventually reversed the tide, they began to punish merchants who had actively supported the revolt on an individual basis. Indeed, even before the revolt was finally crushed, the High Commission pressured bankers and moneylenders to use the Mixed Commercial Court in Damascus to exact loan repayments from certain key merchants, most of whom were already short of cash owing to losses suffered during the economic depression which preceded the revolt. The *Registres Commerciaux* of 1926 were full of cases in which the Mixed Court, whose President was a Frenchman, decided in favor of local bankers and European business establishments against Muslim merchants. No moratorium was granted to these debtors; squeezed to repay but unable to, many went bankrupt.[9]

LANDOWNERS

The wing of the absentee landowning class that contributed its support to the Great Revolt did so for several reasons. Members of this class had been involved in the development of the nationalist movement from the very beginning, serving in a leadership capacity. The ideological rift that developed within the landowning-bureaucratic class in the Syrian provinces before and during World War I was originally expressed by Arabism versus Ottomanism. This class was not only the most socially prestigious and politically influential in Syria, its members were also among the most highly educated, politically conscious, and active. Land merely provided a steady source of income with which to further political ambitions. Landowners were rarely involved in the direct supervision of agricultural production, preferring to reside in the city, where they formed a provincial aristocracy of service to the Ottoman state or the political opposition.

With the establishment of an Arab government in Damascus at the end of the war, the Arab nationalist movement expanded to incorporate elements from other classes, notably the professional middle classes and the

[8] MAE, Syrie–Liban 1918–29. "Les négociations qui suivirent le bombardement de Damas," 10 Feb. 1926, vol. 197, pp. 24–34.

[9] See various cases in MWT, *Registre Commercial* (2 June 1926–28 Dec. 1927). In the case of landowners, the French were known to have confiscated their properties for participating in the revolt. The best known case was that of the Bakri properties near Damascus in Jarmana, al-Qabun, and Mazra'at al-'Amadiyyan. MWT, *Dakhiliyya, qadaya wa hawadith*, 26-2747, 10 Oct. 1927. In some districts, peasants seized the property of landowners. *Ibid., al-Intidab*, 4/784-1202, 24 April 1927.

commercial bourgeoisie. Although the former helped to refine nationalist ideology by secularizing it and the latter served as an important link with the popular classes in the towns, members of prominent absentee land-owning families steered the movement. The leadership role of the land-owning class continued after the French occupation and throughout the Mandate. For instance, both the Iron Hand Society of 1922 and the People's Party of 1925 contained a strong landowning component.

Once the French occupied the Syrian interior, they designed a strategy to defeat the nationalist movement. Besides trying to isolate the movement, the French sought to exacerbate tensions between the nationalist and collaborationist wings of the urban absentee landowning class and between city-based and rural landlords. One method was to deny the nationalists access to state institutions and thus to the reins of power. Another was to break the economic hold of the absentee landowning class over the countryside, by instituting reforms inimical to its interests.

A catalyst for the revolt was the refusal of French authorities to adjust land taxes to the prevailing rate of exchange, which weakened the position of landowners. When, in 1925, French advisers to the Finance Ministry in Damascus decided to systematize tax collection, notably of the *dîme* or tithe, they adopted an average of these taxes in the four preceding years, which was payable in Syrian paper notes. While this measure was in theory sound, in its immediate wake came the collapse of the French franc and the consequent decline of the Syrian pound. To protect the Treasury, the High Commission hastily increased the tax by 87.5 percent and allowed it to be paid in gold. The French maintained the increase mainly to punish the great landed families who were customarily regarded as the backbone of native recalcitrance. The result was that the land tax nearly doubled at a time when harvests were very poor, owing to the destructive frost and drought of the spring and summer. This precipitated considerable discontent among big landlords and small cultivators. Even moderate elements in the landlord class turned against the French, in the process contributing their support to the revolt.[10]

All along the French played the countryside against the city, by promoting rural notables and village *mukhtars* against city-based landlords. They had already used this strategy in 1923, during the first Representative Council elections, when rural districts were permitted to select a disproportionate number of electors in the primaries. Many landlords feared that the revolt might encourage peasants, whose misery had become even more acute owing to the late spring frost and long summer drought, to attack and even seize their property. Most alarmed were members of the

---

[10] See FO 371/3071, vol. 12306. Hole to Chamberlain, 13 June 1927.

landlord class who were openly collaborating with the French. Some were ranking functionaries and ran such important government departments as the land registries and bureaux of taxation. They were the notables who used their access to the French and their government offices to circumvent the High Commission's land reform measures, and even to turn the whole process in their favor at the expense of the peasantry. Nationalists among the landowning class were also alarmed by the potential consequences of a widespread rural revolt. Nevertheless, almost from its inception, the revolt engulfed rural areas. Furthermore, once the French demonstrated their unwillingness to compromise, they drove the nationalist leadership out of the towns. The leadership then had little choice but to root their struggle in the countryside. They did so reluctantly but had sufficient authority to prevent armed peasant bands from seizing property indiscriminately. Instead, they directed peasants against the property of local collaborators. This seizure of land provided rebel bands with their major internal source of material and financial support during much of the revolt. Nationalist leaders, however, were unable to guarantee the security of their own property from French reprisals.

Obviously, such attacks led to an even wider gulf between the nationalist wing of the absentee landowning class and the French. But High Commission policies alienated the class as a whole, driving more and more of its members into the nationalist camp. Landowners contributed money, arms, and their personal followings to the Great Revolt not simply because the landowning class had a strong connection with the nationalist movement from its inception, but because the French attacked their material interests while excluding landowners with nationalist leanings from holding high government office. Had the French acted differently, the contribution of landowners to the revolt might not have been so important.[11]

[11] No less an observer of the political situation in Syria in 1926 than M. de Reffye, the architect of the French strategy to suppress the Great Revolt, explained why the landowning class in the country joined it. For members of the absentee landowning class, the French Mandate signalled material ruination, the result of agrarian reforms which were designed to end the exploitation of rich proprietors and the corruption directly practiced at the expense of an impoverished peasantry. Tax farming was supplanted by a cadastral survey which established a more equitable land taxation system. Such reforms protected small proprietors who, unlike the absentee landowning class, could not bribe tax assessors and other government functionaries who were so often in the service of big landowners. Reffye claimed that French control of the judicial system had already begun to eliminate a process by which the wealthy easily bought off judges. The French attack on the material interests of the ruling class prompted it to undertake the revolt. Reffye concluded that the French Mandate "of honest bureaucrats, will result in the election of deputies who, for the first time, do not owe their nominations to their personal fortunes, which will signal the end of their influence over the country's affairs and over appointments to government." MAE, Syrie–Liban 1918–29. "Reffye Note," Jouvenel to P.M., 29 June 1926, vol. 199, p. 58.

Peasants

Rebel bands were led by city-based nationalists and quarter chiefs and included in their rank and file members of the educated elites, merchants, artisans, and casual laborers. The peasantry added numbers to the bands and, more importantly, provided the environment, including cover and day-to-day material support, for rebel bands to carry on outside their original city base.

For peasants, the revolt was an opportunity to express their anger and frustration at various socio-economic, political, and even cultural changes threatening their traditional way of life.[12] Above all, peasants feared and were hostile to French agrarian policies. Some peasants took up arms at the urging of nationalist leaders, many of whom were big absentee landowners in the rebellious districts. There is evidence that landless peasants and sharecroppers joined the revolt on the understanding that if it were successful, the lands of urban and rural notables who collaborated with the French would be confiscated and divided among the actual tillers of the soil.[13] Others joined the revolt after being driven from their homes by punitive expeditions against villages accused of aiding rebel forces. Yet others, facing the difficulty of making ends meet after the unusually meager harvest of 1925, particularly in those districts engulfed by insurrection, joined the bands for the sole purpose of survival.[14] For many young male peasants the chance to join one of the rebel bands operating between Homs and Damascus, in southern Lebanon, or in the Hawran was one of the few real options available to them, particularly since Damascus and other interior towns were also experiencing the same debilitating economic depression and were in no position to offer either material or psychological security to refugees from embattled rural districts. Indeed, in the early stages of the revolt, population flowed mainly out of the big interior towns and into the countryside or to neighboring countries.

Behind these immediate factors pushing peasants toward rebellion lay

[12] On the role of peasants in politics and why some peasants rebel, see E. J. Hobsbawm, "Peasants and Politics," *Journal of Peasant Studies*, 1 (October 1973), pp. 3–22 and Elizabeth J. Perry, *Rebels and Revolutionaries in North China 1845–1945* (Stanford, 1980), Chapter 1.

[13] The French seemed to believe that peasants in the Ghuta and elsewhere joined the rebels for this reason alone. MAE, Syrie–Liban 1918–29. *Bulletin de Service des Renseignements*, no. 18, 28–30 Dec. 1925, vol. 428.

[14] At the end of 1925, the major villages east and south of Damascus in the Ghuta were in the hands of Nasib al-Bakri's band. The villages of Jawbar, 'Agraba, and Jisrin in the east Ghuta were among the biggest suppliers of rebels to the bands. There were also a number of so-called "neutral" villages and a few "pro-French" villages, usually inhabited by Circassians. One was inhabited by Algerians. *Ibid*.

long-term structural changes in the countryside. In the course of the nineteenth century much of the Syrian countryside entered the transitional stage of capitalism as a result of agrarian commercialization. The cumulative impact of European economic penetration, which had increasingly tied Syria to the world market since the Egyptian occupation of the 1830s, encouraged the Ottoman state to expand its presence in the countryside. Towns and a network of regional market centers which grew up as a result of this commercial development gradually came to dominate the countryside. Economic structures in rural areas were transformed as private landownership supplanted traditional agrarian relations and as the world market introduced new patterns of trade and exchange. This fostered the emergence of a class of landowners, a class of small peasant proprietors, and class of landless peasants. These developments had advanced farthest in the irrigated gardens and fields around Damascus, though they had also taken hold in the grain-producing regions of the Hawran and of Homs and Hama. It was in these areas that capitalist relations had penetrated most deeply and that, in 1925, Syrian rebel bands were most active.

One result of these changes was that the relationship of big landlord to peasant was no longer simply one of patron to client, where the landlord provided social services and physical protection to the peasant who, in turn, produced for the landlord and gave him his allegiance. By the end of the nineteenth century, this relationship in many regions of Syria was now motivated by a combination of extra-economic and purely economic factors, and the latter were clearly in the ascendant.

Another development was the increasing differentiation of village society and the breakdown of traditional village loyalties. The growth of a class of small peasant proprietors was most disruptive to rural society. At the head of this class of wealthier peasants generally stood the *mukhtar*. His middling socio-economic status differentiated him, on the one hand, from the majority of small peasant proprietors and sharecroppers in the village and, on the other, from the big landlord. Unlike the landlord, however, who rarely lived in the village, the power and wealth of the *mukhtar* was a constant irritant to his less fortunate neighbors. In many instances, the *mukhtar* and other rich peasants began to identify their interests more closely with those of the big landlord class and the state, often at the encouragement of the latter and often cutting their support system in the village community from below. In time, the *mukhtar's* interests and those of the village majority, which he was elected or appointed to represent, diverged. This was not always the case, but it was observed with great frequency in the villages around Damascus in the early 1920s. Incidents of villagers trying to overthrow their *mukhtars* were reported with greater frequency on the eve of the revolt. Increased polarization within village society meant the appearance of direct economic conflict between rich peasants and poor and landless peasants.[15]

The revolt threatened to upset the unequal balance of power that had been established in many villages. *Mukhtars* and other wealthy peasants, some of whom had first consolidated their landholdings and offices under the French Mandate, saw little or no reason not to supply the French authorities or their Syrian agents with information as to the whereabouts, movements, and size of rebel bands.[16] Clearly not all *mukhtars* cooperated with the authorities—some feared the wrath of rebel forces—but for those who did, French monetary inducements or other benefits made their path all the sweeter.

A NATIONALIST REVOLT?

The assertion that the Great Revolt had a distinctly nationalist character requires some final elaboration. Although the Druze–People's Party connection is now clear, categorically to fasten a nationalist label to the revolt still requires some consideration of the ideological character of nationalism in Syria in the mid-1920s, of its appeal, and of its specific goals. In 1925, nationalism was the exclusive instrument of Syria's urban upper and middle classes. Although the original proponents of nationalist ideology had spent more than a decade engaged in disseminating this ideology in towns through political organizations and activities and through the spoken and written word, the Syrian masses had yet to acquire a strong nationalist political consciousness. Traditional loyalties of the individual to family, clan, quarter, village, or religious community continued to be stronger than new, ascendant loyalties to the nation or state.

What the nationalist elite did accomplish was to channel the growing frustration and discontent of the masses into an anti-imperialist movement. They successfully blamed the French for unemployment, rampant inflation, and the disruption of traditional ways of life. Nationalism provided a handy mechanism by which to express local grievances; it was both internationally *au courant* and politically useful to a class which was excluded from political power by the French. It was presented and largely accepted as a cure-all for all sorts of economic and social ills across a broad spectrum of society.

Nationalist leaders sponsored a brand of nationalism that had a distinctly secular flavor. They conceived of a secular, independent Arab state

[15] On the selection and functions of *mukhtars* in Palestine in the late Ottoman and mandatory periods see Gabriel Baer, "The Office and Functions of the Village Mukhtar," in Joel S. Migdal (ed.), *Palestinian Society and Politics* (Princeton, 1980), pp. 103–23.

[16] See MWT, *al-Thawra al-suriyya*, 43/9830. Husni al-Barazi (Minister of Interior), 17 May 1926.

built on Western institutions and of an Arab nation cemented together by a common history, language, culture, and territory. Nationalists could not ignore, however, the importance and contribution of Islam to the formation of a national ideal. Islam was clearly the fountain of Arab culture and civilization and equally clearly a natural rallying point for a society threatened by Christian Europe.

And so, although nationalist leaders always presented the idea of a unified and independent Syrian-Arab nation to the French and the League of Nations with a proviso for safeguarding the rights of religious and ethnic minorities, this did not mean that they presented the nationalist idea to the Syrian masses in purely secular terms. In fact, the People's Party leadership relied on Islamic invocation and symbolism as instruments of political mobilization. They called upon the popular classes to revolt in the name of the nation, but also in the name of Allah, the Prophet, and religious solidarity. Mosques and *masjids* were still the most important rallying points in towns and villages, and among the most valuable intermediaries between the nationalist movement and the masses were Muslim preachers and scholars. French imperialism, after all, directed a powerful assault on the values, customs, and way of life of the overwhelming majority in Syria, and this elicited an Islamic response.

The Great Revolt, in the final analysis, incorporated secular ideals and appealed to new classes. It also evoked rooted norms and principles and drew upon the forces of tradition. But, above all, it heralded a new age of politics, though one that would take years to mature.

CHAPTER NINE

FACTIONALISM DURING THE
EARLY MANDATE

THE GREAT REVOLT revealed deep divisions within the national movement which would weaken the struggle for independence in Syria over the next two decades. Factionalism reflected both personal and ideological conflicts within the urban upper classes. It had deep roots, although it was not until the tail end of the revolt that it achieved a fierce intensity.

Arab grievances with the Ottoman imperial government in Istanbul in the last years of the Empire were of sufficient magnitude to add nationalism to the cauldron of effective political ideologies in the Syrian provinces. But it was the Mandate system which ensured that nationalism became the overwhelming flavor of the stew. French control in Syria, contrary to French design, made nationalism the chief political instrument of a large segment of the Syrian political elite. Nationalist slogans—"unity" and "independence"—were used as a crude, lowest-common-denominator appeal to rally the Syrian masses behind this elite. Although the ideological tool to muster support was new, the short-run goal of the Syrian elite was old. It was to achieve a monopoly of political power in the local arena.

The French invasion and capricious policies imposed on Syria in the early years of the Mandate let this new sentiment of nationalism spread faster than ever before at the expense of other loyalties. Yet, the national independence movement was unable to reach a high degree of unity, cohesion, and organization. Not only did the movement become increasingly isolated from parallel movements in Palestine and Iraq, but its leaders became increasingly embroiled in personal and ideological disputes which the French successfully exploited.

The independence movement in the early 1920s was largely a movement in exile. Scores of nationalists had been forced to flee Damascus and other Syrian towns either to avoid death sentences or arrest, or simply because political life under the French quickly proved intolerable. For most Syrian leaders, Amman and Cairo became their temporary bases of operation.[1]

[1] The Anglo-French partition had a different impact on Baghdad and Jerusalem than it had on Damascus. The British offer of ân Iraqi throne to Faysal enabled him to establish a

Amir ʿAbdullah in Amman had set his sights on acquiring a Syrian throne for himself. He was madly jealous that Britain had put his younger brother, Faysal, on an Iraqi throne after the French had unseated Faysal in Syria; for the Syrian Congress had earmarked Iraq for ʿAbdullah in March 1920. ʿAbdullah gathered around him a group of ex-Ottoman functionaries from Syria who ran his administration.[2] Some of these men were radical nationalists belonging to the Syrian Istiqlal Party (Hizb al-istiqlal), an active pan-Arab organization in Damascus during the short-lived period of Arab independence which followed World War I. The party was more or less an amalgamation of leaders from the two pre-Mandate secret nationalist societies, al-Fatat and al-ʿAhd.[3] From the safety of Amman, these Syrian nationalists urged ʿAbdullah to adopt an aggressive policy vis-à-vis the French. But the British, on whom ʿAbdullah grew increasingly reliant, gradually and inexorably forced him to sever his ties with the more radical Syrian members of his entourage. Some were driven out of office and eventually out of Transjordan.[4] By 1922, the Istiqlalis had become ʿAbdullah's declared enemies. As for the British, it had also become clear that they were unwilling, if they ever had been, to support Syrian nationalist aims.

Cairo, by contrast, remained a hospitable refuge. Almost all important exiled nationalists passed through or resided in Cairo at one time or another during the interwar years. Before the outbreak of World War I, Cairo had served as the major coordinating center of the nascent Arab independence movement. Its cultural and political permissiveness and its large Syrian émigré community attracted political exiles.[5] Therefore, it

---

legitimate institution around which Iraqi nationalists (mainly officers in al-ʿAhd) who had been at Faysal's side since the days of the Arab Revolt could rally. Indeed, Baghdad became a place to which these officers could return quite conveniently, despite the presence of the British. Although some Syrian and Palestinian nationalists chose to follow Faysal to Baghdad (such as Rustum Haydar and Satiʿ al-Husri), most did not. For these leaders, Iraq was politically and socially unfamiliar, and geographically distant from the primary focus of their attention. Furthermore, Iraqis had an obvious edge on their own turf; and Faysal's own brand of diplomacy in 1919 and 1920 in Europe, followed by his sudden appearance in 1921 on a British-built throne in Iraq, doubtless weakened his political credibility in the eyes of more than a few hardline Syrian and Palestinian nationalists. Baghdad could and would be looked to for support but it was not a place from which to launch their struggles. Palestinians residing in Damascus during the Faysal interlude also encountered few obstacles to their return. On the short-lived Arab independence era, see Khoury, *Urban Notables*, Chapter 4.

[2] Among those Syrians who held high posts in ʿAbdullah's *diwan* were ʿAli Rida al-Rikabi, Nabih al-ʿAzma, ʿAdil Arslan, Mazhar Raslan, Rashid Taliʿa and Hasan Pasha Abu'l Huda. See Wilson, *King Abdullah*.

[3] See Khoury, *Urban Notables*, Chapter 4.

[4] See Wilson, *King Abdullah*.

[5] See Khoury, *Urban Notables*, Chapter 3.

was Cairo that became the home of the Executive Committee of the Syrian-Palestine Congress, established in Geneva in 1921.

THE SYRIAN-PALESTINE CONGRESS: ORIGINS AND FACTIONS

The origins of the Syrian–Palestine Congress can be traced to the end of 1918, when a number of Syrian exiles in Cairo—several of whom had been connected to the prewar Arab nationalist Ottoman Party of Administrative Decentralization—founded a successor organization, the Party of Syrian Unity (Hizb al-ittihad al-suri). Channeling their energies into support and propaganda work on behalf of the fragile Arab government in Damascus, this Party's leaders were more concerned with a Greater Syria union scheme and with maintaining contact with the British than with espousing pan-Arabist ideas such as those being promoted by more overtly anti-imperialist associations like al-Fatat/Hizb al-istiqlal and the Palestinian-led Arab Club.[6] With the fall of the Arab Kingdom in the summer of 1920, the Party of Syrian Unity offered to coordinate all Syrian and Palestinian nationalist organizations whose activities had consequently been curtailed or reduced. A general Syrian–Palestine Congress was called in early 1921. Its first session took place in June in Geneva, where demands for Syrian unity and independence were presented to the League of Nations. At this session, an Executive Committee was established to coordinate future Congress activities.[7] Not surprisingly, the officials elected to the Executive were also at the helm of the Party of Syrian Unity.

The Congress Executive, though in principle devoted to both Syrian and Palestinian affairs, focused more attention on events in Syria and Lebanon. This concentration reflected the strong Syrian and Lebanese component in the Congress leadership which, incidentally, controlled Congress purse strings.[8] That the Congress soon reproduced many of the

---

[6] Y. Porath, *The Emergence of the Palestinian-Arab National Movement, 1918–1929* (London, 1974), p. 116.

[7] For the activities of the Syrian–Palestine Congress in Geneva, see Marie-Renée Mouton, "Le congrès syrio-palestinien de Genève," *Relations Internationales*, 19 (Autumn 1979), pp. 313–18.

[8] Besides Michel Lutfallah, the Congress Executive included Shaykh Rashid Rida (Vice-President); Najib Shuqayr (Secretary), a Druze from Mount Lebanon; As'ad al-Bakri, son of Fawzi and nephew of Nasib; Dr. Khalil Mishaqa, a Damascene Protestant, members of whose family had served as American Consul and as dragomans at the British Consulate in Damascus in the nineteenth century; al-Hajj Adib Khayr, a wealthy merchant of Damascus; Sa'id Tali'a, a Druze from Mount Lebanon and cousin of Rashid Bey; Shukri al-Quwwatli; As'ad Daghir, a Lebanese Greek Catholic writer; and Khayr al-Din al-Zirikli, a Damascene writer of Kurdish extraction. MAE, Syrie–Liban 1918–29. "Note," 10 Dec. 1926, vol. 211, p. 22; *Salname: suriye vilayeti*, 1302/1885, pp. 98–99.

same divisions and regionalist tendencies which had already surfaced among Syrian, Palestinian, and Iraqi nationalists is understandable. With the collapse of Faysal's Arab Kingdom and the European partition of the Fertile Crescent into separately administered French and British Mandates, the idea of a unitary Arab nation rooted in a common language and culture was forced to compete with the growth of narrower, territorially defined ideas of an Iraqi or a Palestinian or a Syrian nation.[9]

The first major schism occurred in 1922, when Palestinian representatives withdrew from the Congress in protest at the insufficient attention devoted to Palestinian affairs. From the days of the Arab Revolt in 1916, few Palestinian leaders sincerely acknowledged the Hashemites as their legitimate representatives.[10] Faysal's dealings with the Zionist leader Chaim Weizmann just after the war were regarded as a betrayal of their cause. Some Palestinian leaders accused Faysal of trading on Palestine for a secure, internationally recognized Arab monarchy in Syria.[11] The Syrian–Palestine Congress Executive also seemed preoccupied with Syria, to the detriment of the Palestine question. In fact, while the Congress supported the idea of a Greater Syria by stressing the need for a unified Syrian–Palestine front, certain Syrian nationalists in 1921 and 1922 applied pressure on Palestinian leaders to reach an accommodation with the Zionists. Some Syrians even met independently with Zionist leaders in London and in Palestine to discuss prospects for a compromise solution.[12]

The rift between Syrians and Palestinians was by no means absolute; nor was it the only rift to appear in Congress ranks. Personal and ideological differences, stemming from the Arab Revolt or from rivalries formed in Damascus after the war, eventually split the Syrian membership of the Congress in two.

MICHEL LUTFALLAH, the eldest of three politically active sons of Habib Pasha Lutfallah, a Lebanese émigré in Cairo, was perhaps the leading personality on the Congress Executive; he also represented one of the two major competing trends to emerge within the Syrian nationalist movement after 1920. Michel's father, a Greek Orthodox Christian of modest extraction, had made a fortune as a moneylender during the Anglo-Egyptian expedition to the Sudan. He used this fortune to buy cotton plantations, making him one of the wealthiest landowners in Egypt. After 1908, Habib Lutfallah developed close links with Sharif Husayn in the Hijaz, serving as an adviser and banker to his family. Michel grew up in the cos-

---

[9] Albert Hourani, *Arabic Thought in the Liberal Age, 1798–1939* (London, 1962), p. 293.
[10] Porath, *The Emergence*, pp. 121–22. Kedourie, *England*, p. 153.
[11] See Khoury, *Urban Notables*, Chapter 4.
[12] Porath, *The Emergence*, pp. 112–14.

mopolitan atmosphere of Levantine Cairo where he later married the daughter of a rich Syrian Christian merchant of Alexandria. When the Arab Revolt erupted, Michel devoted most of his time to fund raising and publicity work on behalf of the Hashemites.[13] He also began to cooperate with the British authorities, as many Syrians in Cairo did during World War I. Michel's brother, Habib junior, was appointed by Husayn as his personal envoy to Paris in 1919, where he used his family's fortune to publicize the Hashemite cause. King Husayn awarded Habib senior the title of *amir* (prince) in return for his services, a title his sons inherited.

Michel Lutfallah, together with several other Syrian émigrés in Cairo, founded the Party of Syrian Unity at the end of the war; he was also the inspiration behind the Syrian–Palestine Congress. He was elected President of the Congress Executive and he and his other brother, George, were its major financial backers.[14]

Associated with the Lutfallah family was 'Abd al-Rahman Shahbandar, who first met Amir Michel and his brothers during his brief exile in Cairo toward the end of the war. In Cairo, Shahbandar—an outspoken secularist and critic of Young Turk centralization policies in the Syrian provinces—also developed friendly relations with Hashemite representatives as well as British political officers of the Arab Bureau. During his second exile in Cairo in 1920–21, Shahbandar assisted Michel Lutfallah in activating the recently established Executive of the Syrian–Palestine Congress. The first nationalist organization inside Syrian territory, the Iron Hand which Shahbandar founded after his amnesty in 1921, was largely financed by donations from the Congress or, in other words, by the Lutfallah family. Shahbandar spent most of his third exile in 1923–24, which followed his arrest and imprisonment in 1922–23, in Europe and the United States doing publicity work on behalf of the Syrian nationalist movement. During this period, the Congress financed his travels. Similarly, Shahbandar's People's Party, which was so active in the Great Revolt, received its greatest external support from the Congress Executive in Cairo. 'Abd al-Rahman Shahbandar and Michel Lutfallah were linked by more than a financial relationship and a mutual fondness of Cairo. Both men were educated in Western rather than in Ottoman professional schools. Thus neither shared in the high Ottoman-Arab culture of the late Empire or was a member of the Ottoman aristocracy of service. Their social backgrounds and intellectual upbringing placed them

---

[13] MAE, Syrie–Liban 1918–29. "Renseignement," 24 Oct. 1922, vol. 208, p. 68.

[14] George Lutfallah personally contributed £S (Syrian lira) 30,000 (600,000 French francs) to the Congress's permanent delegation in Geneva in 1922; see MAE, Syrie–Liban 1918–29. "Note," 20 July 1925, vol. 211, pp. 94–97.

among the leading advocates of a purely secular nationalism.[15] Owing to their personal interests and their rivalries with other Syrian nationalists, both remained close to the Hashemites and did not sever their ties with the British after 1920.

THE OTHER POLITICAL FACTION in and around the Syrian–Palestine Congress was headed by Shakib Arslan, the leading member of the Congress delegation stationed at the League of Nations. Arslan was born in the Lebanese mountain village of Shuwayfat in 1869, to a family of Druze *amirs*. His father preferred, however, to spend several months each year in Beirut's Musaytiba quarter, enabling his children to grow up in a fairly cosmopolitan Sunni Muslim environment.[16] Indeed, in spite of his Druze origin, Shakib was a proclaimed Sunni. He first attended an American mission school in his village and then the Ottoman Sultaniyya school in Beirut. On completing his education, which included an intensive course of study in Turkish, he spent two years abroad. During this time he paid the first of many visits to Paris and Cairo, before settling down to a career as a poet, essayist and political activist.[17]

Between 1913 and 1918, Shakib Arslan was an elected deputy from the Hawran to the Ottoman Parliament in Istanbul. His refusal to break with the Young Turks highlighted one of his conflicts with the Lutfallah–Shahbandar faction. At the time of the Arab Revolt, Arslan was of the firm conviction that the Arab provinces should not try to break from the Empire, despite the Young Turks' intensified "Turkification" policies, which he did not favor.[18] He sincerely believed that such a rupture would leave the Arab peoples, their territory, and their civilization open to further European assaults and encroachments. Arslan warned that the Empire's breakup would enable the European powers to extend their control over the whole region, including the Holy Places in the Hijaz. Even after the Empire's collapse, Arslan—a cosmopolitan Ottoman-Arab intellectual—looked to Turkey for political support. He regarded Turkey's national struggle against the European powers as critical to the future of the Arab nation. Turkey, after all, was still a Muslim nation bent on protecting its territory against European imperialism and it therefore offered the Arabs an excellent example to follow.[19]

---

[15] Shahbandar had been frequently accused by some of his enemies of being an atheist. See Chapter 23.

[16] This quarter also contained a large Greek Orthodox community of merchants.

[17] Adham al-Jundi, *A'lam al-adab wa al-fann* (Damascus, 1958), vol. 2, pp. 373–75. For the most profound study of Arslan's political and intellectual career, see William L. Cleveland, *Islam against the West. Shakib Arslan and the Campaign for Islamic Nationalism* (Austin, Tex., 1985).

[18] Hourani, *Arabic Thought*, pp. 303–4.

[19] MAE, Syrie–Liban 1918–29. "Renseignement," 24 Oct. 1922, vol. 208, p. 68.

Shakib Arslan's pronounced anti-British tendencies, his reluctance to align with the Hashemites, his use of Berlin as a major center for his propaganda campaign against the French,[20] his interest in gaining Turkish support for the independence of the Arab territories, and his emphasis on an Arab nation whose underlying moral principles were based on the Divine Law of Islam, were bound to clash with the Lutfallah–Shahbandar faction's British and Hashemite links, its suspicion of the Turks, and its secularism. In the early 1920s, however, Arslan kept these conflicts under wraps, mainly because the delegation he headed in Geneva was almost completely dependent on financial subsidies from the Lutfallah family.[21]

In Shakib Arslan's camp were two other prominent personalities, Shaykh Rashid Rida and Ihsan al-Jabiri. Rashid Rida's contribution to the Syrian nationalist movement lay mainly in the intellectual domain, where he concentrated on the ideological articulation of nationalism and particularly on the importance of Islamic content in its formulation. His beliefs and ideas were expressed candidly over the years in *al-Manar*, the periodical he published in Cairo from 1898 (a year after he emigrated there from Tripoli, Syria) until his death in 1935. Rida's link to Shakib Arslan, who was four years his junior, came through their intellectual mentor, Shaykh Muhammad ʿAbduh. Rida and Arslan eventually became friends and in the process discovered a profound intellectual compatibility, despite differences in social background and education. Arslan was absorbed by Rida's powerfully articulate defense of the primacy of Islam for the Arabs, their historic contribution to its birth and expansion, and the need for the nation to be governed by Islam's highest principles.[22]

The two men, however, did not always agree on matters of political strategy. For instance, Arslan was not particularly pleased by Rida's rather harsh attitude toward the Young Turks and his willingness to cooperate with the British during the war to secure Arab independence. But after the war and the European division of geographic Syria, Rida's attitude toward Britain underwent a fundamental change. More important, he became an outspoken critic of the Hashemites, whom he regarded as corrupt, incompetent, and destined to continue to sacrifice the interests of the Arab nation by completely identifying their personal fortunes with those of British imperialists.[23] Thus, Rashid Rida, who was elected Vice-President of the Syrian–Palestine Congress Executive, provided an important check on the activities of the pro-Hashemite faction around Michel Lutfallah.

[20] *Ibid.*

[21] *Ibid.*, Hourani, *Arabic Thought*, pp. 298–307.

[22] Hourani, *Arabic Thought*, pp. 222–24; al-Jundi, *Aʿlam*, vol. 2, p. 374. Arslan was also Rida's biographer.

[23] Rida was President of the General Syrian Congress in Damascus in 1919, though this position was largely ceremonial; see FO 371/3149, vol. 6453. 10 March 1921.

Ihsan al-Jabiri, who was 13 years younger than Shakib Arslan, was also an Ottoman-Arab aristocrat, with an Istanbul education and an advanced degree in law from Paris. He had been a ranking Ottoman bureaucrat, serving in Istanbul and the Syrian provinces, and had remained faithful to the idea of Empire almost until its very end. His family's prominence in Aleppo, where Ihsan had most recently been mayor, his familiarity with Europe, and his willingness to adopt the nationalist mantle, convinced Faysal to make him head of his *diwan* and his Chamberlain in 1918. But, driven into exile by the French, Jabiri devoted himself to propaganda work in Europe while following with great interest news of events in and around his hometown, where the anti-French Hananu revolt raged in 1920–21. Like Arslan, Jabiri believed that an alliance with the Turks, who were also fighting the French, should be encouraged.[24] But, while Arslan emphasized the need for an Islamic front with Turkey against Europe, Jabiri, whose family had strong social ties to Istanbul, was more concerned with reviving commercial relations between Syria and Turkey.[25] This Turkish connection irritated the Lutfallah–Shahbandar group, who despised the Turks against whom they had revolted during World War I and whose territorial designs on northern Syria they seriously feared.[26]

The Arslan faction in the Syrian–Palestine Congress included one other important grouping, members of the pan-Arab Istiqlal Party who had sought refuge in Amman, Cairo, and even in Jerusalem. These men tended to be Syrian activists of a younger generation than Arslan's and Rida's (though not Jabiri's) and of an ultra-nationalist persuasion. Although few Istiqlalis looked to Turkey for salvation or stressed the Islamic character of the Arab nation as espoused by Arslan, Rida, and others—a clear reflection of their age and more secular intellectual formation—all were anti-British, suspicious of the Hashemites (though not necessarily of Faysal), and outspokenly pan-Arab. The Istiqlalis also continued to be intimately connected to like-minded radicals in Palestine who had been active members of the Istiqlal Party and the Arab Club in Damascus after the war.[27]

[24] MAE, Syrie–Liban 1918–29. "La propagande," 19 April 1923, vol. 208. Both al-Jabiri and Arslan used Turkey as a base to make propaganda against the French in the early 1920s. Also see MAE, Syrie–Liban 1918–29. "Sarraut Telegram," 18 Nov. 1925, vol. 210, p. 18.

[25] FO 371/600, vol. 210, 12 Jan. 1923.

[26] Faris, *Man huwa 1949*, p. 78; MWT, *al-Qism al-khass*, 'Abd al-Rahman Shahbandar Papers, no. 7/23. Shahbandar (Baghdad) to Hasan al-Hakim, 15 March 1927; *ibid.*, no.9/25. 28 March 1927.

[27] Notably 'Izzat Darwaza and 'Awni 'Abd al-Hadi. The Arab Club had branches in Damascus and Jerusalem. Until April 1920, the Jerusalem branch was headed by Hajj Amin al-Husayni. See Porath, *The Emergence*, p. 78.

Among the most important Istiqlalis the French forced into exile in 1920 was ʿAdil Arslan, the younger brother of Shakib.[28] Born in 1882 in Shuwayfat, he was educated in French mission schools and in Paris, where he specialized in literature, and graduated from the Mülkiye in Istanbul. Like his brother, he faithfully served the Ottoman state in an official capacity until the end of the War. After the Allied occupation of Syria in 1918, Faysal appointed ʿAdil Bey *mutasarrif* of Mount Lebanon, and just before the collapse of the Arab Kingdom he became Faysal's political adviser and one of his chief intermediaries with the French and the British. During this period he also became an active member of the Istiqlal Party. With French occupation, the younger Arslan took up residence in Transjordan where he and several other exiled Syrian Istiqlalis, including the Damascene Nabih al-ʿAzma, the Director of Public Security in Amman, formed a new branch of the Party. Between 1921 and 1923, ʿAdil Arslan served as an adviser to ʿAbdullah until ʿAbdullah was obliged, under considerable British pressure, to exile him along with his comrades for anti-French activities. Arslan followed ʿAzma, who had also been banished, to the Hijaz.[29]

It was through his brother ʿAdil and other Istiqlalis that Shakib Arslan maintained direct contact with the younger group of radical Syrian nationalists. From different angles, members of the Arslan faction began to challenge Lutfallah and Shahbandar for control of the Syrian–Palestine Congress and the overall independence movement. Although Shakib Arslan and Ihsan al-Jabiri spent most of their time in Europe, both men were looked to by the younger group of ultra-nationalists as leaders of political and intellectual integrity who steadfastly opposed the idea of cooperating with either Britain or France. Equally impressive to the Istiqlalis was that both notables, especially Arslan, refused to shy away from the controversy over Palestine.

RADICALS, HASHEMITES, AND IBN SAʿUD

As early as October 1922, French Intelligence observed that Amir Michel Lutfallah was beginning to lose the direction of the Syrian–Palestine Congress.[30] But it was not until early March 1924, when Sharif Husayn

---

[28] Other members of the Istiqlal Party included Khayr al-Din al-Zirikli, Asʿad Daghir, Riyad Sulh, Rashid al-Husami, Amir Mustafa al-Shihabi, Wasfi al-Atasi, Ahmad Muraywid, Ahmad Qadri, Saʿid Taliʿa, Tawfiq al-Yaziji, Khalid al-Hakim, ʿIzzat Darwaza, Muʿin al-Madi, Shukri al-Quwwatli, and ʿAwni ʿAbd al-Hadi. Two members who dropped out of the informal organization early on were Saʿdallah al-Jabiri and ʿAfif Sulh. See *al-Musawwar* (Damascus weekly youth magazine), no. 14 (9 Sept. 1936), p. 20.

[29] Al-Jundi, *Tarikh*, pp. 240–41, 541.

[30] MAE, Syrie–Liban 1918–29. "Renseignement," 24 Oct. 1922, vol. 208, p. 68.

laid claim to the Caliphate, that lines of division in the Congress and in the overall Syrian national movement became more visible.

Husayn's claim, which immediately followed the abolition of the Caliphate by the Turkish National Assembly, sparked a lively debate. There was no unanimity on the resurrection of the Caliphate—whether the present time was propitious or whether the institution should be resurrected at all. Some Arab religious experts believed that the Caliphate had to be revived because it was the one institution that could provide the Muslim community with unity amidst the wide diversity of its local interests and that control of the institution should be returned to its rightful heirs, the Arabs.[31] But there was no unanimity on whether Sharif Husayn was qualified to become Caliph, despite the publicity campaign he orchestrated in his own support. Significant support for Husayn's claim came from a number of religious leaders in Damascus, Homs, Hama, and Aleppo.[32] But the majority opinion among members of the Arab Muslim religious establishment was that his claim was inopportune and ephemeral.[33] Several prominent religious scholars, including Shaykh Rashid Rida, openly opposed Husayn's bid for the Caliphate. They accused the Hashemites of being intellectually unqualified to deal with critical theological questions in the spiritual domain and of being incompetent, self-seeking, and mercenary. For Rida and other theologians, the very fact that the Hashemites had aligned with Britain to realize their personal ambitions and that they continued to do so long after all promises of independence made to the Arabs had been broken was sufficient evidence to render them ineligible for Islam's most esteemed office.[34]

But rather than political-theological reasoning, it was the sudden shift in the balance of power in the Arabian peninsula which sapped Sharif Husayn's claim of its force. Ibn Saʿud, who had already consolidated his position of political paramountcy in key parts of Arabia, overran the Hijaz in a few months, captured Mecca, and forced the Sharif's abdication. Hu-

[31] FO 684/111/98. Smart (Damascus) to FO, 15 March 1923.

[32] Information on support in Syria for Husayn's claim comes from the following sources: FO 684/111/98. Smart to FO, 15 March 1923; FO 371/2761, vol. 1003. Satow (Beirut) to FO, 15 March 1924; FO 371/4141, vol. 10164. Damascus Consul to FO, 28 April 1924; FO 684/111/121. Smart to FO, 20 March 1924; FO 684/111/208. Smart to FO, 22 April 1924; Alif ba' (15, 16 March 1924); Oriente Moderno, 4 (1924), pp. 236–37; MAE, Syrie–Liban 1918–29. Telegram, 2 Sept. 1922, vol. 274, p. 11.

[33] PRO, Air Ministry/23405. "Note on Pan-Islamism," High Commissioner (Baghdad) to Reed, 14 Nov. 1931.

[34] Muhammad Rashid Rida, al-Khilafa (Cairo, 1341/1922–23), pp. 73 ff., cited in Hourani, Arabic Thought, p. 305. Another prominent critic of the Hashemites was the Damascus religious leader, Shaykh Kamil al-Qassab, who in 1924 was in exile in the Hijaz. He had opposed Hashemite dealings with the British since Faysal's days in Damascus. See, al-Jundi, A'lam, vol. 2, pp. 77–78.

sayn's eldest son and heir, ʿAli, remained in Jidda, but a year later was himself driven out. In January 1926, Ibn Saʿud added Husayn's title, King of the Hijaz, to his own title, Amir of Najd. Although the question of reviving the Caliphate lingered, Husayn was no longer a serious contender. His loss of authority over the Holy Places removed yet another feather from the Hashemite cap.[35]

Ibn Saʿud's victory gave political rivalries within the Syrian nationalist movement and in the Congress greater definition and dimension. His conquest was highly acclaimed in Muslim reformist circles and by secular nationalists in the Istiqlali, anti-Hashemite mold, who regarded him as the one Arab statesman who remained untainted by foreign control.[36] Ibn Saʿud viewed the Hashemites as illegitimate spiritual and temporal authorities and subscribed to and defended a religious ideology and set of dogmas, Wahhabism, which was particularly attractive to radical religious reformers like Rida and his disciples.[37] Meanwhile, younger radical nationalists, aside from being impressed by Ibn Saʿud's ability to prevent Arabia from falling under European hegemony, looked to him as a solid source of political support, especially given their dislike and distrust of the Hashemites and their Syrian allies. Not only did Ibn Saʿud serve as a strong check on Hashemite designs and particularly those of ʿAbdullah in Transjordan, but he seemed to entertain no personal ambitions in Syria.

With respect to the Hashemites, Husayn and ʿAbdullah were the Sharifs most disliked and distrusted by Arslan, Rida, and the Istiqlalis. Husayn was regarded as a collaborator and intriguer; the loss of his mini-kingdom in the Hijaz also proved his incompetence. ʿAbdullah not only continued to serve British interests in the region, but he even began to conciliate the French; his agreement to expel from Transjordan several Istiqlalis was an indication of his lack of pan-Arab solidarity. Soon there-

[35] The Caliphate question was finally set aside in May 1926, when a Caliphate Congress was held in Cairo, attended by delegates from Egypt, Libya, Tunisia, Morocco, the East Indies, British India, the Yemen, the Hijaz, Palestine, Syria, and Iraq, but with no representatives from Turkey, Iran, Afghanistan, the Najd, or the Muslim communities in the Soviet Union. Although the Congress confirmed a continuing need for such an institution, it concluded that conditions were not ripe for its re-establishment. The Caliphate question remained dormant with intermittent agitation for its revival in times of trouble or at subsequent Islamic Congresses. See Wilson, *King Abdullah*; PRO, Air Ministry/23/405. High Commissioner (Baghdad) to Reed, 14 Nov. 1931; A Sékaly, "Les deux Congrès musulmans de 1926," *Revue du Monde Musulman*, 64 (1926), pp. 3–219; Hourani, *Arabic Thought*, p. 184.

[36] Actually, Ibn Saʿud's two governments in the Najd and Hijaz were soon to receive large British subsidies. See Khaldun S. Husry, "King Faysal I and Arab Unity, 1930–1933," *Journal of Contemporary History*, 10 (1975), pp. 328–29.

[37] Hourani, *Arabic Thought*, p. 305.

after, he confirmed the opinion of radical pan-Arabists by failing to come to the aid of the Syrian rebels during the Great Revolt.

The Arslan–Istiqlali faction's attitude toward the other important Hashemite prince, Faysal, was less black-and-white. Faysal was still highly esteemed by many pan-Arabists, particularly by men like Ihsan al-Jabiri[38] and ʿAdil Arslan, who had been part of his inner circle in Damascus. After several years of exile, these nationalists yearned for the re-establishment of an independent monarchy in Syria which they could rally around and hope to guide. As for Faysal himself, he was regarded as more honest and straightforward than his father or his brother, ʿAbdullah. He did not force Syrian nationalists out of Iraq as ʿAbdullah had in Transjordan, and many pan-Arabists did not regard him as a British stooge. In fact, because Faysal had sought in the opening years of the Iraqi monarchy to "interweave" his dynastic ambitions with those of the Arab nationalist movement, the monarchy's interests were seen as "antithetical" to those of the British.[39]

There were other Syrians, however, who because of their age or lack of prominence, or both, had never really known Faysal intimately and could only recall that he was a moderate who had shown a willingness to cooperate with the Europeans to save his monarchy in Syria. Although he lost Damascus, he was now well ensconced in Baghdad, but still harboring ambitions in Syria. To these men, one Hashemite prince was like another: all, in the final analysis, were self-seeking agents of the British. By contrast, Ibn Saʿud, who had no identifiable territorial or dynastic ambitions beyond Arabia and who seemed willing to give "unconditional" support to the Syrian nationalists, was a more acceptable statesman with whom to do business.[40] In any case, many of these younger radical nationalists, frustrated by Hashemite intrigues, had lost their interest in the idea of monarchy. Alhough they did not hesitate to play one Arab monarch against another in their quest for control over the Syrian nationalist movement, republicanism was rapidly overtaking monarchism as their ideal form of government.

By the eve of the Great Revolt, the Arslan–Istiqlali alliance within the Syrian–Palestine Congress had already crystallized. It could be characterized by its pan-Arabism, its reluctance to collaborate with the British in

---

[38] According to one keen observer of political life in Damascus after the war, when Ihsan al-Jabiri was Faysal's Chamberlain, he instructed the Amir in all forms of protocol. "He told him what to say and whether or not to stand when greeting someone in his office" (Kurd ʿAli, al-Mudhakkirat, p. 327).

[39] Batatu, The Old Social Classes, p. 25.

[40] MAE, Syrie–Liban 1918–29. "Interview with Edmond Rabbath," 12 July 1927, vol. 213, pp. 16–24.

the struggle to oust the French from Syria, and its various shades of opposition to the Hashemites.

THE DIVISIVENESS OF REVOLT

Since the French occupation of Syria, Dr. Shahbandar and his closest allies had maintained a monopoly on nationalist organization. Although jailed and exiled for long periods, they had found opportunities to construct a political apparatus through which they could translate the frustrations and grievances of the Syrian urban populace into collective action. By contrast, the Istiqlal group were denied a similar opportunity because the French refused to amnesty them. By October 1925, the latter group had no choice but to throw their full weight behind the revolt, which meant behind the People's Party. Personal rivalries and ideological disputes were submerged for the time being.

It was only after the military balance began to shift irreversibly in France's favor in the spring of 1926 that factionalism became dangerously divisive, splitting the ranks of the independence movement wide open and, in some senses, crippling it for a whole generation. But even before the revolt's prospects soured, two new developments occurred which were eventually to give factionalism fuller expression: one was an unexpected meeting between Shakib Arslan and Henry de Jouvenel, and the other was the establishment of a rival fund-raising organization to the Lutfallah controlled Syrian–Palestine Congress.

In November 1925, Shakib Arslan, the nationalists' chief emissary and publicist in Europe, was invited to an exclusive audience with Jouvenel in Paris, just before the newly-appointed High Commissioner's departure for Beirut. Their candid conversation concerned what Amir Shakib claimed was an "official" Syrian formula for resolving the Syrian question. He proposed that if France granted Syria independence, allowed the Alawite territory to become part of a unified Syria, and permitted the Syrian districts attached to Lebanon in 1920 to choose by plebiscite the state to which they wished to belong (either Syria or Lebanon), then the nationalists would concede to France exclusive economic and strategic advantages in Syria. These included the right to issue loans, train the Syrian Army, establish a naval base on the Syrian coast, and conclude a mutual defense treaty. Never before had a Syrian nationalist leader offered such compromises and demonstrated such moderation. Jouvenel replied that while he could not sign an agreement immediately, he would study Syria's claims carefully and work for an accord.[41]

---

[41] Rabbath, *Courte Histoire*, pp. 8–12. Rabbath was a Syrian student in Paris at the time of the Arslan–Jouvenel rendezvous.

Arslan's proposals created much confusion and consternation back at Congress headquarters in Cairo and in the Jabal Druze where the Provisional National Government was steering the revolt. Both Michel Lutfallah and Shahbandar felt Arslan's maneuvers undercut their own political prestige and influence. Their angry reaction was not so much to Arslan's proposed compromises—though many nationalists felt that he had conceded too much— but rather to his success at securing access to a high-ranking French official, which they had failed to do.

Lutfallah attacked Arslan for approaching Jouvenel without first seeking the Congress Executive's permission and for ignoring its most important principle of "no compromise" with the French. Subsequently, when Jouvenel met Congress leaders during a brief stopover in Cairo at the end of November, Lutfallah saw to it that his faction on the Executive Committee took a hard line; from the first moments of their meeting, the Lutfallah group antagonized the High Commissioner by calling for the immediate evacuation of French troops from Syria, a nationalist demand Arslan had assiduously avoided in Paris.[42]

Michel Lutfallah's motives, however, had little to do with the principle of no compromise. By this time he had lost much of his personal influence over the Congress. His uncritical support of the Hashemites and his reputation for secretly playing politics with any European power or Arab political party that could help realize his own ambitions which, by 1925, included a hereditary throne for himself in Lebanon, damaged his reputation.[43] So did the revelation that the wealthy Sursuk family of Beirut and Cairo, with whom the Lutfallahs were intermarried, had recently sold more fertile land in northern Palestine to the Zionists.[44] Michel Lutfallah harbored more compromising political tendencies than virtually any prominent Syrian nationalist leader. For example, while he publicly called for the return of the territories annexed to Lebanon in 1920, he actually preferred the preservation of a Greater Lebanon in conjunction with his dynastic ambitions.[45] His rather fanciful dreams, when stripped

---

[42] Ibid., pp. 13–16. Before Jouvenel left Cairo for Beirut, the Syrian–Palestine Congress set forth its demands: the formation of a unified Syrian state, and a plebiscite in Lebanon to decide whether it would join the Syrian state; the immediate establishment of a national government and an organic law based on the principles of national sovereignty; elections for a Constituent Assembly by direct universal suffrage; the abolition of the Mandate and a Franco–Syrian accord of limited duration safeguarding the principles of national sovereignty; and the evacuation of the army of occupation. Jouvenel responded with the assertion that these proposals were "perfectly unacceptable" and that France was unable "to forget the obligations she assumed before fifty nations of the League."

[43] Conversation with Sabri Farid al-Bidaywi (Damascus, 9 July 1977).

[44] The Sursuks were also Greek Orthodox merchants. See Porath, The Palestinian Arab, p. 83.

[45] MAE, Syrie–Liban 1918–29. "Interview with Edmond Rabbath," pp. 16–24; ibid.,

of their fancy, were in step with the ongoing crystallization of the Beirut commercial bourgeoisie's support for an independent Lebanon.[46] His enormous wealth and his relations with ʿAbd al-Rahman Shahbandar, rather than his politics, enabled him to retain the Congress presidency.

Shahbandar was equally annoyed by Arslan's diplomatic coup. Later he asserted that Jouvenel's promise to Arslan to scrutinize Syria's claims and to work toward a mutually acceptable solution only "threw dust in the eyes of the nation and dampened the force of upsurging public opinion."[47] But Shahbandar was really perturbed because Jouvenel had decided, even before setting foot in Syria, that he would have no dealings with the revolt leadership. From Shahbandar's perspective, Shakib Arslan was only a paid publicist living comfortably in Europe while he and his comrades were the leaders with whom the High Commissioner had to come to terms.

There is little doubt that had Arslan belonged to the Shahbandar network, his overtures to Jouvenel would have been far less objectionable. But such a liaison had never been possible. Shahbandar intensely disliked Arslan and the feeling was mutual. For years, he had accused Arslan of being an agent of Turkey, one of those who had advised the Turks during the First World War to execute Shahbandar's comrades, the vanguard of the infant Arab nationalist movement. In Shahbandar's view, not only were Arslan's hands stained with Arab blood, but lately he had become a paid agent of the Germans. Arslan, for his part, could no longer hide his suspicions that Shahbandar and the Lutfallahs were British agents and Hashemite propagandists and that in the final analysis they were responsible for inviting the Europeans to occupy and dismember the Arab homeland.[48]

Jouvenel's invitation to Arslan showed a clear French awareness of the different tensions and conflicts within the Syrian independence movement, which they sought to exploit fully. By snubbing Shahbandar, the French made it quite obvious that they had no intention of recognizing and thus legitimizing their main opposition in Syria. To this policy, the French remained faithful throughout the revolt.

"Bulletin d'Information de la Direction du Service des Renseignements," Beirut, 16 Jan. 1927, vol. 201, p. 182; *ibid.*, "Note," 20 July 1926, vol. 211, pp. 94–96; FO 371/4744, vol. 12303. Henderson (Cairo) to Chamberlain, 29 Dec. 1927.

[46] See Chapter 2.

[47] Rabbath, *Courte Histoire*, p. 10.

[48] MAE, Syrie–Liban 1918–29. Beirut, 16 Jan. 1927, vol. 201, p. 182; FO 371/2142, vol. 20849, 6 May 1937. To complicate matters, the Druze clans of Arslan and al-Atrash had been on bad terms for some time. See MAE, Syrie–Liban 1918–29. "Interview with Edmond Rabbath."

THE OTHER MAJOR BONE of contention between the Lutfallah–Shahbandar and Arslan–Istiqlali faction during the Great Revolt concerned the control and distribution of financial assistance. Throughout the early 1920s, fund-raising outside Syria was an integral function of the Syrian–Palestine Congress. Indeed, this had been one of the main reasons for its establishment. Normally, funds collected in the Americas, the Arab countries, and the rest of the Muslim world were sent directly to Congress headquarters in Cairo. Some were then secretly channeled to nationalists in Syria, and some were always reserved to cover the expenses of the permanent delegation of the Congress in Geneva and Congress operations in Cairo, which included financial assistance to political exiles and their families. Other funds and matériel did reach Syria without ever passing through the Congress network, especially from Turkey and Transjordan, but the flow tended to be more erratic than that which came from Cairo.[49]

Before the revolt, it is unclear how dependent nationalists in Syria were on external funding for their various activities. French authorities tended to exaggerate the extent of foreign meddling. They were convinced that nationalist activities were all orchestrated and financed by the Syrian–Palestine Congress, which the Quai d'Orsay felt was little more than a front for the Hashemites and their British patrons.[50] One matter is clear, however: once the revolt erupted and the leadership of the People's Party assumed its direction, there was suddenly a much greater demand for regular external assistance. The Cairo Congress responded by exploiting its existing contacts and exploring new ones in the Arab world and the West.[51]

There was one promising source still to be tapped in the Arab world: Ibn Saʿud. Although the Lutfallahs were in charge of Congress financial affairs, being Christians and close to ex-King Husayn made them unsuitable candidates to approach Ibn Saʿud.[52] Other leaders also found themselves in a poor position to appeal to him. For instance, Dr. Shahbandar and rebel chiefs like the aristocratic Bakri family of Damascus were

[49] MAE, Syrie–Liban 1928–29. "Note," 20 July 1926, vol. 211, pp. 94–96.
[50] Ibid., 1922, vol. 40, pp. 48–49. The French claimed that one of the British "secretaries" at the League of Nations—a former Professor in Cairo, received money for distribution to the Syrian–Palestine Congress from the British Consul in Geneva on Lloyd's Bank of Geneva checks. See ibid., "Note," 10 Dec. 1926, vol. 211, pp. 222–24.
[51] Although accurate figures for the amount of money raised outside Syria for the Great Revolt are unavailable, French sources (see MAE, Syrie–Liban 1918–29. 16 Aug. 1927, vol. 213, pp. 85–86) estimated that at least £E 100,000 was sent to Syria from the United States, Brazil, Iraq, Arabia (including Hijaz), Hyderabad, the Jerusalem Committee, and the Cairo Committee.
[52] In fact when Michel Lutfallah, who had served Sharif Husayn as his banker and adviser, proposed to Ibn Saʿud that he open a bank in the Hijaz after its conquest, he was flatly turned down. See ibid., 27 Jan. 1926, vol. 210, p. 105.

known to be proponents of the idea of an Arab Federation headed by Husayn or possibly his son ʿAli. Shahbandar had already sought Ibn Saʿud's aid personally, when he secretly journeyed from his Jabal Druze hideout to the Hijaz in November 1925; but he returned empty-handed.[53] Ibn Saʿud had little tolerance for friends of the Hashemites.

There were, however, several exiled Syrian activists either on or connected to the Executive Committee who were in contact with Ibn Saʿud and in a strong position to cultivate him. Not surprisingly, all were radical pan-Arabists and anti-Hashemite, the most important being the Istiqlal Party leader, Shukri al-Quwwatli. Quwwatli's access to Ibn Saʿud was facilitated by his family's commercial relations with the Saʿud family, and more immediately through one of Ibn Saʿud's most trusted advisers, Shaykh Yusuf Yasin, himself a Syrian and a former Istiqlali, whom Quwwatli had originally sent to Ibn Saʿud as an aide.[54] Quwwatli was born in Damascus in 1891 into a family of prosperous landowners, merchants, and bureaucrats of the popular Shaghur quarter who made their ascent on to the social and political scene in the city after the mid-nineteenth century.[55] He studied in a Jesuit elementary school in Damascus and then at the city's elite government preparatory school, Maktab ʿAnbar, before going on to Istanbul for advanced training in public administration. However, like other qualified young men of his generation from the Syrian upper classes, he was unable to secure a respectable post in the Ottoman provincial administration. Young Turk policies in the Syrian provinces had limited his possibilities. Toward the end of his student days in Istanbul, Quwwatli came into contact with members of al-Fatat. On his return to Damascus, he joined the secret nationalist society. In 1916, with no stake in the Ottoman state, he joined the Arab Revolt and participated in underground activities with his al-Fatat comrades. Eventually, however, he was arrested and jailed. In prison, he is said to have been tortured for months and even to have attempted suicide rather than divulge any secrets to the Turks. Reports of his heroism, even if apocryphal, vaulted him into the limelight as a nationalist hero.[56]

With the Allied victories and the establishment of the Arab government in Damascus, Shukri al-Quwwatli became an official in local admin-

---

[53] H. St. John Philby Papers. Rosita (McGrath) Forbes to Philby, 23 May 1927, Box 14, File 3, Middle East Centre, St. Antony's College, Oxford.

[54] Yasin was one of several Syrians Quwwatli sent to Ibn Saʿud as aides and advisers. See Patrick Seale, *The Struggle for Syria: A Study in Post-War Arab Politics* (London, 1965), p. 26.

[55] Al-Husni, *Kitab Muntakhabat*, vol. 2, pp. 861–62; *Salname: suriye vilayeti*, 1288/1871–1872, p. 72; *ibid.*, 1308–1309/1890–1891, p. 66; *ibid.*, 1309–1310/1892–1893, pp. 102, 124; *ibid.*, 1312/1894–1895, p. 71.

[56] Faris, *Man huwa 1949*, pp. 6–8; Vacca, "Notizie," p. 490.

istration, though he devoted most of his time to extra-governmental na-
tionalist activities as an official of the Istiqlal Party and as a member of
the Damascus branch of the Palestinian-led Arab Club. Forced to flee
Syria in July 1920 under sentence of death, he took up residence in Cairo.
During the next five years he became a sort of roving ambassador for the
Syrian–Palestine Congress, traveling between the Arab countries and Europe. In Europe, he preferred Berlin where he collaborated with Shakib
Arslan in anti-French propaganda campaigns, causing the French to rank
him with Arslan and Ihsan al-Jabiri as the "most dangerous" Syrians in
exile. In this period, Quwwatli served as the key link between exiled nationalists in Europe and nationalist organizations operating in the Arab
countries.[57]

Quwwatli, who was an avowed anti-Hashemite and who intensely disliked the British, was greatly encouraged by Ibn Saʿud's easy and rapid
conquest of the Hijaz. By the outbreak of the Syrian revolt in 1925, he
had positioned himself as the main intermediary between Ibn Saʿud,
from whom he had received funds, and the Syrian–Palestine Congress; in
the process he posed a challenge to Michel Lutfallah, the Congress's chief
fund-raiser.[58] This challenge assumed serious proportions toward the end
of 1925 when two of Quwwatli's fellow Istiqlalis and close personal
friends, ʿAdil Arslan and Nabih al-ʿAzma, convinced their Palestinian
nationalist ally, Hajj Amin al-Husayni, to establish a special finance committee for the Syrian revolt in Jerusalem. The Jerusalem Committee
(Lajnat al-Quds) was designed to counter the influence of the Lutfallah-
dominated Executive Committee of the Congress, though its founders
justified its creation as critical to the progress of the revolt because of Jerusalem's proximity to Damascus. Indeed, once the new Finance Committee had been set up, both ʿAdil Arslan and ʿAzma moved to Jerusalem
to take over its day-to-day operations and to assist its treasurer, ʿAzma's
older brother, ʿAdil.[59] Meanwhile, Shukri al-Quwwatli, who was already
engaged in smuggling money and arms to rebel leaders in Syria from the
Hijaz, began to divert funds to the Jerusalem Committee.[60]

As long as the Syrian rebels were making progress in their struggle,
personal quarrels and political conflicts between the Congress Executive

[57] MAE, Syrie–Liban 1918–29. 10 Dec. 1925, vol. 210, pp. 38–40.
[58] Ibid., Cairo to Briand, 21 Jan. 1926, vol. 210, p. 93; ibid., Cairo, 24 Aug. 1927, vol.
213, pp. 82–83.
[59] For biographical sketches of the ʿAzma brothers, see al-Jundi, Tarikh, pp. 539–41.
[60] MWT, al-Qism al-khass, Shahbandar Papers, no. 10/26. Shahbandar to Hasan al-
Hakim, 22 April 1927. Quwwatli was assisted by two other Istiqlalis: al-Hajj Adib Khayr, a
wealthy Damascene merchant, and Khalid al-Hakim, an Istanbul-trained engineer from
Homs, who was also instrumental in getting Ibn Saʿud to support the Syrian independence
struggle.

and the Jerusalem Committee were kept to a minimum, so as not to disrupt the revolt's momentum. But once nationalist forces began to suffer setbacks in the spring of 1926 and rebel leaders began to flee to Jerusalem and Cairo, these quarrels and conflicts could no longer be contained. The Lutfallah–Shahbandar faction dominating the Cairo Executive accused the Jerusalem Committee (which by this time had usurped the Congress's financial role) of using its contacts, especially in the United States and Brazil, where large Syrian émigré communities resided, to divert funds collected for the revolt to Jerusalem, in the name of the Istiqlal Party. This enabled Istiqlalis to expropriate funds for their personal affairs instead. Cairo accused ʿAdil Arslan, for example, of banking £E 6,000 raised by his brother Shakib, while Shukri al-Quwwatli was supposed to have pocketed money he raised in Arabia. Cairo also accused him of using funds raised by the Jerusalem Committee to pay a rebel chief to protect the Quwwatli family's extensive apricot orchards near Damascus from banditry.[61]

Rebel leaders, who began to pour out of Syria into Palestine as the revolt was crushed, also joined the attack on the Jerusalem Committee, and specifically on the Istiqlalis. The Bakri family, whose six homes had been destroyed and large estates confiscated, expected financial assistance from their comrades in exile, as did other rebel leaders obliged to flee the embattled areas. Instead, they learned that there was to be little or no aid available for refugees because the Jerusalem Committee had decided to continue financing the revolt.[62] Nationalists who had risked their lives in the name of Syrian independence reacted bitterly as they helplessly watched those who had not carried arms or known the hardships of rebellion dictate strategy. In their estimation, the revolt was a lost cause and it was urgent to cut its losses.

The Great Revolt was a very costly venture with no tangible dividends. The number of Syrians killed, wounded, and uprooted was staggering. At least 6,000 rebels were killed, over 100,000 persons were left homeless, and one-fifth of the homeless flooded into Damascus from devastated rural areas around the Syrian capital. Sections of Damascus were burnt-out shells, the result of French air bombardments and artillery shelling. Hama had been similarly devastated. The immense physical destruction the revolt wrought in the towns and countryside paralyzed the already

[61] MAE, Syrie–Liban 1918–29. Cairo, 24 Aug. 1927, vol. 213, p. 159; Shahbandar Papers, no. 10/26. Shahbandar to Hasan al-Hakim, 22 April 1927. ʿAdil al-ʿAzma was also accused of pilfering a large sum of money as was the Mufti, Hajj Amin al-Husayni. See MAE, Syrie–Liban 1918–29. 16 Aug. 1927, vol. 213, pp. 85–86; Porath, *The Emergence*, p. 203.
[62] MAE, Syrie–Liban 1918–29. French Consulate (Jaffa) to Consul-General (Jerusalem), 10 Oct. 1927, vol. 23, pp. 202–5.

enfeebled economy. Commerce and industry ground to a standstill. Agricultural production was dangerously low, the result of severe winter frost and summer drought exacerbated by damaging French military operations in the Hawran, the gardens around Damascus, and in central Syria near Homs and Hama. The physical and psychological exhaustion produced by nearly two years of full-scale rebellion led to a general demoralization of the Syrian masses. Their natural leaders could no longer rally them to battle. The French government, which had increased the number of French troops in Syria and Lebanon from 14,000 in the summer of 1925 to 50,000 by early 1926, was clearly determined to retain its Mandate despite significant and humiliating military losses, the growing financial burdens of quelling a popular, mass-based uprising, and the attacks of internal and international critics on its handling of the "Syrian question." For the revolt leadership, this all became starkly apparent after the French Army took the military offensive in the spring of 1926 and the Paris government decided that there were to be no diplomatic dealings or political compromises with Syrian nationalists until the revolt had been completely crushed.

Under such conditions, rebel leaders like Dr. Shahbandar and the Bakris, now in exile, viewed all efforts to keep the revolt alive as fundamentally suicidal, both in military and political terms. They accused the Jerusalem Committee and its supporters of being schismatics, men of a "doctrinaire literary type" who had never been in touch with the realities of the revolt. Although Shahbandar and his comrades admitted that they had called off the revolt—an admission that provoked accusations of betrayal and national treason from their critics—they claimed they had had no alternative because the Jerusalem Committee had withheld the funds and provisions required to keep it going.[63] Rebel leaders accused the Jerusalem Committee of misappropriating funds and demanded that a new financial organization be established, one dedicated to assisting those individuals who had actually participated in the revolt and who were forced to take refuge outside the Syrian homeland.[64]

The Jerusalem Committee and its Istiqlal Party supporters replied with an equally venomous series of accusations. They claimed that had the Congress Executive given priority on financial assistance to rebel forces

[63] Shahbandar Papers, no. 7/23. Shahbandar to Hasan al-Hakim, 15 March 1927. The Shahbandar group claimed that when the Jerusalem Committee did send money for the revolt, it went to rebels operating in the gardens around Damascus, and not to the Jabal Druze because it considered the Jabal to be much less critical to the success of the revolt. See MAE, Syrie–Liban 1918–29. 16 Aug. 1927, vol. 213, pp. 85–86.

[64] MWT, al-Qism al-khass, Nazih Mu'ayyad al-'Azm Papers, "Petition of Zu'ama of Ghuta and Damascus," 11 Aug. 1927; ibid., Nasib al-Bakri Papers, no. 30. Nasib al-Bakri to Michel Lutfallah, 12 March 1927.

in Syria trying to keep the revolt alive rather than to exiled rebel leaders, there would have been no reason to establish the Jerusalem Committee. In fact, Jerusalem accused Cairo of doing just what Jerusalem had been accused of—withholding funds earmarked for the Syrian insurgents.[65] To make matters worse, the Istiqlalis bitterly criticized the revolt's leadership for calling it off before the Syrian rebels had been decisively checked and defeated.

The charges hurled back and forth between the two rival factions as to who had diverted, withheld, or pilfered funds designated for the revolt illustrated the depth of division within the Syrian independence movement. The internecine rivalries also reflected the extent of frustration and hopelessness that pervaded the movement as the revolt began to lose its momentum, and its leaders their determination. The nationalist movement was wracked by divisions and it had again lost its territorial base. Defeated, forced outside Syria, its leaders had little to do but argue as to who deserved the blame, and to fight among themselves for control of the movement in exile.

Radical pan-Arabists associated with the Istiqlal Party and Shakib Arslan seized the offensive in their struggle with the Lutfallah–Shahbandar faction on the Syrian–Palestine Congress once the Great Revolt began to lose its momentum. In fact, the Istiqlali call for renewed armed resistance inside Syria at a time when the revolt's leaders were fleeing the country in droves was calculated to discredit these leaders and their allies on the Congress Executive. Thus, it was not an irrational plea made by misinformed individuals who had sat out the revolt on the sidelines and, as Shahbandar and others claimed, were ignorant of the immense military obstacles to keeping it alive. Rather, it was a stratagem employed to gain dominance within the Syrian nationalist movement. There is no evidence to suggest that the Istiqlalis seriously intended to prolong the revolt; they were perfectly aware that such efforts would be wasted.

ON THE SURFACE, differences between the Istiqlalis and the People's Party or the Jerusalem Committee and the Lutfallah-dominated Executive Committee of the Syrian–Palestine Congress reflected little more than the personal ambitions and struggles for power of Syrian nationalist leaders at home and in exile. Although personal rivalries were certainly at play, a closer investigation reveals more profound conflicts underlying these rivalries. These conflicts concerned the diplomatic and political strategy of the Syrian national independence movement, its direction,

[65] MAE, Syrie–Liban 1918–29. Muhammad Trabulsi to 'Adil Arslan and Nabih Bey (most likely al-'Azma), 29 Dec. 1925, vol. 211, pp. 142–50.

and ideological orientation. The Arslan–Istiqlali branch of the movement was avowedly pan-Arabist, anti-Hashemite, and opposed to cooperating with the British. It stood for the complete liberation of all Arab peoples and territories from foreign rule and the establishment of a unitary Arab state. Although for obvious reasons these radical nationalists were more directly concerned with Syrian affairs, they never shirked their "duties" toward Palestine, where by 1925 several of their most important members were based. Shahbandar's People's Party and the dominant faction on the Syrian–Palestine Congress Executive were close to the Hashemites and willing to cooperate with the British to accomplish their more limited goal, the establishment of an independent Syrian state. On the question of Lebanon, the Lutfallah–Shahbandar faction, under the influence of Michel Lutfallah, appeared willing to accept a Greater Lebanon.[66]

These rivalries and conflicts were sufficiently pronounced by the end of 1926 to create permanent lines of division in the Syrian nationalist movement. In early 1927, the movement's leaders—several of whom were now in exile in Cairo—began to wash their dirty linen in public. With the death of Najib Shuqayr, the Lebanese Druze Secretary of the Congress's Executive Committee and the one person who had held its factionalized members together, the Congress began to break apart. The following October Shakib Arslan resigned from the Executive, a move intended to prompt Shaykh Rashid Rida and the Istiqlali wing of the Executive to seize the leadership by deposing Michel Lutfallah. The embittered Lutfallah responded quickly by announcing the formation of his own Executive Committee from among his partisans and the exiled revolt leaders. By December 1927, two separate and antagonistic Committees functioned in Cairo, each one claiming to be the legitimate Executive of the Syrian–Palestine Congress. One was Lutfallah's ʿAbdin Committee (its office was located near the ʿAbdin Palace) which included Dr. Shahbandar and other rebel chiefs; Rashid Rida and various Istiqlalis headed by Shukri al-Quwwatli composed the other. [67]

[66] Ibid., "Notice par Enkiri," 25 Oct. 1927, vol. 214, pp. 18–21; Oriente Moderno, 7 (1927), pp. 564–66. In the early 1920s the Lutfallahs and their in-laws the Sursuks, who were among the wealthiest members of the Lebanese comprador bourgeoisie with branches in Beirut and Cairo, had already begun to engage in joint ventures with French capitalists in Lebanon. For the Lutfallahs, whose activities on the Syrian–Palestine Congress made them personae non gratae with the French High Commission, there was a growing need to mend their fences in order to pursue their various financial ventures unencumbered by travel restrictions and other obstacles which the High Commission may have imposed. See FO 371/ 9712, vol. 10162. Lord Allenby (Cairo) to Beirut Consulate, 8 Nov. 1924.

[67] FO 371/4744, vol. 12303. Henderson (Cairo) to Chamberlain; Oriente Moderno, 7 (1927), pp. 564–66, and 8 (1928), p. 56; conversation with Hasan al-Hakim (Damascus, 12 March 1976); conversation with Nasuh Babil (Damascus, 20 Feb. 1976); Nazih Muʿayyad al-ʿAzm Papers, no. 15. "Diary" (1927). Other members of the "ʿAbdin Committee" in-

The collapse of the Great Revolt led to the final rupture in the Syrian–Palestine Congress and the Syrian nationalist leadership's division into two hostile factions. It also left the Syrian people without an immediately identifiable local leadership and instrument of political expression.

Although radical nationalists associated with Shakib Arslan and the Istiqlal Party now had political leverage over the Lutfallah group and Shahbandar's People's Party, which they had managed to discredit, their political prospects were no more hopeful than those of their bitter rivals. Indeed, without recourse to armed struggle after the revolt's collapse, they watched helplessly as the French reasserted their control over Syria. It soon became obvious to Syrian nationalists—regardless of their political persuasion or ideological perspective—that they could not expect to achieve the consideration they sought from the French unless they abandoned their tactics of direct confrontation.

To be permitted to return to Syria and to participate in political life, nationalists had to resign themselves to playing politics by the rules of the French High Commission. The idea of achieving complete independence immediately was no longer feasible, if it ever had been. The most that could be achieved was a "gradual relaxation" of French control. Nationalists, in a sense, were back to square one. They had to concentrate their energies on discrediting all local rivals, those urban notables whom the High Commission had propped up in the first place. Only then could nationalists gain sole access to the French. This required an assertion of their independent influence in Syrian society and subtle diplomatic bargaining.

Instead of immediate independence, nationalist leaders now aimed to govern alongside the French in anticipation of their eventual departure. The Mandate system, after all, was by its very nature transitional. And though nationalism, with its need for strong and broadly based alliances, still served as the best instrument for diminishing the influence of narrower loyalties to religious community, ethnic group, or region, it nevertheless had to be refashioned to conform to new political and military realities. Whatever revolutionary appeal nationalism had assumed during the Great Revolt, clearly this had to be diluted.

Fortunately, for most Syrian nationalists, the French made the difficult task of seeking a more cooperative spirit easier than they had anticipated. The pressures of the Great Revolt convinced Paris to reconsider its political strategy.[68] Supported by the rise of a new climate of political thought

cluded Hasan al-Hakim, Tawfiq al-Yaziji, Khalid al-Khatib, Tawfiq Haydar, and Niqula Haddad. The Istiqlali "Committee" included Khayr al-Din al-Zirikli, Asʿad Daghir, ʿAbd al-Latif al-ʿAsali, al-Hajj Adib Khayr, Nabih al-ʿAzma, Saʿid Awda, and Saʿid Tarmanini.

[68] Apart from the fact that the Great Revolt took two years to crush, it also taxed French human and material resources. Some 2,000 French troops and auxiliaries were either killed

in postwar French policy-making circles, the older, more costly methods of colonial rule were severely criticized. In the case of Syria, the Quai d'Orsay was prepared to discard these outmoded methods in favor of more "delicate relationships," based on diplomacy rather than the overt threat of continuous military domination.[69] Thus, while the French continued to set the rules of the political game, they also felt pressure to revise them in light of the changing political conditions back in Paris.

---

or reported missing. This figure can be added to the 6,700 French troops who had been killed trying to pacify Syria between the occupation of 1920 and the revolt. In addition, the French Treasury was already stinging from the worst financial crisis France had experienced for over a century and a costly counterinsurgency campaign in Morocco (the Rif Rebellion). See David S. Woolman, *Rebels in the Rif. Abd el Krim and the Rif Rebellion* (Stanford, 1968), who points out that the rebellion cost France in 1925 an estimated 12,000 casualties, and $US 45 million. France maintained 300,000 troops in the country. At the same time, the French Treasury had to contribute nearly 500 million francs to support a greatly reinforced French army in Syria; FO 371/6841, vol. 10851. Crewe to Chamberlain, 7 Nov. 1925; MacCallum, *Crusade*, pp. 214–15; FO 371/5013, vol. 11516. Crewe to Chamberlain, 29 March 1926.

[69] Hourani, "Revolution in the Arab Middle East," p. 70.

PART IV

THE NATIONAL BLOC
AND URBAN LEADERSHIP

CHAPTER TEN

ALLIANCE OF EQUALS

NATIONALISTS WHO MANAGED to remain in Syria after the Great Revolt had an opportunity to assume the leadership of the fragmented independence movement. The People's Party leadership had been discredited in the eyes of some for having tried to halt the revolt, and so pressures from exile groups in Cairo abated.

An opportunity for nationalists still in Syria to pull together arose in the summer of 1927, on the occasion of the first major French policy statement on the future of Franco-Syrian relations since the collapse of the Great Revolt. To put that statement and the nationalist response in proper perspective, it is necessary to go back to late August 1926, when Raymond Poincaré tapped Henri Ponsot to succeed Henry de Jouvenel as High Commissioner.

Ponsot's tenure eventually established a new framework for political life in Syria. Fifty years old when he took up his office, he had been an official in the Ministry of Foreign Affairs since 1904. After serving for some years in Southeast Asia as Consul in Bangkok and for a brief period after the war as Consul-General in Montreal, he was appointed Assistant Chief of the African and Levant Section of the Ministry, a post which he held until his departure for Beirut in early October 1926.[1]

Unlike Jouvenel, who emphasized the liberal intentions of the French government in a continuous barrage of proclamations to the Syrian people, Ponsot followed a deliberately cautious course. He wanted to appear "impenetrable" and "enigmatic" as he studied the various problems and options at hand. During his first five months in the Levant he travelled extensively, with Colonel Catroux at his side, listening to the wishes, programs, and complaints of representatives of Syria's different communities, but never offering an inkling of his own conception of the tasks awaiting him. In Damascus and elsewhere, he heard familiar demands: a general amnesty, Syrian unity, compensation for the losses sustained during the revolt, an organic law to be promulgated by a Constituent Assembly, a 30-year treaty with France similar to the British treaty with Iraq, a national judicial system, and the admission of Syria into the League of Nations.[2] In Aleppo, which he visited in early November, he

[1] FO 371/5074, vol. 11516. Crewe (Paris) to Chamberlain, 30 Aug. 1926; MacCallum, *Crusade*, pp. 194–95.

[2] FO 371/6755, vol. 11508. Hole (Damascus) to Chamberlain, 25 Nov. 1926.

met with two nationalist leaders, Ibrahim Hananu and Dr. 'Abd al-Rah-man al-Kayyali, who complained about the severe economic problems in the country which they blamed on the recent increase (from 11 to 25 per-cent) in customs duties.[3] Between February and June 1927, Ponsot re-turned to Paris to report his findings to the Quai d'Orsay and consider solutions to the Syrian question.

Ponsot's administration undertook few new projects in its first nine months in office.[4] It was not until a month after the High Commissioner returned from his extended visit to France—with a new Secretary-Gen-eral, M. Maugras, in tow—that a formal policy statement was at long last delivered, and then not by the aloof Ponsot, but by Colonel Catroux. Speaking to journalists in Beirut on 26 July 1927, Catroux prefaced his remarks with a firm denial of rumors reported in the international press that France was about to relinquish her Mandate for Syria and Lebanon to the League of Nations. He then went on to say that France intended to integrate outlying districts inhabited by religious minorities (the Druze and Alawite states) with the Arab populated regions, while safeguarding their special interests and rights. France was also willing to allow for an organic law and the devolution of affairs of state onto local heads of gov-ernment. But France would not tolerate any actions that threatened the Mandate's security and the Common Interests, including customs, posts and telegraphs, concessionary companies, and the monetary system. He looked forward to the continued development of the country in collabo-ration with French capital.[5]

The general reaction in Syrian political circles was overwhelmingly negative. No one seriously believed that the High Commissioner in-tended to unite the minority districts with the nationalist heartland. The absence of any mention of a treaty along Anglo-Iraqi lines or the estab-lishment of a national army made it all too clear that the French did not seriously intend to relax their direct control over Syria's domestic affairs. Ponsot's program at this stage did not seem to differ substantially from Jouvenel's.

The timing of Ponsot's declaration coincided with the elimination of the last vestiges of the Great Revolt. To the defeated nationalists who had led the revolt, the High Commissioner's declaration was a natural conse-quence of France's victory. For three months, local nationalists did not utter a word in response as they shuttled between Damascus and Cairo

---

[3] FO 371/6527, vol. 11516. Akras (Aleppo) to Chamberlain, 9 Nov. 1926.

[4] Apart from the formation of a third cabinet in December 1926 under Ahmad Nami Bey. Hasan al-Hakim, *Mudhakkirati*, vol. 2, pp. 162–64.

[5] Rabbath, *Courte Histoire*, pp. 46–50; MacCallum, *Crusade*, pp. 197–98. For a transla-tion of Ponsot's declaration of 26 July 1927, see MacCallum, *Crusade*, Appendix 3, pp. 273–77.

during the long hot summer, consulting on what course ought to be followed. Nationalist leaders realized that their options were few and feud-
ing within the Syrian–Palestine Congress made mapping out a strategy
that much more difficult. Under the circumstances, a more conciliatory
approach was inevitable.

It was no coincidence that the long-awaited nationalist response to
Ponsot's July declaration and the coup against Michel Lutfallah and his
faction on the Syrian–Palestine Congress Executive occurred within days
of each other. Both seem to have been reactions to the ratification, in mid-
October 1927, of a revised constitution for Greater Lebanon.[6]
For nationalist leaders in Damascus and elsewhere in the Syrian interior, the revised Lebanese constitution posed a serious problem. Not only
did it legitimize the existence of a Lebanon, which would remain politically and administratively independent of Damascus, but it also suggested
the characteristics of the constitution or organic law M. Ponsot had promised Syria.[7] Michel Lutfallah, however, avoided voicing any opposition to
the new Lebanese constitution. His acquiescence underscored his mounting interest in establishing a family dynasty in a Lebanon separate from
Syria.[8]
With the crisis over the Lebanese constitution as a catalyst, the nationalist reponse to Ponsot's declaration was issued on October 25. It came in
the form of a statement drafted at the conclusion of a six-day conference
held in Beirut and attended by nationalists from the main towns of Syria
and Lebanon. In ten precise paragraphs the nationalists addressed the
High Commissioner's proposals.[9] Its preamble echoed the unhappiness
and "disillusion" fostered by Ponsot's uncompromising attitude. They
asked if he was sincerely predisposed to conclude a treaty, and why he had
made no mention of the Syrian nation's desire to "exercise her natural
right to freedom of the press and political association."[10] They inquired if
martial law was to be terminated, if a proscription against house arrest
was to be instituted, and if a general amnesty was to be granted. Then
followed the familiar demands for a Constituent Assembly freely elected
by universal suffrage and the reunification of Syria in its entirety. Finally, the nationalist response concluded on a melancholic but highly revealing note:

[6] MacCallum, *Crusade*, pp. 200–201.

[7] *Ibid.*, p. 201.

[8] *Oriente Moderno*, 7 (1927), pp. 564–67.

[9] Amin Sa'id, *al-Thawra al-'arabiyya al-kubra* (Cairo, 1934), vol. 3, pp. 531–36; Muhammad Harb Farzat, *al-Hayah al-hizbiyya*, p. 103; 'Abd al-Rahman al-Kayyali, *al-Marahil fi al-intidab al-faransi wa fi nidalina al-watani* (Aleppo, 1958), vol. 1, pp. 64–67.

[10] Rabbath, *Courte Histoire*, pp. 50–52.

We are certain that in France the nation supports our national cause and desires to re-establish confidence between us. The sentiment of justice of the French people is evidence of this and we believe in the necessity of *collaboration* based on the reciprocity of interests and on the determination of mutual obligations.[11]

With these words a new era in Franco-Syrian relations dawned, labeled by nationalists the era of "honorable cooperation." The Beirut conference had one other important outcome. From it emerged a new nationalist organization in Syria, the National Bloc (al-Kutla al-wataniyya), which would steer the course of the independence struggle in Syria until its completion 19 years later.

FOUNDING FATHERS

The new organization did not begin to sign its name to nationalist proclamations until the autumn of 1931, and did not spell out its organizational principles until a year after that.[12] But the seeds of the National Bloc were planted at the Beirut Conference of 1927 and by the Constituent Assembly elections in the spring of 1928 it had begun to establish an identifiable pattern of political behavior. By 1930, al-Kutla al-wataniyya was a household name in the towns of the Syrian interior.[13]

Fifteen Syrian and Lebanese representatives gathered in Beirut in October 1927 to frame a response to M. Ponsot's July declaration. Seven of these formed the core of the National Bloc: Ihsan al-Sharif from Damascus, Ibrahim Hananu and ʿAbd al-Rahman al-Kayyali from Aleppo, Najib al-Barazi and ʿAbd al-Qadir al-Kaylani from Hama, and Mazhar Raslan and Hashim al-Atasi (the conference President) from Homs.[14] This core group was enlarged by the return to Syria of several revolt leaders pardoned by the French in March 1928. Among those amnestied who immediately joined the Bloc's ranks were Fawzi al-Ghazzi, Lutfi al-Haffar, and Faris al-Khuri from Damascus; Husni al-Barazi from Hama; and

---

[11] *Ibid.*, p. 53.

[12] According to one source, the National Bloc's first proclamation was dated 10 December 1931. See al-Kayyali, *al-Marahil*, vol. 1, pp. 131–35. Also see Dhuqan Qarqut, *Tatawwur*, p. 104.

[13] Conversation with Edmond Rabbath (Beirut, 3 Sept. 1975). For example, *al-Mudhik al-mubki* referred to *al-Kutla al-wataniyya* on several occasions toward the end of 1929.

[14] The other three Syrians were Saʿid al-Jazaʾiri, Yusuf al-ʿIssa (the editor of *Alif baʾ*) from Damascus, and Fakhr al-Jabiri from Aleppo. The Lebanese representatives were Shaykh ʿAbd al-Hamid Karami, Dr. ʿArif al-Baysar, and ʿArif al-Rifaʿi from Tripoli, and ʿAbd al-Rahman Bayhum and Dr. ʿAbdullah al-Yafi from Beirut. Amin Saʿid, *al-Thawra al-ʿarabiyya al-kubra* (Cairo, 1934), vol. 3, p. 531.

Sa'dallah al-Jabiri (whose brother Fakhr had represented Aleppo at the Beirut conference).[15]

The 1928 amnesty helped the National Bloc to broaden its political base by absorbing returning nationalists and to protect itself from other claimants to the nationalist mantle. But, the amnesty had been designed to exacerbate jealousies among Syrian nationalists. Still blacklisted were rebel leaders, notably Dr. Shahbandar, Hasan al-Hakim, Sa'id Haydar, Nazih Mu'ayyad al-'Azm and Sultan al-Atrash, and long-time exiled radical nationalists like Shukri al-Quwwatli, Nabih al-'Azma, Shakib and 'Adil Arslan, and Ihsan al-Jabiri.[16] The growing chasm within the nationalist movement in exile, which pitted Shahbandar's People's Party against the Istiqlal Party, enabled the Bloc to develop along non-revolutionary lines.

At the end of March 1928 a second conference was convened in Damascus to announce that the loosely-knit nationalist coalition would participate in the Assembly elections. At that time several other well-known political activists joined the emerging Bloc. These new additions included Fakhri al-Barudi, Zaki al-Khatib, Ahmad al-Lahham, 'Afif Sulh, Fa'iz al-Khuri, Muhammad al-Nahhas, and Jamil Mardam from the Syrian capital; Tawfiq al-Shishakli from Hama; and Ahmad al-Rifa'i, 'Abd al-Qadir al-Sarmini, Hasan Fu'ad Ibrahim Pasha, and Jamil Ibrahim Pasha from Aleppo.[17] These men, in addition to the original seven from the Beirut conference and the amnestied leaders of the revolt, accounted for most of the leadership of the National Bloc.[18]

It has been argued that the "first coordinated nationalist thrust" in the Arab countries tended to produce a "broad heterogeneous grouping" such as the Egyptian Wafd, the Tunisian Neo-Destour and the Syrian National Bloc. While it is true that the National Bloc emerged as the broadest political grouping in pre-independence Syria in terms of its geographical range, numerical size, and diverse class support, at the leadership level the Bloc, like the People's Party before it, was highly homogeneous.[19] The leadership of the nationalist movement in Syria, from its inception in late Ottoman times, was drawn primarily from the Sunni Arab landowning and bureaucratic class of the interior towns. Land provided a steady source of income to further political ambitions exclusively within an urban environment.

Over 90 percent of the Bloc chiefs were Sunnis and all were permanent

---

[15] *Ibid.*; FO 371/1472, vol. 13074. Hole (Damascus) to Chamberlain, 23 Feb. 1928.

[16] For a complete roster of the 1928 Black List, see *Arrêté*, no. 1817, 14 March 1928.

[17] Farzat, *al-Hayah al-hizbiyya*, p. 110.

[18] *Oriente Moderno*, 19 (1930), p. 369.

[19] See Jacques Berque, "L'univers politique des Arabes," in *Encyclopédie française* (Paris, 1957), vol. 11, cited by Patrick Seale, *The Struggle for Syria. A Study of Post-War Arab Politics 1945–1958* (London, 1965), p. 27.

residents of the interior towns; nearly 50 percent came from Damascus, over 30 percent came from Aleppo, and the remaining 20 percent were divided almost equally between Homs and Hama. The class origins of the Bloc reveal that nearly two-thirds of its leaders belonged either to the landowning-bureaucratic or the landowning-scholarly segments of Syria's traditional upper class. Another quarter were from wealthy or middling merchant families, while 10 percent hailed from a class of unpropertied functionaries.

The Bloc leadership was unusually well educated. More than 90 percent had received a secular education rather than traditional religious instruction, and more than half had acquired advanced professional training in Istanbul in preparation for administrative or military service in the Ottoman Empire; another 20 percent had attended universities in Europe or the Syrian Protestant College in Beirut where they had studied law, public administration, and medicine. The leadership's occupational background shows that 40 percent were "professional politicians." Another third were either lawyers or instructors of law at the Syrian University in Damascus who were actively involved in local politics, while the remaining third included three physicians, two merchants, a religious dignitary, a bureaucrat, and a retired Sharifian officer. Many members had a generous annual income from land rents, which freed them from regular employment to practice politics.[20]

The age structure of the National Bloc and especially of its Damascus members contributed to its homogeneity. The average year of birth of its 25 leading personalities was 1886 (the median was 1887). Although men like Ibrahim Hananu and Hashim al-Atasi belonged to an older generation of nationalists than did Sa'dallah al-Jabiri and Jamil Mardam, over three-fourths of the Bloc leadership were born within a 13-year span, between 1882 and 1895. These men grew up in a similar social and cultural milieu, attended the same schools, and were often related. Many had studied at Maktab 'Anbar in Damascus[21] and then in Istanbul at the Mülkiye, returning to the Syrian provinces after the Young Turk Revolt of 1908 to join the provincial bureaucracy. However, Turkish insensitivity to Arab feelings and aspirations strained their loyalty to the Ottoman state.[22] Before World War I, some future Bloc leaders had already participated in secret nationalist activities. The earliest members of al-Fatat included Fakhri al-Barudi, Nasib al-Bakri, and Jamil Mardam. Many others

[20] Conversation with Hasan al-Hakim (Damascus, 12 March 1976).
[21] For a personal account of life at Maktab 'Anbar, see Fakhri al-Barudi, *Mudhakkirat al-Barudi* (Damascus, 1951), vol. 1, pp. 30–37. At the time the author attended this school, other future nationalist leaders enrolled there included Shukri al-Quwwatli, Muhammad Sa'id al-Ghazzi, Sa'id Haydar, Fawzi al-Ghazzi, and Mazhar Raslan.
[22] See Khoury, *Urban Notables*, Chapter 3.

who eventually became Bloc leaders joined one of the several extra-governmental nationalist societies which dominated political life during the Faysal interlude. Among these were Shukri al-Quwwatli, Fawzi al-Ghazzi, Zaki al-Khatib, Husni al-Barazi, Ihsan al-Jabiri, Tawfiq al-Shishakli, Muhammad al-Nahhas, Nabih and ʿAdil al-ʿAzma, ʿAdil Arslan and Mustafa Barmada. Linked by common political aims and accustomed to working together, these young men had already started to build a loose alliance by the time France occupied Syria.[23] Supporting them in their endeavors were other future Bloc chiefs who played an active political role in governmental life under Amir Faysal, including two Cabinet Ministers (Hashim al-Atasi and Faris al-Khuri); five representatives to the Syrian National Congress of 1919–1920 (Ibrahim Hananu, Saʿdallah al-Jabiri, ʿAbd al-Qadir al-Kaylani, and Mazhar Raslan; Atasi was also a deputy); and members of Faysal's immediate entourage (Fakhri al-Barudi and Ihsan al-Jabiri, who were his Chamberlains, and Colonel Ahmad al-Lahham, his official delegate in Beirut.[24] Thus the National Bloc was a direct descendant of the early nationalist societies of the late Ottoman and Arab independence eras in Syria, and especially of al-Fatat and the Istiqlal Party. (See Tables 10-1 to 10-3 for a biographical analysis of the National Bloc leadership compared with moderate and pro-French politicians and bureaucrats.)

AIMS AND STRATEGY

The National Bloc was considerably less militant than the Iron Hand Society or the People's Party. Its policy of "honorable cooperation" was born out of defeat. The bombardment of Damascus, the almost complete destruction of the Maydan quarter, and the massive sweeping-up operations in the countryside around the Syrian capital and elsewhere were sufficient testimonials to French military superiority and hence to the futility of armed struggle in the future. The personal and financial losses suffered by the absentee landowning class and the old commercial bourgeoisie, especially of Damascus, heightened this reality, and encouraged the Bloc to fashion less confrontational tactics. In addition, the spread of the revolt to the countryside, while it eventually prolonged the revolt, also damaged agrarian productive forces and hurt the material interests of the landowning class, to which many nationalists belonged.

It is equally true that nationalists regarded peasant society as too so-

[23] C. Ernest Dawn, "The Rise of Arabism in Syria," in *From Ottomanism to Arabism* (Urbana, 1973), pp. 174–76.

[24] Najati Sidqi, "al-Haraka al-wataniyya al-ʿarabiyya min al-inqilab al-ittihad ila ʿahd al-kutla al-wataniyya," *al-Taliʿa* (Damascus), 4 (May 1938), no. 6, pp. 419–20. On Lahham's career, see MD, 7N 4190. "Sûreté Générale," Damascus, 5 May 1926.

TABLE 10-1

Characteristics of the National Bloc Leadership Compared with Characteristics of Syrian Government Ministers and Moderate or Pro-French Deputies who did not belong to another Nationalist Organization during the French Mandate

	NB[a]	Other[b]
Average year of birth	1886	1879
	Percentages	
Religion (by sect)		
Muslim: Sunni	92.0	89.0
Christian: Protestant	4.0	3.5
Christian: Greek Orthodox	4.0	3.5
Jew	0.0	3.5
Education		
Advanced Ottoman	56.0	54.0
Advanced Western	20.0	7.0
Local Secondary	16.0	25.0
Traditional Religious Instruction	8.0	14.0
Occupation		
Landowner-Politician	40.0	28.5
Lawyer/University Educator (law)	28.0	11.0
Physician	12.0	0.0
Merchant	8.0	14.0
Religious Dignitary-Bureaucrat	4.0	11.0
Bureaucrat	4.0	32.0
Retired Military Officer	4.0	0.0
Journalist	0.0	3.5
Class Origin		
Landowning-Bureaucrat, Landowner	40.0	43.0
Landowning-Scholar	24.0	18.0
Upper- and Upper-Middle-Class Merchant	12.0	11.0
Middle-Class Professional	8.0	0.0
Bureaucrat	8.0	0.0
Middle-Class Merchant	4.0	3.5
Religious Dignitary	4.0	21.0
Middling Landowner	0.0	3.5

[a] Based on information on 25 leaders in Table 10-2.
[b] Based on information on 28 individuals in Table 10-3.

cially backward and politically dormant to warrant the time and effort needed to mold it into an effective weapon of resistance. Throughout the Mandate, the nationalist leaders focused their attention on the towns which were thought to be more easily mobilized, owing to the higher concentration of people in a finite area and because the political consciousness of the urban masses was already on a more elevated plane than that of rural society.[25]

Without recourse to armed struggle, the emerging National Bloc adopted other tactics. While Bloc leaders always had to demonstrate their independent influence in society to the French, they also had to make themselves more attractive political actors, by showing a willingness to play politics by the rules of the High Commission. They had to strike a delicate balance between strength and moderation. The Bloc's first goal was to discredit all local rivals who had been propped up by the High Commission in the first place in order to gain sole access to the French. Its second goal was to govern alongside the French in anticipation of their inevitable departure.[26] Inevitably this process would have to be slow and evolutionary not to upset the foundations of their independent influence, which made them the most prominent intermediary between the French and the Syrian people.

The push for compromise was not solely on the Syrian side, however. In the aftermath of the Great Revolt, France also adopted a somewhat more balanced and reasoned approach to governing Syria. Already within postwar French policy-making circles there had arisen a new climate of political thought. The older, more costly methods of direct colonial rule had been called into question and were now being discarded in favor of more "delicate relationships" based on diplomatic bargaining rather than on the threat of overt military domination. In the Syrian case, this shift was in part a response to the League of Nations' criticisms of France's handling of the revolt. Above all, it was an internal response to a growing realization that France could no longer afford either to rule directly by means of a large army of occupation or to act out the twin roles of ruler and political mentor in Syria. In order to remain in Syria, the French eventually would have to turn to those native forces with significant independent strength in society to fill the role of political leadership; and those whom the French had propped up in government posts would eventually have to be pushed aside.

Most nationalists had regarded French strategies as inimical to their own interests, mainly because they at first threatened the absentee land-

[25] Conversations with Hani al-Hindi (Beirut, 28 Aug. 1975) and ʿAli ʿAbd al-Karim al-Dandashi (Damascus, 21 Oct. 1975).
[26] Albert Hourani, "Revolution in the Arab Middle East," p. 70.

TABLE 10-2
Biographical Data: The National Bloc Leadership

Name	Year of Birth	Religion	Education	Occupation	Class Origin	Year Joined	Offices
From Damascus							
Nasib al-Bakrī	1888	Muslim: Sunni	Local Secondary (Damascus)	Landowner, politician	Landowning-bureaucratic, ashrāf	1932	Min. 1939: Deputy: 1932, 1936, 1943
Fakhrī al-Bārūdī	1889	Muslim: Sunni	Local Secondary (Damascus)	Landowner, politician	Landowning-bureaucratic	1928	Deputy: 1928, 1932, 1936
Fawzī al-Ghazzī	1895 (d.1929)	Muslim: Sunni	Advanced Ottoman (Istanbul)	Lawyer	Landowning-scholarly, ashrāf	1928	Deputy: 1928
Lutfī al-Ḥaffār	1891	Muslim: Sunni	Traditional religious instruction (Damascus)	Merchant	Upper-middle-class merchants	1928	Min. 1926, 1938, 1939, 1943, 1945. Deputy: 1928, 1936, 1943
Zakī al-Khaṭīb	1887	Muslim: Sunni	Advanced Ottoman (Istanbul)	Lawyer, politician	Prominent religious dignitaries, ashrāf	1928[a]	Min. 1941–42. Deputy: 1928, 1932
Fāʾiz al-Khūrī	1895	Christian: Gr. Orth.	Advanced Western (Paris)	Lawyer, educator	Middle-class professional	1928	Min. 1939, 1941–43. Deputy: 1928, 1932, 1936

Name	Birth	Religion/Ethnicity	Education	Profession	Class background	Year	Offices
Fāris al-Khūrī	1877	Christian: Protestant	Advanced Western (Beirut)	Lawyer, educator	Middle-class professional	1928	Min. 1920, 1926, 1944-45. Deputy: 1936, 1943
Ahmad al-Laḥḥām	1883	Muslim: Sunni	Advanced Ottoman (Istanbul)	Retired Ottoman & Sharifian officer	Upper-middle-class merchants	1928	Deputy: 1928, 1936
Jamil Mardam	1894	Muslim: Sunni	Advanced Western (Paris)	Landowner, politician	Landowning-bureaucratic	1928	Min. 1932-33, 1936-39, 1943-45. Deputy: 1932, 1936, 1943
Shukri al-Quwwatli	1892	Muslim: Sunni	Advanced Ottoman (Istanbul)	Landowner, politician	Landowning-bureaucratic and merchant classes	1932	Pres. 1943. Min. 1936-38. Deputy: 1936, 1943
Ihsān al-Sharif	1893	Muslim: Sunni	Advanced Western (Paris)	Lawyer	Ottoman officials and scholars	1928	Deputy: 1928, 1932, 1936
'Afif Ṣulḥ	1890	Muslim: Sunni	Advanced Ottoman (Istanbul)	Lawyer	Wealthy merchants and bureaucrats	1928	Deputy: 1932, 1936, 1943
From Aleppo							
Najīb Bāqī Zādih	1877	Muslim: Sunni Arabized Kurd	Local Secondary (Aleppo)	Merchant	Ottoman officials	1928	

TABLE 10-2 (cont.)
Biographical Data: The National Bloc Leadership

Name	Year of Birth	Religion	Education	Occupation	Class Origin	Year Joined	Offices
Ibrāhīm Hanānū	1869 (d.1935)	"	Advanced Ottoman (Istanbul)	Landowner	Landowning	1928	Deputy: 1928
Ḥasan Fu'ād Ibrāhīm Pāshā	1879	"	Advanced Ottoman (Damascus)	Physician	Landowning	1928	Deputy: 1936
Jamīl Ibrāhīm Pāshā	1882	"	Advanced Ottoman (Istanbul)	Landowner, politician	Landowning	1928	Deputy: 1928, 1936
Sa'dallāh al-Jābirī	1893	Muslim: Sunni	Advanced Ottoman (Istanbul)	Politician, landowner	Landowning-scholarly, ashrāf	1928	Min. 1936–39, 1943–44. 1945–46. Deputy: 1928, 1936, 1943
'Abd al-Raḥmān al-Kayyālī	1887	Muslim: Sunni	Advanced Western Beirut/SPC-AUB)	Physician	Landowning-scholarly, ashrāf	1928	Min. 1936–39, 1943–45. Deputy: 1928, 1936, 1943
Aḥmad al-Rifā'ī	1887	Muslim: Sunni	Advanced Ottoman (Istanbul)	Lawyer	Landowning-scholarly, ashrāf	1928	Deputy: 1928
'Abd al-Qādir al-Sarmīnī	1877	Muslim: Sunni	Traditional religious instruction (Aleppo)	Religious shaykh	Middling merchant	1928	Deputy: 1928, 1936

From *Hama*							
Ḥusnī al-Barāzī	1893	Muslim: Sunni Arabized Kurd	Advanced Ottoman (Istanbul)	Landowner, politician	Landowning-bureaucratic	1928[b]	Min. 1926, 1934–36, 1942–43. Deputy: 1928
Najīb al-Barāzī	1882	"	Local Secondary (Hama)	Landowner, politician	Landowning-bureaucratic	1931	Deputy: 1932, 1943
Tawfīq al-Shīshāklī	1884 (d. 1940)	Muslim: Sunni	Advanced Ottoman (Damascus)	Physician	Landowning-bureaucratic	1928	Deputy: 1932, 1936
From *Homs*							
Hāshim al-Atāsī	1876	Muslim: Sunni	Advanced Ottoman (Istanbul)	Landowner, politician	Landowning-scholarly, *ashrāf*	1928	Pres. 1936–39. Deputy: 1928, 1932
Mazhar Raslān	1887	Muslim: Sunni	Advanced Ottoman (Istanbul)	Official	Landowning-scholarly, *ashrāf*	1928	Min. 1932–33, 1939, 1943–44. Deputy: 1928, 1932, 1936, 1943

[a] Resigned in 1935.
[b] Resigned in 1931.

TABLE 10-3

Biographical Data: Moderate and Pro-French Politicians and Bureaucrats

Name	Year of Birth	Religion	Education	Occupation	Class Origin	Party, Year Joined	Offices
From Damascus							
Muḥammad ʿAli al-ʿĀbid	1868	Muslim: Sunni	Advanced Western (Paris)	Landowner, politician	Landowning-bureaucratic		Pres. 1932–36. Min. 1922–24, 1932–1936
ʿAṭā al-Ayyūbī	1877	"	Advanced Ottoman (Istanbul)	Bureaucrat	Landowning-bureaucratic[a]		Min. 1922–24, 1925, 1934–35, 1936, 1943
ʿAbd al-Qādir al-ʿAẓm	1881	"	"	Lawyer, educator, bureaucrat	Landowning-bureaucratic		Min. 1926
Ḥaqqī al-ʿAẓm	1864	"	"	Politician, landowner	Landowning-bureaucratic	RP[b]/ 1929	Min. 1920–22, 1932–34. Deputy: 1932
Badiʿ al-Muʾayyad	1870	"	"	Bureaucrat	Landowning-bureaucratic	RP/ 1929	Min. 1920–22, 1930–32
Wāthiq Muʾayyad al-ʿAẓm	1885	Muslim: Sunni	Advanced Ottoman (Istanbul)	Bureaucrat	Landowning-bureaucratic		Min. 1926
Naṣūḥi al-Bukhārī	1881	"	"	Retired army officer	Religious dignitaries		Min. 1920–22, 1926–28, 1939, 1944. Deputy: 1943

Name	Birth	Religion	Education	Occupation	Class	RP/1930	Positions
Shākir al-Ḥanbalī	1876	"	"	Educator, lawyer	Religious dignitaries	RP/1930	Min. 1926, 1930–31, 1931–32
Tāj al-Dīn al-Ḥasanī	1885	Muslim: Sunni	Traditional religious instruction (Damascus)	Religious dignitary, politician	Religious dignitaries		Pres. 1941. Min. 1928–31, 1934–36. Deputy: 1928
Sulaymān Jukhadār	1867	"	"	Religious dignitary, educator, bureaucrat	Religious dignitaries	RP/1930	Min. 1933–34
ʿAbd al-Qādir al-Khaṭīb	1880	"	"	Religious dignitary, bureaucrat	Religious dignitaries, *ashrāf*		Director of *Awqāf*, 1928–34
Nasīb al-Kaylānī	1896	"	Local Secondary (Damascus)	Landowner, politician	Landowning-scholarly, *ashrāf*		Deputy: 1932, 1943
Muḥammad Kurd ʿAlī	1876	Muslim: Sunni	Traditional religious instruction (Damascus)	Journalist, bureaucrat	Middling landowning		Min. 1920–22, 1928–31
Yūsuf Linyādū	1872	Jew	Local Secondary (Damascus)	Merchant	Upper-class merchant		Deputy: 1928, 1932, 1936
Saʿīd al-Maḥāsinī	1885	Muslim: Sunni	Advanced Ottoman (Istanbul)	Lawyer, politician	Religious dignitaries, middling landowners		Min. 1928–29

TABLE 10-3 (cont.)

Biographical Data: Moderate and Pro-French Politicians and Bureaucrats

Name	Year of Birth	Religion	Education	Occupation	Class Origin	Party, Year Joined	Offices
Tawfīq Shāmiyya	1885	Christian: Gr. Orth.	Advanced Western (Beirut/SPC-AUB)	Landowner, merchant, politician	Landowning		Min. 1928–31, 1943–44
Wadī' al-Shishāklī	1888	Muslim: Sunni	Advanced Ottoman (Istanbul)	Landowner, politician	Landowning-bureaucratic		Deputy: 1928, 1932, 1943
Jamīl al-Ulshī	1883	Muslim: Sunni	Advanced Ottoman (Istanbul/Mil. Col.)	Landowner, politician	Upper-middling landowning-scholarly		Min. 1920, 1928–30, 1934–36, 1943
From Aleppo							
Ṣubḥī Barakāt	1889	Muslim: Sunni	Local Secondary (Antioch)	Landowner, politician	Landowning	LCᵈ/ 1931	Min. 1922–26. Deputy: 1932
Henri Hindiyya	1897	Armenian Catholic	Local Secondary (Aleppo)	Merchant, banker	Middle-class merchants	LC/ 1931	Min. 1934–36. Deputy: 1932
Ghālib Ibrāhīm Pāshā	1878	Muslim: Sunni Arabized Kurd	Advanced Ottoman (Istanbul)	Landowner, bureaucrat	Landowning	LC/ 1931	Governor (Aleppo). Deputy: 1932
Salīm Jambart	1873	Christian: Gr. Cath.	Local Secondary (Aleppo)	Merchant	Upper-middle-class merchants	LC/ 1931	Min. 1932–34, 1939. Deputy: 1932

Name	Birth	Religion	Education	Occupation	Social background	Party	Offices
Nabīh Mardīnī	1884	Muslim: Sunni	Advanced Ottoman (Istanbul)	Bureaucrat	Religious dignitaries		Governor (Aleppo)
Ṣafwat Qāṭiraghāssī	1881	Muslim: Sunni	"	Bureaucrat	Landowning-bureaucratic		Governor (Aleppo)
Ṣubḥī al-Nayyāl	1874	"	"	Judge, bureaucrat	Landowning-scholarly, *ashrāf*	LC/1931	Min. 1928–30
Muḥammad Basīm al-Qudsī	1883	"	Local Secondary (Aleppo)	Landowner	Landowning-scholarly, *ashrāf*	LC/1931	Deputy: 1932
Shākir Ni'mat al-Sha'bānī	1871	"	Advanced Ottoman (Istanbul/Mil. Col.)	Politician, journalist	Landowning-bureaucratic	LC/1931	Min. 1926, 1933–34. Deputy: 1932
From Hama							
'Abd al-Qādir al-Kaylānī	1875	"	"	Religious dignitary, bureaucrat	Landowning-scholarly, *ashrāf*		Min. 1928–30. Deputy: 1928

[a] Landowners by marriage.
[b] Reform Party.
[c] Originally from Antioch.
[d] Liberal Constitutionalist.

owning class's economic hold over the countryside and then politically pre-empted nationalists in rural districts. It is unlikely that the nationalist leadership could have prevented the revolt from engulfing the countryside, but there is evidence to suggest that it only supported rural rebellion fully after the French expelled it from the towns. Had the nationalist leadership not turned to the countryside, it would almost certainly have lost its direction of the revolt.

After the revolt, however, the High Commission abandoned its rural strategy of undercutting the material base of the absentee landowning class. Its implementation of land reform measures slowed. Until the late 1930s, therefore, the landowning class was sure of its ascendancy, something which French policy actually reinforced.

Yet, despite a distinct shift in French political strategy, France failed to develop a stable and consistent imperial policy. The new climate in France still suffered from interruptions of foul weather. While political pressure groups against imperial responsibility were growing, they still encountered strong political and ideological opposition from the military establishment and pro-colonial elements in Parliament supported by a small but vocal lobby of financial and religious groups with interests in the Levant. These conflicts, when transferred to the Syrian arena, regularly confounded the National Bloc, making it consistently uneasy about its policy of "honorable cooperation." As long as the High Commission showed a willingness to concede some nationalist demands, the Bloc's moderate wing was able to keep the organization on a steady course. But, whenever the High Commission slowed the pace toward constitutionalism or a treaty, the Bloc's radical wing pushed the organization to a less accommodating stance. Local forces were then mobilized to remind the French of the Bloc's strength. Obviously, in such fluid conditions nationalist political behavior was rarely stable.[27]

Ethos and Aims

Among nationalists throughout the Arab East there existed a common *weltanschauung* or psychology, "a system of ideas which formed the political orthodoxy" of the interwar years.[28] This system was anchored in a common language, education, and political culture and in shared experiences in the schools, barracks, Ottoman Parliament, exile in Cairo, the Arab Revolt, and Faysal's Damascus. But after the European division of the Arab East, the nationalist idea had to be recast to suit the specific conditions of a truncated Syria.

[27] *Ibid.*
[28] Albert Hourani, *Arabic Thought*, p. 293.

One distinctive characteristic of the nationalism subscribed to by the National Bloc was its secular content. Since the end of the nineteenth century nationalism had grown at the expense of other loyalties, particularly of religion. Although the Bloc's brand of nationalism continued to be infused with religious symbolism, the religious expression in its appeal was less pronounced than the territorial and ethno-cultural calls for unity and resistance. The secularization of the Syrian nationalist movement was very much a product of the general secularization of the class interests of its leadership, a process which began in the latter half of the nineteenth century. Concomitantly, the Bloc's secularism would never have been so strong had the influence of the traditional religious leadership in the towns not been in decline for equally as long. The growth of the state in the nineteenth century, the spread of modern learning, the widening of Syria's links with the outside world, and her ongoing integration into a world economy created new forces, new opinions, and a new psychological climate. Relations between Syrians were increasingly governed by the money nexus. Religious solidarity still existed as did other loyalties to the family, clan, ethnic group, town quarter, and village, but all of these had been corroded somewhat by the ascendance of nationalism. In the case of religious solidarity, it no longer governed the intellectual lives and ideological perceptions of Syria's political leadership, even though many Bloc chiefs were more than nominally pious.[29]

The founding principles of the Bloc clearly underscored the leadership's dominant characteristics and class interests. These were first set forth at the Homs Congress in November 1932. There, nationalists officially declared the Bloc a political organization standing for the complete unity, territorial integrity, and independence of Syria (a proviso that Lebanon could "decide her own political fate within her pre-1920 borders" was added). The Bloc also called for "combining efforts with other Arab countries to unite them, providing that their endeavors would not obstruct the specific aims and needs of each country." In comparison with the 1928 draft version of the Syrian Constitution which stated that

> the Syrian territory separated from the Ottoman state constitutes a single indivisible unit and any arbitrary division that has occurred from the end of World War I to 1928 is meaningless,

the 1932 statement was clearly a compromise, framed to conform more closely to existing political realities. The Bloc could not hide the changing territorial frame of reference which the European partition had imposed on Syrian nationalism at the end of the war. And though the Bloc's gen-

---

[29] Conversation with Qustantin Zurayq (Beirut, 10 Jan. 1976). This has also been observed in Iraq: see Hanna Batatu, *The Old Social Classes*, pp. 209–10.

eral principles were phrased in such a manner as to make them seem final, in fact these principles were also liable to redefinition.[30]

The absence of any systematic social or economic program at this time, or at any other time during the interwar years, is revealing. The founding fathers made only brief reference to the question of the religious minorities "whose freedom and equality of rights and obligations were to be honored," and to the various classes in society "whose standard of living was to be raised and in whom culture and nationalism were to be instilled." In the 1932 declaration, the Bloc frankly stated that all the Syrian nation's material and moral power was to be harnessed for the sole purpose of nationalist struggle until the goals of the nation as set forth by the Bloc—which, incidentally, appointed itself as the "guardian of the nation"—were achieved.[31] The Bloc perceived itself as a purely political organization dedicated to opposing all foreign hegemony. But it had little vision itself of the social and economic future and condemned the formation of all other parties as detrimental to the preservation of unity in the face of the colonial power.

The Bloc's very existence was predicated on struggle against foreign occupation, and the organization's leaders rarely looked to active contact with the masses. Their reasoning was that the liberation of Syria from France had to come before the economy and society could be restructured. The "nationalism of the *pashas*" never stretched so far as to include problems of internal social and economic development, which they perceived to be inimical to their own interests.[32] Because the Bloc incorporated several divergent groups, its leaders could claim that it was impossible to press for substantial economic and social gains. Any efforts in this direction, according to the Bloc, diverted the movement's attention from the ultimate goal of independence.

On a more specific and practical level, the aims of the National Bloc in the thirties revealed bourgeois democratic tendencies. The leaders of the Syrian nationalist movement, having failed to dislodge the French, reorganized around the less radical demand for adequate consideration from the ruling system. This entailed convincing the High Commission, by a mixture of peaceful means and occasional demonstrations of popular power, that the Bloc was sufficiently responsible and influential in local society to be entrusted with a share in the management of government. The Bloc's fundamental demands were expressed in Western political

---

[30] The text of these general principles can be found in al-Kayyali, *al-Marahil*, vol. 1, pp. 184–85. Qarqut has analyzed them quite satisfactorily in *Tatawwur*, pp. 104–5.

[31] See al-Kayyali, *al-Marahil*, vol. 1, p. 185.

[32] The use of the phrase "nationalism of the *pashas*" has been coined by Pierre Rondot in, "Du nationalisme des Pachas au nationalisme populaire et unitaire en Orient," CHEAM, no. 3 215 (20 Jan. 1959).

concepts and focused on democratic institutions which were more or less compatible with traditional ways of exercising political power and preserving vested interests.[33] These demands were reasoned and pragmatic and concerned specific concessions, most notably a liberal constitution, representative government, a treaty normalizing relations between Syria and France, positions in the administration and judiciary, and certain economic measures which would benefit the class interests of the Bloc leadership.

For these nationalists, most of whom were quite uncomfortable in a revolutionary situation, a freely-elected Parliament would best serve their interests and those of their class. In such a chamber they could put their political skills to use legally, by working to redress grievances in a situation marked by economic disruption, a sense of personal deprivation, and general weakness vis-à-vis the French. Parliament was a safe place to play out personal rivalries and ambitions. It could be used to discredit rivals, whose political survival was dependent on the High Commission, and it could serve as a suitable arena in which to mediate their own political and personal differences over leadership roles and methods of political action. To most nationalist landlords, the constitutional route to independence and power was much safer and more attractive than one dependent on the mobilization of the masses.

ORGANIZATION

The National Bloc's organization was first spelled out at the Homs Congress of 1932. A Permanent Office (al-Maktab al-da'im) was established, composed of seven elected members: Hashim al-Atasi (President), Ibrahim Hananu (za'im or political chief), Sa'dallah al-Jabiri (vice-President), Faris al-Khuri ('amid or Dean), Jamil Mardam, Shukri al-Quwwatli, and 'Abd al-Rahman al-Kayyali. These men ran the daily affairs of the Bloc and constituted its effective leadership. They were responsible for executing decisions, issuing declarations, lodging complaints, settling differences efficiently, and for convening, at regular intervals, the National Bloc Council (Majlis al-kutla al-wataniyya).[34]

The Bloc Council was the body which set the tone of the organization, determined its principles and strategy, and elected the Permanent Office. It was composed of the Permanent Office members plus 31 others, the most important being Lutfi al-Haffar, Nasib al-Bakri, Ihsan al-Sharif, 'Afif Sulh, Fa'iz al-Khuri, and Fakhri al-Barudi from Damascus; Mazhar

---

[33] See Michael Van Dusen, "Syria, Downfall of a Traditional Elite," in Frank Tachau (ed.), *Political Elites and Political Development in the Middle East* (New York, 1975), p. 130.

[34] See al-Kayyali, *al-Marahil*, vol. 1, pp. 185–86.

Raslan from Homs; Tawfiq al-Shishakli and Najib al-Barazi from Hama; Najib Baqi Zadih, Jamil Ibrahim Pasha and Hasan Fu'ad Ibrahim Pasha from Aleppo; and ʿAbd al-Qadir Shraytih and ʿAbd al-Wahhab Harun, both landowners from Latakia.[35] The Council also named several associates who were resident in Lebanon including Riyad Sulh and ʿAbd al-Rahman Bayhum from Beirut, and ʿAbd al-Hamid Karami from Tripoli. As a token gesture to nationalist unity, the Bloc also inscribed the names of several exiled nationalists on the Council roster. Among them were Dr. Shahbandar, Shakib Arslan, Ihsan al-Jabiri and Nabih al-ʿAzma.[36] These politicians were unable to exercise any influence within or against the Bloc, however, until 1937 when they returned to Syria in the last general amnesty.

Provisions were made for a General Congress (al-Mu'tamar al-ʿamm) to be held at regular intervals and attended by all members of the Council, plus one member from each of the different committees appointed by the Bloc President to handle propaganda, finances, and the like. The Congress, in fact, was conceived as a device to mobilize large numbers of nationalist partisans whenever the Bloc leadership needed to show strength and unity in the face of political setbacks in their struggle and for the right to participate in running the affairs of the country.[37]

The National Bloc did not constitute a political party in the modern sense of the term and the choice of the term "bloc" (*kutla*) is not without significance. Although the Bloc established an internal organization and made provisions for the division of power, the allocation of responsibilities, membership status, finances, and the dissemination of propaganda, in fact its organization was rather feeble. Actually, the Bloc functioned on an informal basis as the personal instrument of a small elite who relied almost completely on shared dedication of purpose and on ascriptive ties of one sort or another such as marriage and kinship, old school friendships, and past participation in other nationalist organizations. On joining the Bloc, each leader brought to it his own network of supporters, who owed him, rather than the Bloc, personal allegiance. This patron–client relationship was one of dependency in which clients offered support in return for certain material benefits or services from patrons. The Bloc did

[35] Other members of the Council were Ahmad al-Lahham, Muhammad Ismaʿil, Nazim al-Qudsi, Rushdi Kikhya, Saʿd al-Din al-Jabiri, Faʿiz al-Khuri, Ismaʿil Kikhya, ʿAbd al-Wahhab Muayssir, Nuri al-Fatih, Naʿim al-Antaki, Edmond Rabbath, Ahmad Munir al-Wifaʿi, Mikhaʿil Ilyan, Ahmad Khalil al-Mudarris, Najib al-Rayyis, Sulayman al-Maʿasarani, Majid al-Din al-Azhari. *Ibid.*, vol. 1, pp. 186–87.
[36] Other associates included ʿAbd al-Latif Baysar, al-Amir Amin Arslan, Saʿid Haydar, Muhammad ʿArif al-Hasan al-Rifaʿi. *Ibid.*, vol. 1, pp. 187–88.
[37] *Ibid.*, pp. 188–90.

not integrate the clientele groups. The Bloc was molded into a symbol of its leaders' independent influence and as a vehicle for the defense and consolidation of their class interests, rather than as an assembly in which interests of a categorical nature could be integrated. Consequently, the Bloc leadership never seriously tried to foster mature public opinion or to politicize systematically the various geographic regions and communities in Syria in order to bring them into the mainstream of Syrian-Arab political thought and culture. Rather than developing a program of mass political education and action which could lead to the formation of a mass-based party with a unified ideology, the Bloc preferred that the masses be mobilized only intermittently, that is, whenever Bloc chiefs found such tactics politically opportune.

If the choice of the term "bloc" is revealing, the use of the term "national" (wataniyya) is ambiguous. Bloc leaders almost completely neglected the rural areas around the four towns of concentrated nationalist activity. The Bloc also failed to make deep political inroads in the regions containing compact minorities. This was especially true of the Territory of the Alawites, but also of the Jabal Druze where the collapse of the rebellion forced those political elements most sympathetic to nationalist aims into exile. Meanwhile, French efforts to foster communal isolation and regional separatism and the comparatively slow integration of these outlying areas into the Syrian market economy hindered the emergence and crystallization of a Syrian political community with a unified national and territorial identity.[38]

The National Bloc's failure to erode the subnational loyalties of Druzes and Alawites, or to oppose the development of local "national" elites jealous of their acquired power under the French and unwilling to lose it in a large Arab entity, was compounded by the fact that nationalist leaders, themselves, continued to be attached to mixed and often conflicting loyalties. Depending on his particular set of circumstances, a nationalist's loyalty might be first to his town before the state or to Islam before Arabism.[39] One thing is certain, however: the loyalties to the Arab nation which all Bloc leaders proclaimed publicly and frequently became in time increasingly circumscribed by the specific socio-economic and political problems facing a truncated Syria governed by France. Political frontiers imposed a new territorial frame of reference and with it new and uncomfortable limits on Syria's market economy. Meanwhile, the National Bloc never became more than a loosely constructed coalition of landlords,

[38] See Moshe Ma'oz, "Society and State in Modern Syria," in Menahem Milson (ed.), Society and Political Structure in the Arab World (New York, 1973), pp. 29–45.

[39] See the incisive article by L. Jovelet [pseûdonym for Robert Montagne], "L'évolution social et politique des pays arabes (1930–1933)," in Revue des Etudes Islamiques (1933), pp. 425–644.

merchants, and middle-class professionals bent on redressing class grievances with the French Mandate in the short term, and ultimately on guaranteeing that their organization stood at the summit of power and authority in Syria when France relinquished control over the country.
The National Bloc was able to develop greater stability, inner momentum, and longevity than other political alliances in Syria because it successfully claimed the guardianship of the Syrian nation in the struggle to
oust its foreign occupiers. The Bloc held together in spite of constantly
shifting cliques, fierce personal rivalries, and regional jealousies, not to
mention French pressures. By establishing a sort of equilibrium with the
French, within which it worked to relax French control over Syria, the
Bloc was able temporarily to keep a lid on other social forces agitating
from below for greater attention from the ruling system. It would be a
gross simplification, however, to assume that Bloc leaders had an easy
time convincing the masses that they had the people's interests at heart,
especially since the Bloc had no socio-economic program to speak of. In
fact, it was only within a framework of conflict with France that the Bloc
could survive. Initially an instrument to wrest political control of Syria
from the French, by the late 1930s nationalism had become a diversionary
instrument which protected the Bloc and its class from mounting internal
tensions. Not surprisingly, once the framework of conflict with France
began to dissolve, the Bloc's fortunes took an irreversible turn for the
worse.

DAMASCUS HEADQUARTERS

Damascus, the capital of the Syrian state, was the Bloc's central headquarters. Located in al-Qanawat was the Bloc's Permanent Office, known
as Bayt al-Diab (Diab House), a building donated by a certain ʿIzzat Diab,
a prosperous merchant of the quarter. There Adib Safadi, the Bloc's official Secretary throughout much of the 1930s, and a small staff of volunteers ran the organization's various operations and issued its irregular
communiqués and manifestos.[40] Most of the Bloc's important political organs were situated in Damascus, including two newspapers which it
owned or financed, al-Qabas and al-Ayyam.
The Bloc's Damascus branch, which was the largest and most active
though not the most militant, included 12 men at the leadership level.
The first to join hands in the late 1920s were Fawzi al-Ghazzi, Jamil Mardam, Ihsan al-Sharif, Fakhri al-Barudi, Ahmad al-Lahham, Lutfi al-Haffar, ʿAfif Sulh, Zaki al-Khatib, Faris al-Khuri, and Faʾiz al-Khuri. Later,
in 1932, Nasib al-Bakri and Shukri al-Quwwatli also joined. With the ex-

[40] Al-Mudhik al-mubki, no. 233 (8 Sept. 1934), p. 4.

ception of the Khuri brothers, all were Sunni Muslims. Their median
year of birth was 1890 and ten of the twelve were born in the eight-year
span between 1887 and 1895. Mardam, Barudi, Ghazzi, Quwwatli, and
Bakri came from the absentee landowning class and also happened to be
the most influential Bloc chiefs. Their families, which had risen to social
and political prominence in the second part of the nineteenth century,
were a springboard into politics and provided them with important networks and contacts.[41] Khatib, Sharif, and Ghazzi were from the religious
establishment. Haffar and Lahham hailed from prosperous merchant
families as did Sulh, whose family originated in Sidon. Sulh, Ghazzi,
Khatib, Lahham, and Quwwatli received advanced professional training
in Istanbul (Lahham at the Military College) while Mardam, Fa'iz al-
Khuri, and Sharif took advanced degrees in Paris. Barudi also studied
briefly in Paris but never completed a degree, while Faris al-Khuri graduated from the Syrian Protestant College in Beirut in 1897. Only Haffar
and Bakri never went past high school. Sulh, Khatib, Ghazzi, Sharif, and
the Khuri brothers were lawyers; Mardam, Quwwatli, Barudi, and Bakri
were—for want of a better category—professional politicians supported
by rents from farm lands and urban real estate; Haffar was a wealthy
merchant and Lahham was a retired military officer and bureaucrat. Several of these men also happened to be related by marriage. For instance,
Barudi and Bakri were cousins and they and Quwwatli were related by
marriage to the Dalati family of the confectionary industry.[42]

Most of the leaders contributed to the Bloc's overall strength in society
by bringing under the organization's sway, when they so chose, their
own personal or family networks, which often extended into crucial sectors of Damascus society. For example, Barudi had the strongest following among the educated youth in the capital and was recognized as their
major patron and benefactor. Bakri commanded great respect among the
bosses (*qabadayat*) of the popular quarters, many of whom had fought
alongside him during the Great Revolt. Haffar, an active officer in the Damascus Chamber of Commerce and a longtime nationalist, had strong ties
to the commercial bourgeoisie of the town, which contributed quite generously to the Bloc's operations. Respected lawyers and educators like
Ghazzi, Sharif, and the Khuri brothers attracted personal followings
among middle-class professionals and activist university students at the
Law Faculty. The Khuris were also able to contribute support from the
Christian community concentrated in Bab Tuma and al-Qassa', and particularly from the Greek Orthodox population. Quwwatli and Khatib

[41] See Khoury, *Urban Notables*, Chapter 2. The exception was the Ghazzi family.
[42] Conversation with Wajiha al-Yusuf (Beirut, 15 Aug. 1975); also Fakhri al-Barudi,
Mudhakkirat al-Barudi (Damascus, 1951), vol. 1.

were both highly acclaimed in the popular quarters, Quwwatli in his native Shaghur and Khatib in the religious ʿAmara and among radicalized youth in the government high school and university. Last but not least, Mardam—a gifted tactician—had followings in the great bazaars, where his family was one of the biggest rentiers, and among the educated youth. He was also the recognized (though not always appreciated) intermediary between the French High Commission and the Bloc.

With the exception of Fawzi al-Ghazzi, who was murdered in 1929, and Zaki al-Khatib, who broke with the Bloc to form his own organization in 1935, the Damascus Bloc clung together, though in the most fragile of circumstances, and stood almost unrivalled in Damascus political circles during the 1930s. The same can be said of its counterpart in Aleppo.

THE ALEPPO BRANCH

The Aleppo branch ranked a close second to the Damascus Bloc in the amount of influence it could bring to bear on nationalist politics.[43] In fact, there were times in the thirties when Aleppo forced the Damascus branch to back off from some preferred strategy or tactic.

Aleppo's effective leadership consisted of eight men: Ibrahim Hananu, Hasan Fuʾad Ibrahim Pasha, Jamil Ibrahim Pasha, Najib Baqi Zadih, Saʿdallah al-Jabiri, ʿAbd al-Rahman al-Kayyali, Ahmad al-Rifaʿi, and ʿAbd al-Qadir al-Sarmini. The first four were Arabized Kurds; all were Sunnis. Their median year of birth, 1879, made them a full ten years older than their Damascus counterparts, which helps to explain their somewhat later conversion to Arab nationalism. Their greater proclivity to stand by the Ottoman Empire until its collapse seems to have been in part a function of their greater political and social security within the Empire. Being older, they had already established themselves in relatively secure positions either in the state bureaucracy or in one of the liberal professions before the Young Turk Revolt of 1908 and the subsequent Turkification policies. Their younger colleagues in Damascus, such as Mardam, Barudi, Bakri, Haffar, and Quwwatli, never had secure positions in the Ottoman system before the Young Turk Revolt, and thus were more easily excluded once policies in Istanbul changed. Interestingly, the first member of the Aleppo Bloc to have made the switch to Arab nationalism also happened to be its youngest member, Saʿdallah al-Jabiri, who was born in 1893. Ihsan, his older brother by eleven years, only switched after the collapse of the Ottoman state.

All leaders in the Aleppo Bloc, with the exception of Sarmini and Baqi Zadih, came from the big landowning aristocracy of the Aleppo province.

---

[43] Al-Kayyali, al-Marahil, vol. 1, pp. 186–87.

The Jabiris, Kayyalis, and Rifaʿis belonged to the local *ashraf* and rose to fame and fortune in the eighteenth century. Although Hananu and the Ibrahim Pashas were big landowners, they acquired their social pedigrees much later than the *ashraf*. As for Sarmini, his social origins were obscure; it seems that he built his own personal following as a popular religious leader in Aleppo. Although the Baqi Zadihs first appeared in the eighteenth century, their fortunes fluctuated in the course of the nineteenth century until Najib converted the family inheritance into a lucrative agribusiness.[44]

The educational backgrounds of the group were mixed. Hananu, Jamil Ibrahim Pasha, Jabiri, and Rifaʿi received advanced training in public administration in Istanbul. The two doctors, Hasan Fuʾad Ibrahim Pasha and Kayyali, studied respectively at the Ottoman Medical Faculty in Damascus and the Medical School of the American Syrian Protestant College in Beirut. Baqi Zadih, an entrepreneur, never went beyond high school, while Sarmini, an ʿalim, received traditional religious instruction in Aleppo. Hananu, Jamil Ibrahim Pasha, and Jabiri may be considered professional politicians, who were supported by their land rents.

Aleppine aristocratic families preferred intermarriage even more than their Damascene counterparts. Families like the Jabiris also showed a preference for Turkish wives. Members of Bloc families not only intermarried, but they also contracted marriages with members of other great political families such as the Qudsis, the Kikhyas and the Mudarrises.[45] During the Mandate, Kayyalis married Rifaʿis, Hananus, and Kikhyas. The Ibrahim Pashas married Jabiris and Hananus. Jabiris married Kikhyas and Mudarrises, just to mention a few. Not only did these family networks help to broaden the political bases of individual Bloc members, but they also helped to preserve a rather stuffy and clubby atmosphere on the local political level.

As with the Damascus Bloc, each Aleppo Bloc chief had his own independent network which he contributed to the organization in addition to his own special skills. Hananu was the senior member and the uncon-

[44] On the history of the Jabiri family, see Muhammad Raghib al-Tabbakh, *Iʿlam al-nubula bi-tarikh halab al-shahbaʾ* (Aleppo, 1923–1926), vol. 7, pp. 40, 154, 241, 308, 386–87, 405, 506, 534, 545–46, 581–82. On the Kayyali family, see *ibid.*, vol. 6, p. 547; vol. 7, pp. 95, 145, 195, 317, 559–60. On the Rifaʿi family, see *ibid.*, vol. 7, p. 43, 163, 277, and Adham al-Jundi, *Tarikh*, pp. 126, 128. On the Baqi Zadih family, see al-Tabbakh, *Iʿlam*, vol. 7, pp. 15–17, 343, 547, and al-Jundi, *Tarikh*, pp. 126–27. For the various offices in the state structure in late Ottoman times which these families and others held, see *Salname: vilayet-i halab*, 1324/1906–1907, pp. 128, 144, 196, 204; *ibid.*, 1314/1896–1897, pp. 155–56; *ibid.*, 1321/1903–1904, pp. 141–45; *ibid.*, 1326/1908–1909, pp. 124, 144, 192–99.

[45] On the Qudsi family, see al-Tabbakh, *Iʿlam*, vol. 7, pp. 172–73, 436–37. On the Kikhya family, see *ibid.*, pp. 584–86, 601–4. On the history of the Mudarris family, see *ibid.*, pp. 253–54, 267, 441–42, 529–30, 555–56.

tested *za'im* of the North, and he commanded immeasurable respect. He was one of the very few Syrian politicians with a national reputation built on his heroic resistance to French occupation in the early 1920s. Jabiri and Kayyali, who were rarely on good personal terms owing in part to the mutual antagonism of their families who vied for top status among aristocratic families in Aleppo,[46] were the sophisticates of the group, closely in touch with the educated elite and professional middle class. Rifa'i, a highly regarded attorney, also had a following in this sector. Jabiri and Kayyali served as Bloc publicists and as intermediaries with the French. Jabiri happened to be closely linked to the Damascus Bloc and his more than occasional proclivity to align with Damascus against Aleppo never sat well with his colleagues at home. Baqi Zadih brought valuable support from Aleppo's disaffected trading classes whose fortunes had plummeted with the erection of high customs barriers, isolating Syria from Turkey and Iraq. The Ibrahim Pashas were the Bloc's chief mobilizers and organizers of the popular classes in the older quarters, where their paternal cousin, Shakib, was a well-known and highly regarded *qabaday* (traditional quarter boss). They also had quite a following among the educated youth of the town, and for a time in the mid-twenties, their maternal nephew, Rashid Rustum, was the top student leader in Aleppo.[47] Sarmini was a natural link to the religious establishment and to the *imams* of local mosques who played an invaluable role in the organization of resistance efforts. There was only one segment of Aleppo society in which the Bloc leadership did not make deep inroads: the large Christian minorities, including the Armenians. In the early thirties, however, they tried to correct this situation by recruiting to the Bloc an important group of young, European-trained intellectuals and professionals, the majority of whom came from the Christian minority.[48]

Although Aleppo was a relative latecomer to nationalism, the Aleppo branch of the National Bloc was generally thought to be more radical, uncompromising, and unified than its Damascus counterpart. This reputation was very much the product of two related factors: the more disruptive impact of French occupation and partition on Aleppo's economy, and Aleppo's lower stature, in spite of its larger population, in the overall Syrian political equation during the Mandate.

In the early twenties, French policy aimed to separate Aleppo from Damascus, by making each town the capital of an autonomous state with a separate administration. While nationalists in both towns rejected this

[46] Conversation with Edmond Rabbath (Beirut, 21 Aug. 1975).
[47] Ibrahim Pasha, *Nidal*, p. 53.
[48] See Chapter 15.

formula, Aleppines were naturally pessimistic about their position in any unified state. Aleppo nationalists always felt the need to assert themselves against Damascus for fear that their town's interests would otherwise be overlooked.

Aleppines had every reason to be concerned. Between 1925 and 1936, for instance, only 11 Aleppines became ministers whereas Damascenes held 23 ministerial portfolios one or more times. Furthermore, whereas three Damascenes were chosen by the High Commission to become Prime Minister in the same period, only one Aleppine was given the same opportunity: Subhi Barakat, who held the position briefly in 1925, and who was really an outsider in Aleppo. Similarly, with the central government located in Damascus, Damascenes were favored for positions at all levels in the bureaucracy. Aleppine nationalists were not only jealous of their Damascus colleagues, who had greater access to the French owing to their favorable location in the capital, they also sensed that the Damascus-framed policy of "honorable cooperation" aimed to get the Damascus leadership into government alongside the French, at the expense of Aleppo's specific interests. In National Bloc congresses and council meetings both branches jockeyed for position, trying to win the two smaller but critical swing votes of Homs and Hama. Throughout the Mandate, there was continuous tension between the two cities, which occasionally escalated to the point of nearly destroying the Bloc. But, the question of independence from French rule always seemed to prevent a complete rupture in nationalist ranks.

FINANCES

The National Bloc administered its financial affairs as it administered everything else, in an unstructured and inconsistent fashion. Most of the money plowed into Bloc political activities came from private donations, either from its own leaders or from affluent merchants and landlords. Certain Bloc partisans in Lebanon, most notably Riyad Sulh, were also generous contributors.[49]

Several prominent merchants in Damascus were well-known Bloc financiers, among them 'Arif Halbuni, the longtime President of the Damascus Chamber of Commerce;[50] Tawfiq al-Qabbani, a sugar industrial-

[49] Unsolicited donations from the masses were not unusual. In times of crisis such as the General Strike of 1936, women were known to have contributed their gold bracelets and other jewelry to help striking workers feed their families. Conversation with Farid Zayn al-Din (Damascus, 14 April 1976).

[50] Halbuni and his two brothers owned a prosperous trading house with branches in Cairo and Istanbul. 'Arif Bey, who ran the Damascus branch, owned a large palace in the Halbuni district of al-Qanawat. On the palace grounds he built his own family *masjid*, known as

ist in al-Bzuriyya, whose permanent residence in Shaghur was a regular Bloc gathering spot; Husni Zayn, a prosperous novelties store owner of Halbuni-Qanawat; Hani Jallad; Hajj Amin Diab of Bab al-Srija; ʿAbd al-Hadi al-Rabbath; and for a while Khalil Maʿtuq, an influential and highly-regarded Christian merchant. In Aleppo a similar group of financiers existed, including Najib Baqi Zadih; Hajj Sami Saʾim al-Dahir, a silk industrialist; and Mikhaʾil Ilyan, the politically active son of a Greek Orthodox landowner and moneylender.[51]

Although these men were generous, they normally made their contributions during times of crisis, and not always to the Bloc's standing Finance Committee but rather on a personal basis, to one Bloc member or another. This hindered the development of a sound financial apparatus since Bloc chiefs tended to distribute money as each saw fit, usually for expanding or deepening their individual patronage networks which, in turn, enabled them to increase their influence within the Bloc. It is also important to note that the merchant class feared a return to the days of armed struggle and consequently preferred to back those Bloc chiefs who called for a moderate, peaceful approach to achieving independence.[52] Meanwhile, Bloc coffers were often empty before 1936.[53]

Only one Bloc chief appears to have taken a sincere interest in shaping a program for national fund-raising and in developing the Bloc's infrastructure. This was Fakhri al-Barudi, a remarkable and much-loved notable whose personal sacrifices for the Syrian independence movement were unrivalled.

The son of an influential absentee landowner whose family came to Damascus from Egypt at the turn of the nineteenth century, Barudi was born in 1889.[54] He studied at Maktab ʿAnbar and then at the local Ottoman officer's school before heading to Paris in 1911 to study agriculture. He never completed his Paris studies, though he did come into contact with the infant al-Fatat. At the outbreak of World War I, Barudi joined the Ottoman Army as a second lieutenant and fought in the Beersheba campaign. He was captured and sent to Egypt where he joined Faysal's Arab Army in 1917. Later, in occupied Damascus, Faysal appointed him Chamberlain and Deputy Chief of Police. Forced to take refuge in Transjordan in 1920, he was allowed to return home by the French amnesty a

---

masjid al-Halbuni, with its own private entrance from his garden. Among his wealthy neighbors was Fakhri al-Barudi.

[51] See *al-Mudhik al-mubki*, no. 300 (8 Aug. 1936), p. 6, and *al-Musawwar*, no. 13 (26 Aug. 1936), p. 11.

[52] Conversations with Mahmud al-Bayruti (Damascus, 10 March 1976) and Farid Zayn al-Din (Damascus, 14 April 1976).

[53] Al-Kayyali, *al-Marahil*, vol. 1, pp. 187–88.

[54] See Khoury, *Urban Notables*, Chapter 2.

year later. For the next few years he maintained a low profile, occupying himself with his estate in Duma. With the foundation of the People's Party in 1925 and the outbreak of the Great Revolt, Barudi resurfaced, becoming one of the revolt's main propagandists. For his participation he was arrested and imprisoned in the Damascus Citadel for several months. In 1927, he again turned away from politics to devote himself to building the Damascus cheese and milk industry, but he was destined to return to politics. With the establishment of the National Bloc, he found new hope and ran on the victorious nationalist list for the Constituent Assembly in 1928.[55]

Fakhri al-Barudi typified the traditional urban patron, one, however, with progressive ideas. He was a dedicated nationalist, a man of sincere conviction who made the greatest pecuniary sacrifice for the cause of national independence. He was also a great humorist with charm and wit, a fiery orator, a renowned patron of the arts and music, and a popular songwriter. He was not without vices, however, being a pederast and a heavy tippler, though his drinks were always served discreetly in teacups.[56] He was probably the most popular politician in Damascus, endowing the National Bloc with the character it desperately needed. Barudi maintained a large personal following among merchants and artisans and among the Damascus intelligentsia, who respected him in spite of his rather limited formal education. His calling card, which he frequently distributed to those in need of work or other services, was guaranteed to open doors. Meanwhile, he always kept the doors of his own spacious home in al-Qanawat open to the public.[57]

Barudi was very conscious of the need to build a national economy independent of foreign control. He was greatly disturbed by the way middle- and upper-class Syrians squandered their money on foreign goods and, in particular, on luxury items. He reacted by initiating several nationwide campaigns featuring songs or jingles written by himself to illustrate his point. One rather famous campaign concentrated on discouraging wealthy families from purchasing European-made wedding dresses, whose average cost in the early twenties was £T 50 gold, a staggering

[55] See al-Barudi, *Mudhakkirat al-Barudi*, vols. 1, 2; Nahal Bahjat Sidqi, *Fakhri al-Barudi* (Beirut, 1974); al-Jundi, *Tarikh*, pp. 555–56; Ahmad Qudama, *Ma'alim*, vol. 1, p. 10; Faris, *Man huwa 1949*, p. 54; Vacca, "Notizie," p. 478.

[56] Conversation with Sir Richard Beaumont (London, 2 June 1975). Beaumont, who was a political officer at the British Consulate in Damascus in the early 1940s, was well acquainted with Barudi.

[57] MWT, *al-Qism al-khass*, Fakhri al-Barudi Papers. These papers indicate that elements from all classes solicited help or assistance from Barudi, including businessmen, lawyers, students, teachers, and peasants. Job placement was the most sought-after service.

sum; instead, Barudi promoted a line of "national," locally-made wedding dresses which were much cheaper.[58]

A more serious Barudi project was his national fund-raising campaign known as the "franc plan," initiated in 1932. It called on each Syrian citizen to donate one franc (5 Syrian piastres) monthly for the support of nationwide educational projects such as the foundation of night schools to educate adults in modern science and national literature, the spread of elementary schools to the countryside, and the creation of recreational facilities for youth in urban areas. The plan enjoyed considerable success before its discontinuation in 1936. But the money collected seems to have fed only one project, the Barudi Bureau for National Propaganda and Publication (Maktab al-Barudi lil di'aya wa al-nashr), which later became known as the Arab National Bureau for Research and Information. In Barudi's own words, this Bureau was dedicated "to achieving a national Arab renaissance and to encouraging internal and foreign propaganda and scientific research."[59]

The Bureau opened in October 1934 and remained active until the Second World War. Located at National Bloc headquarters at Bayt al-Diab, it was the first Arab research institute devoted to the systematic dissemination of Arab propaganda and information. Several researchers worked on different projects, making use of a small library, several local and foreign newspapers, a large map collection, and its own printing press to produce occasional pamphlets on burning political issues facing Syria and her Arab neighbors, such as the Alexandretta Question and, of course, Palestine. But the Bureau also had another purpose. With an ascendant generation of radical Arab nationalists beginning to criticize the rather outmoded and moderate strategy of the National Bloc, the Bureau could channel some of this discontent into less threatening outlets. Barudi saw to it that the Bureau's advisory committee was packed with leaders of this new generation, many of whom were educated in Europe, and he filled its research section with a number of unemployed intellectuals from this elite. The Bureau was but one of several ways the National Bloc kept emerging radical forces in the thirties from eroding its political leadership.[60]

---

[58] Al-Mudhik al-mubki, no. 390 (15 Oct. 1938), pp. 13–14.

[59] Al-Tali'a (1936), pp. 812–15. Sidqi, Fakhri al-Barudi, p. 98. Petty jealousies among Bloc chiefs caused the dissolution of the "franc plan" in 1936.

[60] This information comes from a pamphlet entitled al-Maktab al-'arabi lil-di'aya wa al-nashr: al-nizam al-asasi. It was found in the MWT, Fakhri al-Barudi Papers. Also see Anon., "Etude sur le fonctionnement du Bureau National Arabe de Recherches et d'Information de Damas," CHEAM, no. 350, pp. 1–11. The "advisory committee" included a number of second generation nationalists from Syria and Palestine such as Sulayman al-Ma'asarani, Nazim al-Qudsi, Edmond Rabbath, Farid Zayn al-Din, Shawqat 'Abbas, Kazim Sulh, Fu'ad Khalil Mufarrij (Barudi's secretary), Akram Zu'aytir, Wasif Kamal, Munir al-

There was one other source of funding which needs brief mention: Arab regimes and political parties. Although the Bloc did not keep accurate accounts, it claimed that until 1936 it received no outside funding either from the Syrian–Palestine Congress or from any Arab government.[61] In 1936, the Iraqi government, headed by the Arab nationalist Yasin al-Hashimi, bankrolled the Syrian delegation in Paris during its treaty negotiations with the Popular Front government in Paris.[62] Once the Bloc finally achieved one of its principal aims, the right to govern alongside the French, it relied on the privileges of government, such as the distribution of building or import licenses and lucrative contracts, to secure needed finances.[63]

A NOTE ON THE BLOC'S ECONOMIC ORIENTATION

The National Bloc was made up of two urban-based and intertwined classes—the absentee landlordry and commercial bourgeoisie, and the professional middle class. The economic activities and interests of this combine were not so much dependent upon foreign imperial interests as they were directly threatened by them. Given the class nature of the nationalist leadership, the Bloc was not a progressive force struggling for rapid or revolutionary social and economic change in Syria. On the contrary, its political tactics were tailored to secure only piecemeal gains: in the short run, power-sharing with the French; and, in the long run, supreme political power. In economic affairs the Bloc had two options: it could either join the dominant alliance of French capital and the predominantly Christian comprador bourgeoisie or it could work to undermine this alliance. National Bloc leaders were divided on the issue of economic orientation. There is evidence that a number of Bloc chiefs wanted to break the dominant alliance supporting French imperialism by trying to lay the foundations of a "national economy." It would be premature, however, to suggest that the primary classes represented by the Bloc assumed the fundamental characteristics of a "national bourgeoisie."

On the contrary, the same factors which, during the Mandate, caused

---

Rayyis, and Ahmad al-Samman. In its last year, 1939, the Bureau had 16 full-time employees.

[61] Interview with the late Nabih al-'Azma conducted by Hisham Nashabi in 1952 and cited in "The Political Parties in Syria 1918–1933," M.A. Dissertation (American University of Beirut, 1952).

[62] Conversation with Zafir al-Qasimi (Beirut, 24 July 1975). Hashimi supposedly instructed the Iraqi Minister in Paris to subsidize the Syrian delegation.

[63] 'Adil al-'Azma Papers [Syria], File 116/403. Institute for Palestine Studies, Beirut. Other examples of external funding can be found in Nabih al-'Azma Papers [Syria], File 6/362, 'Azma to 'Abd al-'Aziz Ibn Sa'ud, 20 July 1938. Institute for Palestine Studies, Beirut.

the final extinction of many traditional handicrafts in Syria, also retarded the growth of modern industry, and hence the full development of a national industrial bourgeoisie, at least before World War II.[64] These factors are well known: the partition of the Arab provinces; the creation of national borders; a French-imposed monetary system which pegged the Syrian pound to an unstable franc; the concentration of French finance capital in banking, transportation, and public utilities which facilitated the penetration of French manufactures and the extraction of raw materials most needed by French industry; and the devastating impact of the world depression. Related to these factors were others: widespread political instability during the early Mandate which hindered local capital accumulation by reinforcing the proclivity of the wealthy to invest in short-term projects and in immobile property (lands and buildings); the difficulty of securing loans from European banks; and the prohibitive interest rates charged by local banks and moneylenders.[65]

The development of modern industry in Syria was a response (somewhat delayed by the disruption of the Great Revolt of 1925–1927) to two general tariff increases in 1924 and 1926, which raised customs duties from 11 percent for all countries to 25 percent for members of the League of Nations and to 50 percent for non-members. These adjustments, which included the adoption in 1924 of exemptions from customs duties for industrial machinery and, after 1928, the lowering of duties on imported raw materials for local industry, helped to create the conditions for industrial growth. So did such factors as surplus labor created by the disappearance of traditional handicrafts and migration to the cities during the depression, and cheap local raw materials.[66]

Local industry centered on cement, food processing, cigarettes, cotton-spinning, and textiles, which were labor-intensive and could, up to a point, face foreign competition. Some of these industries had attracted French capital well before the Mandate, in particular the production of raw silk and tobacco. Others, such as cotton-growing and ginning, were financed during the Mandate by French capital in association with local capital. Many of the new industries, for example cement production, preserves, and leather goods, were financed almost entirely by local capital, provided in many cases by the absentee landowning class and the Muslim section of the commercial bourgeoisie. Members of the National Bloc were involved in several of these enterprises.

The appearance of the National Bloc and the first locally financed modern industries occurred in the same year, 1928. Some National Bloc chiefs

[64] On the concept of the "national bourgeoisie," see Alec Gordon, "The Theory of the 'Progressive' National Bourgeoisie," *Journal of Contemporary Asia*, 3 (1973), pp. 192–203.
[65] See Chapter 3.
[66] Hakim, "Industry," pp. 130–31.

were especially concerned about protecting Syria's national wealth from foreign exploitation and about harnessing the nation's resources for sustained economic growth. Mention has been made of Fakhri al-Barudi's rather primitive national savings schemes. More involved in promoting Syrian economic nationalism was Barudi's close friend, Lutfi al-Haffar, the only merchant in the Damascus leadership.

Born in 1891 into an affluent family of textile merchants of the Shaghur quarter, Haffar received his education largely at the feet of private religious tutors in the circle of the reformist Shaykh Tahir al-Jaza'iri, not an unusual way for the son of a city-center merchant to acquire learning. Inspired by his teachers, Haffar and several other future nationalist leaders founded the secret Arab Renaissance Society in 1906, one of the first proto-nationalist parties of prewar Syria. At the time he was only 15 years old. Although his Qur'anic education may not have qualified him for a career in the Ottoman state bureaucracy, it did provide him with a strong command of the Arabic language and he soon won a reputation as a respected orator and authority on classical Arabic literature. His prose style ranked Lutfi among the most admired Syrian writers of his day.[67]

Aside from his early attachment to Arab nationalism and his intellectual prowess, Haffar took a deep interest in the history and former greatness of commerce in the Islamic world and he wrote several articles on the subject. What impressed him most about this past was the ease with which trade flowed throughout the region, unencumbered by forbidding political frontiers and customs barriers. But, while the past offered him some lessons, what inspired him most was the German model of late industrialization, in which government planning and financing combined with private enterprise to develop the country at an accelerated pace. Haffar was convinced that if Syrians could acquire modern industrial techniques, they could eventually produce many of the manufactured goods that until then had to be imported. The know-how would have to come from the establishment of engineering and industrial schools and from regular technical missions to Germany and other European countries.[68]

One of Haffar's ideas was to bring running water to Damascus both for drinking and for industry, and at the same time to free the River Barada and smaller streams for more effective irrigation of the gardens around the city. He had had the good fortune to study the water systems of Egyptian cities in 1920 and to follow the formation of Bank Misr, a dynamic Egyptian financial and industrial complex started by Tala't Harb in the same year. In Egypt, Haffar also came to see the importance of the joint-

---

[67] Lutfi al-Haffar, Dhikrayat (Damascus, 1954), vol. 1, pp. 7–14; Vacca, "Notizie," p. 483; Faris, Man huwa 1949, pp. 18–19; conversation with Zafir al-Qasimi (Beirut, 26 July 1975).

[68] Al-Haffar, Dhikrayat, vol. 1, pp. 15–36, 37, 126–33, 172–76, 204–9.

stock company in developing modern enterprises.[69] Under the Ottoman Empire, such financial combinations had been discouraged because of the difficulty of getting imperial permission to form them.[70]

By 1922, Haffar had come up with a proposal for such a combination which would eventually pipe a regular supply of water into Damascus from a rich source at ʿAyn al-Fija, a spring lying in the foothills to the northwest of the city. Worried that his conservative colleagues in the Damascus Chamber of Commerce (of which he was Vice-President) would balk at a public shareholding scheme, he asked the much-trusted lawyer Faris al-Khuri to investigate all the legal angles beforehand. When Chamber members learned that a French company in Beirut was bidding on a similar project, and that Haffar had been offered a reported £S 10,000 by the same company to withdraw his own bid, they threw their weight behind him. They applied pressure on the Governor of the Damascus state who, in turn, convinced the High Commissioner (Weygand) to grant Haffar the concession. The ʿAyn al-Fija Company was capitalized at £T 150,000 gold and many of the biggest shareholders were merchants in the Chamber and landowners over whose land the aqueduct to Damascus was eventually to pass. By 1932, the aqueduct was complete and running water flowed to the capital. Haffar's idea was a resounding success even though he personally landed in debt and had to take a part-time job as a waterworks inspector in the Damascus Municipality to supplement his income until ʿAyn al-Fija began to pay dividends. Not only did his project bring many advantages to the Damascus public, it was also a great source of pride to those men of land and capital who mustered the skills and resources to carry it out. The timing of its completion also enabled the National Bloc to enjoy much of the credit for ʿAyn al-Fija.[71]

The first big industrial project of the post-revolt era involving nationalists concerned the production of cement. The choice of cement was due to a combination of factors: the region around Damascus was rich in limestone and clay; during the Mandate there was a great increase in use of cement, which was rapidly replacing stone as a building material; political and economic instability made investment in urban real estate and housing construction a safer refuge for local capital; and the raising of tariff barriers allowed local cement to compete with imported cement.[72]

[69] Ibid., pp. 46–53, 89–94; on Bank Misr, see Eric Davis, Challenging Colonialism (Princeton, 1983).
[70] Batatu, The Old Social Classes, p. 226.
[71] Al-Haffar, Dhikrayat, vol. 1, pp. 89–94.
[72] A. S. Bagh, L'industrie à Damas entre 1928–1958. Etude de géographie économique (Damascus, 1961); Hakim, "Industry," p. 157.

In addition, the cost of importing such a bulky product made cement production an eminently sensible import-substitution industry.

On 8 January 1930, several landowners, merchants, and nationalists
headed by Faris al-Khuri founded the National Cement Company on a
joint-stock basis and capitalized it at £T 144,000 gold with 24,000 shares.
The Director of the Company was Khalid al-ʿAzm, scion of the leading
family of Damascus, who, at the age of 35, was at the forefront of the industrialization movement in Syria. The location of the cement factory on
a 154-acre site at Dummar, to the northwest of Damascus, indicated a
growing trend toward the concentration of modern industry on the periphery of the city. The site was near the raw materials and was also able
to make use of waters from ʿAyn al-Fija. Modern transport had made the
movement of labor outside the city possible.

In 1934, the first full year of operation, the factory produced nearly
30,000 tons of cement; by 1938, it produced a Mandate high of 63,500
tons. In no time, Syria was producing nearly 60 percent of its local needs.
Dummar cement was considerably cheaper than foreign cement; in the
year Dummar opened, foreign cement cost £T 4 gold per ton, while by the
end of the same year, the National Cement Company was producing a ton
for £T 2 gold and, by 1936, the local price was down to about £T 1 gold
per ton.[73] Once again, the National Bloc stood firmly behind this project,
from which several leaders profited handsomely.

Another successful industry was food processing. In the Damascus region, the most prized agricultural products were fruits and, in particular,
the apricot (*mishmish*). Syria ranked third in world apricot production.
For generations, the bulk of the crop had been processed by primitive
methods into apricot paste for export.[74] And before the introduction of
modern transport, preserved foods were vital for provisioning the pilgrimage caravan, which originated in Damascus.

Among the biggest fruit orchards in the Ghuta around Damascus were
those belonging to the Quwwatli family. On returning to Damascus after
the French amnesty of 1930, Shukri al-Quwwatli devoted most of his
time and energy to transforming fruit and vegetable processing into a
modern industry. What stimulated Quwwatli was the rapidly rising price
of raw fruit. Already the modernization of the related sugar and confectionary industries of Damascus was under way and gave him a good example to follow. In February 1932, not long before he formally joined the
National Bloc, Quwwatli founded the Syrian Conserves Company.

---

[73] *Dalil al-jumhuriyya al-suriyya 1939–1940* (Damascus, n.d.), pp. 464–65; Bagh, *L'industrie*, pp. 73–76; Hakim, "Industry," p. 157.

[74] Albert Khuri, "Agriculture," in Himadeh, *Economic Organization of Syria*, p. 86.

Backed by several wealthy Damascene merchants and industrialists, including Tawfiq al-Qabbani and Sadiq al-Ghrawi, leaders of the sugar and confectionary industries, Quwwatli was able to capitalize his company at £T 30,000 gold, which was to be divided into 15,000 shares.[75] A dedicated pan-Arabist, Quwwatli sold the shares in Damascus at the local Bank Misr branch and in Palestine at the Arab Bank in order to keep the company a purely Arab enterprise. By the late 1930s, 200 workers (including many women) were producing about 25 tons annually of dried processed fruits and vegetables (tomato paste) which were crated or canned for export to Palestine, Egypt, and Europe. The success of Quwwatli's enterprise brought him much praise and the sobriquet, the Apricot King (*Malik al-mishmish*). Along with the National Cement Company, the Quwwatli enterprise was the pride of the National Bloc in the 1930s. In patriotic circles, it became the fashion to give one or more shares of Conserves' stock as a present to newly-weds and new-born babies.[76]

After 1928 other modern industries began to spring up in Damascus and Aleppo. Some, like the leather and tanning, weaving, and soap industries, concentrated on mechanizing dying handicrafts and in restructuring them to comply with changing patterns of taste and demand. Others, like cement, were completely new. Several modern factories were built during the depression years (1930–1934), when labor costs reached a new low, because of the surplus labor caused by the extinction of many handicrafts and the drying up of emigration possibilities, and because of a decline in foreign imports. By 1934, there were reportedly 63 modern factories in Damascus and 71 in Aleppo,[77] and by the end of 1936, Damascus alone had 7 registered joint-stock companies with a total capital investment of £S 12,625,000.[78] Yet the scale of Syrian industrialization by the Second World War was not very large. On the contrary, Syria continued to import most of its manufactured goods in the 1930s. And many of the modern industries that grew up before the war were decidedly lightweight. Industries like fruit preserving and flour milling "slightly" transformed "agricultural products to a state better adapted for consump-

---

[75] Later these figures rose to £T 49,500 gold and 22,500 shares.

[76] The Conserves Factory purchased one-half of the Quwwatli family's fruit crop annually. *Dalil*, pp. 468–70; *Oriente Moderno*, 12 (1932), pp. 376–77; *al-Musawwar* (30 May 1936), p. 7; Nabih al-ʿAzma Papers [Syria], File 2/10; conversation with Nadim Demichkie (London, 25 June 1975); Demichkie, the son of a Beirut notable with strong family links to Damascus, became Managing Director of the Conserves Company in 1941 just after completing his education at the American University of Beirut.

[77] *Revue International du Travail* (Geneva Monthly) (1934), cited by Farra, *L'industrialisation*, p. 169.

[78] Bagh, *L'industrie*, p. 46.

tion" in the local or regional market.[79] Others, like cement, were simply import substitution industries. Finally, the size of mechanized plants and the number of workers organized in them remained small and they were unable to absorb surplus labor with any rapidity.

A nascent industrial bourgeoisie was in formation in the thirties but it was still difficult to draw a sharp line between industrialists, landowners, merchants, and moneylenders, for the same individuals or families were often in more than one branch of the economy. The Quwwatli family, for example, were first landowners and merchants. Their Conserves Company was possible because the family possessed both raw materials and ties to the marketplace.

Ideas of economic nationalism came naturally to those directly engaged in the development of modern industry and the creation of national markets. Since some of these incipient industrialists were also in the Bloc leadership, such ideas were slowly but unsystematically incorporated into the strategy and program of the National Bloc. By the mid-1930s, the Bloc was increasingly committed to undermining the dominant alliance of French capital and the comprador bourgeoisie through the vehicle of nationalism. But just as industry did not take great strides forward in the thirties, neither did the Bloc. Both would have to await the special circumstances of the Second World War to register significant victories; the former to dissolve some of the bonds impeding industrial growth and the latter to weaken France's hold on the administration of the country.

Despite the obstacles Syrian industry faced in the 1930s, economic nationalism served the National Bloc and the classes it represented on an even more important level. It effectively blunted the class contradictions arising from the spread of capitalist relations by keeping the attention of other classes riveted on the question of independence from the French. Although class consciousness spread in this decade, as long as the French were in Syria national struggle took priority over class struggle.

Economic nationalism blended nicely with the brand of nationalism sponsored by the Bloc. It highlighted an emerging Syrian national identity which Bloc leaders embraced in the face of mounting pressures from radical pan-Arabist forces in the 1930s. The partitions of 1920 and the imposition of political boundaries and customs barriers around Syria (and Lebanon) helped to reshape the country's territorial frame of reference. The specificity of French rule forced the growth of a Syrian identity and destiny which the expansion of a national market reinforced. A similar trend could be observed in Iraq and Palestine. Just as the National Bloc demanded that the French offer greater protection for Syrian industry, so nationalist organizations in Iraq and Palestine demanded the same of the

[79] Hakim, "Industry," pp. 130–35.

British. Although the call for Arab political and economic unity continued to resound in each country, the appeal of unity grew weaker as small
state economies emerged.

The most vivid example of the mounting tension between pan-Arabism and Syrian nationalism involved Palestine. For the Syrian economy,
the Palestine market was of immense importance during the Mandate.
Owing to its location, this was especially true for Damascus. Palestine received more Syrian exports than any other country and Syrian laborers
in Palestine regularly remitted money to their families back home. Syrian manufactures, such as cement, conserves, and textiles, were mainly
exported to the Arab market in Palestine and penetrated quite easily in
the mid-1930s, owing in part to the greater structural weaknesses in Palestinian industries and in part to the Arab boycott of highly competitive
Jewish products. But while Syrian industrialists profited from the Palestinian Arab boycott of Zionist goods and tried to keep them off the Syrian
market as well, some, with highly competitive goods, also showed a keen
interest in finding markets in the Jewish sector of Palestine.

No Syrian nationalist leader commanded greater respect in Palestinian
nationalist circles than Shukri al-Quwwatli. His commitment to the liberation of Palestine from Zionist colonization and British rule was unde-
niable. Yet, in October 1935, six months before the outbreak of the rebellion in Palestine, Quwwatli visited the country to explore the possibility
of establishing branches of his Conserves Company "to win Jewish
clients."[80] The rebellion stymied Quwwatli's desire. Nevertheless, even
the staunchest of pan-Arabists in the Syrian National Bloc would not let
Arab nationalist politics interfere with the expansion of his material interests. Indeed, Quwwatli's discreet inquiries in 1935 foreshadowed the
ambivalence of the National Bloc government toward the Palestinian rebellion of 1936–1939. Syrian nationalism, however inarticulate in the
mid-thirties, had already begun to overtake Arab nationalism.

[80] Nabih al-ʿAzma Papers [Syria], File 3/119. ʿIrfan Jallad to al-ʿAzma, 15 Oct. 1935.
Jallad, a member of the Syrian Istiqlal Party, was to be Quwwatli's agent and ʿAzma, his
advertising or public relations man.

CHAPTER ELEVEN

PATRONS, CLIENTS, AND QUARTERS

URBAN LEADERSHIP was the basic building block of political influence in Syria. At the heart of urban politics were the quarters, the traditional domain in which political leadership operated and from which it derived much of its support.

The Syrian city retained several of its important medieval focal points during the Mandate period: a cathedral mosque, a citadel, a central marketplace, and a complex of ancient residential quarters. Artisans remained loosely organized in corporations (asnaf), each craft grouped together, often on a single street or alley. The religious minorities, Christians and Jews, were also clustered in their own quarters with their own places of worship. "Except for a very small number of educated [and wealthy] people, they [quarter residents] were pretty much absorbed in the narrowness of their life, and seldom if ever thought of the community at large or of its interests. . . ." In some senses, the most acute cleavages were those between the independent quarters, which were separated from one another by walls with gates locked tight at dusk by watchmen. This physical separation had come about for many reasons, but was above all "an expression of the innate impulse for protection through unity."[1]

Quarters retained their distinctiveness in the early twentieth century.[2] But their cohesiveness had begun to be eroded as a consequence of structural changes in the Middle East since the early nineteenth century— changes in administration and law; in commerce, industry and agriculture; in the movement of goods, peoples and ideas; and, most notably, in the Ottoman state's relations with Europe. New loyalties to the city, the state, and ultimately to nationalism began to corrode traditional ties to the quarter, family, clan, and confessional group. Under the Mandate, political leaders were obliged to broaden the range of their operations beyond the quarters in order to retain their independent power and influ-

---

[1] Batatu, The Old Social Classes, pp. 19–22. Scholars are not in agreement on the question of how much should be attributed to "insecurity" as a factor in the creation of the walled quarter in the Arab or Islamic city. See T. H. Greenshields, " 'Quarters' and Ethnicity," in G. H. Blake and R. I. Lawless (eds.), The Changing Middle Eastern City (London, 1980), p. 124. For further discussion of this question and related ones, see Philip S. Khoury, "Syrian Urban Politics in Transition: The Quarters of Damascus during the French Mandate," International Journal of Middle East Studies, 16 (November 1984), pp. 533–35.

[2] Scholars are far from agreement on a precise definition of the term "quarter" in the Arab, Middle Eastern or Islamic city. See Greenshields, " 'Quarters,' " p. 124.

ence. Nationalism produced movements and organizations of greater complexity and territorial scale.

The older quarters—marked by their small mosques, fountains and baths, small shops, and cafés—could not remain unaffected by the changing circumstances. Some maintained a certain stability but many others did not. Ironically, as quarter inhabitants attained higher levels of political consciousness and organization, the influence of quarters over urban politics and the active forces of society waned. Outside the quarters, modern institutions and classes claimed greater amounts of the urban leadership's attention and time, becoming in the process new and dynamic focal points for nationalist resistance. Although the quarters remained one of the crucial foundations of urban politics, during the French Mandate the center of political gravity in Syrian cities began to shift irreversibly.

THE QUARTERS OF DAMASCUS

There is no more important or suitable city in which to examine the changing character of Syrian urban politics than Damascus. In its capacity as the premier metropolis, capital, and center of the national independence struggle against the French, Damascus embodied, shaped, and reflected nearly all the major political trends of the period. In terms of the erosion of old urban patterns and the formation of new ones, the experience of Damascus is representative of the experience of other major Syrian cities during the interwar years.[3]

Much of the population of Damascus and most quarters were on the southern bank of the River Barada, the original source of water for the

[3] On the structure of Damascus in the late nineteenth and twentieth centuries, see Samir Abdulac, "Damas: les années Ecochard (1932–1982)," *Les cahiers de la recherche architecturale*, 10/11 (April 1982), pp. 32–43; Anne-Marie Bianquis, "Damas et la Ghouta," in André Raymond (ed.), *La Syrie d'aujourd'hui* (Paris, 1980), pp. 359–84; René Danger, "L'urbanisme en Syrie: la ville de Damas," *Urbanisme* (revue mensuelle) (1937), pp. 123–64; K. Dettmann, *Damaskus. Eine orientalische Stadt zwischen Tradition und Moderne* (Nürnberg, 1967); N. Elisséeff, "Dimashk," *Encyclopaedia of Islam* (new edition); Safuh Khayr, *Madinat dimashq. Dirasa fi jughrafiyya al-mudun* (Damascus, 1969); J. M. Proust-Tournier, "La population de Damas," *Hannon. Revue Libanaise de Géographie*, 5 (1970), pp. 129–45; Muhammad Saʿid al-Qasimi, *Qamus al-sinaʿat al-shamiyya*, ed. by Zafir al-Qasimi (Paris, 1960), 2 vols.; ʿAbd al-Qadir Rihawi, *Madinat dimashq* (Damascus, 1969); J. Sauvaget and J. Weulersse, *Damas et la Syrie sud* (Paris, 1936); Linda Schatkowski Schilcher, *Families in Politics. Damascene Factions and Estates of the 18th and 19th Centuries* (Stuttgart, 1985); R. Thoumin, "Damas. Notes sur la répartition de la population par origine et par religion," *Revue de Géographie Alpine*, 25 (1937), pp. 633–97; Thoumin, "Deux quartiers de Damas: Le quartier chrétien de Bab Musalla et le quartier kurde," *Bulletin d'Etudes Orientales*, 1 (1931), pp. 99–135; Jacques Weulersse, "Damas. Etude de développement urbain," *Bulletin de l'Association de Géographes Français*, no. 93 (January 1936), pp. 5–9.

town and the irrigated gardens (known as al-Ghuta) to its east and west.[4] By the 1930s, Damascus contained nearly 40 identifiable quarters (see Table 11-1 and Map 2), although several were no more than neighborhoods within larger quarters on the city's northwest and south. For the sake of convenience, however, the city can be divided into four sections or districts.

The first section is the old city (see Table 11-1, Group 1), a maze of ten quarters encircled by the ancient wall. Some quarters (like ʿAmara and Shaghur) were subdivided, part of each falling inside the wall and part lying just outside.[5] The residents of the Muslim quarters were active in the traditional religious, political, and commercial life of the city, to which the neighboring Great (Umayyad) Mosque, Citadel, and suqs of al-Hamidiyya and Midhat Pasha (also known as Suq al-Tawil or The Street Called Straight) were central. Because quarters were almost exclusively residential (they did contain non-specialized shops and markets [suwayqa] and some limited craft production), many of their male inhabitants were employed elsewhere, usually nearby in the old commercial district. This also held true for the two quarters containing the ancient religious minorities of Damascus: Bab Tuma, which housed 60 percent of the Christian community of the city, and the Jewish Quarter (Hayy al-Yahud), in which nearly all Jews resided during the Mandate. The central bazaars, in addition to their prosperous shopkeepers and traders, comprised a vast array of productive activities—mostly handicrafts such as clothing, household goods, metal wares, and jewelry—each located along a single street or alley.[6] It is not clear whether these corporations ever provided a sense of solidarity and organization strong enough to allow them to be used for political purposes in the Mandate era. Most had been under direct state supervision in the last decades of the Ottoman Empire, a situation that French Mandatory authorities sought to reinforce. The great bazaars frequently went on strike during the Mandate era, but whether they did so of their own volition or because the nationalist leadership forced them to is a question worthy of further investigation.[7]

[4] Thoumin, "Deux quartiers," p. 99.
[5] Referred to as *jawaniyya* (inner) and *barraniyya* (outer). See René and Raymond Danger, Paul Danger, M. Ecochard, "Damas: Rapport d'enquête monographique sur la ville 1936" Unpublished, Table 13.
[6] In the case of Damascus, some of the quarters of the old city seem to have been economically and socially homogeneous, while others, including the Christian and Jewish quarters, were not. The more recently established quarters (between the fourteenth and the nineteenth centuries), which encircled the old city, were more easily identifiable by their major class component.
[7] Information on the labor movement in Syria during the French Mandate can be found in ʿAbdullah Hanna, *al-Haraka al-ʿummaliyya fi suriyya wa lubnan 1900–1945* (Damas-

TABLE 11-1
The Quarters of Damascus and Their Population by Religious Community,
circa 1936

Quarter	Muslims	Christians	Jews	Total
Group 1				
al-Qaymariyya	5,817	241		6,058
Bāb Tūmā		6,750		6,750
[Bāb Sharqī]				
Ḥayy al-Yahūd			9,706	9,706
al-Kharāb	1,849			1,849
Madhnat al-Shaḥm	7,750			7,750
al-Jūrra	1,378	591		1,969
Bāb al-Barīd	1,715			1,715
Bāb al-Salām	1,599			1,599
ʿAmāra jawāniyya	4,044			4,044
Shāghūr jawānī	6,383			6,383
Group 2				
Sūq Sārūja	6,868			6,868
ʿUqayba	5,095			5,095
Bahṣa Sanjaqdār	2,655	310		2,965
al-Qaṣṣāʿ		1,872		1,872
ʿAmāra barrāniyya	7,980			7,980
Masjid al-Aqṣāb	6,900			6,900
Shāghūr barrānī	12,332			12,332
al-Qanawāt	8,625			8,625
Bāb al-Jābiyya	1,933			1,933
Bāb al-Srīja	12,000			12,000
Qabr ʿātaka	8,027			8,027
Birka ḥaṭṭāb	2,020			2,020
al-Suwayqa	5,620			5,620
Tayāmna	—	—	—	—
Group 3				
Mūṣallī	2,826			2,826
Sūq al-Maydān	7,015			7,015
al-Haqla	1,493			1,493
Maydān fawqānī	10,595			10,595
Maydān taḥtānī	1,730			1,730
al-Qāʿa	3,400			3,400
al-Sāḥa	3,040			3,040
Bāb Muṣalla	5,279	1,217		6,496
Group 4				
al-Akrād	6,650			6,650
Sharkasiyya	9,610			9,610
Abū Jarash	9,600			9,600

TABLE 11-1 (*cont.*)
The Quarters of Damascus and Their Population by Religious Community,
circa 1936

Quarter	Muslims	Christians	Jews	Total
al-Ṣālḥiyya	2,622	182	10	2,814
al-Muhājirīn	3,442			3,442
TOTAL	177,892	11,163	9,716	198,771

SOURCE: René and Raymond Danger, Paul Danger, M. Ecochard, "Damas: Rapport d'enquête monographique sur la ville 1936" (unpublished), adapted from Table 13.

Some quarters had a significantly higher concentration of wealthy residents than did others—in particular, ʿAmara (home of the local religious aristocracy) and al-Qaymariyya (known for its wealthy merchants)—and several displayed a certain economic homogeneity, although this was not true of the Christian and Jewish quarters. Residents of some exclusively Muslim quarters seem to have formed communities because of their involvement in similar occupations or trades. However, these individuals did not necessarily belong to the same ethnic group or come from the same place of origin. Their fairly high level of collective consciousness and purpose resulted from occupational and kinship ties that had developed over long periods of permanent residence in the quarter. Ties of descent and residence encouraged neighborhood and even quarter-wide solidarity and disposed local residents toward collective action.[8]

The quarters of the old city are characterized by their walls, narrow and crooked streets, and inward-looking houses built around courtyards. By the mid-1930s, the old city contained about one-fourth of the Damascene population. But with rapid demographic growth in the interwar period, and the city's physical expansion to the northwest, old Damascus's share of the city's total population diminished considerably.

The second section of Damascus includes the quarters and subquarters on the northern, western, and southern peripheries of the old city, which lay just outside the ancient wall. This section contained 40 percent of the city's population in the mid-thirties. Most of its quarters were medieval outgrowths of the old city which eventually were fully integrated into the life of the town. Several were exclusively residential and catered to the wealthy classes. Suq Saruja dated from the fourteenth century and in the nineteenth became known as "Little Istanbul," owing to its popularity with the class of Ottoman functionaries; al-Qanawat was established as

cus, 1973) and Elisabeth Longuenesse, "La classe ouvrière en Syrie. Une classe en formation," 3ème cycle Dissertation (Ecole des Hautes Etudes en Sciences Sociales, Paris, 1977).

[8] On the foundation of these quarters and their density during the Mandate, see Danger, "L'urbanisme," pp. 129, 136; Abdulac, "Damas," pp. 32–33.

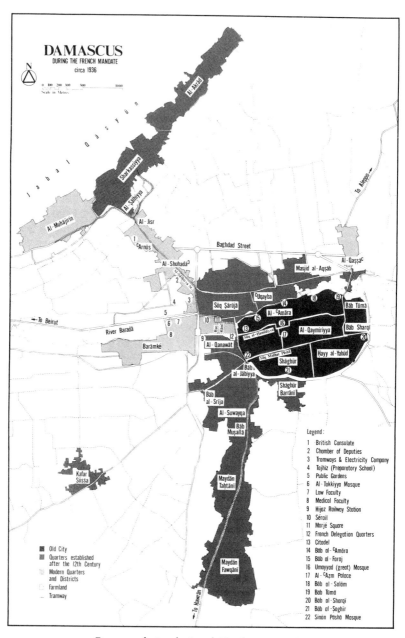

DAMASCUS
DURING THE FRENCH MANDATE
circa 1936

N

0   100   200   300   500   1000
Scale in Metres

Jabal Qasyūn

Al-Akrād

Sharkasiyya

Al-Şālihiyya

Al-Muhājirīn

Al-Jisr

ᶜArnūs

Baghdad Street

Al-Shuhadāᵓ

Al-Qaṣṣāᶜ

Masjid al-Aqṣāb

ᶜUqayba

Sūq Sārūjā

Al-ᶜAmāra

Bāb Tūmā

To Beirut

River Baradā

Barāmké

Al-Qanawāt

Sūq al-Ḥamīdiyya

Al-Qaymiriyya

Bāb Sharqī

Hayy al-Yahūd

Bāb al-Jābiyya

Sūq Midḥat Pāshā

Shāghūr

Shāghūr Barrānī

Bāb al-Srīja

Al-Suwayqa

Bāb Muṣallā

Kafar Sūssa

Maydān Taḥtānī

Maydān Fawqānī

To Ḥawrān

To Aleppo

Legend:

1 British Consulate
2 Chamber of Deputies
3 Tramways & Electricity Company
4 Tajhiz (Preparatory School)
5 Public Gardens
6 Al-Takkiyya Mosque
7 Law Faculty
8 Medical Faculty
9 Hijaz Railway Station
10 Sérail
11 Marjé Square
12 French Delegation Quarters
13 Citadel
14 Bāb al-ᶜAmāra
15 Bāb al-Faraj
16 Umayyad (great) Mosque
17 Al-ᶜAzm Palace
18 Bāb al-Salām
19 Bāb Tūmā
20 Bāb al-Sharqī
21 Bāb al-Saghīr
22 Sinan Pasha Mosque

Old City
Quarters established after the 12th Century
Modern Quarters and Districts
Farmland
Tramway

Damascus during the French Mandate, circa 1936

early as the sixteenth century but only assumed a cosmopolitan character in the nineteenth century. Both housed officials and prominent political leaders of the late Ottoman and Mandate periods. Others, like ʿUqayba, which was north of the old city and became in the 1930s one of the centers of modern industry, were less exclusive.[9] Al-Qassaʿ, to the northeast, became an appendage of Bab Tuma in the early twentieth century, housing wealthier Christian families who had found life in Bab Tuma's crowded ancient dwellings increasingly difficult.[10] The greater security provided by the Ottoman state after the 1860 massacres in Damascus certainly contributed to the development of this new quarter beyond the old fortified walls of Bab Tuma.

The third section of Damascus, popularly referred to as al-Maydan, is actually a long, narrow series of quarters and subquarters extending southwards toward the grain-producing Hawran. It took shape as a suburb after the Ottoman conquest in the sixteenth century.[11] It did not have as high a population density as the quarters closer to the old city, and its commercial and residential buildings were rarely more than one storey high. But it accounted for nearly a fifth of the city's population in the mid-thirties. It was the most heterogeneous quarter, with Hawrani peasants, Druze highlanders, Arab tribes in winter, and a small Christian community of artisans and merchant-moneylenders (in Bab Musalla). It was also one of the poorest quarters, though it did house a wealthy community of Muslim grain and livestock dealers which had grown out of the local Janissary forces (*yerliyye*) that dominated the Maydan until the mid-nineteenth century. As the wholesale provisions market of the city, the Maydan contained few bazaars or industries. Rather, its distinctive features were the numerous *hawasil* (storehouses) that handled the grain and livestock trade coming from the Hawran and Palestine and provisioned the annual pilgrimage to Mecca which originated in Damascus.[12] Beginning in the nineteenth century, al-Maydan became slowly integrated into Damascus as the forces of agrarian commercialization in Syria developed, but during the Mandate it was still characterized by sharp social conflicts and a high crime rate. Because its largely immigrant population came from ethnically and geographically diverse origins, al-May-

[9] Danger, "L'urbanisme," p. 143.

[10] Greenshields writes that in Middle Eastern cities ". . . the partial or complete departure of an ethnic group [he includes religious communities in his definition of ethnic groups] from its original quarter . . . leaves a vacuum which in many cities is filled by the invasion of new population elements, often of a different group, and results in an intermixing of populations . . ." " 'Quarters,' " p. 131. This process had begun to take place during the Mandate era in the Hayy al-Yahud as Jews began to emigrate to Palestine or to the West. See Danger, "L'urbanisme," pp. 123–64.

[11] Bianquis, "Damas," p. 362.

[12] Danger, "L'urbanisme," pp. 136, 143.

dan was unable to develop a single collective consciousness, let alone a single identifiable political leadership. Certain communities in al-May-dan actively participated in nationalist resistance efforts during the Mandate, but it was virtually impossible to organize for collective action.

The fourth section of Damascus lying to the northwest of the old city up to the slopes of Jabal Qasyun was also its most sparsely and its most recently settled section. In the mid-1930s it housed only 15 percent of the city's population. Several quarters within this section deserve special mention owing to their distinctive characteristics. Closest to old Damascus physically and socially was al-Salhiyya. Originally a medieval village, it enjoyed a renaissance in the late nineteenth century. Here could be found the typical array of pious foundations, mosques, and *madrasas* (religious schools) common in the older quarters across the Barada.[13] Between al-Salhiyya and old Damascus several modern garden quarters (the best known being al-Shuhada', 'Arnus, and al-Jisr) were created during the Mandate. These housed French officials and other members of the town's small European community in addition to a growing number of wealthy Muslim families. Built in this area were new government schools, the Parliament, European-style hotels and social clubs, and a burgeoning modern commercial district along the now-famous al-Salhiyya Street. Closest to the old city were Marjé Square and the various buildings housing the French administration, including the Sérail. This new center of urban life was well laid out with paved roads. The absence of walls created a sense of openness and security.

Further up the hill lay al-Muhajirin, a distant suburb settled by Muslim refugees from Crete in the late nineteenth century, which began to attract the local upper class by the early twentieth century. The other significant quarter in section four was the Hayy al-Akrad, originally a village established by Kurdish settlers during the reign of Saladin, which became a refuge in the nineteenth century for immigrant Kurds who were not especially welcome further inside Damascus. In contrast to the well-planned al-Muhajirin with its prosperous inhabitants and its streets laid out at right angles, the Kurdish quarter was generally poor and its streets were a maze for protective purposes. In time the Kurds, who engaged in farming and the livestock trade, lost many of their particular customs and even their language as they became more fully a part of Arab Damascus. Their clan structure, however, was not as easily dissolved. Clan heads continued to exercise much local influence in the quarter even after some moved further inside the city into wealthier residential quarters like Suq Saruja in the last half of the nineteenth century.[14]

[13] See *ibid.*, pp. 129, 136.
[14] See Jean Sauvaget, "Esquisse d'une histoire de la ville de Damas," *Revue des Etudes*

ALTHOUGH DAMASCUS NEVER attracted the large European-settler population which the cities of French North Africa did, French architects and planners were obviously influenced by French urban experiments in Morocco. Two approaches were followed. In the old city, the French made concerted efforts to preserve its ancient physical character and the "supposed harmonies of a traditional way of life," basically by leaving it alone. But, in the newer districts which were taking shape during the Mandate, they sought to establish a cultural synthesis between local tradition and modern urban form. Here, they set up new zoning regulations and constructed wide, tree-lined boulevards along which were built small, separate residential dwellings of four to five storeys. And they blended into these "local ornamental motifs . . . together with architectural adaptations to the climate such as courtyards," especially for the new government buildings. But the French master plan for Damascus, which René Danger and Michel Ecochard drew up in the mid-1930s, was only partially completed before independence, owing to cost factors and the advent of World War II.[15]

URBAN LEADERSHIP

The older quarters remained important focal points of social and political organization, despite various external pressures which broke through their self-contained and isolated structures. Moreover, each quarter tried to preserve its own personality during the Mandate. A typical older quarter had its own local leaders, including a *mukhtar* (headman, called *agha* in some quarters), the *imams* of the local mosque, and the *wujaha'* (notables) who were usually the quarter's wealthy landowners and merchants. Together they sat on the council of the quarter (*majlis al-hayy*) which acted as a mini-government to protect quarter residents from excessive state interference, to represent the quarter in disputes with other quarters, and to mediate internal conflicts. Often one of these traditional leaders could be found on the Municipal Council (*majlis al-baladi*) of Da-

---

Islamiques, 8 (1934), pp. 473–74; Greenshield, " 'Quarters,' " p. 122; Bianquis, "Damas," p. 374; Thoumin, "Deux quartiers," pp. 116–20, 131; Khoury, *Urban Notables*, Chapter 2.

[15] On French urban experiments in Morocco (and other areas of the French Empire), see the sensitive study of Gwendolyn Wright, *At Home and Abroad: French Colonial Urbanism, 1880–1930* (forthcoming). I wish to thank Professor Wright for making available to me the draft of a forthcoming article which synthesizes some of the arguments found in her book. It is entitled "Tradition in the Service of Modernity: Architecture and Urbanism in French Colonial Policy, 1900–1930." I have quoted from pp. 12, 25–26. On urban planning in Damascus in the 1930s, see René and Raymond Danger, Paul Danger, M. Ecochard, "Damas: Rapport d'enquête monographique sur la ville 1936" (unpublished), and Abdulac, "Damas: les anneés Ecochard (1932–1982)," pp. 32–35.

mascus. At the lower end of the quarter's social scale, community life revolved around kinship groups, religious associations, and street gangs.[16]

Protection from government agents was one of the most important services that secular and religious dignitaries rendered their neighbors, friends, and clients. Tax collectors in Damascus during the Mandate were accompanied not only by a police officer but also by the *mukhtar* and the *imam* of the quarter. In fact, in certain quarters, tax collectors were not allowed to conduct their investigations unless they secured the agreement of the *majlis al-hayy* or its leading notable beforehand. In the case of Suq Midhat Pasha, which received protection from the militant Shaghur quarter, custom dictated that tax collectors had to go to the home of the notable to request ("often beg for") a written introduction before entering the suq. Without this document, the tax collector could conduct no official business there.[17]

During the Mandate, the older quarters also maintained informal *diwans* (councils) where local dignitaries met with delegations from all classes, communities, and interest groups to discuss the critical issues of the day. These *diwans* were usually held in the outer salons (*madafa* or *salamlik*) of the great residences of the quarter belonging to its wealthy landowning-bureaucratic and mercantile families. Such gatherings contributed far more than newspapers and other media to the formation and reinforcement of public opinion. Since the Mandate authorities frequently censored or suspended publication of newspapers and magazines, the *diwan* served as a great storehouse of much fresher and more confidential information. Public political consciousness in the cities was advanced far beyond the level of education of the common people, who were largely illiterate and thus had little direct need for newspapers.[18]

The contribution of prominent families in the quarter to the political life of the city was considerable. They were instrumental in mobilizing local forces in protest or in support of the government. They organized public gatherings in squares, cafés, theaters and gardens; circulated petitions; boycotted elections and also foreign concessions and goods; shut down the great bazaars; raised funds; disseminated political information;

---

[16] Ahmad Hilmi al-ʿAllaf, *Dimashq fi matlaʿ al-qarn al-ʿashrin*, ed. by ʿAli Jamil Nuʿiysa (Damascus, 1976), pp. 41–43.

[17] J. Grellet, "Mémoire sur la fiscalité municipale en Syrie," CHEAM, no. 331, n.d., pp. 31–32.

[18] There was another informal council which met in the quarters. It was called *majlis al-shiyukh* (Council of Shaykhs), composed of leading intellectuals who met in different homes to discuss political strategy. Occasionally, quarter notables would attend in order to learn how to explain to the common people what was going on at the summit of nationalist politics. Conversation with the late Farid Zayn al-Din (Damascus, 14 April 1976).

and gauged the pulse of the city for the "beys" (begawat)—the appellation given the nationalist leadership during the Mandate.[19] These notable families had traditionally played the role of patron and broker, intervening on behalf of their clients with the government or mediating their personal disputes. By offering services to their neighbors and friends, they guaranteed loyalty and support and, in return, created for themselves an advantageous stability in the quarter. Their access to the state depended on their ability and willingness to maintain the social peace, which in turn depended on the degree of their independent influence in local society. Patronage was the source of this independent influence.[20]

Because the population of Damascus nearly doubled in the two decades following the French occupation of Syria in 1920, the older quarters began to lose their intimacy and warmth, and their emotional support systems broke down. They became crowded and increasingly impersonal, owing to an unprecedented in-migration of peasants and tribes from outlying areas and to improved health conditions and facilities which lowered infant mortality rates.[21] The delicate balance of forces in the quarters and the positions of influence of the notable families were upset by the pressure of increased population. The great families found it increasingly difficult to absorb the growing number of newcomers to Damascus into their personal networks. Patronage became a more complex and competitive operation, which a number of the notable families could no longer manage satisfactorily. Feeling increasingly claustrophobic and threatened by the changing character of their quarters, especially their growing face-

[19] Zafer Kassimy [Zafir al-Qasimi], "La participation des classes populaires aux mouvements nationaux d'indépendance aux XIXᵉ et XXᵉ siècles: Syrie," in Commission internationale d'histoire des mouvements sociaux et des structures sociales (ed.), Mouvements nationaux d'indépendance et classes populaires aux XIXᵉ et XXᵉ siècles en Occident et en Orient (Paris, 1971), p. 348.

[20] I have been deeply influenced by the theoretical and empirical studies on patron–client relations of James Scott and, in particular, his "Patron–Client Politics and Political Change in Southeast Asia," American Political Science Review, 66 (March 1972), pp. 91–113. More of Scott's work and that of a number of prominent social scientists can be found in Ernest Gellner and John Waterbury (eds.), Patrons and Clients in Mediterranean Societies (London, 1977). On the political and social behavior of urban notables in the Middle East, see Albert Hourani, "The Islamic City in the Light of Recent Research," in A.H. Hourani and S.M. Stern (eds.), The Islamic City (Oxford, 1970), pp. 9–24; Hourani, "Ottoman Reform and the Politics of Notables," in W.R. Polk and R.L. Chambers (eds.), Beginnings of Modernization in the Middle East: The Nineteenth Century (Chicago, 1968), pp. 41–68; and Khoury, Urban Notables, pp. 1–55.

[21] The population of Damascus in 1922 (beginning of Mandate) was estimated at 169,000. In 1943 (end of the Mandate), it was estimated at 286,000, meaning that the population increased 1.7 times in 21 years. The increase in the 1930s was more rapid than it was in the 1920s. Similarly, the population of Aleppo doubled (2.05 times) in the same period. For statistical information and sources on the population of the cities (and countryside) in Syria during the French Mandate, see Introduction.

lessness, some of the wealthier families in the old quarters left for the new garden suburbs to the town's northwest.[22]

Contributing to this flight during the Mandate was the widening social and cultural gulf between the modern educated and European-clad upper and upper-middle classes, which produced the urban leadership, and the largely unlettered and tradition-bound masses. The sweeping structural changes, initiated in the nineteenth century, helped to erode patronage systems, promoting instead an increasingly differentiated class structure. As class distinctions became more obvious, the wealthier and European-ized classes found reason to distance themselves from the popular classes. One simple way was to move out of their ancestral quarters into the cleaner, safer, and more spacious areas on the outskirts of Damascus. Muslim notable families who linked their interests to the Mandate authorities or to European commercial enterprises were among the very first to leave. They could do so since their political influence was no longer dependent on building and maintaining patronage networks in the popular quarters.

A related factor precipitating this flight was the growing inadequacy of the ancestral courtyard house in the old quarter.[23] It became in time less able to accommodate the changes taking place in the structure and orientation of the upper-class family. In the course of two or three generations (that is, by the early twentieth century), the extended family or clan had developed its own distinct economic branches. Within the extended family, a hierarchy of power and influence became established and rival branches emerged.[24] Members of the wealthier branches preferred to move into their own homes, designed along European lines and reflecting the new patterns of social relations between the sexes and the generations. The availability of space in the gardens to the northwest of the city was ideally suited to their needs. Moreover, improved technology brought new advantages for the privileged, such as running water and other sanitary devices, which could not easily be installed in older homes. At the same time, paved roads and motorized vehicles brought the city-center within reasonable reach of outlying areas.

Not all wealthy families found it convenient to make such a move.

[22] See N. Elisséef, "Dimashk," *Encyclopaedia of Islam* (new edition), p. 290.
[23] On the changing architectural style and social functions of houses in Syrian cities, see R. Thoumin, *La Maison syrienne dans la plaine hauranaise, le bassin du Barada et sur les plateaux du Qalamoun* (Paris, 1932); A. Abdel-Nour, *Introduction à l'histoire urbaine de la Syrie Ottomane (XVI–XVIIIe siècle)* (Beirut, 1982); Jean-Charles Depaule, "Espaces lieux et mots," *Les cahiers de la recherche architecturale*, 10/11 (April 1982), pp. 94–101; and Jean-Claude David and Dominique Hubert, "Maisons et immeubles du début du XXe siècle à Alep," *Les cahiers de la recherche architecturale*, 10/11 (April 1982), pp. 102–11.
[24] See Khoury, *Urban Notables*, Chapters 2 and 3.

Landed families who already owned the garden districts, which were to become modern Damascus, had a distinct advantage and interest in doing so. But an important determinant was the source of a family's wealth. Many could meet the financial demands of moving but were unable to leave because of the source of their livelihood. For instance, merchants whose enterprises depended on their daily presence in the city-center could not risk moving. By contrast, families who lived off farm or urban real estate rents (and who thus had much less of a need to be in daily contact with the old commercial center of the city) could more easily afford the comforts of suburban life. Merchants in traditional businesses not directly linked to European commercial interests also tended to be those who had not acquired a modern education, Ottoman trappings, or European tastes, and who therefore were set apart from the absentee landowning-bureaucratic families that had served the Ottoman state as a provincial aristocracy of service.[25] Muslim merchant families tended to be more tradition-bound and, hence, more quarter-bound. Meanwhile, a cosmopolitan, landed upper crust, with a new attitude toward property relations, and newly acquired European tastes in dress and creature comforts, encouraged intimate social relations only with the wealthiest and most sophisticated merchant families, and increasingly with members of the educated middle class. The exclusive social and cultural proclivities of the members of the landed class encouraged them to live together at a distance from the rest of urban society.[26]

By the mid-1930s, not only had several of the great families in regular collaboration with the French moved out of their ancestral quarters but eight of the ten principal nationalist leaders had also done so. Most had moved to the northwestern suburbs. Jamil Mardam, the architect of nationalist strategy in the 1930s, had left the Suq al-Hamidiyya area where the Mardam-Beg Palace was situated; Shukri al-Quwwatli and the only merchant in the Bloc leadership, Lutfi al-Haffar, had moved out of the popular Shaghur quarter. Only Fakhri al-Barudi and Nasib al-Bakri continued to be permanent fixtures in their quarters: Barudi in al-Qanawat, which was still a very comfortable residential quarter and conveniently located for his many political and economic enterprises, and Bakri in the

[25] *Ibid.*, Chapter 2.

[26] This information and analysis is based on conversations with Wajiha al-Yusuf (Beirut, 15 and 29 Aug. 1975), and with ʿAli ʿAbd al-Karim al-Dandashi (Damascus, 9 March 1976), Mahmud al-Bayruti (Damascus, 10 March 1976), and Fuʾad Sidawi, and George Sibaʿ (Damascus, 13 Feb. 1976). One of the most prized of the creature comforts found in the new homes constructed in the bourgeois suburbs of towns like Damascus or Aleppo was the modern (private) bathroom. Another such creature comfort for the wealthy was the modern kitchen. See David and Hubert, "Maisons," pp. 64–65 and Muhammad Roumi, "Le hammam domestique: nouvelles pratiques et transformations de l'espace," *Le cahiers de la recherche architecturale*, 10/11 (April 1982), pp. 74–79.

old city, to service better his personal network, which consisted of popular quarter bosses and veterans of the Great Revolt of 1925.[27]

Unlike those notables who collaborated with the French, the most influential nationalist leaders were careful not to sever ties with the popular quarters. They retained large personal followings which cut across class and even confessional lines. However, their actual physical presence became more infrequent. At election time, on feasts, and at other commemorative occasions, such as the annual Maysalun memorial or the Prophet's birthday, Jamil Mardam and Shukri al-Quwwatli could always be seen amongst the common people in the old quarters, where they opened the outer salons of their family residences to supporters and well-wishers. Nationalist chiefs always listed their ancestral quarters as permanent residences and in election primaries they ran on their quarter's list. Because their new suburban houses were inconveniently and sometimes inaccessibly located, it was necessary to maintain their traditional homes for social and political purposes.[28] On lesser occasions, nationalist chiefs were rarely present. Surprisingly, the task of organizing strikes, demonstrations, and nationalist rallies did not require their presence.

During the Mandate period, a growing division of labor developed within the independence movement, particularly after the failure of the Great Revolt and the nationalist elite's decision to adopt the radically different but clearly more comfortable strategy of "honorable cooperation." This strategy placed a greater emphasis on diplomacy, supported by carefully orchestrated strikes, boycotts, and demonstrations which aimed to discredit rival factions of notables collaborating with the French High Commission and to convince the French that the nationalists alone should be invited to form a national government in Syria.[29]

In each town, the National Bloc was an alliance of like-minded political leaders, each heading an autonomous machine which was used in the common cause of national independence.[30] A combination of elements

[27] MWT, *al-Qism al-khass*, Fakhri al-Barudi Papers, "al-Barudi File 1922–47."
[28] The first President of the Syrian Republic, Muhammad 'Ali al-'Abid, saw to it during his tenure in office (1932–36) that a tramway line connected the center of Damascus with the bourgeois suburb of al-Muhajirin where the 'Abid family had moved during the Mandate, after leaving Suq Saruja. This enabled the 'Abids, one of the most prominent notable families and possibly the wealthiest family in Damascus, to service their original clientele in Suq Saruja, in addition to the poorer residents of their new district, especially during the holy month of Ramadan when they fed hundreds of people nightly at their al-Muhajirin palace. Conversation with Nasuh [Abu Muhammad] al-Mahayri (Damascus, 10 March 1976).
[29] See Chapter 9.
[30] See Chapter 10.

drawn from the traditional and modern sectors of urban society powered these political machines. Although the lines between the traditional and modern sectors were often blurred because urban society was still evolving gradually and unevenly, one distinction was clear: the support of the traditional sectors of society stemmed less from ideological considerations than did the support of the modern sectors. In his own quarter, the Bloc chief built and reinforced his personal network by using his inherited wealth and family connections to funnel crucial benefits and services to a broad array of individuals from classes beneath his own. Despite an ongoing process of class polarization and hence an increased opportunity for class conflict, society in the popular quarters was still organized according to relations of personal dependence. At the top of the social pyramid stood the great urban-absentee landowning families such as the Mardam-Begs, Quwwatlis, Barudis, Bakris, and Ghazzis from which the nationalist leadership of Damascus emerged.

As National Bloc chiefs became increasingly preoccupied with diplomatic bargaining at the summit of politics, they were obliged to leave the day-to-day task of organizing and maintaining their patronage systems to members of their families, personal secretaries, and other prominent personalities in their political orbit. In other words, as Bloc leaders began to distance themselves socially and physically from the city-center, they turned to other intermediaries who could more conveniently maintain face-to-face contacts and purvey the material benefits and services which buttressed each leader's personal network. Prominent merchants and religious leaders in the quarters were two such natural intermediaries.

Merchants and *imams* in the popular quarters supported the National Bloc for a variety of reasons, but mainly because they perceived foreign rule as the primary cause of their misfortunes. The French-imposed banking and tax systems were inimical to the financial interests of the Muslim commercial bourgeoisie. The partition of Greater Syria severely damaged commerce and industry, and the French were either unwilling or unable to permit merchants and industrialists to have access to foreign capital, giving them few investment outlets. Many, although by no means all, saw the French as robbers of Syria's national wealth and the major obstacle to economic development.[31] At the same time, the upper layers of the Muslim commercial bourgeoisie were closely intertwined

---

[31] Naturally, not all merchants were anti-French. Numerous merchants engaged in the import-export trade with Europe, many of whom belonged to the religious minorities, collaborated rather freely with the French. Furthermore, the structural constraints of colonial rule necessitated some degree of collaboration with the mandatory authorities by nearly everyone engaged in commerce and industry. The question is: to what degree did merchants and industrialists collaborate? The answer is to be found in the character and orientation of the enterprises they ran.

with the absentee landowning class in the Syrian capital from which the major National Bloc leaders emerged. They maintained social and financial relations through marriage and joint ventures. Merchants provided loans to landowners and often handled the distribution of their crops. They generally responded promptly to the Bloc's call for strikes and boycotts. The new strategy developed by the Bloc in the wake of the Great Revolt, with its emphasis on patient diplomacy, appealed to a commercial bourgeoisie that had suffered considerable financial misfortune during the revolt and therefore feared continued political instability. The merchant classes had reason to support the Bloc's new tactics. However, although merchant families supported the National Bloc with funds and their own personal networks of artisans, small shopowners, and peddlers in the quarters and bazaars, rarely did they become official members of the Bloc or of any other nationalist organization. Their participation in nationalist politics came about through their personal association with individual nationalist leaders.[32]

Muslim religious leaders in Damascus, a number of whom belonged to mercantile families, were also of invaluable service to the nationalist movement. In general, the religious establishment's interests and influence had been declining for several generations, owing to increased government control over their institutions and a much altered intellectual climate. Traditional ideas—historically the monopoly of the 'ulama'—began to lose their grip on the minds of the educated elites, and the traditional activities of the 'ulama', as interpreters of the law, educators, and heads of the mystic orders, declined in social value. Less and less significance came to be attached to posts in the religious institutions whereas greater wealth, power, and status accrued to those individuals in the new, modern branches of administration, and from large-scale landownership.[33] Religious leaders suffered further humiliations under the French, who, as a Christian power, tried to impose direct supervision over such religious institutions as the awqaf (pious trusts), which often provided a major portion of their incomes. Equally damaging to their interests was the French effort to denigrate the influence of Islam by relegating it to the status of one religion among many. For these reasons, the religious establishment, ranging from ranking legal scholars and judges to preachers in the local mosques, supported the resistance to foreign hegemony in Syria.

Although the influence of religion and the status of religious leaders had declined, these individuals had not lost their ability to shape public

---

[32] Conversations with 'Ali 'Abd al-Karim al-Dandashi (Damascus, 9 March 1976) and Mahmud al-Bayruti (Damascus, 10 March 1976).
[33] See Khoury, Urban Notables, Chapter 3 and Conclusion.

opinion among the illiterate and the uneducated in the popular quarters. For most urbanites, the mosque and *masjid* continued to be the central institution in their lives, giving preachers the opportunity to argue for resistance to the French and defense of traditional society in religious terms. To the common people, nationalism was still only a code word for the defense of Islam against foreign aggression, despite ongoing efforts by secular nationalists, including the National Bloc leadership, to dilute the Islamic content of nationalist ideology. As long as Islam had a strong hold on the minds of the common people, religious leaders were able to maintain their own positions as guardians of the faith and the culture, if not of the nation.[34]

Wealthy merchants and *imams* recruited clients, financed various na-tionalist activities, and helped to organize their quarters and the bazaars on a political footing. But, neither group was able to pose a challenge to the National Bloc's control over nationalism or its domination of local politics during the Mandate. Whereas merchants and *imams* remained bound up in the closeness of quarter life, the marketplace, and the mosque, the nationalist leadership was able to devote its undivided atten-tion to politics on a grander scale. Because many nationalist chiefs could live off land rents collected by their families, they had little need to seek full-time employment. It was during the Mandate that a class of profes-sional politicians arose in Damascus and other Syrian towns. Hailing from affluent families, with a long history of administrative service and with a common upbringing, education, and set of political experiences, the nationalist elite was eminently (and almost exclusively) qualified to represent Damascus at the summit of politics. Therefore, as long as urban society continued to regard these individuals as the "natural" leaders of the opposition to the French, they could expect the continued support of merchants and the religious establishment.

Merchants and *imams* enhanced their personal status by associating with nationalist chiefs. But this enhancement alone was not sufficient to ensure their long-term loyalty. It was also expected that once a national-ist leader reached the heights of goverment, he would reward his follow-ers. Hence allegiance might be offered with the knowledge that returns in the form of government contracts, licenses, jobs in the central adminis-tration and municipality, new mosques, paved roads, sewage systems, and other facilities might be in the offing in the long run.

There was fierce competition among nationalists for access to the French. Only this access would give a leader the most valuable form of patronage. Competition for clientele networks was equally fierce, for

---

[34] Conversation with Zafir al-Qasimi (Beirut, 24 and 26 July 1975). Al-Qasimi's father was the leading religious figure of Bab al-Jabiyya during the Mandate.

only these networks could prove a leader's local power and indispensability to the French. Competition in both arenas was closely intertwined; success in the one depended on success in the other.

QABADAYAT

One figure in the quarters who could give the nationalist leader a decisive edge in the competition for clientele was the local gang leader, the *qabaday* or, in the patois of Damascus, the *zgriti*.[35]

Probably no individual with independent influence in the quarters was closer to the common man than was the *qabaday*. He was something akin to an institution. Each quarter had its own set of historical figures who were glorified from one generation to the next. In time, an ideal type was formed, one that characterized the *qabaday* as strong, honorable, the protector of the feeble and the poor as well as of the religious minorities, the upholder of Arab traditions and customs, and the guardian of popular culture. He was hospitable to strangers, always pious and a clean liver.[36] This image placed far less emphasis on the *qabaday*'s darker side, his shady dealings, his preference for physical coercion, and even his "mortal" crimes for personal gain. The common people clearly differentiated between the *qabadayat* and the *zu'ran* or hoodlums who ran protection rackets (*khuwa*) in the quarters and bazaars, although in reality such distinctions were hazy.[37]

A *qabaday* might eventually become fairly well-to-do, but what distinguished him from the dignitaries of the quarter were his significantly lower social origins, his general want of formal education, his outspoken preference for traditional attire and customs, and the much narrower range of his interests and contacts, all of which accorded him a less exalted

[35] See al-'Allaf, *Dimashq*, pp. 244–47. According to the author, who wrote during the early Mandate, *al-zgritiyya* is a Turkish word referring to the "courageous of the quarter."

[36] These characteristics have been isolated in an inspiring article on the power structure in Beirut's Muslim quarters in the early 1970s, and in particular the role of *qabadayat* in these quarters. See Michael Johnson, "Political Bosses and Their Gangs: Zu'ama and Qabadayat in the Sunni Muslim quarters of Beirut," in Ernest Gellner and John Waterbury, (eds.), *Patrons and Clients in Mediterranean Societies* (London, 1977), pp. 207–24. Conversation with Fu'ad Sidawi, *qabaday* of the Christian quarter of Bab Tuma during the Mandate (Damascus, 13 Feb. 1976). A list of some nineteenth and early twentieth century *qabadayat* of Damascus is provided by al-'Allaf, *Dimashq*, pp. 247–51.

[37] *Zu'ran* featured prominently in the medieval Muslim city (see Ira M. Lapidus, *Muslim Cities in the Later Middle Ages* [Cambridge, Mass., 1967], Chapter 5); in Damascus during the Mandate (al-'Allaf, *Dimashq*, p. 244); and in Beirut during the Lebanese civil war of the 1970s (based on my personal observations). Also see Johnson, "Political Bosses," p. 212.

status than that enjoyed by merchants or religious leaders.[38] He survived best in the traditional milieu of the self-contained quarter with its inwardness and narrowly defined interests. There he was needed to provide physical protection from hostile external forces and extra-legal mechanisms for settling personal disputes. But by the time of the Mandate, the *qabaday* had begun to feel threatened by the pressures of change created by rapid urbanization, the growth of a market-oriented economy, and the rise of new classes and institutions outside the popular quarters. This period was a transitional phase in the life of the Syrian city, and in the organization and functions of its quarters; the *qabaday* survived it, although not without difficulty.

A *qabaday* might rise to leadership in the quarter by several different paths, and it is difficult to separate myth from reality when tracing the emergence of any particular strongman. It is, however, possible to trace the career of at least one prominent *qabaday* of the Mandate period in Damascus.

Abu ʿAli al-Kilawi [al-Gilawi][39] claims to have been born in 1897, in Bab al-Jabiyya, an old popular quarter situated near the entrance to Suq Midhat Pasha and which included the charming Mosque of Sinan Pasha. The origins of the Kilawi family are obscure. They seem to have first settled in al-Maydan some time in the early nineteenth century where they were engaged in the transport of wheat from their native Hawran to flour mills in al-Maydan. They may have belonged to one of the tributaries of the Rwala Bedouin who roamed southern Syria, and it is known that they were on close personal terms with the Rwala chieftains of Al Shaʿlan before the Mandate.[40] The Kilawis also claimed descent from Abu Bakr, the Prophet's companion and first Caliph, and billed themselves as members of the *ashraf* (descendants of the Prophet), although the great religious families of Damascus did not recognize their claim. According to Abu ʿAli, the family's surname had originally been al-Bakri until the end of the nineteenth century, when his father died unexpectedly and the family dropped al-Bakri for some inexplicable reason and adopted instead the surname of Abu ʿAli's maternal grandfather. During the Mandate, the Kilawis were not regarded as members of the aristocratic al-Bakri family

---

[38] Conversations in Damascus with Abu ʿAli al-Kilawi (3 March 1976), ʿAli ʿAbd al-Karim al-Dandashi (9 March 1976), and Mahmud al-Bayruti (10 March 1976).

[39] The following information on the personal life and career of Abu ʿAli al-Kilawi is based on several days of conversations with him and with several other *qabadayat* of the Mandate and early independence eras whom I met at his home in Bab al-Jabiyya (Damascus, 14 Feb., 3 and 15 May 1976).

[40] On the Al Shaʿlan, see Khoury, "Tribal Shaykh," pp. 183–85.

of Damascus; however, they were very partial to the Bakris and especially close to Nasib Bey of the National Bloc.[41]

Abu ʿAli had two older brothers. He happened to be much closer to the oldest, Abu Hasan, who assumed the leadership of the family upon their father's death, and under whose wing Abu ʿAli grew up learning the ways of the quarter. Abu ʿAli attributes his rise to the status of a *qabaday* to several factors, all of which suggest that he did not inherit the title. One factor was his own physical strength, which he displayed early in life despite his slight build. The youth of Bab al-Jabiyya and other quarters engaged in different forms of informal competition which could help to lay the groundwork for the rise of a *qabaday*. Abu ʿAli, for example, excelled in wrestling *(musaraʿa)*. To the beat of two drums, the youth of the quarter would congregate in an open field or garden where wrestling matches were staged between boys dressed in leather shorts worn above britches. By the age of sixteen, Abu ʿAli was reputed to be the best wrestler in his quarter.[42]

By this age, the youth of the quarter had already begun to practice the martial arts and in particular swordsmanship. Wielding a long, silver-handled sword in one hand and a small metal shield *(turs)* in the other, two young men would face each other, twirling their swords through different orbits over and around their heads while interspersing blows against their own shields and those of their opponents in a complicated cadence.[43] The boy who could handle his sword most adeptly and innovatively advanced in the competition, and the best five or six contestants were asked to form a troupe. This troupe would then have the honor of performing on all festive occasions in the quarter, such as at weddings, and on the Prophet's birthday.[44] In his day, Abu ʿAli was the leader of such a troupe of swordsmen and from it he began to build his own personal following.

Horsemanship was Abu ʿAli's other forte. After their father's death, Abu Hasan decided to use his family's relations with the Bedouin tribes south of Damascus to convert the Kilawi transport business into a horse-breeding and trading concern. The center for their new activities was a small stud farm which the family owned just south of al-Maydan. In time, the Kilawis became renowned horse-dealers throughout the Arab East, purveying purebred show animals and race horses to the royal families of Transjordan and Saudi Arabia, and to other Arab dignitaries. By

---

[41] For the rise of the Bakri family, see Khoury, *Urban Notables*, pp. 34–35.

[42] See al-ʿAllaf, *Dimashq*, pp. 242–43.

[43] *Ibid.*, pp. 240–42.

[44] Kilawi was also an accomplished Arabic musician who played a three-stringed guitar, and sang popular Bedouin ballads. His dialect reflected his long years of association with tribes south of Damascus.

the time he was 20, Abu ʿAli was considered to be the best horseman in his quarter, a reputation which soon spread throughout Damascus and the rest of Syria. By the mid-1930s, the Kilawi stable of show horses had become an attraction in all national parades, at the head of which Abu ʿAli always rode.[45]

Successful business enterprises helped to vault the Kilawi family into the social limelight of Bab al-Jabiyya. Neighbors began to ask for favors or assistance and in no time they built a solid core of followers and clients from among the poorer elements of the quarter, some of whom were personally loyal to Abu ʿAli. The result was that Abu ʿAli was able to put together his own gang, composed mainly of unemployed youth and casual laborers.

In the early 1920s, as the Kilawis began to accumulate capital, they were able to purchase a fairly large apartment with a special salon for entertaining in the heart of their quarter. This salon also was used as an informal courtroom where the Kilawis, now much trusted in Bab al-Jabiyya, served as administrators of extra-legal justice, arbitrating or mediating disputes between individuals and families who for one reason or another were not comfortable going before the religious or civil courts. The Kilawis also lent their salon to poorer families for wedding parties and other social functions, and it eventually became one of the meeting places of the roving *diwan*. Abu ʿAli claimed that he and his brothers never asked for money or other material rewards for their hospitality and services. But they did expect personal loyalty to the family, which they acquired as the Kilawi network grew and the family name came to be mentioned with both reverence and fear.

One of the most prominent features of urban life in Damascus were the ʿarada or traditional parades held in the quarters to celebrate religious events such as a circumcision, the return of the pilgrimage, or the Prophet's birthday. These occasions allowed the youth of one quarter to compete with the youth of neighboring quarters in wrestling matches, sword games, horseraces, and the like. The honor of the quarter was always at stake in these events, as were specific controversies over turf and freedom of movement. Certain quarters were known to be long-standing rivals, most notably Suq Saruja and al-Salhiyya, and Shaghur and Bab al-Jabiyya.[46] Yet another way in which Abu ʿAli al-Kilawi reinforced his status in the quarter was to lead his stalwarts in street fights against rival gangs of Shaghur.

---

[45] As late as 1976, Abu ʿAli was still riding and showing his horses in national parades in Damascus, despite his antipathy toward the Syrian Baʿthist regime.

[46] Al-ʿAllaf, *Dimashq*, pp. 259–62.

By the early twentieth century, however, the parades had begun to assume secular dimensions as they came to mark political events such as the election of a deputy, the return of an exile, the Young Turk Revolt of 1908, or the Italian invasion of Libya in 1911.[47] This politicization accelerated during the Mandate. But, as political consciousness rose in the quarters, the fierce rivalries between them were transformed into an alliance of quarters against the French. The narrowness and insularity of quarter life began to break down as the scope for political activity widened.

The Great Revolt of 1925 hastened the erosion of traditional rivalries between quarters and helped to bind them together in a common front against the French. There is little doubt that the many stories of individual heroism which quickly became part of the local history of the revolt helped many a young man to enhance his reputation in the popular quarters and achieve the status of *qabaday*. In fact, there was a noticeable turnover of *qabadayat* at this time, owing to the emergence of new heroes during the revolt who replaced those who had been killed. Probably the most respected and esteemed *qabaday* of his day was Hasan al-Kharrat, the nightwatchman of Shaghur, who led a rebel attack on French positions in the Syrian capital and was later killed by French troops.[48] His elimination permitted another rising young star of the revolt, Mahmud Khaddam al-Srija, to assert himself as the undisputed strongman of Shaghur.

Abu ʿAli al-Kilawi frankly admitted 50 years after his own participation in the Great Revolt that it also enabled his family to consolidate their position as the *qabadayat* par excellence of Bab al-Jabiyya.[49] When the revolt erupted, the Kilawis and their armed gang prepared their quarter for insurrection against the French. Abu ʿAli joined the rebel band of Nasib al-Bakri, whose family had patronized the Kilawis for some time. After the French regained control of most of Damascus in October, Abu ʿAli followed Bakri's forces into the gardens around the Syrian capital. One particular episode at this time (among several) contributed to his immortalization in the minds of future generations. Seriously wounded in a single-handed attempt to liberate his rebel comrades imprisoned in the

[47] On the transformation of *ʿarada* into political manifestations in the twentieth century, see J. Lecerf and R. Tresse, "Les ʿarada de Damas," *Bulletin d'Etudes Orientales*, 7/8 (1937–1938), pp. 237–64; al-Qasimi, *Watha'iq*, pp. 63–74; MAE, Syrie–Liban 1930–40. Martel to MAE, 5 July 1935, vol. 491, pp. 31–33.
[48] On al-Kharrat and other hero/martyrs of the revolt, see al-Jundi, *Tarikh*.
[49] Besides the Kilawis, other noted *qabadayat* of the Mandate era were Abu Ghassim ʿAbd al-Salam al-Tawil (al-Qaymariyya quarter); Abu Rashid Khuja (al-Kharab); Abu'l Haydar al-Mardini (Bab al-Srija), Mahmud Khaddam al-Srija (Shaghur); and Abu ʿAbdu Dib al-Shaykh (ʿAmara).

Citadel of Damascus, he managed to flee on horseback, taking refuge among his traditional enemies in Shaghur. Two days later, a weak but determined Abu ʿAli al-Kilawi recruited some young men of Shaghur and rode back with them to Bab al-Jabiyya, where he rounded up more followers and returned to the Ghuta to rejoin the Bakri band.[50]

As National Bloc leaders grew more distant from their ancestral quarters, they came to depend heavily on intermediaries to dispense favors and services to the large mass of poorer residents. *Qabadayat* were typically more important to a nationalist leader's political machine in the quarters than were merchants or religious figures. Merchants, whose status was based on wealth, philanthropy, and religious piety, were among those intermediaries who had assumed this function for the politicians. But as class differentiation evolved during the Mandate, merchants increasingly began to take less and less interest in the poor and their individual problems. They neither found ample time for, nor were they well disposed toward, the poor. Philanthropy, after all, did not require regular contact with the lower classes. Some members of the Muslim religious establishment also placed a greater distance between themselves and the common people. Others, however, including preachers in the popular quarters, actually strengthened their influence among the destitute and the illiterate. Although leading religious dignitaries and lower-ranking *imams* generally supported the nationalist chiefs, they also formed religious benevolent societies (*jamʿiyyat*) which assumed a militant anti-Western and anti-secular political character by the mid-1930s and which eventually posed an unwelcome challenge to the authority of the nationalist leadership in the quarters.[51]

The *qabaday*, in contrast, posed no such threat. He hailed from the common people, was under the protection of the *bey*, was often indebted to him for loans and services, and, in any case, lacked the education, status, and statesmanlike qualities to reach the *bey*'s level of political leadership. Thus, while the National Bloc leader, assisted by his personal secretary and family, policed the core of his patronage network, the *qabaday* looked after its periphery, servicing it directly whenever possible and guaranteeing its support when the *bey* required it.[52] The *qabaday* was an

---

[50] Information on the Great Revolt and Abu ʿAli's role in it comes from his personal memoir which his eldest son, ʿAli, had recorded, and which Abu ʿAli kindly made available to me. The memoir is entitled: *Thawra ʿamma 1925. Al-Faransiyyin fi suriyya* (Damascus, n.d.).

[51] The *jamʿiyyat* were the prototype for the Syrian Muslim Brethren (founded in the 1940s). See Johannes Reissner's groundbreaking study, *Ideologie und Politik der Muslimbrüder Syriens* (Freiburg, 1980). Also see Chapter 23.

[52] See Johnson, "Political Bosses," pp. 214–20.

important link in the chain of clientele, so important that he had direct access to the *bey*'s immediate entourage, in particular to his personal secretary. In this way, the *qabaday* could count on preferential treatment and a few more privileges than could the average client on the periphery of the *bey*'s network.[53] Although the scope for social mobility was not wide, a number of *qabadayat* did manage to enrich themselves through connections with their patrons.

At any given time the residents of a quarter might refer to several individuals as *qabadayat*. A quarter could support more than one strongman, although it was not uncommon to associate the *qabadayat* with a single family. Residents of Bab al-Jabiyya referred to "*wilad al-Kilawi*" (the sons of al-Kilawi) as frequently as they did to any one member of the family. It was the family, through its connections, which provided protection and assistance to the quarter. Abu ʿAli did make a name for himself in particular, but he frankly admitted that his oldest brother, who had some education, made the family's major decisions, ran its business, and dealt with the National Bloc politicians and their deputies. Abu ʿAli was in effect Abu Hasan's lieutenant, prepared to execute his commands. When Abu Hasan died, the leadership of the Kilawi family passed to Abu ʿAli (his other brother was regarded as a high-liver and a playboy, which disqualified him), who had already begun to educate his eldest son to fill the role of family lieutenant.[54]

Part of the mythology surrounding the *qabaday* was that he never took money from politicians or their secretaries, or from merchants in the quarter for carrying out various instructions, such as mobilizing the youth of the quarter to demonstrate or enforcing a strike or boycott. Abu ʿAli did admit that the Bloc offered him money at various times and cited several attempts by merchants close to the Bloc to pay him to keep the General Strike of 1936 going.[55] Defending the ideal image of a *qabaday*, he also claimed that to accept such offerings ran against his honor. He did not deny, however, that some *qabadayat* broke this code by accepting cash and other benefits for fulfilling their duties. For example, after the National Bloc took office in 1936, Shukri al-Quwwatli, the Minister of Finance and National Defense, saw to it that Mahmud Khaddam al-Srija received a regular stipend from a *waqf* originally designated for the poor in his native Shaghur. Srija was the most renowned *qabaday* of the decade and had performed valuable services for Quwwatli during the General Strike of 1936.[56]

[53] *Ibid.*, pp. 218–20.
[54] Conversation with Abu ʿAli al-Kilawi (Damascus, 3 March 1976).
[55] On the General Strike of 1936, see Chapter 17.
[56] MWT, *Registre des jugements correctionnels*, 5 Oct. 1932–8 Feb. 1934, pp. 216–18.

Each National Bloc chief relied on a combination of resources to fuel his political machine and support within the quarters of Damascus was only one component among several. A politician like Nasib al-Bakri, who cut a much more socially and religiously conservative figure than did his more cosmopolitan Bloc comrades, and who had the religious prestige of his family behind him, moved easily among the tradition-bound masses of the popular quarters, was extremely well-connected to numerous *qaba-dayat* like the Kilawis, the Dib al-Shaykh family of the ʿAmara quarter, and to other veterans of the Great Revolt in which he had featured so prominently. By contrast, Shukri al-Quwwatli, Jamil Mardam, and Fakhri al-Barudi (the other major Bloc figures in Damascus), although they were all extremely influential in their respective quarters and particularly with merchants, could not claim large personal followings in other quarters. Unlike Bakri, however, they serviced much more diversified political machines; each had a significant following in the modern sectors and institutions of Damascus, especially among the educated youth and emerging middle classes.[57]

No National Bloc chief could claim to have considerable influence in the two popular quarters on the periphery of Damascus, Hayy al-Akrad and al-Maydan. In the Kurdish quarter, where clan loyalties persisted, the great Kurdish families of Yusuf and Shamdin still held sway. Although Arabized in the course of the nineteenth century, they were never particularly well-disposed toward Arab nationalism which threatened to erode the ethnic and clan loyalties on which their influence was in part based. Furthermore, the role that Kurdish auxiliary troops had played in suppressing the Great Revolt strained relations between nationalists and the Kurds of Damascus for the duration of the Mandate.[58]

In the long, narrow, socially heterogeneous al-Maydan to the city's south, the Bloc's problems were of a different order and magnitude. There, the social tensions and dislocations produced by the unsettling effects of increasing in-migration kept political power fragmented. Al-

---

[57] On the formation, composition, and operation of individual political machines in Damascus during the Mandate, and in particular those of Shukri al-Quwwatli and Jamil Mardam, see Chapters 15–17.

[58] On the origins of the Kurdish notable families of Damascus in the nineteenth century, see Khoury, *Urban Notables*, Chapters 3 and 4. This information has been supplemented by conversations with Wajiha al-Yusuf [Ibish], daughter of ʿAbd al-Rahman Pasha al-Yusuf, the leading Kurdish notable of Damascus in the late nineteenth and early twentieth centuries, and wife of Husayn Ibish, the leading Kurdish notable of the Mandate era, and the biggest landowner in the province of Damascus (Beirut, 15 and 29 Aug. 1975). Another political force to draw support from the Kurdish quarter by the late 1930s was the Syrian Communist Party. Indeed, the Party rank and file in Damascus included a number of Arabized Kurds owing to the fact that its leader, Khalid Bakdash, was a Kurd from the quarter. See Batatu, *The Old Social Classes*, Chapter 24.

though the Maydan, unlike Hayy al-Akrad, contributed heavily in blood
and sweat to the cause of independence (the French bombarded it from the
air twice during the Great Revolt, nearly destroying the entire quarter),
influential Maydani families were never closely linked to the National
Bloc. Some, like the great merchant *aghawat*, Sukkar and al-Mahayni,
assisted the Bloc only when they wanted to. Others, like the Hakim family, opposed the National Bloc, supporting instead the major rival faction
headed by Dr. ʿAbd al-Rahman Shahbandar.[59]

Although there is no single explanation for why the Maydan eluded
the influence of the National Bloc, the Bloc was clearly ill-equipped to
mitigate the Maydan's social contradictions or to ameliorate its poverty,
and hence to integrate and organize its population for political action.
This left the area vulnerable to politicization by more socially conscious
forces, ranging from Muslim benevolent societies to modern radical political organizations like the Communist Party and the nascent Baʿth
Party. In a wider context, the rapid pace of urbanization during the Mandate was not accompanied by the kind of industrialization that could have
provided the growing pool of unskilled labor with jobs which would have
led to some form of social and political organization and control.

BEYOND THE QUARTERS

Although the popular quarters remained important units of political and
social organization despite changes in internal structure during the Mandate period, their importance to the independence movement continually
declined. The advancement of urban political life gradually led to new focal points outside the quarters. These were the modern institutions which
were closely identified with the growth of a professional middle class
whose fundamental interests lay beyond the quarters. The dominant sentiments of this class of lawyers, doctors, engineers, educators, journalists,
and other members of the intelligentsia transcended the narrowness of
quarter life; their primary loyalties were to the city, state, and the nation
rather than to the family, clan, confessional group, or quarter.

The importance of the modern middle class to the development of the
independence movement in Syria grew with time. Although this class
was intimately involved in the birth of the Arab nationalist movement in
the last years of the Ottoman Empire and its members could be found in
all secret nationalist societies before and during World War I, it really
only began to have a dramatic impact on political life in the 1930s.[60]
Many factors lay behind its ascent at this time, all of which were con-

[59] See Chapters 9 and 22.
[60] On the contribution of this class to the independence movement, see Chapters 15–16.

nected to changes in the structure of Syrian society that had been occurring since late Ottoman times. Among the most important factors was the development of modern secular education, which had only become available to social strata below the upper class during the Mandate period. The addition of a professional middle class to the ranks of the nationalist movement added a generation younger than the leadership of the National Bloc. This generation was not as touched by the Ottoman experience and legacy, and it possessed a higher level of education.

The number of primary and secondary school students in government institutions nearly doubled between 1924 and 1934.[61] The Syrian University also expanded in this period, and opportunities opened for the brightest high school and university graduates to go to France on scholarships for advanced studies in a wide variety of fields (in particular, law, medicine, and teacher-training). These opportunities certainly played a role in broadening the horizons of the urban youth and in shifting the focus of their activities out of the quarters and into modern institutions and structures. But, although modern education paved the way for social mobility and afforded middle-class status, middle-class incomes were not guaranteed. The rising but unfulfilled expectations of the newly educated created a vast reservoir of frustration and antagonism which the Syrian nationalist leadership had to channel to its own ends. Otherwise, the nationalist leadership stood to sacrifice its potential influence in what was rapidly becoming the most dynamic sector of Syrian society. The National Bloc also recognized that the newly educated cadres were in need of leaders with whom they could identify socially, culturally, and intellectually. Traditionally educated and attired merchants and religious leaders, and the unlettered qabadayat of the popular quarters, were bound to be ineffective as role models for the rising middle classes. A new set of leaders, more closely attuned to their needs and conscious of their aspirations, had to emerge to service the educated youth.

The National Bloc discovered early on that the major source of disaffected, educated youth in Damascus (and in other cities) was the expanding government school system. There, already grouped together, were thousands of students being inculcated daily with patriotic ideals by Syrian instructors and, as a result, drifting away from the influence of the traditional quarters with their increasingly archaic and outmoded social and cultural norms. School life temporarily freed these young people from the entanglements of family obligations and careers.[62] Their growing political awareness, coupled with their youthful lack of inhibitions,

---

[61] See MAE, *Rapport à la Société des Nations sur la situation de la Syrie et du Liban*, 1924, Appendix 4, p. 95; FO 371/625, vol. 19022. MacKereth to FO, 7 Jan. 1935.

[62] Conversation with Qustantin Zurayq (Beirut, 10 Jan. 1976).

could be translated into major support for the National Bloc. All that was wanting was some force to harness their unbridled energy.

Not long after the establishment of the National Bloc, it began to turn its attention to developing a youth wing from among high school and university students. In 1929, such an organization was born—the Nationalist Youth (al-Shabab al-watani). The force behind the Nationalist Youth was Fakhri al-Barudi.

Barudi's interest in the educated young stemmed from several sources. His own fairly broad intellectual interests in literature, the arts, and Arabic music enabled him to stay in close touch with the main intellectual currents and fashions that attracted the young between the wars. His personal inheritance, which included large revenues from his family's farms near Damascus, allowed him to offer patronage to young talented journalists, poets, and musicians whom he encouraged to frequent his large home in al-Qanawat. Barudi preferred to spend much of his time cultivating the young, the educated, and the talented. Unlike his cousin and major rival in the National Bloc, Nasib al-Bakri, who based his political position on relations with *qabadayat*, Barudi was neither as conservative nor as rigid as Bakri and, although conscious of Arab traditions, he was much more discriminating in his choice of those he emphasized. He was clearly a politician with a vision of the future as well as one of the past.[63]

In addition, Fakhri Bey's immediate environment conditioned his decision to cultivate the educated youth. Al-Qanawat was largely populated by upper and upper-middle class Muslim families, like the Barudis, who afforded their children the best local education available in Arabic. It seems that Barudi was impressed by the youth of his quarter and especially by their social and political awareness. He held out great hope for the coming generation of leaders. But he also felt that it was incumbent upon his generation to develop the talents and direct the energies of the educated youth who grew up in a tension-ridden and unsettling era of foreign dominion. For Barudi, the National Bloc had a very important role to play alongside the educational system in developing and refining the national consciousness of Syrian youth.

Immediately after the Great Revolt, Barudi began to devote greater attention to the problem of forming a youth organization affiliated to the National Bloc. Meanwhile, efforts to mobilize students in the government schools were already underway, especially at the *tajhiz*, the major

---

[63] On Barudi's upbringing and career, see Chapter 10; Fakhri al-Barudi, *Mudhakkirat al-Barudi* (Beirut/Damascus, 1951–1952), 2 vols.; Nahal Bahjat Sidqi, *Fakhri al-Barudi* (Beirut, 1974).

government preparatory school in Damascus.[64] The central figure in this activity was Mahmud al-Bayruti, a man in his late twenties who had already acquired a reputation in Damascus for leading several important demonstrations and strikes, always with a small personal following of elementary and high school students at his side.

Bayruti, the son of a low-ranking functionary in the Damascus municipality (al-baladiyya) from Suq Saruja, was born in 1903. He belonged to a new generation of nationalists. From an early age, he aspired to a military career and, on completing his primary education, he enrolled at the War College (al-Kulliyya al-harbiyya), graduating just before the French occupation in 1920. Although qualified to become a second lieutenant, Bayruti was unwilling to cooperate with French military authorities. Instead, he joined a group of school chums in secret political activities against the French which were soon uncovered. To avoid arrest, Bayruti took refuge in Amman, where he tried to become an officer in Amir ʿAbdullah's army, only to discover that his political record in Damascus and his want of proper connections disqualified him. Fortunately, he was able to return home after the French granted their first general amnesty in 1921. By now, Bayruti had developed a fairly high degree of political consciousness which he ascribed to his career setbacks and to the patriotic ideals instilled in him by his instructor at the War College, Nuzhat al-Mamluk, an Istanbul-trained army officer who was to play a key role in organizing the National Bloc's paramilitary wing in the mid-1930s.[65]

Like other young men of his generation whose dreams had been shattered by the political convulsions rocking Syria, Mahmud al-Bayruti expressed deep disappointment over the lack of effective political leadership in Damascus. His hopes were temporarily raised in 1922 by the founding of the nationalist Iron Hand Society under the leadership of Dr. Shahbandar. But these hopes too were dashed later the same year when the French broke up the Iron Hand organization and arrested its leaders. Bayruti was among the many young men who spent the next two years interned with the nationalist leadership. After his release, he decided to resume his education and enrolled at the Damascus Law Faculty, but the outbreak of the Great Revolt in 1925 disrupted this plan. His participation in the revolt led to a brief stint in prison. Disappointed by the outcome of the revolt, he decided not to resume his studies and opted for a career in com-

[64] On the contribution of the *tajhiz* of Damascus to the independence movement, see Chapter 15.

[65] Information on Bayruti's upbringing and career comes from a long conversation with him in Damascus on 10 March 1976, and from conversations with other youth leaders of the Mandate era, including ʿAli ʿAbd al-Karim al-Dandashi. I have also depended on *al-Mudhik al-mubki*, no. 18 (1929), p. 12; and Faris, *Man huwa 1949*, pp. 70–71. On Mamluk's career, see Faris, *Man huwa 1949*, p. 429.

merce. With a small family stake he established a novelties store on the rue Rami in the immediate proximity of the Sérail (French High Commission headquarters) and Marjé Square. His store could not have been more conveniently located, for most nationalist manifestations during the Mandate focused on the Sérail. To attract students, Bayruti added a small library on the second floor of his shop, and in no time it became a popular meeting place. Its location beyond the quarters also afforded youngsters a certain degree of freedom from the watchful eye of the family, of traditional religious figures, and of *qabadayat*.

Eventually Bayruti began to encourage small groups of students to gather at his store after school where they met older students from the university, especially the Faculty of Law. There they listened to discussions of critical political issues, talked over common problems, and read newspapers and the regular decrees of the High Commissioner. At these gatherings and under Bayruti's guidance, various courses of political action were plotted. By the late 1920s his shop had become a springboard for student demonstrations. With the Sérail nearby, protestors did not have to go far to make their opinions heard.

As his following increased with each political activity born on the rue Rami, Bayruti felt a greater need to offer his students some regimentation. Impressed by the *esprit de corps* of the one Boy Scout troop in Damascus, the Ghuta Scouts, but unhappy that its leaders refused to engage the troop in political activities, Bayruti and an activist medical student from al-Maydan, Midhat al-Bitar, formed their own Umayyad Scouts in early 1929. Many of the young visitors to Bayruti's store became the troop's first members.

News of this development delighted Fakhri al-Barudi who had already begun to hear good things about Bayruti's activities with students. Soon thereafter, Barudi began to extend personal invitations to Bayruti and his followers through one of his minions, a law student from al-Qanawat, Khalid al-Shiliq. Bayruti quickly developed a warm relationship with Fakhri Bey and began to reap the benefits of his patronage. With Barudi's encouragement, Mahmud al-Bayruti, assisted by Khalid al-Shiliq, established the Nationalist Youth (al-Shabab al-watani), putting it under the direct responsibility of the National Bloc.[66]

Mahmud al-Bayruti, who visibly prospered through his National Bloc connection, virtually monopolized the leadership of the Nationalist Youth in Damascus until the mid-1930s, when his Bloc patrons decided that his organization desperately needed a new, more attractive image. By that time, rival political organizations led by a rising generation of

[66] Conversation with Mahmud al-Bayruti (Damascus, 10 March 1976); Faris, *Man huwa 1949*, pp. 70–71; *al-Mudhik al-mubki*, no. 103 (21 Nov. 1931), p. 14.

radical nationalists were bidding for the support of the growing student population in Damascus and other towns. Bayruti had performed an important service, but the National Bloc had to provide a more authentic role model for the educated youth if it intended to retain its grip on the independence movement, especially after the Bloc gained control of government in the late 1930s and was more subject to criticism from rival nationalist organizations.[67] It therefore became necessary to turn to a group of articulate, young, European-schooled lawyers, doctors, and engineeers for the critical task ahead.

Despite a comparatively limited education, and a certain roughness around the edges, Mahmud al-Bayruti lived and operated in a social and political milieu more akin to that of the National Bloc leadership than that of a *qabaday* like Abu ʿAli al-Kilawi. Clad in European clothes and proudly sporting the fez of the *effendi* class of politicians and bureaucrats, Bayruti was literate and ideologically motivated. With a political base outside the popular quarters among the young educated elites, he was an early representative of the forces of political modernization in Syria which had begun to shift the center of political life out of the popular quarters and into new, more sophisticated institutions and structures such as the government schools, the university, and various youth organizations. Unlike Abu ʿAli and other *qabadayat*, Bayruti was a "party man."

Mahmud al-Bayruti and Abu ʿAli al-Kilawi held each other in low esteem. Bayruti saw Abu ʿAli as a relic, an obstacle to progress; Abu ʿAli saw Bayruti as a party hack, a man whose highest commitment was to an elitist organization, not to the common people.[68] Interestingly, as other youth leaders began to eclipse Bayruti in importance, he became more dependent on individual Bloc chiefs, especially Jamil Mardam, for patronage and, in this sense, he began to resemble the *qabaday*. Yet, he remained closely linked to and identified with the Bloc organization which he continued to serve. Although his age and lower social origins prevented him from joining the Bloc's inner political circle or participating in critical strategy sessions, he nevertheless operated on a higher political level than did any *qabaday* and was duly accorded greater recognition from his Bloc mentors. Like the *qabaday*, he served as an intermediary, but more for the Bloc organization as a whole than for any single individual in it. Unlike the *qabaday*, his base of operations was fundamentally outside the popular quarters among the educated elites. Consequently, he worked in

[67] Conversation with Munir al-ʿAjlani (Beirut, 2 Sept. 1975). On the development of the new "nationalist youth" leadership, see Chapters 15–17.

[68] Conversations with Abu ʿAli al-Kilawi (Damascus, 14 Feb. 1976) and Mahmud al-Bayruti (Damascus, 10 March 1976).

a milieu that ultimately proved to be more important to the future of the Syrian national independence movement and to urban politics in general.

The Mandate years were a critical transitional phase for urban political life in Syria. Rapid population growth, an inflated cost of living, the spread of agrarian commercialization, the accelerated collapse of traditional industries and the retarded development of new ones, the growing polarization of class forces, and the shaping of a new intellectual climate contributed to a rearrangement of social and political forces in Damascus and in other cities. Physical and psychological barriers between the older residential quarters began to break down. In some instances, the walls separating the quarters literally came tumbling down, as during the Great Revolt, when the French bombarded a large area in the old city (al-Hariqa) and large sections of al-Maydan.[69] The political realities of life under an "illegitimate" and capricious foreign ruler sharpened the political awareness of the common people. It also allowed the urban leadership of Damascus to divert the attention of the popular quarters away from their traditional rivalries and new class conflicts by channeling their competitive energies toward the goal of national independence. In aligning together, quarters contributed to the growing scale of urban politics.

However, the focus of political activity gradually moved outside the quarters altogether, to French High Commission headquarters and to other symbols of foreign control and influence, highly visible to all Syrians.[70] When individuals from the popular quarters demonstrated they did so by quarter, chanting traditional slogans and carrying traditional banners, but they marched alongside men (and now women) from other quarters, demonstrating for a common purpose.[71] This was a new wrinkle in urban political life.

The *qabadayat* seemed to enjoy a new lease on life and a new importance in politics during the Mandate period. They remained an important component in the *beys'* political machines at a time when nationalist lead-

---

[69] See Chapter 7.

[70] The Franco-Belgian owned Société des Tramways et d'Electricité was the most visible foreign concession visited by nationalist demonstrations during the Mandate. The cinemas, located in the modern districts, were another focal point. On the one hand, political organizations that wished to start a demonstration could find a ready-made crowd afternoons and evenings coming out of films. The Roxy Cinema was used most frequently. On the other hand, some Muslim benevolent societies led demonstrations against cinemas which permitted the attendance of women. Most cinemas happened to be Christian-owned. 'Adil al-'Azma Papers (Syria), File 16, no. 398, 7 Feb. 1939 and File 16, no. 398a, 9 Feb. 1939.

[71] See R. Tresse, "Manifestations féminines à Damas aux XIXᵉ et XXᵉ siècles," in *Entretiens sur l'évolution des pays de civilisation arabe, III* (Paris, 1939), pp. 115–25.

ers required extraordinary support to remain in the political game orchestrated by the French. But, in fact, the *qabaday* was merely enjoying a reprieve from political obsolescence. This could perhaps best be seen in the changing composition and character of demonstrations against the French in the 1930s. By that time, young men, organized by Boy Scout troop or by political affiliation, were at the head of these demonstrations. Everything about these young men seemed different, from their secular slogans denouncing French imperialism and invoking pan-Arab unity, national liberation, and (by the end of the Mandate) even socialism, to their European dress and modern uniforms.[72] Many of these youth belonged to the rising middle classes and hailed from the wealthier or newer quarters of Damascus. But even those who did not marched under the banner of their youth organization or school, and not with their quarter. Although the national independence movement, headed by the National Bloc, formed a set of broad alliances which linked together different elites, classes, and confessional groups, by the thirties the dynamic element in the movement had become the new modern educated classes whose base and activities were beyond the older popular quarters and even the ancient commercial district.

The rise of this new elite threatened the National Bloc leadership. In order to survive, nationalist leaders not only had to adjust to the changes taking place in the older quarters, but even more particularly to the new institutions and organizations of urban political life that had arisen alongside the quarters, creating in the process a new balance of local power. By the end of the Mandate era, to maintain control of the independence movement and of the reigning idea of nationalism required, above all, a concentration of attention and resources in these new areas. The traditional style and methods of urban politics had slowly but surely begun to give way.

[72] The Nationalist Youth was transformed into a uniformed paramilitary organization in 1936. See Chapter 17.

British Minister Major-General Spears presenting his credentials to the Syrian government, Damascus, 1941. To the right of Spears is Shaykh Taj al-Din al-Hasani, the Syrian President

President Shukri al-Quwwatli and party listening to Syrian gendarmerie playing Syrian National Anthem, Damascus, 1944. To the right and left of Quwwatli are Sa'dallah al-Jabiri and Faris al-Khuri

Ceremony of thanksgiving for the return to health of the Syrian President, Shukri al-Quwwatli; Quwwatli addressing his well-wishers from the balcony of the Sérail, Damascus, June 1944

American Minister Wadsworth presenting his credentials to President Shukri al-Quwwatli and Jamil Mardam. Damascus, 1943

Official Syrian visit to Egypt in 1943. Fourth from right is Egyptian Prime Minister Nahhas Pasha. To his right and left are Jamil Mardam and Sa'dallah al-Jabiri

Jamil Mardam

Syrian Parliament in Damascus after it was shelled by the French in May 1945

PART V

HONORABLE COOPERATION, 1928–1933

CHAPTER TWELVE

CONSTITUTIONAL EXPERIMENTS

WHEN THE NATIONAL BLOC agreed to participate in elections for a Syrian Constituent Assembly, it became crucial to the French that they be conducted smoothly, without the scandalous incidents of previous elections. One obvious obstacle to such a process was Ahmad Nami. The Circassian aristocrat, who was much disliked in nationalist circles for having assumed office at the height of the Great Revolt, had presided over three cabinets since becoming Prime Minister in April 1926.[1]

What finally sparked Ahmad Nami's ultimate downfall was his bid to make himself King of Syria. After becoming Prime Minister he had lobbied actively toward this end at the High Commission and through the vehicle of a propaganda campaign orchestrated by his trusted adviser and fellow-Mason, Yusuf al-Hakim.[2] It was apparently on Hakim's advice that Ahmad Nami began to squander vast sums on "semi-royal etiquette," which widened the breach between himself and republican-minded nationalists and severely strained his relations with the High Commissioner who had been pressing him unsuccessfully to give his Ministry a more nationalist complexion in time for the elections.[3] On 2 February 1928 the Nami government resigned, discreetly pushed by Ponsot who politely announced that it "did not possess sufficient confidence to preside over elections with complete disinterest."[4]

Ponsot's choice of a successor to Ahmad Nami came as no great surprise. Eight days after his resignation, Shaykh Taj al-Din al-Hasani was invited to form a "provisional government," whose immediate task was to oversee the elections.[5]

[1] Edmond Rabbath, *Courte Histoire* ("L'expérience Ponsot"), pp. 53–54.
[2] The son of a Greek Orthodox physician of Latakia, Hakim was born in 1883 and educated at the American mission school in his hometown and later at the Sultaniyya in Beirut. His public career mainly in the Ottoman and Mandate judiciaries had by the mid-1920s already been long and illustrious. During the Mandate, he served as President of the Court of Appeal until 1926 when the Damad made him Justice Minister, a post he held in his three cabinets. Conversation with Yusuf al-Hakim (Damascus, 21 Feb. 1976); FO 371/1472, vol. 13074. Hole to Chamberlain, 23 Feb. 1928. Also see Yusuf al-Hakim, *Suriyya wa al-'ahd al-'uthmani* (Beirut, 1966) and *Suriyya wa al-'ahd al-Faysali* (Beirut, 1966), for his activities in late Ottoman times and in Damascus under Faysal.
[3] Rabbath, *Courte Histoire*, p. 54.
[4] *Ibid.*
[5] Conversation with Yusuf al-Hakim (Damascus, 21 Feb. 1976); Rabbath, *Courte Histoire*, pp. 54–55.

Although reared in the conservative religious atmosphere of *madrasa* and mosque and surrounded by his noted father's disciples from all over the Islamic world, the 43-year-old Taj was neither well educated nor pious. His one proven skill was his ability to use his father's popularity "to feather his own nest." Behind his rather comic appearance—he was short, expansively stout, and lame—lay a shrewd intriguer, a personality well suited for survival in the ruthless French game of divide and rule.[6]

Taj had realized early on that to be invited by the French to head a government, it was necessary to find that almost unattainable balance between outright collaboration and rejection of French rule. By early 1928, he had managed to do just that. The High Commissioner picked him because of his moderate nationalist stance and his good family connections, even though privately the French regarded him as a "conceited puppet."[7] Apparently prepared to "truckle to anybody," Taj had frankly stated that he was willing "to take office on any terms as a representative of any party that would support him."[8]

Taj's cabinet was in no way remarkable. It was obviously meant to have some conciliatory effect on middle-of-the-road nationalists, for it included one member each from Aleppo and Hama (though no one from Homs to Hashim al-Atasi's consternation), and its formation was timed to accompany the High Commissioner's declarations that martial law and press censorship were to be lifted and that an amnesty for Syrian rebels would soon be granted.[9] But its members had little independent political influence although they set the fashion of riding around Damascus in chauffeur-driven automobiles.[10]

The new government included both old and new faces. Probably closest to Taj was Jamil al-Ulshi, the Minister of Finance, a capable but cunning and unscrupulous politician who had retired from politics after briefly heading the first French-appointed government in the fall of 1920. Regarded in nationalist circles as the betrayer of Faysal, Ulshi had recently attached himself to Taj, his distant relation and neighbor in the Qaymariyya quarter of Damascus.[11] He was a close personal friend of Wathiq al-Mu'ayyad, who accepted from Taj the post of Director of the Syrian Land Registry. Together, Taj, Ulshi, and Mu'ayyad formed a triumvirate which dominated government for two and a half years.[12]

---

[6] FO 371/2142, vol. 20849, 6 May 1937. Conversation with Zafir al-Qasimi (Beirut, 26 July 1975). *Al-Mudhik al-mubki*, no. 1 (1929), p. 3.

[7] *"Fantoche vaniteux."* MAE, Syrie–Liban 1918–29. Briand to Poincaré, 9 Aug. 1928.

[8] FO 371/2142, vol. 20849, 6 May 1937.

[9] Rabbath, *Courte Histoire*, p. 55.

[10] *Al-Mudhik al-mubki*, backcover, no. 20 (1929); *Oriente Moderno*, 10 (1930), p. 533.

[11] Faris, *Man huwa 1949*, pp. 40–41.

[12] FO 371/1472, vol. 13074. Hole (Damascus) to Chamberlain, 23 Feb. 1928.

Other members of Taj's cabinet from Damascus were Muhammad Kurd 'Ali, also a resident of Qaymariyya, who had presided over the prestigious Arab Academy since March 1922 and who now returned to the post of Education Minister after a six-year absence from government;[13] Tawfiq Shamiyya, a wealthy Greek Orthodox politician of Bab Tuma and a founder of the nationalist People's Party as Minister of Public Works;[14] and Sa'id al-Mahasini, a newcomer to government, as Interior Minister. A rather colorless personality, Mahasini hailed from a prominent religious family whose fortunes had for some time been declining. He had attended the Mülkiye in Istanbul, becoming a respected attorney, professor of civil law, and leading light in the Lawyers' Union. He was thought to be a moderate nationalist.[15]

The remaining two ministries were filled by non-Damascenes, both newcomers to the highest level of government. From Aleppo, Taj selected Subhi al-Nayyal, a wealthy landowner from the religious aristocracy of the town and a prominent trustee (nazir) of its various Ottoman religious endowments. Generally regarded as well-disposed to the French, Subhi Bey became Justice Minister.[16] Shaykh 'Abd al-Qadir al-Kaylani of Hama assumed the portfolio of Agriculture and Commerce. A religious dignitary who belonged to the wealthiest and most prominent landowning-scholarly family in Hama, Kaylani cut an odd figure wearing a traditional long outer garment over a European-cut business suit. He was the only committed nationalist to join the new government. His overwhelming popularity in Hama was threatening enough that Taj preferred to have him as a minister in Damascus.[17]

Shaykh Taj outlasted all members of his original cabinet, by hanging on to the Prime Minister's seat for nearly four years. All this attested to his uncanny ability to survive in what continued to be a very unstable political environment. His reign can be compared to the reigns of earlier Prime Ministers in its dominant features. First, Taj had no significant administrative experience before taking office; the same could be said of Subhi Barakat and Ahmad Nami. Secondly, Taj selected ministers and ranking bureaucrats of very different caliber. Like Haqqi al-'Azm, Taj won a scandalous reputation for packing the bureaucracy—which included nearly 8,000 Syrian employees[18]—with incompetent notables who

[13] The Arab Academy of Damascus was founded in 1919 and Muhammad Kurd 'Ali was one of its earliest members. Faris, *Man huwa 1949*, pp. 372–73.

[14] Conversation with Jubran Shamiyya (Tawfiq's son) (Beirut, 29 July 1975).

[15] FO 371/2142, vol. 20849, 6 May 1937.

[16] *Al-Mudhik al-mubki*, no. 102 (14 Nov. 1931), p. 14.

[17] FO 371/2142, vol. 20849, 6 May 1937; *al-Mudhik al-mubki*, no. 2 (1929), p. 3.

[18] Kayyali gives the figure of 7,833 employees. Al-Kayyali, *al-Marahil*, vol. 1, pp. 239–40.

had lost their fortunes and friends. He had a strong proclivity to appoint Damascenes over Aleppines, which caused much discontent in the North,[19] and his real favorites were the ʿulama' of Damascus on whom he lavished extraordinarily high salaries, in many cases retroactively. After all, Taj and his renowned father, Shaykh Badr al-Din, had their roots in the religious establishment and Taj's greatest challenge came from the secularist National Bloc. Ironically, however, Taj harbored much disrespect for the ʿulama', who, he felt, were only good for nurturing the superstitions of the masses.[20] Nevertheless, he permitted mediocrity to pervade the Ministry of Education. According to Kurd ʿAli, only seven of the forty-five religious teachers on the Ministry's payroll were considered "competent teachers."[21]

Of all the religious leaders under Taj's regime, one received preferential treatment and in the process gained great notoriety. Shaykh ʿAbd al-Qadir al-Khatib was a relative of both Shaykh Taj and Jamil al-Ulshi.[22] After a brief career as a nationalist, ʿAbd al-Qadir crossed over to the side of the Mandate with the collapse of the Great Revolt. By early 1927, he was an outspoken supporter of Shaykh Taj.[23] Once Taj assumed office, his reward was the lucrative post of Inspector-General of Waqfs which he, like others before him, quickly debased by embezzling endowment funds. There is good reason to believe that Khatib embezzled funds with the knowledge and even the complicity of Shaykh Taj. It is known that Taj used his influence with Khatib to have income from charitable endowments paid directly to himself.[24] Syrian politics were such that the weaker or more fragile a politician's independent influence in society, the greater his need for large sums of money for patronage purposes, and Shaykh Taj was neither a popular leader nor particularly affluent. Khatib was eventually forced to take a compulsory leave of absence, but he was never prosecuted.[25]

Shaykh Taj was a source of embarrassment to his colleagues in government for other reasons as well. At official functions he appeared in frock

[19] Kurd ʿAli, al-Mudhakkirat, vol. 2, pp. 323–39.
[20] Ibid. According to Kurd ʿAli, the ʿulama' ". . . were only trumpets for the Prime Minister and his father to blow upon."
[21] Ibid.
[22] MAE, Syrie–Liban 1918–29, 1 May 1928, vol. 204, p. 67. Interestingly, Taj's father, Shaykh Badr al-Din, had been the prize pupil of ʿAbd al-Qadir's uncle, Shaykh Abu'l-Khayr al-Khatib, the noted preacher at the Umayyad Mosque in the second half of the nineteenth century. Oriente Moderno, 15 (1935), p. 382; Muhammad Adib Taqi al-Din al-Husni, Muntakhabat, vol. 2, p. 350.
[23] MAE, Syrie–Liban 1918–29, 1 May 1928, vol. 204, p. 67.
[24] Conversation with Zafir al-Qasimi whose father eventually replaced Shaykh ʿAbd al-Qadir al-Khatib as Inspector-General of Waqfs. (Beirut, 26 July 1975); Kurd ʿAli, al-Mudhakkirat, vol. 2, pp. 323–39.
[25] FO 371/5398, vol. 13802, 26 Aug. 1936.

coat and turban and was prone to inebriation and to chasing the wives of visiting dignitaries.[26] Obviously interested in going down in history as a great builder, he had his name inscribed on every station, wall, government office, mosque, and school built or repaired during his tenure of office.[27] Kurd 'Ali, to whom Taj offered the handsome sum of £S 1,000 to compose a panegyric on his achievements,[28] related one story which best summed up his personal style of governing. Wanting to celebrate publicly his recovery from an illness but warned by his advisers that there were no adequate resources available, Taj nevertheless went ahead with his plan. Relying on his influence in religious circles, he mobilized popular shaykhs and the heads of dervish orders attired in their "green turbans and party-colored gowns," to take to the streets, "raising their banners, beating their drums, brandishing their long rosaries and carrying their 'serpents.' " After several hours the celebrants finally ended their march in front of the Sérail where they congratulated the Prime Minister. In return for such "devotion," Taj paid off the leaders with public health funds allotted for the treatment of tubercular patients.[29]

ELECTIONS—1928

Despite his shortcomings, Taj had been appointed to hold the fort during elections for a Constituent Assembly, as government candidates, independents, and "Kutlawis" spent winter and early spring vigorously campaigning for the elections scheduled for April 10 and 24. Most active and certainly most visible among the candidates was Taj himself. In March he made a tour of the country which met with such enthusiasm that he must have paid royally for the necessary arrangements. On returning from the campaign trail he was received in Damascus with such a fanfare that one old resident was heard to comment that neither Faysal nor Kaiser Wilhelm II before him "had been received like this."[30] Meanwhile, M. Ponsot and his Secretary-General, Maugras, continued to search for notables who were willing to cooperate with the High Commission but who, at the same time, represented public opinion.[31]

A partial amnesty granted to Syrian insurrectionists by the High Com-

---

[26] *Ibid*. Kurd 'Ali, *al-Mudhakkirat*, vol. 2, pp. 323–39. Like Haqqi al-'Azm, Taj was concerned about ministerial dress codes. He instructed his ministers to dress in frock coats at official functions and balls. Kurd 'Ali told Taj that frock coats were worn by "porters."

[27] *Ibid*.

[28] This Report was published by Taj's government. See *al-Hukuma al-suriyya fi thalath sinin min 15 shabat 1928 ila 15 shabat 1931. 'ala al-'ahd ri'asa sahib al-fakhamat al-sayyid Muhammad Taj al-Din al-Hasani* (Damascus, 1931); Kurd 'Ali, *al-Mudhakkirat*, vol. 2, pp. 323–39.

[29] *Ibid*.

[30] *L'Asie Française*, no. 260 (May 1928), pp. 203–4.

[31] Rabbath, *Courte Histoire*, pp. 57–58.

missioner in mid-March was accompanied by the publication of a "Black List" containing the names of 64 persons, including Dr. Shahbandar, Shukri al-Quwwatli, and Sultan al-Atrash, who were forbidden to return.[32] Among the surprises on the amnestied list were Faris al-Khuri, Fawzi al-Ghazzi, Husni al-Barazi, Lutfi al-Haffar, Sa'dallah al-Jabiri, and Nasib and Fawzi al-Bakri.[33] By granting only a limited number of pardons, the High Commission and the native government it supported aimed to exacerbate divisions among nationalists.

Those pardoned were generally not militants, nor were they overtly identified with British or Hashemite interests. The one exception, of course, was the Bakri brothers whose influence among the chiefs of the popular quarters of Damascus was unrivalled. The Bakris, who proudly but gracefully affected many of the characteristics of traditional urban patrons such as generosity and piety, had never been particularly fond of Dr. Shahbandar whom they regarded as egocentric, intellectually arrogant, stingy, and, most offensive to their conservative tastes, much too Westernized. By the end of the Great Revolt when nationalist leaders were forced to seek refuge in Palestine or Egypt and ugly accusations were being hurled back and forth as to who was responsible for the "disaster," relations between the Bakris and Shahbandar foundered. The Bakris, who had ended up penniless and in exile in 1927, were especially embittered by the Istiqlalis' financial dealings through the Jerusalem Committee. But they also withdrew their support from Shahbandar when he used funds secured from Iraqi sources to open a private clinic in Cairo in 1927.[34] Quick to capitalize on such splits, the French now saw a golden opportunity to isolate Shahbandar and his followers by wooing the financially destitute Bakris back to Damascus with the offer of a full pardon including the return of their vast properties in and around the capital. After his return, Fawzi al-Bakri surprised the High Commissioner beyond his wildest dreams by deciding to stand as a candidate for the Assembly on the government ticket headed by Shaykh Taj.[35] The Prime

[32] Categories A and B of the Black List divided leaders from the rank and file of the revolt. Other Syrian leaders who were not amnestied included Hasan al-Hakim, Shaykh Kamil al-Qassab, Nabih and 'Adil al-'Azma, Ihsan al-Jabiri, Nazih Mu'ayyad al-'Azm, Fatih al-Mar'ashli, Muhammad 'Izz al-Din al-Halabi. There were six Lebanese on the list including Shakib and 'Adil Arslan and Fawzi al-Qawuqji. The rest of the list contained two from the Alawite territory and 25 lesser-known rebels. See MWT, al-Intidab al-faransi. 80/943/1864, 14 March 1928, citing Arrêté, no. 1817, 14 March 1928; FO 371/1567, vol. 13037. Air Ministry to British Liaison Officer (Beirut), 19 Feb. 1928.

[33] FO 371/1472, vol. 13074. Hole to Chamberlain, 23 Feb. 1928.

[34] MAE, Syrie–Liban 1918–29, 24 April 1927, vol. 213, pp. 85–86.

[35] MWT, al-Qism al-khass, Nazih Mu'ayyad al-'Azm Papers, no. 68, M. Fakhri (Jaffa) to Mu'ayyad al-'Azm, 30 March 1928.

Minister, a long time friend, had worked hard to ensure the return of the 43-year-old Bakri. In return, Fawzi promised Taj his support.[36]

The High Commission had scored a major coup. Shahbandar was both jealous and irate, claiming from his Cairo headquarters that those "so-called" nationalists who had been amnestied had achieved their pardons in underhanded ways.[37] Indeed, with the Bakris' defection, demoralization in nationalist ranks deepened perceptibly.

On the eve of the elections, the National Bloc in Damascus and Shaykh Taj had worked out a "tacit alliance." Both parties agreed to submit a joint list of six government and four nationalist candidates for the second round.[38] But, when it became known that the French-backed government was using the public services at its disposal to procure the return of its nominees in the primaries, nationalist leaders were incensed. They accused Saʿid al-Mahasini, the Interior Minister, and Taj himself of bribing candidates and having police tamper with ballot boxes in their respective quarters of residence, Suq Saruja and al-Qaymariyya. In both quarters, the National Bloc had experienced setbacks. On the day after the primaries Shaykh Taj had rallies organized on his behalf in Suq Saruja, in an effort to prove that nationalist charges were groundless. However, the nationalists were not about to let Taj absolve himself. On April 12, Fawzi al-Ghazzi, a nationalist candidate and popular figure in local politics, led much larger demonstrations against Taj and his government in the aristocratic Suq Saruja and in Shaghur, a hotbed of opposition to French rule.[39] Despite a voter turnout of 60 percent,[40] the highest ever, the alliance between the National Bloc and the government had completely dissolved.

Nationalists then altered their strategy by submitting an independent

[36] FO 371/1887, vol. 13074. Hole to Chamberlain, 15 May 1928. Fawzi al-Bakri who was born in 1885 (the same year as Shaykh Taj), had been educated at the Lazarist mission school in Damascus and then at Maktab ʿAnbar. He was married to an ʿAzm of Damascus, from the most prestigious branch of the family (Asʿad line). Faris, *Man huwa 1949*, p. 67; Conversation with Wajiha al-Yusuf [Ibish] (Beirut, 29 Aug. 1975). Fawzi al-Bakri was an even closer friend of Shaykh ʿAbd al-Qadir al-Khatib, Taj's relative and the Inspector-General of Waqfs.

[37] MWT, *al-Qism al-khass*, Nazih Muʿayyad al-ʿAzm Papers, no. 68, Fakhri to Muʿayyad al-ʿAzm, 30 March 1928. Dr. Shahbandar was especially perturbed when it was reported to him that Nasib al-Bakri had proposed to the High Commission that, with his brother, Fawzi, he be allowed to resurrect the People's Party.

[38] Muhammad Harb Farzat, *al-Hayah al-hizbiyya*, p. 110; FO 371/2401, vol. 13074. Hole to Chamberlain, 10/13 April 1928; FO 371/2683, vol. 13074. Hole to Chamberlain, 25 April 1928.

[39] FO 371/2401, vol. 13074. Hole to Chamberlain, 10/13 April 1928; *Oriente Moderno*, 8 (1928), pp. 196–97.

[40] FO 371/2740, vol. 13034. Air Ministry to British Liaison Officer (Beirut), 25 April 1928.

list in the second round; one, however, which included Shaykh Taj. Their object was to placate the Prime Minister in hopes of isolating him from his natural allies and limiting the repressive measures the government was expected to take. On the day of the final vote, April 24, Taj, who had placed himself at the top of all lists, made strenuous efforts to buy the votes of electors from villages in the Ghuta, which was traditionally an electoral precinct of Damascus. Varying sums (around £T600 according to the British Consul) were allotted to each uncommitted village, ostensibly as relief money for damages inflicted during the Great Revolt. These funds were driven out and distributed in government cars—by now a trademark of Taj's Ministry—which were then supposed to transport electors back to Damascus. But the government was clearly too late in distributing its largesse; the cars all returned empty, the bribe money untouched.[41]

In Damascus, Taj asked Fawzi al-Bakri to marshal a gang of stalwarts armed with staves to ensure the peaceable conduct of the elections. But the presence of these city toughs only aroused the hostility of National Bloc partisans who despised Bakri for aligning with Taj. Clashes between Bakri's gang and spontaneously organized nationalist youth at Marjé Square led to the intervention of the Gendarmerie on the side of government supporters.[42] Other disturbances occurred at voting booths in Shaghur and Bab Sharqi.[43]

In spite of these troubles, the elections in Damascus came off smoothly. The results were very favorable to the nationalists. Of the nine elected deputies from Damascus, seven were members of the National Bloc. Only Shaykh Taj himself, who polled 539 of the 690 maximum electoral votes, and Yusuf Linyadu, a Jewish merchant who was unanimously elected as his community's representative, could not be considered committed nationalists, though at least in Linyadu's case the Bloc was confident that he would not cause them difficulties in the Assembly.[44] As for Taj's supporters, two of his ministers who ran in Damascus were soundly defeated: Sa'id al-Mahasini and Tawfiq Shamiyya.[45]

[41] FO 371/2683, vol. 13074. Hole to Chamberlain, 25 April 1928; *Oriente Moderno*, 8 (1928), pp. 247–48.

[42] *Ibid.*

[43] Records of *Majlis al-sha'b* (Damascus, Syria).

[44] For the second degree election results, see *Oriente Moderno*, 8 (1928), pp. 196–97, 247–48.

[45] The Bloc ran Fa'iz al-Khuri against Shamiyya. Fa'iz al-Khuri was raised as a Protestant but became a Greek Orthodox in 1923 for political purposes. Because his older brother, Faris, was the leading Protestant politician in Damascus, for Fa'iz to break into politics he needed to find the support of another community. Most Protestants in Syria and Lebanon were converted in the nineteenth and twentieth centuries from the Orthodox rite. In fact, the reason Faris did not run in the elections was because the Protestant community of Da-

In Aleppo the National Bloc also predominated, although only 35 percent of the registered voters turned out in the primaries. This figure was up from 1926, but was significantly below the Damascus turnout. It seems that Subhi Barakat, always a political force to contend with, although he was presently in favor with both the High Commission and the National Bloc, had tried to bribe Christian leaders to see that their communities nominated electors sympathetic to him. When Shaykh Taj's supporters caught wind of Barakat's activities, they physically threatened these same Christian leaders, who were originally thought to have been favorably disposed to the government list. In the end, Christian leaders decided to play both sides of the fence: they accepted Barakat's bribes and then they discreetly discouraged their communities from going to the polls. The absence of Christian voters in the primaries left an almost completely Muslim constituency to elect nine deputies and the National Bloc list won easily.[46]

Nationalists were also swept into the Constituent Assembly from Homs and Hama, which registered a 50 percent voter turnout in the primaries. Only three, however, were members of the National Bloc.[47] Yet, when all the tabulations were in, French authorities were not displeased. As was anticipated, French Intelligence officers had managed to get elected a large group of small-town and rural notables from predominantly agricultural districts in the interior and the Sanjak of Alexandretta where the nationalists were poorly organized. And the nationalists elected from the urban sectors held only 22 of the 70 Assembly seats, a little less than one-third.[48] The High Commission's post-election euphoria was heightened in May when government candidates, including Fawzi al-Bakri and Shaykh ʿAbd al-Qadir al-Khatib, won hotly contested elections to four special seats in the Chamber.[49]

FRENCH OPTIMISM, however, dissipated once the Constituent Assembly opened. The spectacle at the Sérail on June 9 was something to behold. Gathered together were members of what seemed to be two alien worlds: one was old and conservative, rural, and coarse; the other, by comparison,

---

mascus was so small that it did not qualify for representation. Conversations with Suhayl al-Khuri, the son of Faris and the nephew of Faʾiz (Damascus, 8 Feb. 1976), and Jubran Shamiyya (Beirut, 29 July 1975).

[46] FO 371/2866, vol. 13037. Air Ministry to British Liaison Officer, 6 May 1928; Faris, *Man huwa 1949*, p. 27.

[47] FO 371/2740, vol. 13037. Air Ministry to British Liaison Officer, 25 April 1928.

[48] Rabbath, *Courte Histoire*, p. 60.

[49] FO 371/3338, vol. 13074. Hole to Chamberlain, 8 June 1928; FO 371/4149, vol. 13074. Hole to Chamberlain, 27 July 1928.

was modern and radical, urban and sophisticated. Here, traditionally attired rural notables and Bedouin chiefs sat across from their urban nationalist colleagues in fezzes and European business suits. These contrasts
were greatly accentuated by the fact that the "moderates" had come to
represent the will of the High Commission, but found themselves on hostile ground with no mechanisms through which to resist the pressures of
more skilfull nationalist deputies, who were clearly in their element.[50]

At the inaugural session on June 9, nationalist deputies responded confidently, if not indignantly, to the introductory speeches of M. Ponsot
and Shaykh Taj.[51] Instead of striking an accommodating pose, they demanded the resignation of the "provisional government" headed by Taj.
They also wanted the four government candidates elected in special session to resign, owing to the illegal and coercive measures used by the
Government to procure their seats.[52]

As the tension mounted in the Grand Sérail, Ponsot looked to the so-
called "majority of moderates" from rural districts and the Sanjak for a
strong rebuttal to the nationalist demands. However, his tongue-tied
clients remained frozen on their benches, no match for the more articulate and better organized National Bloc deputies seated across the hall.[53]
With no party program or apparatus, these moderates were easily divided, isolated, and then individually intimidated by the nationalist minority. The result was that Hashim al-Atasi, instead of Shaykh Taj, was
elected President of the Chamber. Ibrahim Hananu was elected Chairman
of the Assembly Committee to draft the Syrian constitution. Joining him
were 26 other deputies, most of whom were nationalists. This Committee, in turn, elected two of its most qualified members, Fawzi al-Ghazzi
and Fa'iz al-Khuri, to its editorial subcommittee. Both were prominent
attorneys and lecturers at the Faculty of Law.[54] Thus, from the outset, the
Constituent Assembly was an official institution opposed to the French-
appointed government.[55]

When the direction of the Chamber of Deputies became clear, M. Ponsot began to search for ways to counter the drift. Privately he blamed the
overly-confident Shaykh Taj for having misled him as to what could be

[50] Rabbath, *Courte Histoire*, p. 60.
[51] See French text in FO 371/3435, vol. 13074. Hole to Chamberlain.
[52] FO 371/4149, vol. 13074. Hole to Chamberlain, 27 July 1928.
[53] *Ibid.*
[54] Rabbath, *Courte Histoire*, p. 61; FO 371/3435, vol. 13074. Hole to Chamberlain, 12
June 1928; Ghazzi and Khuri taught international law and Roman law, respectively.
[55] Ibrahim Pasha, *Nidal*, p. 47; FO 371/4149, vol. 13074. Hole to Chamberlain, 27 July
1928; FO 371/3435, vol. 13074. Hole to Chamberlain, 12 June 1928.

expected from an Assembly filled with "moderates"; publicly, he was compelled to give the Prime Minister his unqualified support.

Even before the Chamber opened, ranking French military officers in his administration had voiced their disgust with Ponsot for allowing nationalists to undermine the Mandate. The criticism voiced by officers from the elite Service des Renseignements was particularly vicious. They reported to their superiors in Paris that they found it especially "irksome" to work under the "indecisively impartial" civilian High Commissioner and his excessively liberal Secretary-General, Maugras. Several high-ranking Intelligence officers had already left Syria or had requested transfers, among them, Georges Catroux.[56]

<h2 style="text-align:center">THE SYRIAN THRONE QUESTION</h2>

The mounting criticism from within his administration and, after the opening of Parliament, from the military party and right-wing press in France gave M. Ponsot no choice but to interfere in Assembly politics. After consulting Maugras, he decided to slow down the constitutional process by raising the question of a Syrian throne. His decision came just as nationalists were preparing to focus on the critical issues of Syrian unity and the return of the districts that had been annexed to Lebanon in 1920. By raising such an awkward issue, Ponsot sought to split the Assembly into small and jealous factions; he obviously was more than just a liberal diplomat, as his understanding of the fragility of Syrian political life revealed.[57]

Creating a Syrian monarchy had never been a central concern for French policy-makers. Since the dismantlement of Faysal's Arab Kingdom in 1920, it had occasionally surfaced in the form of rumors in the Syrian or French press either planted by a hopeful candidate or possibly even by the Quai d'Orsay itself. The most active claimants had been the Hashemites and the French feared that a Hashemite throne would introduce the hand of British influence in the country. But, in 1928, the French themselves raised the question of a Syrian monarchy.

Ponsot wrote Foreign Minister Briand that the vast majority of Syrians wanted such an institution because it would "assure stability, protect national traditions, and safeguard the prestige of the country." He added a list of candidates. Included were Amirs Zayd and ʿAli (the brothers of Faysal and ʿAbdullah), ʿAli Haydar or his son Amir ʿAbd al-Majid (whose branch of the Hashemites had been the principal rival to that of Sharif Husayn's for the post of Sharif of Mecca in 1908), Amir Faysal

[56] FO 371/3188, vol. 13037. Air Ministry to Chamberlain, 23 May 1928.
[57] FO 371/3338, vol. 13074. Hole to Chamberlain, 8 June 1928.

(son of Ibn Saʿud), Amir Yusuf Kamal of Egypt, Amir Saʿid al-Jazaʾiri, and, of course, the Damad. Ponsot then asked Briand to consider the question seriously; a monarchy in his opinion could protect the state from the "rivalries and intrigues" that generally fostered instability in government and might well give French rule in Syria a permanent pillar of support. He concluded, however, with a word of caution: the success of a monarchy hinged almost completely on the personality of the individual selected for the position.[58]

In the meantime, King Faysal of Iraq, who had never lost his appetite for Syrian politics or the question of a throne, intervened both in the Syrian Assembly and at High Commission headquarters in Beirut. The appearance in Beirut and Damascus of three emissaries from Baghdad in June 1928 certainly helped to bring the Syrian throne question to the fore.

To Damascus, Faysal sent his most trusted adviser, Rustum Haydar, a Sorbonne-educated member of a powerful Shiʿi feudal family of Baʿlabakk. Haydar learned of serious divisions on the issue of a monarchy. Those who seemed favorably disposed to the idea of a Syrian throne belonged to one of two professional groupings: the religious establishment or the class of retired military officers. Both, however, cast their defense of this institution in religious terms, claiming that Islam knew no other form of government. More importantly, both saw many potential benefits were a monarchy to be re-established in Syria. The ʿulamaʾ believed that a monarchy would help to stem the tide of secularism which had been eroding their social prestige and political influence. A monarch was perceived as someone akin to a Caliph, both a spiritual and a temporal leader whose position required religious legitimization and from whom they could expect protection and other benefits. There was no unanimity on a candidate for the throne, however, or on whether the Caliphate ought to be revived.[59] As for the ex-Sharifian officers, they observed the situation of their Iraqi counterparts who now exercised considerable political influence in Baghdad, and hoped for the same in Syria. For this group, a Hashemite prince was clearly preferred.[60]

The opponents of a Syrian throne, Rustum Haydar discovered, included "moderate" urban notables in Damascus, who had managed to fill the upper echelons of the state bureaucracy and to hold most of the ministerial portfolios since occupation. The installation of a king threatened their position. Moreover, bitter memories of the Faysal era, when many

[58] MAE, Syrie–Liban 1918–29. Ponsot to Briand, 10 May 1928, vol. 204, pp. 96–97.
[59] Oriente Moderno, 8 (1928), pp. 249, 347.
[60] Ibid., pp. 402, 525.

of this old guard were driven to the margins of political life, were still vivid.[61]

But, what really mattered to Rustum Haydar was the attitude of the nationalist leaders in the Constituent Assembly and at National Bloc headquarters; and their reaction to the prospect of a Hashemite monarch for Syria[62] was overwhelmingly negative. While certain nationalist leaders in Syria and in exile still had much sympathy and admiration for King Faysal,[63] the commanding presence of Ibn Saʿud, untainted by foreign influence and surrounded by Syrian advisers, was very attractive to others.[64] Few nationalists, however, seriously entertained the idea of a Syrian throne in 1928, despite their penchant to play politics with different Arab monarchs, including, in the case of Shahbandar and his supporters, Amir ʿAbdullah. These highly educated and sophisticated politicians were avowedly republican by this time, ironically inspired by the democratic system of the French republic and the liberal bourgeois ideals of the French revolution. Secularists and civilians, they feared that the installation of a monarchy might revive the religious and military establishments in Syria. They also feared that the king, most probably an outsider whose final choice depended on French pleasure, was likely to become a pawn in French hands. Or, an imported monarch might split nationalist ranks by constituting a third political force in the country, as had happened in Egypt and Iraq.[65]

After his visit to Damascus, Rustum Haydar moved on to Beirut to join Faysal's two other emissaries, Nuri Saʿid and Yasin al-Hashimi—both ex-Sharifian officers and prominent Iraqi politicians. There, toward the middle of June, they were granted an audience with Ponsot, who informed them that he personally favored a monarchy and would consider only a Hashemite candidate. But the Iraqi emissaries realized that with both the National Bloc and the French-picked government of Shaykh Taj unequivocally committed to the idea of a Syrian republic, Ponsot was on shaky ground in respect to the imposition of a monarchy. The idea had

---

[61] Al-Mudhik al-mubki, no. 3 (1929), p. 8.

[62] Most probably Amir Zayd. FO 371/3567, vol. 13076. Hole to Chamberlain, 21 June 1928.

[63] Such as Hashim al-Atasi and Ihsan al-Jabiri. Ibid.

[64] Such as Shukri al-Quwwatli and Jamil Mardam. Of Ibn Saʿud's three principal advisers, two were from geographical Syria. Fuʾad Hamza, a Lebanese Druze who was intimately involved in Saʿudi foreign affairs; and Yusuf Yasin from the Latakia region, the King's private secretary, who was particularly close to Quwwatli and the Istiqlal Party of Syria. See Ahmad M. Gomaa, The Foundation of the League of Arab States. Wartime Diplomacy and Inter-Arab Politics 1941–1945 (London, 1977), pp. 73–74.

[65] FO 684/5/2. C. H. F. Cox (Transjordan) to High Commissioner (Palestine). 22 Jan. 1921.

the support of only the religious establishment, whose fortunes were on the wane, a small and uninfluential group of disaffected military officers mostly in retirement, and a handful of Bedouin chiefs. French officials themselves were split on the issue[66] and the High Commissioner had to drop it.

CONSTITUTIONAL CONFUSION

It took the Constituent Assembly less than two months during the summer of 1928 to write a draft constitution of 115 articles. Inspired by European democratic systems, it adopted a parliamentary republic "with a single Chamber to be elected, for four years, by universal suffrage exercised in two stages."[67] The constitution was a modern, sophisticated document reflecting not only the finely tuned legal minds of its main authors, Fawzi al-Ghazzi and Fa'iz al-Khuri, but also the democratic elitism of the National Bloc. What satisfied the French most was the reaffirmation of equality for all citizens of all religious persuasions, "with freedom of religious observance and for the community schools."[68] In fact, the constitution contained only one article which was considered outmoded in some political circles.[69] Executive power was to be vested in a President who was required to be a Muslim. Had the nationalists extended the concept of religious equality to the very top of the governmental hierarchy, they would undoubtedly have faced a violent reaction in conservative religious circles and among the Syrian masses, who were still very much attached to and guided by their religious beliefs and practices and who regarded the nationalists as defenders of the faith and guardians of culture. Syrian nationalist leaders almost always sided with the religious establishment and the Muslim majority on critical religious issues, many of which became important symbols of opposition to French rule. To have done otherwise would have undercut the support system on which their power and influence rested.

The constitution did contain six articles which were bound to raise more than eyebrows in Paris. These declared that Syria, including Lebanon, Transjordan, and Palestine, was one and indivisible, that the Syrian government was to organize its own national army, and that the President of the Republic was empowered to conclude treaties, receive ambassadors, grant pardons, and declare martial law.[70] The mandatory authority could scarcely accept these articles without the restraint of a special

---

[66] FO 371/3666, vol. 13076. Hole to Chamberlain, 28 June 1928.
[67] Ibid.
[68] Longrigg, Syria, p. 184.
[69] Ibid.
[70] Rabbath, Courte Histoire, p. 61.

treaty, something still far off in the future. Nonetheless Maugras, who had been in frequent and cordial contact with nationalist deputies, assured them toward the end of July that the French government would accept the draft constitution almost as it stood.[71] But then, on August 3, he unexpectedly did an about face. In an emotionally charged speech he asserted that the six articles in question were against the international accords of the Mandate and concluded that the High Commissioner was unable to promulgate the constitution in its present form.[72] The incensed Assembly was further aggravated by Shaykh Taj who, on behalf of his French patrons, recommended that the Assembly accept the High Commissioner's demands. This provoked a bitter attack led by Fakhri al-Barudi who accused Taj, quite accurately, of squandering public revenues for personal ends.[73] After Taj stormed out of the Chamber, the Assembly issued a declaration claiming that the suppression of these articles was equivalent to "amputating the constitution," because it denied Syria's rights to sovereignty and independence.[74] Ignoring a French warning, the Chamber proceeded to pass the draft version on August 7 and prepared to debate and vote on each article, one by one, on August 9.[75] The new era of cooperation and understanding, inaugurated between the National Bloc and the High Commission only a few months earlier, faced its first major crisis.

From all accounts, it appears that pressures from higher up in Paris had forced the High Commissioner suddenly to reverse his direction. The same right-wing factions that had put obstacles in the way of his predecessor, Jouvenel, and that had so viciously attacked General Sarrail, now focused on Henri Ponsot. His opponents among the top French officers in the Armée du Levant and the Service des Renseignements had for some time been communicating their criticisms of the civilian High Commissioner to their colleagues in right-wing military circles in France. These criticisms, in turn, were fed to the French press which began a violent and calumnious campaign against the High Commission. Critics claimed that France's abdication from the "Orient" had begun with the establishment of a Syrian Constituent Assembly which was determined to elude the "imperative character of France's international obligations."[76] Ponsot

---

[71] FO 371/4390, vol. 13074. Hole to Chamberlain, 9 Aug. 1928.

[72] Rabbath, Courte Histoire, pp. 62–63. The six articles were nos. 2, 73, 74, 75, 110, and 112.

[73] FO 371/4390, vol. 13074. Hole to Lord Cushendun, 9 Aug. 1928.

[74] Rabbath, Courte Histoire, p. 63.

[75] MAE, Syrie–Liban 1918–29, 9 Aug. 1928, vol. 205, p. 10; Rabbath, Courte Histoire, p. 61.

[76] Ibid., pp. 61–65; FO 371/4390, vol. 13074. Hole to Lord Cushendun, 9 Aug. 1928.

342   HONORABLE COOPERATION

was accused of bargaining away what France had secured with her own
"sweat and blood."[77] The High Commissioner's enemies, by once again
stirring up French public opinion over the question of Syria, wanted to
convince the Quai d'Orsay to veto the proposed constitution.[78]

Ponsot's dilemma was complicated by several tactical errors and political miscalculations. Although he had closely followed the progress of the
Editorial Committee and was fully cognizant of what was being written
into the constitution, he did not anticipate that the Chamber might publish the draft version to an "astonished world" without allowing him to
take a long, hard look at it beforehand.[79] He had also neglected to keep his
superiors in Paris informed of the details of some of the more controversial articles. But in retrospect his chief failing was his misunderstanding
of what the whole Syrian constitutional process, including the drafting of
the six controversial articles, actually represented to the colonial party in
France. Acceptance of the draft version of the constitution symbolized a
lack of French commitment to empire.[80] Its passage threatened to initiate
a new era in France's relations with her colonies—an era that the colonial
lobby, made up of business groups, members of the military establishment, and certain conservative forces in Parliament,[81] was struggling to
avoid.

Ponsot, in his capacity as High Commissioner of a Mandate, was a
transitional type of colonial official who found himself almost helplessly
entangled in the long, arduous struggle to resolve a postwar crisis of
French identity. He stood between two poles of identity. One glorified
what had once been great but were now worn, impractical, and blind traditions of empire. The other stressed the new, stark realities of economy,

[77] FO 371/4429, vol. 13037. Air Ministry to FO, 25 Aug. 1928.
[78] *Ibid.* FO 371/3928, vol. 13074. Hole to Chamberlain, 7 Aug. 1928.
[79] Rabbath, *Courte Histoire,* p. 64; FO 371/4429, vol. 13037. Air Ministry to FO, 25 Aug.
1928.
[80] A few months before the draft Constitution was published, *L'Asie Française,* the
mouthpiece of French political, economic, and cultural interests in Syria, reiterated, as it so
often did, why France had to remain in Syria. The basic arguments had not changed at all.
However, the article did begin with the claim that French obligations differed from those of
Britain's in Iraq (a highly defensive point as the French watched Iraq approach independence
under British tutelage). French patrimony was exclusively one of protecting minorities, of
culture, and of economy. The article admitted that French rule was temporary, but that it
would not end until a sound administration and government were devised. It also admitted
French faults; too many changes of men at the top; the inability to rule indirectly because
of few well-trained or efficient native bureaucrats (which has to do with the nature of the
"Oriental"). Indeed, the author admitted that even collaborators were lacking in ability.
Anonymous, "La politique du Mandat français—Irak et Syrie," *l'Asie Française,* no. 257
(Feb. 1928), pp. 66–67.
[81] William L. Shirer, *The Collapse of the Third Republic* (New York, 1971), pp. 169–71.

restrictionism, even withdrawal, as France prepared to enter the long, harsh years of the world depression.

ADJOURNMENT AND SUSPENSION

Annoyed with the High Commissioner and under considerable pressure from right-wing groups and the conservative French Parliament, the Quai d'Orsay reacted at once to developments in Damascus. It demanded an explanation from Ponsot and, at the same time, condemned the six controversial articles.[82] It was Maugras' speech on August 3 which Ponsot had used to convey Paris opinion to the Constituent Assembly and the Syrian nation. Immediately afterwards, Ponsot was assured by Shaykh Taj that a majority of deputies would vote for acceptance of the French demands. But Taj's grasp of the situation was little better than Ponsot's and both were shocked and disappointed by the Assembly's vote on August 7. On August 11, Ponsot adjourned the Chamber for three months.[83]

The entente between France and Syria had seemingly ruptured. But neither Ponsot nor the Assembly was really to blame. The colonial party in Paris had scored yet another victory, diverting, as it had done before, the High Commission from its task of developing a consistent policy in Syria.

The adjournment of the Chamber caused greater tension in Damascus and in other nationalist towns than at any time since the revolt. Fearing massive disturbances, the French increased the number of troops posted in the capital. But, nationalist deputies had given Ponsot their promise not to provoke disturbances and, aside from a few isolated incidents, calm was maintained. The last official statement issued by the Assembly indicated the National Bloc's frame of mind.

> The Assembly, animated by a desire to proceed with the policy of loyal collaboration and not to lose in vain the efforts already made on the road to 'entente' and in view of realizing the wishes of the country, welcomes its adjournment, voluntarily, but with resignation. It maintains its complete rights intact hoping that after this adjournment obstacles will be ironed out and its wishes realized.[84]

[82] FO 371/4429, vol. 13037. Air Ministry to FO, 25 Aug. 1928.

[83] Rabbath, *Courte Histoire*, pp. 62–63; FO 371/4488, vol. 13074. Hole to Lord Cushendun, 15 Aug. 1928. Actually Ponsot had already begun to think of Taj as a "liability" after the Prime Minister's defeat in the election for President of the Constituent Assembly. See MAE, Syrie–Liban 1918–29. Ponsot to Briand, 12 June 1928, vol. 204, pp. 126–27. Adjournment by *Arrêté*, no. 2,063, 11 Aug. 1928.

[84] Rabbath, *Courte Histoire*, p. 64; FO 371/4488, vol. 13074. Hole to Lord Cushendun, 15 Aug. 1928.

But, whether these admirable sentiments were a sign of magnanimity or an admission of weakness was debatable.

Soon afterwards, Ponsot proceeded to Paris to face the wrath of the Quai d'Orsay. Following on the High Commisioner's heels was a small delegation of Syrian moderates associated with Shaykh Taj who hoped to work out an acceptable constitution. At first the National Bloc refused to send its own delegation. Eventually, however, Jamil Mardam was dispatched to see Ponsot and ranking members of the Quai d'Orsay. It was also hoped that Mardam would convince the High Commissioner to allow Ihsan al-Jabiri, who had not yet been amnestied, to return to Syria. But neither Taj's emissaries nor Jamil Mardam could influence what was, in effect, a struggle for France's soul.[85]

In Syria the situation remained remarkably quiet. Having discouraged violent protest, the National Bloc decided that the best way to maintain a high profile was to stage large but peaceful public rallies in the interior towns. On August 26, one such nationalist gathering took place in Aleppo. Held in the grounds of a popular café near the town center, 6,000 participants turned out, among them nationalist youth, quarter chiefs, religious shaykhs, merchants, and artisans. Only those notables in open collaboration with the French were not among the crowds. The main speakers were Ibrahim Hananu, Dr. Kayyali, Fathallah Asiyun, and, from Damascus, Fa'iz al-Khuri. Each spoke about the six controversial articles of the draft constitution, warning the gathering that certain self-styled nationalists—namely Shaykh Taj and his ilk—had actually sided with the High Commission in refusing to accept the articles. While Kayyali urged his audience to turn a deaf ear to the arguments of the National Bloc's enemies (alluding to the absent Aleppine notables), Khuri preached the need for patriotic solidarity between Christians and Muslims and advised his Christian brothers not to be misled by either French or British offers of protection since the constitution, which he, a Christian, had helped to write, clearly respected the rights of religious minorities; in fact, he added, it accorded them more rights than any Mandate government could possibly provide.

But aside from similar meetings, little of importance transpired in Syria until news spread that Ponsot, in Paris, had renewed the decree adjourning the Assembly for another three months. This news set off some

---

[85] FO 371/4488, vol. 13074. Hole to Lord Cushendun, 15 Aug. 1928. The moderate wing of the Bloc wanted to buttress its influence in Aleppo where the less compromising faction of Bloc politicians around Ibrahim Hananu had the upper hand over Sa'dallah al-Jabiri, Ihsan's younger brother. See MAE, Syrie–Liban 1918–29. Atasi to Ponsot, 5 Oct. 1928, vol. 215, p. 25; Rabbath, *Courte Histoire*, p. 65; FO, 371/5308, vol. 13037. Air Ministry to FO, 13 Oct. 1928.

minor disturbances in the towns as Syrians awaited news of Ponsot's return to the Levant, or his dismissal.

Ponsot was allowed to return, and his first act was to invite Hashim al-Atasi, the Bloc President, to Beirut to compare Syria's revised formula for a constitution with his own. But, their differences of opinion proved insurmountable. Ponsot was bound by political considerations in Paris and the most Atasi was prepared to concede was the addition of an article which would accord France special rights through the conclusion of a treaty.[86] This formula might have satisfied Ponsot in August 1928, but in January 1929 he was unable to accept it. Even last minute concessions arranged by Shaykh Taj and accepted by the National Bloc were too late to avert a total breakdown of relations. On February 5, the High Commissioner decreed that the Constituent Assembly was to be prorogued *sine die*.[87]

[86] Rabbath, *Courte Histoire*, pp. 65–67; FO 371/5766, vol. 13074. Tyrrell (Paris) to Chamberlain, 3 Dec. 1928.

[87] By *Arrêté*, no. 2,385, 5 Feb. 1929.

CHAPTER THIRTEEN

THE ROCKY ROAD TO PARLIAMENT

THE COVER OF AN April 1929 issue of *al-Mudhik al-mubki* featured a revealing cartoon. Hashim al-Atasi, with Fakhri al-Barudi next to him, was
tugging on a long rope coming out of the mouth of the High Commissioner, himself looking unconcerned. The caption read: "Help me pull
harder, Fakhri Bey, maybe we can extract a word from M. Ponsot." The
cartoon captured the essence of the first sixteen months of the second
phase of Ponsot's rule in Syria. During this period Ponsot reverted to the
style he had adopted on first arriving in the Levant—one of aloofness,
distance, and studied inscrutability.[1] He pretended to be disinterested in
all political issues, substituting instead a preoccupation with Syria's economic development. Mundane political decisions were left to the new
Delegate in Damascus, M. Solomiac, whom Ponsot had transferred from
Lebanon where his reputation had been that of a "skillful maneuverer."
Solomiac's task was to fragment the ranks of the National Bloc. In the
interim, Ponsot's liberal and like-minded Secretary-General, M. Maugras, had quietly taken leave of Syria, reportedly in disgrace.[2]

As for Shaykh Taj, the National Bloc's recent setback gave him another
opportunity to entrench himself and his government. But, it was not easy
to live down his reputation as the most unpopular politician in Syria.
Whenever he appeared in public he was booed and hissed. He could find
no solace even in prayer, for each time he entered the Great Mosque in
Damascus he could expect to hear himself denounced from the pulpit as
the "traitor of traitors."[3] His main hope for survival hinged on Ponsot's
reluctance to hand the political ball to nationalists, whom the High Commissioner continued to regard as too uncompromising.[4]

The National Bloc, unable to advance the independence movement at
all, turned to building and broadening the base of its organization. The
mainstream of the Bloc leadership was still committed to bringing about
a gradual relaxation of French rule through accommodation. As a consequence, political life in Syria in this period was characterized by fairly

---

[1] *Al-Mudhik al-mubki*, no. 16 (1929), cover.
[2] *Rapport à la Société des Nations sur la situation de la Syrie et du Liban, 1929*, p. 1;
Rabbath, *Courte Histoire* ("L'expérience Ponsot"). Maugras surfaced a little later as Minister in Teheran.
[3] MAE, Syrie–Liban 1918–29. Ponsot to Briand, 3 Jan. 1929, vol. 205, pp. 160–61.
[4] *L'Asie Française*, no. 269 (April 1929), p. 136.

regular negotiations between nationalists and the High Commission interspersed with remarkably mild public rallies and demonstrations. These were designed both to remind the French of the Bloc's influence and to reinforce its position among Syrians.

The mildness of political activity over Syrian affairs was shattered by events in Palestine. There, mounting tensions between Arabs and Jews broke out in to violent riots in August 1929,[5] which captured the attention of Syrian Muslims and pan-Arabists alike.[6]

The National Bloc played a peculiar role in these events. Bloc leaders discouraged manifestations of any sort against Britain for fear of jeopardizing any future British support against the French. Bloc leaders did not want the attention of the Syrian masses diverted from the most pressing problem of all: how to ease the French out of their country.[7] Thus, the nationalist leadership increasingly sacrificed pan-Arab sentiments to local self-interest.

When Henri Ponsot returned from a visit to Paris at the end of October, there was a noticeable crescendo in diplomatic activity in Syria. Nearly all factions sent delegations to Beirut to present their programs to the High Commissioner.[8]

Immediately after a National Bloc Congress in late October, Hashim al-Atasi reiterated his call for a Franco-Syrian treaty. Now, however, he stressed the progress being made between Britain and Iraq and called for France to follow an identical course.[9] But Ponsot was still unwilling or unable to reply. In December a series of meetings held between Atasi and the High Commission achieved no positive results.[10] At the end of 1929, there was talk among radical nationalists of scrapping the Bloc strategy of "honorable cooperation" altogether.

A MODIFIED CONSTITUTION

The second decade of French rule in Syria began with a series of episodes which reflected the rapidly deteriorating political and economic conditions in the country. There were several strikes in the winter of 1930

[5] For details on this series of incidents, see Porath, *The Emergence*, pp. 258–73.
[6] *L'Asie Française*, no. 273 (Sept.–Oct. 1929), pp. 313–14; Jean Gaulmier, "Notes sur le mouvement syndicaliste à Hama," *Revue des Etudes Islamiques*, 6 (1932), p. 116.
[7] Rabbath, *Courte Histoire*, p. 71.
[8] MAE, Syrie–Liban 1930–40. "Note confidentielle sur la situation politique en Syrie," vol. 477, pp. 232–33.
[9] On 31 October 1929. See Atasi letter in *La Syrie* (Beirut), 5 Nov. 1929, cited in USNA, Syria. 890d./296. Beirut Consul to Secretary of State.
[10] FO 371/231, vol. 14553. Satow (Beirut) to Henderson, 19 Dec. 1929.

against the imposition of an indirect tax, the *octroi,* which fell most heavily on the commercial, industrial, and professional classes that supported the nationalist movement.[11] The constant stream of nationalist and moderate politicians to Ponsot's Beirut headquarters in the meantime generated no progress toward a treaty. Hashim al-Atasi, under immense pressure from nationalist quarters, published a statement on April 15 entitled "An Appeal to the Syrian Nation," in which he refuted charges that he was pandering to the French. In words carefully chosen for their moderate tone, he placed the burden of responsibility for the lack of progress on the High Commission, but avoided mentioning Ponsot.

With the situation degenerating, Ponsot finally broke his long silence and met with Atasi. Atasi warned of a possible upheaval, convincing Ponsot to accelerate political momentum in Syria.[12] Several weeks later, Ponsot signed six important decrees: the Organic Laws of the governments of Latakia, the Jabal Druze, and the Sanjak of Alexandretta, Common Interests, and the long-awaited Lebanese and Syrian constitutions. He even accepted the Syrian constitution's six controversial articles, in a slightly modified form. But, an additional article safeguarded the position of the mandatory power in all cases where the constitution might prove to be in opposition to its rights and obligations under the Mandate. This article and the six decrees in general sanctioned the status quo established by General Gouraud.

The new constitution was not received enthusiastically. It looked even worse a month later when Iraq, considered by Syrian nationalists as culturally and socially inferior, was given a treaty by the British and promised entry into the League of Nations. Politically frustrated, National Bloc leaders left for their cottages in the gardens around the towns or to the resorts of Bludan and Sofar for the summer. Popular attention turned toward the economic sphere.[13]

The economic and financial picture in Syria in 1930 was dismal. Real wages were falling in certain trades and unemployment reached new heights, owing to a combination of factors, not least of which was the continued decline of traditional handicrafts.[14] Conditions were aggravated by the seasonal nature of many Syrian industries, the onset of the world depression which slowed the building cycle and the construction of public

[11] The *octroi* tax was introduced in *Arrêté,* no. 1,894, 24 Feb. 1930, by Shaykh Taj al-Din al-Hasani and approved by the High Commissioner. See J. Grellet, "Mémoire sur la fiscalité municipale en Syrie," CHEAM, no. 331, n.d.; FO 371/4036, vol. 15365.

[12] MAE, Syrie–Liban 1930–40. "Direction politique et commerciale," 15 April 1930, vol. 478, pp. 87–99.

[13] FO 371/3486, vol. 14554. Hole to Henderson, 27 May 1930.

[14] Longuenesse, "La classe ouvrière," p. 39.

works, the institution of new municipal taxes, and the depreciation of the Turkish *mejidi* (silver piece) often used to pay wages.[15]

Consequently, the summer of 1930 was marked by strikes of a more purely economic nature.[16] In Hama, where one strike against the depreciation of Turkish silver had already been conducted at the end of January, the town literally closed down on June 19, to protest a new bread tax.[17] In Aleppo, workers in the traditional sector of the textile industry struck for higher wages at the very end of July.[18] Later, in Homs where the number of employed artisans was falling, and wages in the textile industry had been cut three times in as many months, 600 recently organized textile workers struck on September 20.[19] Meanwhile, Damascus was in the midst of a strike that had begun in mid-July among thousands of textile workers led by the activist Union of Weavers.[20] The nature and sophistication of the demands put forth to factory owners by the "committee of workers"—higher wages, better working conditions, shorter work days—signalled the progress being made by the emerging workingmen's associations. But, relations and conflicts between workers and manager-owners were rarely allowed to take their normal course. In fact, workers' struggles were regularly submerged by the unions which included both workers and patrons and which were often headed by National Bloc partisans.[21]

The development of class conflict in Syria was remarkably gradual during the interwar period, owing in part to the common front of workers and the young bourgeoisie against French economic policies. The dominant position of foreign goods and especially of French goods on local markets, supported by low duties, posed a direct challenge to local production and hurt both small producers and workers, whose wages were already very low. The growing conflict of interests between workers and

[15] George Hakim, "Industry." Saʿid B. Himadeh (ed.), *Economic Organization of Syria* (Beirut, 1936), pp. 172–73.

[16] The last major workers' strikes took place in 1926 in conjunction with the Great Revolt: in textile factories, among public utility workers such as those of the D-HP, the tramways and electricity concessions, the tobacco concession, and in the weaving industry. These strikes were essentially against the lowering of wages. See Hanna, *al-Haraka al-ʿummaliyya*, pp. 338–43; Chafiq Sanadiki, "Le mouvement syndical en Syrie," Doctorat en Droit Dissertation (University of Paris, 1949), p. 54; Longuenesse, "La classe ouvrière," p. 43.

[17] Gaulmier, "Notes sur le mouvement syndicaliste à Hama," pp. 115, 117.

[18] Hanna, *al-Haraka al-ʿummaliyya*, pp. 384–85; Longuenesse, "La classe ouvrière," p. 49

[19] *Ibid.*

[20] The Union of Weavers, the first modern Syrian union, was established in Damascus in 1925, and at the time included only four factories and 52 workers. See Hanna, *al-Haraka al-ʿummaliyya*, pp. 338–43.

[21] *Ibid.*, pp. 350–51.

employers was impeded by the small size of shops and factories and the slight differentiation between classes, but above all by the nature of the struggle between the Syrian population and French hegemony.

RETURN OF THE BLOC

Although National Bloc leaders did not view the constitution with favor, its promulgation did make new elections inevitable. Ponsot proposed to Paris that elections be held in October 1930. But, after his blunder with the constitution back in 1928, the Quai d'Orsay watched the Syrian political scene and the movements of their High Commissioner much more carefully, and his proposal was vetoed by his superiors at the Quai d'Orsay. They argued that with the election campaign falling during the summer, few French officials would be available to organize elections in a fashion favorable to France.[22] The earliest possible date for elections would be the spring of 1931.

It appears from the unusually low profile maintained by the National Bloc during the summer and fall of 1930[23] that it, too, was no more anxious for elections than the Quai d'Orsay. Shaykh Taj alone appeared to be preparing the electoral ground. He reshuffled his cabinet three times in this period, clearly in order to construct a viable front of "moderates" to strengthen his hand with the High Commission and consolidate his position against the far more popular National Bloc.

By New Year, 1931 the National Bloc's interest in major political issues had revived, undoubtedly in reaction to Taj's recent intrigues but also owing to the Anglo-Iraqi Treaty of June 1930. Hashim al-Atasi and Jamil Mardam declared, in back-to-back interviews in the third week of January, that the Bloc was willing—with regret and some reservations—to swallow the High Commissioner's "interpolations" in the constitution and to participate in elections provided that guarantees were made "against illicit interference" by the Syrian government and its French patrons. In addition, the Bloc chiefs demanded the conclusion of a treaty along the lines of the one between Britain and Iraq.[24] These concessions,

[22] MAE, Syrie–Liban 1930–40. Note (internal MAE), 5 May 1930, vol. 478, pp. 189–90. For Ponsot's economic plans, see MAE, Syrie–Liban 1930–40. Ponsot to MAE, 18 Feb. 1930, vol. 477, pp. 168–75.

[23] The general silence noticed during the fall and early winter of 1930 may have been, in part, related to the enforcement of a new High Commission decree in September which forbade any worker or employee of the government either to write manifestos or participate in any political gathering, meeting, demonstration, etc. The penalty was either the loss of job or imprisonment or both. The decree was signed by Shaykh Taj al-Din al-Hasani. *Arrêté*, no. 2,449, 20 Sept. 1930 in MWT, *Qararat mukhtalifa.*

[24] Atasi interview in *L'Orient* (Beirut), no. 93, 19 Jan. 1931; Mardam interview in *L'Orient*, no. 95, 21 Jan. 1931.

however, were not accepted by all Bloc members. Criticism of Mardam
was particularly strong. Even though he was more adamant than Atasi in
his desire to have the broad lines of a future treaty made public before the
nationalists took part in elections, his protest against Article 116 (which
guaranteed for France control of all internal Syrian security and the execution of her international obligations for the duration of the Mandate)
was regarded as perfunctory.[25] And even though Mardam had been
obliged to publish a *mise au point* in response to his critics, his own political coloring and pragmatism had begun to distinguish him from his other
colleagues both in Bloc councils and before the French. Indeed, it was at
this time that Solomiac, in the absence of Ponsot, met regularly and almost exclusively with Mardam to try to reach an agreement with the National Bloc about election procedures.

In Aleppo, nationalists took a dim view of Mardam's dealings in the
Syrian capital. French maneuvers in the North were already well under
way to prevent the Bloc from scoring a major victory in forthcoming elections. The proximity of elections had aroused political parties in Aleppo
to new activities. At a meeting held on February 2 in the home of Ibrahim
Hananu, and attended by Sa'dallah al-Jabiri, Dr. Kayyali, and Edmond
Rabbath, a young, Paris-educated lawyer and intellectual, the general
tenor was one of violent opposition to the Mandate and particularly to the
still-to-be-announced elections. Only Kayyali advised prudence because
he was currently engaged in secret negotiations with Shakir Ni'mat al-
Sha'bani, in hopes of keeping him out of the clutches of the very persua-
sive French Delegate in the town, M. Lavastre. The meeting broke up
without reaching a final decision when reliable reports were brought in
that the Governor of Aleppo, Nabih Bey Mardini, was soon to be replaced
by Wathiq al-Mu'ayyad, one of Shaykh Taj's closest allies and, of late, his
main political mouthpiece. Both Taj and Lavastre were worried about the
mild-mannered Mardini's resolve to persuade community leaders in
Aleppo to vote for French-backed candidates. For Lavastre, who was both
a hardliner and upwardly mobile in the French administrative network,
this task was a minimum prerequisite of any "obedient servant" of the
Mandate.[26]

THE SYRIAN THRONE QUESTION REVISITED

The prospect of new elections always seemed to bring certain politically
charged questions out of the closet and into the limelight in Syria and
elsewhere in the Arab world and Europe. As always at such "critical mo-

[25] FO 371/656, vol. 15364. Hole to Henderson, 30 Jan. 1931.
[26] *Al-Mudhik al-mubki*, no. 59 (10 Jan. 1931); *ibid.*, no. 62 (31 Jan. 1931).

ments," the Syrian throne question resurfaced. The nationalists did not raise the question, but rather found themselves confronted with the problem of having to present a unified response to it.

The names of interested Hashemites always emerged at these moments. In early 1930, a semi-official report from Palestine reached the Colonial Office in London that the French were again concerned about the possibility of a monarchical form of government for Syria and that 'Ali, the ex-King of the Hijaz and the older brother of Faysal and Abdullah, was being considered for the post. But on checking the veracity of the report in Paris, the British soon learned that the French, in their own search for a "solution to the Syrian problem," were not yet convinced of the utility of a monarchy.[27] One year later, King 'Ali's name cropped up first in regard to the question of a Syrian throne on the eve of his surprise visit to Beirut at the invitation of the French High Commission.[28] It seems that the French had once again put out feelers. Their main agent was a certain Paul Lepissier, who had become French *chargé d'affaires* in Baghdad in 1930, after serving five years as French Consul and Assistant Secretary-General to the High Commissioner in Beirut. Lepissier, like his former boss, Henri Ponsot, was impressed by the progress made by the British toward normalizing their relations with Iraq and felt that his government ought to follow a similar path.[29] Like Ponsot, Lepissier was interested in the possibility of a monarchy in Syria.

Even before 'Ali left Baghdad for Amman, Beirut, and Damascus, Lepissier asked him about what demands any prospective Hashemite candidate for a Syrian throne might make before accepting the position. At this time, King Faysal smelled "an odor of oil," and advised the British High Commissioner in Iraq that the French government sought to draw him "into some kind of conditional acceptance of the throne" which would strengthen its hand in the current negotiations over an outlet through Syria for Iraqi crude.[30] No detailed record of what took place between 'Ali and the French during his visit to Beirut on January 11 and 12 is available, but it is certain

[27] FO 371/5186, Wigram (Paris) to Monteagle (FO), 29 Oct. 1928. Ponsot himself had supplied this information to Wigram at a Paris dinner party. Quwwatli had been a supporter of Faysal ibn Sa'ud as early as 1926. *Oriente Moderno*, 8 (1928), p. 347.
[28] Later the name of the ex-Khedive of Egypt, 'Abbas Hilmi II, also circulated. On his activities concerning a throne and his December 1931 visit to Syria see MAE, Syrie–Liban 1930–40. Chargé d'Affaires (Cairo) to Briand, 2 June 1931, vol. 480, p. 95 and Fleurian Telegram, 23 Dec. 1931, vol. 480, pp. 187–88; CO 732/59117—34, "Memorandum," n.d.; FO 371/441, vol. 14557. CO to FO, 23 Jan. 1930.
[29] CO 732/98059—54, Cox to High Commissioner, 16 Dec. 1931.
[30] Khaldun S. Husry, "King Faysal I and Arab Unity, 1930–33," *Journal of Contemporary History*, 10 (1975), p. 325. FO 371/206, vol. 15364. Humphreys (Baghdad) to Colonial Secretary, 10 Jan. 1931.

that he did not confer with Ponsot, who was still in Paris.[31] What is known is that ʿAli's reception in Damascus, where he made a one-night stopover on his way back to Baghdad, was a low-key affair. No nationalists or government officials called upon him at his hotel,[32] indicating that both the National Bloc and Shaykh Taj were resolutely opposed to a monarchy for Syria.

ʿAli's only visitors were a number of ex-Sharifian officers, among them Rida al-Rikabi, who still cherished the monarchical idea and its promise of future employment.[33] Several of these officers had already formed their own royalist party (Hizb al-umma al-malaki) in the summer of 1928. This party later merged with another faction of royalist veterans headed by ʿArif Pasha al-Idlibi, an Ottoman-trained officer who had fought with the Turks in the Dardanelles and then with the Sharifian Army of Faysal around Aleppo. A member of the secret society of officers *al-ʿAhd*, Idlibi had been a major supporter of King Faysal under whom he became a General. He and his colleagues were keenly interested in a constitutional monarchy for Syria which they believed would eventually lead to a union with Iraq and a treaty with France.[34] In the months following ʿAli's visit, royalists assumed that Ponsot would put ʿAli on the throne, despite signs to the contrary. But, stalwart republicans considered talk of monarchy a French diversion to lessen Syrian hostility to the Mandate or an expedient to assist the settlement of the pipeline problem with Iraq which would be disavowed as soon as the pipeline matter was resolved.[35]

The Syrian throne question received more attention in Syria and Europe in the aftermath of King Faysal's meeting with the Director-General of the Quai d'Orsay, M. Berthelot, in early September 1931.[36] According to Faysal's understanding of the exchange, France, while wishing to leave the actual choice of a ruler to the Syrian people, welcomed Faysal's return to Syria as King. Faysal also gave some indication of his idea of a united

[31] There seems little doubt that Faysal, and probably ʿAbdullah, knew of ʿAli's invitation from the French, FO 371/206, vol. 15304. Cox (Amman) to High Commissioner, 12 Jan. 1931.

[32] FO 371/356, vol. 15364. Hole to Henderson, 14 Jan. 1931.

[33] *Ibid.*; MAE, Syrie–Liban 1930–40. "Note confidentielle," vol. 477, pp. 232–58.

[34] *Oriente Moderno*, 8 (1928), p. 402; Farzat, *al-Hayah al-hizbiyya*, pp. 117–118; Faris, *Man huwa 1949*, p. 19. It was Idlibi who spearheaded the moderate opposition to Shaykh Taj's government as early as July 1929. MAE, Syrie–Liban 1930–40. Fleurian Telegram, 23 Dec. 1931, vol. 480, pp. 187–88.

[35] FO 371/3916, vol. 15364. Hole to Henderson, 29 June 1931.

[36] Faysal had met Berthelot at least once before, in November 1925, over the throne issue. On this occasion, he was asked for advice on how to deal with the Syrian Question. Faysal advocated a constitution similar to Iraq's and hinted that a monarchy with a Hashemite prince was preferable. See FO 371/5485, vol. 15364. Parkinson Memorandum, 3 Nov. 1931.

Syria and Iraq. Under his kingship, each country would have its own parliament and he (Faysal) would reside half a year in each, appointing a regent in his absence.[37] On returning to Baghdad, Faysal gave the impression to the acting British High Commissioner that the whole question was settled: that he was to be King of Syria and Iraq, that the French government had extended an offer of a Syrian throne, and that the British government was not opposed to such a development.[38]

London, in fact, was not at all predisposed to the idea of a Syrian-Iraqi confederation or union ruled by Faysal. It was feared that if he divided his time between Iraq and Syria, his already weak position in Baghdad would further deteriorate. Moreover, since the locus of Faysal's power and interests was bound to shift in the direction of Syria, given her higher state of development and more advanced urban culture, French influence in Syria might eventually threaten or even supplant British influence in Iraq. For these reasons, the British discouraged Faysal from pursuing a Syrian throne.[39]

From the French perspective, Faysal had "gravely misrepresented" their attitude to the British. According to Ponsot, the King had interpreted his cordial reception in Paris as an official declaration that France was prepared to accept him as King of Syria, a construction that was, in Ponsot's words, "entirely fantastic."[40] In fact, from all reports, the French government seemed quite content to leave the choice of Syria's form of government to the Syrian people, particularly insofar as it might split the nationalist movement. Already by June 1931, the Quai d'Orsay had stated before the Permanent Mandates Commission of the League its intention to conclude a treaty with the governments of Syria and Lebanon along the lines of the Anglo-Iraqi Treaty. This would entail the selection of a President or a King, but France did not specify which. Faysal may have been sounded out,[41] but this did not mean that Paris seriously entertained the idea of a Syrian throne or a union of Syria and Iraq. On the contrary, France feared that the importation of Faysal or any other Hashemite monarch would strengthen the hand of Britain in Syria and the region, possibly even leading to France's displacement altogether.[42]

[37] CO 732/59117—34, 1931.

[38] Ibid. No one was more disturbed by and jealous of Faysal's bid for a throne than Amir ʿAbdullah, who sent a nasty and accusatory letter to Faysal in which he reminded him of familial promises which were not kept. See CO 732/89059—47, Kirkbride to High Commissioner (Palestine), enclosing letter from ʿAbdullah to Faysal.

[39] FO 371/5872, vol. 15364. Cunliffe-Lister to Humphrys (Baghdad), 27 Nov. 1931.

[40] Ponsot's remarks were made to the British High Commissioner of Iraq during the latter's visit with the French High Commissioner in late October 1931. FO 371/5483, vol. 15364. FO to Clerk (Angora), 4 Nov. 1931.

[41] FO 371/5872, vol. 15364, 27 Nov. 1931; CO 732/59117—34, n.d.

[42] FO 371/5872, vol. 15364. Cunliffe-Lister to Humphrys, 27 Nov. 1931.

By broaching the subject of a Syrian throne at this time, the French were certainly trying, on the one hand, to encourage the Iraqi government to grant a favorable settlement regarding the pipeline and, on the other, to create confusion in the Syrian political arena as elections neared. Posing the question forced Syrian nationalists to engage in private debate which might create new divisions in their ranks. Ponsot had employed this stratagem in 1928; though it had backfired that time, the High Commissioner was running out of stalling tactics.

While the Syrian throne question generated much euphoria in pro-Hashemite and royalist circles in Damascus, it was more than an annoyance to Syrian nationalists and even to some moderates in and out of government.[43] For one thing, it highlighted divisions within the nationalist movement, both at home and in exile, on the questions of Syrian independence and pan-Arab unity. At least four overlapping factions could be discerned at this time. Two of these were committed first and foremost to Syrian independence and paid increasingly less attention to the idea of Arab unity, particularly of the Syrian-Iraqi variety. One faction revolved around Jamil Mardam and the moderate wing of the National Bloc; the other looked to Dr. Shahbandar and the exiled 'Abdin wing of the Syrian–Palestine Congress in Cairo. While the Bloc faction was staunchly republican and was unwilling to tolerate any Hashemite interference in Syrian affairs, the Shahbandarists were, by and large, royalists. Their ties were with Amir 'Abdullah of Transjordan, however, rather than with Faysal.[44] The two other nationalist factions were composed of radical pan-Arabists. They were not as easily distinguished from one another as were the National Bloc and Shahbandar groupings: one was identified with Shukri al-Quwwatli, whom the French had amnestied in July 1930,[45] and the other with Shakib Arslan and Ihsan al-Jabiri, who both remained in exile.

[43] Both Shaykh Taj and his coterie and Haqqi al-'Azm's Reform Party were annoyed by Ponsot's courting of Faysal on the question of a future Syrian throne, either for himself or for his brother 'Ali. Al-Mudhik al-mubki, no. 82 (27 June 1931), ran a cartoon on its front cover showing Taj, with Jamil al-Ulshi next to him, remarking to Ponsot that "while we [the Syrians] are under a French Mandate, it appears that you [the French] are under a British Mandate!"

[44] For instance, among the Bloc leaders, Ibrahim Hananu was opposed to a throne because "a strong personality would play into foreign hands and thus could divide the Syrian nation." IPS, Nabih al-'Azma Papers [Syria]. Ibrahim Hananu to al-'Azma, 28 Oct. 1931, File 3/57.

[45] See Oriente Moderno, 10 (1930), p. 369. Others included in the amnesty were Sami Sarraj, Shaykh Kamil al-Qassab, both of whom were close to Quwwatli and the Istiqlal Party, and 'Uthman al-Sharabati and Nazih Mu'ayyad al-'Azm, who were close to Dr. Shahbandar.

The two pan-Arabist factions were devoted to the idea of Arab unity and, unlike the mainstream of the National Bloc, were more or less of the opinion that Syrian independence was not a necessary stepping-stone to the achievement of this larger ambition. Nevertheless, the idea of using a Syrian throne as a vehicle to achieve greater Arab unity presented a problem for both. On the one hand, Shakib Arslan and Ihsan al-Jabiri, who had been stationed in Europe for most of the previous decade, were both interested in bringing about a Syrian-Iraqi union as quickly as possible and advocated consolidating this union by a Hashemite throne. For Jabiri, who had been Faysal's Chamberlain in Damascus, Faysal was unquestionably the most suitable candidate for a joint throne. For Arslan, who tended to lean more in the direction of Ibn Saʿud on ideological grounds (he favored Ibn Saʿud's reformist brand of Islam and his more independent role vis-à-vis the British) and who had deep reservations about the usefulness of the Hashemites in achieving Arab unity, Faysal was also the only qualified candidate, especially since Ibn Saʿud had no immediate interest in Syria.

What really mattered to Arslan was that monarchy and union went hand-in-hand. By his lights, the republican form of government did not embody any of the supreme governing principles of the shariʿa. In contemporary terms, he emphasized that Iraq under monarchy had achieved greater progress on the road to full independence than Syria or any other mandated territory. Yet, Arslan was not an unqualified supporter of monarchy. He understood that Faysal was not and could not be an absolute ruler either in Iraq or in Syria and that, at best, Faysal could become a constitutional monarch whose power would be circumscribed by local political forces. Faysal looked even better to Arslan after February 1930, when he and Ibn Saʿud met for the first time. This reconciliation, in Arslan's opinion, was another good reason to pursue his strategy.[46]

The younger group of Syrian Istiqlalis led by Shukri al-Quwwatli in Damascus and including members of the Istiqlal-led Executive Committee of the Syrian–Palestine Congress in Cairo, was not well disposed to the idea of a theocratic state or a constitutional monarchy, at least in Syria. Nor were they particularly enamored of the Hashemites, including Faysal. In fact, they had already demonstrated strong republican tendencies. They were, however, just as committed as Arslan and Jabiri to the idea of greater Arab unity, and had cooperated with them toward this end. Indeed, both the National Bloc and the exiled leadership of Shahbandar's People's Party viewed the Istiqlalis and the Arslan–Jabiri group as a relatively unified political faction within the overall Syrian national movement.

[46] Husry, "King Faysal I," pp. 327–28.

Personal relations between Quwwatli and Arslan were particularly close. They had worked together in Berlin in the early twenties and during the Great Revolt, when Quwwatli was the main link between Syrian nationalists throughout the Arab world and the permanent delegation of the Syrian–Palestine Congress at Geneva. Soon after the revolt was crushed, Quwwatli returned to Berlin where Arslan, among his myriad activities,[47] was preparing to embark on a new project: the establishment of a cohesive Islamic-Arab movement that would serve on one level as a common front against the European Powers and on another level as a mechanism by which to realize the specific aims of different nationalist struggles in the Arab East. To inaugurate this project, Arslan sent Quwwatli back to Cairo in November 1928, to spearhead the unity campaign from the inside.

Quwwatli's initial tasks were two. First, he was to try to heal the breach in the Syrian–Palestine Congress between the Lutfallah-Shahbandar and the Rida–Istiqlal Executive Committees. Arslan, while still distrustful of Lutfallah and Shahbandar (the feeling was mutual), had been prompted by financial considerations to try to regain the support of the wealthy Lutfallah family. In this first endeavor the impatient Quwwatli failed.[48] Because of his Sa'udi ties and his deep distrust of the Hashemites, he was the wrong man for the job. His second task was to strengthen the bonds between nationalist parties in Egypt, Palestine, Transjordan, Iraq, and Arabia, with the assistance of Shaykh Rashid Rida and 'Adil Arslan. From December 1928 until July 1930, when he returned to Damascus, Quwwatli quietly pursued Shakib Arslan's master plan, moving between Jerusalem, Cairo, and the Hijaz, widening his contacts in an effort to set the Arab nationalist movement on a surer footing.[49]

Quwwatli and the Istiqlalis were strongly in favor of a Syrian-Iraqi union. However, they had great difficulty accepting Shakib Arslan's enthusiasm for a union cemented together by a Hashemite king. From their perspective (and Rashid Rida's[50] but not 'Adil Arslan's, who was aligned with his older brother)[51] Faysal's personal ambitions were not only intol-

[47] On the Quwwatli-Arslan link in the 1920s, see Chapter 9 and MD, 7N 4185. Renseignements spéciaux, no. 1,591, 27 Sept. 1921. For Arslan's activities in Europe, the Arab East, and North Africa in the early 1930s, see *ibid.*, 7N 4191. 2ᵉ Bureau, 12 Nov. 1933, and MAE, Syrie–Liban 1930–40. "Note de renseignement," 17 Aug. 1930, vol. 479, pp. 220–24. The French were especially concerned about Arslan's and Quwwatli's ties to Germany and German Intelligence.

[48] FO 371/1020, vol. 13749. Eastern Department "Political Report," 22 Feb. 1929.

[49] *Ibid.*

[50] IPS, Nabih al-'Azma Papers [Syria]. Rashid Rida to al-'Azma, 22 March 1932, File 3/67.

[51] 'Adil Arslan had an intense admiration for King Faysal. He had also made his new base Baghdad after being expelled from Egypt for anti-Italian agitation in 1931. There, in Iraq,

erable in principle, but they were also dangerous. In a long letter to a fellow Istiqlali, Quwwatli summarized the Istiqlalis' strong reservations: France sought to exploit Faysal's ambitions for her own ends and would discard them before consummation. Even Faris al-Khuri, who had long been an advocate of a Syrian-Iraqi union and who had traveled to Switzerland in the summer of 1931 to confer with Faysal and Arslan on the subject of a throne just before Faysal's Paris visit,[52] finally judged that Faysal's motives were purely selfish.

While Quwwatli acknowledged that the idea of a Syrian-Iraqi union signalled the advent of a new era in the struggle for greater Arab unity, he felt that at the present stage it was hopeless to think of unity when nationalists could not even be assured of winning a majority of seats in the upcoming parliamentary elections. What bothered Quwwatli most was that committed nationalists could talk about union when a mass-based popular front against the French Mandate in Syria and Lebanon had yet to be organized. He wrote to Nabih al-ʿAzma that

> as long as the French were still able to convince the Druzes of the benefits of independence from Syria, then it was useless to try to unite Beirut with Basra and Baghdad with Damascus.[53]

Yet, the main question remained: what policy should the Istiqlal Party adopt publicly on the question of a throne? If the Istiqlalis openly opposed the idea of a throne, which seemed to go hand-in-hand with a Syrian-Iraqi union, they might damage their relations with Arslan and Jabiri as well as possibly discredit themselves in the eyes of the Syrian masses who could not but be aroused by the idea of union. Quwwatli offered a solution that pinned its success on the National Bloc. Even though Istiqlalis disapproved of the compromising techniques of the Bloc's moderate wing headed by Jamil Mardam, Quwwatli believed that they should try to capitalize on the Bloc's staunch republicanism. His idea was to keep radical nationalists silent, leaving the Bloc to lead the opposition to a Syrian throne. Quwwatli realized that as long as the Bloc pursued its policy of "honorable cooperation" with the French and simultaneously opposed a monarchical form of government in Syria, there was little chance of a throne being established. At the same time, Quwwatli proposed that amnestied Istiqlalis work quietly to penetrate the Bloc organization with the

---

he was to build up considerable commercial interests as the representative of a very large firm of British contractors. FO 371/2142, vol. 20849, 6 May 1937.

[52] *Al-Mudhik al-mubki*, no. 78 (30 May 1931), p. 13. *Al-Mudhik* suggested the factors of Iraqi oil and enhanced stability in Syria which could be had with a Syrian throne.

[53] IPS Nabih al-ʿAzma Papers [Syria], File 3/60. Shukri al-Quwwatli (Damascus) to ʿAzma (Palestine), 19 Nov. 1931.

aim of forcing it to adopt a more radical stand on the questions of independence and Arab unity.[54]

THE NATIONAL BLOC AND PAN-ARABISM

Along the campaign trail in 1931, the National Bloc led the drive for a republican government in Syria while it discreetly worked to upset Faysal's project for a Syrian throne. Ironically, its efforts in this direction were indirectly aided by the coalition government of Shaykh Taj, which was adamantly opposed to monarchy and Hashemite interests. But the year 1931 also happened to usher in a wave of pan-Arabist activities that the National Bloc preferred to avoid. Indeed, the Bloc leadership maintained a low profile on all issues not directly related to elections. The Damascus Bloc, in particular, was committed to a policy of "honorable cooperation" with the French and wanted to circumvent all issues that might cause a rupture with the French and possibly the cancellation of elections. At the many large public rallies staged in solidarity with different Arab and Islamic struggles in the months before the elections, Bloc leaders purposely avoided the limelight. Because they were the only nationalist leaders recognized by the High Commission, they were clearly interested in playing down all sentiments that were thought to be connected to royalist or radical nationalist interests in Syria. At this stage, pan-Arabism directly conflicted with National Bloc strategy.

Therefore, the Bloc did not participate actively in demonstrations in late April 1931 in Damascus and Aleppo against Italian atrocities in Libya and against ʿAdil Arslan's deportation from Cairo for anti-Italian activities, even though the French did not discourage this agitation since Italy was still thought to have designs on Syria.[55] What was surprising was the conspicuous absence of Bloc leaders at the May 6 anniversary of the hanging of Syrian leaders by the Turks in 1915–16, an anniversary which had gained the full status of an official holiday in Damascus largely owing to Bloc activities over the years. In fact, at this ceremony the Bloc was criticized (along with the government of Shaykh Taj) in the keynote address delivered by the former government attorney, ʿArif Bey Nakadi, an ally of Shukri al-Quwwatli and the Istiqlal Party. This much-respected nationalist chastised Bloc leaders for their cooperativeness and for their failure to broaden the base of their struggle to include the countryside, whose population needed "to be taught their rights and duties."[56]

[54] *Ibid.*

[55] FO 371/2629, vol. 15364. Monck-Mason to FO, 22 April 1931; FO 371/2507, vol. 15364. Monck-Mason to FO, 1 May 1931; FO 371/2603, vol. 15364. Monck-Mason to FO, 4 May 1931.

[56] FO 371/2689, vol. 15364. Hole to Henderson, 9 May 1931.

The National Bloc's refusal to assume a pan-Arab program in Syria became starkly clear when it did not participate in demonstrations in Damascus at the end of October to commemorate the execution of the Libyan resistance leader, 'Umar Mukhtar, on the customary fortieth day. Instead of Bloc leaders, Sa'id al-Jaza'iri was at the head of the tumultuous anti-Italian procession through Damascus. He was trying desperately to rehabilitate his image in time for the elections, for not only was he disrespected for his willingness to deal with any party, foreign or local, that could help him further his personal ambitions in Syria, he was also accused, quite accurately, of having sold some of his vast landholdings in Palestine to the Zionists.[57]

Jaza'iri also managed to steal the Bloc's thunder later when he seized the leadership of the first major boycott of the Franco-Belgian owned Damascus Electricity Company (Société des Tramways et d'Electricité), whose rates were increased just as the impact of the world depression had begun to be felt in Syria. This boycott started in April 1931, and was connected to a similar boycott begun in Beirut two weeks earlier. It lasted throughout the long hot summer and fall, attracting the support of students, the illegal trade union movement, and the nascent Communist Party. It was marked by violence—students placed bombs under tramcars and forced store owners to switch from electric current to petrol—and it was successful. Eventually the Belgian concessionaire had to lower the rate by a piastre.[58] Jaza'iri presided over the steering committee of 41 members, composed largely of moderate notables on the Municipal Council and the Chambers of Agriculture and Industry, but which also included a few Bloc stalwarts, notably Fakhri al-Barudi.[59]

FRENCH ELECTION STRATEGY

Although Henri Ponsot did not set an election date until his advisers judged that the country was ripe for such an event, French agents had been silently preparing for elections since the promulgation of the Syrian Constitution in May 1930. Messrs. Solomiac in Damascus and Lavastre in Aleppo, with the collaboration of two Assistant Delegates, M. Durieux in Alexandretta and Colonel Trenga in Dayr al-Zur, pursued a strategy of continued "wear and tear" against the National Bloc. The successive adjournments of the Constituent Assembly and its eventual suspension, Ponsot's vacillations, his occasionally lenient policies, his temporary clo-

---

[57] FO 371/5574, vol. 15364. Napier to Marquess of Reading, 29 Oct. 1931.

[58] MAE, Syrie–Liban 1930–40. Ponsot Telegram, 16 April 1931, vol. 578, p. 147; *ibid.*, 7 May 1931, vol. 578, pp. 174–75.

[59] *Ibid.*; *Oriente Moderno*, 11 (1931), p. 590; MAE, Syrie–Liban 1930–40. Solomiac to Ponsot, 6 July 1931, pp. 33–36.

sures of the many newspapers and magazines which had been allowed to publish (or in many cases to reappear) after the Great Revolt,[60] all tended to dull political enthusiasm and to create weariness and discouragement. The High Commissioner also managed to "tame" many hardline nationalists by continually extolling the Bloc and its sincere interest in a spirit of reconciliation and *détente*.

Ultimately, the French aim was to find a group of docile candidates dependent on a special electoral corps. The High Commission staff discovered an inordinate number of men of various appetites but without deep influence in Syrian society, who were rivals for the same lucrative posts. They were selected for their passivity in the face of the most flagrant Mandate abuses. The National Bloc's own political inactivity had established a certain milieu in which these candidates could operate under French direction in the towns and especially in the countryside.[61] Besides these clients, the French had older and more reliable ones: the Christian minorities of the interior towns, especially those of Aleppo and the Sanjak of Alexandretta,[62] and the rural notability among whom the National Bloc had failed to amass a significant following.

In Aleppo, where Christians constituted 35 percent of the population, the Uniate communities had profited from the political, commercial, and cultural penetration of the European Powers in the nineteenth century. They were allowed to play the role of "natural" intermediaries between Europe and northern Syria. As usurers and commission agents, they became the predominant force in the region's finance and commerce. With the French occupation, they depended on French patronage and protection to continue their domination of trade (as importers of European and American goods) and of finance (as moneylenders and bankers). In fact, their position was reinforced because their major interests were not as severely affected as were those of the Muslim commercial bourgeoisie by the postwar partition and subsequent loss of markets in Turkey and Iraq.[63] Therefore, in Aleppo a significant fraction of the Christian busi-

[60] Among the Syrian newspapers and journals which first began to appear or to reappear during M. Ponsot's tenure were the following: (Damascus) *al-Jil* (24 May 1927), *al-Istiqlal* (25 June 1927), *al-Sha'b* (1 July 1927), *al-Nizam* (25 August 1927—twice weekly), *Baradi* (1 May 1928), *al-Akhbar* (26 July 1928), *al-Qabas* (1 Sept. 1928), *al-Ayyam* (7 March 1931); (Aleppo): *al-Jihad al-'arabi* (24 December 1927), *al-Jama'at al-islamiyya* (17 June 1929), *al-Taqaddum* (4 Jan. 1919). See *Dalil al-suri lil-jumhurriyya al-suriyya 1947–48* (Damascus, n.d.), pp. 668–69; *A Post-War Bibliography of the Near Eastern Mandates* (Beirut, 1933), pp. 43–51.

[61] Rabbath, *Courte Histoire*, pp. 75–76

[62] *Ibid.*, p. 76.

[63] For instance, the *Bulletin Annuel de la Chambre de Commerce d'Alep* (Aleppo, 1922) each year listed the Chamber membership by rank. Merchants and financiers were ranked by class (first, second, third, fourth) which was determined by the amount of their capital.

ness classes was generally ill-disposed to the aims of Syrian-Arab nationalism which directly threatened its material interests. In addition, France
fed their already obsessive fears of persecution at the hands of the Muslim
majority. Lavastre, whose tactics were far less subtle or sophisticated
than those of Solomiac in Damascus, built an insidious propaganda campaign which stressed that if Christians did not align with their traditional
protector, elections would consign them to a "sea of Islam." Indeed, for
many Christians the major political struggle in Syria continued to be expressed in terms of "cross versus crescent" rather than in terms of European domination versus national independence.[64]

M. Ponsot returned to Syria in November 1931 with some big surprises— surprises, however, that had been in the making long before his
return. Almost immediately after his welcoming reception (the first one
ever attended by Syrian nationalists) he announced by letter to Shaykh
Taj on November 20 that his services were no longer needed.[65] The subsequent dissolution of Taj's cabinet did not "meet with even a whimper
from the most mercenary of Syrian politicians."[66] What followed were
three decrees which embodied Ponsot's pre-election game plan. First, he
established a consultative council to advise him on the application of the
constitution. Next, he made provisions for carrying on the administration of the State of Syria until the elections by putting the business of
government in the hands of a Secretary-General and the remaining
members of Taj's cabinet (minus Jamil al-Ulshi). Finally, Ponsot assumed
the functions of the Chief of State himself for the purpose of the elections, which were now officially scheduled for 20 December 1931 and 4
January 1932.[67]

Although happy to see the last of Shaykh Taj, the National Bloc was
not particularly happy with Ponsot's interim arrangements. The Consultative Council read like a "Who's Who" of *intidabis*.[68] Of the ten members, only one—Hashim al-Atasi—belonged to the Bloc. And Ponsot
continued to make an irritating distinction between nationalists and what
he referred to as the "true representatives" of the country.[69]

In 1922, 25 merchant houses were listed as "first class": 4 were foreign, 18 were local Christian or Jewish (although they may have held foreign citizenships), and only 3 were Muslim
in ownership.
[64] Rabbath, *Courte Histoire*, pp. 76, 82–83.
[65] *The Times* (London), (23 Nov. 1931).
[66] Rabbath, *Courte Histoire*, p. 77.
[67] FO 371/5980, vol. 15364. Hole to Simon, 23 Nov. 1931.
[68] Literally "belonging to the Mandate," a term coined by the Bloc to refer to pro-French
collaborators. See FO 371/6020, vol. 15364. Monck-Mason to FO, 25 Nov. 1931. FO 371/
5980, vol. 15364. Hole to Simon, 23 Nov. 1931; *Almanach Français* (1932), p. 171.
[69] Rabbath, *Courte Histoire*, p. 79.

As for the appointment of a Secretary-General, there was apprehension that it would merely disguise direct and autocratic government by the High Commission, and that the chief role in the Secretariat would be played by a French official. These fears were partially allayed by the appointment of Tawfiq al-Hayani—at the time the *mutasarrif* of the Hawran. Hayani, a member of a prominent landowning-bureaucratic family of Aleppo, had trained at the Mülkiye in Istanbul and had served in various posts in the Ottoman provincial administration. The French occupation did not force him into the ranks of the unemployed; in need of good administrators, the High Commission was happy to keep him on. He became Chief of Police of his home town, a post which he held for several years before becoming *qa'immaqam* of Idlib in 1924, and then of Duma during the Great Revolt (from where he seems to have supplied French Intelligence with regular reports on the activities of rebel bands in the district). Before assuming his new position, he had been stationed in the Hawran for two years. What impressed the nationalists about Hayani was his reputation as an honest, fair, and capable administrator. Although he had no definable political leanings, he was thought in some circles to be secretly sympathetic to the National Bloc.[70] Some nationalists recalled that Hayani had been a member of *al-Fatat* in 1920.[71]

On December 7, the new Consultative Council convened to listen to one of Ponsot's rare speeches. In his address, which he unmistakably directed at the National Bloc, he rejected its demand that the broad outlines of a treaty be spelled out before the elections and its proposal that the electoral law, with all its admitted imperfections, be modified at so late a date.[72] The Bloc responded by declaring its strong reservations about the election process. It protested that popular national patriots like Dr. Shahbandar, Shakib Arslan, and Ihsan al-Jabiri had not been allowed to return to stand as candidates (though Bloc leaders like Jamil Mardam breathed much more easily in their absence), and that the French were manipulating the elections in many subtle and diverse ways.[73] Yet, despite these reservations, which were strongest among Aleppine leaders, the Bloc still decided to participate in the elections.[74]

The High Commission employed a mixture of heavy-handed and subtle methods to control the elections. For instance, the authorities kept nationalist candidates under surveillance until election day, certain news-

[70] Faris, *Man huwa 1949*, p. 140.
[71] C. Ernest Dawn, "The Rise of Arabism in Syria," in *From Ottomanism to Arabism. Essays on the Origins of Arab Nationalism* (Urbana, 1973), p. 176.
[72] FO 371/6291, vol. 15365. Hole to Simon, 11 Dec. 1931.
[73] Rabbath, *Courte Histoire*, p. 86.
[74] George Antonius File, no. 21. Antonius (Jerusalem) to Rogers, 12 Feb. 1932, Middle East Centre, St. Antony's College, Oxford.

papers and magazines supporting nationalist candidates were suppressed, and several editors, intimidated by security agents, refused to publish nationalist manifestos and declarations.[75] From rural districts came reliable reports that French agents were exerting great pressure to secure malleable electors in the primaries there.[76] In Aleppo, where the Armenian community of 50,000 formed the largest minority in the city, the High Commission was fast at work trying to guarantee that a collaborator would go to Damascus.

Most Armenians were recent settlers in Aleppo, having come from Turkey as refugees at the end of the First World War. The French, whose policy showed a strong favoritism toward minorities, gave them Syrian nationality *en masse*. For this reason alone Armenians, who were forced to compete with Arabs for jobs in sluggish economic times and who on occasion aroused the wrath of the local populace,[77] were generally subservient to the interests of the High Commission. The election of a nationalist candidate in the 1928 elections had been a shock, and the brazen M. Lavastre wanted to avoid a repeat. The Armenian community was politically divided between the Dashnak Party with its strength among the Armenian bourgeoisie, small shopowners, and priestly class, and the Henchak, a significantly smaller but well-organized revolutionary party with Communist leanings, based among intellectuals and workers. While it was the general policy of both parties to avoid any friction with native Syrians which might cause a backlash detrimental to the welfare of the Armenian community, the Henchak specifically sought to promote amicable relations with the Arab population. It supported Syrian national liberation and joined the struggle of the Syrian people against French interests in the country. Such an attitude clearly conflicted with Lavastre's minority strategy for the upcoming elections. To prevent the Henchak from undermining his strategy, he saw to it that the Party was smeared with pro-Communist and pro-Soviet epithets and even arrested a group of 20 influential Henchak partisans before the elections, a crude but successful means of intimidation.[78]

[75] Rabbath, *Courte Histoire*, p. 84.

[76] FO 371/6291, vol. 15365. Hole to Simon, 11 Dec. 1931.

[77] Occasionally, manifestos or proclamations would appear in Aleppo denouncing the Armenians. One such proclamation was known to have circulated in October 1928, signed by the "Committee for the Independence and Liberation of Syria," stating: "We Syrians, who bravely withstood the Turks, seem now to be the prisoners of the Armenians." See FO 371/5338, vol. 13074. Monck-Mason to Cushendun, 30 Oct. 1928.

[78] Rabbath, *Courte Histoire*, pp. 77, 84. As early as July 1930, the Henchak (Bell) seem to have spread its ideas in a series of notices printed in Arabic and distributed in Aleppo under the name of the "Regional Committee of the Syrian Socialist Party" (similar notices appeared at the time in Damascus, Beirut, Tripoli, Latakia, and Alexandretta). These notices attacked the French for ruining the economy of Syria, the constitution, and all those influ-

Among the subtler methods employed by the High Commission were the reapportionment of electoral districts and the reshuffling of deputies. For example, the turbulent anti-French Maydan quarter of Damascus, which returned some 170 electors in the 1928 elections, was suddenly discovered to have a much smaller population than previously reported. Consequently, it was allowed to elect only140 electors in the primaries. Similarly, the demand of the Greek Catholic community in Damascus that by its size (approximately 5,000) it deserved its own elector, was denied because it had voted nationalist in 1928.[79]

ELECTIONS—1931-32

The first-round elections were hotly contested. In the capital, four political factions competed: Shaykh Taj and his followers still in government, the moderate and republican Reform Party (Hizb al-islah) of Haqqi al-ʿAzm, the monarchists led by Rida Pasha al-Rikabi, and the National Bloc.[80] One week before the primaries, the French managed to form a loose coalition of the three other factions to stand against the Bloc. Their list included Taj, Haqqi al-ʿAzm, Rikabi, Badiʿ al-Muʾayyad, who had been working closely with M. Solomiac to promote pro-French candidates, and Nasib al-Bakri, among others.[81] Yet, even before election day, nationalist complaints against the interference of police and other government agents electrified the political atmosphere, leading to gang wars between supporters of Taj and the Nationalist Youth (al-Shabab al-watani). Police intervention was anything but impartial, confirming nationalist accusations. The Chief of Police, Bahij al-Khatib, and the Acting Governor of Damascus, Wathiq al-Muʾayyad, were keen supporters of Taj's faction. Over the previous month they had packed local security

---

ential Syrians who accepted it for betraying their country. In the notices, Russia is called the "Savior of the oppressed" though the word "communist" does not appear. Special criticism however, was reserved for the National Bloc's moderate wing. It seems that the Aleppo cell of the Communist Party was purely Armenian and dependent on Beirut, where the Communist Party leader Fuʾad Shamali resided. The Henchak was the forerunner of the Communist Party in Syria. Aleppo was of particular importance because of the waves of Armenian immigrants coming into the town between 1915 and 1922. Some members of the Party, which was founded in the late nineteenth century in the Turkish provinces of the Ottoman Empire and in Switzerland, were among these immigrants. See Batatu, *The Old Social Classes*, pp. 373–74. FO 371/1188, vol 15364. Monck-Mason to FO, 5 Feb. 1931.

[79] FO 371/6291, vol. 15365. Hole to Simon, 11 Dec. 1931.

[80] On the French attitude to Rikabi, see MAE, Syrie–Liban 1930–40. "Note confidentielle sur la situation politique," vol. 477, pp. 232–58.

[81] *Al-Mudhik al-mubki*, no. 108 (26 Dec. 1931), p. 2. Nasib al-Bakri was aligned with Taj but still sympathetic to the idea of a Syrian throne for a Hashemite prince. FO 371/6399, vol. 15365. Hole to Simon, 17 Dec. 1931.

forces, including the fire brigades, with their personal henchmen and dismissed regular police without explanation.[82]

Three days of strikes and demonstrations followed the gang wars.[83] On election morning, the government unveiled its plan for rigging the voting. The moment the voting booth opened in the Qaymariyya quarter, where Taj and Jamil al-Ulshi were candidates, voters were forcibly turned away by police and gendarmes. Then, paid agents protected by local security forces appeared, stuffed the boxes with papers carrying the names of electors chosen by the government, and quickly disappeared. When nationalist leaders later appeared and tried to inspect the boxes they were told that this had already been done. They immediately called for a total boycott of the fraudulent elections, which *qabadayat* and the Nationalist Youth promptly enforced. Fighting broke out all over the city. In Shaghur, one of the great seats of anti-Mandate activity and where Lutfi al-Haffar was a candidate, and in Suq Saruja, the home base of several leaders of the Nationalist Youth, violence was widespread. In al-Qanawat, Zaki al-Khatib, one of the Bloc candidates, insisted on remaining at the polling station to discourage voters from casting their ballots. But Wathiq al-Mu'ayyad ordered the police to throw him out, which caused Khatib to deliver an impromptu speech which sparked a large march on Marjé Square and government headquarters. There, firemen tried to disperse the marchers with their water pumps which were soon put out of action by the rioters who then set upon the firemen with slingshots and stones. The police opened fire, pumping the crowds with live ammunition, before retreating to the Municipality building where officials were busily counting votes. This last incident brought the French Army into the streets. Solomiac announced the suspension of the elections in Damascus, strategic points were occupied by the army, a curfew was imposed, and special measures were taken to defend al-Salhiyya, where most of the French community resided.[84]

Five persons were killed and 50 injured in the rioting. The following day large crowds congregated at the Umayyad Mosque to hear nationalist leaders attack Shaykh Taj and his accomplices. The possibility of renewed violence, however, dissipated under the judicious policing of the Nationalist Youth commanded by Fakhri al-Barudi.[85] By contrast, elections in the rural areas adjacent to Damascus went smoothly in all but one dis-

---

[82] *Ibid.*; FO 371/171, vol. 16085. Hole to Simon, 22 Dec. 1931.

[83] *Oriente Moderno*, 12 (1932), pp. 52–53.

[84] *Ibid.*; MWT, "Registre des jugements du Tribunal de 1ère Instance Correctionnelle de l'année 1931 et 1932," uncatalogued, pp. 281–86. Many of the arrested were leaders of the Nationalist Youth, including Mahmud al-Bayruti, the organization's chief. See also FO 371/171, vol. 16085. Hole to Simon, 22 Dec. 1931; Rabbath, *Courte Histoire*, p. 86; *The Times*, 23 Dec. 1931.

[85] FO 371/172, vol. 16085. Hole to Simon. 23 Dec. 1931.

trict. In most constituencies, there was only one candidate to choose from, causing *al-Mudhik al-mubki* to comment that voters had been discouraged long in advance from exercising their legal rights by election officials who reassured them that they would gladly do the voting for them.[86]

The one place where the elections were contested was in Duma, the second largest town in the Damascus governorate. Situated in a very fertile region, 25 percent of Duma's cultivable land was owned by five families,[87] among them the Shishaklis and the Kaylanis. Wadiʿ al-Shishakli and Nasib al-Kaylani were, without a doubt, the two most politically active landlords in the district. Together they controlled Duma's Administrative Council and the Department of Land Registry. Both men had long been in collaboration with French agents and with the local *qa'immaqam*.[88] Two other interesting features of Duma should be mentioned. One was that several National Bloc leaders also owned large tracts of land there, among them Fakhri al-Barudi and Jamil Mardam, although unlike Shishakli and Kaylani, they spent most of the year in Damascus where they stood as candidates for election. The other was that the town had begun to develop a small but active number of trade unions, headed in many cases by partisans of the National Bloc. Elections in Duma were rigged well in advance and French authorities did not anticipate any difficulties. But on December 20, an organized crowd of about 1,500 men— many belonging to the unions—attacked the voting booths in the town, stoning the election officials and gendarmes guarding them. Demonstrators then made their way to the town's central mosque where they battled with gendarmes and mounted police who fired bullets into the crowd. The army was obliged to intervene and voting was suspended.[89]

The primaries in Hama produced scenes analogous to those in Damascus and Duma. There, the political situation was very much tied to the growth of an active but illegal trade union movement and to the group of

[86] *Al-Mudhik al-mubki*, no. 108 (26 Dec. 1931).

[87] Duma's population at the time was 12,000. In the district of Duma, the landownership structure was roughly as follows: 25 percent of the cultivable land was held by five families; 50 percent was held by one peasant clan which included over 100 heads of families; 25 percent belonged to middle-sized and small landowners. There was also a growing number of landless peasants who were primarily sharecroppers but who also included wage laborers. The land was irrigated in many areas and those who produced a surplus on 10–15 acres were considered wealthy peasants. See Allen Tower, *The Oasis of Damascus* (Beirut, 1935), pp. 45–46.

[88] Shishakli had headed the Administrative Council of Duma since 1922. He was also Duma's deputy to the Constituent Assembly in 1928, supported by the French. Faris, *Man huwa 1949*, p. 248. Kaylani, who was born in 1896, was also aligned with the French. He was married to the sister of Khalil Mardam Bey, the cousin of Jamil. *Ibid*.

[89] MWT, *Dakhiliyya* (Intikhabat): 8/-973/8. Qa'immaqam (Duma) to Director of the Ministry of Interior, 20 Dec. 1921.

young, middle-class intellectuals and professionals who had helped to in-
spire it. The patron and major personality of the union movement was
Nawras al-Kaylani, a locally educated aristocrat and religious leader who
had served as *mufti* of Hama between 1919 and 1921 and then as its *mutasarrif* until his dismissal by the French on the eve of the Great Revolt.
After the revolt, Kaylani was elected as Council President of Hama's only
government secondary school, a post which he used to build a following
among young teachers and professionals. The men closest to him included a pharmacist, four Damascus-trained lawyers, a schoolteacher, and
a well-known physician. All of these men came from prominent families
of the town, though often from branches whose fortunes were, for one
reason or another, in decline. Most also belonged to either of the two Masonic lodges of Hama, the Orontes and the Abu'l Fida.[90]
    Under the direction of Nawras al-Kaylani and his closest aid, 'Abd al-
Hamid Qumbaz, 21 unions were formed in Hama between 1928 and
1931. By the end of 1930, a Higher Council of Trade Unions (Majlis al-
niqabat al-a'la) was established, incorporating 20 of these unions. It was
presided over by Qumbaz, with the blessing of Nawras al-Kaylani.[91] But,
although the unions and the Higher Council uniting them focused on
various economic issues (shorter working days, weekly days of rest, protective tariffs, higher municipal taxes, and the depreciation of the local
currency) and encouraged boycotts, strikes, and shutdowns against foreign goods and concessions, they were only transitional institutions between the traditional guild structures and class-based trade unions. Both
workers and patrons joined the unions and more often than not their statutes, which never mentioned class struggle, favored the patron over the
worker, betraying their petty bourgeois character.[92] Their activities also
betrayed their more pronounced political, as opposed to economic, orientation.
    In 1928, Hama had elected two deputies to the Constituent Assembly,
'Abd al-Qadir al-Kaylani and Husni al-Barazi, a National Bloc leader
who had served for a very short period in 1926 as the Interior Minister
under Ahmad Nami before the French arrested and deported him for pro-
testing their bombing and burning of the Maydan quarter in May of that
year. Barazi's tenure in the National Bloc was brief. Although he was one
of several lawyers who drafted the constitution, he eventually took the
side of Shaykh Taj in agreeing to the French reservations about the controversial "six articles." After August 1928, his relations with the Bloc

---

[90] Founded in 1922 and 1925 respectively. Gaulmier, "Notes sur le mouvement syndicaliste à Hama," pp. 99–100.
    [91] *Ibid.*, pp. 103–5. Among the most prominent unions were those for tailors, shoe-
makers, and barbers.
    [92] *Ibid.*, pp. 106–12.

began to deteriorate to the point, in 1931, where he was no longer considered a member. By then he had formed his own party of big landlords in Hama in preparation for parliamentary elections.[93]

The major question facing the National Bloc in Hama was who to run on its list. In order to counter Husni al-Barazi's influence, the local chapter of the Bloc convinced Najib Agha al-Barazi, Husni's cousin and also a wealthy landlord, to join the nationalist list. Najib Agha, the son of a former adviser to the Ottoman *mutasarrif* of Hama, had pursued a local administrative career in the Ottoman state until 1915, when the Turks exiled him to Anatolia for Arab nationalist activities. With the establishment of the Arab government in Damascus in 1918, he returned to Hama to become its mayor, a position which he retained until 1925 when the French arrested him for assisting rebel forces in and around the town.[94] Although he was considered a moderate, the Bloc was nonetheless pleased to have the popular Najib Barazi on board.

Because the High Commission—employing one of its numerous pre-election tricks—allowed a total of three deputies to be elected from the district of Hama, the Bloc was still in need of a strong second candidate to help neutralize Husni al-Barazi's list. One of the most promising of the group of rising young political stars associated with Shaykh Nawras al-Kaylani was 'Abd al-Hamid Qumbaz. In his capacity as President of the Higher Council of Trade Unions, the 34-year-old pharmacist had led local demonstrations, strikes, and boycotts focusing on local economic grievances such as the high price of electricity (supplied by the Société d'Electricité de Homs) and the influx of French goods, and on pan-Arab issues such as Palestine and Libya (by boycotting Italian products in 1931).[95] By February 1931, Qumbaz and Ra'if al-Mulqi, who headed the local branch of the Nationalist Youth, announced their decision to oppose the party of big landlords and notables headed by Husni al-Barazi. In fact, the ambitious Qumbaz decided to promote his own candidacy before receiving the official support of the National Bloc. He claimed to have the backing of all the trade unions and most villages in the district.[96] The Bloc, however, was not particularly pleased with many of Qumbaz's radical ideas and his independent cast of mind. Furthermore, the Bloc seriously doubted whether Qumbaz could effectively challenge the power of the big landlord class in Hama; there was no evidence, for instance, that he had any following in the villages adjacent to Hama which voted in the town. Un-

---

[93] FO 226/233/31. Spears to Eden, 28 April 1942; conversation with Zafir al-Qasimi (Beirut, 26 July 1975); Faris, *Man huwa 1949*, p. 58.

[94] *Salname: Suriye vilayeti*, 1308–1309/1890–1891, p. 116; Faris, *Man huwa 1949*, p. 60.

[95] Gaulmier, "Notes sur le mouvement syndicaliste à Hama," pp. 115–17.

[96] *Ibid.*, pp. 118–19.

like most of the other young politicians with whom he was associated and
who claimed to represent the people against the feudalists, Qumbaz had
no personal ties to the land. But there was another reason why the Bloc
was not well-disposed to Qumbaz: neither he nor his mentor, Nawras al-
Kaylani, had joined the Bloc. They could not, therefore, be counted on to
support major Bloc decisions and strategy taken in Damascus and, in fact,
the Bloc wanted to break their grip on nationalist political life in Hama.

There was another very promising nationalist in Hama who, while associated with Kaylani, was influential enough to mount a serious challenge to Husni al-Barazi: Tawfiq al-Shishakli. Shishakli had purposely
drawn closer to the National Bloc in 1931, having his eye on a parliamentary seat. He had already played a long and active part in Arab nationalist
politics, and had even run on the nationalist ticket in 1928, though the
French rigged the elections against him.[97] Born in 1884 into a family of
middling landowners, his early education was in Homs where his father
was a civil servant. He then went to school in Hama and finally enrolled
at Maktab 'Anbar in Damascus. Afterwards, he became a student at the
Ottoman Medical Faculty in Damascus, which had been founded in 1903,
becoming President of the Society of Medical Students in 1908 and graduating in 1911 as an eye specialist.[98] An early supporter of the Young
Turk movement, Shishakli fought with the Ottoman Army as a captain,
later serving as a surgeon in Medina in 1917 and as the chief physician of
a nursing home in Zahla (Lebanon) in 1918.[99] On returning to Hama in
1919 he joined the local branch of al-Fatat and became involved in nationalist politics. He supported the Hama uprising in 1925 and was exiled by
the French for his complicity with the rebels. He was amnestied in 1928.
His first experience with the Syrian electoral process was a bitter one. The
French singled him out as dangerous, owing to his oratorical skills and his
consistent championing of radical political and social causes. It was at this
time that Dr. Shishakli began to publish a newspaper in which he expressed his different views on social, economic, and political conditions in
Hama and the vicinity. Although the Damascus Bloc regarded him as a
left winger—indeed, a "socialist"—his landowning background, popular
appeal and reputation as one of the few honest politicians around made
him an obvious choice for its slate.[100] The Bloc asked 'Abd al-Hamid
Qumbaz to withdraw as a candidate in order to make way for Dr. Shi-

---

[97] Al-Jundi, *Tarikh*, pp. 259–60.
[98] *Ibid.*, pp. 259–60; Vacca, "Notizie," p. 490; United States: American Consulate General at Beirut, "Education in the States of the Levant under French Mandate" (unpublished
report for the Office of Education, Department of the Interior—on file at the Jafet Library
of the American University of Beirut), Beirut, 1 Nov. 1933, p. 19.
[99] Al-Jundi, *Tarikh*, pp. 259–60.
[100] *Ibid.*

shakli, a request to which the younger trade union leader reluctantly acceded.[101]

In the face of the usual electioneering fraud encouraged by the French and their local agents, Qumbaz convinced the Higher Council of Trade Unions to call for a complete boycott of the primaries. Shishakli and Ra'if al-Mulqi brought the Nationalist Youth to the streets, which led to violent clashes between protesters and the gendarmerie in which four townsmen were killed. The Trade Union Council maintained the boycott for two more days and singled out merchants suspected of voting against the nationalist list.[102] The elections were suspended.

Hama had to wait several more months before getting a second crack at electing deputies to Parliament. For Tawfiq al-Shishakli this respite proved ultimately valuable. He was able to expand his personal influence at the expense both of Husni al-Barazi and the landlord party, and of 'Abd al-Hamid Qumbaz and his mentor, Nawras al-Kaylani.

Homs and Aleppo were the only nationalist centers in Syria that managed to complete both the primary and second-round elections on schedule. However, the conditions in each were radically different. In Homs, the political fief of Hashim al-Atasi, the National Bloc list won easily. Joining Atasi in Parliament were two other Bloc partisans, Mazhar Raslan and Rafiq al-Husayni.[103] In Aleppo, the opposite was true. The National Bloc was defeated by the French-backed "Liberal Constitutionalist Party" in a bitterly contested race.

The elections in the northern capital were a confusing series of incidents.[104] M. Lavastre, unlike his counterpart in Damascus who believed in a supple, flexible policy of entente with the Bloc, preferred to employ harsh and devious procedures against the nationalists. Over the previous year he had managed to piece together a group of moderates—many of whom were ranking functionaries and ex-Ministers—to oppose the Bloc. His major coup was to mold two loosely knit coalitions of notables into a single political organization which came to be known as the "Liberal Constitutionalists." Its leaders were Subhi Barakat and the 62-year-old Shakir Ni'mat al-Sha'bani (the publisher of the Ahali newspaper).[105] Although their program called for Syrian unity and independence to be consecrated in a treaty with France and by admission into the League of Na-

---

[101] Gaulmier, "Notes sur le mouvement syndicaliste à Hama," pp. 118–19.

[102] Ibid.

[103] L'Asie Française, no. 299 (April 1932), p. 146; Rabbath, Courte Histoire, p. 87.

[104] For the French version, see MAE, Syrie–Liban 1930–40, vol. 480, pp. 225–33, 245–56, 260–70.

[105] Al-Mudhik al-mubki, no. 102 (14 Nov. 1931), p. 14. The Bloc had been trying since 1930 to strike a deal with Sha'bani.

tions—standard platforms for all parties in Syria in the early thirties—
the Liberal Constitutionalists were prepared to collaborate with the High
Commission.[106] Among its members were Ghalib Ibrahim Pasha, the current President of the Municipality (and the cousin of Jamil and Dr. Hasan
Fu'ad);[107] Muhammad Basim al-Qudsi, a wealthy landowner from a
noted religious family and the older brother of Nazim al-Qudsi, the most
militant of an ascendant group of young nationalist lawyers in Aleppo
connected to the Bloc;[108] and Latif al-Ghanima, a Syrian Catholic lawyer
who had won his religious community's seat in the Assembly in 1928 by
running on a nationalist ticket, but whom the Liberal Constitutionalists
had recently managed to co-opt through the help of their French friends.

M. Lavastre had few problems in winning to his side the large Christian minority in Aleppo, including many Armenians, by playing on fears
of religious persecution. His task was made easier by the Aleppo Bloc's
rather complacent attitude toward the Christian vote, which it all but ignored. Meanwhile, in order to help ensure a victory for the Barakat-
Sha'bani list in the second round, M. Lavastre made no effort to prevent
the Liberal Constitutionalists, in collusion with the local government,
from stuffing ballot boxes in the primaries with the names of Aleppines
who had long been deceased.[109]

The National Bloc was not oblivious to such methods of fraud and deceit; disturbances at voting booths attested to its awareness. But, with
Ibrahim Hananu ill and confined to his bed, the nationalists seemed unable to take charge and organize a boycott. By the evening of December 20,
the Bloc had been stung by the election results. Of the several hundred
individuals nominated to elect Aleppo's future parliamentarians, the majority were committed to the government list. Troubles continued for the
next few days, reaching a climax on December 25. Just after noon prayers
on Friday, an enormous crowd burst out of the Great Mosque into the
main arteries and converged on Lavastre's headquarters in the town center. But the French Army, on alert, charged the crowd and broke it up.
Some demonstrators were killed and several dozen arrested. For the next
22 days Aleppo was a theatre of repeated violence, its bazaars and shops
closed tight as all economic life came to a dead halt. Many more citizens

[106] See Samy, "I Partiti," pp. 104–5. The Liberal Constitutionalist program also called for administrative reforms.

[107] Faris, Man huwa 1949, p. 10; Almanach Français (1932), p. 219.

[108] Faris, Man huwa 1949, p. 349; al-Mudhik al-mubki, no. 110 (9 Jan. 1932), p. 6, mocked the Qudsis, by asking how such a young, intelligent nationalist like Nazim could tolerate his older brother's partying with the pro-French clique of Barakat and Sha'bani.

[109] Conversation with Edmond Rabbath (Beirut, 21 Aug. 1975). Rabbath, a Christian, re-members inciting many Muslims to break electoral boxes. For his participation, he was ex-iled to Beirut.

were arrested including several nationalist leaders, among them Najib Baqi Zadih, the wealthy merchant and Hananu partisan, who had been the main instigator of the strike.[110] Elections were not suspended in Aleppo where the French held the upper hand.

On 4 January 1932, the final round of elections was held amidst intense security precautions, especially in Aleppo, which resembled a garrison town. But trouble never materialized. When it became evident that there was no chance of defeating the government list, Saʿdallah al-Jabiri, under instructions from the convalescing Ibrahim Hananu, withdrew the National Bloc list. The moderate collaborators had clinched an unusually deceptive victory, and as one nationalist candidate was heard to remark on learning the results: "the proof that the elections were fixed is that I was not elected!"[111]

Lavastre's policy of confronting the Aleppo Bloc head on, rather than working toward a compromise solution, as M. Solomiac had done in Damascus, was clearly a success. Commended by the Quai d'Orsay, Lavastre enjoyed a much better reputation at High Commission headquarters in Beirut than Solomiac whose prestige had been deflated. Not only had he lost Ponsot's respect, but the military brass in Syria, who were especially harsh on civilian officials, sharply criticized him for his failure to carry the primaries of December 20 by force.[112]

While Lavastre's method of rule was enshrined in Aleppo through a decree announcing stiff penalties and long terms of imprisonment for the slightest disturbance of public order,[113] in Damascus Solomiac held fast to his belief that a legitimate regime (even if at first erratic!) was better than the use of martial law. More farsighted than his rival in Aleppo, Solomiac clearly preferred a half success to an unstable victory as he moved for the resumption of negotiations with the Bloc in the Syrian capital and new elections in Damascus, Duma, and Hama.

In the interim, nationalist leaders did their utmost to refrain from exciting public feelings, in spite of the precarious circumstances in which they found themselves at the beginning of the New Year.[114] The Bloc refused to give its stamp of approval to a large, violent demonstration and 16-day strike, which began on January 10 when elementary and high school students protested the imprisonment of a number of their colleagues who had participated in the December disturbances.[115] But

[110] Rabbath, *Courte Histoire*, pp. 87–88; al-Jundi, *Tarikh*, pp. 126–27.

[111] Rabbath, *Courte Histoire*, pp. 88–89.

[112] FO 684/5/4/26. Hole to FO, 8 April 1932.

[113] *Arrêté*, no. 4, 12 Feb. 1932. Rabbath, *Courte Histoire*, p. 89.

[114] FO 371/271, vol. 16085. Hole to Simon, 4 Jan. 1932.

[115] MWT, "Registre des jugements du Tribunal de 1ère Instance Correctionnelle de l'année 1931 et 1932," uncatalogued, 12 February 1932, pp. 263–65, 268–70.

though the Damascus Bloc seemed to be accommodating, the overall organization was inclined to boycott fresh elections.

Jamil Mardam, ignoring his colleagues' criticisms in and outside of Damascus, accepted Solomiac's offer to resume discussions on a compromise solution.[116] From mid-February, lengthy negotiations ensued, but in secret, a tactic that was rapidly becoming a Mardam trademark. Ultimately, a deal was struck: elections would be free if the nationalists guaranteed not to present more than six candidates for the nine contested seats, the remainder being reserved for three moderates.[117] After a long struggle with the leaders of the National Bloc in Aleppo, Mardam's compromise solution prevailed. Primaries were held as scheduled in Damascus, Duma, and Hama. Solomiac held up his end of the bargain and there were no serious disturbances.[118]

In Damascus, fortified by Senegalese troops concentrated around the single polling station at the municipal building next to Marjé Square, everything went smoothly. As anticipated, the Jewish candidate, Yusuf Linyadu, running unopposed, received the maximum number of votes (607), followed by the six National Bloc candidates, led by Jamil Mardam (542 votes). Only two of the three candidates whom the High Commission hoped to see elected managed to secure the necessary majority of votes: Muhammad ʿAli al-ʿAbid and Haqqi al-ʿAzm. Solomiac's favorite candidate, Rida al-Rikabi, was placed second behind Nasib al-Bakri on the list of those who had failed to gain a majority. To the Bloc, Bakri was preferable to the avaricious Rikabi, and on April 9, he won a special run-off election for the remaining seat by a large margin.[119] Shaykh Taj, who had been told by Ponsot not to bother to enter his name, suffered a humiliating defeat.[120]

The moderate wing of the National Bloc, under Jamil Mardam's guidance, had scored an important victory. The election returns from Hama raised the number of avowed nationalist deputies to 17, out of a total of 69. Mardam was confident that the vast majority of deputies, being "nonentities" from rural constituencies, could be swung around to the nationalist perspective, at least on controversial issues, as had happened in the Constituent Assembly.[121] His conclusion, however, rested on the Bloc's ability to keep moderates and hardliners united in the months to come.

[116] George Antonius File, no. 24. Antonius to Rogers, 9 April 1932.

[117] FO 371/1046, vol. 16085. Hole to Simon, 11 Feb. 1932.

[118] FO 684/5/4/26. Hole to FO, 8 April 1932; Rabbath, *Courte Histoire*, p. 91; George Antonius File, no. 19. Antonius to Rogers, 9 April 1932; *ibid.*, no. 24. Antonius to Rogers, 13 May 1932.

[119] FO 684/5/4/26. Hole to FO, 11 April 1932.

[120] For Damascus election results, see FO 684/5/4/26. Hole to FO, 8 April 1932.

[121] *Ibid.*; George Antonius File, no. 19. Antonius to Rogers, 9 April 1932.

CHAPTER FOURTEEN

FAILURE OF DIPLOMACY

THE CONCLUSION OF ELECTIONS did not remove the bad feelings raised by them. In Aleppo, the defeated left wing of the National Bloc organized a mini-terror campaign against the Liberal Constitutionalists. A leading supporter of the latter who had denounced the violent tactics of the Bloc was assassinated in May and an attempt was made on the life of Subhi Barakat, the anti-French rebel leader from Antioch turned self-seeking Aleppine politician and French collaborator. Rumors spread that many Aleppo deputies were considering resigning their seats before the opening session of Parliament unless they were afforded adequate government protection.[1]

But even more dangerous than the bitter political situation in Syria was the growing impatience of commercial and agricultural sectors which had to shoulder most of the burden of high taxation just as the depression was being felt most heavily. Aleppo textile workers went on strike in early June against France's failure to protect the local market against the influx of Japanese goods.[2] In the Syrian countryside the small peasant proprietor, sharecropper, and wage laborer suffered under a harsh taxation system rendered intolerable by fluctuations of exchange. A succession of four years of poor harvests had not been compensated by any serious concessions, such as tax moratoriums. The failure of winter rains and a late ground frost in the spring of 1932 entirely destroyed hill crops and vineyards in the plains; whole districts now faced the prospect of starvation.[3] Unorganized and inarticulate, rural society's grievances were customarily ignored.

Against this background of economic grievance and continued political dissatisfaction, Parliament opened on the morning of 7 June 1932 under heavy police protection. The deputies from Aleppo barely reached the Chamber, having been liberated only moments before from their hotels

[1] MAE, Syrie–Liban 1930–40. "Procès-verbal sommaire," 14 May 1932, vol. 481, pp. 119–27, 128–34.

[2] Hanna, al-Haraka al-ʿummaliyya, pp. 384–85; MWT, uncatalogued materials from the French adviser to the Ministry of Finance (Aleppo), S. Martin to Demeulenaere, 2 July 1934. At the time, Saʿim al-Dahir owned 22 silk-weaving workshops in Aleppo in the Jamiliyya quarter; Longuenesse, "La classe ouvrière," p. 49.

[3] MAE, Syrie–Liban 1930–40. Helleu (Beirut) to MAE, 5 Aug. 1932, vol. 484, pp. 13–14; FO 371/2645, vol. 16085. Hole to Simon, 7 May 1932.

where angry protestors had imprisoned them. In Aleppo itself, the bazaars were shut down by the local branch of the National Bloc to protest
the convocation of the fraudulently elected Parliament. Similar scenes
took place in all nationalist centers.[4]

Aside from the 68 deputies, several French observers attended, including the rival Delegates, Messrs. Solomiac and Lavastre. After the text of
the decree convening Parliament was read, the oldest deputy, Muhammad Yahya al-'Adali of Antioch, assumed the task of Speaker *pro tem-
pore*. But before he could reach his chair, Fakhri al-Barudi called upon the
Chamber to observe two minutes of silence in memory of the late Fawzi
al-Ghazzi, the author of the much-contested constitution, who had been
poisoned by his wife three years earlier. Barudi then encouraged his colleagues to act in Parliament according to their consciences and not to fear
external pressures. Shakir Ni'mat al-Sha'bani sarcastically expressed his
wholehearted agreement; he was one of those Aleppine deputies recently
imprisoned in his hotel.[5]

As the Acting Speaker tried to proceed with business, Zaki al-Khatib,
taking Barudi's suggestion literally, interrupted with a long speech and
would not be seated in spite of the Speaker's injunctions. Soon, the long-
winded Fa'iz al-Khuri joined in and a general uproar ensued. The Speaker
ordered a policeman to remove Khuri from the Chamber but he refused
to budge, aptly quoting Mirabeau: "We are here by the will of the people
and we will not leave except by the force of bayonets." Instead, the policeman was ejected and the Speaker adjourned the meeting for twenty
minutes until relative calm was restored.[6]

When the session was reopened lemonade was served to all to calm
down feelings before the Chamber moved on to the business of electing a
Speaker. The results of the first ballot were inconclusive. Subhi Barakat
received 28 votes, Haqqi al-'Azm, 23, and Hashim al-Atasi, 17. Since no
candidate had secured a simply majority, a second ballot had to be cast.
The nationalists, sensing the inevitable, decided to abstain, enabling Barakat to poll 30 votes to 'Azm's 23.[7]

From the Speaker's chair, Subhi Bey's first utterances in halting Arabic
rang of hypocrisy. One moment he announced his commitment to work
harmoniously with all parties and, in particular, the National Bloc. The
next he turned around and placed his followers from the North in all the
important parliamentary posts.[8]

[4] Rabbath, *Courte Histoire* ("L'expérience Ponsot"), p. 94.
[5] Ghazzi had been murdered by his wife in 1929 after he discovered that she had committed adultery! FO 684/5/436. Hole to FO, 8 June 1932.
[6] *Ibid.*
[7] *Ibid.* Rabbath, *Courte Histoire*, p. 94.
[8] FO 684/5/436. Hole to FO, 8 June 1932.

But the real test in Parliament was still to come: elections for President of the Republic. Barakat, backed by his bloc of 28 northern deputies, was the odds-on favorite. But Solomiac, who had been sitting quietly in the gallery, sensed a threat to his own strategy, which was to get the only committed pro-French candidate, Haqqi al-'Azm, elected. Catching the eye of one of his clients in the Damascus delegation, he signalled him to move for an adjournment; this request immediately drew the support of the nationalist deputies who also realized that their candidate had no serious chance of winning. But Shakir Ni'mat al-Sha'bani and others opposed the motion. Subhi Barakat had to announce a 30-minute recess. When the deputies returned, Sha'bani unexpectedly withdrew his objection and it was agreed to postpone the election for four days. In bringing this action-packed opening meeting to a close, Barakat announced that postponement was conditional upon deputies no longer being imprisoned in their hotels.[9]

By the time Parliament reassembled on June 11, several days of fierce political intrigue had elapsed. In order to defeat M. Lavastre's Aleppine candidate, Subhi Barakat, M. Solomiac and the Bloc gave up their respective candidates, Haqqi al-'Azm and Hashim al-Atasi, and agreed to support Muhammad 'Ali al-'Abid.[10] That same morning 'Abid was elected the first President of the Syrian Republic, defeating Barakat by a slim margin of four votes. He was then escorted to his new headquarters by a very enthusiastic crowd patrolled by the Nationalist Youth. There, he received a 17-gun salute and witnessed the unfurling of the new Syrian flag. Like the Hashemite flag flown over the Syrian Congress of 1920, it had three horizontal bars of green, white and black (representing the Fatimid, Umayyad and Abbasid dynasties, respectively). But across the white bar were added three red stars, indicating Syria's wish to distance herself from Hashemite influence.[11]

MUHAMMAD 'ALI AL-'ABID belonged to the old school of Ottoman diplomats and politicians for whom the complex questions of European imperial penetration and hegemony could not be treated by force of arms. He hailed from a line of well-connected merchants and landowners of Damascus who spanned four generations in the service of the Ottoman Empire, and who, with their relations, the 'Azms and the Yusufs, constituted the cream of Ottoman-Arab society. Muhammad 'Ali's great-great-grandfather, 'Umar Agha, had played an important humanitarian

[9] Rabbath, *Courte Histoire*, p. 95.
[10] MAE, Syrie–Liban 1930–40. Ponsot Memorandum, 30 May 1932, pp. 148–53.
[11] FO 684/4/529. Hole to Simon, 16 June 1932.

role during the 1860 disturbances in Damascus; his grandfather, Hawlu Pasha, had been a *mutasarrif* in various districts, eventually becoming the President of the Administrative Council of the Syrian Province in the 1890s. His father, Ahmad 'Izzat Pasha, was Sultan Abdülhamid's "second secretary," one of his closest confidants, the inspiration behind the Hijaz Railway scheme, and probably the most influential Syrian in the Ottoman administration during the last years of the Sultan's long reign. Muhammad 'Ali grew up in an aristocratic milieu in Istanbul and was educated at the Galata Sérail School and in Paris.[12] On returning to Istanbul in 1905, he joined the Ottoman Ministry of Foreign Affairs, advancing rapidly to become Minister to Washington in 1908. But his stay there lasted only six weeks, cut short by the Young Turks' July Revolt which ousted many of the Sultan's influential advisers, including 'Izzat Pasha al-'Abid. Muhammad 'Ali Bey and his wife[13] sailed for Europe to join his family in political exile. In Paris he and his brother helped their father manage his many financial interests. There, the cultivated Muhammad 'Ali also found ample time to pursue his favorite pastime, reading French and Arabic literature. During the war years he also had the good fortune to mix with many distinguished Europeans, an opportunity few of his fellow Syrians ever enjoyed. He returned to Damascus in 1919, but spent the following decade on the margins of political life, accused by many nationalists of being a Francophile.[14]

Muhammad 'Ali al-'Abid was reputed to be the wealthiest man in Damascus, if not in the whole of Syria.[15] In the latter half of the nineteenth century his grandfather had converted some of the family's Maydan business enterprises into Suez Canal Company shares and fertile agricultural lands, including several villages in Duma, the Ghuta, and in the gardens of al-Qanawat. Aside from these holdings and large assets in European and American banks, the 'Abid family owned valuable real estate in Damascus, most notably the Victoria Hotel in the town center—a family *waqf* established by 'Izzat Pasha, which yielded a handsome yearly income in rent.[16] He was also reputed to be miserly and unpatriotic. News-

---

[12] Al-Zirikli, *al-A'lam*, vol. 7, p. 197; *Les Echos de Syrie*, no. 149 (12 June 1934).

[13] Muhammad 'Ali al-'Abid and his brother, 'Abd al-Rahman, were married to sisters of 'Abd al-Rahman Pasha al-Yusuf. Conversations with Wajiha al-Yusuf (Beirut, 15 and 29 Aug. 1975).

[14] Kurd 'Ali, *al-Mudhakkirat*, vol. 2, pp. 323–45. Conversation with Zafir al-Qasimi (Beirut, 26 July 1975).

[15] *Al-Mudhik al-mubki* (Damascus), no. 33 (12 April 1930), p. 5.

[16] The Victoria Hotel was originally called the Hawlu Pasha al-'Abid Hotel after Muhammad 'Ali's grandfather. Muhammad 'Ali also owned a large tract of land in the Shaghur quarter. The Damascus properties of the family which yielded a considerable rent, especially the farm lands and the Victoria Hotel, were continuously in court litigation over ownership after the death of 'Izzat al-'Abid in 1924. In the courts his sisters and nieces fought Mu-

papers and magazines regularly criticized him for keeping so much of his capital abroad, reported in the late twenties to be about £1 million gold, and for deserting his family's traditional residence in Suq Saruja for a new modern palace in the suburb of al-Muhajirin.[17] But he did not neglect his family's old clients in Suq Suruja or its new ones; on the contrary, the ʿAbids assisted the poor and the destitute especially during Ramadan, when they fed hundreds of people every evening of the month.[18] ʿAbid also saw to it that a tramway line was built to al-Muhajirin. Still, there was a certain amount of truth to the accusation that he refused to repatriate his capital. To get him to invest money in Syria he had to be prodded, and only the National Bloc was able to do that by persuading him to become a major shareholder in the National Cement Company, a Bloc enterprise.[19] ʿAbid was also an early backer of the nationalist newspaper, *al-Ayyam*, which he helped to subsidize with a grant of £S 5,000 in 1930.[20]

Ironically, President ʿAbid invited Haqqi al-ʿAzm to form a government on 15 June 1932. One of the unresolved mysteries surrounding the Presidential election deal was whether the High Commissioner had offered ʿAzm the consolation prize of Prime Minister for his quiet withdrawal in favor of ʿAbid. There was no mystery, however, as to who chose the other cabinet members. It was Messrs. Ponsot and Solomiac. They chose Salim Jambart, Mazhar Raslan, and Jamil Mardam.

The inclusion of Raslan and Mardam in the ʿAzm government suggests that the National Bloc and M. Solomiac may have struck a secret deal before the parliamentary election re-run the previous spring. The appearance of these two nationalists in ministerial posts seemed to be an important French concession. Moreover, they had two ministries each, whereas the moderates had only three ministries (two for ʿAzm and one for Jambart), which certainly required the High Commissioner's approval.[21]

Jambart, at 59, was a prosperous Greek Catholic merchant from Aleppo

---

hammad ʿAli and his brother. See MWT, *Registres des jugements civils*, 28 July 1928–14 Oct. 1929; 15 Oct.–16 April 1930; 2 June 1926–15 Feb. 1928; 13 Dec. 1930–25 Aug. 1932. *Ibid., Registre commercial*, no. 6 (1934).

[17] *Al-Mudhik al-mubki*, no. 43 (27 June 1930), p. 14; Kurd ʿAli, *al-Mudhakkirat*, vol. 2, pp. 323–45. *Al-Mudhik al-mubki* sarcastically commented that ʿAbid left Suq Saruja without even "saying good-bye" and wondered how his clients would ever find him cloistered away on a big hill? No. 152 (3 Dec. 1932), p. 7.

[18] Conversation with Nasuh (Abu Muhammad) al-Mahayri (Damascus, 10 March 1976).

[19] *Al-Mudhik al-mubki*, no. 33 (12 April 1930), p. 5.

[20] *Ibid.*, no. 45 (19 July 1930), p. 4.

[21] ʿAzm, in addition to being Prime Minister, took the important Interior portfolio, a standard procedure for Prime Ministers. Raslan was given Justice and Education while Mardam received Finance and Agriculture. Jambart was left with Public Works. Longrigg, *Syria*, p. 192

and a Liberal Constitutionalist, though he had not approved of the electioneering methods used by his northern colleagues.[22] Raslan, a 45-year-old bachelor and notable of Homs whose family were religious scholars and bureaucrats of middling landed status, already had had a long and rewarding political and administrative career. After graduating from the Mülkiye, he held a number of posts in the Ottoman provincial bureacracy. After World War I, he began to serve Amir Faysal, ending up as the *mutasarrif* of Salt. In 1920, he was also elected to the Syrian Congress from Homs. After Faysal was overthrown, Raslan formed an Arab government in Salt and Amman, one of several short-lived governments which appeared in Transjordan at this time. With the establishment of ʿAbdullah's government at Amman in 1921, he became one of ʿAbdullah's advisers. In August of the same year he formed a government which lasted until March 1922 when he was replaced by Rida Pasha al-Rikabi. He headed another government between February and September 1923 and left Transjordan in May 1924 for Syria. Implicated in the Great Revolt, he was jailed at Arwad Island and then exiled until the amnesty of 1928. A month later he was elected a deputy from Homs to the Constituent Assembly. A member of the moderate wing of the National Bloc, he was, nonetheless, regarded as a dedicated nationalist who spent generously on its activities.[23] As for Jamil Mardam, he remained the principal strategist of the Bloc policy of "honorable cooperation." It was Mardam who publicly labeled the new cabinet, the "Ministry of mutual understanding and honor,"[24] and who was the center of controversy in the new government.

From its first day in office, the ʿAzm government faced a barrage of criticism from all corners in Syria, and for a variety of reasons. Steadfast opposition to compromise and collaboration was an easy way to score popularity points, especially at a time when the country was saddled with a devastating economic depression. The commemoration of the Battle of Maysalun on July 24 furnished clear evidence of the rifts which had emerged in nationalist ranks since Mardam first enunciated the National Bloc's policy of "honorable cooperation." On the same occasion just two years before, he had violently denounced the government of Shaykh Taj, and extolled the Bloc as the apostle of complete unity and independence. In 1932, he did not even attend the ceremony. Had he, he would have heard himself denounced by a man destined to be his chief rival on the national political scene, Shukri al-Quwwatli. Quwwatli, who had focused

[22] Faris, *Man huwa 1949*, p. 96; Rabbath, *Courte Histoire*, p. 96.
[23] Faris, *Man huwa 1949*, p. 479; *al-Mudhik al-mubki*, no. 246 (9 March 1935), p. 9; FO 371/2142, vol. 20849, 6 May 1937.
[24] "*Wizarat al-tafahum al-nazih.*" See al-Kayyali, *al-Marahil*, vol. 1, pp. 179–83.

most of his attention since his amnesty on various economic enterprises, most notably on laying the groundwork for his National Conserves factory, had only recently adopted a public profile. In an inflammatory speech, he accused Mardam and other nationalists of treachery and deceit, of leading the country into slavery for motives of pure personal gain.[25]

Problems in Aleppo continued unabated. Political malaise was aggravated by the deepening of the world depression. In the summer, a series of boycotts culminated in a massive strike of workers and employers in the local textile industry against low tariffs for Japanese imports. Although this agitation forced the French to double the tariff, the subsequent refusal of employers to raise their workers' wages resulted in two more weeks of strikes. At the time, the National Bloc leadership revealed its bourgeois character by defending managers and owners, many of whom were Bloc partisans, against workers.[26] Bloc headquarters distributed propaganda calling for the solidification of national ranks against the French, the true enemy of the Syrian people. The Aleppo Bloc tried but failed to turn its economic grievances against Mardam and Raslan. Not even popular demonstrations staged at the end of August in Damascus calling for their resignation managed to shake them out of office. Instead, police surrounded Bloc headquarters at the center of the capital on August 31, arresting thirty local leaders who were later tried for plotting against the security of the state. Mardam nonetheless had begun to feel the pressure and he decided to take refuge in Lebanon for the rest of the summer.[27]

The Treaty of 1933

The French elections of May 1932 returned the Left to power after an eight-year absence and finally enabled France to address the question of a treaty with Syria. Not only did elections give the Chamber a leftist tinge, they also put Edouard Herriot in the office of Prime Minister. A brilliant professor of literature turned passionate radical politician, Herriot was an acknowledged connoisseur of Mediterranean culture and was even regarded by some Syrians as a sincere friend.[28]

Herriot (who also held the Foreign Ministry portfolio) instructed his vacationing High Commissioner to initiate a scheme which would put Syria on a more rapid schedule toward emancipation. His inspiration, like Ponsot's and the National Bloc's, was Britain's successful treaty with

[25] MAE, Syrie–Liban 1930–40. Helleu to MAE, 5 Aug. 1982, vol. 484, pp. 9–11.
[26] Al-Qabas (11–15 Aug. 1932), cited in Hanna, al-Haraka al-'ummaliyya, pp. 392–93; Longuenesse, "La classe ouvrière," p. 49.
[27] Rabbath, Courte Histoire, pp. 97–98.
[28] Shirer, The Collapse of the Third Republic, p. 139.

Iraq. He realized that France would inevitably face great troubles if she did not match Britain's generosity.[29] There was considerable speculation in Syrian political circles that Ponsot might actually return with a draft treaty in hand. The Bloc convened one of its irregular general assemblies at the Lebanese mountain resort of Sofar, a favorite vacation spot of the Damascene notability, to consider treaty possibilities. The meetings were long and strenuous, revealing the extent and depth of divisions within the Bloc over strategy.[30]

The High Commissioner finally reached Syria on October 21. Arriving in Aleppo, his first gesture was calculated to sweeten nationalist hard-liners. He instructed the French Attorney General who had been respon-sible for the mass arrests and trials of dissidents in August to declare the immediate release of all political detainees in the town. Then, as if he were trying to make up for lost time, Ponsot rushed on to Damascus. At the Rayak train depot, just outside the Syrian capital, he discovered an excellent opportunity to make another gesture of goodwill. To a group of moderate deputies who had journeyed there to greet him, he announced the commencement of negotiations toward a treaty which he described only as being more "liberal" in content than the Anglo-Iraqi Treaty.[31]

In the days to follow, Ponsot repeatedly reaffirmed his desire to enter into negotiations with government representatives of all political parties. But the Bloc leadership—still in session in Sofar—reached a nearly unan-imous agreement which forbade nationalist deputies from returning to Parliament before the High Commissioner defined in writing what the official bases of the treaty were to be. They added, moreover, a minimum demand that the treaty's concessions must match those granted by Brit-ain to Iraq. Behind the Bloc's rigid, no-nonsense stand stood Ibrahim Hananu and the Aleppo hardliners, supported by Hashim al-Atasi who, since his uncontested electoral victory of the past spring in Homs, had aligned with the abstentionists. Meanwhile, Jamil Mardam and Mazhar Raslan—advocates of "honorable cooperation"—had no choice but to concur, though they did so reluctantly.

Many Bloc chiefs were unconvinced that France really wanted to con-clude a treaty. Of late, they had received mixed and confusing signals. While Ponsot announced on a visit to Suwayda' that the "independence" of the Jabal Druze was unrealistic and thus impermanent, the language of

---

[29] FO 371/5349, vol. 16085. Smith (FO), 14 Oct. 1932. Also see Rabbath, *Courte His-toire*, p. 99.

[30] See *al-Ayyam*, no. 276 (29 Oct. 1932); *Ibid.*, no. 279 (1 Nov. 1932).

[31] Ponsot had received his instructions to start treaty negotiations on October 12, before his departure from Paris. Iraq had been admitted to the League of Nations on October 3. MAE, Syrie–Liban 1930–40. Note of MAE, 28 March 1933, vol. 484, pp. 10–11. Rabbath, *Courte Histoire*, p. 99.

the Parisian press was far less reassuring. For instance, the influential *Le Matin* categorically denied all rumors that a treaty was to be substituted for the Mandate. In the newspaper's opinion, the question of ceding the Mandate was a very distant eventuality.[32]

By October 29, the day Parliament reconvened, no progress had been made toward breaking the impasse. A letter from Ponsot on the same day to President ʿAbid and the ʿAzm cabinet did little to change the general mood of pessimism and doubt in Syria. Aside from Mardam and Raslan, only one Bloc deputy dared to enter the Chamber. This was Faʾiz al-Khuri, who had made it known in Sofar that he had been elected to defend his country from the "pulpit," not from the "street."[33]

Despite the absence of 15 nationalist deputies, the atmosphere in the Chamber was charged with tension and apprehension. Subhi Barakat was easily re-elected Speaker, but acrimonious debate ensued, the most vicious remarks being those of the Liberal Constitutionalist leader, Shakir Niʿmat al-Shaʿbani, who reviled Ponsot for permitting a cabinet of strong nationalist complexion to run the country's daily affairs when Parliament was, in fact, dominated by northern moderates. Before the session turned into a free-for-all, Barakat wisely adjourned it.[34]

In the meantime, although the High Commissioner remained mute, his advisers did not. In particular, the Secretary-General, the Chief of the Political Bureau, and the new Delegate to Damascus, M. Weber, stepped up contacts with President ʿAbid, Hashim al-Atasi, and other Bloc leaders. These officials made plain their desire to see the Bloc preserve its policy of "honorable cooperation." M. Weber was especially frank, producing more formal assurances of French sincerity but without being any more precise than his boss. He encouraged the Bloc to trust Ponsot, promising that this time the Quai d'Orsay had empowered him to treat the Syrian Question in its entirety.[35]

Yet another National Bloc Congress took place in Homs, between November 2 and 4, ostensibly for reorganization purposes, but also to reassess the strategy of "honorable cooperation." The Homs Congress was the nastiest and most perilous in the National Bloc's brief history. Although the complete story of what transpired in the inner sanctum of the Bloc Council remains shrouded in secrecy, two critical maneuvers seem to have been undertaken. The first brought Shukri al-Quwwatli, the Is-

[32] MAE, Syrie–Liban 1930–40. Helleu (Damascus) to MAE, 9 Dec. 1932, vol. 482, pp. 219–20; Rabbath, *Courte Histoire*, pp. 101–2.

[33] *Ibid.*, pp. 102–3; FO 371/6246, vol. 16085. Napier (Damascus) to Simon, 2 Nov. 1932; *al-Ayyam*, no. 279 (1 Nov. 1932).

[34] FO 371/6246, vol. 16085. Napier to Simon, 2 Nov. 1932.

[35] Rabbath, *Courte Histoire*, p. 103.

tiqlali leader, into the ranks of the Bloc and onto its Council.[36] In theory, this should have strengthened Bloc hardliners against Jamil Mardam, thereby reinforcing the Sofar decisions. But Quwwatli's appearance was almost nullified by the second maneuver: the sudden and unexpected defection of a faction of Aleppo nationalists to the side of Jamil Mardam. The elegant Sa'dallah al-Jabiri, whose differences with Ibrahim Hananu were thought to have been patched up in November 1929,[37] broke with his rival and aligned with Jamil Mardam as he had in 1928. It appears Jabiri did so in order to win the Bloc vice-presidency. Hashim al-Atasi saved the Bloc from a fatal rupture, by effecting a new accord between Jabiri and Hananu. The Homs meeting reversed the Bloc's decision to boycott Parliament, but if immediate progress in negotiations were not made, then Jabiri would cease to support nationalist participation in Parliament and government.[38]

Of course, Atasi's public explanation of the Bloc's sudden shift in direction was made to sound as if the Bloc no longer suffered from any differences of opinion or violent clashes of personality. He announced that the

nationalists accepted to participate in the electoral process with the aim of concluding with the French government a treaty assuring the independence of the country and its unity. Because for five months we [the National Bloc] have not heard the goodwill of France on modifying the form of the regime, we had decided not to participate in Parliament until we received a treaty no less satisfying than the Anglo-Iraqi. But at the most recent discussion of the Bloc [in Homs] and its two nationalist ministers, we became convinced that the provisional continuation of a politics of conciliation would aid the claims of the nationalists. This is why we have judged that it is opportune to be patient and to re-affirm the good faith of the nationalists in the hope of obtaining a solution to the present crisis and to independence and unity. We hope the French will appreciate our attitude and respond with goodwill.[39]

---

[36] Al-Kayyali, al-Marahil, vol. 1, p. 185.

[37] MAE, Syrie–Liban 1918–29. "Sûreté Générale," Aleppo, 28 Nov. 1929, vol. 215, pp. 212–18. Through Riyad Sulh's intervention. Sulh's ties to Aleppo were especially strong. Although he came from a family of merchants of Sidon, he grew up partly in Aleppo where his father, Rida Bey, had been an Ottoman official. Later Riyad married the daughter of Nafi' al-Jabiri, an uncle of Sa'dallah and Ihsan, and the leading notable of the town around the turn of the century. Nafi' Pasha was also an elected deputy to the 1908 Ottoman Parliament in Istanbul. See Salname: vilayet-i halab, 1326/1908–1909, p. 192.

[38] Jabiri had aligned with Mardam in support of Hashim al-Atasi, rather than Hananu, for the President of the 1928 Constituent Assembly. Hananu removed his name as a candidate in order not to divide nationalist ranks. Rabbath, Courte Histoire, p. 105; MAE, Syrie–Liban 1930–40. Ponsot (Beirut) to MAE, 11 Nov. 1932, vol. 482, pp. 133–39.

[39] Rabbath, Courte Histoire, p. 105.

These remarks were soon echoed in Parliament by the returning Bloc deputies. They formally demanded that the Chamber grant President ʿAbid authority to negotiate a treaty "regulating the future relations between France and Syria in harmony with the desires of the country," and in preparation for the entrance of Syria into the League of Nations. The Chamber's vote on this motion was nearly unanimous; only the embittered Shakir Niʿmat al-Shaʿbani cast a negative vote.[40] With the Liberal Constitutionalists now supporting the idea of a treaty and the Bloc's left wing momentarily quiescent, a major breakthrough seemed to have been made, indicating a triumph for Jamil Mardam and the policy of "honorable cooperation."

M. Ponsot decided to handle the French end of negotiations himself. Before leaving for Geneva to address the League on the subject of the treaty, he took the opportunity to discuss with the entire ʿAzm cabinet and President ʿAbid the outlines of such an agreement, though he remained, as always, purposely vague on the question of Syrian unity.[41]

Ponsot prefaced his remarks in Geneva with praise for Iraq's recent acceptance into the League. He then went on to spell out his proposal. In brief, he suggested that the territory under French Mandate be divided into two zones, one a "treaty zone" to comprise the State of Syria and the other a "Mandate zone" to include Greater Lebanon, the Alawite state and the Jabal Druze.[42] When the PMC Chairman questioned him on the subject of Syrian unity, Ponsot responded by stressing the need for political evolution before the absolute integration into Syria of the Alawite and Druze minorities, owing to their political underdevelopment. In his speech, Ponsot also made reference to the different nationalist elements in Syria, purposely passing over the National Bloc's "legitimate" claim to the Syrian leadership.[43]

Syrian nationalists reacted to Ponsot's speech with disappointment and anger. Not only had he refused to accord the National Bloc the full recognition it demanded and deserved, but he had also clumsily side-stepped the issue of Syrian unity. Initially the High Commissioner received the heaviest criticism from Shakib Arslan and Ihsan al-Jabiri in Geneva in their periodical, *La Nation Arabe*.[44] A wave of petitions flooded League headquarters throughout early 1933, mostly in support of "unity." There were serious problems concerning unity, however, which nationalists and their supporters either papered over or ignored. For instance, during the Bayram feast at the end of Ramadan a minor incident in La-

[40] *Ibid.*, pp. 105–6.

[41] *Ibid.*, p. 106.

[42] Longrigg, *Syria*, p. 193.

[43] Rabbath, *Courte Histoire*, p. 112.

[44] *The Times* (London), (4 Jan. 1933), cited in FO 371/120, vol. 16973.

takia developed into a violent confrontation between Alawite troops and Sunnis, in which one person was killed and twenty others injured. Each sect blamed the other, but Sunni leaders intervened to make it appear that their community harbored no ill-feelings against the Alawite minority; they feared that sectarian conflict would obstruct their path toward Syrian unity.[45]

On returning to Beirut at the beginning of February, Henri Ponsot published the various statements he had made in Geneva in order to give the Syrian public some idea of his government's intentions.[46] He also resumed negotiations with President ʿAbid and the ʿAzm cabinet.

Meanwhile, the Central Council of the National Bloc called for a special session, this time in Aleppo on hardliner turf, at the home of Ibrahim Hananu. At the end of nine days of intense discussion, Hashim al-Atasi issued a manifesto denouncing the High Commissioner's proposals.

> Syrian nationalists, anxious to achieve the rights and interests of their country, proclaim to the people of the coast and the interior, their unwavering attachment to the principle of national unity. No treaty is to be signed and no negotiations are to be undertaken with France except on this basis.

The Bloc was explicit: there was to be no separation of the question of unity from the application of the treaty, and no member of the Bloc was to negotiate until the High Commissioner accepted the Bloc's position.[47] But Bloc hardliners were unable to prevent Jamil Mardam from straying from the line adopted in Aleppo. On his return to Damascus, he made secret contacts with Ponsot via Messrs. Chauvel, the French Chief of the Political Bureau, and Weber, in a bid to keep negotiations alive.[48]

[45] These disturbances had a social dimension which confessionalism masked. Not only was the big landowning class Sunni Arab and resident in Latakia while the cultivators were mainly poor Alawite peasants, but Alawites had been moving since the start of the Mandate from the countryside (mountain) to Latakia, where they began to form their own artisanal and professional classes. This threatened the Sunni absentee landowning class. MAE, Syrie–Liban 1930–40. Ponsot to MAE, 10 Feb. 1933, vol. 483, pp. 124–25; FO 371/957, vol. 16973. Satow to Simon, 9 Feb. 1933.

[46] See L'Orient (Beirut), 3 Feb. 1933; al-Kayyali, al-Marahil, vol. 1, pp. 202–7.

[47] Al-Kayyali, al-Marahil, vol. 1, pp. 207–9; Rabbath, Courte Histoire, pp. 113–14. It was at this time that an expanded and more detailed version of the National Bloc response to the High Commissioner was published in pamphlet form, first in Arabic and then in French, and bound together in one volume for distribution at the League of Nations. Its principal author was Dr. Kayyali who claims that it first appeared on 16 February 1933. See ʿAbd al-Rahman al-Kayyali, Radd al-Kulta al-wataniyya ʿala bayanat al-mufawwad al-sami (Aleppo, 1933), French version: A. Keyyali, Réponse à Ponsot, Haute-Commissaire de la République Française en Syrie et au Liban (Aleppo, 1933); MAE, Syrie–Liban 1930–40. "Manifeste du BN," vol. 482, pp. 210–11.

[48] FO 371/2092, vol. 16974. MacKereth to Simon, 31 March 1933.

Wearing glasses and dressed in rumpled suits, appearing always to be absorbed in deep contemplation, Mardam cut the figure of an intellectual rather than that of a political intriguer absorbed in the art of diplomacy. But, utilizing his nearly flawless French to great advantage, he had established himself as the one nationalist politician in Syria eminently qualified to move between the nationalists and the French, trying to effect a balance.[49] He did so to advance his own career, yet at the same time he believed that his approach to the French was the only feasible one; the Bloc and its predecessors had exhausted all other options. Despite his proven political skills, he soon discovered that the task he had set himself was impossible, at least in 1933. Syria, after all, was still under colonial rule and any politician who staked his fame and fortune on his commitment to national liberation and independence—as all Bloc leaders did— had only a narrow space in which to maneuver between a reasonable degree of cooperation with the French and out-and-out collaboration. And though no nationalist had stretched this space in as many directions as had Jamil Mardam, by the end of March 1933 it appeared that even he could no longer maintain his own equilibrium between the two competing forces of the Mandate and the nationalist movement.

Mardam continued to negotiate secretly with the High Commissioner and his staff in early April. But, since Ponsot's return to Beirut in February, a rejectionist campaign to force Mardam and Raslan to resign had been building up steam. From his seat in Aleppo, Ibrahim Hananu declared the Mandate illegal and formally demanded the resignation of the Bloc Ministers. Desperate, Mardam began to vascillate. He begged Ponsot to reconsider the question of unity, but Ponsot, as was his habit, reverted to silence, and Paris refused to depart from the line laid down at Geneva.[50]

Hananu, Hashim al-Atasi, and the Damascus-based Istiqlalis feared that Mardam would queer the abstentionist campaign by proposing an eleventh hour deal, which could redivide the fragile Bloc. Or, they feared, he might try to convince his moderate supporters to carry out negotiations independently of the Bloc. The Aleppo Bloc's distrust was so deep that when rumors spread that a treaty had been signed, the ailing Hananu rushed to Damascus to reverse what had not occurred.[51] Such was the condition of the National Bloc in 1933.

Actually, Jamil Mardam had some time earlier reached the conclusion that he did not have the weapons to confront Bloc intransigence. Nor did

[49] Al-Mudhik al-mubki, no. 137 (30 July 1932), p. 4.
[50] Rabbath, Courte Histoire, p. 115.
[51] FO 371/4055, vol. 16974. Todd, Quarterly Report, April–June 1933, 1 July 1933.

he see any advantage in bringing about the Bloc's demise by leading a breakaway faction. There had been considerable talk in Aleppo of expelling Mardam and Raslan from the Bloc and by mid-April Hananu was still inclined in this direction. It was at this time, however, that word reached the Aleppine leader that Mardam had accepted the demands of his colleagues and would resign but needed to have a way to step down with "honor." Despite his intense dislike of Mardam, Hananu willingly softened his position. He now believed that to expel Mardam before he could resign would only give the French another opportunity to exploit the schism in nationalist ranks.[52]

Just two days before Parliament was to reconvene to debate the treaty proposals, Hananu arrived with Jamil Ibrahim Pasha in Damascus to make certain that Mardam resigned, and with dignity. Ibrahim Pasha met with a group of Nationalist Youth and arranged for a demonstration in honor of Mardam to coincide with his resignation. At the appointed time on April 20, Mardam announced his departure and was carried from his office at the Sérail to his residence on the shoulders of a cheering crowd, as if he were a hero.[53] Not long after this rather astonishing spectacle, Mazhar Raslan submitted his resignation.[54] Efforts to get President 'Abid to step down as well failed; he wanted to carry on negotiations in the hope of stealing all the glory.[55] Nevertheless, under the daring leadership of Ibrahim Hananu, the National Bloc appeared triumphant. Although scarred by recent events, the Bloc continued to steer the independence movement.

In preparation for the reopening of Parliament, Damascus was well fortified, braced for major disturbances. From the southern suburbs an "array of military camps, aerodromes, barracks, and artillery parks [lined] the road along the stretch of one and one-half miles into the heart of the city."[56] On April 22, the day Parliament reopened, the French cut all telephone lines within the city and to the outside world to prevent the circulation of rumors. Police and gendarmes in steel helmets were on the streets, but French troops remained confined to their barracks. Machine guns were mounted on street corners and armored cars circulated slowly

---

[52] Al-Mudhik al-mubki, no. 181 (12 Aug. 1933), p. 4: MAE, Syrie–Liban 1930–40, vol. 484, pp. 64–71.

[53] Ibrahim Pasha, Nidal, pp. 62–63.

[54] Rabbath, Courte Histoire, p. 116.

[55] FO 371/2354, vol. 16974. MacKereth to FO, 24 April 1933. The Bloc also tried to force, unsuccessfully, the resignation of President 'Abid's chef de cabinet, Najib al-Armanazi. The 35-year-old Paris-trained political scientist happened to be Jamil Mardam's brother-in-law.

[56] George Antonius File, no. 29. Antonius to Rogers, 18 April 1933.

and "menacingly." "Groups of demonstrators harangued the already converted and crowds sang national songs."[57] In this atmosphere Parliament met. Although nationalist deputies stayed away, a quorum of two-thirds was mustered.

Jamil Mardam had in the meantime published a "curious statement" praising the French for their generous attitude during the negotiations and claiming that he had resigned for personal reasons. For some time it had been bazaar gossip that the French had "bought" Mardam, whose liquid assets were suddenly enormous, and his *volte face* perplexed some members of the National Bloc who "indignantly dubbed him" a "traitor."[58]

On May 3, Prime Minister Haqqi al-ʿAzm managed to come up with a new government. He retained the Ministry of Interior and Salim Jambart took on the Education portfolio, in addition to that of Public Works. The newcomers to government were Muhammad Yahya al-ʿAdali of Antioch (Agriculture and Commerce); Shaykh Sulayman Jukhadar of Damascus, who had made an unsuccessful bid for a parliamentary seat on the Reform Party slate in 1932 (Justice); and the provocative Shaʿbani (Finance).[59] On May 8, with Damascus still closed, the nationalist boycott of Parliament still in effect, and Parliament still protected by bayonets, the Chamber reassembled to hear Haqqi al-ʿAzm present his new government for a vote of confidence. The Prime Minister promised to carry on treaty negotiations and stressed his commitment to achieving unity and implementing other important reforms. However, his words rang of Mandate jargon, suggesting that the High Commission had drafted his speech. Nevertheless, nearly all of the 44 deputies in attendance gave their support to the government, the "Liberal Constitutionalists" happily leading the way with two of their own now in office.[60]

Parliament met until the end of May. Little was accomplished, however, and by the time of the summer recess, prospects of a Franco-Syrian treaty were as remote as ever.

A TREATY POST-MORTEM

Although treaty negotiations continued till the end of 1933, after Mardam and Raslan had resigned from government they were little more than an exercise in futility. Ponsot adopted a rigid position, increasing surveillance of nationalist leaders and suspending the publication of its two major papers in Damascus, *al-Ayyam* and *al-Qabas*. But, in late

[57] FO 371/2354, vol. 16974. MacKereth to FO, 24 April 1933.
[58] FO 371/2354, vol. 16974. MacKereth to FO, 24 April 1933.
[59] Hasan al-Hakim, *Mudhakkirati*, vol. 2, p. 169.
[60] FO 371/2851, vol. 16974. Acting Consul Todd (Damascus) to Simon, 10 May 1933.

May he was stricken with phlebitis. Confined to bed for several weeks, he finally regained enough strength for his annual vacation in France at the beginning of July. After he had made a full recovery he learned that he was to be transferred to Morocco.[61]

At the time, several opinions—and many rumors—were offered to explain Ponsot's transfer. British observers noted that he had become so involved in local politics that he had completely neglected other matters, such as the administration of justice, and fiscal and customs policies.[62] Some French officials claimed that the symptoms of agitation in Morocco, a country of far greater importance to France, urgently required an expert of his stature whose keen administrative and political skills would insure the French presence in North Africa. Still others believed that he was removed because of a failure to uphold France's traditional *politique orientale*, which stressed the promotion of Franco-Lebanese friendship through good relations with the Maronite Patriarch and clergy. An astute observer of the Lebanese political scene, he had indeed noticed that Maronite clerics were suffering a steady loss of power and influence; consequently, he paid less attention to them. It was rumored that some prelates had voiced their dislike of him to certain Paris ministers who, when the opportunity arose, prevented him from returning to Beirut. Finally, there were even rumors that French Zionists had conspired against him, because he was hostile to Zionist ambitions in Palestine.[63]

Ponsot's approach to the nationalist movement in Syria had been to exploit its deep divisions, which had surfaced in the wake of the Great Revolt. By isolating those nationalists who showed no interest in cooperating with the French, and cultivating others who believed that some degree of cooperation was the last option available, he attracted to his side a small but influential group of ambitious and intelligent nationalist politicians, headed by Jamil Mardam. Using this strategy he had been able to get an Organic Law written and ratified. But, a dangerous flaw marred his strategy and caused it to founder over the issue of treaty negotiations. This was the split between the Damascus and Aleppo Bloc leaders, aggravated by the different policies of the French Delegates in those towns. In the 1931–32 elections, Damascus Bloc chiefs eventually gained entry to Parliament. In Aleppo, the primaries were fixed by the French to exclude the Bloc. The manipulated results generated cynicism in Aleppo and nationalist leaders there consequently doubted that anything acceptable could

---

[61] *Ibid.*; Rabbath, *Courte Histoire*, pp. 117, 142. Ponsot was not the last French High Commissioner to serve in Syria and then in Morocco. Gabriel Puaux, High Commissioner in 1939–1940, became Resident in Morocco in 1943, but with no previous knowledge of conditions in the country; see also, *L'annuaire diplomatique* (1938), pp. 329–30.

[62] FO 371/4159, vol. 16974. Todd to Simon, 20 July 1933.

[63] Rabbath, *Courte Histoire*, pp. 142–43.

be gained by following the conciliatory course mapped out by the Damascus Bloc. Aleppine nationalists were also visibly jealous of their Damascus colleagues, whom the High Commission had courted for several years. Lacking a stake in either Parliament or government, Aleppo nationalists had nothing to lose by adopting a purist, uncompromising political line. Hananu and other leaders felt that as long as they were not part of the political equation, then Jamil Mardam and his more moderate colleagues had to be prevented from effecting the type of compromise that would allow them to reap all the political benefits.

Ponsot had wooed the Mardam faction in Damascus because he found it to be fairly accommodating. He hoped that by drawing out Jamil Mardam and his allies, they would, in turn, attract greater numbers of hardliners to their conciliatory position. But Ponsot was ultimately unable to divide the Bloc or to offer the sort of concessions that would allow negotiations to continue. His task had also been made more difficult by a long period of political instability in France during which conservatives had the upper hand until 1932, when they were replaced by the Center-Left, which was itself deeply divided and preoccupied with the painful effects of the world depression. During the whole period of his tenure, he faced attacks by conservative French parliamentarians and from the military who used their influence to restrict his diplomatic maneuverability. His bargains with the Bloc's moderate wing alienated many French officials both on his own staff and in Paris. These, swayed by a small but vocal number of interest groups concerned with Syrian affairs, feared that the attention Ponsot lavished upon the nationalists would lead to a premature French evacuation of the country.[64] When Ponsot finally left Syria, he also left the Syrian Question nearly where he had found it on first coming to the Levant seven years earlier.

PONSOT'S REPLACEMENT, Comte Damien Joseph Alfred Charles de Martel, arrived in Beirut on 12 October 1933. He was the sixth High Commissioner of France to Syria and Lebanon. Previously Ambassador in Tokyo, Martel was an aristocrat, a pragmatic politician, and a courtly diplomat.[65] He was also a man of action and within two days of his arrival he pro-

---

[64] George Antonius File, Antonius to Rogers, 16 May 1933. The French Chief of the Political Bureau, M. Chauvel, reported this reaction of French officials to Antonius.

[65] Martel's appointment was made by the Daladier government in July 1933. The government fell on October 24. FO 371/2141, vol. 20849, 6 May 1937. Conversation with Sir Geoffrey Furlonge (London, 26 March 1975) who described Martel as a cynic, who was much more of a politician than a diplomat or Quai d'Orsay official. Furlonge in the late thirties served as a British political officer in the Beirut Consulate; see also, L'annuaire diplomatique (1938), p. 307.

392   HONORABLE COOPERATION

ceeded to Damascus with the sole aim of accomplishing what Ponsot had failed to do: negotiate a treaty. His approach to the treaty, however, was not at all similar to Ponsot's. He saw the issue of the treaty as a stumbling block which had to be removed one way or another in order to free himself for the more important task of laying the foundations of an economic revival in a country suffering from the world depression. During the following month, Martel worked closely with the ʿAzm government to elaborate the terms of the treaty and to convince deputies to vote for it, sometimes even by financial inducements from the High Commission's *fonds secrets*.[66]

This sudden flurry of diplomatic activity[67] did not elicit a strong response from the National Bloc, chiefly owing to news from Palestine of violent demonstrations by the Arab population of Jaffa against Jewish immigration.[68] For some time Syrian nationalists had refrained from engaging in mass political activities,[69] but the Palestine issue at this moment was an excellent focus for such activities. The fear that Jewish colonization would expel the Arab population of Palestine from the land provided fertile ground on which pan-Arab agitators could sow seeds of resistance not just to the Zionist movement and Britain, but to all foreign occupation.[70]

On this occasion, the National Bloc found it convenient to cooperate with two recently established Muslim organizations: the Society of Islamic Civilization (Jamʿiyyat al-tamaddun al-islami) and the Society of Islamic Guidance (Jamʿiyyat al-hidaya al-islami). Both organizations were led by the religious establishment in Damascus. Their members were small shopkeepers, teachers, lawyers, doctors, workers, and students; their primary focus was a desire for Muslim education based on a mixture of modernistic and *salafi* or religious reformist ideas, by which Muslim ethics and morals, nationalism, and anti-imperialist feelings could be spread.[71] Previously these two societies were known to have engaged in anti-French protests against French control of the *Awqaf* administration and of the Muslim-owned Hijaz Railway.[72]

At a meeting on November 1, the ʿulama' of Damascus, in conjunction with the National Bloc, decided to use the occasion of the anniversary of

[66] FO 371/7071, vol. 16974. *The Times* (London), (21 Nov. 1933).

[67] Even radical nationalists paid visits to Martel, including Ibrahim Hananu who made a special trip from his village to greet him when he passed through Aleppo on October 20. MAE, Syrie–Liban 1930–40. Martel to MAE, 20 Oct. 1933, vol. 486, pp. 223–25.

[68] Porath, *The Palestine Arab National Movement*, vol. 2, p. 45.

[69] For example, the annual commemoration of the Battle of Maysalun had passed on July 24 with very little commotion.

[70] FO 371/6825, vol. 16932. MacKereth to Simon, 1 Nov. 1933.

[71] See Chapter 23.

[72] *Oriente Moderno*, 14 (1934), p. 438.

the Balfour Declaration to hold a massive demonstration. A complete closure of the bazaars followed on November 2. Attacks upon the central police station and attempts to enter the Jewish quarter in the old city and the British Consulate resulted in numerous arrests and injuries, and a few deaths.[73]

In Aleppo, ʿAbd al-Rahman al-Kayyali called for a march on the British Consulate in that town; but, in a surprising move, Ibrahim Hananu vetoed the proposal, claiming that at this stage demonstrations were likely to do more harm than good to the nationalist cause. A second attempt on November 3 to emulate events in Damascus failed when M. Lavastre let it be known that he would not tolerate such actions. As the Aleppo Bloc well knew, the French Delegate was not an individual to be crossed.[74]

By the time the nationalists had a chance to regain their composure, the new High Commissioner had already persuaded Haqqi al-ʿAzm to sign the treaty, which he did on November 16.[75] Two days earlier the National Bloc had received warnings from Salim Jambart that ʿAzm would sign. After a dramatic scene in a Damascus church in which Jambart prayed for his own personal salvation and that of the Syrian nation, he resigned from government.[76] The terms of the treaty were too unfavorable, even for this moderate Aleppine merchant. Martel's next move was to send the treaty to Parliament where Shakir Niʿmat al-Shaʿbani was rumored to be distributing cash from the *fonds secrets* to deputies, to insure a favorable vote.[77]

The text of the treaty was introduced to Parliament on November 21. Inside the Chamber, guards were posted in the event of an outbreak of violence. In attendance was the National Bloc's delegation of 17 deputies, who had agreed to suspend their boycott of Parliament. Anticipating the worst, M. Weber interrupted the discussion of the treaty to read out an edict of prorogation. But before he could finish, the nationalists managed to swing a majority of deputies to vote against the treaty. Weber, under instructions from Martel, refused to accept the legality of the vote and suspended the Chamber for four months.[78]

---

[73] FO 371/7505, vol. 13976. MacKereth to FO, 9 Nov. 1933.

[74] FO 371/7010, vol. 16392. P. Cowan (Aleppo) to FO, 9 Nov. 1933.

[75] MAE, Syrie–Liban 1930–40. Martel Telegrams, 18-22 Nov. 1933, vol. 487, pp. 55–82. FO 371/7245, vol. 16974. MacKereth to Simon, 29 Nov. 1933.

[76] Conversation with Edmond Rabbath (Beirut, 3 Sept. 1975). Jambart was immediately replaced by another Uniate from Aleppo, Latif al-Ghanima, who was also a deputy.

[77] It was rumored that Shaʿbani received £S 20,000 from the High Commission. See FO 371/525, vol. 17944. MacKereth to Simon, 4 Jan. 1934.

[78] MAE, Syrie–Liban 1930–40. Martel Telegrams, 18–22 Nov. 1933, vol. 487, pp. 43–44; FO 371/525, vol. 17944. MacKereth to Simon, 4 Jan. 1934. For the French analysis (version) of why the treaty was rejected, see MAE, Syrie–Liban 1930–40. Martel (Damascus) to

Apart from the well-known articles concerning the gradual transfer of authority from France to the Syrian Republic over the next four years, the treaty met few of the National Bloc's demands. Its terms were vague, creating ample room for suspicion that France was not resolved to relinquish her hold on Syria. The military clause in Article 5, for instance, was insubstantial, causing fears that the newly built fortification on the heights west of the city meant continued French domination. Article 6 allowed France a generous number of its own advisers and magistrates. And, by Article 3 of Protocol B, France would also be allowed to keep a tight hold on Syria's purse strings. But most offensive was France's refusal to compromise on the question of Syrian unity.[79] By a series of letters attached to the treaty, the Alawite and Druze states were to remain detached from the Syrian state and administered separately by France.[80]

Despite France's attempt to prolong the life of the treaty by suspending Parliament, the treaty was dead. Already after only two months of hard work at his new post, M. de Martel returned to France for a long vacation.[81]

MAE, 24 Nov. 1933, vol. 487, pp. 106–9; *Ibid.*, "Note du Chauvel," 3 Feb. 1934, vol. 488, pp. 50–60.

[79] FO 371/202, vol. 17944. MacKereth to Simon, 8 Dec. 1933.
[80] Longrigg, *Syria*, p. 197.
[81] FO 371/2547, vol. 17944. MacKereth to Simon, 3 April 1934.

PART VI

NEW APPROACHES, 1933–1936

CHAPTER FIFTEEN

RADICALIZATION

By 1933, Syria was deep in the clutches of the depression. Between 1930 and 1934, 150,000 men were unemployed in the French mandated territories, or the equivalent of 15 to 20 percent of the labor force.[1] According to the Damascus Chamber of Commerce, the collapse of handicrafts had caused the unemployment of some 77,000 Syrian men, women, and children.[2] Meanwhile, the local tanning and dying industries were in decline, with only 14 out of 30 shops in Damascus working anywhere near capacity. The town's renowned confectionery industry also faced severe competition from Palestine, which received sugar duty free. Whereas in 1932 there were between 700 and 750 trades operating in Damascus, by 1933 the number had fallen to 400.[3] Moreover, the growth of new, modern industries—also a feature of the depression years in Syria—was not fast enough to absorb this unemployment.[4]

Industry was not the only sector of the Syrian economy to suffer. Marketing and commerce were hard hit by the devaluation of the French franc, the decline in European and American production for export, the almost complete cessation of remittances from abroad and the reversal of the emigration cycle, and the inability and/or refusal of Syrians of all occupations to repay their loans on schedule. Many local business and financial concerns went bankrupt.[5] The value of Syria's total exports between 1929 and 1933 fell by one-half, while the value of imports fell by 38 percent, increasing the trade deficit by 18 percent.[6] Among Syria's leading exports, wool fell by 86 percent, cocoons and raw silk by 81 percent, and locally manufactured textiles by 56 percent.[7] Furthermore, between 1931 and 1933, Syria's agricultural imports rose 19 percent while agricultural exports, normally three-fourths of total Syrian exports, fell by 47 percent.[8]

[1] Hershlag, *Introduction*, p. 231.

[2] Al-Nayal, "Industry," p. 69.

[3] FO 371/4055, vol. 16974, 1 July 1933.

[4] George Hakim, "Industry," pp. 172–73.

[5] Himadeh, *The Monetary and Banking System*, p. 219; also see various MWT, *Registres commerciales* (uncatalogued), 1930–1934.

[6] Calculated from *Statistiques Générales du Commerce Extérieur des Etats du Levant sous Mandat Français* (1930–1933).

[7] See Appendices in Himadeh (ed.), *Economic Organization of Syria*, pp. 418–19.

[8] Calculated from Table XVI in Albert Khuri, "Agriculture," in Himadeh (ed.), *Economic Organization of Syria*, p. 111.

The depression did not loosen, in any perceptible way, France's economic hold over Syria. As long as the Syrian pound was still pegged to the franc, the Syrian economy had little room to engage in its own development free of French controls. The modern, Syrian-owned industries that emerged during the depression were either import substitution industries, like cement, or industries uncompetitive with French production.[9]

The French argued that Syria weathered the depression years better than most countries because it was largely an agricultural country in which the majority of the population consisted of self-sufficient peasants. By the early thirties, however, the agrarian sector in Syria had been sufficiently commercialized to be drawn into the world market; since peasants produced cash crops and bought food with the proceeds, they too suffered.[10] Peasants also suffered from a crippling climatic crisis during this time, which drastically reduced production levels. To counter the drought, the Ministry of Interior issued a most unusual decree. The yo-yo, a popular children's toy which had recently been introduced in Syria, was banned. According to the Mufti of Damascus, who had sponsored the decree, the yo-yo's "exasperating motion" was responsible for the drought. Three days after the ban it rained, elevating the Mufti's reputation to new heights among the ignorant and superstitious.[11] For Syrian agriculture, however, the rains had come too late. Since the fall of 1932, peasants from the Hawran and other agricultural areas had been migrating to Damascus in a steady stream, increasing the population of beggars in the capital.[12] This exodus followed the severest drought since World War I (some said "in living memory").[13] People and animals were dying of thirst. The government sent water twice a week by train to Hawrani villages along the railway line, which was sold for £S 3 per 15 tons; but this did little to improve conditions in a region whose water resources, even in normal times, were scarce.[14] The drought greatly aggravated the situation of the southern Syrian tribes, which now had to send for water three or four hours away from their encampments. Already the increase in motorized transport was eroding their staple trade in camels and their flocks of sheep were declining in number. Reports of Bedouin parents

[9] See the informative study of A. S. Bagh, *L'Industrie à Damas entre 1928 et 1958. Etude de géographie économique* (Damascus 1961).

[10] Norman Burns and Allen D. Edwards, "Foreign Trade," in Himadeh (ed.), *Economic Organization of Syria* , pp. 241–55.

[11] FO 371/2092, vol. 16974. MacKereth to Simon, 21 March 1933.

[12] *Ibid.*

[13] E. Epstein [Elath], "Notes from a Paper on the Present Conditions in the Hauran," *Journal of the Royal Central Asian Society*, 23 (1936), pp. 612–13; FO 371/2092, vol. 16974, 31 March 1933.

[14] Epstein, "Notes," pp. 612–13.

selling infant girls as domestics in the towns to provide for further means of existence abounded.[15] Indeed, famine began to reach alarming proportions and, with the almost complete lack of fodder, the price of livestock fell sharply. Wheat, which was Syria's most important crop—half of cultivated land was given over annually to its production—fell by 16 percent in 1932–1933, and by much more in the worst stricken areas of the Hawran.[16] In the Ghuta and Qalamun, a severe late frost and violent winds damaged 60 percent of the apricot trees in mid-March 1933, badly affecting the spring harvest of this most valuable export.[17]

Peasants who had been unable to pay back either the interest or principal on outstanding loans from town moneylenders were now denied fresh loans. Taxation in previous years had been so heavy that even rich farmers found themselves without reserves.[18] In Damascus and other cities, where the economic "crisis" had already created a large glut on the labor market, the influx of peasant refugees from the countryside exacerbated a deteriorating situation. There was a marked increase of brigandage in the countryside and of larceny in the towns. Trade was almost stagnant. Owing to high prices and lower customs duties in neighboring countries, an increase in smuggling was reported, particularly from Palestine and Transjordan. In February 1933, cotton piece-good merchants in Damascus called for the government to patrol the Syrian borders more vigilantly,[19] and on March 8, flour millers of the Maydan quarter (who were often big grain merchants and moneylenders in the Hawran) went on strike against the recent reduction of import duties on flour.[20] Already one of the largest mills in Damascus had shut down in November 1932.[21] A member of the Jewish National Fund reported that in the spring some 25,000 to 30,000 Hawranis fled their lands, 90 percent to Palestine (the remainder to Damascus and Beirut). In Palestine, these refugees were absorbed into the Jewish-controlled sector of the labor market, though by October, 30 percent had returned home. The same source claimed to have saved the peasants from starvation, and Syria from massive upheaval.[22]

[15] FO 371/525, vol. 19744. MacKereth to Simon, 4 Jan. 1934.

[16] FO 371/2092, vol. 16974, 31 March 1933; also see Table II in Khuri, "Agriculture," p. 78.

[17] FO 371/4055, vol. 16974. Todd (Quarterly Report, April–June 1933), July 1933.

[18] Epstein, "Notes," pp. 612–13.

[19] A great deal of smuggling was also reported from Syria into Turkey where customs rates were much higher. FO 371/6220, vol. 16976. Satow to FO, 10 October 1933.

[20] Syria imported five times more flour than she exported. FO 371/2092, vol. 16974, 31 March 1933; Khuri, "Agriculture," Tables XVII, XIX, pp. 113, 114.

[21] The Shaykh and Mahayni Mill. MWT, "Rapport de la liquidation de la Société Sheikh et Mahayni," Damascus, 4 July 1937, Dossier 170/1934. Tribunal de Ière Instance: Affaire commerciale.

[22] Epstein, "Notes," pp. 612–14; FO 371/2547, vol. 17944. MacKereth to Simon, 3 April 1934.

The most serious political crisis of 1933 was a crisis of confidence in the National Bloc. In the six years since its appearance, the Bloc had managed to keep the nationalist movement almost exclusively on a political footing by fixing the attention of Syria's urban masses on the activities of the French who, despite new signs of weakness in their imperial order, remained the final source of authority in the country. By the summer of 1933, however, the Bloc was no closer to solving the critical political question than it had been in 1928, when it began to follow its evolutionary strategy of "honorable cooperation." Not only had the Bloc been unsuccessful in the political arena so far, but other than political problems were now coming to the fore. The Bloc had no social or economic reform program to meet these new issues.

THE LEAGUE OF NATIONAL ACTION

On 19 August 1933, a party of young men traveling by car from Damascus crossed the Lebanese frontier and stopped to rest at Shtura. Following instructions, they opened a sealed envelope which they had been careful to conceal while going through the border checkpoint. The instructions were explicit: "Move to Qarna'il, the conference begins tomorrow." The following day, the opening session of what proved to be the most important interwar gathering of radical pan-Arabists was held shrouded in secrecy in this Lebanese mountain village.[23]

Preparations for the Qarna'il Conference had been made well in advance by a committee of three based in Damascus.[24] But French Intelligence caught wind of some of the committee's plans and was on the lookout for known political agitators. In fact, some men had been prevented from entering Syria from Iraq, Palestine, and Transjordan, though the majority of those invited managed to reach Qarna'il. The conference got under way as planned on August 20. In attendance was an elite group of nearly 50 radical Arab nationalists from all over the Arab East.[25] These men were united by one aim: to set the national independence movements in the Arab territories on a firmer footing by systematically coordinating their activities.[26]

After four days of rigorous discourse, the participants at Qarna'il announced the formation of a new political organization which was to be

[23] Conversation with Akram Zu'aytir (Beirut, 6 Aug. 1975). Zu'aytir was one of the young men traveling from Damascus to Qarna'il.
[24] The three men were 'Abd al-Razzaq al-Dandashi, 'Irfan Jallad, and Shafiq Sulayman. Conversation with Zu'aytir (Beirut, 6 Aug. 1975).
[25] For a list of participants, see Akram Zu'aytir, "Ittifaq al-'arab 'ala wada' lubnan al-khass," al-Hawadith (Beirut), no. 978 (Aug. 1975), p. 66.
[26] Conversation with Zu'aytir (Beirut, 6 Aug. 1975).

based in Syria but connected to similar parties in the neighboring Arab territories. Its name: the League of National Action (ʿUsbat al-ʿamal al-qawmi). The new organization embodied the beliefs and ambitions of a new generation of angry young nationalists which had begun to emerge throughout the Arab East. The term *qawmi* (literally: belonging to a nation) was indicative of the League's orientation; nationalists used *qawmiyya* to mark a "feeling of loyalty to the whole Arab nation" and thus distinguished it from the term *wataniyya*—the preference of the National Bloc—which denoted an attachment to the fatherland, the specific country of one's birth.[27] Its goals were Arab sovereignty, independence, and comprehensive Arab unity, and it particularly emphasized the need for economic development and integration in order to wage a successful struggle against the exploitation of foreign powers and against feudal landlords. With specific reference to Syria, the program demanded the rejection of the policy of "honorable cooperation" and of all attempts to get the people to accept the fraudulently elected Parliament and French-appointed government. Finally, it warned that all promises of treaties made at this time (August 1933) were, in fact, synonymous with the extension of imperialism.[28]

From its program, it is clear that the League of National Action was neither socialist nor Marxist-Leninist. For class struggle it substituted nationalist struggle. It was reformist and, in some ways, populist. The League's program also revealed a strong tendency toward authoritarianism.

The roots of Qarnaʾil can be traced to the autumn of 1929 when Farid Zayn al-Din, a brilliant 23 year-old student of economics in Paris and the head of the Arab student organization of France, traveled to Geneva to meet two like-minded men, Darwish al-Miqdadi, a Baghdad schoolteacher of Palestinian origin who had graduated from the American University of Beirut in 1922 and Nafiʿ Chalabi, an Aleppine whom Zayn al-Din had known when both were students in Berlin. At the meeting, Zayn al-Din, a Druze of Lebanese origin whose father had been an Ottoman civil servant, had little trouble convincing his colleagues of the urgent need to form a clandestine organization of Arab nationalists with branches in each of the Arabic-speaking countries. The idea of a secret society was certainly not foreign to these young men; they were inspired by al-Fatat and al-ʿAhd. And they all had some previous experience as

---

[27] For a fuller discussion of these terms see: S. G. Haim, "Islam and the Theory of Arab Nationalism," in W. Z. Laqueur (ed.), *The Middle East in Transition* (London, 1958), pp. 287–98.

[28] ʿUsbat al-ʿamal al-qawmi, *Bayan al-muʾtamar al-taʾsisi*. Pamphlet (Damascus, 24 Aug. 1933). Also see Farzat, *al-Hayah al-hizbiyya*, pp. 138–40.

student leaders, particularly Zayn al-Din, on whom the French Sûreté kept a watchful eye.[29] Its first name was the Arab Liberation Society. Among its rather ambitious aims, three were of particular importance: to establish relations with key pan-Arab nationalist leaders; to set up clandestine branches of their organization in the Arab territories; and to establish a series of frontal organizations.[30]

Shukri al-Quwwatli was one of the first key pan-Arabists with whom the Liberation Society had links. Zayn al-Din had been introduced to Quwwatli in Berlin in 1927, by another Lebanese Druze, Shakib Arslan,[31] and a warm friendship developed between the two. Zayn al-Din viewed Quwwatli as a sincere and dedicated pan-Arabist; Quwwatli at the time was about to embark on Arslan's new project for the unification of the Arab countries.[32] Through Quwwatli, the Arab Liberation Society gained access to other Syrian Istiqlalis, most notably Nabih al-'Azma, residing in Palestine. The other senior radical nationalist looked up to by the Arab Liberation Society was Yasin al-Hashimi, an ex-Sharifian officer, a noted military strategist, a member of al-'Ahd, and, for a short while, Faysal's Chief of Staff in Damascus. Hashimi also was one of the loudest Iraqi critics of the Anglo-Iraqi Treaty of 1930, which he felt granted but tenuous independence to his country.[33]

The Arab Liberation Society's second strategy was to establish a central coordinating committee with branches throughout the Arab world. Between the end of 1929 and the Qarna'il Conference, contact organizations were formed, first in Beirut and Baghdad and then in Syria, Palestine, Transjordan, Tunisia, Morocco, and Yemen. But the effective core was concentrated in Iraq, Lebanon, Syria, and, to a lesser extent, in Palestine. Zayn al-Din headed a secret Executive Committee that included Darwish al-Miqdadi and Wasif Kamal, a Palestinian intellectual from Nablus; Mahmud al-Hindi, an Iraqi army officer of Syrian origin; Ahmad al-Sharabati, an American-trained engineer and the son of the nationalist merchant, 'Uthman al-Sharabati; and 'Ali 'Abd al-Karim al-Dandashi, a Boy Scout leader. Inspired (according to Zayn al-Din) by Communist

[29] Conversation with Farid Zayn al-Din (Damascus, 18 Oct. 1975); Faris, *Man huwa 1949*; AUB, *Directory of Alumni, 1870–1952* (Beirut, 1953), p. 165. Darwish al-Miqdadi was born in 1899 in Taybih, Palestine. He was first a teacher and then a director of secondary schools in Baghdad and Mosul in 1926–1936, before doing postgraduate work in Berlin in 1936–1939. *Ibid.*, p. 142.

[30] Conversation with Farid Zayn al-Din (Damascus, 18 Oct. 1975).

[31] Like Arslan, Zayn al-Din was much closer to being a Sunni Muslim. In fact he denied his Lebanese heritage, claiming to be originally from the Jabal Druze in Syria. He also married into Sunni Muslim society in Damascus by taking the hand of an 'Azm. *Ibid.*

[32] *Ibid.*

[33] *Ibid.* Also see Batatu, *The Old Social Classes*, pp. 195–205; Khaldun S. Husry, "King Faysal I," p. 327. Hashimi had come out behind Faysal's Syrian throne plans in 1932–1933.

Party organization in Europe, the Executive Committee saw to it that cells were established in the different territories, each one composed of two to five men, with only one member serving as the contact with other cell informants. In this way, members of regional cells never knew the members of other cells or the central leadership of the Arab Liberation Society.[34] Together these cells, which were instructed to follow one of three designated programs, known as the yellow, green, and red books, formed the base of a pyramid structure which linked cell informants to one another and to individual members of the anonymous Executive.[35]

All cells had one common strategy: to infiltrate existing pan-Arabist organizations and to encourage the formation of frontal parties whose activities the Arab Liberation Society Executive could steer. In 1932, two such organizations were active and ripe for penetration: the Ahali group in Iraq and the Istiqlal Party of Palestine.

The Ahali group had coalesced around the Baghdad newspaper of the same name in January 1932. It included among its members two young lawyers, 'Abd al-Fattah Ibrahim and Muhammad Hadid, who had known Farid Zayn al-Din during their student days in the mid-twenties at the American University of Beirut. Inspired by a mixture of ideas, including Fabian socialism, Marxism, and Darwinism, the radical nationalist Ahali group emphasized "popular reformism." It also supported parliamentary democracy and rejected "class struggle" for "national unity." Sometime in the summer of 1932, Farid Zayn al-Din, who the year before had re-

[34] Conversations with Farid Zayn al-Din (Damascus, 18 Oct. 1975); 'Ali 'Abd al-Karim al-Dandashi (Damascus, 9 March 1976). Other Syrians connected to the Executive Committee were Qustantin Zurayq, a Damascene Professor of History at the American University of Beirut, and Jubran Shamiyya, an AUB graduate and lawyer trained in Geneva, who was the son of Tawfiq Shamiyya.

[35] The information provided on the Arab Liberation Society (ALS) and its contribution to the Arab nationalist movement is sketchy and therefore probably only a small part of the story. I first learned of the organization from Farid Zayn al-Din during a conversation with him in Damascus on 18 October 1975. After supplying some details for about an hour, he suddenly turned the discussion to an unrelated subject. When I tried to return to the topic of the "Liberation Society," he told me that he was vowed to secrecy but suggested that perhaps 'Ali 'Abd al-Karim al-Dandashi had something to say. Three days later, on October 21, I visited Dandashi, the Syrian Boy Scout leader, at his Damascus headquarters where he was still active. He added a few more details including the names of Qustantin Zurayq, George Tomeh, and Jubran Shamiyya. He also mentioned the oath of secrecy but intimated that the whole story could be told by Zayn al-Din. (It should be mentioned that in an earlier interview in July with Jubran Shamiyya, he made no mention of the Society.) On returning to Damascus, I tried again to elicit a response on the topic of the Society from Dandashi and Zayn al-Din. Dandashi now criticized Zayn al-Din for somehow steering the ALS off course in the late thirties. He provided no details, however. I returned to Zayn al-Din twice in April 1976; although he was quite revealing about certain nationalists, particularly Shukri al-Quwwatli, he remained tight-lipped on the subject of the Arab Liberation Society. Zayn al-Din has since died.

turned from Paris to become an economics instructor at the American University of Beirut, resigned his post and moved to Baghdad to become a schoolteacher, a respectable cover for his covert political activities. His post was arranged by Darwish al-Miqdadi.

Young political activists in the Arab countries knew no national or colonial boundaries. Zayn al-Din was welcomed into the Ahali group[36] and he, along with four Iraqi comrades in Baghdad, formed the Iraqi delegation to the Qarna'il Conference in August 1933.[37] After the Qarna'il Conference, the Ahali group founded two cultural fronts: the Association for Combatting Illiteracy and the Baghdad Club. Less than two years later a new organization, Nadi Muthanna (Muthanna Club), appeared and absorbed the Baghdad Club, its founders including Farid Zayn al-Din and other members of the Iraqi delegation to Qarna'il. Nadi Muthanna's commitment to "disseminating the spirit of Arab nationalism, preserving Arab traditions, strengthening the sense of Arab manhood in youth, and creating a new Arab culture which would unite to the Arab heritage what is worthy in the civilization of the West" clearly echoed the program of the League of National Action and the ideas of men like Farid Zayn al-Din.[38]

The Istiqlal Party in Palestine had its origins in a general Islamic Congress held in Jerusalem in December 1931. Called for by the Mufti, Hajj Amin al-Husayni, the Congress was designed to display pan-Islamic solidarity against Zionist colonization and British imperialism in Palestine, and to boost Husayni's own prestige.[39] In addition to the various religious dignitaries from the Arab-Islamic world, the Congress brought together nearly 40 members of al-Fatat/al-Istiqlal,[40] including several Syrian radical nationalists, such as Shukri al-Quwwatli, Nabih al-'Azma, already in Palestine, Khalid al-Hakim, at the time resident in Saudi Arabia, and Khayr al-Din al-Zirikli of the Executive Committee of the Syrian–Palestine Congress in Cairo.[41] Together with their Palestinian comrades, such as 'Izzat Darwaza, Subhi al-Khadra, and 'Awni 'Abd al-Hadi, they proposed that a general Arab Congress based on the principles of Arab unity and anti-regionalism be held in the coming year in Baghdad. This congress never materialized, mainly because the Iraqi government, under

[36] Conversation with Farid Zayn al-Din (Damascus, 18 Oct. 1975). AUB, *Directory of Alumni*, pp. 142, 163.

[37] Sadiq al-Bassam, Naji Ma'ruf, 'Abd al-Majid al-'Abbas, and Sa'id Fahim. See, Zu'aytir, "Ittifaq al-'arab," pp. 64–66.

[38] Conversation with Farid Zayn al-Din (Damascus, 18 Oct. 1975); Batatu, *The Old Social Classes*, pp. 298–99.

[39] Porath, *The Palestine Arab National Movement*, vol. 2, p. 12.

[40] *Ibid.*, p. 123.

[41] FO 371/5584, vol. 16086. H. P. Rice (CID Palestine), 21 Sept. 1932.

British pressure on the eve of Iraq's acceptance into the League of Nations, refused to host such a gathering.[42]

Denied a pan-Arab platform, a more exclusively Palestinian group was formed called the Istiqlal Party. It was established in August 1932 by a group of radicals of the professional middle class and provincial notability of Palestine, several of whom had been behind the abortive Arab Congress idea, and who were closely linked to Shukri al-Quwwatli and Nabih al-ʿAzma. Like the older Syrian Istiqlalis, Palestinian Istiqlalis were pan-Arabist, anti-imperialist, and militantly anti-Zionist. They were also not Jerusalemites; their leading members—Darwaza, ʿAbd al-Hadi, and Akram Zuʿaytir—came from the Nablus area where the term "southern Syria" was still fairly widely used in everyday political parlance. Nor were they supported by the prominent political and aristocratic families of Jerusalem or encouraged by Hajj Amin's party. Their youthfulness and idealism, however, proved to be very attractive to such organizations as the Boy Scouts and the Young Men's Muslim Association, both of which came to be largely influenced by the Istiqlal Party.[43]

The formation of the Palestine Istiqlal Party gave the Arab Liberation Society two needed links: Nabih al-ʿAzma and Wasif Kamal from Nablus. Kamal was a member of the clandestine Liberation Society Executive. Although he refrained from joining political organizations—in theory, a requirement of all Executive members—and thus never belonged to the Istiqlal Party, he did maintain regular contacts with Istiqlalis.[44] Nabih al-ʿAzma was much admired by the Arab Liberation Society Executive as well as by Palestinian Istiqlalis, particularly ʿIzzat Darwaza, whom ʿAzma had cultivated since their first meeting in Damascus at the end of the First World War. Through Darwaza, Akram Zuʿaytir met and came to admire ʿAzma.[45] Akram Zuʿaytir headed the Palestine delegation to Qarnaʾil. Wasif Kamal was also on the delegation.[46]

For the Arab Liberation Society, there still remained the problem of setting up a frontal organization in Syria. The key, as it turned out, rested with a young intellectually motivated lawyer named ʿAbd al-Razzaq al-Dandashi, a member of a large and prosperous clan of feudalists whose fief was Tall Kalakh. Dandashi himself grew up in Tripoli. In 1929, when Farid Zayn al-Din first embarked on his "revolutionary program," the 30-year-old Dandashi was studying law in Belgium, where he also partic-

---

[42] Porath, *The Palestine Arab National Movement*, vol. 2, p. 124.

[43] *Ibid.*, pp. 125–26.

[44] Conversation with Farid Zayn al-Din (Damascus, 18 Oct. 1975).

[45] Conversation with Akram Zuʿaytir (Beirut, 11 Aug. 1975); FO 371/5584, vol. 16086. Rice (CID Palestine), 21 Sept. 1932.

[46] Zuʿaytir, "Ittifaq al-ʿarab," pp. 64–66.

ipated in Arab student politics. On his return to Syria, he settled in Damascus to practice law.

By 1932, the slight, bespectacled Dandashi had already won a reputation as a courageous and uncompromising champion of the Arab nationalist cause. He was an impassioned orator, whose popularity with high school and law students, young journalists, and café intellectuals was growing daily. The Damascus cell of the Arab Liberation Society carefully cultivated him to prepare the groundwork for Qarna'il. He eventually became Chairman of the three-man preparatory committee of the conference and the first elected Secretary-General of the League. Yet, he never even knew of the existence of the Arab Liberation Society.[47]

The League of National Action which came out of the Qarna'il Conference took over the coordination of pan-Arab activities from the amorphous Arab Liberation Society. Based in Damascus, it naturally had to take a stand on National Bloc strategy and activities. Radicalized intellectuals and political activists, like ʿAbd al-Razzaq al-Dandashi, were alarmed by the National Bloc's activities. First, the Bloc was preoccupied with day-to-day political affairs and had no time to conceive of the social and economic basis of the new state once independence finally came. Secondly, the ties binding the older generation of nationalists were largely based on personal relations and thus had a tendency to loosen over time, especially as Syria remained exposed to the vagaries of French Mandate policy. Indeed, this new generation expressed profound fear that the National Bloc had drifted away from its heritage of pan-Arabism, rooted in the secret societies and personal experiences of the past, and toward a local Syrian nationalism. The Bloc's policy of "honorable cooperation" was the best indication of this break with the past and with the original principles of the movement.

Given the age of the founders of the League of National Action and their lack of a political organization among the urban masses, the only way they could express their dissatisfaction with the well-entrenched leadership of the Syrian independence movement was to mount a challenge to the Bloc's youth wing, the Nationalist Youth.

YOUTHFUL STRUGGLES

The Nationalist Youth (al-Shabab al-watani) had begun to take shape in 1929, at the encouragement of Fakhri Bey al-Barudi whose reputation as a patron of educated youth in Damascus was unrivalled. Barudi's large house in the Qanawat quarter served as a regular meeting place for high school and university students. But the actual day-to-day politicization

---

[47] Conversations with Farid Zayn al-Din (Damascus, 18 Oct. 1975); Akram Zuʿaytir (Beirut, 6 Aug. 1975); ʿAli ʿAbd al-Karim al-Dandashi (Damascus, 9 March 1976).

and organization of this elite (as distinguished from the youth of the poorer neighborhoods of Damascus, who were more closely linked to the traditional quarter chiefs or *qabadayat* and who tended to be much less inspired by intellectual or articulate ideological considerations) were carried out by a group of young men who were not much older than their students, headed by Mahmud al-Bayruti, the novelties store owner on the rue Rami, and Khalid al-Shiliq, an unemployed lawyer from al-Qanawat. But, by the end of 1931, signs of a split within the Nationalist Youth over the Bloc's policy of "honorable cooperation" and its neglect of pan-Arabism surfaced, first in the Boy Scout movement and, by the end of 1932, among student leaders. These splits enabled the League of National Action to build its own political base in the capital and elsewhere in the country.

The history of the Boy Scout movement in Syria dates from 1912 when two Indian Muslims studying at the Syrian Protestant College founded a troop in Beirut. Two years later another troop of Muslim Scouts (al-Kishaf al-muslim) was established in Damascus, though the war curtailed its activities. In 1919, the Muslim Scouts were reactivated in Damascus, this time for a duration of seven years, until the Great Revolt forced their suspension. In Aleppo, a troop of Muslim Scouts had been established which collapsed in 1924. It did not reappear on an official basis until 1931.[48]

Not long after the end of the Great Revolt, the Muslim Scouting movement was revived in Damascus. In July 1927, a new organization called the Ghuta Troop was formed with the blessing of the High Commission.[49] Its founders were three youth leaders: ʿAli ʿAbd al-Karim al-Dandashi (a cousin of ʿAbd al-Razzaq);[50] Ahmad al-Shihabi, a law student who came from a prominent family of south Lebanon;[51] and Faʾiz al-Dalati, a law student from a poorer branch of one of the principal families engaged in the Damascus confectionery industry.[52] None of these scout masters was willing to affiliate with the National Bloc, and eventually Fakhri al-Barudi saw to it that a new troop, the Umayyad, was formed as an appendage of the Nationalist Youth in 1929. For Barudi, who strongly believed that the nationalist movement required its own militia, the Umayyad Troop was to be the prototype of the future Syrian National Army. Over the next two years it also became a bitter rival of the independent Ghuta Troop.[53]

[48] *Ibid.*; Anonymous, "Note sur le Scoutisme musulman en Syrie et au Liban," CHEAM, no. 684 (Beirut, 4 April 1944), pp. 1–2.
[49] *Ibid.*, p. 2.
[50] Conversation with ʿAli ʿAbd al-Karim al-Dandashi (Damascus, 9 March 1976).
[51] Conversation with the Amir Ahmad al-Shihabi (Beirut, 21 Jan. 1976).
[52] Anonymous, "Le Scoutisme musulman," p. 2.
[53] Conversation with ʿAli ʿAbd al-Karim al-Dandashi (Damascus, 9 March 1976). Dan-

In 1929, both the Ghuta and the Umayyad Troops became affiliates of the Beirut Scouting movement, which had received international recognition in 1922. By 1931, the Umayyad Troop, headed by Mahmud al-Bayruti and comparatively well-financed by the National Bloc, ran into considerable difficulty and disintegrated by the end of the year; some of its scouts defected to the Ghuta Troop.[54]

Earlier that summer, the Ghuta Troop had decided that the time was ripe to federate Muslim Scouts throughout Syria, which would then enable the country to be represented on International Scouting Councils. To this idea, the High Commission in Beirut offered no opposition.[55] The first and only President of the Syrian Federation of Scouts during the Mandate was Dr. Rushdi al-Jabi, the son of an ex-Ottoman bureaucrat.[56] The daily affairs of the Federation, however, were left to its Executive Director, ʿAli ʿAbd al-Karim al-Dandashi.[57]

Before federating, the Muslim Scouting movement had been small and not particularly well organized. Most efforts were spent on training bright high school students as troop leaders. But soon the patience and diligence of the movement's leadership began to pay dividends. By 1933, the Muslim Scouts, now grouped into several troops concentrated in Damascus and in most big towns in Syria, numbered 3,000 members.[58] All of these troops were self-financed through dues and private contributions. Indeed, during the Mandate the Syrian government never officially sponsored the Boy Scouts.[59] By 1935, when the Scouting leadership opened its ranks to the religious minorities, membership had risen to 15,000.[60] Three years later, after divisions for Cub Scouts (ages 7–12) and Rover Scouts (18 and over) were added, the number of scouts in Syria swelled to 38,000.[61]

Three of the leaders of the Syrian Scouting movement, ʿAli ʿAbd al-Karim al-Dandashi, Rushdi al-Jabi, and Ahmad al-Shihabi, were among the founding members of the League of National Action in 1933.[62] But

---

dashi claims that at this time he and his colleagues made every effort to keep the Ghuta Troops out of partisan politics.

[54] Anonymous, "Le Scoutisme musulman," p. 2; Conversation with ʿAli ʿAbd al-Karim al-Dandashi (Damascus, 9 March 1976).

[55] Ibid.

[56] Faris, Man huwa 1949, p. 82; AUB, Directory of Alumni, p. 145.

[57] Conversation with ʿAli ʿAbd al-Karim al-Dandashi (Damascus, 9 March 1976).

[58] Anonymous, "Le Scoutisme musulman," p. 2.

[59] Conversation with ʿAli ʿAbd al-Karim al-Dandashi (Damascus, 9 March 1976).

[60] Ibid. By 1931, the Scouting movement was much more pan-Arab than pan-Islamic in character.

[61] Ibid. The figure of 15,000 was given by an anonymous French official in "Le Scoutisme musulman," p. 3.

[62] Jabi was President of the Qarnaʾil Conference.

there is still another thread in the story of Qarna'il, the foundation of the League of National Action, and the Syrian Scouting movement which needs to be tied, that of the Damascus *tajhiz*, the government high school in the capital.

There were two types of schools under the Mandate. One was the private foreign schools, which were mostly French and belonged either to one of the religious orders, such as the Lazarists or Jesuits, or to the *mission laïque*. These catered to the religious minorities and to the old Muslim bourgeois families of the towns, who preferred that their children not be raised in a popular milieu. In addition, each confessional group maintained its own schools which attracted children from its community and, in the case of the Christian minorities, competed with foreign mission schools. The other type of school was government-run and catered to the Muslim (and some Christian) elites.[63] In these schools, which were organized on a French model "with a twelve-year ladder of general education involving a primary-certificate examination," followed by *brevet* and *baccalauréat* examinations, direct French influence was less pervasive. Nevertheless, each government school had one director of French studies and French occupied a "prominent place in the curriculum," although the language of instruction was Arabic.[64] Government schools were also comparatively inexpensive. By 1933, tuition in all primary schools was free while secondary schools, which charged a yearly fee, also provided some assistance to the needy.[65]

During the Mandate, enrollment in the government school system grew at a quicker pace than it did in private and foreign schools. Growth, however, was not dramatic. Public education was still restricted to an elite and almost exclusively to boys. Whereas in 1924, 47 percent of all primary and secondary school students (23,783) in Syria were in government schools,[66] by 1934, a year after primary education became free, this proportion had risen to only 50 percent (37,786).[67] The increase was faster after 1929, when the budget for education began to rise steadily. For example, between 1925 and 1929 the average expenditure by the government on public education as a percentage of the Syrian budget was

[63] R. Montagne, "L'évolution de la jeunesse arabe," CHEAM, no. 244, n. pl. (21 June 1937).

[64] Roderic D. Mathews and Matta Akrawi, *Education in the Arab Countries of the Near East* (Washington, 1949), p. 325.

[65] Montagne, "L'évolution," p. 8; Mathews and Akrawi, *Education*, p. 340.

[66] MAE *Rapport à la Société des Nations sur la situation de la Syrie et du Liban, 1924,* Appendix 4, p. 95.

[67] FO 371/625, vol. 19022. MacKereth to FO, 7 Jan. 1935.

only 8 percent, whereas between 1930 and 1934 it averaged 12 percent, and rose to an average of 15.5 percent in the late thirties.[68]

The government school system rather than the private and foreign schools inculcated students with national ideals, thereby helping to fuel the independence struggle. Politicization took place at both the primary and secondary school levels, though it was in the secondary or preparatory schools, known as the *tajhiz*, that this process was most intense.

Compared to the few government secondary schools of the late Ottoman period in Syria which serviced the Muslim notability exclusively, the Mandate witnessed the critical extension of public instruction; the number of secondary schools increased from two in 1920 to fourteen in the early 1930s. In addition, the provision of scholarships and the modernization and expansion of school facilities now enabled the children of the professional middle classes in the towns, and an increasing number of children from the petty bourgeoisie, most notably the sons of small shop-owners and traders, to attend.[69] The model for secondary schools throughout Syria was, without a doubt, the Damascus *tajhiz*.

In late Ottoman times, there had been only one government secondary school in Damascus, Maktab ʿAnbar, which was located on the inner edge of the Jewish quarter in the old city. Conceived of as a national school, Maktab ʿAnbar produced the vanguard of the national independence movement during the Mandate.[70] In the winter of 1918, Maktab ʿAnbar officially became known as the *tajhiz*. It remained on the grounds of the ʿAnbar Palace and maintained its status as the elite secondary school of Damascus.[71] In 1932, long after it had exhausted its limited space, the *tajhiz* moved to new spacious quarters with modern laboratories and other facilities in the Europeanized and still sparsely-settled Salhiyya district, not far from the new Parliament building. At that time, the school's enrollment increased by nearly 40 percent to between 650 and 700 teenage boys.[72]

The Damascus *tajhiz* accepted boarders from as far away as Hama and Homs, and most of its graduates went on to study law or medicine at the Syrian University, or in Paris; many became teachers in smaller towns and villages throughout the country. Since students paid a nominal sum

[68] See Syria: Ministry of Education, *Statistical Abstract* (Syria, 1956), p. 60.

[69] Montagne, "L'évolution, " p. 9; Ahmad Hilmi al-ʿAllaf, *Dimashq*, pp. 169–71; FO 371/625. vol. 19022. MacKereth to FO, 7 July 1935.

[70] See Zafir al-Qasimi, *Maktab ʿAnbar* (Beirut, 1967). ʿAnbar was a wealthy Jewish merchant whose large home became the school.

[71] Al-Rayyis, *al-Kitab al-dhahabi*, p. 102.

[72] United States. American Consulate at Beirut, "Education in the States of the Levant under French Mandate" (Report for Office of Education, Department of Interior) (Beirut, 1 Nov. 1933), p. 321.

of £S 19,[73] the *tajhiz*, unlike its predecessor Maktab ʿAnbar, was not as prohibitive for the middle and lower-middle classes. Twenty percent of the students in 1933, for example, were exempted from all fees.[74] Nevertheless, education during the Mandate retained its elitist status; this was patently obvious in a country where in 1931 the literacy rate was still only 28 percent, and only 4 percent of the population had a secondary school education.[75]

The majority of the *tajhiz's* full-time faculty of 26 were trained in Paris and offered their students excellent instruction in literature, history, mathematics, and sciences, all in the medium of Arabic. In fact, the one area on which the curriculum placed little emphasis was athletics,[76] a void filled by the Boy Scout movement and other youth organizations.

The *tajhiz* was one of the principal centers of nationalist activity during the Mandate. The influence of the school's highly trained teachers upon the intellectual and ideological formation of many a bright young mind had already begun to have an impact by the time Syria entered the 1930s. Aside from the study of modern sciences, European philosophy, and literature, students were encouraged to commit to memory the nationalist poetry of well-known Arab poets such as Ahmad Shawqi of Egypt. The history of the Arabs and their great contribution to the progress of world civilization were taught in the most exacting national terms. No glories or wonders of the Arab heritage were left unmentioned in the classroom. Since Syria did not enter the interwar years with a host of local intellectuals to whom this young generation could turn, the educated youth had to look to Egypt and elsewhere in the Arab world for intellectual nourishment, which reinforced a national identity reaching beyond Syria's newly imposed frontiers. As this generation reached maturity in the early 1930s, pan-Arabism appeared to undergo a revival.[77]

This spirit of pan-Arabism alive in the *tajhiz* was at odds with the spirit of the Nationalist Youth controlled by the Syrian-bound National Bloc. This issue of pan-Arabism also gave ideological shape to the amorphous disillusionment widespread among the Syrian youth with the National Bloc's policy of "honorable cooperation" and its failure to achieve any-

---

[73] *Ibid.*, p. 321. When the *tajhiz* moved to Salhiyya, it also began to take a limited number of boarders from beyond Damascus at the cost of £S 181.50 per year.

[74] *Ibid.*, p. 321.

[75] This figure covers only the State of Syria. For instance, in the Jabal Druze the literacy rate in 1931 was 6 percent. *L'Asie Française*, no. 287 (Feb. 1931), p. 63.

[76] Conversation with ʿAli al-Dandashi (Damascus, 9 March 1976). Later, in the thirties, the growth of sporting clubs offered the youth of the towns athletic opportunities.

[77] These remarks are based on a careful reading of *al-Mudhik al-mubki* in this period, and on conversations with graduates of the *tajhiz* who had studied there in the 1930s. Among them were Amin al-Nafuri (Damascus, 22 Feb. 1976) and Nuzhat Mamluk (Damascus, 15 July 1977).

thing in the way of political autonomy or economic development. At a
General Student Congress held in Hama in February 1932, none of the
various resolutions included any references to the National Bloc or the
Nationalist Youth.[78]

At the head of this new movement of disaffection a new leader emerged
to challenge the founders of the Nationalist Youth. Shafiq Sulayman was
a graduate of the *tajhiz* when it was still known as Maktab ʿAnbar and,
having later taken a law degree, he was much more respected among students at the *tajhiz* than Mahmud al-Bayruti, the shopowner who had
failed to acquire a university education.[79] The two grew up together in
Suq Saruja and, for a while, were good friends. Sulayman was a regular
visitor to Bayruti's novelties shop and small library on the rue Rami,
often coming with students from the *tajhiz*.[80] But, by the autumn of
1932, relations had cooled between them. Bayruti's refusal to criticize
Jamil Mardam and other National Bloc moderates, particularly during the
first big showdown between the Aleppo Bloc and Damascus over whether
nationalist deputies should return to Parliament, angered Sulayman. He
had also fallen under the influence of ʿAbd al-Razzaq al-Dandashi and
was especially enamored of Dandashi's radical pan-Arabism. Meanwhile,
many students at the *tajhiz* had, for some time, been disenchanted with
the Mardam faction's unflagging pursuit of "honorable cooperation,"
even when all political signs pointed in another direction.[81] Sulayman had
also heard rumors that Bayruti had refused to let the Nationalist Youth
criticize Mardam publicly because he was now on Mardam's payroll.[82]

A month before Qarna'il, *al-Mudhik al-mubki* noted the appearance of
a new political circle in the capital.[83] The satirical weekly was able to point
out some of the characteristics distinguishing this clique from the leadership of the Nationalist Youth. Whereas the National Bloc and the Nationalist Youth continued to congregate at their favorite café, the Globe,
the young men around ʿAbd al-Razzaq al-Dandashi and Shafiq Sulayman had designated the Ghazi café as their "official" gathering spot.[84]
Many *tajhiz* students also began to frequent a new bookstore, Maktabat
al-ʿummumiyya (The Public Library), which had recently been opened
by Hajj Adib Khayr, a wealthy merchant and Istiqlali. His bookstore came

[78] J. Gaulmier, "Congrès Général des étudiants tenu à Hama, 1932," CHEAM, no. 46, n.
pl. (1936), p. 2. One plank was for all students to boycott foreign religious schools.
[79] Conversation with Mahmud al-Bayruti (Damascus, 10 March 1976).
[80] *Ibid.*
[81] Various articles and columns in *al-Mudhik al-mubki* in late 1932 mentioned the negative reaction of *tajhiz* students to the moderate wing of the National Bloc led by Jamil Mardam.
[82] *Al-Mudhik al-mubki*, no. 163 (11 March 1933), p. 4.
[83] *Ibid.*, no. 179 (29 July 1933), p. 8.
[84] *Ibid.*, no. 193 (11 Nov. 1933), p. 8.

to rival Mahmud al-Bayruti's nearby shop as a magnet for educated youth.[85] Finally, in traditional Middle Eastern manner, headgear distinguished the two groups. Men like Dandashi, Sulayman, Ahmad al-Shihabi, Rushdi al-Jabi, and more and more Boy Scouts began to sport the Iraqi *sidara*, the army headgear invented by King Faysal, instead of the familiar *tarbush* (fez), a National Bloc symbol worn by Bayruti and others.[86]

By July 1933 the struggle moved beyond symbolism when tensions between Bayruti and Sulayman escalated into student gang wars in Suq Saruja.[87] Although neither faction claimed a decisive victory, the *tajhiz* thereafter was more closely identified with the breakaway faction of Nationalist Youth and their new comrades at the Ghazi café.[88]

Closely associated with the *tajhiz* was the Damascus Law Faculty, established in 1919. *Tajhiz* graduates regularly went on to study at the Law Faculty and many law graduates became activists in the League of National Action. They, in turn, politicized the younger *tajhiz* students. Shafiq Sulayman had followed this route.

Students at the *tajhiz*, however, seemed to be much more in the political limelight than their older brothers and cousins at the Law Faculty. One reason for this was the sheer difference in size. The Law Faculty student body was minuscule, with rarely more than 100 students in residence at any given time. Both the League of National Action and the Nationalist Youth found it more rewarding to focus their mobilization efforts on the *tajhiz* and government primary schools where there was a higher concentration of students. And because younger students were not yet burdened by career pressures, they were less inhibited about taking to the streets. Moreover, nationalist leaders were fully aware that the French had a much more difficult time confining minors in prisons (though they did on occasion) than young professionals who had already reached their majority.[89]

The League of National Action was, nonetheless, swamped with law-

---

[85] *Ibid.* Conversation with Hasan al-Hakim (Damascus, 21 March 1976).

[86] *Al-Mudhik al-mubki*, no. 191 (28 Oct. 1933), p. 2. Wearing the *sidara* was not only a way of criticizing the Bloc, but also of rejecting the fez because it was a foreign-made product, imported mainly from Czechoslovakia. Later, the League switched from the *sidara* to the *kufiyya*, traditional Arab headdress. See M. [Raymond] O'Zoux, "Les insignes et saluts de la jeunesse en Syrie et au Liban," *Entretiens sur l'évolution des pays de civilisation arabe*, vol. 2 (Paris, 1938), p. 100. Fakhri al-Barudi actually tried to promote a scheme for the development of a native Syrian hat that would replace the fez.

[87] *Al-Mudhik al-mubki*, no. 191 (28 Oct. 1933), p. 2.

[88] Zu'aytir, "Ittifaq al-'arab," pp. 64–66.

[89] Conversation with Qustantin Zurayq (Beirut, 10 Jan. 1976).

yers who made up a majority of its leaders.[90] Law was an honorable
profession, but it was neither particularly lucrative nor even a sure road
to steady employment. This was particularly true in Damascus, the hub
of government and political life, where more than half of the licensed
lawyers in Syria resided.[91] As a consequence, the cafés of Damascus and
other towns did a brisk business, filled with idle, unemployed, young
professionals. Like the preceding generation of Istanbul-trained professionals who, not finding work in Damascus, became nationalists, this
generation also formed an "avant-garde" of political upheaval and
change.[92]

COMPOSITION AND ORGANIZATION

The League of National Action was actively engaged in nationalist political life until World War II, when it was forced to go underground; its
leaders, however, maintained influence with the Boy Scouts and other
youth organizations through the war.[93] Because the League maintained a
floating membership, it is difficult to estimate accurately the number of
its active members at any given time. Suffice it to say that the range of its
influence among the young, educated elites in Syria in the thirties was
considerable, certainly much greater than its numbers indicate.

Between 1933 and 1936, when the League suffered its first major internal schism, its effective leadership was in the hands of two dozen like-
minded men[94] whose age, educational background, and intellectual formation betrayed a strong professional middle class identity. Nearly
three-fourths of the League leaders were at Qarna'il.[95] (For characteristics

[90] Among the League's lawyers were Sabri al-ʿAsali, ʿAbd al-Razzaq al-Dandashi, Jamil
al-Jabi, Fahmi al-Mahayri, Ahmad al-Shihabi, Shafiq Sulayman, Farid Zayn al-Din, Ghalib
al-ʿAzm, Muhsin al-Barazi, Mustafa Hawrani, and ʿAdnan, Makram and Hilmi al-Atasi.

[91] Calculated from lists of the various unions of lawyers in Syria in Dalil al-jumhuriyya
al-suriyya, 1939–1940, pp. 514–15. There were approximately 400 lawyers registered in
1939. Also see Donald M. Reid, Lawyers and Politics in the Arab World, 1880–1960 (Minneapolis, 1981), p. 225.

[92] Al-Mudhik al-mubki made regular reference in the early thirties to the great numbers
of unemployed lawyers in the country. Also see Edmond Rabbath, "Esquisse sur les populations syriennes," Revue Internationale de Sociologie, 46 (1938), pp. 508–9.

[93] FO 226/233/31, vol. 236. "Beaumont Table on Syrian Political Parties," 7 Oct. 1942.

[94] These were Sabri al-ʿAsali, ʿAbd al-Razzaq al-Dandashi, ʿAli ʿAbd al-Karim al-Dandashi, Rushdi and Zaki al-Jabi (brothers), Fahmi al-Mahayri, Ahmad al-Sharabati, Ahmad
al-Shihabi, Shafiq Sulayman, Farid Zayn al-Din, Ghalib al-ʿAzm, Muhsin al-Barazi, Mustafa Hawrani, ʿAdnan, Hilmi, and Makram al-Atasi (cousins), Zaki al-Arsuzi, ʿAbd al-
Karim al-ʿAʾidi, Abuʾl Huda al-Yafi, ʿIrfan Jallad, Munir al-ʿAita, and Mazhar al-Quwwatli.

[95] Zuʿaytir, "Ittifaq al-ʿarab," pp. 64–66.

of the leadership of the League and the Nationalist Youth, see Tables 15-1–15-3.)

Like the Nationalist Youth, the League incorporated a second generation of Syrian nationalists who were, on the average, 20 years younger than their Bloc counterparts. In fact, at the time of its establishment in 1933, the League's oldest active member, Makram al-Atasi, was only 34. The average age of the leadership was 29. As for educational backgrounds, all of the League's leaders had advanced training, half in Europe (mostly in France) and the other half at the Syrian University in Damascus.[96] By contrast, only 20 percent of the National Bloc leadership had an advanced Western education, while 56 percent were trained in Istanbul in preparation for the Ottoman Empire's civil service; 16 percent never went further than secondary schooling. These educational differences, when coupled with the generation gap, placed the League's leadership on a more sophisticated intellectual footing than its National Bloc elders. Whereas the Bloc leadership had a shared Ottoman-Arab cultural experience colored with some European cultural influences, the next generation of nationalist leaders in Syria shared a much stronger and more purely Arab cultural identity which was reshaped by their modern Western educations.

In the front rank of the League stood men from the professional middle class, merchant backgrounds, or the old aristocracy of officials. Some leaders also hailed from the big landlordry. But the vast majority were either from the poorer branches of these families or were unpropertied, unlike the leadership of the National Bloc of which more than 60 percent belonged to the urban absentee landlord class. In fact, League leaders were almost completely dependent on their salaries in the liberal professions for their livelihood. Seventy percent were either practicing lawyers or instructors of law; the remainder was divided among the other professions. By contrast, 45 percent of the Bloc leadership lived off agricultural and urban rents, while only 40 percent were licensed professionals, 30 percent of these being lawyers.[97]

From the outset, the League of National Action attempted to organize itself along the lines of a modern political party. It had a central political council which provided for the division and distribution of power and the allocation of responsibilities. It had a core of regular dues-paying members, governed by a set of party rules. It also had a political program and its own political mouthpiece, a weekly newspaper called al-ʿAmal al-

---

[96] See Tables 15-1 and 15-2 for a comparison of the League and the Nationalist Youth.

[97] For a comparison of the League and the National Bloc look at Table 10-1, Chapter 10, and Table 15-1.

TABLE 15-1
Characteristics of the Leadership of the League of National Action ('Usbat al-
'amal al-qawmi)[a] and the Nationalist Youth (al-Shabab al-watani)[b]

	NY	LNA
Age (average by year of birth)	1904.0	1904.0
Religion (by sect)		
Muslim: Sunni	76.0%	82.0%
Muslim: Shi'ite	0.0	6.0
Druze	0.0	6.0
Alawite	0.0	6.0
Christian: Gr. Orthodox	14.0	0.0
Christian: Syrian Catholic	5.0	0.0
Christian: Armenian Catholic	5.0	0.0
Education		
Advanced Western	57.0	41.0
Local Secondary	29.0	6.0
Advanced Local	14.0	53.0
Occupation		
Lawyer	52.0	47.0
Lawyer/University Educator	0.0	23.0
Schoolteacher	0.0	6.0
Dentist	0.0	6.0
Merchant	5.0	6.0
Youth Leader	0.0	6.0
Physician	0.0	6.0
Landowner	19.0	0.0
Journalist	19.0	0.0
Engineer	5.0	0.0
Class Origin		
Landowning-Bureaucrat	24.0	23.0
Bureaucrat	9.5	23.0
Landowning-Scholar	9.5	18.0
Large Landowner	0.0	12.0
Middling Landowner	0.0	12.0
Upper and Upper-Middle Merchant	24.0	6.0
Religious Dignitary	5.0	6.0
Middle-Class Merchant	29.0	0.0

[a] Based on information in Table 15-2.
[b] Based on information in Table 15-3.

TABLE 15-2
Biographical Data: League of National Action ('Usbat al-'amal al-qawmi)

Name	Year of Birth	Religion	Education	Occupation	Class Origin	Offices
From Damascus						
'Abd al-Karim al-'A'idi	1909	Muslim: Sunni	Advanced local (Damascus/Syrian University)	Dentist	Religious scholars	
Sabri al-'Asali[a]	1904	"	"	Lawyer, youth leader	Upper-middle land-owning-bureaucratic	Min. 1945–46 Deputy: 1936, 1943
'Abd al-Razzāq al-Dandashī[b]	1905 (d. 1935)	"	Advanced Western (Brussels)	Lawyer, youth leader	Landowning	
'Alī ' Abd al-Karīm al-Dandashī[b]	1908	"	Local secondary (Beirut)	Youth leader (Boy Scouts)	Landowning	
Rushdi al-Jābi	1900	"	Advanced Western (Paris)	Physician, youth leader (Boy Scouts)	Ottoman officials	
Fahmī al-Mahayrī	1902	"	Advanced local (Damascus)	Lawyer, youth leader	Ottoman officials	
Ahmad al-Sharabāti	1905	"	Advanced Western (Boston/Germany)	Merchant/Ind. politician	Upper-class merchants	Min. 1945 Deputy: 1943

TABLE 15-2 (*cont.*)

Biographical Data: League of National Action (ʿUsbat al-ʿamal al-qawmi)

Name	Year of Birth	Religion	Education	Occupation	Class Origin	Offices
Ahmad al-Shihabiᶜ	1905	Muslim: Shiʿite	Advanced local (Damascus/Syrian University)	Lawyer	Landowning-bureaucratic, *amīrs*	
Shafiq Sulaymānᵈ	1903	Muslim: Sunni	Advanced local (Damascus/Syrian University)	Lawyer	Ottoman officials	
Farīd Zayn al-Dinᵉ *From Hama*	1907	Druze	Advanced Western (Beirut/AUB, Berlin, Paris)	Educator, lawyer, bureaucrat	Ottoman officials	Director of Ministry: 1937–39
Ghālib al-ʿAẓm	1905	Muslim: Sunni	Advanced local (Damascus)	Lawyer, landowner	Landowning-bureaucratic	Deputy: 1943
Muḥsin al-Barāzī	1904	Muslim: Sunni Arabized Kurd	Advanced Western (Paris)	Lawyer, educator	Landowning-bureaucratic	Min. 1943
Muṣṭafā Ḥawrānī	1902	Muslim: Sunni	Advanced local (Damascus/Syrian University)	Lawyer	Middling-landowning	

From Homs						
'Adnān al-Atāsī	1905	"	Advanced Western (Geneva)	Lawyer, educator	Landowning-scholarly, *ashrāf*	Deputy: 1943
Ḥilmī al-Atāsī	1902	"	Advanced local (Damascus/Syrian University)	Lawyer, youth leader	Landowning-scholarly, *ashrāf*	Deputy: 1943
Makram al-Atāsī	1899	"	Advanced Western/local (Beirut/AUB, Damascus/Syrian University)	Lawyer, educator	Landowning-scholarly, *ashrāf*	Deputy: 1936
From Antioch						
Zakī al-Arsūzī	1901	Alawite	Advanced Western (Paris)	Schoolteacher	Middling landowning	

[a] Joined National Bloc in 1936.
[b] From Tall Kalakh.
[c] Originally from Hasbaya, Lebanon.
[d] Resigned from Nationalist Youth in 1932.
[e] Originally from Mount Lebanon.

TABLE 15-3

Biographical Data: The Nationalist Youth (al-Shabab al-watani)

Name	Year of Birth	Religion	Education	Occupation	Class Origin	Offices
From Damascus						
Munīr al-ʿAjlānī	1905	Muslim: Sunni	Advanced Western (Paris)	Lawyer, politician, journalist, youth leader	Landowning-scholarly, *ashrāf*	Deputy: 1936 Min. 1942–43
Naṣūḥ Bābīl[a]	1905	"	Local secondary (Damascus)	Journalist	Middle-class merchants	
Mazhar al-Bakrī	1900	"	Advanced Western (Grenoble)	Landowner	Landowning-bureaucratic, *ashrāf*	
Mahmūd al-Bayrūtī	1903	"	Local secondary (Damascus)	Merchant, youth leader	Middle-class merchants, bureaucrat	
Wajīh al-Ḥaffār	1912	"	Advanced local (Damascus/Syrian University)	Journalist	Upper-middle class merchants	
Shafīq Jabrī	1898	"	Local secondary (Damascus)	Journalist	Ottoman officials	
Sayf al-Dīn al-Māʾmūn	1905	"	Advanced Western (Paris)	Lawyer, youth leader	Middle-class merchants, bureaucrats	

Name	Birth	Religion	Education	Profession	Class background	Political positions
'Abd al-Wahhāb al-Mālkī	1898	"	Advanced Western (Paris)	Engineer	Landowning-bureaucratic	
Rashīd al-Malūḥī	1902	"	Local secondary (Damascus)	Journalist	Middle-class merchants	
Khālid al-Shiliq	1902	"	Advanced local (Damascus/Syrian)	Lawyer, youth leader	Middle-class merchants	
Aḥmad al-Sammān	1907	"	Advanced Western (Paris)	Lawyer, educator	Upper-middle class merchants	
From Aleppo						
Na'īm Anṭākī	1903	Christian: Gr. Orth.	Advanced Western (Beirut/Paris)	Lawyer	Upper-middle class merchants	Min. 1943, 1945; Deputy: 1943[b]
Fathallāh Asīyūn	1899	Christian: Armen. Cath.	Advanced Western (Cairo)	Lawyer	Upper-middle class merchants	Deputy: 1936, 1943
Ma'rūf al-Dawālibī	1908	Muslim: Sunni	Advanced Western (Paris)	Lawyer, educator	Middle-class merchants	
Mikhā'il Ilyān	1905	Christian: Gr. Orth.	Local secondary (Aleppo)	Landowner, politician	Landowning	Min. 1945–46; Deputy: 1943
Rushdī al-Kīkhyā	1900	Muslim: Sunni	Local secondary (Aleppo)	Landowner, politician	Landowning-bureaucratic	Deputy: 1936, 1943

TABLE 15-3 (*cont.*)
Biographical Data: The Nationalist Youth (al-Shabab al-watani)

Name	Year of Birth	Religion	Education	Occupation	Class Origin	Offices
Nāzim al-Qudsī	1906	Muslim: Sunni	Advanced Western (Beirut/Geneva)	Lawyer, politician	Landowning-scholarly, *ashrāf*	Deputy: 1936, 1943
Edmond Rabbath *From Hama*	1904	Christian: Syr. Cath.	Advanced Western (Paris)	Lawyer, politician	Upper-middle class merchants	Deputy: 1936
Ra'īf al-Mulqī	1902	Muslim: Sunni	Advanced local (Damascus/Syrian University)	Lawyer, youth leader	Ottoman officials	Deputy: 1943
Muhammad al-Sarrāj *From Homs*	1910	"	Advanced Western (Paris)	Lawyer, bureaucrat	Religious dignitaries	
'Abdullāh Farkūh	1905	Christian: Gr. Orth.	Advanced Western (Paris)	Landowner	Landowning, merchants	Deputy: 1936, 1943

[a] Resigned (1933).
[b] Elected from Damascus.

qawmi (the National Action).[98] However, the League was anything but a mass-based party, nor did it ever encourage anything of the sort. Rather it was distinctly elitist, well-organized in government schools, the university, and in institutions such as the Boy Scouts, whose leaders, Rushdi al-Jabi and ʿAli ʿAbd al-Karim al-Dandashi, also became members of the League's inner circle.

It was the League's self-styled elitist character which prevented it from widening its base beyond the schools and university into the popular quarters of the towns and the countryside.[99] This was, in part, because its young, gifted, but often aloof leaders were, with few exceptions, not street-wise. They depended, instead, on attracting a following in the institutions from which they themselves had emerged—the *tajhiz* and Faculty of Law in Damascus. In fact, the League adopted a rather cliquish demeanor, characterized by the young man in a sports jacket sitting at the League's favorite café, proudly displaying the latest available edition of the prestigious Cairo newspaper, *al-Muqattam*, or maybe the literary and scientific journals, *al-Hilal* and *al-Muqtataf*. At the café he sipped coffee and plotted a course of action against the most recent French decree with his companions. The average Leaguer, in short, lived in a world quite foreign to the one most Damascenes inhabited.[100] Like the National Bloc, the League pictured political life in its own image. But, more than the Bloc, it was committed to moving urban political life out of the popular quarters and into the government schools and other modern institutions in which it would have automatic influence. But though this shift was well under way by the early 1930s, it was far from complete. The older and more experienced National Bloc leaders, whose own styles were a mix of traditional city patron and modern party man, were not nearly as impatient as their younger counterparts in the League and they preserved their links with the popular quarters controlled by religious shaykhs, merchants, and *qabadayat*.[101]

League Outreach

The League of National Action had several branches linked to its Central Council in Damascus. The one locale in which it had a decisive political

[98] Its chief editors were Abu'l Huda al-Yafi and ʿUthman Qasim. Conversation with Akram Zuʿaytir (Beirut, 11 Aug. 1975).

[99] Conversations with Farid Zayn al-Din (Damascus, 22 April 1976); ʿAli ʿAbd al-Karim al-Dandashi (Damascus, 9 March 1976).

[100] This image derives from a conversation with Zafir al-Qasimi (Beirut, 26 July 1975). Qasimi never joined the League but was intimately connected to it through his relationship with Sabri al-ʿAsali. By 1935 the two men had become law partners.

[101] Conversation with Munir al-ʿAjlani (Beirut, 2 Sept. 1975).

edge was Homs, the third largest town in Syria. At the time of the
League's foundation, Homs had a population of approximately 70,000
and was the capital of a district containing 148,000 inhabitants.[102] Nearly
55 percent of the privately-owned land of this district belonged to a small
group of landlords, among them the Atasi, Durubi, Raslan, Jundi, Husayni, Akhrass, Farkhuh, Suwaydan, and Dandashi families. Most were
urban absentee landowners resident in Homs. These families not only
owned large tracts of land, reported in 1938 to be about 125,000 hectares,
and all or part of 110 villages, they also owned the most fertile lands,
more than 1,000 hectares of Orontes-irrigated fruit farms around the
city.[103]

Homs was commonly referred to as Hashim al-Atasi's fief. But, although Atasi had been President of the National Bloc since its foundation,
he had become increasingly frustrated by the Bloc's failure to make any
substantial progress toward independence by the route of "honorable cooperation." His adept handling of the 1931–32 parliamentary elections in
Homs, the one nationalist stronghold where Bloc candidates swept the
board after waging a fierce struggle against French interference, freed
him to assume a more radical posture. That stance in turn helped him to
attract the Istiqlal Party leader, Shukri al-Quwwatli, to the Bloc Council
in late 1932.

It is unlikely that the League of National Action would have made such
deep inroads in Homs had Hashim al-Atasi not given it leeway from the
very beginning.[104] Atasis controlled the League in Homs, receiving the
patronage of their much respected family head. Among them was Hashim's son ʿAdnan, also a law partner of ʿAbd al-Razzaq al-Dandashi in
Damascus; and two cousins, Makram and Hilmi.[105] But there was another equally important factor behind the League's strength in Homs. It
concerned the town's largest religious minority, the Greek Orthodox.

The Greek Orthodox community was influential in the town's principal industries—silk- and cotton-weaving, and leather and tanning—and
in the distribution of their products. Homs's traditional handicrafts historically depended on exports to Anatolia and northern Iraq by land, and
to Izmir and Istanbul by sea from its principal port, Tripoli, to which it

[102] The census of 1932 listed Homs's population at 68,000. In 1922, it was reported to be
approximately 70,000. See Le Commandant Le Boulanger, "Homs," in L'Asie Française,
(Documents économiques, politiques et scientifiques, no. 6 [Nov. 1922], p. 138). In 1903,
the date of the second and last census under the Ottomans of the population of Homs, it was
given at 51,082. The first census was in 1881.

[103] P. Berthelot, "Notes sur la mise en valeur de la Région du 'Caza' de Homs," CHEAM,
no. 249 (Feb. 1938), pp. 22–23. These families owned 65 villages completely.

[104] Conversation with Farid Zayn al-Din (Damascus, 22 April 1976).

[105] Faris, Man huwa 1949, p. 14.

was connected by rail just after the turn of the century. The collapse of the Ottoman Empire, followed by the erection of new and hostile customs barriers, had severed Homs from its traditional markets. On the eve of World War I Homs had nearly 4,000 small workshops producing handi- crafts, but by 1922 this number had been drastically reduced to 1,000.[106] A decade later, the depression exacerbated what was already a static eco- nomic situation. The Greek Orthodox community in Homs, unlike other religious minorities, does not seem to have developed strong links to for- eign capital; as a consequence, the community unequivocally perceived French hegemony and European economic penetration to be a direct threat to its material existence. Illegal unions, like those in Hama, aligned with students and held demonstrations and strikes against low wages and foreign competition, most notably that of Bata Shoes of Czechoslovakia, in July 1932.[107]

The Greek Orthodox saw themselves as an integral part of the region, a community whose identity and culture was Syrian-Arab, and Greek Orthodox schools helped to reinforce this identity and cultural aware- ness.[108] With their fortunes on the downgrade, Greek Orthodox artisans supported the National Bloc's various political activities in the late twen- ties and early thirties. But, with the ascent of the League of National Ac- tion, whose brand of Arab nationalism was more convincingly "secular," many younger members of the community shifted their allegiance to the League.[109]

League of National Action chapters also emerged in Tall Kalakh,[110] Dayr al-Zur, Antioch, and Hama. Three lawyers in their late twenties headed the League in Hama: Ghalib ʿAbd al-Qadir al-ʿAzm, born into a prosperous landowning family and a graduate of the Damascus *tajhiz* and Law Faculty;[111] Mustafa Hawrani, the son of a middling landowner and

---

[106] Boulanger, "Homs," pp. 139–40.

[107] Hanna, *al-Haraka al-ʿummaliyya*, pp. 382–416; Longuenesse, "La classe ouvrière."

[108] The Greek Orthodox Patriarch in the 1920s was Gregorius Haddad (1859–1928) who had become Patriarch of Antioch and the East in 1907. He was much admired by his own community and by Muslims as well. His love of Islamic history and law was renowned. He was also an active pan-Arabist. At the time of his death he was referred to as the "Patriarch of the Muslims." See Qudama, *Maʿalim*, pp. 285–86.

[109] Still others hooked up to the nascent Communist Party at this time, though its follow- ing remained much smaller than that of either the League or the Bloc. Conversation with Farid Zayn al-Din (Damascus, 22 April 1976).

[110] Tall Kalakh was the home of the Dandashi family. See *al-Musawwar* (Damascus weekly), no. 9 (29 July 1936), p. 3.

[111] Faris, *Man huwa 1949*, p. 306. ʿAzm's father had been a member of the Administra- tive Council of the *Liwaʾ* of Hama in the 1890s. *Salname: suriya vilayeti*, 1309–1310/1892– 1893, p. 171.

'Azm's senior by three years at the Law Faculty;[112] and Muhsin al-Barazi, the son of one of the most distinguished notables of Hama, Khalid al-Darwish al-Barazi.[113] After graduating from Paris with a doctorate in law, Muhsin became an instructor at the Damascus Law Faculty, serving as a link between the Hama branch of the League and Damascus. Meanwhile, 'Azm and Hawrani focused their activities on the Hama *tajhiz* and the local Boy Scouts. In Hama, youth leaders could not escape the clutches of the radical National Bloc leader, Dr. Tawfiq al-Shishakli, who kept a tight rein on the Nationalist Youth. Because Shishakli was recognized as a populist and a pan-Arabist, he was able to contain potential conflict between the League and the local Bloc chapter. In fact, under his patronage, the two were loosely allied until early 1939, when the Hama branch of the League disintegrated with Ghalib al-'Azm's and Mustafa Hawrani's defection to a new organization, al-Shabab al-hamawi (Hama Youth), composed of local *tajhiz* students and Boy Scouts, militantly opposed to the National Bloc. This organization was headed by two other members of the Hawrani family: 'Uthman, a forty-year-old schoolteacher at the local *tajhiz*, and Akram, a full-time political activist.[114]

Until this late development, the League–Bloc alliance remained intact and opposed to two radically different trends which also surfaced in Hama in the early 1930s. One trend was embodied in the Syrian Social Nationalist Party founded by the Lebanese intellectual Antun Sa'ada, which spoke of a "natural" Syrian nation and opposed the pan-Arab doctrines of the League and the Bloc. Up until the appearance of al-Shabab al-hamawi, one of the leading members of the SSNP was Akram Hawrani, who had come into contact with it during his days as a student at the Medical Faculty of the Jesuit University in Beirut.[115] For the League and the Bloc, the second trend was even more menacing; it was inspired by a religious organization known as Shabab Muhammad (Muhammadan Youth), one of the forerunners of the Muslim Brethren in Syria.[116] This phenomenon of a religiously inspired movement led by popular shaykhs and middle-

---

[112] Gaulmier, "Notes sur le mouvement syndicaliste à Hama," p. 100.

[113] Qudama, *Ma'alim*, p. 116; al-Jundi, *Tarikh*, pp. 595–96.

[114] MWT, *al-Intidab al-faransi: al-Ahzab. Nadi al-'arabi*, 135/346–450, Chief of Police (Hama) to Muhafiz (Hama), 28 Feb. 1939. Faris, *Man huwa 1949*, p. 139; Qudama, *Ma'alim*, p. 352.

[115] On the Syrian Social Nationalist Party (or as the French referred to it, the *Partie Populaire Syrien*) see MAE, Guerre 1939–45 (Londres CNF). Secret Report on "Le Parti Populaire Syrien (P.P.S.)," Beirut, April 1942, vol. 40, pp. 16–21; Labib Zuwiyya Yamak, *The Syrian Social Nationalist Party: An Ideological Analysis* (Cambridge, Mass., 1966). Qudama, *Ma'alim*, p. 352; Akram Hawrani had been expelled from the Jesuit Medical Faculty by the French, accused of being involved in an assassination attempt on Subhi Barakat in Beirut in the spring of 1932.

[116] See Chapter 23.

class professionals was bound to be strong in a religiously conservative town like Hama, of which the saying went

> while in Aleppo it takes only three men to make the Bloc, and in Homs only three men to make the League, and in Damascus only three men to start a demonstration, in Hama, it takes only three men to get the town to pray.[117]

The other League chapters were much smaller than those of Damascus, Homs, and Hama. In Dayr al-Zur, the League was led by a young landowner, Jalal Sayyid—a graduate of the Damascus *tajhiz* and the Law Faculty.[118] Sayyid had been one of the League's founding members at Qarna'il. In Antioch the chapters were headed by Zaki al-Arsuzi, a Sorbonne-educated schoolteacher of Alawite origin whose father was a lawyer and middling landowner. Both Jalal Sayyid and Arsuzi broke with the League in 1939, Arsuzi to form his own political organization which he later fused with an emerging movement of intellectuals in Damascus headed by two teachers at the *tajhiz*, Michel ʿAflaq and Salah al-Din al-Bitar. The result was the birth of the Baʿth Party.[119]

Opposition in Aleppo

Aleppo was the one nationalist center in Syria which actively but discreetly opposed attempts by the League of National Action to establish a base. Aleppine delegates were conspicuously absent from Qarna'il in August 1933; apparently Ibrahim Hananu had passed the word that no one in his organization was to accept the invitation.[120] Hananu's reservations were strong though not clear or consistent. He argued that because nationalist ranks were still divided on the "treaty question" and the Bloc's policy of *tafahum* (mutual understanding), another splinter might damage the independence movement irreparably. His fear seemed to blind him to the fact that the League, like Hananu and the Aleppo Bloc, adamantly opposed the "dirty" dealings of Jamil Mardam and company. Hananu was also excessively concerned about the League's strong Iraqi connections and seemingly pro-Faysal tendencies, which he understood as "unity at any price," even a Hashemite throne. For hardline republicans like Hananu, although unity was always to be encouraged, a mon-

---

[117] *Al-Mudhik al-mubki*, no. 291 (6 June 1936), p. 9.
[118] Conversation with Akram Zuʿaytir (Beirut, 11 Aug. 1975).
[119] *Al-Mudhik al-mubki*, no. 293 (20 June 1936), p. 14; Batatu, *The Old Social Classes*, pp. 722–24. Jalal Sayyid was one of the Baʿth Party's earliest leaders.
[120] *Al-Mudhik al-mubki*, no. 184 (2 Sept. 1933), p. 5. When Nazim al-Qudsi, a young Bloc youth leader, was asked to join the League, he replied: "I must ask Hananu." Conversation with Akram Zuʿaytir (Beirut, 11 Aug. 1975).

archy was anathema.[121] In this sense, Hananu expressed the opinion held by almost all Bloc leaders.[122] For example, at the 40-day-after ceremony commemorating King Faysal's death in September 1933, the National Bloc sent only two representatives; the League, however, sent a large contingent to Baghdad.[123] Hananu, furthermore, observed the strength of the League's following in Damascus and its connection with Shukri al-Quwwatli, who, at the time, was maneuvering the Istiqlal Party into an alliance with the Bloc. Hananu was obsessed by fears that such an alliance would ultimately give the Damascus Bloc decisive political leverage over Aleppo.[124]

Under Hananu's direction, the Aleppo Bloc had successfully kept its ranks unified, amidst challenges from the French-sponsored Liberal Constitutionalists, from the Damascus Bloc itself, and, last but not least, from Saʿdallah al-Jabiri. But Hananu had been able to clip Jabiri's wings, bringing him back into line; and his faithful strongmen, the Ibrahim Pashas, still controlled the educated youth and the popular quarters and kept the Boy Scout movement small and semi-independent.[125] Hananu also had nurtured a group of loyal young activists—the exact contemporaries of the League leadership—who, had they been resident in any other town, would doubtless have joined the radical pan-Arabist organization (see Table 15-3). The attachment of young nationalist activists in Aleppo to their National Bloc elders kept the Aleppo Bloc comparatively cohesive throughout the thirties—a claim no other Bloc chapter could make. This loyalty to the Aleppo Bloc ultimately stopped the spread of the League of National Action to the northern capital.[126]

THE LEAGUE AND THE BLOC

To understand how the League of National Action and the National Bloc were related within the structure of the Syrian nationalist movement, it is necessary to return to the question of the class backgrounds and inter-

---

[121] There is also reason to believe that Hananu personally disliked and distrusted Faysal for having offered the French Army of Occupation in the North of Syria military assistance against his revolt in 1920, in the hope of forestalling or appeasing French territorial ambitions in the Syrian interior. See Chapter 4.

[122] One notable exception was Hashim al-Atasi, who still harbored monarchist sympathies.

[123] Fakhri al-Barudi and Najib Rayyis (editor of the National Bloc newspaper, *al-Qabas*).

[124] Conversation with Farid Zayn al-Din (Damascus, 22 April 1976).

[125] Ibrahim Pasha, *Nidal al-ahrar*, p. 53; Anonymous, "Le Scoutisme musulman," p. 11. There were only about 650 scouts in Aleppo.

[126] These young nationalist leaders included Nazim al-Qudsi, Rushdi Kikhya, Naʿim Antaki, Mikhaʾil Ilyan, and Edmond Rabbath. For details on their careers see Khoury, "The Politics of Nationalism," Chapter 12, and Tables 15-1 and 15-3.

ests of both organizations. Although the leaderships of the League and the Bloc were socially differentiated, they were not representative of rival economic classes. In fact, the League, like the Bloc, represented fractions of economic classes whose interests overlapped or whose elements found themselves for the most part aligned against the actual financial and political decision-makers in Syria: the French.

The men of capital in Syria during the Mandate and in the preceding half-century did not form a homogeneous or stable class. They were divided according to status between old landed and mercantile interests and nouveaux riches, and according to religious loyalty into Sunni Muslims, Christians and Jews, and, economically, into elements whose predominant interests were either intrinsically incompatible or compatible with foreign, and particularly French, commercial and financial interests.

Much of the upper and upper-middle strata of the mercantile and moneyed classes in Syria during the Mandate were intimately associated with foreign and, in particular, French capital. They were also largely members of minority communities and were often protected by European citizenship. Thus, politically and economically they were effectively cut off from the mass of Syrians. Their political and economic concerns were met directly by the High Commission itself. Muslim merchants, however, who constituted a small fraction of the same strata, found it somewhat more difficult to cooperate with the French directly because of religious and cultural barriers. Their political representatives tended to be one of the loosely-knit and often feeble coalitions of Muslim notables and bureaucrats headed by politicians such as Subhi Barakat, Haqqi al-ʿAzm, or Shaykh Taj al-Din al-Hasani, whom the High Commission had put in power in the first place. The landed and old mercantile fraction of the Syrian upper class, which under the Mandate had been denied access to foreign capital or was struggling to assert an effective claim to adequate consideration from the French, had the National Bloc as its representative. Indeed, the Bloc leadership was mainly drawn from this segment of the upper class. As for the League of National Action, its leadership constituted the vanguard of an ascendant political elite which was rooted in the professional middle class, the intelligentsia, educated youth, and the middle levels of the bureaucracy. Its interests stood in direct contradiction to the Mandate system for a variety of reasons, not least of which was that the system's rewards did not satisfy its growing appetites and expectations.

Although the League of National Action was at odds with the National Bloc at its inception, in time mutual frustration with French political and economic policies brought the two together. The League, while it was more truly a political party than the Bloc, was rather more distant from Syrian realities. Despite its active campaigns for pan-Arab economic in-

tegration, it failed to build relations with bazaar merchants and it neglected the artisans and the unemployed in the popular quarters, with
whom the National Bloc had close connections. The League also failed to
make significant inroads in the countryside, despite its accusation that
the older generation of nationalists purposely avoided politicizing the
peasantry to protect their own wealth and power. In fact, the League's
leadership was at least one and, in many cases, two or more generations
removed from the land and its urbane, cosmopolitan character made it ill-
suited for political work in rural districts. It is true that a number of
League partisans began their careers as village teachers, but the transla-
tion of these countryside linkages into peasant organizations struggling
against the established order would not be realized until after independence, that is, long after the League had been supplanted by its direct descendant, the Ba'th Party.

The League was also unable to build bridges to another potentially important segment of the professional middle class, the Syrian officer corps.
Unlike in Iraq, where the ex-Sharifian officers constituted the most important element of the political elite under the monarchy and where radical Arab nationalist organizations such as Nadi Muthanna[127] aligned
with factions of the officer corps in the thirties, in Syria the army officers
had little impact on politics. The French, on occupation, dismantled the
Sharifian Army and jailed or exiled many Syrian officers, denying them
the opportunity to practice their profession. At the same time, republican
nationalists disapproved of the royalist (mainly Hashemite) proclivities
of ex-Sharifian officers. In fact, for nearly a century there had been a noticeable absence of a strong military tradition in Syria. The Syrian upper
classes disdained military careers and used their wealth and connections
to purchase exemptions for their sons. As for the new native officer corps
of the Troupes Spéciales, the French controlled its membership, encouraging it to acquire a distinctive minority and rural complexion.

As long as the French ruled Syria, the League was destined, albeit
grudgingly, to collaborate with the National Bloc in the day-to-day
struggle for independence in order to survive. Not only was its leadership
too young and inexperienced and its political base too narrow to pose an
effective challenge to the Bloc's influence, but its links outside Syria,
mainly with similar political organizations in Iraq, were insufficiently developed to allow complete independence from the Bloc. From the start,
the League found itself able, at best, to engage in a push and pull battle
with the Bloc leadership, to force the Bloc's radicalization along League
lines.

The League emerged on the political scene in Syria at a critical moment

---

[127] Batatu, *The Old Social Classes*, pp. 298–99.

for the National Bloc. The forced resignation of Jamil Mardam and Mazhar Raslan in 1933 polarized Bloc ranks and threatened to lead to its complete disintegration. In Shukri al-Quwwatli's opinion, such a danger had
to be averted at all cost. He had joined the Central Council of the Bloc—
the only Istiqlali to do so—because, by the time the French had granted
him and other radicals amnesties, the Bloc was already in full operation
and was unrivalled in its control of the Syrian independence movement.
Quwwatli believed that he could best practice politics under the cover of
the Damascus Bloc, which the French recognized as a legitimate organization because of its moderate position. Quwwatli realized that only by
penetrating Bloc ranks could he hope to put it on a less compromising
course; by remaining locked outside in direct opposition to the Bloc he
would be a marginal political actor, particularly with French Intelligence
keeping close tabs on him at all times. Indeed, the Bloc, at least in 1932–
33, provided him with shelter.

Quwwatli was of the opinion, however, that if the Bloc planned to be in
the driver's seat come independence, then the Damascus branch should
not be allowed to break party ranks. For this reason alone, he aligned with
Aleppo, Homs, and Hama against Jamil Mardam and company. Yet, he
was perfectly aware that like most other nationalists his power base lay in
one city, in his case, Damascus. Therefore, to fulfill his own personal ambitions, the balance of power within the Bloc could never be allowed to
pass out of the hands of the Damascus branch. For this reason, Quwwatli
had to delicately undermine his Damascene colleagues, reserving his
most hostile criticisms for Jamil Mardam in the hope of permanently im-
pairing Mardam's, but not the Bloc's, political credibility.

To counterbalance the refined Mardam, whose attractiveness to the
French High Commission was unparalleled among his Bloc colleagues,
Quwwatli had to develop his own patronage system into one that could
rival Mardam's. The divisions that appeared in Nationalist Youth ranks
in 1931–32 and the subsequent emergence of the League of National Action the following year were not purely fortuitous. Indeed, it seems that
Quwwatli and his Istiqlali partisans discreetly encouraged such a schism,
one which they could turn to their advantage.

Shukri al-Quwwatli was informed in advance of plans for the Qarna'il
Conference from his comrade Hajj Adib Khayr, whose bookstore had be-
come a popular gathering spot for young radical nationalists. Just two
days after Qarna'il, Quwwatli made his first known overtures to the
League by inviting some of its leaders to his home to meet Shaykh Fu'ad
Hamza, Ibn Sa'ud's adviser on foreign affairs and, himself, a Lebanese
Druze. A longtime critic of the Hashemites, Quwwatli was disturbed by
the blind devotion of many young Syrian pan-Arabists like Dandashi and
Sulayman to King Faysal and to the idea of an immediate union with

Iraq.[128] The appearance at this time of young radicals wearing the *sidara* made him very uneasy. The meeting with Hamza was meant to cast Ibn Saʿud in a favorable light and eventually to reorient the League's perspective on Arab unity away from Faysal. Whether Quwwatli would have been able to reorient the League had Faysal not suddenly died in Switzerland on September 7, just two weeks after Qarna'il, must be left to conjecture. There is no doubt, however, that Faysal's death was a heavy blow to the dreams of the League leadership; it also allowed Quwwatli to breathe a bit more easily at this critical juncture of his own rising political career in Syria.

At Qarna'il, the League advocated a hardline stance of no compromise with the French and an active display of hostility to any party prepared to cooperate with the colonizers. Its members vowed not to accept any government posts as long as foreigners remained in control of Syria. During the first three years of its existence, Shukri al-Quwwatli, assisted by Adib Khayr and other Istiqlalis, quietly cultivated the League. He maintained close contact with these young radicals, consciously trying to keep them within his political orbit. He devoted considerable attention to the League's strongmen and even bankrolled its one serious financial enterprise, a national land development company.[129] When this failed, he placed some of the League's chiefs on the board of directors of his own National Conserves Company, and granted them favorable stock options.[130] But, while he could support the League on the one hand and encourage it to take pot shots at Jamil Mardam and the Nationalist Youth which was under Mardam's control, he could not permit the League to tarnish the Bloc as a whole. In other words, Quwwatli had to find ways to channel the League's energies into productive support activities for the National Bloc.

In the period 1934–35, the League of National Action grew in membership. It was also during this period that the National Bloc, having failed miserably in its attempt to negotiate a treaty with France, seemed to lay its strategy of "honorable cooperation" to rest. Indeed, it chose to adopt an unusually low profile at the highest level of politics. In the process, it shifted to a less compromising stance, helping to bring to the surface the growing forces of radicalism in Syria best represented by the League of National Action.

[128] *Al-Mudhik al-mubki,* no. 183 (26 Aug. 1933), p. 6. A deputation including some future League leaders was sent to Amman in June 1933 to visit Faysal who was on his way to Europe. The National Bloc did not want to associate with this group but felt obliged to send two representatives as a courtesy. The delegation asked the King to intercede with France on Syria's behalf. See FO 371/4055, vol. 16974. Todd to FO, 1 July 1933.

[129] *Al-Mudhik al-mubki,* no. 233 (8 Sept. 1933), p. 5.

[130] Conversation with Nadim Demichkie (London, 25 June 1975).

But as the National Bloc traveled leftwards along the political spectrum, the League's strategy automatically came up for reconsideration. Some members came to agree with Quwwatli that the best way to bring the Bloc around to the League's way of thinking was to work within its framework. They argued that the League could never hope to have a lasting impact on nationalist politics unless it, too, penetrated the mainstream of the nationalist movement, just as their mentors, the Istiqlalis, had done. Others on the League's Central Council—and they seem to have been in the majority—wanted to stay out of daily government-level politics, and let the burden of the nationalist struggle fall on the Bloc's shoulders, while the League remained faithful to its hallowed principles and worked to reconstruct the nation on an Arab and not on a Syrian basis.[131] By 1934, a dangerous controversy was brewing within the ranks of the League of National Action. When the controversy matured, the League suffered a serious setback and with it the forces of radicalization in Syria.

[131] Conversation with Qustantin Zurayq (Beirut, 10 Jan. 1976).

CHAPTER SIXTEEN

CRISES BEFORE THE STORM

THE GROWING ATTRACTIVENESS of the League of National Action in the government schools, university, and Boy Scouts indicated that the National Bloc's influence among the educated youth of Damascus was on the wane. The National Youth's day-to-day chiefs, Mahmud al-Bayruti and Khalid al-Shiliq, were no match for the sophisticated and intellectually-oriented League leaders.[1] Although they had not outlived their usefulness, their rather haphazardly-run organization needed a change. It had to have a more refined and dynamic leadership and a broader base than Bayruti's little novelties shop and library. The image of small gangs of Nationalist Youth partisans, cigarettes dangling from their mouths, perpetually hanging around the corner store waiting for instructions to challenge a group of League partisans or the Syrian Social Nationalists,[2] or to attack a passing tramcar, had to be changed. Greater order and discipline were called for.

More than any other Bloc chief in Damascus, Jamil Mardam saw the need to give the Nationalist Youth a facelift. He needed to broaden his political base in the capital after his recent setbacks, by tying the Nationalist Youth more tightly to his own political network. His first step was to cultivate Mahmud al-Bayruti, whom he had inadvertently neglected after joining the government in 1932. Bayruti had demonstrated his loyalty to Mardam during the Bloc's various disputes, which had wracked the Nationalist Youth and the Boy Scout movement in this period. Mardam began to lavish attention upon Bayruti, putting his family's diverse resources and connections at his disposal. By his own admission, Bayruti could not have been more thrilled and honored. A close association with one of the National Bloc *beys* helped to brighten his own image, tarnished

---

[1] Conversation with ʿAli ʿAbd al-Karim al-Dandashi (Damascus, 9 March 1976).

[2] Intermittent gang wars between students associated with the Nationalist Youth and the League of National Action were reported in 1933 and 1934 at the *tajhiz* of Damascus and in Suq Saruja, the residence of Bayruti and Sulayman. The Nationalist Youth also skirmished with the Syrian Social Nationalist Party which was based in Damascus and Hama, and which by 1936 had 120 members. See A. de Boucheman, "Les chemises de fer," CHEAM, no. 6[bis], n. pl., 1936, pp. 16–18. By the spring of 1935 the Nationalist Youth and the Syrian Social Nationalist Party were looking for a reconciliation. Fakhri al-Barudi, however, opposed a rapprochement on the grounds that the SSNP's ideology asserted a specifically Syrian race and not an Arab race. In July 1935, the SSNP conducted large demonstrations in Damascus against the High Commission for jailing its leader, Antun Saʿada.

after his struggle with the League of National Action.[3] But Bayruti's re-vitalized relationship with Mardam did not mean that he became part of the Bloc decision-making process. Class and education clearly distin-guished him from the *beys*; patronage was still a dynamic form of politi-cal association and mobilization in Syria's towns and face-to-face contacts were an important cement in such a system.

Mardam had a second purpose in cultivating Bayruti. He wanted to avoid ruffling Bayruti's feathers as he introduced into the Nationalist Youth leadership a group of young, sophisticated personalities who were, by social background and intellectual formation, more akin to the League's leadership.

He found two such young men in Munir al-ʿAjlani and Sayf al-Din al-Maʾmun. Of the two, Maʾmun was the first to be swept into the Mardam orbit and the last to be dislodged from it. Born in 1905, into a family of middle-level functionaries in the Ottoman administrative order, he stud-ied at the American University of Beirut and then in Paris, where he received a doctorate in law.[4] Upon his return to Damascus he joined the Nationalist Youth and, by 1932, was already identified in *al-Mudhik al-mubki* as a "Mardam man."[5] In terms of loyalty, Mardam could not have made a better selection. Furthermore, Maʾmun's dapper style and attrac-tive personality contributed to the Nationalist Youth's facelifting.[6]

On paper, Munir al-ʿAjlani resembled Sayf al-Din al-Maʾmun in sev-eral respects. They were the same age and were trained in Paris as law-yers. There, however, the likeness ended. ʿAjlani was born into an old aristocratic family of *ashraf*, who had controlled the position of *naqib* (doyen) throughout much of the nineteenth century.[7] The ʿAjlanis were also wealthy, owning hundreds of hectares of irrigated fruit farms in the Ghuta and in the district of Duma.[8] ʿAjlani's father—a resident of Sidi ʿAmud in the Shaghur quarter—was a prominent religious shaykh and big landowner. His uncle had served as a judge on the Court of Appeals, as a member of the Council of Education in the 1890s, as President of the Damascus Municipality, and as an elected deputy to the Ottoman Parlia-ment.[9]

[3] Conversation with Mahmud al-Bayruti (Damascus, 10 March 1976).

[4] Faris, *Man huwa 1949*, p. 398.

[5] Along with Bayruti, Shiliq, Najib al-Armanazi, Rashid al-Maluhi, and Husni Tillu. *Al-Mudhik al-mubki*, no. 136 (23 July 1932), p. 1.

[6] The fastidious Maʾmun, considered the "second best-dressed man" in Syria in the 1930s, spent profusely on his wardrobe. He seems to have emulated Saʿdallah al-Jabiri, who was regarded as the "best-dressed man" in Syria, and who later cultivated Maʾmun.

[7] See Khoury, *Urban Notables*, Chapters 1, 2.

[8] Communiqué from Ramez G. Tomeh.

[9] *Salname: Suriye vilayeti*, 1309–1310/1892–1893, pp. 107, 120; 1312/1894–1895, p. 88; also see *Khoury, Urban Notables*, Chapter 3.

Munir was educated at the *tajhiz* and the Damascus Law Faculty before going to Paris. In Paris, his various political activities as Secretary of the Arab Association and later the Association of Arabic Culture (Jam'iyyat al-thaqafa al-'arabiyya) got him into trouble with the police. Eventually, he was suspended from the University of Paris for distributing printed matter meant to enlighten French public opinion on Syrian affairs and for writing an article critical of French policy in Syria in the Paris newspaper, *Le Soir*. After a brief exile in Switzerland, he was allowed to return to Paris where he completed his doctorate in constitutional law. Along the way he also picked up a diploma in journalism and followed courses at the Sorbonne in literature and philosophy.

On his return to Damascus, Munir al-'Ajlani's first impulse was to put his intellectual capacities to full use in the world of journalism. He began writing provocative articles on politics and society for the National Bloc newspaper, *al-Qabas*, and for other papers. He also joined the Nationalist Youth.[10]

By virtue of his status in Damascus society and his financial independence, Munir al-'Ajlani, unlike most of his contemporaries, had the potential to become his own "free agent." In 1934, only his age seemed to stand in his way. To the leadership of the National Bloc his qualifications were impeccable and it is possible that Jamil Mardam looked on him at first as his protégé. Although 'Ajlani's greater lateral political mobility had to be carefully watched, in 1934 he appeared willing to cooperate with the Bloc.

'Ajlani saw that the educated youth of Damascus were by the early thirties looking for an outlet into politics. He also noted, with regret, that the primary mechanisms of political mobilization in the capital still rested in the hands of traditional and often illiterate *qabadayat* in the quarters. Not only were these mechanisms primitive, they were no longer respected by the educated youth who wanted to break away from these popular personalities. 'Ajlani differed, however, from Farid Zayn al-Din and 'Abd al-Razzaq al-Dandashi in one important way: he was more attracted to the disciplinary side of political organization and mobilization. Indeed, early on in his career he betrayed instincts akin to authoritarianism. He believed, for instance, that the salvation of the youth and the nation could best be secured through the formation of a paramilitary organization with an "independent voice and impact upon society."[11] It is likely that 'Ajlani, who remained in Europe later than other Syrian nationalists, had a chance to witness first-hand the mushrooming "rightist anti-

[10] Vacca, "Notizie," pp. 486–87; Faris, *Man huwa 1949*, p. 284; conversation with Munir al-'Ajlani (Beirut, 2 Sept. 1975); *al-Mudhik al-mubki*, no. 202 (27 Jan. 1934), p. 7.
[11] Conversation with Munir al-'Ajlani (Beirut, 2 Sept. 1975).

parliamentary Leagues" in Paris or even the paramilitary Black Shirts in Italy and Brown Shirts in Germany[12] who featured so prominently in the daily headlines in Europe. He certainly admitted to having been impressed with their high level of organization, discipline, and *esprit de corps*. On ʿAjlani's return to Damascus he discovered a small but attentive audience—among whom were Jamil Mardam and Fakhri al-Barudi—to listen to his appraisal of the nationalist movement's ills and his remedies. Two years passed, however, before the time was propitious and the resources available for ʿAjlani's ideas to materialize.

In the meantime, Jamil Mardam encouraged ʿAjlani and Sayf al-Din al-Ma'mun to take charge of the Nationalist Youth. He also encouraged Bayruti and Khalid al-Shiliq to concentrate on what they did best—recruiting youth from the quarters and pursuing their bitter rivalry with League strongmen, such as Shafiq Sulayman. Under this division of labor the Nationalist Youth experienced a mini-revival as its new leaders endowed it with much greater respect at the *tajhiz* and Law Faculty.[13] In the same year, a new Boy Scout outfit, known as the Maysalun Troop, appeared in Damascus, led by a medical student and former Umayyad trooper, Midhat al-Bitar. The son of a prosperous Maydani merchant, Bitar had been in and out of jail between 1931 and 1933 for his role in various nationalist demonstrations and strikes. Dissatisfied with attempts by ʿAli ʿAbd al-Karim al-Dandashi and Rushdi al-Jabi to keep the Ghuta Troop out of the political limelight, Bitar turned his troop into a militant political arm of the Nationalist Youth. Not long afterwards, the Sûreté Générale suspended the Maysalun Troop for disturbing the peace in the Syrian capital by clashing with the Ghuta Troop. The Maysalun Scouts, however, clung together, taking refuge in the Nationalist Youth, from which they would again emerge.[14]

The Nationalist Youth's new image had two other important consequences. It began to receive greater financial backing from merchants sympathetic to the National Bloc, among them Tawfiq al-Qabbani, the wealthy sugar industrialist and a prominent resident of Shaghur, and Amin al-Dalati, a landlord and the owner of the biggest lumber yard in Damascus, who in 1935 donated all the building materials for the Nationalist Youth's first clubhouse in al-Qanawat.[15] And it began to attract members of the intelligentsia. However, the choice made by many young men to join the Bloc's youth wing rather than the League of National Action was one of strategy, not ideology. The young intelligentsia were in-

---

[12] Shirer, *The Collapse of the Third Republic*, pp. 178–79.

[13] *Al-Mudhik al-mubki*, no. 202 (27 Jan. 1934), p. 7; MAE, Syrie–Liban 1930–40. Martel to MAE, 11 May 1934, vol. 488, pp. 159–65.

[14] Anonymous, "Le Scoutisme musulman."

[15] *Al-Mudhik al-mubki*, no. 273 (16 Nov. 1935), p. 5.

terested in radicalizing the Bloc, but they saw the need to cooperate with their elders in the urgent political circumstances of the day. The new Nationalist Youth recruits believed that the League's pan-Arab ideals failed to correspond to the day-to-day realities of steering an independence movement whose territorial demands, indeed horizons, were rapidly shrinking.

Of the many young men who had gravitated toward the Nationalist Youth by 1935, several deserve mention: ʿAbd al-Wahhab al-Malki, an engineer in the Department of Public Works who hailed from a landowning family of Damascus;[16] Shafiq Jabri, a 33-year-old journalist and rising nationalist poet who descended from a *yerliyye* (local janissary) family of the Shaghur quarter and whom the Lazarists had educated;[17] Ahmad al-Samman, the scion of a prosperous merchant family of Damascus who had a doctorate in law from Paris and who, on returning to Damascus, joined the prestigious law firm of the Bloc chief, Ihsan al-Sharif;[18] and Mazhar al-Bakri, the younger brother of Fawzi and Nasib.

Born in 1900, Bakri completed his secondary studies in Damascus before going to Grenoble to study agricultural engineering, one of several younger members of big landowning families to be sent to France or Britain after World War I for training in the agricultural sciences.[19] Mazhar returned to Syria just in time to participate in the Great Revolt. By the end of 1926, he had to flee the country with his brothers. Mazhar and Fawzi ended up in Cairo while Nasib took refuge in Jaffa.

During the Great Revolt the nascent Palestine Communist Party had assisted the rebel bands in the Ghuta with funding,[20] in a bid to establish ties between the Comitern and the Syrian national movement.[21] Although the Party Vice-Chairman Elie Teper had contacts with Nasib al-Bakri, ʿAdil Arslan, and other leaders, the Palestine Communist Party's pronounced Jewish component made the Arabs generally wary.[22] It succeeded, however, in getting Nasib Bey and Rashid al-Taliʿa to go to Cairo in January 1927, to meet Soviet agents.[23] In the next month, Mazhar al-

---

[16] De Boucheman, "Les chemises de fer," p. 3.

[17] Qudama, Maʿalim, vol. 1, p. 230.

[18] Faris, Man huwa 1949, p. 214.

[19] Ibid., p. 477.

[20] The Palestine Communist Party contributed the sum of £E 80. MAE, Syrie–Liban 1918–29. 17 June 1927, vol. 213, pp. 26–34. This same report stated that the aid contributed by the "Secours rouge de Palestine" and the Soviet government was much more substantial.

[21] MAE, Syrie–Liban 1918–29. "Note au sujet du communisme au Levant," Commandant Terrier, vol. 433, pp. 4–8.

[22] Hanna Batatu, The Old Social Classes, Appendix One, pp. 1151–52.

[23] It seems that ʿAdil Arslan, who was in Cairo at this time, was also contacted. MAE, Syrie–Liban 1918–29. 17 June 1927, vol. 213, pp. 21–34.

Bakri, who had also been in contact with Palestine Communist Party members in Vienna and Berlin,[24] surfaced in Brussels as the Syrian delegate to the Comitern-backed "International Congress of the League Against Imperialism and Colonial Oppression and for National Independence." Intended to coordinate the activities of anti-colonial struggles, the League set up a "Secretariat" for the Arab countries and chose Mazhar as its head. But he never completed his task of setting up regional committees in the Arab territories under Mandate. His contacts in Baghdad, where he went first, were almost exclusively with members of the big landowning class, identified as pro-British.[25] Soon thereafter the deal his brothers struck with the French in return for complete repatriation made Mazhar suspect in Arab nationalist circles. In August 1928, the delegate from Syria and Palestine to the Sixth Congress of the Communist International identified the Bakris as part of the "National reformist bourgeoisie" of Syria, and not as part of the "radical" or "extreme" opposition.[26] Mazhar had obviously been the wrong man for the Comitern's assignment.

Mazhar al-Bakri's re-emergence in Damascus in the early thirties as a Nationalist Youth leader indicated that his family had returned to the mainstream of the independence movement. Already Nasib had been brought on to the National Bloc Council in November 1932, after the organization supported his bid for a seat in Parliament earlier that year. His political views, tempered in the years after the Great Revolt, were definitely an asset to Jamil Mardam; indeed, the older Bakri supported wholeheartedly the policy of "honorable cooperation." Another asset was his virtually unsurpassed influence in the quarters among qabadayat and popular religious shaykhs, many of whom were veterans of the revolt who had served alongside him.

Political life in the quarters was not as vibrant in the thirties as it had been in the previous decade, nor was it as vital to the continuation of the

---

[24] Ibid., "Bouchede Note," 14 March 1927, vol. 212, pp. 125–29.

[25] Batatu, The Old Social Classes, pp. 1152–53.

[26] In his Report, the delegate ranked the "National Reformist Bourgeoisie" just ahead of the "Compradors" such as the Lutfallahs, Sursuks, and, surprisingly, Shahbandar. The Bakris were listed with Shaykh Taj al-Din al-Hasani as part of the landlord, commercial bourgeoisie and high bureaucratic class who wanted re-unification of Syria with Lebanon and democratic liberties. The other two categories were the "radical opposition" and the "extreme opposition." The former included the remnants of the People's Party, the industrial bourgeoisie, petty bourgeoisie (merchants and artisans), intellectuals (liberal professions). The latter included emigrant Syrians. The delegate claimed that this group was not class-oriented, and included Sultan al-Atrash, Shakib Arslan, Ihsan al-Jabiri, Shukri al-Quwwatli, and Riyad Sulh. MAE, Syrie–Liban 1918–29. "Report of the Syrian Delegate to the Sixth Congress of the Communist International, Moscow," 18 July 1928–30 Aug. 1928, vol. 215, pp. 69–82.

independence struggle. But a nationalist politician's influence was still measured by the extent of his patronage network among the mass of un-educated and unemployed residents in the popular quarters, the small merchants and artisans, and the religious leadership. For instance, Jamil Mardam may not have moved as comfortably among the masses as Fakhri al-Barudi or Nasib al-Bakri, but he always worked to diversify his patron-age network through face-to-face contacts. He also knew that one way to strengthen his bargaining position with the French was to rely on popular leaders who were willing to support him by putting their own patronage networks at his disposal. By 1935, Mardam could claim to include in his political network the Nationalist Youth, important elements of the absen-tee landowning class and traditional commercial bourgeoisie, and quarter chiefs and popular religious shaykhs. On the level of city politics, this di-verse base gave him a clear edge over his rivals, particularly Shukri al-Quwwatli, in spite of the independence movement's radicalization after 1933.

On the level of national politics, the persistent rivalry between the Da-mascus and Aleppo Blocs continued to threaten Jamil Mardam's pre-em-inent position. The Aleppo Bloc, on the surface more unified than the Da-mascus Bloc, nonetheless was criss-crossed by subterranean currents of family and political factionalism. For example, the Hananu-Ibrahim Pasha faction still did not completely trust Saʿdallah al-Jabiri. Jabiri was not on good terms with the Qudsis who had been at odds with his family over personal matters for years, not least of which was the social rebuff received by young Nazim al-Qudsi, a Bloc stalwart, when he asked for the hand of Saʿdallah's niece. Meanwhile, a bitter rivalry was brewing be-tween the two physicians, Hasan Fuʿad Ibrahim Pasha and ʿAbd al-Rah-man al-Kayyali. Ibrahim Pasha, a popular personality with the masses, among whom he built up quite a large following through his distribution of free medical services to the needy and his family's diverse personal connections among the educated youth and *qabadayat*, was deeply irri-tated by Kayyali's loquaciousness, arrogance, and aloofness. For his part, Kayyali scarcely concealed his disrespect for Ibrahim Pasha's medical training, which he thought inferior to his own American University of Beirut training.[27] Finally, Kayyali and Jabiri were not always on good terms. Not only were their respective relatives rivals for the same reli-gious posts, but Jabiri was especially disdainful of Kayyali's long-wind-edness and his acute impetuosity, which in his opinion regularly led Kayyali to lose sight of the day-to-day realities of struggle against the French.[28]

[27] *Al-Mudhik al-mubki*, no. 227 (6 Oct. 1934), p. 18.
[28] Conversation with Edmond Rabbath (Beirut, 21 Aug. 1975).

But Mardam did not use any of these conflicts to engineer a split in the Aleppo Bloc to his own advantage. Rather, in a most unorthodox move, he began to promote Subhi Barakat as a potential Bloc member. He claimed that Barakat, the ex-Prime Minister and Speaker of Parliament, had mended his ways. It was true that Barakat had distanced himself from the High Commission when he was passed over for the Presidency of Syria in 1932, that he had voted against the French-sponsored treaty in November 1933, and that he had begun to criticize the French openly when he was passed over for the Prime Ministership in March 1934. Barakat, however, was despised in Aleppo for his chameleon-like political style. If anything, Mardam's championship of Barakat helped to close Bloc ranks in Aleppo, where the thought of collaborating with him bordered on treason.[29] Mardam failed in this attempt to breach Aleppine unity, though some felt his real aim had been to exploit Barakat's connections with the Quai d'Orsay for his own ends. Mardam did visit Paris later in 1934, though the use he made of his new ally's friends in high circles there did not bring him anything substantial in return.[30] But Mardam was a calculating man, always trying to peer into the future.

THE COURSE OF FRENCH POLICY in Syria shifted with political changes in Paris. Although the Syrian people unequivocally expressed their opinion of the treaty in the 1933 parliamentary vote, the High Commission's decision to drop all negotiations did not come until after the fall of two French governments in early 1934, the scandal-ridden Chautemps ministry at the end of January[31] and the Daladier ministry several days later. These events were accompanied by bloody street battles in Paris between rightist Leagues and leftists; indeed, the very existence of the Third Re-

---

[29] The Bloc Congress in February 1934 revealed two opposing factions: the radicals led by Ibrahim Hananu and including Hashim al-Atasi, Zaki al-Khatib, Ihsan al-Sharif, Riyad Sulh, Tawfiq al-Shishakli, and, by the end of the Congress, Sa'dallah al-Jabiri; and the moderates led by Jamil Mardam and including Mazhar Raslan, Fakhri al-Barudi, 'Afif Sulh, Faris and Fa'iz al-Khuri, and Dr. Kayyali. At the Congress, Mardam wanted to have the Bloc's statutes revised so that a simple majority was required to take any decision; to create a permanent office for the Bloc in Damascus; and for reopening contacts with the High Commission. But Mardam and his supporters got nowhere. Not only were Atasi and Hananu elected President and Vice President of the Bloc, respectively, but the Bloc's political program again demanded that Syrian unity include the four contested "cazas" (districts) which the French attached to Lebanon in 1920, and that national sovereignty, administrative, political and economic unity, and a general political amnesty be granted. Furthermore, there was to be no contact with the Mandate authorities until the High Commissioner returned to the Levant. MAE, Syrie–Liban 1930–40, vol. 488, pp. 72–80.

[30] Al-Mudhik al-mubki, no. 269 (5 Oct. 1935), p. 18.

[31] The scandal was the Stavisky Affair. See Shirer, The Collapse of the Third Republic, pp. 184–90.

public seemed in jeopardy. What followed was another flimsy coalition
cabinet. It discarded the superficially liberal policy toward Syria initiated
in the spring of 1932 by Edouard Herriot.[32] In official French circles in
Damascus, this policy change was supposedly attributed to the "lesson
British benevolent rashness in Iraq holds for others tempted to follow
along the same path."[33]

Before his return to Beirut in March 1934 from a lengthy vacation in
Paris, the Comte de Martel had been handed several instructions: one was
to renew for another six months the decree suspending Parliament; another was to make a clean sweep of French advisers and delegates; a third
was to dismiss the government of Haqqi al-ʿAzm. Martel was also instructed to ask the pliable, though unreliable, Shaykh Taj al-Din al-Hasani to form a new government. Shaykh Taj himself deserves at least part
of the credit for his own selection. He too had gone to Paris the previous
summer in search of support for his return to politics, after an absence of
more than two years. There, he was assisted by the "persistent canvassing" of Ben Ghabrit, "the *eminence grise* at Rabat and at one time the
'chaouch' in the French Legation at Tangiers," who was Taj's patron in
Paris.[34]

Taj's re-emergence forced the cooperative wing of the National Bloc to
drop once and for all the idea of resuming negotiations. In the mind of the
Syrian public, his name elicited one response: "treason." As news of his
appointment spread on March 17, the bazaars in the interior towns shut
down automatically.[35]

Taj's new cabinet included two of his closest associates: Jamil al-Ulshi,
one of the most distrusted politicians in Syria, and Husni al-Barazi of
Hama, the renegade nationalist who had all but broken with the National
Bloc by 1931. Other appointees were the respected Damascene notable,
ʿAta al-Ayyubi, the Antioch deputy, Muhammad Yahya al-ʿAdali and
the Armenian Catholic deputy of Aleppo, Henri Hindiyya.[36]

Taj's government lasted nearly two years. It took no major initiatives

[32] *Ibid.*, pp. 190–211.
[33] FO 371/625, vol. 19022. MacKereth to FO, 7 Jan. 1935. The growth of radical anti-
British movements in Iraq was watched closely by the French, as were the Assyrian massacres.
[34] *'Chaouch'* or *shawish* (councillor). On the Algerian Khaddour Ben Ghabrit's activities
in Franco-Moroccan politics, see Edmund Burke, III, *Prelude to Protectorate in Morocco.
Precolonial Protest and Resistance, 1860–1912* (Chicago, 1976), pp. 168–69; FO 371/2395,
vol. 17944. MacKereth to Simon, 19 March 1934.
[35] FO 871/2395, vol. 17944. MacKereth to Simon, 19 March 1934. Taj was denounced as
an "enemy of Allah" for breaking the Ramadan fast by eating lunch with the High Commissioner on his visit to Damascus.
[36] Hasan al-Hakim, *Mudhakkirati*, vol. 2, pp. 170–71.

during this period and, in fact, was regularly passed over by the High Commission and his staff. The Comte de Martel devoted most of his attention to economic matters, ostensibly in an effort to lay the foundations of an economic revival in Syria as the great depression began to recede. As a matter of principle, he steadfastly refused to talk politics.

The new government, however, did receive the attention of Syrian nationalists.[37] For example, Aleppo greeted Taj's first official visit to the city with a spate of bombings, strikes, and demonstrations. During his visit, 188 persons were arrested, 57 of whom were sentenced to prison terms of up to eight months. Among those jailed were three Aleppo Bloc leaders: Sa'dallah al-Jabiri, Dr. Hasan Fu'ad Ibrahim Pasha, and Shaykh 'Abd al-Qadir al-Sarmini.[38]

Such episodes were repeated frequently and with even greater intensity once Martel suspended Parliament *sine die* on 2 November 1934. The National Bloc reacted with a strongly-worded declaration issued by the "Committee for the Defense of Parliamentary Institutions," an *ad hoc* group of Bloc leaders which protested "France's illegal dictatorship," the continued partition of Syria, her misappropriation of the funds of the Common Interests, and her "irregular methods of financial and political administration."[39]

The High Commissioner's suspension of Parliament helped to unify the Bloc. Jamil Mardam, who returned to the Syrian capital on November 3, after a month-long fact-finding mission in Paris, which he made without the permission of the Bloc, reported to his colleagues that they should not expect a change in the French government's attitude.[40] After his discouraging trip, during which he met only low-ranking officials of the Quai d'Orsay,[41] Mardam personally apologized to his colleagues for his earlier deviations from National Bloc tenets. First, he held a special meeting of the Damascus Bloc at his home on November 17, at which time he sponsored an internal resolution calling for a Bloc congress to be held in Aleppo and to coincide with the anticipated release from prison of Sa'dallah al-Jabiri and Hasan Fu'ad Ibrahim Pasha at the end of the

[37] FO 371/2142, vol. 20849, 6 May 1933.

[38] Al-Kayyali, *al-Marahil*, vol. 2, pp. 200–3; FO 371/3609, vol. 17944. Cowan (Aleppo) to FO, 26 May 1934; FO 371/3862, vol. 17944. Todd to FO, 5 June 1934; MAE, Syrie–Liban 1930–40. Martel Telegrams, 25 May 1934, vol. 488, 171–74.

[39] For the Arabic text, see *al-Ayyam*, no. 645 (7 Nov. 1934). A French text is included in FO 371/790, vol. 19022. MacKereth to Simon. It is also translated into English; MAE, Syrie–Liban 1930–40. Martel to MAE, 2 Nov. 1934, vol. 489, pp. 138–39.

[40] Al-Kayyali, *al-Marahil*, vol. 2, pp. 271–72, 277; MAE, Syrie–Liban 1930–40. Martel to MAE, 26 Oct. 1934, vol. 489, pp. 115–17.

[41] *Ibid.*

month.[42] Then, he led his colleagues on a silent march to the Sérail in Marjé Square to protest French political intransigence. Joining nationalist leaders were scores of veiled women, who had begun to play a more active role in nationalist demonstrations and other political activities. The police, however, were little more polite to women than they were to men on such occasions. When the women refused to disperse, eleven were arrested. In Aleppo similar incidents occurred and many women from the notable families of the town were also jailed.[43]

For the Syrian nationalist movement, the years 1934–35 were not perceptibly active ones at the uppermost levels of politics, largely because of the treaty stalemate and breakdown in negotiations. But the movement's survival required constant activity on other political fronts. Now, more than ever, the National Bloc had to make the French feel its independent influence in society; and this required a supple shift from a policy of cooperation to one of measured confrontation. This shift was easy enough for the aristocratic members of the National Bloc who regarded most French officials as incompetents who had been unable to make it at home. And though much of the financial corruption and speculation engaged in by French officials in the first years of the Mandate had been cleaned up by the mid-thirties, Syrians still widely believed that many French officials continued to line their own pockets. As for the personal character of recent High Commissioners, Jouvenel was regarded as a "windbag and hypocrite"; Ponsot had the reputation of being "indolent and tactless"; and Martel, though more energetic and enterprising than his predecessors, had allowed his private life to become an "open scandal."[44] He was a frequenter of cafés and cabarets in Beirut, and was indiscreetly engaged in a relationship with the Russian wife of a foreign consular official.[45]

THE BLOC, PALESTINE, AND PAN-ARABISM

The Bloc, having decided to shift to a more confrontational style of politics, also became more engaged in pan-Arab issues. In 1933 and 1934 the sale of land to Zionist organizations in Palestine emerged as one of those

[42] *Les Echos de Syrie.* no. 6, (17 Nov. 1934), cited in FO 684/7/1/3, MacKereth to Simon.
[43] *The Palestine Post* (25 Nov. 1934), cited in FO 684/7/13, MacKereth to Simon; MAE, Syrie–Liban 1930–40. Martel to MAE, 23 Nov. 1934, vol. 489, pp. 183–86; *ibid.*, Telegram of 23 Nov. 1934, vol. 489, p. 194.
[44] FO 371/2220, vol. 20065. J. G. Ward (Eastern Department) Memorandum, 22 April 1936.
[45] FO 371/2142, vol. 20849, 6 May 1937. Martel's wife arrived in Beirut in the winter of 1935. Intensely keen on horseracing, her colors were seen regularly at the weekly races in Beirut.

issues. Until the late 1920s, most of the land purchased by Jews in Palestine was uncultivated and often sold in absentia by Lebanese and Syrian owners. Although Syrian landowners and Lebanese merchants had sold lands to Jews in Palestine, most notably the Amir Saʿid al-Jazaʾiri who unloaded some of his lands in Tiberias in the early twenties,[46] and the Sursuk family of Beirut who between 1921 and 1925 parted with vast tracts of land in Marj bin ʿAmir,[47] Syrian nationalists were largely indifferent to such sales. Palestinian Arabs themselves only began to make concerted efforts to block land sales to Jews after 1929, when "a growing percentage of the lands which the Jews acquired was purchased from local landowners and was generally cultivated."[48] Indeed, there seems to have been no sustained opposition to such sales until 1934.[49]

The timing of the first major reaction in Syria to land sales coincided with the resumption of large-scale purchases of lands from Palestinian and other Arab owners in 1933, after an appreciable decrease in Jewish land purchases between 1930 and 1932.[50] Rumors circulated in Damascus in March 1934 (originating from the Istiqlal Party of Palestine) that the biggest landowning family in the Syrian capital, the heirs of the late ʿAbd al-Rahman al-Yusuf, had sold their large property, al-Btayha, on the Syrian shore of Lake Tiberias, to the Jewish National Fund.[51]

ʿAbd al-Rahman Pasha al-Yusuf's eldest son, Muhammad Saʿid, an Austrian-educated aristocrat, had accumulated large debts between 1926 and 1933 and was about to be foreclosed by a group of local Christian financial establishments including the Ernest Asfar Bank and the Asfar & Sara Bank.[52] The Yusufs, like several other big landowning families of

---

[46] See Chapter 9.

[47] Also known as the Jezreel Valley. Kenneth W. Stein, *The Land Question in Palestine, 1917–1939* (Chapel Hill, 1984), pp. 54–59; Y. Porath, *The Palestinian Arab National Movement*, vol. 2, p. 83.

[48] *Ibid.*

[49] The Zionists developed a thirst for Syrian and Lebanese waters early on. According to the French report on "The Modifications of the Syro-Palestinian Frontier" of 1 April 1926, they requested that the High Commissioner Henry de Jouvenel place the Yarmuk Falls and the Litani in their hands, so that they might better exploit the Ruthenberg Monopoly, which included the Palestine Electric Company concession, and to furnish new lands for Jewish colonization in the regions of Dirʿa, Qunaytra, Tyre, and Sidon. MD, 7N 4171.

[50] Porath, *The Palestinian Arab*, p. 83.

[51] FO 684/7/25. MacKereth to Simon, 24 March 1934; FO 371/2398, vol. 17946. MacKereth to Simon, 24 March 1934.

[52] The British Consul in Damascus reported the amount of debts at £T 12,000 gold. The £T 14,000 gold figure of Yusuf indebtedness comes from the following sources: MWT, *Registre Commercial de Damas* (4 Jan. 1928–19 Dec. 1928). £T 2,865; *Ibid.* (24 Dec. 1928–30 Oct. 1930). £T 8,000 (11 Nov. 1928); *Ibid.* (4 Jan. 1928–30 Oct. 1930). £T 479 (18 Dec. 1926–31 July 1927); *Ibid.* (30 Oct. 1929–3 Dec. 1930). £T 471 (5 Nov. 1929); *Ibid.* £T 660

Damascus, were heavily mortgaged by the early thirties, owing, on one hand, to the great losses in land rent because of the collapse of world food prices during the depression (which incidentally the widespread drought in southern Syria exacerbated in 1933–34) and, on the other, to their proclivity to live extravagantly, indulging in exceedingly expensive pleasures. At least for a while, landed families like the Yusufs could borrow large sums, using their lands as collateral. In the process they became heavily mortgaged to local Christian and Jewish banking houses. With no end to the depression in sight, these bankers grew increasingly reluctant to lend, having already experienced difficulty in collecting both the interest and the principal on earlier loans. The Yusuf family had to ask their in-law, Husayn Ibish, another big landowner whose credit rating was still sound, to borrow money on the family's behalf.[53]

Court registers in the late twenties and early thirties reveal a high incidence of declared bankruptcies in commercial and banking establishments in Damascus, and heavy landlord indebtedness to these concerns. Registers also point to a high incidence of conflict over inheritance and other property rights within large landowning families.[54] The absentee landowning families of Damascus faced increasing financial paralysis as a result of their social decadence. Formerly powerful and tightly knit, some now lived not only on borrowed money but on borrowed time. Many landowners still viewed their lands as only good to provide rents, security, and prestige. Rarely did families reinvest in the agricultural productivity of their lands or in agricultural-based industries.[55] Rather, they

(2 Oct. 1929); *Ibid.* £T 185 (27 June 1929); *Ibid.* £T 411 (3 Jan. 1930); *Registre Civil,* no. 6 (14 June 1934–18 July 1935). £T 179 (5 Nov. 1929). £T 534.5 (12 March 1930); *Ibid.* (16 Dec. 1937–5 July 1939). £T 350 (30 Nov. 1931).

[53] *Ibid., Registre Commercial,* no. 9 (26 Oct. 1933–12 April 1934), Hussein [Husayn] Ibish borrowed from Antoine Siouffi, sum of £T 487 gold (three years), on behalf of Fa'iza al-ʿAzm al-Yusuf (wife of ʿAbd al-Rahman Pasha al-Yusuf). Husayn Ibish (b. 1885) was educated at the Syrian Protestant College in Beirut. He was the son of a prosperous Kurdish livestock merchant and married Wajiha al-Yusuf, daughter of ʿAbd al-Rahman Pasha, and at the time bought some of the Yusuf lands known as Bitariyya in Duma. By the 1940s Ibish was the biggest landowner in the Damascus province. See AUB, *Directory of Alumni,* p. 74; MWT, *Registre Civil* (19 Feb. 1942–26 Nov. 1942); conversation with Wajiha al-Yusuf (Beirut, 15 Aug. 1975); communiqué from Ramez G. Tomeh.

[54] Especially conflicts within the ʿAbid and ʿAzm families. On the ʿAbids see MWT, *Registre Civil* (31 Dec. 1930–25 Aug. 1932), pp. 191–200; *Ibid.* (19 Feb. 1942–26 Nov. 1942). On the ʿAzms see *ibid., Registre Civil* (25 Feb. 1929–21 Dec. 1930); *Ibid.* (19 Feb. 1942–26 Nov. 1942). *Registre Commercial* (6 Dec. 1930–8 Dec. 1931), pp. 171–74.

[55] For instance, Syrian landlords rarely sold their lands, preferring to mortgage them. MWT, *Registre des jugements du Tribunal de 1ère Instance Correctionnelle de l'année 1931 et 1932,* pp. 22–25.

preferred to spend their earnings on conspicuous consumption in the towns.

The Yusuf family's financial troubles became public knowledge in 1933, when the Asfar & Sara Bank won the right in court to foreclose on the buildings and some lands of the family in al-Btayha, the Jawlan, and Duma, if the Yusufs did not immediately repay in full the sum of £T 3,892 gold.[56]

The Yusuf family thought of selling their Btayha property first. The 300,000 dunam tract (approximately 75,000 acres) lay farthest away from Damascus,[57] much of it was uncultivated despite its renowned fertility,[58] and the Jewish National Fund had long been interested in acquiring the frontier holdings of the Yusufs and other families like the Jaza'iris, their Beirut in-laws the Bayhums, and the Sursuks.[59] The Fund certainly knew that the Yusufs desperately needed capital and al-Btayha promised to fetch a high price, one which the Fund promised to pay in gold.[60] What the Yusuf family never anticipated was the loud outcry in Damascus against such a deal.

In February 1934, Damascus merchants, frustrated by the prolongation of the depression, by increased competition from Jewish textiles and the Palestine-Jewish owned confectionery industry, and by the continued smuggling of Zionist goods into Syria,[61] initiated a boycott of Zionist products. Many boycott leaders, including Tawfiq al-Qabbani, were National Bloc partisans. Initially by word of mouth and eventually by the circulation of anti-Zionist manifestos and the staging of large rallies, the boycott spread. Popular enthusiasm for it was flamed by rumors of the Yusufs' sale of al-Btayha to the Jewish National Fund. In early March, large stocks of Jewish-manufactured cloth were publicly burnt in Suq al-Hamidiyya.[62] Then, on March 12, the Damascus Police disbanded several

[56] MWT, *Registre Civil* (14 June 1934–18 July 1935).

[57] *Oriente Moderno*, 15 (1935), p. 268.

[58] Conversation with Wajiha al-Yusuf (Beirut, 15 Aug. 1975).

[59] *Les Echos de Syrie* (10 April 1934), cited in FO 684/7/25. MacKereth to Simon. This newspaper claims that Zionists wanted Yusuf lands (500,000 dunams); Jaza'iri lands (100,000 dunams); Sursuk and Bayhum (15,000 dunams); and the heirs of Mansur Pasha (50,000 dunams) and 'Izz al-Din Sulayman (15,000 dunams). The size of these holdings are inflated.

[60] Conversation with Wajiha al-Yusuf (Beirut, 29 Aug. 1975). MAE, Syrie–Liban, 1930–40. Sharife Abed to MAE, 26 June 1935, vol. 491, pp. 13–14; *ibid.*, Martel to MAE, 28 June 1935, p. 28; *ibid.*, Jamil Mardam-Beg (Damascus) letter, 16 July 1935, pp. 51–53[B]; *ibid.*, Haqqi al-Azm letter, 18 July 1935, pp. 54–56; *ibid.*, Lagarde (Beirut) Telegram, 6 September 1935, p. 87.

[61] FO 371/2236, vol. 16976, Satow to Simon, 17 March 1935.

[62] *L'Asie Française*, no. 317 (Feb. 1934), p. 64; FO 371/2547, vol. 17944. MacKereth to Simon, 3 April 1934.

Jewish societies that had been actively smuggling Jewish settlers into Palestine, on the grounds that by spreading Zionist propaganda they were
disturbing public order.[63] Meanwhile, several Syrian nationalist committees were hastily formed to intensify the anti-Zionist propaganda
campaign[64] and to encourage the peasants of al-Btayha to resist evacuation. There was serious concern that the Jewish organizations would oust
the Arab peasantry to make room for their own immigrants, as they were
known to have done in Palestine.[65]

Shukri al-Quwwatli encouraged the National Bloc to pressure the
French High Commission to halt the sale, which, it turned out, had yet to
be consummated. The result was, for a change, positive. On March 20,
the High Commission announced two decrees which prohibited the sale
to foreigners of lands on the frontiers of Syria-Lebanon with Palestine-
Transjordan.[66] To make certain that these decrees had their desired impact, they were conveniently predated to 18 January 1934, that is, before
the Yusuf–Jewish National Fund deed of sale was signed. It was obvious
that the High Commission, which had little sympathy for the Zionist
movement to start with, intended to block the sale of the Yusuf properties
and to prevent future Zionist purchases of Syrian land near the Palestine
frontier.[67]

Syrians had little reason to trust the High Commission and two alarming developments in the following week spawned a new Syrian nationalist offensive against the sale. The first was a controversial article in the
influential *Le Commerce du Levant* of Beirut, a Jewish-owned publication, which, in debating the pros and cons of Jewish immigration into Palestine, concluded that Syria stood to profit from Jewish investments in
the country and from increased tourism.[68] The other development was
the appearance in Damascus two days later of Chaim Weizmann, who had
come to the Yusuf home to complete the Btayha purchase.[69] In reaction,
especially to the Weizmann visit, a "Society for the Exploitation of the
Village of Btayha" was formed under President ʿAbid's auspices; he happened to be married to one of the Yusuf heirs, a sister of the late ʿAbd al-
Rahman Pasha. Assisted by several prominent political and business

[63] *Ibid.*
[64] *L'Asie Française*, no. 317 (Feb. 1934), p. 64.
[65] FO 371/2547, vol. 17944. MacKereth to Simon, 3 April 1934; also see Porath, *The Palestinian Arab*, pp. 87–90.
[66] Nos. 16/LR and 17/LR. FO 371/2398, vol. 17946. MacKereth to Simon, 24 March
1934.
[67] FO 371/2547, vol. 17944. MacKereth to Simon, 3 April 1934. By preventing the sale,
the French also wanted to prevent the British from incorporating the frontier areas under
the Mandate into Palestine. See Stein, *Land Question*, p. 200.
[68] *Le Commerce du Levant*, no. 317 (18 April 1934).
[69] *Les Echos de Syrie*, no. 114 (21 April 1934).

leaders, the Society sought funds to match the price being asked by the Yusufs for al-Btayha,[70] the staggering sum of £T 150,000.[71]

Over the next few months, the "Btayha Society" desperately tried to raise money, but the economic situation in the country hindered its efforts. Eventually, it was forced to adopt a new approach. On August 16, President ʿAbid issued a decree (no. 2,813) approving the formation of the Syrian Agricultural Company Ltd., of Damascus. Obviously inspired by the success of two other nationalist enterprises, the National Cement Company and the National Conserves Company, its founders wanted to purchase and then exploit the agricultural lands of al-Btayha and other frontier properties in order to "preserve the wealth of the country in the hands of her children." The Company's capital was fixed at £T 150,000 to be divided into 50,000 shares at £T 3 each; however, it was only to be formed when one-tenth of its capital was subscribed, and it would only begin to develop the lands when one-third of its capital had been collected.[72] The Syrian Agricultural Company's board of directors was composed of ten members; nine prominent Syrians[73] and one Palestinian, Ahmad Hilmi Pasha, the Company's Chairman and one of the founders of the recently-established Arab Bank, a Palestinian-owned institution.[74]

Although the Syrian Agricultural Company was a joint venture supported by the National Bloc, the League of National Action, and the Istiqlal Party, it, too, failed to raise the required capital. By the end of 1935, it was dissolved and its shareholders reimbursed. Meanwhile, the spendthrift Yusufs remained heavily in debt and still under Zionist pressure to sell al-Btayha. Nevertheless, the Syrian government and the High Commission refused to lift the veto which they had placed on the sale of these lands; a stand which in no small part was due to continued nationalist pressure. The Yusufs were eventually forced to find another means of solving their financial woes,[75] while the Jewish National Fund soon had to turn its attention to the disturbances which broke out in Palestine in 1936.

The role played by the National Bloc in the Btayha campaign indicated a slight but perceptible shift to a broader pan-Arab position. But it was

[70] *Le Commerce du Levant*, no. 321 (2 May 1934); *L'Orient* (Beirut), no. 62 (25 Sept. 1934).

[71] FO 371/2398, vol. 17946. MacKereth to Simon, 24 March 1934.

[72] *Le Commerce du Levant*, no. 349 (10 Oct. 1934).

[73] *Ibid.* Syrian directors were Nasuhi al-Bukhari, Nuri Ibish, Wasfi Zakariyya, Shamsi and Tawfiq al-Malki, Amin al-Dalati, Ihsan al-Quwwatli, Muhammad Nahhas, ʿAbd al-Razzaq al-Dandashi.

[74] *Oriente Moderno*, 15 (1935), p. 268.

[75] FO 371/6091, vol. 19022. MacKereth to FO, 1 Oct. 1935.

not only the Bloc leadership's anxiety about Zionist penetration into Syria which provoked its pan-Arab response.[76] Once its strategy of "honorable cooperation" had been diagnosed as bankrupt, the Bloc had to adopt a more confrontational approach toward the French; this entailed, among other things, placing a greater emphasis on pan-Arab politics. Of course, pressures from the Bloc's own left wing in Damascus and Aleppo as well as from radicalized youth organizations, such as the League of National Action, were also at play. On one level, the Bloc had to accommodate these more radical forces in order to retain its control of the overall nationalist movement. On another level, its chiefs had to strengthen their ties to the Arab world, both to prevent the Istiqlalis and the League of National Action from monopolizing the pan-Arab card which had become more important after the Bloc leadership lost its access to the High Commission. Jamil Mardam's abrupt turn toward the Arab world after 1933 was the best indication of the Bloc's changing needs.[77]

The years 1934-35 were full of active travel for Syrian nationalist leaders, who moved from one Arab country to the next, seeking support for personal and national aims. Jamil Mardam went on a personal mission to Saudi Arabia in May 1934, as head of the Syrian Red Crescent Society, to assist casualties of the Saʿudi-Yemeni War. Ostensibly, his mission was one of charity and was reportedly self-financed, but in fact his real object was to seek Ibn Saʿud's active support for Syrian nationalist strategy.[78] Later in July, Hashim al-Atasi met with Nahhas Pasha, the leader of the Egyptian Wafd Party, who was summering in Alexandria, to get the Wafd to actively support the Bloc.[79] By the end of the year, Nuri Saʿid, the Iraqi Foreign Minister, visited Damascus on his way to Geneva and

[76] In this period, the local Syrian press devoted considerable attention to Zionist activities in Palestine. It also began to report with alarming regularity rumors of various Zionist schemes to purchase and develop Syrian lands. For instance, local newspapers reported that the Syrian government was approached by a Palestinian Jewish group represented by one Joseph Levi, "with an offer to drain marshes on condition that they should be given all land reclaimed for agricultural exploitation over a period of 50 years. Labour, both for the actual work on the drainage of the marshes of Amq and for the subsequent exploitation of the territory, was to be provided by Zionist immigration." FO 371/2864, vol. 19024. Parr (Aleppo) to FO, 28 April 1935.

[77] The Bloc's renewed emphasis on pan-Arab policies in 1934 was part of the new political program worked out at the Homs Congress in February. The Congress participants adopted a motion calling for Arab unity with Iraq, Transjordan, and Palestine. At the time, Mardam opposed the motion on the grounds that it was "too hazardous" given the Bloc's rather weak position inside Syria. MAE, Syrie–Liban 1930–40. Martel Telegram, 3 Feb. 1934, vol. 488, pp. 42–49.

[78] MAE, Syrie–Liban 1930–40. Martel to MAE, 6 June 1934, vol. 488, pp. 230–34; FO 684/7/45. MacKereth to Simon, 10 May 1934.

[79] MAE, Syrie–Liban 1930–40. "Communiqué," 1 Aug. 1934 (Ramleh), vol. 489, pp. 27–28.

took the opportunity to tell Mardam and other Syrian leaders to seek a positive understanding with France, as Iraq had with Britain.[80] In Nuri's opinion, this was Syria's only hope for salvation. Later, in March 1935, Mardam, Fakhri al-Barudi, and Shafiq Jabri visited Baghdad and then Saudi Arabia to try once again to persuade Ibn Sa'ud to adopt a less platonic attitude toward pan-Arabism.[81]

TAXING NATIONALIST NERVES

Several other developments in 1934–35 aggravated the mounting tensions between Syrian nationalists and the French. One was the question of Assyrian migration. Since the fall of 1933, Assyrian refugees had been entering northeast Syria from Iraq where their rebellion against the newly independent Baghdad government had been ruthlessly squashed. Syrian nationalists supported the Iraqi government's actions against the Assyrians who had doubtless received encouragement from their erstwhile patrons, the British. Syrians had every reason to oppose the Assyrian influx into their country. For one thing, they feared that the Assyrians would become a fifth column and likened their coming to that of the Armenians after World War I. When the French government announced in 1934 that on humanitarian grounds France would help to settle this refugee community of some several thousand Christians in homes in the Jazira, the National Bloc was livid.[82] Nationalists justifiably asked how the Syrian government could offer financial assistance and even build homes for Assyrians on Syrian soil when it had neglected to lift a hand on behalf of the thousands of Syrian citizens in the Hawran and elsewhere who, because of the devastating drought, had been forced to quit the land and even the country, "leaving their fields and agricultural work prey to sterility and barrenness." But the Bloc's protests went unheard as more and more Assyrians were settled under the supervision of the League of Nations and granted full Syrian citizenship by the Mandate authority.[83]

Another sensitive issue straining Syrian nationalist nerves was the reintroduction of the Tobacco Monopoly on 1 March 1935. In the twenties, the Régie de Tabac remained a French-owned and administered monopoly;[84] but in 1930, when the monopoly elapsed, it was replaced by the

---

[80] FO 371/625, vol. 19022. MacKereth to FO, 7 Jan. 1935.

[81] FO 684/8/8(563). Humphrys to Simon, 13 March 1935. *Ibid.*, A. C. Kerr to Simon, 11 April 1935. MAE, Syrie–Liban 1930–40. Lagarde (Beirut), to MAE, 15 March 1935, vol. 490, pp. 109–11; also see MAE, Syrie–Liban 1930–40. Paul Lepissier (Baghdad) to Martel, 12 and 19 April 1935, vol. 490, pp. 14–18.

[82] Longrigg, *Syria*, p. 213.

[83] See *al-Ayyam*, no. 595 (10 Sept. 1934).

[84] See PMC, *Minutes*, 5/14/333, 31 Oct. 1924, p. 108. A useful summary of the history

banderole system, whereby the growing of tobacco and the manufacture
of cigarettes belonged to privately-owned establishments under license,
whose products were taxed (40 percent in Syria and 25 percent in Lebanon)[85] according to the *banderole* label "attached to the package in the
factory."[86] Under this system, production and pricing were not regulated; consequently, when the depression of the early thirties began to
have an impact, the tobacco industry suffered from overproduction causing prices to fall sharply. In September 1932, the various governments
under French Mandate decided to limit the maximum level of production
in each territory.[87] The replacement of the *banderole* system by a modified version of the *Régie* angered both producers and consumers, largely
because this new monopoly was granted to a privately-owned Franco-
Lebanese combine, the Compagnie Libano-Syrienne de Tabacs, which, in
turn, adopted an arbitrary pricing policy.[88] Although the loudest protests
against the new monopoly were heard in Lebanon—the biggest producer
of tobacco—protests were also registered throughout Syria. When the
monopoly was first announced in late November 1934,[89] the National
Bloc immediately led the opposition to it. Early in December, a large protest rally was held in the Umayyad Mosque in Damascus, at which time
Fakhri al-Barudi delivered a violent diatribe against the monopoly and its
authors.[90]

   Syrian nationalist reaction to the tobacco monopoly, however, was not
entirely economic in nature. Syrian protests happened to coincide with
developments in Lebanon, where the Maronite Patriarch had become the
center of opposition to the High Commission. Visibly annoyed by
France's refusal to take measures to reduce the economic burdens of the
depression and its refusal to grant Lebanon "true independence," Mon-
signor Arida used the tobacco issue to raise other political issues.[91] His
surprising overture to the National Bloc, whose leaders he visited in February 1935, raised hopes for a Muslim-Christian *entente* and for the unification and consolidation of opposition to the French. From the French

---

of the Tobacco Monopoly in Syria and Lebanon during the Mandate can be found in the
MAE, Gabriel Puaux Papers. Carton 35, "Note."
   [85] Hershlag, *Introduction*, p. 240.
   [86] Longrigg, *Syria*, p. 268.
   [87] Khuri, "Agriculture," pp. 81–82.
   [88] Hershlag, *Introduction*, p. 255.
   [89] *Arrêté*, no. 275/LR, 27 Nov. 1934.
   [90] MAE, Syrie–Liban 1930–40. "Note," 20 April 1935, vol. 500, pp. 210–11; FO 371/625,
vol. 19022. MacKereth to Simon, 7 Jan. 1935.
   [91] FO 371/2554, vol. 19022. MacKereth to Simon, 1 April 1935; Longrigg, *Syria*, pp.
206–7. Tobacco producers in Lebanon had applied pressures on Arida when they began to
fear losing their influence. See MAE, Syrie–Liban 1930–40. "Note," 20 April 1935, vol.
500, pp. 210–11.

perspective, there was considerable reason to worry about the implications of such a *rapprochement*.

The clearest expression of the nationalists' growing willingness to confront the French was a new boycott of the Damascus Tramway and Electricity Company, which began in June 1935. A vestige of Damascus's Ottoman past, this French-capitalized, Belgian-based concession was one of the most visibly annoying reminders of the European exploitation of Syria. In the summer of 1924, it first came under nationalist fire for doubling tram fares without warning. Local notables and religious leaders organized a boycott which lasted nearly three months.[92] Another boycott took place in 1931, just before the parliamentary elections, when electricity prices were again raised.[93] Throughout the period of Mandate government isolated incidents against the Company occurred, some of which were violent. By the thirties, it was the Nationalist Youth who led the attack, which usually consisted of overturning tramcars and setting them on fire, sometimes during the course of a demonstration.[94] The 1935 boycott was called for by the National Bloc. Fakhri al-Barudi inspired it, and by accusing the Company of selling electricity at prohibitive prices he had little difficulty keeping the boycott alive for several months. It was a peaceful and effective boycott, but even though it reportedly cut the company's receipts by more than half, the controlling group in Brussels refused to capitulate, fearing that any show of weakness might encourage the repetition of the same tactics on future occasions. A settlement was finally reached in November.[95]

The boycott was one sign among many that the mood among nationalists was changing from frustration to deep-seated anger during the summer of 1935. Ten years had elapsed since the start of the Great Revolt and there had been little progress toward independence. On the anniversary of the Prophet's birthday in early July, nationalist leaders refused to allow the Prime Minister and other Ministers of State to enter the special enclosure in the Umayyad Mosque reserved for members of government.

[92] FO 371/8546, vol. 10165, 17 Sept. 1924. On the Company's financial foundation see MAE, Syrie–Liban 1930–40. Belgian Ambassador (Paris) to Briand, 23 April 1931, vol. 578, pp. 161–62.

[93] Hanna, *al-Haraka al-ʿummaliyya*, p. 149.

[94] Conversation with Mahmud al-Bayruti (Damascus, 10 March 1976). For the role of public transport in city insurrections, see E. J. Hobsbawm, "Cities and Insurrections," in *Revolutionaries* (London, 1977), pp. 220–33.

[95] MAE, Syrie–Liban 1930–40. Martel to MAE, 14 June 1935, vol. 580, pp. 178–80; *ibid.*, Lagarde (Beirut) to MAE, 9 Aug. 1935, vol. 580, p. 184. According to the French, store owners in Damascus, fearing nationalist reprisals if they didn't comply with the boycott, resumed using *"lampes luxes,"* which they had held in reserve since the last boycott. Oil merchants, of course, were delighted by this opportunity to increase their sales to store owners. MAE, Syrie–Liban 1930–40. Martel to MAE, 21 June 1935, vol. 491, pp. 3–5.

After the service, several nationalists addressed the large crowds and then were carried by their "enthusiastic followers out of the Mosque" and through Suq al-Hamidiyya, "amidst cheering by orderly spectators."[96] Denunciations of Shaykh Taj as the "enemy of Allah" followed by praise for the Maronite Patriarch were chanted in the bazaars and streets.[97] But what was most impressive on this day and again on July 20 at the annual commemorative services for the "martyrs" of Maysalun was the ability of the National Bloc to exercise almost complete control over these large crowds; the Bloc had never before demonstrated such organizational skills, at least not in Damascus.[98] All this was doubtless frightening to behold, for the French and for their Syrian collaborators.

But, the nationalists suffered a loss with the death on August 31 of Dr. ʿAbd al-Razzaq al-Dandashi, the much-beloved and esteemed chief of the League of National Action. Ironically, Dandashi, who on that day was late for an appointment in the Maydan, had taken a tram, even though the boycott he had actively supported was still in effect. When some of his followers along the route noticed him, catching his attention, he leaned out of the car to return their greetings only to be cut down by a pole he had failed to notice in the road.[99] His death not only stunned nationalists in Syria but in Iraq and Palestine as well.

Then, on November 21 Ibrahim Hananu died after a long illness. No name was more familiar to children growing up in Syria in the twenties and thirties; stories of his heroics were standard bedtime fare. He had kept the ranks of the Aleppo National Bloc unified and had saved the independence movement from making damaging compromises with Syria's masters. His selfless dedication to Syrian independence was unrivalled. Just ten weeks before his death he wrote to Nabih al-ʿAzma in Palestine, confessing that for the past five years he had been heavily in debt, owing to his personal sacrifices for the nationalist movement. He was even planning to sell some of his lands—something Syrian landlords resorted to only when desperate. Although he specifically asked ʿAzma, a leading Arab nationalist fund-raiser, to keep his financial problems confidential, ʿAzma knew better. He immediately dispatched a letter to Ibn Saʿud, asking him to subsidize Hananu, whose debts totaled about £T 4,500 gold. But before Ibn Saʿud could respond, Hananu had died.[100]

---

[96] FO 371/6099, vol. 19022. MacKereth to Hoare, 1 Oct. 1935; FO 371/4614, vol. 19022. MacKereth to Hoare, 3 July 1927.

[97] J. Lecerf and R. Tresse, "Les ʿarada de Damas," *Bulletin d'Etudes Orientales*, 7/8 (1937–1938), p. 263.

[98] FO 371/4614, vol. 19022. MacKereth to Hoare, 3 July 1927.

[99] Nabih al-ʿAzma Papers [Syria]. File 5/ 274; conversation with Akram Zuʿaytir (Beirut, 11 Aug. 1975).

[100] Nabih al-ʿAzma Papers [Syria]. Ibrahim Hananu to al-ʿAzma, 12 Sept. 1935. Ha-

The deaths of then two eminent and much-loved men cast a shadow over the nationalist movement in Syria and in the other Arab lands. At the same time, clouds were gathering over Europe, for the League of Nations had been unable to prevent the Italian invasion of Ethiopia. With the demise of the international order, rumors began to circulate that a new "world war" was imminent. It was argued in some nationalist quarters that a war would ultimately improve Syria's chances for liberation.[101] Similar sentiments were expressed throughout the Middle East.[102] In general, however, Arab nationalists had little hope for assistance from Mussolini, despite the flirtations of such respected leaders as Shakib Arslan with Il Duce. Italy's reputation in the Arab world had long been impaired by her ruthless colonial rule in Libya and by bitter memories of her bombardment of Beirut in 1912. The National Bloc vehemently protested the recruitment of Syrian laborers by Italian building contractors for Italy's various enterprises in her East African colonies.[103] Related, if only indirectly, to these anti-Italian sentiments was the recurring question of Zionist penetration in Palestine. The Bloc strongly protested Zionist arms smuggling into Jaffa and Tel Aviv,[104] and the purchase of Syrian grain by Jews in Palestine on behalf of the Italian government.[105] Meanwhile, rumors of a new war created a state of great nervousness in the Syrian business community. Banks began calling in credits with alarming velocity and no new loans were being made. At the same time, the prices of essential commodities rose sharply.[106]

In Egypt, Italy's takeover of Ethiopia encouraged nationalists "to press

---

nanu's death and funeral created the opportunity for an important political demonstration in Aleppo. The bazaars and places of entertainment closed. The funeral was attended by delegations from all over Syria. "A notable feature was the public association of Christians and Muslim clergy and the fact that Christian as well as Muslim symbols were used in the designs of the floral tributes carried in the procession," which consisted of about 30,000 persons and stretched for two kilometers. There were no disorders however, as only Syrian police were on duty and the troops of the garrison were confined to their barracks. French residents were warned by the High Commission not to show themselves in public at the time of the funeral. FO 371/7126, vol. 19022. Parr (Aleppo) to Hoare, 29 Nov. 1935. In 1934, Hananu has taken seriously ill with tuberculosis. MAE, Syrie–Liban 1930–40. Martel to MAE, 24 Aug. 1934, vol. 489, pp. 29–31. Earlier in 1932, he had been wounded in an attempt on his life in the Sanjak of Alexandretta, the result of a dispute over landownership. There were demonstrations in all the major cities when news of this incident spread. MAE, Syrie–Liban 1930–40. Helleu (Beirut) to MAE, 9 Sept. 1932, vol. 482, pp. 34–45.

[101] FO 371/609, vol. 19022. MacKereth to Hoare, 1 Oct. 1935.

[102] Porath, The Palestinian Arab, p. 140.

[103] FO 371/6099, vol. 19022. MacKereth to Hoare, 1 Oct. 1935.

[104] FO 371/6174, vol. 19022. Villians to Rendel, 14 Oct. 1935, included in a dispatch from Kirkbride (Amman) to Law (Jerusalem), 2 Sept. 1935.

[105] FO 371/6099, vol. 19022. MacKereth to Hoare, 1 Oct. 1935; Alif ba', no. 4453 (23 Oct. 1935).

[106] FO 371/6099, vol. 19022. MacKereth to Hoare, 1 Oct. 1935.

for the restoration of the suspended Constitution and for achieving independence for their country." Egyptian nationalists were both frightened at the prospect of further foreign control in the region and hoped Britain would be frightened enough of Italian competition to concede some Egyptian demands. When the British responded by bolstering their military presence, anti-British riots broke out, which lasted a week.[107] One month later, the Egyptian constitution was restored. The National Bloc, sizing up the same international configuration of forces, could not fail to learn from the success of Egypt's militant posture.

[107] Porath, *The Palestinian Arab*, p. 159; MAE, Syrie–Liban 1930–40. "National Bloc Manifestos Praising the Wafd," 15 Dec. 1935, vol. 491, pp. 208–9.

CHAPTER SEVENTEEN

ASCENT TO POWER

LIKE COUNTLESS YEARS BEFORE, 1935 ended on a sour note; for the National Bloc it was especially dissonant. France was unprepared to resume treaty negotiations, the Syrian Parliament remained shut, the much discredited government of Shaykh Taj al-Din al-Hasani was still in office, and the Syrian economy had yet to revive from the long years of debilitating depression. Meanwhile, the Bloc's internal wounds—created by the internecine warfare between Aleppo and Damascus—had not yet healed, and the League of National Action's assaults upon the Bloc's strategy of "honorable cooperation" had risen above the mark of irritation.

Under such conditions, the Bloc's survival seemed to hinge on taking some dramatic political action that could reunify nationalist ranks. The question was, of course, what sort of action? Bloc leaders found the option of an armed insurrection, like the one ten years earlier, unattractive. A more measured action was called for. But there was also the question of a precipitating factor. This, the High Commission conveniently provided.

GENERAL STRIKE

On January 20, disturbances erupted in Damascus in reaction to the closing down of the National Bloc Office in al-Qanawat and the arrest of Fakhri al-Barudi and the Nationalist Youth leader, Sayf al-Din al-Ma'mun. Bazaars shut down and a crowd of students and quarter youth gathered in front of Nasib al-Bakri's home to prepare for a march to the Sérail. Led by Bakri, Jamil Mardam, and Shukri al-Quwwatli, the demonstrators never got past the end of Bakri's street where a "cordon of police" was posted. The police fired into the air dispersing the crowd and arrested several students. In Aleppo, Hama, and Homs demonstrations were reported on the same day.

The following day, the French sent their much-loathed Moroccan *spahis* and Senegalese troops into the old city of Damascus to break up a student rally at the Great Mosque. In the mêlée, four persons were killed. In Aleppo, security forces raided the residence of the late Ibrahim Hananu, which had been used by nationalists as a "house of the nation" (*bayt al-umma*)—an echo of Sa'd Zaghlul's "houses of the nation" in Egypt—and confiscated all documents. In retaliation, leaders declared the closure

of the town's mammoth bazaar and rallied their supporters to demonstrate. The arrest of demonstrators caused further demonstrations and by
the end of the day two persons had been killed. Rioting continued for two
more days and another 150 protestors were arrested. On January 22,
20,000 persons marched in Damascus in the funeral of the four protestors
who had fallen on the previous day. But when the procession turned to
violence, French troops swept in, taking the lives of two more demonstrators and arresting 187 others. In Homs, where bazaars had been closed for
two days, French troops killed three demonstrators and wounded another
twenty.[1] Syria was on the verge of a complete shut-down.

The National Bloc was not in charge of the situation in Damascus.
Rather, student leaders, mostly from the League of National Action, and
qabadayat in the quarters were at the forefront of political agitation. In
fact, at Friday noon prayers in the Umayyad Mosque on January 24, Nasib al-Bakri and Hani Jallad, a prosperous merchant connected with the
Bloc, made pleas for the restoration of calm. But students were not ap-
peased. Instead, their leaders organized a march from the Mosque to the
Sérail, then up to al-Salhiyya and back to the Mosque, calling for national
unity and the continuation of the strike. Under immense pressure, Jamil
Mardam led a delegation of trade union chiefs, 'ulama', and members of
the Chamber of Commerce to a meeting on January 26 with the French
Delegate in the capital, in a bid to defuse the explosive situation. But neither this meeting nor the direct intervention of Damascene notables with
the High Commissioner brought any tangible results. On January 27,
Mardam, in the name of the National Bloc, called for a General Strike to
last until the High Commission restored constitutional life to Syria.
While many young enthusiasts applauded the Bloc's action, in effect a
General Strike had been under way by workers, shopkeepers, students,
and government functionaries for nearly a week. Until January 27, the
Bloc had been following rather than leading the urban masses. Even after
that date, the National Bloc tried to end the General Strike before its objectives had been met. While it adopted an uncompromising stance in
public, behind the scenes it continued to make conciliatory overtures to
the French.

Despite the half-hearted attitude of the Bloc, for the coming 36 days,
Syria was almost completely paralyzed by a strike of proportions never
witnessed before in the towns, not even during the Great Revolt. Most
shops were shut and commercial life came to a standstill. Public services

---

[1] Details on the General Strike have been culled from Anwar al-'Ish, *Fi tariq al-hurriyya
min i'tiqal al-Barudi ila safar al-wafd ila Paris* (Damascus, 1936); *Oriente Moderno*, 16
(1936), pp. 61–65, 125–37; *L'Asie Française*, no. 337 (Feb. 1936), pp. 74–78; FO 371/863,
vol. 20065. MacKereth to Eden, 27 Jan. 1936; FO 371/702, vol. 26005. Parr (Aleppo) to
Eden, 29 Jan. 1936.

were unable to function and attendance in schools and university was down to a trickle. Militant students and radical nationalists, capitalizing on the spontaneity of the urban mob, kept Bloc leaders from effecting any compromise. For example, on February 2 merchants linked to the Bloc tried to reopen the *suqs* of Damascus and on the following day the Bloc dispatched Hani Jallad to the Great Mosque to appeal for an end to the strike. But, when student leaders called for the strike's continuation, the Bloc denied that Jallad had been speaking on its behalf and publicly supported the students' declaration. Bitter, the humiliated and discredited Jallad resigned from the Bloc.[2]

Students, Bloc leaders, and '*ulama*' then met in the Great Mosque to formulate their demands: a general amnesty for the hundreds who had been recently arrested; the revocation of the decree expelling all students from school who demonstrated; and the re-opening of the National Bloc Office. When the French rejected an amnesty, demonstrations broke out again. At their head were town merchants who, the day before, had formed a committee to organize the distribution of flour and funds to the poor and striking workers.[3] In the meantime, demonstrations had spread to other towns.

In Hama, which had managed to avoid violent incidents in January, grave anti-French disorders erupted on February 4. Two days later the local Bloc leader, Dr. Tawfiq al-Shishakli, was arrested. In retaliation, a crowd attacked a cavalry troop, which opened fire killing seven of its assailants and wounding another forty.[4] Responding to the Hama incidents, nationalists in Homs renewed their agitation, leaving three more dead on February 8. By February 10, violence had spread as far as Dayr al-Zur, where French troops killed five demonstrators.[5]

There had been some signs of French vacillation in Syria in early February, a natural response to the recent change of government in Paris. The rightist complexion of the outgoing government had enabled the High Commissioner to ignore nationalist leaders. But, with the assumption of the Premiership by the Radical-Socialist Senator Albert Sarraut, Martel's "solos became dissonant." Even as the strike built up steam, his new superiors requested him to avoid all incidents and to discourge any newspaper report that might rekindle in the minds of left-wing parties in France "those altruistic urgings that led to the drafting in 1932 of the

---

[2] *Oriente Moderno*, 16 (1936), p. 65; conversation with Mahmud al-Bayruti (Damascus, 10 March 1976).

[3] *Oriente Moderno*, 16 (1936), pp. 126–27.

[4] FO 371/1941, vol. 20065. MacKereth to Eden, 4 April 1936.

[5] *Oriente Moderno*, 16 (1936), pp. 128–29.

treaty of independence for Syria."[6] But the High Commissioner's actions between February 10–16 erased all signs of vacillation. Events moved quickly and unfavorably for the National Bloc. On February 10, Martel passed the task of restoring order on to General Huntzinger, the Commander of the Armée du Levant, who immediately applied martial law to Damascus. From his temporary headquarters at the Orient Palace Hotel, heavily guarded by Senegalese sentries, Huntzinger issued his proscriptions. He forbade assemblies in the streets of more than three persons and warned the population that his soldiers would return blow for blow.[7] On February 11, Jamil Mardam and Nasib al-Bakri were arrested and deported, Mardam to the Syrian-Turkish borders in the Sanjak of Alexandretta and Bakri to A'zaz. On the next day, the French imposed martial law in the other towns and reinforced their garrisons in the surrounding countryside as reports spread of the appearance of armed bands similar to those that had operated during the Great Revolt. In Damascus, the two most actively resistant quarters, Bab al-Jabiyya and Bab al-Sharqi, were inundated with French troops and the homes of the most influential Bloc leaders not under arrest—Shukri al-Quwwatli and Lutfi al-Haffar—were surrounded. On February 13, French troops arrested the principal Bloc leaders of Aleppo: Sa'dallah al-Jabiri, Hasan Fu'ad Ibrahim Pasha, 'Abd al-Rahman al-Kayyali, and Na'im Antaki. On February 16, in an attempt to break the back of the Damascus nationalist leadership, the High Commission forced the Khuri brothers to resign their teaching posts on the Faculty of Law.[8]

The High Commissioner and his staff believed that the merchants and shopkeepers of Damascus and Aleppo would be only too happy "to resume normal activity provided that they could be protected" from nationalist violence. A large delegation of Damascene merchants headed by 'Arif Halbuni, the mild-mannered President of the Damascus Chamber of Commerce, and Khalid al-'Azm, the Managing-Director of the National Cement Company, disabused him of this belief by refusing to "resume trading" until he redressed some of the Syrian grievances.[9] Five days later, Martel unexpectedly asked the much disliked Shaykh Taj to resign. 'Ata al-Ayyubi was asked to form a new government,[10] in which

    [6] FO 371/1135, vol. 20065. MacKereth to Eden, 10 Feb. 1936; Shirer, *The Collapse of the Third Republic*, p. 240.
    [7] FO 371/1941, vol. 20065. MacKereth to Eden, 4 April 1936.
    [8] *Oriente Moderno*, 16 (1936), pp. 129–31. For a list of those arrested in Damascus during the General Strike see MWT, *Registre Civil: Commandes* (1936): *Tribunal de 1ère Instance de Damas* (Jan.–Feb. 1936).
    [9] FO 371/1434, vol. 20065. MacKereth to Eden, 24 Feb. 1936.
    [10] *Oriente Moderno*, 16 (1936), p. 134.

he included three moderate nationalists.[11] The choice of Ayyubi, a Mül-kiye-trained notable from an old and well-to-do Damascene family, who had considerable administrative experience dating from late Ottoman times, was not thoughtless. Regarded as honest, though possibly a bit too well-disposed to the French, he commanded considerable respect in nationalist circles.[12] So did his ministers. Yet, the Bloc's public reaction to the new government, which released some detainees and proposed a return to parliamentary life, was publicly negative. It renewed its call for the continuation of the strike, and for the boycott of all foreign goods and public utility companies,[13] and disturbances were reported in all major towns.

On February 26, prison doors were opened for all those who had been arrested but had not been brought before a court. But there remained 3,080 persons who had been sentenced by military and civil courts to terms of imprisonment in connection with the strike since January 20.[14]

On February 28, Hashim al-Atasi, in his capacity as President of the National Bloc, issued a strongly-worded declaration claiming that the nationalist program was the only acceptable solution to the Syrian Question. This led to a massive demonstration in the Syrian capital. Protestors clashed with police who opened fire, killing four and wounding scores.[15] But these disturbances proved, surprisingly, to be the last serious ones of the General Strike.

Over the next two days Bloc leaders and the Ayyubi cabinet were locked away in Beirut with the High Commissioner trying to hammer out a mutually satisfactory agreement. On March 2, Hashim al-Atasi announced that a Syrian delegation would proceed at once to Paris to negotiate a treaty, that political prisoners and exiles would be freed, and that nationalist newspapers would be restored.[16] It seems that the Quai d'Orsay had peremptorily dictated the agreement after failing to prevent the Foreign Affairs Committee of the French Chamber and the Leftist press from attacking Martel for his poor handling of the Syrian disturbances.[17]

The following day, after the release of the imprisoned leaders, the National Bloc declared an official end to the 43-day-old strike. A large,

---

[11] Mustafa al-Shihabi (Education), Edmond Homsi (Finance), and Sa'id al-Ghazzi (Justice). Hasan al-Hakim, *Mudhakkirati*, vol. 2, p. 171.

[12] Ayyubi was on the Board of Directors of the National Cement Company and was married to a woman from the landowning Jaza'iri family. See FO 226/240/9/3/119. Gardner to Chancery, 27 March 1943; Faris, *Man huwa 1949*, p. 49.

[13] FO 371/1711, vol. 20065. MacKereth to Eden.

[14] FO 371/1941, vol. 20065. MacKereth to Eden, 4 April 1936.

[15] *Oriente Moderno*, 16 (1936), p. 135.

[16] FO 371/1744, vol. 20065. MacKereth to Eden, 31 March 1936; *L'Orient* (5 March 1936).

[17] FO 371/1437, vol. 20065. MacKereth to Eden, 4 March 1936.

peaceful procession composed of artisans, quarter youth, Bedouin, and the various religious minorities and Muslim sects passed by each released Bloc leader's home to pay their respects and to reaffirm their fidelity to the cause of Syrian emancipation.[18] Later, Bloc leaders reassembled in front of the bazaars to cut the green cords which had been strung across their entrances, symbolizing that only the National Bloc had had the power and authority to reopen the Syrian capital.[19] In Aleppo appeals were made in the Great Mosque for order, loyalty to the National Bloc, and a resumption of business, as the strike quickly began to wind down.[20] Cautiously, but optimistically, nationalist leaders prepared for their voyage to Paris.

THE GENERAL STRIKE of 1936 was clearly the National Bloc's biggest triumph to date. Taking the Egyptian Wafd's lesson to heart, the Bloc adopted a course of action which revitalized its image and enabled its leaders to re-establish a monopoly over the Syrian independence movement.

Ironically, the strike enabled the Bloc leadership to salvage, in less than two months, its strategy of "honorable cooperation." Furthermore, the Bloc was able to place this strategy on much sounder footing. "Honorable cooperation" now meant a treaty "not inferior to the Anglo-Iraqi" treaty[21] and ultimately the right of the Bloc to share power with the French. Bloc leaders had never really bargained for anything more. Diplomacy supported by intermittent displays of its independent influence in the towns were the Bloc's preferred tools. At best these could gradually relax French control in Syria. Armed struggle as a vehicle to power had been ruled out with the failure of the Great Revolt of 1925–27.

But, while the General Strike helped to restore the reputation of the National Bloc, it also severely taxed the Syrian economy and the livelihood of the mass of townspeople. The six-week strike had a devastating impact on life in Syrian towns of the interior as well as in Beirut and Palestine. Business was at a standstill throughout the strike, sales were restricted to immediate necessities, and almost all shops and big business houses were adversely affected. With students and *qabadayat* enforcing the shutdown, few shopowners dared go against the prevailing current. In Muslim quarters, only the bakeries stayed open. Even in the European and Christian quarters, most shops remained partially closed. As a consequence, food prices soared, stocks of perishable goods rotted, hoarding took place, money was scarce, salaries and other financial commitments

[18] FO 371/1437, vol. 20065. MacKereth to Eden, 4 March 1936.
[19] *L'Asie Française*, no. 337 (Feb. 1936), pp. 77–78.
[20] FO 371/1397, vol. 20065. Parr to Eden, 7 March 1936.
[21] Longrigg, *Syria*, p. 218.

were not met, and Beirut merchants, who also suffered big losses, were asked to delay consignments of goods ordered before the strike. Vast numbers of people were forced out of work.

Yet, the spirit in the towns was high throughout the strike and the Syrian people had never seemed more united or more committed. Town quarters banded together to assist one another. The National Bloc, backed by voluntary associations of merchants, made funds available to the very poor and set up distribution centers for food, oil, and clothing which were badly needed to offset the glacial winds and rains which struck Syria during that particularly harsh winter. With trade to the Syrian interior paralyzed and Damascene and Aleppine merchants unable to honor their engagements, unpaid bills accumulated. The National Bloc, however, persuaded banks to grant renewals on loans and prolong credit facilities. The urban rentier class was also pressured into foregoing the collection of rents on business premises for the strike's duration. The responsiveness of the Bloc and its wealthy partisans to the needs of a public obviously exhausted by sacrifice could not fail to be noticed. As the perceptive British Consul in Damascus observed, "a notable feature of the general strike . . . was the remarkable degree of obedience shown to the leaders and the powers of organization and command that these leaders displayed in controlling the crowds." There could no longer be any question in the minds of the High Commissioner and his staff that the Bloc, like the Wafd in Egypt, was the most powerful political influence in the country. Indeed, from the French perspective, it was bad tactics to persist in publicly flouting it.[22]

In addition, the strike aroused expressions of sympathy in adjoining territories. When martial law was imposed on the towns of the interior, Latakia, Tripoli, Beirut, and Sidon all closed down in protest.[23] Merchant groups in the Lebanese capital, though suffering from the prolongation of the strike, raised money to assist the Damascus strike committee.[24] In Iraq, lead articles in Baghdad newspapers condemned French policy and expressed the sympathy and solidarity of the Iraqi people with their Syrian brothers in their struggle against "imperialism." Messages of support

[22] FO 371/961, vol. 20065. Parr to Eden, 15 Feb. 1936; FO 371/1109, vol. 20065. Parr to Eden, 22 Feb. 1936; FO 371/1362, vol. 20069. Parr to Eden, 27 Feb. 1936; FO 371/1289, vol. 20065. Parr to Eden, 29 Feb. 1936; FO 371/4121, vol. 20069. Havard to Eden, 24 June 1936. Conversations with Fu'ad Sidawi and George Siba' (Damascus, 13 Feb. 1976); Suhayl al-Khuri (Damascus, 8 Feb. 1976); Anwar al-Baba (Damascus, 8 April 1976); Nasuh Babil (Damascus, 20 Feb. 1976); Abu 'Ali al-Kilawi (Damascus, 14 Feb. 1976). These conversations were with participants in the General Strike.

[23] FO 371/962, vol. 20065. Havard to Eden, 13 Feb. 1936.

[24] *Oriente Moderno*, 16 (1936), p. 130.

from the Union of Baghdad Lawyers were received in Damascus and petitions from Iraq to the League of Nations condemning French actions
were sent.[25] But, it was in Palestine that the strongest anti-French protests were registered. Several large meetings, demonstrations, and
strikes—sponsored by the Istiqlal Party—were held to express solidarity
with the Syrian people and to condemn French methods. Money was collected for the victims of the strike and telegrams were sent to Syria expressing the solidarity of the people of "southern Syria," a term which
radical pan-Arabists often preferred to "Palestine."[26] It was very closely
watched in Palestine and for good reason. Just as the Egyptian Wafd had
provided a valuable example for the National Bloc, so the Syrian General
Strike provided a paradigm for action to the Palestinians.[27]

PARIS NEGOTIATIONS

Considerable discussion and debate within nationalist circles prefigured
the selection of the Syrian negotiating team that was sent to Paris. The
final composition of the delegation was dominated by four National Bloc
leaders—Hashim al-Atasi, Jamil Mardam, Saʿdallah al-Jabiri, and Faris
al-Khuri, and included two government ministers—Amir Mustafa al-
Shihabi, a French-trained agronomist, and Edmond Homsi, an Oxford-
educated Greek-Catholic banker from Aleppo. At the last moment an
attempt from outside the Bloc to draft the exiled Syrian leader, Dr. Shahbandar, was squashed by the French, who did not favor his return to Syrian politics. The Bloc was secretly pleased. Attached to the delegation
were two secretaries, the European-educated lawyers Edmond Rabbath
and Naʿim Antaki, both from Aleppo, and several other young political
advisers, including, by the summer, the Syrian Communist Party leader,
Khalid Bakdash. On March 21, the delegation left Damascus amidst
scenes of great public enthusiasm.[28]

Negotiations opened on April 2 with a French team headed by Foreign
Minister Pierre-Etienne Flandin. The road to a treaty was not to be as
smooth as the Syrian delegation had anticipated. From the outset, the
Syrians faced an inflexible and unacceptable French bargaining position

[25] FO 371/853, vol. 20065. Kerr (Baghdad) to Eden, 5 Feb. 1936; FO 371/979, vol. 20065.
Kerr to Eden, 13 Feb. 1936.

[26] George Antonius File, no. 17. Antonius memorandum (Jerusalem), 8 Feb. 1936, Middle East Centre, St. Antony's College, Oxford; FO 371/1293, vol. 20018. Palestine CID to
Colonial Office, 18 Feb. 1936.

[27] Porath, The Palestinian Arab, p. 160; FO 371/1515, vol. 20018. Air Ministry Headquarters (Palestine) to FO, 26 Feb. 1936.

[28] FO 371/1624, vol. 20065. MacKereth to Eden, 17 March 1936; FO 371/1941, vol.
20065. MacKereth to Eden, 4 April 1936.

which insisted *inter alia* on retaining the semi-autonomous regimes and French governors in the Alawite territory and Jabal Druze. Fortunately for the Syrian team, it was just able to avert a complete breakdown after M. Flandin presented a patently unacceptable draft proposal toward the end of April. Then, general elections in France on April 26 sealed the Sarraut government's fate: it was replaced by a left-wing coalition headed by the Socialist Party leader, Léon Blum. But because this progressive coalition—known as the Popular Front—could not constitutionally assume office until the beginning of June, treaty negotiations were suspended for the month of May, allowing Syrian delegates to enjoy some of the pleasures of springtime in Paris, and on the expense account of the Iraqi government.[29]

If French workers and white collar employees were thrilled by the dramatic victory of the Popular Front—a coalition of Radical Socialists, Socialists, and Communists which promised long overdue social and economic reforms—so were nationalist leaders throughout the French Empire.[30] One of the most encouraging signs of a diplomatic breakthrough was the appointment of a second French negotiating team, headed by Pierre Viénot, the Popular Front's new Undersecretary of State for Foreign Affairs in charge of Morocco, Tunisia, and the Levant Mandate. A past member of Joseph Paul-Boncour's Socialist group and a former collaborator of Lyautey, Viénot was a "sensitive listener" whose own conception of Mandate was refreshingly realistic and forward looking. Whereas previous official thinking about the Mandate focused on how to bend its underlying principles, Viénot sought to work honestly within the framework of the Mandate charter. In his opinion, the French Mandate in the Levant was "transitory," and thus France's role there could be no more than that of a "tutor." France would have to accept the fundamental rights of Syrian nationalism and the absorption by the Syrian state of the autonomous Druze and Alawite districts (of course with the proviso that their minority rights be recognized and protected). Otherwise French influence was likely to be surpassed by one of France's European allies or rivals.[31]

Viénot's comparatively enlightened perspective did not mean that the Popular Front was prepared to accept all the Syrian delegation's demands.

[29] FO 371/2749, vol. 20065. Peake (Paris) to Eastern Department (FO), 14 May 1936; FO 371/3008, vol. 20069. Nuri Pasha (Sa'id) to FO, 22 May 1936.
[30] W. B. Cohen, "The Colonial Policy of the Popular Front," *French Historical Studies,* 7 (Spring 1972), pp. 368, 378.
[31] J. Henry-Haye and Pierre Viénot, *Les relations de la France et de la Syrie* (Paris, 1939); Pierre Viénot, Article no. 2 in *Le Populaire* (Paris), 12 Jan. 1939; Hourani, *Syria and Lebanon,* pp. 168–69.

466   NEW APPROACHES

The Blum government had its own built-in limits and it also faced pressures from French right-wing parties and special financial and cultural interest groups which vehemently opposed granting Syria any concessions. Indeed, once negotiations resumed in late June, the Blum government demonstrated considerable firmness, at the same time making it perfectly clear that there was unlikely to be any French government in the near future which would be more accommodating.[32] As always, the tricky points of contention were the future of the Alawite and Druze territories and the general question of the definition of Syrian unity.[33]

As negotiations proceeded through the summer months of 1936, news filtered back to France of demonstrations in Latakia, the Jabal Druze, and elsewhere for and against union with Syria.[34] In the Jabal Druze, opposition to unity with Syria was less pronounced than it was in the Alawite territory where Alawites expressed their grave doubts about unity, principally in sectarian terms. By contrast, the Jabal Druze was not divided along sectarian lines because the landowning class and the peasantry were both Druze.[35] Demonstrations on July 12 in Sidon in favor of union with Syria turned into a riot in which four protestors were killed.[36] In the Sanjak of Alexandretta, the Turkish minority had begun to agitate more openly for secession and unity with Ankara.[37]

Despite the confusion, anxiety, and clash of interests over the Paris negotiations, it soon became evident that the new treaty would have to include the Alawite and Druze districts in the Syrian state.[38] By the second

[32] FO 371/3794, vol. 20066. Sir G. Clerk (Paris) to Eden, 22 Jan. 1936. Syrian nationalists had hoped that Martel who had returned to Paris to participate in the negotiations, would be replaced by the Blum government with someone more liberal in outlook. This did not happen. FO 371/4416, vol. 20066. Ogden (Damascus) to Eden, 4 July 1936.
[33] MAE, Syrie–Liban 1930–40. Martel "Note," 3 June 1936, vol. 492, pp. 156–59; ibid., "Note," 15 Oct. 1936, vol. 495, pp. 5–7.
[34] FO 371/3794, vol. 20066. Clerk to Eden, 22 June 1936. FO 371/4416, vol. 20066. Ogden to Eden, 20 July 1936. Longrigg, Syria, pp. 219–20.
[35] See MAE, Syrie–Liban 1930–40. "Note," 27 Oct. 1936, vol. 495, pp. 49-56; ibid., "Note," 11 June 1936, vol. 492, pp. 195–97; ibid., Ali M. al-Atrash to Léon Blum, 4 July 1936, vol. 493, pp. 143-44; ibid., "Note," 24 July 1936, pp. 151–53. In the case of the Alawite territory, French officials made a strong case for attaching it to Lebanon. See MAE, Syrie–Liban 1930–40. "Aide mémoire," 20 Aug. 1936, vol. 493, pp. 181–84. For the Syrian delegation's reaction to the French treaty proposals of June, see MAE, Syrie–Liban 1930–40. "Etude critique du Project Français," signed by H. al-Atasi, 11 June 1936, vol. 495, 14 pages.
[36] FO 371/4804, vol. 20066. Furlonge (Beirut) to Eden, 20 July 1936; MAE, Syrie–Liban 1930–40. Meyrier Telegram, 15 July 1936, vol. 501, pp. 109–10.
[37] Longrigg, Syria, p. 220.
[38] In a note on the treaty, the French orientalist Louis Massignon wrote: "Because we are in Syria for cultural ends and to maintain our promises to the Christians, it is necessary that we reposition the defense of minorities in the framework of a frankly pro-Arab political cul-

week of September, an agreement was reached, enabling the Syrian delegation to return home triumphant.

The draft of the new treaty,[39] while following the general lines of the 1933 treaty which the Syrian Parliament had "unceremoniously rejected," indicated a far greater acceptance by the French government of the Syrian point of view. The Popular Front appeared to have overcome the much less generous attitude of the military party, special interest groups in the Levant, and permanent officials at the Quai d'Orsay. The Syrian Treaty (and the Franco-Lebanese Treaty which had been more smoothly and rapidly negotiated after the Syrian Treaty, in the fall of 1936, and which the French Chamber had ratified on November 17) was loosely modelled on the Anglo-Iraqi Treaty. There was one noticeable inclusion, however: specific provisions for the protection of the religious minorities which, according to French officials, were inspired by Britain's failure to ensure the protection of Iraq's minorities, especially the Assyrian community.[40]

The Syrian Treaty provided for "peace," "friendship," and "alliance" between France and Syria. It was to commence as soon as Syria was accepted into the League of Nations and was to last for 25 years. Apart from the treaty's main articles, which merely formalized the general guidelines of Franco-Syrian relations and were never really in dispute, there were a number of attached documents defining France's military position in Syria, her rights and obligations, and the Syrian state's relations with the Druzes, Alawites, and other minorities, and with Lebanon.

The military clauses provided for French assistance to protect Syrian sovereignty, yet limited the aid Syria would have to give France to aid within Syria's frontiers. The Syrian government also agreed to equip and maintain an army consisting of at least one division of infantry and a cavalry brigade, presumably on the French scale. France was allowed to maintain two military air bases at mutually agreed locales, not less than 25 miles from any one of the four interior towns. France was also given all transport and harbor facilities needed in connection with these air bases and French garrisons. Some of these garrisons, of undetermined strength, were to be stationed in the Alawite and Druze districts for a period of five years from the coming into force of the treaty. These two districts were to be incorporated formally into the Syrian state, but were to

---

ture . . . this way we will win the Syrian *wafd* [delegation] to our side and reach an agreement" MAE, Syrie–Liban 1930–40. 5 June 1936, vol. 492, pp. 161–62.

[39] For the text of the "Treaty of Friendship and Alliance between France and Syria," see Hourani, *Syria and Lebanon*, Appendix A, pp. 314–33.

[40] FO 371/6132, vol. 20066. U.K. Delegation at Geneva to FO, 27 Sept. 1936; FO 371/6599, vol. 20066. Eastern Department (FO), 6 Nov. 1936; MAE, Syrie–Liban 1930–40. Martel "Note," 3 June 1936, vol. 492, pp. 156–59.

retain a limited measure of administrative and financial autonomy, similar to that enjoyed by the Sanjak of Alexandretta.

The treaty contained no formal acknowledgment of the separate existence of the Lebanese Republic, although the four "cazas" added to Lebanon in 1920 remained in Lebanon by her separate treaty with France. As for the regulation of outstanding questions between Syria and Lebanon, including the administration of the controversial Common Interests, these were to be negotiated by the Syrian and Lebanese governments.[41] Finally, France relinquished the right to obtain from Syria the reimbursement of the cost of its administration and protection of the country during its exercise of the Mandate.[42]

ASSUMPTION OF POWER

When news reached Syria on September 10 that the treaty had been initialled in Paris, all government departments closed for the day and many were "bedecked with flags and electric lights." For the first time, National Bloc offices displayed the flags of France and Syria side-by-side. The Bloc's new paramilitary wing, the Steel Shirts, paraded in the streets to the delight of the populace.[43] But the real fanfare did not begin until the Syrian delegation arrived three weeks later in Aleppo, after passing through Turkey where it had been shocked to learn that "Turkey still had her eyes firmly" set on the Sanjak of Alexandretta.[44]

In Aleppo, elaborate demonstrations were staged to advertise the solidarity and the spontaneity of nationalist sentiment in northern Syria as well as the organization and discipline of the Steel Shirts, who assisted the Bloc leadership in bringing into the town between 30,000 and 40,000 villagers from the surrounding area. To the casual observer, it certainly appeared that executive authority in the country had already passed into the hands of the nationalists. Police arrangements during the demonstrations and celebrations seemed to have been largely in their own hands. Since the General Strike, the nationalists had established their own organizations in the various quarters for dealing with local administrative matters. They even set up their own "tribunal" to which an increasing number of civil disputes and complaints of any but the gravest crimes were referred. The British Consul in the town added that "no secret is made of their [the nationalists'] intention to boycott the native administration and

---

[41] FO 371/6599, vol. 20069. Eastern Department (FO), 6 Nov. 1936; FO 371/6896, vol. 20066. MacKereth to Eden, 26 Oct. 1936. Hourani, *Syria and Lebanon*, pp. 200–4; Longrigg, *Syria*, pp. 222–24.

[42] FO 371/6896, vol. 20066. MacKereth to Eden, 26 Oct. 1936.

[43] FO 684/9/632/1. Ogden, 10 Sept. 1936.

[44] FO 371/6968, vol. 20066. MacKereth to Eden, 27 Oct. 1936.

there has been a certain amount of agitation in the local press to the effect that those Syrians who have accepted posts under the French should be penalised when independence is obtained." Another indication of this trend was that the Governor of Aleppo was invited to the festivities only at the insistence of one of the members of the returning delegation; and then he was virtually ignored.[45]

Similar parades and demonstrations greeted the delegation as it passed through Hama and Homs on its way to Damascus, where it arrived on September 29. There, nationalists staged all the activities but, unlike in Aleppo, the Steel Shirts, assisted by the Boy Scouts, could not control the crowds that had gathered at the Hijaz Station for the victory march to the Sérail. Celebrations lasted four solid days.[46]

There seemed to be some hesitation on the part of the French and Syrian delegations to publish the terms of the treaty immediately. The full text was not made public in Syria until October 27 and then it was issued along with a manifesto signed by Hashim al-Atasi, which was cleverly composed for Syrian as well as French audiences. On one hand, Atasi stressed the need to develop a corporate national consciousness and the "ideal of inter-Arab brotherhood," and, on the other, he praised the "free men of France in foregoing the refund of the cost to them of the Mandate, which reached many millions of francs." Yet, while the reception of the treaty was generally favorable, nationalists could not completely conceal their dissatisfaction with its military clauses. As for the Druzes, they seemed to feel no need for protection, whereas the Alawites expressed mixed feelings.[47]

Immediately after the celebrations, the National Bloc began to lay the groundwork for the implementation of the treaty. First, it prepared for general elections, which were still conducted in the customary two stages. They were executed relatively smoothly on November 14 and 30. As anticipated, the Bloc won landslide victories throughout the country, though in Aleppo not before violent clashes between Muslims and Christians.

Earlier in the year, there was a Muslim boycott of Aleppo's cinemas and cafés, in which Muslim youth brigades from the popular quarters were stationed in front of their entrances to discourage patronage. Because the affected establishments were Christian-owned (Muslim enterprises were spared), sectarian tensions heightened in the town. Aggravating the situation was a Muslim boycott of Christian weaving establishments because they distributed home work only to Christian

[45] FO 371/6468, vol. 20066. Parr to Eden, 5 Oct. 1936.
[46] FO 371/6716, vol. 20066. Ogden to Eden, 3 Oct. 1936.
[47] FO 371/6968, vol. 20066. MacKereth to Eden, 27 Oct. 1936.

weavers whereas Muslim enterprises used both Muslims and Christians.[48]

In response to the resurgence of communal strife and to news that the National Bloc had succeeded in Paris, a Christian nationalist organization called the White Badge emerged in Aleppo. Headed by an ex-military officer, ʿAbbud Qumbaz, it called for Aleppo's separation from Damascus and mainly attracted Catholics. It aimed to organize a paramilitary force of 5,000 Christians and in no time it established a presence in the Jazira where it also pressed for separation from Damascus.[49]

Almost immediately the National Bloc's Steel Shirts clashed with the White Badge. The most violent Muslim-Christian clash occurred in mid-October at Aleppo's Sunday Market (Suq al-ahad) which resulted in eight deaths and 150 injured. A dispute over the price of vegetables, which like other retail goods had risen to figures unjustified by the recent depreciation of the French franc, allowed the White Badge to provoke the incident. The Bloc firmly believed that the French authorities had prior knowledge of White Badge plans and it was observed that the disturbances occurred when the whole French garrison was away from Aleppo on maneuvers.[50] Although the White Badge created more trouble for the Bloc, it proved to be only a minor irritant because many Christian dignitaries in the town refused to support the Badge's extremist position.[51]

The Bloc approached each elector in Aleppo chosen in the primaries, handing him its printed list of candidates for whom he was "required" to vote. This method of canvassing was so successful that of the 510 voting papers handed in, 495 were unanimously in favor of Bloc nominees.[52] In most rural districts and minority enclaves, the nationalists did not try to install their own candidates. Rather, they permitted local candidates, mainly rural landowners, tribal shaykhs, and minority leaders to declare themselves "nationalists." The elections demonstrated overwhelming support for the treaty and hence for the National Bloc.[53]

Eighty-two representatives (three were absent) packed into Parliament in Damascus on December 21 to distribute the highest offices of state. Once again Muhammad Yahya al-ʿAdali, the eldest parliamentarian, oc-

[48] MWT, M. Demeulenaere Correspondence (uncatalogued). Demeulenaere (Adviser to Aleppo Municipality) to French Delegate (Aleppo), 13 May 1936.

[49] Oriente Moderno, 16 (1936), pp. 565–66, 683.

[50] FO 371/6610, vol. 20066. Parr to Eden, 13 Oct. 1936; Oriente Moderno, 16 (1936), p. 613.

[51] Ibid., p. 613.

[52] FO 371/7613, vol. 20067. MacKereth to Eden, 1 Dec. 1936; FO 371/7876, vol. 20067. David (Aleppo) to Eden, 10 Dec. 1936.

[53] For a list of elected deputies, see Records of the Syrian Parliament: 1936 Elections (Damascus); also see Longrigg, Syria, p. 220.

cupied the Speaker's Chair until Faris al-Khuri was elected Speaker by a near unanimous vote. There was little debate over the election of Hashim al-Atasi, the senior member of the National Bloc, as the next President of the Republic. He garnered 74 votes. Atasi then asked Jamil Mardam to form the Syrian Republic's first nationalist cabinet. Aside from the Premiership, Mardam assumed the portfolio of National Economy. He asked Saʿdallah al-Jabiri to become Minister of Foreign Affairs and the Interior, Shukri al-Quwwatli to take over Defense and Finance, and ʿAbd al-Rahman al-Kayyali to become Minister of Justice and of Education. Aleppo had never before been so satisfactorily represented in a Syrian cabinet.[54] These arrangements were the result of long discussions among Bloc leaders at Jamil Mardam's home, before Parliament convened.[55]

One of the first things the Mardam government did upon assuming office was to begin to repay its many political debts by packing central and regional administration with partisans and supporters. Two of the most sensitive posts, the governorships of Latakia and the Jabal Druze, went to two Bloc stalwarts, Mazhar Raslan and Nasib al-Bakri, respectively. Raslan was an experienced bureaucrat whom the French thought highly of, and no Damascene politician commanded greater respect among Druzes than Bakri.[56]

On December 22, Jamil Mardam and Pierre Viénot met in Damascus to sign the Franco-Syrian Treaty in a pleasant and friendly ceremony. Four days later Mardam sent the treaty to Parliament for debate. With the only opposition to the treaty coming from the League of National Action and Zaki al-Khatib's pro-Shahbandar organization, the National Unity Front, both of which were unrepresented in Parliament, the Bloc secured its ratification by a unanimous vote on December 27.[57]

STEEL SHIRTS

The resounding success of the General Strike followed by the advent of the Popular Front in France had assured the National Bloc an exclusive place at the summit of politics in Syria, alongside the High Commission. The ease, however, with which the Bloc took over the reins of government at the end of 1936 was in part attributable to new developments within the Syrian nationalist movement which had occurred during the absence of the Syrian delegation in Paris. These were the Bloc's creation

[54] FO 684/9/99/1. MacKereth to Eden, 23 Dec. 1936.

[55] *Ibid.*; FO 371/8024, vol. 20067. MacKereth to Eden, 21 Dec. 1936; MAE, Syrie–Liban 1930–40. Martel to MAE, 19 Nov. 1936, vol. 501, pp. 255–59.

[56] *Dalil al-jumhuriyya al-suriyya 1939–1940* (Damascus, n.d.).

[57] FO 371/6968, vol. 20066. MacKereth to Eden, 27 Oct. 1936; Longrigg, *Syria*, p. 221.

of its own paramilitary force and its success at dividing the leadership of the rival League of National Action.

Since the establishment of the Nationalist Youth in the late 1920s, Fakhri al-Barudi, among others, dreamed of transforming it into the nucleus of a future national army. Some of the ground was cleared for such a development when the Bloc reorganized the Nationalist Youth leadership in the face of new challanges from radicals and, in particular, from the League of National Action. The Bloc's first real opportunity to mold its youth wing into a paramilitary force came in the aftermath of the General Strike, when French military control was relaxed somewhat in the cities, giving nationalists greater freedom of action than ever before.

Already Bloc and Nationalist Youth leaders had been watching with great interest political events in Europe: the rise of Nazi Germany and Fascist Italy, Mussolini's Ethiopian adventure, and the Spanish Civil War. Of general interest was the prospect that the French and British hold over the region might be shaken loose by the challenge of Germany and Italy. Of particular interest was the rise of right-wing and Fascist leagues in Europe. Numerous articles began to appear in the local press and in popular Syrian youth magazines explaining and glorifying how these leagues guarded the moral values of society and instilled discipline among the youth, contributing, in the process, to nationalist struggles.[58] That these leagues were often composed of middle and upper-middle class youths from schools and universities made it that much easier for Syria's Nationalist Youth leaders to identify with their aims and purposes.

For Bloc elders, European youth movements provided several valuable lessons. Most important, perhaps, was that they offered the discipline and *esprit de corps* required to make excellent instruments for executing orders from above, for enforcing decisions, checking rivals, and rapidly launching strikes, boycotts, and demonstrations. On a more metaphysical level, the European leagues provided an example of how to instill a corporate national consciousness where organized cadres in the cities sublimated their interests to the national idea, an idea that by 1936 the Bloc could again claim to monopolize. In fact, by this time the Bloc did not have to look too far to see the advantages of creating a paramilitary wing. A nationalist youth brigade, the Blue Shirts, was already operating successfully in Cairo.[59]

[58] *Al-Musawwar* was one of the short-lived youth magazines which first appeared in Damascus in the spring of 1936. It was largely devoted to chronicling youth activities in Syria and, in particular, the rise of the Steel Shirts. It ran a series of articles extolling the role of European youth brigades and suggested how they could serve as a model for Syrian youth in the independence struggle. Its editor, Habib Kahhala, was also the publisher of the satirical Damascene weekly, *al-Mudhik al-mubki*. See *al-Musawwar*, no. 5 (1 July 1936), p. 12.
[59] De Boucheman, "Les chemises de fer," p. 7.

The Steel Shirts (al-Qumsan al-hadidiyya) first appeared in Damascus on March 8, several days after the National Bloc called off the General Strike. In no time branches appeared all over Syria. By April the program of the Steel Shirts had been spelled out. It called for the unity of Syria within its natural boundaries, was dedicated to being at the forefront of the independence struggle, and was based on "moral," "humanitarian," and "patriotic ideals." It members were to receive athletic and military training, both of which "encouraged talents," and "strengthened character." Headquartered in the Syrian capital and guided by the idea of sacrifice, devotion, and service to the nation, the Steel Shirts were to form the elite cadre of the Nationalist Youth, obedient to its Executive Council. Not long after the announcement of the April program a second and more detailed program for the training of infantry brigades, a cavalry, and a volunteer army was issued.[60]

The patron of the Damascus branch of the Steel Shirts was Fakhri al-Barudi who, after his release in early March, actively sought to realize his dream of a national army. Effective leadership of the organization, however, belonged to Munir al-ʿAjlani, its Secretary-General, and Sayf al-Din al-Maʾmun, its Director of Finance, whose takeover of the Nationalist Youth was now complete. The other members of the Executive Council only underscored the elitism of the Steel Shirts. They included ʿAbd al-Wahhab al-Malki, Dr. Ahmad al-Samman, and Dr. Muhammad al-Sarraj, a young Paris-educated lawyer from Hama who resided in Damascus. Although united in the aim of checking all rivals, and especially the League of National Action which was in the process of setting up its own paramilitary force, the "Lion Cubs of Arabism" (ashbal al-ʿuruba), the Executive Council was not free of internal political and tactical differences. Most noticeable was the growing rivalry between its two chiefs. ʿAjlani whose strong, uncompromising tendencies were directed at protecting the independence of the Steel Shirts competed with Maʾmun, who was devoted to keeping the organization closely attached to Bloc leaders, especially Jamil Mardam and Fakhri al-Barudi. What bothered ʿAjlani and the radical circle was the growing menace of egocentrism and opportunism at the leadership level of the National Bloc, reflected most clearly in the intensifying rivalry between Fakhri al-Barudi, whose influence among the educated youth in Damascus was unrivalled, and Nasib al-Bakri, the most influential Bloc zaʿim in the popular quarters of the capital, who faced a mounting challenge from Barudi. Indeed, by July 1936, Munir al-ʿAjlani, who would soon be elected to Parliament on the Na-

[60] Al-Ayyam (7 April 1936) cited in Oriente Moderno, 16 (1936), p. 265; also see MD, 7N-4190, Dossier 1.

tional Bloc list in Damascus, made the first of several bids to get the Steel
Shirts to break with the Bloc.[61]

Branches of the Steel Shirts were quickly formed in other towns in the
spring of 1936. In Homs, where the League of National Action held the
upper hand, the Steel Shirts were headed by ʿAbd al-Hadi al-Maʿsarani,
an activist lawyer, and Farid al-Mawsili, its military commander. In
Hama where the Nationalist Youth were especially active, the paramilitary wing was overseen by the Bloc leader, Tawfiq al-Shishakli, who was
assisted by Mustafa Hawrani, a young lawyer, and his cousin, Hadi, the
head of the local Boy Scout organization. The Aleppo branch, known as
the National Guard (al-Haras al-watani), was completely subservient to
the National Bloc. By July 1936, the National Guard numbered 1,200
uniformed youth under the leadership of Jamil Ibrahim Pasha, who was
assisted by Dr. Maʿruf al-Dawalibi, a young Paris-trained Islamic legal
scholar, and Jamil al-Ghazzi, a popular religious shaykh. Smaller outfits
also appeared in Latakia, Jarablus, and Dayr al-Zur. Some efforts were
made to set up branches in rural areas, particularly in the Damascus Governorate (muhafaza)—in Duma, Qatana, and in al-Qunaytra, but these
were not successful. By the end of 1936, the Executive Committee of the
Steel Shirts claimed to have 15,000 recruits; French and British officials
in Syria gave slightly lower estimates. By July 1936, there were as many
as 3,000 members in Damascus, and by the end of the year, this figure had
swelled to more than 4,500.[62]

The Damascus Steel Shirts formed sections in most popular quarters
during 1936: in the upper and lower Maydan, Shaghur, ʿAmara, al-Qaymariyya, Masjid al-Aqsab, al-Salhiyya (which included Suq Saruja, al-
Muhajirin, and Hayy al-Akrad), and in al-Qanawat. These sections were
given the names of popular figures in Syrian history such as Salah al-Din
al-Ayyubi (Saladin), Abi ʿUbayda, and Yusuf al-ʿAzma. The Maydan
branch, known as Maysalun, was the best organized and most militant.
Headed by Dr. Midhat al-Bitar, its members were Scouts from the suppressed Maysalun Troop, elementary school students, apprentice tailors,
and barbers. No qabadayat, however, joined.[63] In the Syrian capital and
elsewhere the Steel Shirts' Executive made special efforts to stress the or-

[61] De Boucheman, "Les chemises de fer," pp. 1–2; MAE, Syrie–Liban 1930–40. Meyrier
to MAE, 18 July 1936, vol. 493, pp. 140–41.

[62] Al-Musawwar, no. 1 (30 May 1936), pp. 5, 12; ibid., no. 2 (9 July 1936), p. 7; ibid.,
no. 4 (24 June 1936), pp. 1, 3, 5; ibid., no. 7 (15 July 1936), p. 14; ibid., no. 8 (22 July 1936),
p. 11; Jamil Ibrahim Pasha, Nidal al-ahrar, p. 71; FO 371/6716, vol. 20066. Ogden to Eden,
3 Oct. 1936; MAE, Syrie–Liban 1930–40. Meyrier to MAE, 18 July 1936, vol. 493, pp. 140–
41.

[63] De Boucheman, "Les chemises de fer," p. 4; Sidqi, Fakhri al-Barudi (Beirut, 1974), p.
96.

ganization's non-sectarian line by actively recruiting Christians into its ranks. A special committee, made up of two Muslim and five Christian youth leaders, including Faris al-Khuri's son, was established to direct these efforts.[64]

The uniforms worn by the Steel Shirts were steel grey shirts and trousers, a black tie, the *sidara* popularized by the Iraqi Army, and a belt. Although not all recruits were properly attired, by July 1936 at least 800 had received complete wardrobes in Damascus. The Steel Shirts' insignia, which was proudly displayed at all times, was a torch-bearing hand; their salute resembled that of the Nazi *Heil*. In the beginning, training consisted of one weekly session with local section leaders who, themselves, received instruction twice weekly from a group of retired army officers headed by Colonel Nuzhat al-Mamluk, the former War College instructor and a National Bloc partisan.[65] The Bloc much preferred relying on ex-officers of proven nationalist persuasion to newer French-trained recruits.[66]

Funding came from several sources. Each recruit was asked to pay a two franc initiation fee and was encouraged to pay an optional monthly fee as well. A special finance committee was set up in Damascus composed of leading merchants. Each quarter sponsoring a section was asked to contribute £S 400 for equipment. Before the Barudi "franc plan" folded, it contributed heavily to the Steel Shirts. Other funds also came from the 'Ayn al-Fija water works, the National Cement Company, and from emigrants' remittances. Finally, special theatrical exhibitions and the passing of collection plates in cinemas brought in funds.[67]

Throughout 1936 the Steel Shirts maintained a high visibility in the towns of Syria. Apart from their instrumental role in staging the "victory" celebrations which greeted the Syrian delegation on its return from Paris, they were to be found at the head of all national demonstrations, parades, and commemorative services, at which they proudly displayed their new uniforms and marching techniques. Their ubiquity, especially at voting urns in November, was not without influence over a poll that showed that nationalist candidates obtained 98.5 percent of the total vote.

The National Bloc encouraged the Steel Shirts to organize and participate in all "national events." In the summer months of 1936 the youth of

[64] De Boucheman, "Les chemises de fer," p. 4. Conversation with Suhayl al-Khuri (Damascus, 8 Feb. 1976).

[65] De Boucheman, "Les chemises de fer," p. 5; O'Zoux, "Les insignes et saluts de la jeunesse," vol. 2, pp. 98–99.

[66] See Michael H. Van Dusen, "Intra- and Inter-Generational Conflict in the Syrian Army," Ph.D. Dissertation (The Johns Hopkins University, 1971), pp. 153–54.

[67] De Boucheman, "Les chemises de fer," p. 5.

Syrian cities were treated to a spate of sporting events, including bicycle races and soccer matches, which led to the proliferation of sporting clubs and also helped to fill the ranks of the Steel Shirts. The Bloc also staged large gatherings (*haflat*) at various residences in the quarters of Damascus and Aleppo, at which the Steel Shirts were treated to nationalist speeches, music, and poetry recitations by the likes of Shafiq Jabri and the Aleppine national poet, ʿUmar Abu Rishi. Usually Jamil Mardam and Fakhri al-Barudi attended these gatherings, using them to demonstrate their personal influence over the independence movement. In Aleppo, Saʿdallah al-Jabiri and the Ibrahim Pashas played the same role. Although the organization and discipline of the Steel Shirts had not reached a sophisticated level by the end of 1936,[68] the organization's non-sectarian character, successful recruitment policy, growing influence among the educated youth in the towns, and its militaristic orientation could have only been viewed as a dangerous innovation at High Commission headquarters.

THE BLOC AND THE LEAGUE

At the same time that the Steel Shirts were beginning to take shape, the League of National Action faced its first major internal schism. Before the Syrian delegation departed for Paris in March, the National Bloc appointed Shukri al-Quwwatli as its Vice President in charge of the organization's internal affairs. No Bloc chief held as much influence with the League leadership as Shukri Bey; he had encouraged it at its earliest stages and was one of its leading patrons despite his official position in the Bloc. In the intervening months, he had dedicated himself to two related tasks: to keep the patriotic flames burning, in case the Syrian delegation failed to bring home a treaty,[69] and to unify nationalist ranks in Syria by bringing the League under the Bloc's wing. Ultimately, Quwwatli wanted to form a single national party, but he realized that many of the League's younger and more militant leaders were still unprepared to join ranks with the National Bloc, preferring to stick by the League principle of non-participation in government-level politics. Therefore, his tactics focused on splitting the League leadership over this issue. Although Quwwatli had courted several important leaders over the years,[70] he now focused

---

[68] FO 371/697, vol. 20848. MacKereth to Eden, 5 Jan. 1937; FO 371/6716, vol. 20066. Ogden to Eden, 3 Oct. 1936.
[69] MAE, Syrie–Liban 1930–40. Meyrier (Beirut) to MAE, 3 July 1936, vol. 493, pp. 41–45.
[70] Quwwatli's younger brother, ʿAdil, was a League member. Conversation with Akram Zuʿaytir (Beirut, 11 Aug. 1975).

most of his attention on Sabri al-ʿAsali, who had replaced the late ʿAbd al-Razzaq al-Dandashi as the League's Secretary-General.

Born in 1904, ʿAsali hailed from a family of Maydan quarter notables who had long been associated with Arab nationalist politics. After completing his elementary schooling in Damascus, his studies were interrupted by the events of 1916, when the Turks executed his uncle Shukri along with his nationalist comrades. The ʿAsali family was exiled from Damascus to Anatolia, and young Sabri completed his high school education in Konya. Repatriated at the end of the war, he eventually pursued legal studies, completing his law degree in Damascus in 1924. Another interruption in his career occurred with the Great Revolt, in which he and several of his ʿAsali cousins participated. Forced to take refuge in Palestine after the failure of the Ghuta campaigns in 1926, he developed there his first contacts with agents of the Saʿudi monarchy and was invited to represent the Saʿudis in negotiations with Transjordan on tribal and frontier questions. By 1927, he was in Cairo where he joined the Istiqlal wing of the Syrian–Palestine Congress and drew close to another partisan of the Saʿudis, Shukri al-Quwwatli. Although nearly a generation apart, they became good friends and worked together to convince Ibn Saʿud to increase his support for the cause of Syrian independence.[71] Indeed, ʿAsali and Quwwatli had many characteristics in common. Both came from notable families in the two most popular and politically-active quarters of Damascus and, unlike many nationalist leaders, they moved comfortably between the upper level of politics and the urban masses.

One of Sabri al-ʿAsali's first moves on taking over the League of National Action was to try to broaden its base by forming branches in Tripoli and Beirut. In this endeavor, which met with success, he received the full assistance and cooperation of his friend and mentor, Shukri al-Quwwatli.[72] At the same time, Quwwatli tried to expand the minority trend within the League, which leaned toward greater direct penetration of mainstream nationalist politics. It seems that sometime before the end of 1935, Quwwatli's Istiqlal group and the League of National Action had secretly coordinated plans for a new revolt in Syria, which was to be armed by the Iraqi government. But, by the time plans reached their final stage in the spring of 1936, disturbances had erupted in Palestine and Iraqi arms were hastily diverted there. Although a Syrian uprising never materialized, several League leaders, including ʿAsali, began to stress the importance of working closely with Quwwatli and the Istiqlal wing of the National Bloc.[73]

[71] Al-Jundi, *Tarikh* , pp. 486–87; Vacca, "Notizie."
[72] *Al-Mudhik al-mubki*, no. 293 (20 June 1936), p. 4.
[73] Conversation with Farid Zayn al-Din (Damascus, 22 April 1976).

In the meantime, while more moderate Bloc members were in Paris, Quwwatli moved quickly to infuse the Bloc with more radical elements. For example, he invited Sabri al-'Asali, Ahmad al-Sharabati, and Farid Zayn al-Din, who had returned from Baghdad, to join the National Bloc Council in the summer of 1936. His aim was to keep these young militants informed of the treaty negotiations in order to convince them that the delegation in Paris was not compromising Syrian national and territorial integrity.[74] To everyone's surprise, 'Asali accepted the invitation, precipitating a serious crisis within the League. After strong efforts to woo him back to the fold, the League Executive expelled him from the Secretariat and soon thereafter from the organization itself. In November, 'Asali ran successfully on the National Bloc's electoral list in Damascus and won a seat in Parliament. The first important League leader to stray from the party line, he started a dangerous trend. Soon Quwwatli used the bait of government posts to lure other young radicals into the Bloc. By early 1937, 'Adnan al-Atasi agreed to represent the National Bloc government in Ankara and Farid Zayn al-Din accepted the Directorship of the Ministry of Foreign Affairs,[75] thereby breaking one of the cardinal principles of the League and the clandestine Arab Liberation Society which he had helped to found several years earlier. Not only had Shukri al-Quwwatli managed to weaken the League of National Action, thus making the National Bloc's ascent to government that much smoother, he had also managed to strengthen his own position at the expense of his main nationalist rival in Damascus, Jamil Mardam.

The Task of Governing

Although the National Bloc's capture of government in Syria had been comparatively quick and easy after the General Strike, many of the major problems it encountered during its tenure in office had already surfaced before the Bloc could begin to enjoy the long-awaited fruits of its struggle.

First, there was the question of the ratification of the Franco-Syrian Treaty by the French Parliament, something that was definitely beyond the control of the new nationalist government in Syria. All seemed to hinge on the Popular Front's ability to convince Parliament to accept the treaty. But, from the beginning, an active political campaign to force the French Chamber to reject the concessions made to Syria had been underway in the right-wing French press. Led by a coalition of rightist politi-

---

[74] MAE, Syrie–Liban 1930–40. Meyrier to MAE, 2 and 8 Aug. 1936, vol. 493, pp. 185–89.

[75] *Dalil al-jumhuriyya al-suriyya 1939–1940* (Damascus, n.d.), pp. 253–54.

cians, the military party, and special financial and cultural interest groups, and quietly supported by some permanent officials of the Quai d'Orsay,[76] this campaign opposed the treaty on several grounds: it reflected French vacillation and weakness abroad, it prevented France from recovering her investments in Syria, and "it imposed a unitary regime upon an actually diverse territory,"[77] dissolving the protection system the French had established for the religious minorities.

Secondly, the treaty negotiations and the prospect of nationalists coming to power in Syria renewed the drive for minority separatism in the Jabal Druze and the *muhafaza* of Latakia. In the remote Jazira, Kurdish tribes and Christian townsmen, secretly encouraged by French officials in the region, agitated against government interference in their affairs. Most threatening, however, was the Turkish government's encouragement of a growing separatist movement in the Sanjak of Alexandretta whose large Turkish minority sought Alexandrettan independence from Syria and, in the case of the most extreme factions, unity with Turkey.[78] As for Lebanon, the reception of the Franco-Lebanese Treaty in November 1936 had been stormy in the Muslim parts of Beirut and in Tripoli where the sentiment for unity with Syria remained considerable. Pro-Syrian demonstrations caused the loss of several lives and the arrest of the principal Lebanese leaders at a time when the National Bloc had accepted, albeit reluctantly, the *de jure* existence of a Greater Lebanon.[79]

Thirdly, there was the rebellion in Palestine whose outbreak almost coincided with the end of the General Strike in Syria and the beginning of treaty negotiations in Paris. The Palestinian Revolt placed the National Bloc in a very awkward situation. Although Bloc sympathy was in the main with the Palestinian Arabs, open espousal of the revolt threatened to incur the strong displeasure of the mandatory authorities, both in Syria and in Palestine, and to prejudice the Paris negotiations. But, failure to support their Palestinian-Arab brethren might be interpreted by radical nationalist forces in Syria as indifference to the wider aspects of the Arab cause, something the Bloc had been accused of on more than one occasion. Complicating matters was the economic danger of the Palestine Revolt. Whereas during the General Strike in Syria, Damascus merchants had been able to send some of their surplus goods to Palestine where a ready market was found (even in the Jewish sector), the Palestine

---

[76] Nabih al-'Azma Papers [Syria], File 3/101, French Report of 1 Nov. 1936.

[77] Longrigg, *Syria*, p. 224.

[78] See FO 371/6832, vol. 20067. Morgan (Istanbul) to Eden, 1 Nov. 1936.

[79] George Antonius File, no. 12. Antonius (Jerusalem) to Charles R. Crane, 17 Dec. 1936, Middle East Centre, St. Antony's College, Oxford; FO 371/7315, vol. 20066. Furlonge (Beirut) to Eden, 17 Nov. 1936; FO 371/7488, vol. 20066. Havard (Beirut) to Eden, 24 Nov. 1936. MAE, Syrie–Liban 1930–40. Martel to MAE, 27 Nov. 1936, vol. 502, pp. 90–94.

Revolt seriously impeded Syrian-Lebanese trade with Palestine, causing heavy losses to merchants. This situation was aggravated by the inability of Palestinian agents to repay their bills as they fell due. The Bloc, caught between some of its strongest partisans—the merchants of Damascus who wanted the disturbances in Palestine curtailed and pan-Arabist forces—faced a difficult dilemma.[80]

Finally, the forever sluggish Syrian economy demanded Bloc attention. The economy barely had a chance to catch its breath and get rolling again after the General Strike when it found its most lucrative export market, Palestine, in the midst of a national uprising. During the summer of 1936, some of the worst bankruptcies since the world depression occurred, aggravated by unusually poor harvests in the Hawran.[81] But most serious of all was the Popular Front's fateful decision in the last days of September to devalue the French franc after nearly a decade of relative stability.[82] Prices of almost all commodities began to rise steeply. By the end of 1936, the cost of living index in Syria had risen by not less than 30 percent and continued to climb throughout 1937, so that 12 months after the devaluation it had more than doubled.[83] Wholesalers and middlemen who had to pay the producers of grain and other goods in gold raised their prices to retailers. These retailers, both of local goods and of imports from countries with non-depreciated currencies, in turn raised their prices to the consumer. Retailers of French goods were then also able to raise their prices. Meanwhile, house rents which were also negotiated in gold, rose accordingly.[84] Local Chambers of Commerce immediately demanded a rise in tariffs on competitive imports, while salaried employees in government and in the private sector who received their wages in the official currency, the Syrian paper pound, went on strike for wage increases.[85] As the brunt of Syrian resentment and criticism focused on continued French control of the Syrian economy and, in particular, on the banking, monetary, and customs system, the Mardam government would eventually have to raise with the French such important issues as the modification of the "Exchange of Letters no. 9" of the treaty which continued to provide for "monetary parity" between the French and the Syrian cur-

[80] FO 371/4416, vol. 20066. Ogden to Eden, 4 July 1936; FO 371/5149, vol. 20069. Ogden to Eden, 14 Aug. 1936; FO 684/9/1956/2. Ogden Memorandum, 21 Aug. 1936; FO 371/6716, vol. 20066. Ogden to Eden, 3 Oct. 1936.
[81] FO 371/6899, vol. 20069. Furlonge to Eden, 27 Oct. 1936.
[82] Kemp, *The French Economy*, pp. 122–23.
[83] Haut-Commissariat de la République Française en Syrie et au Liban, *Bulletin Economique Trimestriel*, no. 3 (1936), p. 313 S; *ibid.*, no. 4 (1936), p. 633 S; *ibid.*, no. 2 (1937), pp. 135–39, *graphiques*, nos. 1–3, pp. 207–9; *ibid.*, no. 4 (1937), pp. 799 S–811 S; Youssef Khoury, *Prix et monnaie en Syrie* (Nancy, 1943), p. 91.
[84] FO 371/6899, vol. 20069. Furlonge to Eden, 27 Oct. 1936.
[85] *Oriente Moderno*, 16 (1936), pp. 605–6.

rencies.[86] And the whole question of renewing the much-criticized Banque de Syrie concession, which was scheduled to come up in 1938, was already predicted to be a big headache for the National Bloc.

But even before these serious problems could be addressed, there existed the haunting question of whether a loosely-knit, indeed, fragile organization of nationalist politicians with little or no prior experience in governing could even hope to rule effectively.

[86] See text of "Exchange de Lettres, no. 9," in Appendix A, Hourani, *Syria and Lebanon,* p. 330.

PART VII

NATIONALISTS IN GOVERNMENT, 1937–1939

CHAPTER EIGHTEEN

THE TREATY THAT NEVER WAS

IN ONE SENSE, the history of the French Mandate was the history of failed diplomacy. Ever since Henry de Jouvenel proposed that the best solution to the Syrian Question would be the substitution of a treaty for the Mandate, diplomatic relations between France and Syria had been animated by this idea.[1] What normally prompted France to consider negotiating a treaty with Syrian leaders was sustained political unrest, as in 1925 and 1936. What prevented a treaty from seeing the light of day had as much to do with changing French perceptions of the place of Syria in the French Empire as it had to do with Syria's unwillingness to compromise on the sensitive questions of security for minorities and France's relations with Syria after independence.

It seems clear in retrospect that a treaty was by no means a foregone conclusion once the French government decided to negotiate in 1936. The narrow interest groups that composed the French colonial party voiced deep concern over the negotiations. But once the Popular Front swept into office in June, the colonial party temporarily lost influence at the Quai d'Orsay. The Blum government seemed committed to a treaty and the men assigned to write it were of a liberal and accommodating persuasion.[2]

The terms of the treaty required a three-year probationary period before French ratification. Its opponents, therefore, had time to build a case against it. Parliamentary opposition to the treaty was strong enough to prevent the Blum government from submitting it for ratification, and when Blum fell from power in June 1937, the colonial party launched a press campaign (in newspapers like *République* and *Paris-Soir*) against it.[3] At the center of this opposition were approximately sixty French commercial and industrial establishments with offices in Beirut and elsewhere in Lebanon and Syria. Some of the more influential of these originated,

---

[1] Pierre Viénot, "Le Traité Franco-Syrien," *Le Populaire* (11 Jan. 1939).

[2] In a perceptive article, William B. Cohen argues that although the accession of the Popular Front raised the hopes of independence movements throughout the French Empire, these hopes were "totally unrealistic." None of the three parties that formed the Front (Radical Socialists, Socialists, and Communists) "were unconditionally anticolonial and . . . even their devotion to reform was at best equivocal." Not only did the Front accord a "low priority" to colonial questions but Blum, himself, was disinterested. Cohen, "The Colonial Policy of the Popular Front," pp. 369, 388.

[3] 'Adil al-'Azma Papers [Syria], File 3/101. "Etude," 1 Nov. 1937.

not surprisingly, in Lyons and Marseilles, the two French cities with the strongest ties to the Levant.[4] Among them were the D-HP, the Société du Chemin de Fer Nord-Syrie, the Régie Générale des Chemins de Fer et Travaux Publics de Paris, the Sociétés des Tramways et d'Electricité of Beirut, Damascus, and Aleppo, the Banque de Syrie, and the IPC Group for oil exploration in the Jazira.[5]

Their concerns were familiar.[6] France had to stay in Syria to maintain her traditional influence in the region; to remain a great Muslim power; to prevent the spread of pan-Arabism to North Africa; to protect Lebanon from Syrian irredentism and the religious minorities in Syria from the tyranny of the Muslim majority; and to protect her commercial ventures and financial investments and her routes of communication to the Far Eastern parts of her Empire. Otherwise, Britain or some other power would snatch Syria away.[7]

The colonial party naturally was pleased by the political shift to the right that occurred with the formation of a new French government in 1937 headed by the Radical Socialist, Edouard Daladier, and, in particular, by its commitment to the empire. The Radical Socialists vowed to ''. . . defend [France's] menaced colonial empire, the security of French territory [and] French communications in the Mediterranean.''[8] The new French Foreign Minister explained to High Commissioner Martel in September 1937 that as long as Parliament continued to question the goodwill and sincerity of the Syrian government, the treaty would never be ratified.[9]

There was growing fear in French foreign policy circles, even among liberals, that because of growing tensions in Europe, France should take no steps that might upset her position in the eastern Mediterranean. Her naval and air bases on the Syrian-Lebanese coast, according to one French Admiral, required complete political security in the Syrian hinterland.[10] One perceptive French expert on Syrian affairs wrote in 1937 that

the Arab world has developed all around us much faster than we should have wished, and we have been brought to face in the last few

---

[4] MAE, Syrie–Liban 1930–40. Meyrier (Beirut) to MAE, 3 June 1936, vol. 492, pp. 154–55; *ibid.*, President of Marseilles Chamber of Commerce to MAE, 18 June 1936, vol. 492, pp. 240–42; *ibid.*, Air France to MAE, 9 July 1936, vol. 493, p. 105.

[5] MD, 7N 4190, Dossier 1. ''Etude sur les possibilités actuelles de la politique syrienne,'' 1 Dec. 1937.

[6] Neither the interests of the *parti colonial* nor its demands vis-à-vis Syria had changed significantly since World War I. See Andrew and Kanya-Forstner, *The Climax*, pp. 23–32 *passim*.

[7] MAE, Syrie–Liban 1930–40. ''Etude de René Favre,'' 19 June 1936, vol. 493, pp. 4–6.

[8] The Radical Socialists adopted this policy at a Party Congress on 29–30 Oct. 1937.

[9] MD, 7N 4190, Dossier 1. Bonnet to Martel, 20 Sept. 1937.

[10] MD, 7N 4190, Dossier 1. ''Etude,'' 1 Dec. 1937.

months a Treaty of Independence for Syria . . . which obviously
does not correspond to our original ideas.[11]

The Radical Socialist government, actively encouraged by the colonial
party, spent the next two years undoing the treaty of 1936. Articles in the
French press played on the sympathies of the French public by positing
that the treaty would severely jeopardize France's pre-eminent cultural
position in the Levant. Debates were staged in Parliament over the nature
of the minorities in Syria, which France, according to French rhetoric, had
entered the Levant to protect in the first place. Sympathetic French officials in Syria quietly promoted separatist movements in regions with
large minorities like the provinces of Latakia, the Jabal Druze, and Jazira
in order to challenge the National Bloc government's claim to represent a
unified Syria. In France, colonial groups publicized the frequent disturbances in these regions. Syrian minority leaders who opposed the treaty's
provisions for Syrian unity were invited to Paris to publicize their opposition; Cardinal Tappouni of Aleppo, the head of the Syrian Catholic
Church, was an especially effective critic.

The Quai d'Orsay also undercut the position of the Bloc government
by persuading Jamil Mardam, who had staked his government's credibility on the application of the treaty, to agree to several unfavorable
amendments to the original treaty of 1936. As a result, nationalist opponents of the Bloc government increased their efforts to undermine Mardam, arguing quite convincingly that the amendments called into question France's good-will toward Syria by offering the Syrian people
something far short of political independence and unity.

Mardam had not only staked his reputation on the treaty but he also
understood better than his nationalist colleagues the changing mood in
France. Therefore, to allay French fears, especially in the wake of violence
against Christians in the Jazira and Cardinal Tappouni's visits to the Vatican and to Paris to plead for increased minority protection,[12] Mardam
agreed to negotiate on those issues which required greater elaboration
and clarification. His visit to Paris in November 1937 resulted on December 11 in an exchange of letters with M. de Tessan, the Undersecretary of
State at the Foreign Ministry, which provided an additional Syrian guarantee for minority rights, and an affirmation that Syria would rely on
French technical cooperation for the organization of her public services.[13]

[11] Robert Montagne, "French Policy in North Africa and Syria," *International Affairs*
(March–April 1937), p. 272.
[12] MAE, Syrie–Liban 1930–40. Martel (Beirut) to MAE, 11 Dec. 1937, vol. 519, pp. 108–
15; *L'Asie Française*, no. 356 (Jan. 1938), p. 31.
[13] Pierre Viénot, *Le Populaire* (13 Jan. 1939); FO 371/7509, vol. 20849. Phipps (Paris) to
Eden, 21 Dec. 1937. For text of letters see Hourani, *Syria and Lebanon*, Appendix A.

The announcement of the Syrian guarantees caused demonstrations in Damascus where on December 11 a group of former *mujahidin* (freedom fighters) of the Great Revolt publicly condemned Mardam, declaring that they had spilled their blood for independence and therefore would reject the treaty by resorting to violence if it compromised Syria's national aspirations.[14] Opposition to Mardam's dealings in Paris did not come directly from National Bloc quarters, however; and when Mardam returned at the end of December 1937, Shahbandar supporters rather than Bloc partisans demonstrated against him. At this stage, Mardam still believed that he had considerable nationalist backing and argued confidently that the treaty was now as good as gold. A month later, an equally optimistic Martel reported that French Intelligence saw no chance of the nationalist opposition either bringing Mardam and his government down or even causing him serious political difficulty.[15]

But after a fortnight, Mardam began to lose his confidence. Mounting criticisms pushed him to lash out at his detractors. He ordered security forces to incarcerate 15 members of the Shahbandar group after manifestoes appeared in Damascus calling for the extermination of all despots and traitors. Anti-government forces organized a protest demonstration on the following day, only to face a counterdemonstration on January 18 at which 10,000 National Bloc "supporters" appeared, including members of the Communist Party which, taking its cues from French Communists, backed the treaty. One week later, a Damascus court found Munir al-ʿAjlani, Zaki al-Khatib, and Nasuh Babil—the leaders of the Shahbandar Party—guilty of public disturbances, illegal political reunions, and seditious discourse; each received a six-month prison term.[16]

Not long afterwards, Mardam faced his first serious cabinet crisis. Two issues that provoked controversy in Syrian nationalist circles were the question of oil exploration rights by a foreign company (the Petroleum Company Ltd) and the renewal of the Banque de Syrie concession, both of which had been under negotiation since early 1937. That Mardam kept the terms of the renegotiation of the Banque de Syrie concession secret, even from members of his own government, certainly did not help him when he announced at the end of February 1938 that the government had signed conventions for both concessions.[17] This prompted Shukri al-Quwwatli to resign his cabinet post in early March. Quwwatli had been looking for such an opportunity for several months under considerable

[14] *L'Asie Française*, no. 356 (Jan. 1938), p. 31.
[15] MAE, Gabriel Puaux Papers, Carton 34. Martel to MAE, 2 Feb. 1938.
[16] *L'Asie Française*, no. 357 (Feb. 1938), pp. 65–66 and no. 358 (March 1938), p. 93; *Oriente Moderno*, 18 (1938), pp. 118–19.
[17] MAE, Gabriel Puaux Papers, Carton 35, "Note" on BSL, n.d.; FO 371/1686, vol. 21915. MacKereth to Halifax, 9 March 1938.

pressure from Istiqlalis who had opposed the treaty from the beginning and from the affiliated League of National Action. Adding to the controversy were rumors that Mardam had agreed to unfavorable secret clauses in the Banque de Syrie convention when he was most recently in Paris.[18] Naturally, the Bloc government still had to submit both conventions to the Syrian Parliament for ratification and could do so only after the French Parliament ratified the treaty.

The next six months were extremely critical for the treaty and hence for the Bloc government. Quwwatli's defection, Shahbandar's attacks,[19] continued disturbances in Jazira, heightened tensions between National Bloc representatives and separatists in the Jabal Druze and the Latakia *muhafaza*, the growth of strong pan-Arab sentiment in support of the revolt in Palestine, renewed disagreement with the Lebanese government over the Common Interests, and, above all, the entrance of Turkish troops into the Sanjak of Alexandretta virtually paralyzed the Mardam government. Meanwhile, with the degeneration of the international situation, anti-treaty forces in France stepped up their campaign to protect her position in the eastern Mediterranean.

Under heavy pressure, Jamil Mardam made one last effort to save his precious treaty. In August 1938 he returned to Paris where he spent the next three months negotiating new arrangements that were intended to allay the French government's apprehensions. On November 14, Mardam and M. Bonnet, the Minister for Foreign Affairs, signed an agreement which, in addition to reaffirming the exchanges of 1937, promised to renew the Banque de Syrie privileges, permit oil exploration, guarantee the place of the French language in the Syrian education system and a permanent cadre of French agents in Syria, and ensure the rights of minorities, in particular Christians. From its side, the French government now agreed to 30 September 1939 as the date when the treaty would go into effect and promised to submit it for ratification to Parliament.[20]

Despite signs of good-will from both parties, the treaty was in a sense already doomed. While Mardam was in France, two factions began to mount opposition to his government and to the treaty: the group around Dr. Shahbandar, who had returned to Damascus after being in forced residence in Bludan; and the Istiqlalis who had been, until the fall of 1938, preoccupied with events in Palestine but now, as the revolt became a spent force, turned their attention to domestic politics. The announcement in Paris on October 22 that Gabriel Puaux would replace Martel as High

---

[18] *L'Asie Française*, no. 358 (March 1938), p. 93; Longrigg, *Syria*, p. 232; *al-Mudhik al-mubki*, no. 402 (14 Jan. 1939), p. 14.

[19] *Oriente Moderno*, 18 (1938), pp. 76–77.

[20] MD, 7N 4190, Dossier 1. "Note," 15 Nov. 1938; Hourani, *Syria and Lebanon*, pp. 219–20.

Commissioner seemed to indicate a reversal of French policy and the placement of the treaty on the "scrap heap."[21]

Although Mardam's return to Damascus on December 20 was met by large Bloc-sponsored demonstrations, the Bloc still had to pay dearly to ensure an adequate reception.

> Party leaders in different quarters of the town received sums of money for distribution to demonstrators, each of whom is reported to have been paid the princely sum of 2 piastres for cheering the PM. Cars were also provided and hotel accommodations reserved in Beirut for the more important supporters of the National Bloc to enable them to welcome Mardam on his arrival.[22]

Nevertheless, "these time honoured methods of producing a spurious popularity" were far from successful. Newspapers openly criticized the government and although Mardam, once back home, made speeches justifying his policy, he was accused of all kinds of sins. To refute claims that he was a "lion in Damascus and a fox in Paris," he tried to rally the National Bloc but was too late.[23] Several Damascus leaders asked him to resign. When he refused, they defected to the Shahbandar camp.[24]

Even before Jamil Mardam arrived back in Syria, the foreign affairs committees of both houses of the French Parliament produced their reports (on December 14) which expressed serious doubts about the treaty, even with its modifications. The Daladier government was not especially disappointed: M. Bonnet told M. Bergeron, the reporter for the committee in the Chamber of Deputies, that his government did not want the treaty presented to Parliament "at the present time."[25] Although some officials at the Quai d'Orsay felt that all was not lost because the treaty had come before the two committees at "an awkward moment when the whole question of the Mediterranean was causing a certain amount of excitement,"[26] neither the international situation nor the sentiments of Syrian opponents of the treaty could be reversed.

On December 31 the Syrian Parliament debated the current status of the treaty and after six hours produced a motion of confidence in the Mardam government but a condemnation of the French attitude. On the surface, the motion seemed rather mild and, indeed, it owed much to earlier deliberations among the leaders of the National Bloc when Mardam con-

---

[21] FO 371/6597, vol. 21914. MacKereth to FO, 29 Oct. 1938.

[22] FO 371/925, vol. 23276. MacKereth to Baxter, 28 Dec. 1938.

[23] *Ibid.*

[24] *Al-Mudhik al-mubki*, no. 400 (31 Dec. 1938), p. 14; no. 402 (14 Jan. 1939), p. 14; no. 403 (22 Jan. 1939), p. 8

[25] *Le Temps* (16 Dec. 1938).

[26] FO 371/390, vol. 23276. Wright (Paris) to Eastern Dept., 31 Dec. 1938.

vinced them that "there was nothing to be gained by forcing the pace of [Syrian] opposition to the change in French policy."[27] Yet, the Syrian Chamber made it perfectly clear that it rejected the terms of all agreements signed by Mardam after the original treaty of 1936.[28] Thus, the French had burnt the Mardam government's candle at both ends. The French Parliament refused to ratify the treaty, even with the concessions agreed to by Mardam; and the Syrian government refused to accept any of the compromises Mardam had conceded to France in 1937 and 1938. The treaty was a dead letter.

POST-MORTEM

Why did the French not ratify the treaty of 1936? Its supporters and opponents were in fundamental agreement over the reasons. When the French agreed in 1936 to a probationary three-year period they had expected to be able to ratify the treaty in 1939 without any trouble. But, events intervened. First, regional developments posed new problems. In Iraq, there were minority revolts, a coup d'état, and a brief military dictatorship; in Egypt, authoritarianism had grown and potentially menaced Syria; there was the rebellion in Palestine; and Turkey threatened Syria. And with world war approaching, the possibility of foreign intervention by France's enemies increased. The French found it increasingly difficult to give Syria full independence out of fear that she was still unprepared to cope with the various pressures around her. Secondly, the minorities question had not eased after the National Bloc took over government. The French accused Damascus of using the superior demographic position of the Sunni community to dominate the compact minorities, which destabilized the country. In such circumstances, a treaty jeopardized French interests in Syria, the welfare of Syria's minorities, and the special position of Lebanon. Moreover, a treaty would be viewed in North Africa as a French retreat and would certainly give the Arab population there ideas about demanding independence as the Syrians had.[29]

Where supporters and opponents of the treaty were in disagreement was over whether to re-open the treaty issue at a later date and, if not, what should replace the treaty. Some opponents, like French Senator Henry-Haye, suggested that the best solution was a military occupation which would stabilize Syria for two to three years. This would give France time to reconstruct a Syrian government on other bases. Henry-

[27] FO 371/235, vol. 23276. MacKereth to Halifax, 4 Jan. 1939.

[28] MAE, Gabril Puaux Papers, Carton 36, Dossier S-3-5. Montagne to Puaux, 1 April 1939.

[29] Ibid., MAE, Gabriel Puaux Papers, Carton 36, Dossier S-3-5. "Montagne note sur le Traité Franco-Syrien," 27 April 1939.

Haye also believed that a number of Senators would favor this proposal and would vote increased financial credits to the High Commission. Other opponents proposed a federated Syrian state system to include the governorates of Damascus, Aleppo, the Jabal Druze, Latakia, and the Jazira and which would enable the Sunni majority and the minorities to co-exist. These states would have local autonomy including regional financial control but they would come under a federal system which would be responsible for the internal and external security of the entire federation.[30]

A more enlightened view held that some regions contained elements which were too politically unsophisticated to form administrative cadres of their own in each state; this would continue to render certain states dependent on elements from outside, especially from the nationalist strongholds of Damascus and Aleppo. This view suggested instead a de-centralized system which, if allowed to evolve slowly, would inculcate a broad Syrian-Arab identity and ultimately a *rapprochement* between the minorities and the Sunni majority.[31]

Robert Montagne, a gifted French Arabist and adviser to the High Commission in Syria and Lebanon, articulated this last position, perhaps most systematically. He claimed that although Syria was the only republican government among the Arab states, the general "lack of public education" and the considerable influence of popular forces in Damascus indicated that the Syrian political system was insufficiently developed to accommodate these various pressures. The Syrian political and constitutional structure, if it hoped to ensure national security, required modification. The French government therefore had to rethink the treaty. Montagne suggested that given the minorities' "desire for autonomy, it seems impossible henceforth . . . to accept the principle of Syrian unity, centralized at Damascus. At the same time, Syrian unity cannot be achieved except by slow and prudent steps." He admitted that in Syria

with time [and] with the advancement of public education and administration, the most extreme particularisms will no longer persist, as has been the case in the great western civilized countries [where] religious opinions and provincial tendencies have been protected by laws and values.[32]

In Montagne's opinion, Syria could "profit from a short delay of one year . . . to develop the essential institutions to permit her to benefit from her independence and from internal peace." Then, the French government

[30] *Ibid.*
[31] *Ibid.*
[32] *Ibid.*

"should deliver a solemn declaration to the Syrian government affirming the will of France to assume the mission confided in it by the League of Nations, and, to conclude an equitable treaty."[33]

This divergence of opinion itself suggested how varied French views of Arab nationalism were. Hardliners opposed to the treaty regarded Arab nationalism as an artificial creation, an idea manipulated by agitators to weaken France's position in the eastern Mediterranean. In particular, they continued to hold Britain responsible for the development of Arab nationalism and its extensive activity against French interests.

The minority of politicians and officials who supported treaty ratification based their arguments on a radically different interpretation of Arab nationalism. They held that Arab nationalism appeared before World War I and was "a phenomenon of imitation caused by the modernization of the Orient under the influence of western nationalisms."[34] Rather than accuse the British of creating Arab nationalism, they suggested that the British were the first to utilize it to deepen their influence in the Middle East. By accommodating moderate nationalist leaders such as the Hashemite kings and by tying their interests to British interests, the British were able to play moderates against more dangerous radical nationalist elements in a policy of divide and rule. Frenchmen of this opinion, who included the principal negotiator of the 1936 treaty, Pierre Viénot, recognized Arab nationalism for what it was—one of those great historical movements which were not only political but cultural and whose ideas appealed to a broad spectrum of Arab society. Like the British, they believed that by developing public education in all the Arab states, the barriers separating the minorities from the Sunni majority would eventually break down and the minorities would ultimately embrace Arabism. They realized that a "Syrian edifice whose base is the minorities [was] passé."[35] But their voices remained unheard for the duration of France's stay in Syria. Other forces still had to intervene for Syria to acquire independence.

[33] Ibid.
[34] MAE, Gabriel Puaux Papers, Carton 36, Dossier S-3-5. Montagne to Puaux, 1 April 1939.
[35] Ibid.

CHAPTER NINETEEN

THE LOSS OF THE SANJAK

NOTHING DAMAGED the reputation of the National Bloc more severely than its failure to prevent the step-by-step separation of the Sanjak of Alexandretta from Syria and its transfer to Turkey. For the Mardam government, the loss of the Sanjak was the most humiliating development to occur during its tenure.

The force of separatism in Alexandretta gained strength only after it seemed likely that the nationalists would secure a satisfactory treaty from France and a mandate to govern. Parallels can be drawn with the rise of separatism in the spring and summer months of 1936 in the Jabal Druze, the Latakia province, and the Jazira. But, what allowed the separatist movement in Alexandretta to advance as far as it did was the external hand of Turkey and France's willingness to sacrifice Syria's territorial integrity for France's larger international interests. In retrospect, there seems little doubt that the Turks capitalized on the "deteriorating international situation, particularly the Italian menace in the eastern Mediterranean," and on increased Turkish prestige and strength derived from the recent Turkish acquisition of "complete sovereignty over the Straits," to swallow the entire Sanjak in 1939.[1] In the face of an aggressive Turkish government and hampered by French control, there was little the Syrian nationalist government could do to prevent its loss.

SITUATED IN THE angle formed by the eastern shore of the Mediterranean and the Turkish-Syrian frontier, the region known during most of the Mandate as the Sanjak of Alexandretta consisted of a narrow coastal plain backed by a chain of mountains and the lower valley of the Orontes River to the southeast. Along the coast was Alexandretta with its natural harbor and in the valley rested Antioch, the Sanjak's largest town. During the Mandate, the ethno-religious and social composition of the Sanjak was as mixed as in any of the peripheral regions of Syria; indeed, one could argue more so. The major social and political divisions were between Turkish speakers and Arabic speakers, and between Christians and Muslims, although divisions also fell along a rich–poor axis.

On the other hand, the severe ethnic and religious conflicts that char-

[1] Avedis K. Sanjian, "The Sanjak of Alexandretta (Hatay): Its Impact on Turkish-Syrian Relations (1939–1956)," *Middle East Journal* (Autumn 1956), p. 381.

acterized political life in the Sanjak in the late 1930s were not nearly so sharp in the 1920s and early 1930s. To a certain extent, they were blunted by a measure of local prosperity which was heightened by the fairly high level of economic interdependence of the Sanjak's numerous communities. But, the dramatic slowdown of the Sanjak's economy owing to the world depression, coupled with the rapid spread of Turkish and Arab nationalist ideologies in the early 1930s, destroyed the harmony of communal interests there and helped to set the stage for the explosion of ethnic conflict in 1936.

On one level, the conflict in the Sanjak was one of numbers: not only did each community have its own statistics but statistics could be and were interpreted differently, depending on the categories being used. The most reliable estimates are probably those provided by the French High Commission in 1936. Of a total population of approximately 220,000 in the Sanjak, 39 percent were ethnic Turks, 28 percent were Alawites, 11 percent were Armenians, 10 percent were Sunni Arabs, 8 percent were other Christians (principally Greek Orthodox), and the remainder were divided between Kurds, Circassians, and Jews (approximately 4 percent).[2] The Turkish government disputed the French statistics, claiming that Turks numbered anywhere from 150,000 to 240,000 and that the Sanjak's total population was more like 300,000.[3] The Turkish claim was inflated.

Although the Turks constituted the single largest ethnic community, Arabic speakers, who included Alawites, Sunni Arabs, and most of the non-Armenian Christians, were more numerous than Turkish speakers. As for the religious composition of the Sanjak, nearly 80 percent were Muslim (and 20 percent were Christian). However, Sunni Muslims formed barely half of the local Muslim population, the Alawites making up the difference. The Christian minorities were mainly concentrated in the towns and formed a significant component of the artisanal and mercantile classes, as they did in the Jazira and Latakia provinces. A large part of the Armenian community were refugees from Cilicia, and spoke Turk-

---

[2] Cited in FO 371/7773, vol. 20068. Parr to FO, 14 Dec. 1936; FO 371/7819, vol. 20068. Viénot Memo. to FO, 12 Dec. 1936; Sanjian, "Sanjak," p. 380.

[3] FO 371/196, vol. 20845. Ward (FO), Memo., 11 Jan. 1937. On this history, also see A. Alexandre, "Conflits de l'arabisme et des nationalismes voisins. Le conflit syro-turc du Sandjak d'Alexandrette d'octobre 1936 à juin 1937, vu d'Antioche," in Entretiens sur l'évolution des pays de civilisation arabe, II, (Paris: Centre d'Etudes de Politique Etrangère, 1938), pp. 105–41; Majid Khadduri, "The Alexandretta Dispute," American Journal of International Law, 39 (1945), pp. 406–25; Jacques Thobie, "Le nouveau cours des relations franco-turques et l'affaire Sandjak d'Alexandrette, 1929–1939," Relations Internationales, 19 (Autumn 1979), 355–74; Elizabeth Picard, "Retour au Sanjak," Maghreb-Machrek (Jan.-Feb. 1983), pp. 47–64; Edward Weisband, "The Sanjak of Alexandretta, 1920–1939: A Case Study," in R. Bayly Winder, ed., Near Eastern Roundtable, 1967–68 (New York: New York University Near Eastern Studies Center, 1969), pp. 156–224.

ish in addition to Armenian. Also resident in the towns was a portion of the landowning aristocracy; although divided between Turks and Sunni Arabs, the Turkish element was wealthier and more influential. The vast majority of the Sanjak's inhabitants were impoverished peasants who worked either their own plots of land or, more often, the land of big absentee landowners. The most significant and downtrodden peasants were the Arabic-speaking Alawites who, like their co-religionists in the Jabal Ansariyya to the south, faced the exploitation of a Sunni landowning class, in this case mainly Turkish in composition.[4] Alawites could also be found in Antioch where they engaged in trades associated with food production but they were less influential in commerce than the Armenian and Arabic-speaking Christians. Political loyalties in the Sanjak generally followed ethnic and religious lines, but each community had its own internal socio-economic divisions, which cut across communal lines, making political life quite complex.

When in 1920 the Treaty of Sèvres fixed the Turkish-Syrian frontier too far north for the liking of Turkish nationalists, they rejected it and heavy fighting between Turkish rebel bands and French forces resulted in a new delineation of the line further to the south by the Franklin-Bouillon Agreement of October 1921. This agreement also called for the establishment of a special administrative regime for the district of Alexandretta. The Turkish language was given official recognition and M. Franklin-Bouillon wrote a letter to the head of the Turkish delegation which stated that the French government would, as a general rule, appoint Turkish officials in those regions with a Turkish majority and would set up schools for the promotion of Turkish culture. In a signed protocol, he also promised to recommend to the French government that it accept the Turkish claim that the Sanjak be allowed a special flag and that an area in the port of Alexandretta be leased to Turkey for the handling of goods in transit to Turkey. The frontier laid down between the new Turkish state and Syria in 1921 was confirmed by Article 3 of the Lausanne Treaty of 1923. By Article 16 of the same treaty, Turkey renounced "all rights and title whatsoever over or respecting the territories to the south of this frontier." Later, in May 1926, France and Turkey signed a treaty which supplemented and clarified the provisions of the 1921 agreement.[5]

The French basically upheld their promises to the Turks and a limited measure of administrative and financial (but not political autonomy) was

---

[4] On the Alawites of the Sanjak, see Jacques Weulersse, *Le pays des Alaouites*. On the towns of the Sanjak, especially Antioch, see Weulersse, "Antioche, essai de géographie urbaine," *Bulletin d'Etudes Orientales*, 4 (1934), pp. 27–79; Pierre Bazantay, *Enquête sur l'artisinat à Antioche*. (Beirut, 1936), p. 4.

[5] FO 371/196, vol. 20845. Ward (FO), Memo., 11 Jan. 1937.

granted the Sanjak. Yet, the Sanjak formed an integral part of the State of Syria; in this sense, it was unlike the Latakia province and the Jabal Druze, which, although to some extent associated with Syria, were formally detached from Syrian sovereignty until 1936. Indeed, the regime in the Sanjak, as prescribed by the Statute of 1930, required that the governor and the local judges of the Sanjak were the appointees of the government in Damascus. But, it also provided for a measure of local control over the appointment of subordinate administrative officials, for an Administrative Council with a majority of elected members possessing the power to vote a local budget, and for limited financial autonomy.[6]

Although the Sanjak had considerable agricultural potential, especially for cotton production, the sources disagree over the extent of the Sanjak's prosperity under French rule. British officials in Syria reported that the French rather conspicuously neglected its development except for a certain amount of road construction, land reclamation, and some smaller public works. They claimed that the execution of drainage schemes to open up new agricultural lands and the question of harbor works were almost entirely ignored during the 1920s. By contrast, French officials and observers asserted that the relative domestic tranquility in this decade owed much to sustained improvement in the Sanjak's general financial health. Comparisons were made with other regions of Syria in terms of increased budget surpluses and agricultural production, and improvements in the overall balance of trade. The French High Commission pointed with pride to its successes in land reclamation, in bringing electricity to the towns, and in road-building, supporting its claims with a wealth of statistical data. Conversely, it demonstrated how unproductive expenditures on the military and other forms of security decreased in this period.[7]

The British undoubtedly underestimated French achievements in the Sanjak; yet, there is no doubt that these were, in turn, exaggerated by the French. The High Commission was unable to attract the capital investment it had hoped to, making the completion of a number of development projects impossible. This contributed to the perception in the Sanjak and

[6] Ibid.

[7] For British views, see FO 371/9057, vol. 12160. Aleppo Consul to FO; FO 371/106, vol. 13072. Satow to FO, 2 Dec. 1927; FO 371/956, vol. 12804. Monck-Mason to FO, 1 Feb. 1929. For French views, see MAE, Rapport sur la situation de la Syrie et du Liban (Paris, 1922–23, 1924–31); Raymond O'Zoux, Les états du Levant sous Mandat français (Paris, 1931); and Paul Du Véou, Le Désastre d'Alexandrette (Paris, 1938). A summation of the French argument can be found in a paper by Robert B. Satloff. In it he provides a fascinating revisionist interpretation of the Sanjak's communal relations in the 1920s and early 1930s. It is entitled: "Prelude to Conflict: Communal Interdependence in the Sanjak of Alexandretta 1920–1936" (Harvard University, June 1984). His paper is to be published in a forthcoming issue of Middle Eastern Studies.

elsewhere in Syria that the French were neglecting the Sanjak's welfare. Moreover, the Sanjak's political future in the twenties was sufficiently ambiguous to create considerable apprehension among Syrian politicians, especially in Aleppo (whose principal commercial outlet was the port Alexandretta) that eventually the French would cede the region to the Turks. Their fears were fueled by Iraqi statesmen who warned of Turkish expansion toward Aleppo and even into northern Iraq.[8]

At the same time, the Turkish press helped to foster this impression. Throughout the period there were more than occasional references to the hope that Turkey would one day recover Antioch and Alexandretta and to the unfavorable treatment of ethnic Turks in the Sanjak. Before the mid-thirties, however, there was no indication that the Turkish government actually wished to rule the Sanjak. Rather, its interest was most probably strategic. It wanted to hold both sides of the Gulf of Alexandretta and to embrace all sections of the railway from Adana to Nisbin.

It was not until 1934 that the question of the Sanjak's future began to receive more serious attention, both in Turkey and among Syrians. It was observed, for example, that the Turks had halted construction on the port at Mersine, perhaps because of the possibility of grabbing Alexandretta. Similarly it was asked why France had developed Tripoli instead of Alexandretta.[9] In March of that year, the Turkish *vali* (governor), of ʿAyntab (across the Turkish border) passed through Antioch where Kemalist supporters organized a huge demonstration and sparked the first major disturbances between Turks and Arabs in the Sanjak. From that time on, all major Turkish feast days were celebrated with a flourish in the Sanjak. The 5th Battalion of the Syrian Legion stationed at Antioch and composed largely of Alawites and Armenians reacted with displeasure to the growth of pro-Turkish sentiment[10] which was channeled through a Kemalist organization established at the time and known as the People's Party.[11]

Arab nationalists in the Sanjak—now sensing their political weakness—pressed for its complete integration into the Syrian state and launched a press campaign accusing the French of favoring Turkish irredentism. The Turkish press responded with strong denials of the Arab accusations while it pressed for greater attention to the needs of the Sanjak's Turkish community. The evidence suggests that the Turkish government was still quite willing to accept the status quo in the Sanjak

---

[8] FO 371/229, vol. 16086. Clerk (Constantinople) to Simon, 8 Jan. 1932; FO 371/4063, vol. 16086. Rendel Memo., 20 Aug. 1932.

[9] FO 371/6996, vol. 16976. Morgan (Angora) to FO, 11 Nov. 1933; FO 371/3272, vol. 17947. Morgan to FO, 12 May 1934.

[10] Alexandre, "Conflits," p. 110.

[11] Thobie, "Le nouveau," p. 360.

and that before 1936 few serious disputes actually arose. Apart from French checks on the spread of Kemalist propaganda, which the Turks claimed was merely an effort to promote Turkish culture, Turkish elements in the Sanjak seem to have been rather favorably treated.[12]

STAGE I

Direct Turkish involvement in the question of the Sanjak began after the announcement in September 1936 that a draft treaty had been agreed upon in Paris and, in particular, after the head of the Syrian delegation, Hashim al-Atasi, on his way home via Ankara, announced that the Sanjak would remain autonomous under Syrian sovereignty. Articles appeared in the Turkish press in Ankara and Istanbul declaring that Turkey could never accept a Sanjak under Arab domination. The general line of Turkish argument was that under the new circumstances if the Sanjak did not receive an independent political status then Turkish privileges in the region, as outlined back in 1921, would be jeopardized. Special criticism was reserved for the French whom the Turks accused of packing local administration with their favorite minority, the Alawites, to the exclusion of Turks. They singled out M. Durieux, who was in his eleventh year as Assistant Delegate in the Sanjak, for purposely obstructing the promotion of Turkish culture and rights.[13]

The Turkish press clearly echoed the sentiments of the Turkish government, which did not take long to demand a clarification of the Sanjak's future status. In fact, because the terms of the draft Franco-Syrian Treaty did not contain specific provisions for the continuance of the special autonomous regime in the Sanjak, the Turkish government put forward its own demands. These appeared in a Note handed by the Turkish Ambassador in Paris to the Quai d'Orsay on October 10, requesting a treaty granting the Sanjak full independence. Although Pierre Viénot and other officials at the Quai were visibly disturbed by the Turkish proposals, it was becoming increasingly obvious that the Turkish government now attached great importance to the future of the Sanjak.[14] Two speeches in early November by Ataturk—one before the National Assembly—in which he spoke of Alexandretta as the burning issue of the day, reflected this heightened Turkish interest.[15]

Although the French government was unwilling to accept the idea of an independent Sanjak, it had to respond to Turkish pressures and, at the end of November, it came up with the counterproposal that both parties

---

[12] Alexandre, "Conflits," p. 111.
[13] Ibid., pp. 112–13; FO 371/6183, vol. 20067. Morgan (Istanbul) to Eden, 12 Sept. 1936.
[14] Thobie, "Le nouveau," p. 361.
[15] FO 371/7357, vol. 20067. Fox Note, 25 Nov. 1936.

submit their differences to the Council of the League of Nations. The Turkish government eagerly agreed. By the end of 1936, the Turkish government had revealed no official interest in the annexation of the Sanjak, only in its independence. The most generous explanation offered of Turkish aims was that the Sanjak should become a pro-Turkish, autonomous, and neutralized buffer between Turkey and Syria. Popular sentiment, however, was less benign. A spirited debate in the Turkish National Assembly on November 27 produced strong criticism of French treatment of the Sanjak's Turkish population and deputies threatened to seize the Sanjak by force, no matter what the outcome of the League Council deliberations. According to the British Ambassador in Ankara,

> some deputies described the Sanjak as Turkey's Alsace-Lorraine and demanded immediate abolition of the unnatural frontier which separated Turk from Turk, the annexation of the sanjak to the mother land, and the creation of a new frontier from the Orontes to the Euphrates.[16]

On the other side of the frontier there was a growing sense of alarm that Turkey planned to absorb the Sanjak through the application of steady pressure on the French and on the Arab population in the Sanjak. Already in mid-November, election primaries "tore off the veil behind which the animosity of the various groups in the Sanjak . . . were hidden." Elections were a failure with only 8 percent of the electors voting and the pro-Turkish party abstaining altogether. The Turks sent agents into the Sanjak to stir up the Turkish population against the Arabs and arms were reported to have been smuggled in on a large scale for the pro-Turkish element.[17] Then, on November 30, Turkish elements attacked the houses of the three newly elected deputies to the Syrian Parliament. French military intervention resulted in the death of three Turkish demonstrators; seventeen others were injured.[18]

Syrian nationalists in Aleppo and Damascus firmly believed by this time that France and Turkey had already settled the question of Alexandretta and that the deliberations of the League Council were "a mere formality designed to render the bitter pill of dismemberment less unpalatable." There seems little doubt that in recent years the High Commission staff in the Sanjak had been encouraging and pampering the Turkish minority as part of the general French policy of divide and rule, and this policy seems to have been stepped up around the time of the treaty ne-

---

[16] FO 371/7611, vol. 20068. Lorraine to Eden, 2 Dec. 1936.
[17] FO 371/413, vol. 20845. Catoni (Aleppo) to Eden, 24 Nov. 1936.
[18] FO 371/7759, vol. 20068. Parr (Aleppo) to FO, 13 Dec. 1936.

gotiations. However, as was the case in the other peripheral Syrian provinces, once the Quai d'Orsay committed itself to the treaty, there arose the inevitable divergence of points of view between French High Commission headquarters and local French officials. While the High Commissioner and his immediate staff had to accept directives from Paris, local officials were less inclined to do so because the full implementation of the treaty would inevitably mean the loss of their importance and eventually their posts. They had become quite attached to their districts and had built up local clients whom they did not wish to see sacrificed—a typically paternalistic attitude of the colonial official in the field. Such a situation had already developed in the Latakia province where the French governor and his supporters did their best to stir up the Alawites to agitate for the retention of Alawite autonomy outside a Syrian administrative framework. The High Commissioner, in order to live up to his government's pledge to restore that territory to Syria, had to retire the governor and to transfer most French officials from the territory.[19]

In Damascus Jamil Mardam expressed skepticism about the sincerity of Turkish intentions. He was convinced that Turkey wanted to expand territorially into Syria and he told the British Consul that the Syrian government would "never consent to the removal of the Sanjak from Syrian sovereignty," if only because it would bring disaster to the Aleppo district which had already been severed from its natural Turkish hinterland in 1920.[20]

Whether Turkey seriously wanted something more than the Sanjak's independence by the end of 1936 is debatable. But, the fact is that an independent Sanjak had little prospect of standing alone, given its economic dependence on its neighbors and its lack of national and linguistic cohesion. As the British Foreign Office suggested:

if it were set up as an independent unit, it would inevitably become a tempting field for irredentist ambition, both in Turkey and in Arabia, and since the Turks, after the interest they have taken in the question, could hardly leave Arab activity and propaganda a clear field, they would presumably be almost obliged to embark on similar activities themselves. Indeed, if only in order to prevent the Sanjak from falling back into Syria they would have to attract it towards themselves, and it is not difficult to imagine a situation in which the area would gradually be forced into increasing independence on, and eventually almost automatic absorption, by Turkey.[21]

[19] FO 371/371/969, vol. 20846. Baggalay (FO) to Perowne (Paris), 25 Feb. 1937.
[20] FO 371/88, vol. 20845. MacKereth to Eden, 31 Dec. 1936.
[21] FO 371/7666, vol. 20067. Eastern Dept., 12 Dec. 1936.

ALTHOUGH ON THE SURFACE the Sanjak controversy assumed a dominant
Franco-Turkish coloration, its internal dimensions have rarely received
the weight they so rightly deserve. Indeed, it is unlikely that the Sanjak
would have been severed had the force of Turkish nationalism not been
more dynamic than the force of Arab nationalism and had it not received
greater reinforcement from across the Turkish frontier than Arab nationalism received from Damascus. Therefore, to understand the nature of
conflict in the Sanjak and how this conflict ultimately ended, it is necessary to examine the Sanjak's various political forces as they interacted
during the different phases of the Sanjak's alienation from Syria.

On a political level, the internal history of the Sanjak in the interwar
period can be interpreted in terms of two linguistic, cultural, and national
blocs, each vying for access to French patronage. By the mid-1930s, these
two adversarial blocs had also developed diametrically opposed radical
wings: one called for the reattachment of the Sanjak to Kemalist Turkey
and the other demanded the full integration of the Sanjak into Syria. The
important point to underscore, however, is that both blocs had their own
profound divisions which colored the political scene.

Among the Turkish-speaking population, three political factions
emerged: the autonomists who were favorably disposed to cooperate with
Damascus provided that the Sanjak retained a considerable measure of
administrative autonomy; those who sought an independent Sanjak with
strong ties to Turkey; and Turkish irredentists who wanted the Sanjak
completely integrated into Turkey. Of the three groups, the most influential were the autonomists, who consisted of the great Turkish landowning families of the region and the Turkish-Muslim religious establishment. Socially and religiously conservative, they had never been drawn
into the whirlwind of modern Turkish nationalism as embodied in the
Kemalist movement and, indeed, were increasingly intimidated by the
force of this movement.

As for the two Turkish nationalist groups, both subscribed to the socio-
political and cultural theories of Kemalism; the difference separating
them was more one of strategy than of ideology. They drew their suste-
nance from across the frontier with Turkey and owed their cohesion to
the structural changes which the Sanjak experienced in the twenties and
early thirties. Many Turkish nationalists in the Sanjak were products of
the expanding local Turkish educational system which became infused
with the ideas of Kemalism. These same young men were to experience a
severe blow to their material expectations and employment opportunities
in the early thirties as a consequence of the world depression. With their
prospects for social mobility now diminished, they looked to Turkey for
support as their interest in a re-arrangement of power relations in the
Sanjak sharpened. Standing in their way, of course, was the Turkish land-

owning aristocracy whose moral authority they sought to weaken. Armed with the Kemalist ideology, they attracted to their side Turkish merchants and artisans who had also witnessed an erosion of their economic bases. In Antioch where the ethnic Turkish elite was strongest, their vehicles of expression were a Turkish newspaper (*Yeni Gün*) and a youth sporting club (*Genç Spor Klübü*). By the mid-1930s, the emerging Turkish nationalist movement in the Sanjak not only threatened the status of the local Turkish upper class but also posed a serious danger to the power of the Arab bloc.[22]

Increasing polarization among the Turkish minority became obvious at the end of January 1937, when the League Council, after considerable debate, adopted a proposal providing for the Sanjak's transformation into a separate, demilitarized entity, with full control over its internal affairs. Other terms in the proposal stated that Syria would be responsible for the conduct of the Sanjak's external relations and both Syria and the Sanjak would be bound by the same customs and monetary system. Turkish would be an official language alongside Arabic.

On the one hand, the Turkish landed classes were relieved that the Sanjak was not incorporated into Turkey

at least as much as they are that they are not to pass under Arab rule. Though they are anxious to preserve their Turkish traditions, language and culture, they have no desire whatsoever to become citizens of the Turkish Republic, a change that would involve the forcible abandonment of many customs and religious institutions which [they] are still old-fashioned enough to venerate. The proposed autonomous régime satisfies all their aspirations.[23]

On the other hand, thousands of Turkish separatists and irredentists had already taken to the streets of Alexandretta and Antioch in early January, demanding the Sanjak's independence. Although these demonstrations faced even larger Arab counterdemonstrations, Turkish protestors were emboldened by reports of Turkish troop movements on the borders and by direct assistance from recently established Hatay [literally Hittite] Independence Committees in Istanbul and other Turkish towns, consisting of natives of the Sanjak living in Turkey and of university students and schoolboys. These committees had their own flag and anthem which unmistakably resembled the Turkish national flag and anthem.[24]

The Arabic-speaking population in the Sanjak also had its divisions. And, as with the Turcophone population, these were accentuated by the

[22] Alexandre, "Conflits," pp. 108–9.

[23] FO 371/902, vol. 20846. Davis to Eden, 4 Feb. 1937.

[24] FO 371/209, vol. 20845. Lorraine to Eden, 5 Jan. 1937; FO 371/336, 20845. Davis to Eden, 5 Jan. 1937; FO 371/449, vol. 20845. Davis to Eden, 13 Jan. 1937.

rise of new educated elites, armed with the dominant idea of Arab nationalism and poised to challenge the traditional communal leaders
among the Arabophones.

Religion separated the Alawite, Sunni, and Christian communities,
and each community had its own internal political differences. Some desired the French Mandate to be extended indefinitely and looked to the
French for protection. Others sought the Sanjak's complete unity with
Syria and were connected to the National Bloc in Aleppo and Damascus.
Still others viewed Syrian independence only as a first step toward the
creation of a larger Arab nation; they belonged to the Antioch branch of
the radical, pan-Arab League of National Action. As was the case among
the Turkish factions, National Bloc and League of National Action supporters had much more in common than either had with the Syrian autonomists. However, the Arabic-speaking party was less cohesive than
the Turkish-speaking one, owing to its greater religious and social diversity. And even with the political tide in the Sanjak shifting quite palpably
away from the Arabs, which encouraged all Arabic-speaking factions to
declare themselves Arab, the coalition they formed was at best fragile and
ultimately ineffective.

The autonomist faction of Arabic speakers consisted principally of the
Alawite farming community and the Christian minorities in the towns.
Joining them were the Armenians who bitterly distrusted the Turks under whom they had suffered extensive human and material loss, but who
were also wary of Arab nationalist forces. The Syrian unionists attracted
a growing number of the Sunni Arab landowning class in the Sanjak, who
had strong social and economic ties to Aleppo. The radical pan-Arabists
were led by a Sorbonne-educated intellectual of Alawite provenance,
Zaki al-Arsuzi, and drew support from the growing Arabic-speaking
intelligentsia—mainly Sunnis and Christians—in the towns of the Sanjak. Although the League of National Action's principal focus was on preventing a Turkish takeover in the Sanjak and on continuing the anti-imperialist struggle, it was also committed to breaking the hold of the Sunni
landowning class and, in particular, its dominant Turkish element, over
the predominantly Alawite peasantry.[25]

Like the Turkish landowning class in the Sanjak, Alawite communal
leaders, who were also landowners, welcomed the League of Nations' January proposals and the prospect of local autonomy. These traditional
leaders feared full incorporation in a Syrian state dominated by Arab nationalists in which they would become a comparatively unimportant

[25] Alexandre, "Conflits," pp. 109–10. For an example of the considerable Syrian unionist
publicity generated by the National Bloc in the late 1930s and especially by Fakhri al-Barudi's Arab Bureau see Bureau National Arabe de Recherches et d'Informations, La vérité sur
la question d'Alexandrette (Damascus, n.d.), 12 pages.

elite. The Armenians also breathed a sigh of relief because they deeply resented the idea of being ruled again by Turks, though they were not particularly keen on Arab rule either. In general, the local, Arabic-speaking Christian commercial classes feared that any change in the status of the Sanjak would cut off their extremely valuable trade with Aleppo, which was more developed than their trade with Turkey.[26] Sunni Arab landowners, on the other hand, were extremely worried by the League's proposals. In recent years, they had become increasingly concerned about their future in the Sanjak. Not only were they dominated by the Turkish section of the landowning class but the Arabic-speaking 'ulama' were also less influential than the Turkish-speaking 'ulama' of the Sanjak. If the Sanjak developed a pronounced Turkish orientation, as they expected it would, then the local Arab elite would inevitably become less politically influential than the larger Turkish landowning elite. Their inclination therefore was to press for the Sanjak's full integration into Syria where they could expect to have their greatest influence, owing to their ties with the nationalist leadership in Aleppo and Damascus.

This then is the way the various local classes, nationalities, and rites lined up on the question of the Sanjak, as its fate was being decided in the late 1930s. There is little doubt that the effects of the world depression had eroded the Sanjak's traditional economic system of communal interdependence, fostering intense ethnic conflict between an increasing number of Arabs and Turks, and especially between the modern educated elites of each community. Yet political divisions along ethnic lines were not as sharply drawn for all the Sanjak's communities; they continued to cut across communal and class lines. Indeed, in one sense, three identifiable political blocs operated at this time, especially in Antioch, the principal center of Sanjak political life and the seat of local government. Although they could be distinguished from one another in several ways, the easiest way was by the dress code each chose to adopt. The Kemalist Turks, like their allies across the frontier, wore Western clothes, in particular a melon-colored sports jacket and Western cloth hats. The pan-Arab League of National Action youth brigades, like their comrades to the south, sported the sidara, popularized by the late King Faysal. Positioned between both blocs were the Turkish and Alawite notables, the Armenians, and the Greek Orthodox Christians, all of whom wore the fez.[27]

---

[26] FO 371/902, vol. 20846. Davis to Eden, 4 Feb. 1937.

[27] By the spring of 1937, the Turkish government was flooding the Sanjak with cloth caps for their supporters. See FO 371/2188, vol. 20846. Ward Memorandum no. 2, 19 April 1937. Also MAE, Syrie–Liban 1930–40. Martel to MAE, 21 July 1937, vol. 469.

THE LEAGUE OF NATIONS' January report, which also called for a Franco-Turkish Treaty to determine the manner in which the two states would guarantee the territorial integrity of the Sanjak, was received with alarm in Damascus. To the nationalist government, it was obvious that the French were not prepared to shed any blood to uphold the principles of the Mandate. However, Jamil Mardam's commitment to keeping the Sanjak a part of the Syrian state was not all that strong, despite his various outward manifestations of solidarity with the Arab peoples of the region. Mardam was much more concerned with whether his government's treaty with France would be ratified.

Rumors had begun to spread that since the Syrian delegation had left Paris French officialdom had re-asserted its 'imperialistic' influence with the Blum government and was seeking a repudiation of the Treaty in the [French] *Chambre* [of Deputies].[28]

Ostensibly, Mardam had made his February 1937 trip to Paris to argue the Alexandretta Question. But secretly his intention was to lobby "his political friends" to speed up the treaty ratification process. In fact, it is likely that Mardam had already written off the Sanjak and chose to use it as a bargaining point to extract further concessions from the French. One matter that needed resolution was the question of a full amnesty for Syria's large number of political exiles. On his return to Damascus in mid-April, the one piece of good news Mardam had to report was that a general amnesty for 42 political activists was forthcoming.[29]

The months and days leading up to the establishment of a new regime in the Sanjak were marked by laborious negotiations between Turkey and France in Geneva, a series of violent incidents between Turks and Arabs in the Sanjak, and a growing mistrust of the French in Damascus.[30] The High Commission appears to have promised the Syrian government that French diplomacy would lead to a favorable interpretation of the League's January proposals.[31] But the League's acceptance of the report on 29 May 1937 and the Franco-Turkish accord that followed indicated nothing of the sort. The French were accused of duplicity and the Syrian Parliament voted against the Geneva accords and the new statute in May and again in December, after the establishment of the newly independent regime in the Sanjak on November 29. Nevertheless, the French prepared the San-

[28] FO 371/2159, vol. 20848. MacKereth to Eden, 8 April 1937.
[29] FO 371/2294, vol. 20848. MacKereth to Eden, 20 April 1937.
[30] MD, 7N 4190, Dossier 6. Etat-Major de l'Armée, "Note," 7 May 1937; *ibid.*, 7N 4190, Dossier 6, "Note," 8 May 1937.
[31] FO 371/2429, vol. 20847. Lorraine to FO, 1 May 1937; FO 371/5509, vol. 20847. Davis to FO, 24 Aug. 1937.

jak's population for the new regime, in the face of mounting Turkish interference and increasingly violent Arab protests.[32]

STAGE II

With the establishment of the new regime, the first stage of the Sanjak's separation from Syria was complete. The second stage focused on the organization of elections in the Sanjak, as called for by the League of Nations. Turkish objections to the draft electoral regulations—on the ground that they had been devised by the League Council and the French but not in consultation with Turkey—led to a new compromise. In January 1938, the League appointed a new electoral commission, including Turkish and French representatives, to be sent out to the Sanjak to supervise registration. It also modified the registration procedure. Registrants no longer had to provide evidence of their religious or ethnic origin. Arab protests against a religious division of categories, which separated Alawites from Sunni Arabs, were ignored.[33]

It was within this electoral framework that the Turkish and Arab parties squared off for their major showdown. And it was in these circumstances that the French government acquiesced to Turkish pressures and indicated quite openly its willingness to break its commitment to the Mandate charter by opting for what it perceived to be the higher national interests of France—that of preventing Turkey from being drawn toward the Rome–Berlin axis.

Turkish strategy was again played out on two fronts: in the Sanjak and with the French at Geneva. The Turks actively intrigued in the Sanjak with the "thinly disguised object of producing a situation which would lead to its annexation." The Turks knew all along that they would be unable to secure an absolute majority unless they resorted to a policy of intimidation and coercion. One popular method was for Turkish landowners to require their Arab peasants to register as Turks or else be driven off the land. Whole Arab villages were known to have dissolved under such pressures. Another method was to pay Turks born in the Sanjak but who had moved to Turkey to return to the Sanjak to register.

There was little doubt that in the growing struggle between Turks and Arabs, the Turks, although fewer in number, had the advantage. In part, this was because they were dealing with a more compact, disciplined and better educated body of supporters who responded to the well-orches-

---

[32] MAE, Syrie–Liban 1930–40. "Note," 29 Sept. 1937, vol. 495, pp. 210–11; Hourani, *Syria and Lebanon*, pp. 208–9.

[33] Khadduri, "Alexandretta Dispute," pp. 420–22.

trated activities of the specially appointed Turkish consular representatives in Antioch and Alexandretta. As a British diplomat observed

their clubs and youth organisations are well organised and ready for the fray. Their migrants residing in Turkey proper, at least 3,000 in number, are even now returning to the Sanjak, each of them receiving from Turkish authorities a free passage and 25 liras for expenses.[34]

By contrast,

the very new and rather inchoate Arab state [at Damascus] with organisation and resources distinctly inferior to those of the Turks, and with its hands full of thorny problems, has failed to produce an effective union among the various sections of the non-Turk majority or to organise them for the coming electoral campaign. Its appeal to natives of the sanjak residing in Syria and elsewhere to return to Alexandretta and register themselves as voters has passed unheeded. Its efforts to organise Arab clubs and Arab youth movements to counterbalance those of the Turks have met with scant success. The administrative officials in the Sanjak, formerly more or less dependent on Damascus and inclined to support the Arab cause, have deserted the sinking ship . . .[35]

But also hindering the development of Arab resistance was a Syrian government which tacitly accepted the Geneva settlement of May 1937, even though the Syrian Parliament remained bitterly opposed to it. On his return in December from his second trip to Paris since becoming Prime Minister, Jamil Mardam passed through Ankara where, as a distinguished visitor, he had the requisite night out in a restaurant with Ataturk. There they discussed Alexandretta. The Turkish leader claimed that he had no intention of annexing the Sanjak and that all Turkey wanted was a measure of room for the Turkish population in the Sanjak to develop freely within its boundaries. It is unlikely that Mardam took Ataturk seriously, but at the same time he felt powerless to do anything. He had not placed his trust in Turkish good will but rather relied on French and, particularly, British influence with the Turks to secure a just settlement.[36]

French reaction to Turkish strategy was mixed. In the Sanjak itself, a new Delegate, M. Garreau, brought in troops to try to reduce Turkish pressure. At the same time, he closed down the League of National Ac-

[34] FO 371/311, vol. 21909. Davis (Aleppo) to FO, 23 Dec. 1937.
[35] Ibid.
[36] FO 371/122, vol. 21914. Davis to FO, 30 Dec. 1937; FO 371/29, vol. 21909. Lorraine to FO, 1 Jan. 1938.

tion's headquarters in Antioch and arrested its leader, Zaki al-Arsuzi, on the grounds that the League was formenting ill-feeling between Turks and Arabs.[37] Neither Turks nor Arabs appreciated this French even-handedness and both criticized the High Commission. From the perspective of the Quai d'Orsay, the French and their European allies could not afford a direct confrontation with Turkey as the international situation degenerated. With Italy holding the Dodecanese and eyeing the eastern Mediterranean, Turkish neutrality, if not friendship, was a must. But Paris also felt that if the Turks did not get their way in the Sanjak, they were quite capable of disregarding all their treaty obligations and militarily occupying the territory. The French, while not prepared to resist such an occupation, wanted to avoid the appearance of weakness at this crucial time.[38]

When registration resumed in early May 1938, all indications were that Turkish methods of intimidation had backfired, despite their superior organization, considerable funds, and the "failure of the Arabs to sink their differences."[39] Battles between Turks and Arabs continued, especially in Alexandretta, but neither bribery nor coercion worked. By this time, "the prospects of the Turks obtaining a majority at elections . . . [were] considered to be nil." Only 5 percent of the Arabs, no Armenians, and no Syrian Christians registered as Turks. Meanwhile, many conservative Turks, mainly landowners, were registering themselves as Sunnis rather than as Turks. The situation had grown so alarming that an additional 1,000 Moroccan troops from Damascus were sent into the Sanjak.[40]

In fact, the High Commission made concerted efforts to curtail Turkish activities; Garreau's antipathy toward Turkish interference with his jurisdiction was more than a simple irritant. Moreover, an immense amount of personal hostility existed between the High Commissioner, Martel, and his predecessor, Ponsot, who was now French Ambassador in Ankara and quite well-disposed to Turkish ambitions in the Sanjak. But, in spite of the High Commission's resistance and increased Alawite solidarity and the defection of conservative Turks in the face of Turkish interference, persistent Turkish pressures on the French at Geneva and in Paris ultimately forced the French government to interpret the last Franco-Turkish accord in Turkish terms. The die had already been cast in Geneva in March 1938 when the Turkish Prime Minister and the French Foreign Minister concluded a private arrangement which promised the

[37] FO 371/7409, vol. 20848. Rendel Memo, 15 Dec. 1937; FO 371/7546, vol. 20848. Davis to FO, 17 Dec. 1937.
[38] FO 371/550, vol. 21909. Rendel Note No. 2, Geneva Discussions with M. Lagarde (Head of the Africa and Levant Department of the French Foreign Ministry), 27 Jan. 1938.
[39] FO 371/2472, vol. 21910. Havard to FO, 29 April 1938; FO 371/2620, vol. 21910. Davis to FO, 5 May 1938.
[40] FO 371/2764, vol. 21910. Davis to FO, 12 May 1938.

Turks a simple majority of 22 deputies out of a total of 40.[41] Although this deal outraged French officials in Syria and member states of the League of Nations, the outcome of the elections was now a foregone conclusion. Throughout May and June, violence between Turks and Arabs escalated. As the League's electoral commission tried to run the elections in accordance with the Geneva regulations, an aggressive Ankara and a rather passive Paris rendered their efforts futile. Garreau and his French staff, in the absence of direct support from Paris, tried desperately to save the situation by forming a short-lived party of "national union" of all ethnic and religious elements to back the current regime, but failed. The Arabs refused to cooperate in any scheme that supported the status quo and the Turks flexed their muscles both within the Sanjak and outside with troop movements on the borders. By early June, Garreau had received instructions from the High Commission to summon the heads of the non-Turkish communities and urge them to persuade their members not to register. But, when he leaked his instructions to the League's electoral commission, he was replaced by Captain Collet, who was known to be much more sympathetic to Turkish interests in the Sanjak.

Not long afterwards, in mid-June, Collet cracked down on the major force of Arab resistance, the League of National Action, again arresting Zaki al-Arsuzi. The Arab quarter of Antioch shut down completely in protest, Moroccan troops were sent in, Turkish atrocities against the Arab and Armenian populations increased, and the nationalist press in Aleppo accused the French of complicity. The French Commandant of the Gendarmerie resigned in protest against the removal of Arabs and Armenians from his command and their replacement by Turks. In the all-important district of Antioch, Captain Collet had done his best to ensure a result favorable to the Turks. He placed a pro-Turk as *mutasarrif* of the district, he recruited Circassian gendarmes to guard voting bureaux which were under the surveillance of Moroccan units, he replaced pro-Syrian Alawite officials by pro-Turkish Alawites, and he increased pro-Turkish propaganda among the minorities in order to foil League of Nations' measures to ensure proportional representation according to the number of registered voters.[42]

The situation had grown so uncontrollable that the frustrated League's electoral commission actually closed down its operation and left the Sanjak toward the end of June. The admission of a Turkish military mission into the Sanjak was the final blow to the electoral process. The French military command agreed to allow Turkish troops to enter the Sanjak in

[41] FO 371/3008, vol. 2191. Lorraine to FO, 22 May 1938.

[42] MD, 7N 4190, Dossier 6. Collet (Antioch) to High Commission, 4 June, 5 June, 9 June 1938; *ibid.*, 7N 4190, Dossier 6. Riemers (Antioch, League Commission in Sanjak) to Collet (Antioch), 7 June 1938.

return for a Franco-Turkish Friendship Treaty which provided that neither country would enter into any political or economic combination directed against the other, that if one of the parties became a victim of aggression the other would lend no help to the aggressor, and that, in case of any threat to the territorial integrity of the Sanjak, both parties would collaborate in carrying out their responsibilities under the agreement of 29 May 1937.[43] The friendship treaty went into effect on July 4. The next day, Turkish troops marched into the Sanjak.

Under the threat of Turkish bayonets, registration results were announced. The Turks received their expected 22 seats and thus a majority. Arabs and Armenians, though fearful of Turkish rule, reserved their bitterness for the French who,

> having led them to believe that there were to be free elections and having encouraged them to organise themselves and vote against the Turks, have now handed them over body and soul to their adversaries.[44]

Stage III

The inaugural meeting of the recently elected Assembly of the Sanjak, now renamed the *Hatay*, took place on September 2. Held in a local cinema in Antioch and attended by various European officials in addition to the 40 deputies, it was a sight to behold. As the British Consul observed:

> the proceedings opened with the playing of the Turkish National Anthem, and in fact it was hard to realize that we were not on Turkish soil. . . . True, the Marseillaise was played later, but so unobtrusively that no one paid much attention to it. . . . From beginning to end the proceedings were entirely in Turkish. The officers elected [all Turks] were then duly installed and the deputies took the oath of fidelity to the Constitution, some of them not without difficulty as they either did not know Turkish or could not read and write.[45]

It did not take long for the Turkish unionists to press their case. And when they did so, they encountered pathetic resistance. The radical pan-Arabist League of National Action had been shut down and its leader, Zaki al-Arsuzi, had taken up residence in Damascus. The notables belonging to the old Turkish families of Antioch, including Subhi Barakat, were completely ignored by the new regime which filled all important posts with émigrés who had returned to the province from Turkey. And

---

[43] FO 371/3981, vol. 21912. Morgan to FO, 5 July 1938.
[44] FO 371/4296, vol. 21912. Davis to FO, 11 July 1938.
[45] FO 371/5474, vol. 21913. Davis to Halifax, 9 Sept. 1938.

though the French continued to support Turkish notables who stood for true autonomy under joint Turkish and French guarantees and French officials whom the new Hatay government had dismissed, their commitment was at best weak.[46] On the economic front, there was now free and increased trade between Turkey and the Hatay, while free trade between Syria and the Hatay was "already becoming a thing of the past." The French enforced customs frontiers between the two while they diverted Aleppo's import and export traffic from its normal route via Alexandretta to Latakia and Tripoli. In these circumstances, both Aleppo and the Hatay suffered economic recessions. Aleppo had to pay for the greater cost of transport to these more distant ports, which incidentally had much less developed shipping facilities than had Alexandretta. The Hatay lost heavily with the dramatic decline in the transit trade to Aleppo. Whereas the busiest road in Syria used to be the Aleppo–Alexandretta motorway, where 300 vehicles used to pass daily, now less than 20 vehicles made the journey on any given day.[47]

By February 1939, the Hatay had become part of Turkey. Turkish administration and law were in force and all previous legislation like the shari'a, Ottoman law codes, and High Commission decrees were "declared inoperative." Turkish nationals could enter and leave the Hatay without passport or visa. In mid-March, Turkish currency became the legal tender in the Hatay, required for all official transactions, and the President and Premier of the Hatay became members of the Turkish Parliament. In the meantime, the Turkish government in Ankara had approached the French government with the request that the Hatay be incorporated in Turkey.[48] As was expected, French reaction to the Turkish request was on the whole negative, but French pragmatists at the Quai d'Orsay eventually gave in. High Commissioner Gabriel Puaux—recently ensconced in Beirut—opposed the idea of ceding Alexandretta because it would have "heavy and dangerous consequences for France's prestige in Syria," and because what the Turks offered in return had "no value." Puaux was not simply echoing the fears of nationalist leaders like Jamil Mardam and Dr. Shahbandar when he reported extensive Turkish propaganda in northern Syria, especially in Aleppo where Turkish agents were everywhere, and the growing alarm that Turkey would also annex

[46] FO 371/6911, vol. 21913. Davis to FO, 17 Oct. 1938.
[47] FO 371/6938, vol. 21913. Davis to FO, 14 Nov. 1938; FO 371/614, vol. 27277. Davis to FO, 23 Dec. 1938.
[48] FO 371/2630, vol. 23277. Davis to FO, 18 March 1939; FO 371/2578, vol. 23277. Phipps, (Paris) to Halifax, 6 April 1939.

Aleppo and the Jazira.[49] And for some French politicians such as Senator Gautherot who toured the Hatay in the spring, there was considerable concern about the weak French military presence there; in a letter at the beginning of May to the Quai d'Orsay, he asked "are we abdicating?"[50] The answer by then could have only been "yes."

The French formally relinquished their control over the Hatay toward the end of June 1939. In return for the right of annexation, the Turkish government promised not to seek additional Syrian territory and to respect the Syrian frontier. The Hatay's Assembly was dissolved and within a short time the region became a province of the Turkish Republic.

With the completion of this third and final stage of the Sanjak's separation from Syria and its incorporation into Turkey came one of those ugly and wrenching episodes that had visited itself on the peoples of northwestern Syria and southern Turkey so often in recent years, the exodus of large numbers of refugees, in this case of non-Turkish communities into Syria. Just two months after the Sanjak's transfer, Syria had already received some 50,000 refugees. The largest number were Armenians—as many as 22,000—who fled their homes even before French troops had pulled out, many for a second time in less than 20 years. In addition, some 10,000 Alawites, 10,000 Sunni Arabs (including tribes), and 5,000 Christian Arabs also left. Those who chose to remain were Sunnis and Alawite peasants who were attached to the land and who, unlike the merchant and artisanal communities, had few opportunities to resettle in Syria.[51]

ALTHOUGH THERE WAS both division and disbelief over French acquiescence to Turkish demands in France, among the Allies and in Syria, French official thinking on the matter was perhaps best expressed in the pages of *L'Asie Française*, the mouthpiece of the French colonial party. In an article just after the Sanjak's cession we find one author stating that the Alexandretta question "is an affair whose judgment must be left to history." It was a weighty matter to let it go, but it was done for the preservation of the European alliance.[52] There is no doubt that the French

---

[49] MAE, Gabriel Puaux Papers, Carton 33, "Relations avec la Turquie," 1939. Puaux to Diplomatie (Paris), 18 Feb. 1939; MAE, Syrie–Liban 1930–40. Puaux Telegram, 5 October 1939, vol. 473, p. 191.

[50] MAE, Syrie–Liban 1930–40. Gautherot to MAE, 1 May 1939, vol. 469, pp. 119–22.

[51] MAE, Syrie–Liban 1930–40. Puaux to MAE, 4 July 1939, vol. 471, pp. 33–35; *ibid.*, Grosson (Alexandretta) to MAE, 23 Sept. 1939, vol. 473, pp. 150–53; FO 371/7354, vol. 21913. M. J. Kunzler Report from Syria on Refugees, 8 Nov. 1938.

[52] *L'Asie Française*, no. 372 (July–Aug. 1939), pp. 25–26.

were especially worried in the late 1930s about Italian designs on the eastern Mediterranean. Apart from the Italian military presence in the Dodecanese, the Italians actively disseminated their propaganda through their Middle Eastern Consulates, especially in Cairo, through the print and wireless media, and through Italian philanthropic, educational, scholarly, and financial institutions such as the Franciscan Terre Santa College in Tripoli and the Banco di Roma. The role of Radio Bari and of radical Syrian politicians with ties to Italy, such as Shakib Arslan, caused the Quai d'Orsay and High Commission considerable worry in the late 1930s.[53] A neutral or friendly Turkey could serve as an important bulwark against Italian penetration and, by French calculations, the Sanjak happened to be an obstacle to an alliance with Turkey. Thus, the French took a controversial political decision and rationalized it by suggesting that the sacrifice of the Sanjak was "ultimately in the interest of Syrian independence."[54]

But, in July 1939, with the National Bloc out of power, the Franco-Syrian Treaty now a dead letter, and the *muhafazat* of the Jabal Druze, Latakia, and the Jazira no longer under the authority of Damascus, no one in Syria seriously believed that Syrian independence was still on the French agenda.

[53] MD, 7N 4190, Dossier 3. 2ᵉ Bureau Note, Beirut, 7 April 1938; MAE, Syrie–Liban 1930–40. Puaux to MAE, 27 June 1939. vol. 470, pp. 197–98.
[54] *L'Asie Française*, no. 372 (July–Aug. 1939), p. 26.

CHAPTER TWENTY

DRUZES, ALAWITES, AND OTHER CHALLENGERS

SEVERAL OTHER DEVELOPMENTS on the Syrian periphery in the late 1930s helped to undermine the credibility of the nationalist government in Damascus. Among the most grave was the challenge posed to its authority by separatist movements in the Jabal Druze, the Alawite territory, and the Jazira, where a combination of factors hindered the political unification and the crystallization of a Syrian national identity. These included sectarianism and tribalism, geography, comparative political and socioeconomic underdevelopment, continued domination of urban groups over rural groups, and intra-elite and class conflict. In addition, France promoted autonomous movements among the compact minorities. Given the ideology of Arab nationalism, which in the hands of the Sunni-absentee landowning class demonstrated a particular insensitivity to the needs of Syria's minorities, the seeds of separatism planted by the High Commission fell on fertile ground.

THE INCREASED MANIFESTATION of separatist sentiment and activity in the Jabal Druze and Latakia provinces correlated with the administrative unification of these two regions under the National Bloc government in Damascus. The Druzes and Alawites had much in common: both were a mountain or hill people, both belonged to small, rather mysterious sects that were offshoots of Shiʿite Islam, both were Arabic-speaking, both had enjoyed generations of relative isolation from central government authority, and both were engaged in agriculture and were comparatively impoverished. At the same time, both communities were internally divided along tribal or clan lines and between an emerging educated stratum and a traditional elite, each vying for support among the mass of poor peasants. But the Druze and the Alawite communities also had different characteristics and faced different conditions, which gave political life in each a specific coloring.

DRUZE SEPARATISM

The collapse of the Druze rebellion in 1927 and the exile of the most important Druze leaders enabled France to keep the Jabal administratively autonomous for another ten years. It could not, however, be insulated from the nationalist sentiments radiating from Damascus or from the political activities of Hashemite agents across the border in Transjordan, where a number of Druze settlements were located. The lure of Damascus was especially strong for educated Druzes, some of whom began to fill administrative posts at Suwayda' and Salkhad. Yet, in nationalist politics the Druze had closer ties to Dr. Shahbandar and the People's Party leadership than to the National Bloc. Exiled Druzes, like Sultan al-Atrash, who were disposed to integrate the Jabal into the Syrian state, had come down on the side of Dr. Shahbandar and pro-Hashemite Syrians in the intense factional struggles that developed at the end of the revolt. Many, though by no means all, Druze unionists remained loyal to Sultan Pasha and through him to the Shahbandar wing of the independence movement. Their proclivity was reinforced when Dr. Shahbandar, Sultan al-Atrash, and other Great Revolt leaders returned to Syria in May 1937 after a decade in exile.

Even before the completion of treaty negotiations in Paris and the formation of Syria's first nationalist government, there was growing agitation in the Jabal Druze concerning the governorate's future. Some Druze notables, including members of the Atrash clan, claimed that the vast majority of Druzes wanted Syrian unity; others, also led by some Atrash chiefs, claimed the opposite.[1] Once the negotiations were over, the National Bloc, to reduce the anxiety of those Druzes opposed to the transfer of the reins in the Jabal from French hands to the new nationalist government's, gave its full assurances to Druze skeptics that many benefits would accompany full union with Syria. It promised that the entire annual tax yields in the Jabal would be respent there and that the number of non-Druzes employed in the Jabal "would be exactly counterbalanced by the number" of Druzes "employed in other parts of the republic." It also agreed to undertake important public works concerned with water conservation and road-building, which the French had neglected in recent years.[2]

These efforts at conciliation were marred by the appointment of Nasib al-Bakri as governor of the Jabal. Although no member of the National Bloc had a wider appeal in the Jabal, owing to his role in the Great Revolt, from the vantage point of Druze opponents of Syrian unity, Bakri's appointment indicated that Damascus planned to deny Druzes authority over their own affairs.[3]

---

[1] *Oriente Moderno*, 16 (1936), pp. 267–68, 398; FO 684/9/722/1. Manifesto of Druze Youth Congress (Damascus, 27 March 1936).
[2] FO 371/697, vol. 20848. MacKereth to Eden, 5 Jan. 1937.
[3] FO 371/2159, vol. 20849. MacKereth to Eden, 8 April 1937.

Actually, the problems surrounding Bakri's appointment were quite complicated. At least three Druze opinions weighed in at the time. Opposing the Damascus government was a faction of Druze notables headed by the influential Amir Hasan al-Atrash, who argued that it was an insult to Druze integrity and tradition if the governor was not a "son of the mountain." That Amir Hasan wanted the governorship for himself is certain. While he also had considerable backing from his own branch of the Atrash clan, other Atrash branches were not behind him. His major rival was ʿAbd al-Ghaffar al-Atrash who had strong ties to Damascus and to Amman and who was himself a candidate for governor.[4]

Supporting the government's choice was the ʿAmr clan from the northern Jabal, the traditional rivals of the Atrash, and an emerging group of young educated Druzes associated with Muhammad ʿIzz al-Din al-Halabi. Halabi was especially close to the radical Istiqlal wing of the National Bloc. He opposed the idea of a Druze governor on the grounds that only an outsider could rise above endemic Druze factionalism and hence prevent the French, who had exploited these conflicts between the Druze clans for years, from regaining direct control of the Jabal. The ʿAmr were opposed because they knew that, given the distribution of power in the Jabal, a Druze governor would inevitably be an Atrash.[5]

The third opinion was the least clear: it belonged to Sultan al-Atrash who, despite his continued exile at Kerak, retained a large personal following in the Jabal. For Bakri to be effective, Sultan Pasha's support was necessary. Although there were still personal bonds between him and Bakri, Sultan Pasha was not on particularly good terms with the National Bloc. He felt that the Bloc had ignored him and his followers during their long years of exile and he was not therefore inclined to acquiesce automatically to the Bloc's wishes. To remind the Bloc of his personal influence, he ordered that elections were not to be held in the Jabal until his return.[6]

The Bloc's tactic was to appeal both to Sultan Pasha's vanity and to his purse to get him to drop his opposition to Bakri's appointment. Bloc representatives encouraged him to assume his natural role as the leading Druze statesman by standing above petty Druze factionalism. To help convince him of the importance of statesmanship, Sabri al-ʿAsali brought him much needed funds which Nabih al-ʿAzma, the master Syrian fundraiser, provided. The result was a compromise. Sultan al-Atrash con-

[4] Nabih al-ʿAzma Papers [Syria], File 5/197. Shukri al-Quwwatli to Nabih al-ʿAzma, 12 Jan. 1937; ibid., File 5/198. ʿAli ʿUbayd to ʿAzma, 16 Jan. 1937.
[5] Ibid., File 5/219. Muhammad ʿIzz al-Din al-Halabi to Nabih al-ʿAzma, 3 April 1937. Also see Faris, Man huwa 1949, pp. 129–30.
[6] Nabih al-ʿAzma Papers, File 5/217. Ahmad Adib Khayr to ʿAzma, 25 March 1937.

vinced his cousin, Amir Hasan, to drop his opposition to Bakri, with the understanding that Bakri's appointment was only for six months.[7]

The compromise did not prevent trouble in the Jabal. The return of Sultan al-Atrash after the French amnesty of May 1937 was met by demonstrations for and against complete union with Damascus. Sultan Pasha's popular following was still immense, but his ten-year exile had allowed new leaders to emerge and new factions to form. Amir Hasan[8] had become a serious rival to Sultan Pasha and nationalist forces in the Jabal had fractured. The Halabis and their followers among the Druze intelligentsia identified with the radical wing of the National Bloc and thus supported the government in Damascus as long as the Istiqlalis did. Sultan al-Atrash remained close to the Shahbandar faction and was susceptible to Hashemite influences.

In mid-June, Dr. Shahbandar undertook to mediate between rival Druze factions and the government. Finally it was agreed that Bakri would be replaced after six months by Tawfiq al-Atrash, a 50-year-old ex-Ottoman functionary who was a ranking official in the Jabal's administration.[9] At election time Tawfiq al-Atrash was replaced by a Syrian bureaucrat *par excellence*, Bahij al-Khatib, who served as interim governor.[10] Once elections were over in December 1937, Khatib left the Jabal. Mardam appointed Amir Hasan al-Atrash as governor the following February. Mardam clearly wanted to avert the possibility of renewed disturbances over the issue of Druze autonomy, at a time when he was trying to clinch French ratification of the 1936 treaty.

After Amir Hasan's appointment, the Jabal Druze was unusually quiet for several months, although beneath the surface conflict between separatists and unionists continued. Non-Druze officials retained a certain amount of authority and real trust between Amir Hasan and the Mardam government was never fully established. By the summer of 1938, separatists renewed their agitation for greater autonomy from Damascus, which Druze unionists and non-Druze officials countered. In December, signs of a complete breakdown of order surfaced in the Jabal when French judges replaced Syrian judges after a strike by the latter. A rather tactless reference by a leading government supporter in the Syrian Chamber of Deputies to ʿAbd al-Ghaffar al-Atrash as a French stooge (after some Druze notables had called for the total separation of the Jabal from Syria

---

[7] *Ibid.*, File 5/205. Sabri al-ʿAsali to Nabih al-ʿAzma, 25 Jan. 1937; *ibid.*, File 4/175. Mustafa Bushnaq to Nabih al-ʿAzma, 10 Dec. 1936; *ibid.*, File 4/170. ʿAdil al-ʿAzma to Nabih al-ʿAzma, 22 Nov. 1936.

[8] He became head of his branch of the Atrash clan in 1926 and participated in the Great Revolt. He was amnestied in 1928. See al-Jundi, *Tarikh*, p. 235.

[9] *Ibid.*, p. 239; FO 371/2295. MacKereth to FO, 21 April 1937.

[10] MAE, Syrie–Liban 1930–40. "Note," 29 Sept. 1937, vol. 495, p. 213.

and for strong ties with France), led Druze deputies to withdraw from the Chamber. A series of demonstrations all over the Jabal followed at the precise moment when the Mardam government faced the heaviest pressure from the nationalist opposition to end its cooperation with the French.[11]

To complicate matters, the new High Commissioner, Gabriel Puaux, paid his first visit to the Jabal Druze where he encountered demonstrations for and against Druze union with Syria. At the entrance of the villages he visited, truckloads of Bloc-organized demonstrators, draping Syrian flags over the trucks, denounced the French and sang patriotic songs. Further inside, separatist demonstrators waving French flags greeted him. Puaux personally believed that more than two-thirds of the Druzes wanted autonomy, but that the Atrash and 'Amr clans, each with its own clientele, remained bitter contestants for the leadership of an autonomous Druze state. A remaining third of the Druze population supported the nationalists and union with Damascus, though even they wanted a measure of autonomy and demanded that the Jabal be staffed solely with Druze officials, that the Jabal receive a larger share of the national budget, and that taxes be reduced.[12]

Syrian nationalists in Damascus and elsewhere were not wrong to suggest that the arrival of Puaux in the Levant meant an end not only to the idea of a treaty but to Syrian unity. The case of the Jabal Druze was illustrative. After his visit, Amir Hasan al-Atrash stepped down as governor and a French colonel, Bouvier, replaced him at Suwayda'. A house-to-house search for nationalist sympathizers followed. A number of Druze notables with ties to Damascus were jailed on the grounds of failing to pay their taxes.[13] Sultan al-Atrash was conspicuously silent during this period. He, like so many other prominent Syrian leaders, was a committed opponent of the government in Damascus by the beginning of 1939.[14] Several months after the Mardam government resigned,[15] the Jabal Druze was again put under an administration autonomous from Damascus.

[11] *Palestine Post* (4 Jan. 1939). In fact, 'Abd al-Ghaffar was at the time trying to arrange through Consul MacKereth in Damascus British support for an independent Jabal Druze and its eventual annexation to Transjordan, a proposal that Amir 'Abdullah took a lively interest in. See FO 371/ 185, vol. 23276. MacKereth to FO, 30 Dec. 1938 and FO 371/811, vol. 23276. Cox (Transjordan) to British High Commissioner, 7 Jan. 1939.

[12] MD, 7N 4190, Dossier 1. "Voyage de M. Puaux au Djébel Druse," Feb. 1939. The French claimed that the National Bloc distributed 50,000 francs to its supporters in the Jabal to protest Puaux's visit.

[13] FO 684/12/106/1. Petition to Druze Youth of Suwayda' to HMG Consul, 23 Feb. 1939.

[14] *La Chronique* (28 Jan. 1939).

[15] FO 371/837, vol. 23276. MacKereth to Baxter, 28 Jan. 1939; *Palestine Post*, (4 Jan. 1939); Longrigg, *Syria*, p. 247.

The renewal of separatism in the Latakia governorate at the time of the
National Bloc's ascent to government had paralleled the increased separatism in the Jabal Druze. But, it was also more intense and more complex. Power struggles in the province were not principally between factions of the same religious community, as was the case in the Jabal Druze,
but between different communities. Although the Alawites were internally divided, when they were threatened with domination by a more
powerful urban absentee Sunni landowning class which supported unity
with Damascus, they responded as a "sect-class."[16]
    The Latakia region contained a more heterogeneous population than
the Jabal Druze. The key societal division was along religio-cultural lines
and took the form of a struggle of town against countryside. The bureaucratic elite belonged to the great landowning families of the port of Latakia and was Sunni, as was nearly 80 percent of the town's population.
Orthodox Christians formed the second largest community in Latakia.
The town, however, contained less than 10 percent of the total population
of the province, an indication of the low level of urbanization in the region. Sixty-two percent of the province were impoverished Alawite peasants in the mountains and plains behind the coastal towns.[17] A significant
portion of the land farmed by Alawites was owned by Sunnis from Latakia and Hama.[18] Consequently, divisions of wealth exacerbated religious divisions.
    Under Ottoman rule, the Latakia region had enjoyed a largely autono-
mous existence, though the port of Latakia and the coastal plain were

----

    [16] This is the term used by Hanna Batatu to describe the Alawite community. See "Some
Observations on the Social Roots of Syria's Ruling, Military Group and the Causes for Its
Dominance," *Middle East Journal*, 35 (Summer 1981), pp. 331–344.
    [17] The total population of the Latakia province was 261,162 in 1922 and 335,454 in 1943.
Alawites were (and still are) the second largest religious community in Syria: approximately 11.5 percent of the total Syrian population in 1945 (Sunnis were 68 percent of the
total). Eighty-six percent of the Alawite population of Syria lived at this time in the Latakia
governorate. The French coined the term Alawite ('Alawi). It became widespread during
the Mandate and referred to a member of the Nusayri religious sect. This sect developed in
the mountainous region of northwestern Syria well before the appearance of the Ottomans.
Nusayri doctrine includes a strong Shi'ite strain. See Sir Alexander Gibb and Partners, *Economic Development*, p. 3; Jacques Weulersse, *Les pays des Alaouites* (Tours, 1940), pp. 51–
58; Great Britain: Naval Intelligence Division, *Syria* (London, April 1943), p. 160; Albert
Hourani, *Minorities in the Arab World* (London, 1947); Lieutenant-Colonel Paul Jacquot,
L'état des Alaouites. Guide, 2nd. ed. (Beirut, 1931); Muhammad Amin Ghalib al-Tawil,
Tarikh al-'alawiyyin (Beirut, 1966).
    [18] Weulersse, *Alaouites*, pp. 362–66. [Gaulmier], "Note sur la propriété foncière dans la
Syrie centrale," *L'Asie Française*, no. 309, (April 1933), p. 133.

more vulnerable to external influences than the rugged mountain behind, with its preponderant Alawite population. The Jabal Ansariyya, like the Jabal Druze and other mountains in geographical Syria, allowed a compact minority to live in relative seclusion and to preserve its heterodox beliefs and practices.[19] The Alawites, like the Druzes, were capable of putting up fierce resistance to external interference in their communal affairs. This they did between 1919 and 1921 when the French tried to establish hegemony over the mountain.

In response, the French applied their Moroccan strategy of divide and rule. In September 1920, the two former Ottoman *sanjaks* of Latakia and Tartus were formally incorporated into a single territory which was administered separately from the rest of Syria. In addition, the French weakened the economic base of the Sunni latifundia and promoted certain Alawite tribal leaders.[20]

French governors, assisted by a large French staff of native affairs officers and cooperative local elements, ran the daily affairs of the Alawite state from 1920 till the end of 1936. Frenchmen also presided over directorates of Justice, Posts, and Customs.[21] Although the Sunni landowning elite supported Syrian unity and was structurally and morally tied to the nationalist leadership in the interior towns, it was unable to effectively oppose French policy in the province. The French strengthened the rural-based Alawite elite and played it against the Sunni elite of the towns, while they administratively insulated the entire province from the national independence movement. As one French scholar-official of the period observed, about the only concession accorded the nationalists in the region before 1936 was a change of name: in 1930, the rather provocative "Alawite state" became known by the less offensive designation, "the Government of Latakia."[22]

Various disputes between Alawites and Sunnis had punctuated political life in the province in the early 1930s and presaged the heightened conflicts which followed the Bloc's assumption of governmental power. But these were isolated incidents, and small in scale.[23] As was the case in the Jabal Druze, movements for and against union with Syria grew in the region once the Syrian delegation embarked for Paris in the spring of 1936.

[19] Weulersse, *Alaouites*, pp. 58–59; al-Jundi, *Tarikh*, pp. 26–27.

[20] An interesting analysis of Alawite tribal structure *circa* 1920 can be found in Colonel Niéger, "Choix de documents sur le Territoire des Alaouites," pp. 1–69. The author was one of the first French governors of the Alawite state.

[21] Longrigg, *Syria*, p. 120. On regaining its independence from the Syrian state in 1925, the Alawite state began issuing its own postage stamps. FO 371/145, vol. 10850. Beirut Consul to FO, 9 Jan. 1925.

[22] Weulersse, *Alaouites*, p. 121.

[23] Longrigg, *Syria*, p. 210.

On the one hand, Alawite separatists launched a propaganda campaign with sectarian implications which the French governor of the province, M. Schoeffler, may have orchestrated. He had been in charge for years and was a committed opponent of union with Damascus. On the other hand, a number of intellectuals and professionals formed a League of Alawite-Muslim Youth to combat separatism and to push for Syrian unity.[24] It included members of two Sunni absentee landowning families (Harun and Shraytih), a sprinkling of Christians of the Orthodox rite, and the ʿAbbas clan, wealthy chiefs of the Alawite tribe of Khayyatin. By virtue of education, profession, class background, and economic interests, the League was well disposed to the National Bloc. It was through this unity party that the first nationalist governor sent out from Damascus in January 1937 tried to extend his government's authority.[25]

By the time Mazhar Raslan assumed the governorship at Latakia, political lines in the governorate had been drawn. Alawite autonomists and some of their allies in the local Christian community pressed their demands, which included Raslan's replacement by a local governor. In the fall of 1937, Raslan had to make all sorts of compromises over Sunni protests in Latakia, in order to get the elections to Parliament underway. Fifteen deputies, including nine Alawites and three Sunnis, were eventually elected.[26] The Mardam government then replaced Raslan with an even more distinguished notable, the Aleppine Ihsan al-Jabiri, who had returned to Syria after many years in Europe publicizing the Syrian national cause.[27]

Political tensions mounted after the elections and his appearance at Latakia, exacerbated by French efforts to subvert Jabiri's authority by arming Alawite tribes and promoting Christian factions in the towns.[28] On the side of union stood Munir ʿAbbas, a Paris-trained lawyer with an extensive French culture, and a major political force in the province. A calm, reflective man of enormous personal means, ʿAbbas was chief of the Khayyatin tribe and of the local unionist faction. He represented a growing educated Alawite elite who believed that Syrian unity was both inevitable and in his community's interest, but that the governorate should be accorded a certain measure of administrative autonomy over its internal affairs.[29] Such ideas of national integration had their parallel in the

[24] Known as the *Rabitat al-shabab al-muslim al-ʿalawi*. See *Oriente Moderno*, 16 (1936), p. 267.
[25] MAE, Syrie–Liban 1930–40, vol. 494, pp. 67–71.
[26] MAE, Syrie–Liban 1930–40. "Note," 29 Sept. 1937, vol. 495, p. 212.
[27] Longrigg, *Syria*, p. 244.
[28] *Oriente Moderno*, 18 (1938), p. 79.
[29] MAE, Guerre 1939–45. "Alger," vol. 1004. "Notice," 25 Oct. 1945 (Damascus); FO 371/7048, vol. 27314. (French personality report, 1941); Faris, *Man huwa 1949*, p. 275.

Jabal Druze among the rising educated elite associated with the Halabi clan. Munir 'Abbas refused to join the National Bloc, but he was one Alawite chief with wide influence who lent the idea of Syrian unity credibility in the Latakia region.

Although separatist sentiments among Alawites were strong, the Alawites did not speak with anything like one voice on the question of independence or autonomy. One factor barring the emergence of a common Alawite front was the community's inability to produce an independent cohesive political leadership, a familiar problem faced by traditional peasant communities in many parts of the developing world.[30] The majority of Alawites were peasants exploited by a predominantly Sunni landowning class resident in Latakia and Hama. They were divided by tribal affiliation (al-Khayyatin, al-Matawira, al-Kalbiyya, al-Haddadin), by religious subsect or ties (Qamaris, Shamsis, Murshidiyyin), and by geography (the more fiercely independent peasant highlanders and the more "submissive" peasants of the plains).[31] Alawites were just as apt to be bogged down in their own internal disputes as they were to take collective action against outside interference in their internal affairs.[32] Thus there was a wide range of separatists and of unionists, rather than two simple and distinct parties. Apart from separatists whom the French High Commission courted and unionists with ties to the mainstream of the Syrian independence movement represented by the National Bloc, there were other movements and trends in the Latakia governorate. The most important one during the Mandate was associated with Sulayman al-Murshid.

In 1923, Murshid, a penniless shepherd still in his teens, had begun his rise on the political scene in his remote village of Jabet Burghal, high up in the impoverished northeastern mountain, in Khayyatin territory. Afflicted by epilepsy, he lapsed into long states of semiconsciousness during which he claimed to have received messages that "the end of the world was approaching" and "the Mahdi would appear."[33] Soon, he won a reputation as a prophet and a miracle worker and attracted a following. The curious and the needy converged on Jabet Burghal, secret meetings took

---

[30] See Hobsbawm, "Peasants and Politics," pp. 2–23.

[31] See Batatu, "Some Observations," pp. 331–36.

[32] The fact that the Alawite community was at this time a sect-class "in itself" (although not "for itself") indicated that it might in the future find the opportunity to form a revolutionary peasant movement, but only on a regional scale. Here, sectarianism, geographic isolation, and relative political ignorance were obstacles to Alawites linking their fortunes to peasant movements among Sunni Arabs outside their region. Hobsbawm has written that ". . . peasant movements all appear to be regional, or coalitions of regional movements . . . unless sponsored or organized by the state authorities, they are unlikely to be simultaneous or to have the same political characteristics or demands." "Peasants and Politics," p. 9.

[33] Weulersse, *Alaouites*, p. 334; Rabinovich, "Compact Minorities," p. 704.

place, peasants armed themselves, and villages withheld their taxes. In no time, Murshid had alarmed Alawite religious leaders of the majority Qamari subsect, Alawite landowners in his district, and the French. His arrest and brief imprisonment only enhanced his reputation, and his reappearance in 1924 marked a period of growth for his movement. *Murshidiyyin* missionaries appeared in the southern region of the mountain, in the Jabal Hilu, which became a major propaganda center, and as far away as Homs and Hama.[34]

Not long afterwards, the French again arrested Murshid and several of his followers, exiling them to Raqqa on the Euphrates. After his release and return, Murshid toned down the more militant aspects of his movement and sought greater respectability among Alawite tribal leaders and religious shaykhs. He used the marriage bed to consolidate his influence with Alawite notables, and at one time he had 13 wives. By the 1930s, he and the French High Commission had worked out a *modus vivendi*, although the French kept a close eye on him while they quietly promoted his rivals. Murshid was by now a wealthy man and headed a revivalist movement reportedly with more than 40,000 adherents.[35]

The treaty of 1936 provided for a relaxation of direct French control in the Latakia province and its administrative attachment to Syria. Local leaders with independent influence in the region now found the opportunity to engage in politics on the national level and to represent their community's specific interests in the Syrian capital. Sulayman al-Murshid was elected to the Syrian Parliament and proved to be a fairly effective deputy. He did not adopt a strong separatist line but rather worked within the framework of a unified Syria while he attempted to broaden his base among Alawites. But his willingness to cooperate lasted only as long as the French government remained committed to a treaty. Once it broke this commitment and the Mardam government's political fortunes collapsed, Murshid retreated into the bosom of separatist sentiment and drew closer to the French. Murshid's political flexibility hinged in large measure on the strength of his popular following and his enormous landed wealth.[36]

After the Latakia province was again rejoined to Syria during World War II, Murshid became quite an irritant to the new nationalist government in Damascus through the Alawite lobby he headed in Parliament. But his strength and that of his movement lasted only as long as the French remained in Syria. The independent Syrian government executed

[34] Khayr al-Din al-Zirikli, *al-Aʿlam*, vol. 3, p. 70; Batatu, "Some Observations," p. 334; Weulersse, *Alaouites*, p. 335.

[35] Weulersse, *Alaouites*, p. 336.

[36] FO 371/7687, vol. 21914. MacKereth to Baxter, 10 Dec. 1938; also see Rabinovich, "Compact Minorities," pp. 704–5.

him less than a year after the French withdrawal in 1946, for crimes against the nation.

There were two other institutions which were to have more lasting impact on the Latakia province and the Alawite community than the Murshidiyyin. One was the emerging radical nationalist organization known as the Hizb al-qawmi suri or, as the French called it, the Parti populaire syrien (PPS) and the other was the military. The PPS, with its strongly secular ideology, appealed first to the Christian Orthodox community of the province, as it did in Lebanon, but it also appealed to Syria's other minorities. The Alawite intelligentsia found the party attractive because it rejected Arabism and religion altogether. It also stressed the values of village life over those of the city where Arab nationalism had its deepest roots.[37]

The other institution was the army. For a poor community like the Alawites it was the only means available for social advancement. Moreover, the French preferred to recruit from minorities, for obvious reasons. Though even under French control, the military could not avoid instilling national values.[38] Both the army and the PPS promoted in different ways the process of Alawite integration into Syria; yet their influence with Alawites also obstructed the expansion of the National Bloc's authority in the Latakia region.

DISTURBANCES IN THE JAZIRA

The conclusion of treaty negotiations in 1936 had severe repercussions throughout Syria but perhaps nowhere more acutely than in the Jazira. In many ways, this remote, sparsely settled triangle formed by the east bank of the Euphrates river and Syria's frontiers with Iraq and Turkey—with its Arab and Kurdish tribes and its largely Christian urban communities of Armenians, Jacobites, and Assyrians—belonged more to traditional Mesopotamia than to Syria. In 1920, the Jazira was cut off from its natural commercial center at Diarbakir in eastern Turkey, and for the following 15 years Syrian politicians ignored developments there.

The Jazira's immediate administrative incorporation under the authority of a nationalist government at Damascus was fraught with prob-

[37] The PPS officially named itself the Syrian Social Nationalist Party (SSNP). MAE, Guerre 1939–45 (Londres CNF), "Le Parti populaire syrien (P.P.S.)," vol. 40, Beirut, April 1942. Also see Labib Zuwiyya Yamak, *The Syrian Social Nationalist Party: An Ideological Analysis* (Cambridge, Mass., 1966).

[38] See Michael H. Van Dusen, "Intra-and Inter-Generational Conflict in the Syrian Army," Ph.D. Dissertation (The Johns Hopkins University, 1971), and Hanna Batatu, "Some Observations," pp. 341–43.

lems.[39] For one thing, French officials in the Jazira fiercely guarded their positions of local influence built up over a decade and a half. They argued for gradual administrative integration in order not to arouse local antagonisms. But their superiors at the Quai d'Orsay had agreed to terms that relegated the French to observer status in the province, giving Syrian functionaries a fairly free administrative hand.

The complex social and cultural landscape of the Jazira clearly contributed to its political instability during the Mandate. The difficulty of stabilizing Syria's frontiers with Turkey and Iraq, which took nearly a decade, and the influx of various refugee populations from these two neighbors aggravated the situation. The appearance of Kurdish tribes in 1926, escaping Turkish attacks, disrupted the traditional balance of nomadic and semi-nomadic Kurdish and Arab tribes. Not only were some of the incoming Kurdish chieftains imbued with Kurdish nationalist sentiments, which began to influence the older Kurdish tribes, but their tribes readily took up farming which encouraged Arab tribes to follow suit. In fact, Kurdish and Arab tribes came increasingly into contact especially in spring when they both competed for water in the same districts. Conflicts arose over grazing and farming lands but were not easily resolved. Syrian functionaries from the towns, whom French officers of the Services Spéciaux installed and supported, tried unsuccessfully to maintain the peace. Ignorant of the Kurdish language and Kurdish customs, these bureaucrats were distrusted by the immigrant tribes. That these same bureaucrats also proselytized Arab nationalism added to the tensions between Kurds and Arabs.[40]

Also upsetting the balance in the Jazira was the influx of the various Christian minorities who were principally engaged in commerce and who clustered in the towns. The single most important commercial center of the province was Qamishli, which was literally a creation of the Mandate. Located on the frontier with Turkey, it mushroomed after the frontier was stabilized in the late 1920s. By 1939, its population exceeded more

---

[39] See L. Dillemann, "Les Français en Haute-Djezireh—Une réussite ignorée en marge de l'échec syrien," CHEAM, no. 50538, n.d., 72 pages. A partial version of Dillemann's study has been published as "Les Français en Haute-Djezireh (1919–1939)," *Revue Française d'Histoire d'Outre-Mer*, 66 (1979), pp. 33–58. The population of the Jazira in 1943 was 146,000 of which only 18 percent were urban dwellers. Approximately 68 percent of its population were Sunnis (divided between Arab and Kurdish tribes and Arab townsmen); 22.5 percent were Syrian Catholics and Assyrian Christians; and 7 percent were Armenians. For a historico-geographic account of the Jazira, see Roupen Boghossian, *L'Haute-Djézireh* (Aleppo, 1952).

[40] Lieutenant Ayme, "La rivalité arabo-kurde en Djeziré Syrienne," CHEAM, no. 223 (Dec. 1937), pp. 1–6; Victor Müller, *En Syrie avec les bédouins* (Paris, 1931); FO 371/220, vol. 14553. Monck-Mason to FO, 18 Dec. 1929; FO 371/1144, vol. 16975. Monck-Mason, (Aleppo) to Simon, 20 Dec. 1932; Dillemann, "Les Français en Haute-Djezireh," CHEAM.

than 15,000. Because Dayr al-Zur, the provincial capital, was too far from the upper Jazira's agricultural heartland and Hassaja was deprived of a railroad connection, Qamishli benefitted most from the Jazira's economic prosperity. It was linked by train to Aleppo and it flourished because of its commercial ties with Aleppo. Qamishli gathered and sent off to Aleppo Jazira's raw materials and foodstuffs and it distributed Aleppine manufactures in the province. One indication of the importance of the Qamishli–Aleppo tie was that after 1929, Khan al-Jazira in Aleppo became one of the most active commercial depots in that city.[41]

Armenians were attracted to Qamishli and were pioneers in the opening up of the Jazira. They provided the liberal professions of the town—from doctors and lawyers to pharmacists—and they also formed the small artisanal class of mechanics, blacksmiths, and *carduers de laine*. Also at this time, Christian merchant-moneylenders—Armenians and Syrian Catholic settlers from Aleppo and elsewhere—began to buy up mortgages and to collect debts in the form of lands from Bedouin chiefs and peasants. In this way, Christians and Kurdish and Arab tribes came into contact and increasingly into conflict, based on their economic or financial relations. Other refugee populations like the Assyrians from Iraq and the Kurds provided new sources of labor and became farmers and sharecroppers.

The growth of separatism in the Jazira reflected its comparative sociocultural and political underdevelopment, where the principal loyalty of its mixed population was to family, clan, tribe, ethnic and religious community, locale, or some combination thereof. The idea of a unified Syrian state and nation was foreign to most of the Jazira's inhabitants. The minority who favored centralization were young high school graduates imbued with nationalist ideals and in search of positions in the local bureaucracy. They quite naturally looked to a sympathetic nationalist government in Damascus for support. Nationalist forces opposed French efforts to resettle the Kurdish tribes and Christian refugee communities which would upset the communal balance and check nationalist ambitions there. The opening up and settling of the Jazira also revealed its enormous economic potential and therefore its importance to the future of a unified and independent Syria. Regionalists, on the other hand, were local minority leaders wishing to retain their traditional influence and autonomy under French protection. They feared a diminution of their power under a nationalist government and even of being unseated by local nationalist upstarts.

Political life in the Jazira was subdued during the early 1930s. Once the nationalists assumed control of government, however, the major political factions, which had formed the heart of all disputes since the late 1920s,

---

[41] *Ibid*; FO 371/1144, vol. 16975. Monck-Mason to Simon, 20 Dec. 1932.

became more active. The General Strike of 1936 had encouraged a handful of nationalist intellectuals and functionaries in Hassaja to close the bazaars in solidarity. To do so, nationalists had to rely on the Arab tribes surrounding Hassaja because they had little support in the town itself, where two-thirds of its 6,000 inhabitants were Christians, who since 1933 had agitated for an autonomous province under a French governor and locally-recruited officials. In response to the growth of nationalist activity, separatist forces led by the Christian mayor of Qamishli and two prominent Kurdish tribal leaders—Hajo Agha of the Hufrakiyya and Mahmud Bey of the Milliyya—launched their own autonomous movement in the middle of February 1936, demanding administrative and financial autonomy, the continuation of the French Mandate, and the appointment of local functionaries under a French governor. Supporting them were several Kurdish tribes and even some Arab ones like the Baggara and Sharabiyyin, who worked for town-based Christian merchant-moneylenders as shepherds and therefore who were dependent on them for their livelihoods or, like the Tayy, who were politically divided between partisans and opponents of Daham al-Hadi, the powerful chieftain of the Arab Shammar al-Khursa.[42]

Local nationalists immediately responded to the eruption of a separatist movement with a smear campaign against the separatists, claiming that they were anti-nationalist and agents of the French. This forced the Christian minority in the region to modify their demands. They now emphasized only administrative and financial autonomy, in a bid for support from Arab tribes. But they were largely unsuccessful. Their failure to consult the ambitious Daham al-Hadi encouraged him to throw his considerable weight behind unionist forces and, indeed, to assume their leadership. Nationalists received added encouragement by the resignation toward the end of February of Shaykh Taj al-Hasani in Damascus and the announcement that the French had agreed to initiate treaty negotiations in Paris.

The Jazira's autonomy program rallied nearly all of Qamishli behind it and considerable effort was spent on publicizing it at the High Commission in Beirut, at the League of Nations, and in Paris, where the Rabbi of Qamishli appealed to Léon Blum, on the grounds of their common faith, to support the autonomy movement. However, Kurds and Christians had little reason to be hopeful that the Jazira would be accorded a status analogous to that of the Sanjak of Alexandretta. By the fall of 1936 all factions found themselves preparing for parliamentary elections.

[42] Ayme, "La rivalité," pp. 8–10; FO 371/7401, vol. 20066. Walters (League of Nations) to Ward (FO), 25 Nov. 1936. The demands of the regionalist alliance in the Jazira can be found in an anonymously authored pamphlet titled "La Question syrienne. La vérité sur les événements de la Djézireh," CHEAM, no. 212078 (1937), pp. 5–33.

The primaries of mid-November were conducted without incident but the second degree elections were not without their difficulties. Only Daham al-Hadi, representing the nomadic tribes of the Jazira and running on the nationalist list, won easily. But the other three seats, which were designated for two Sunnis representing the sedentary tribes and a Christian, were hotly contested. The National Bloc supported several undistinguished candidates—a rich Sunni landowner of Qamishli, a chief of a lesser section of the Jabbur tribe, and an obscure Christian of Hassaja. Although at issue was nothing more than a clash of personalities, the victors were all sympathetic to the autonomy program. So, to complicate matters, Daham al-Hadi, who had inscribed on his calling card the title "chief of the chiefs of the tribes of Jazira" vigorously lobbied his colleagues in the overwhelmingly nationalist Chamber of Deputies in Damascus in order to get them to reject the credentials of the other elected Jazirans. But, when Hajo Agha and his allies threatened a massive rebellion against the Mardam government if the credentials of the still unseated deputies were not accepted, the Chamber finally validated them, in mid-April 1937.[43]

The new *muhafiz* sent out from Damascus in February was Amir Bahjat al-Shihabi, an Istanbul-educated lawyer of considerable intellect and authority but who also displayed all the arrogance of a Damascus notable. He had little previous administrative experience, but he did have the complete backing of his government, which wanted to compensate for its ineffectiveness in confronting the Turks in Alexandretta by imposing its will in the Jazira. Shihabi's task was to disarm the local population in the towns, to encourage peasants from southern districts of Aleppo, Homs, and Hama to emigrate to the Jazira in order to strengthen the Sunni Arab majority, to dismiss local officials hostile to Syrian unity, to pack local administration with elements sympathetic to the Mardam government, to improve security in the towns by increasing the police force, and to snuff out growing Turkish propaganda in Qamishli and elsewhere in the province. Meanwhile, the local minorities of the Jazira, despite their deep-seated hatred of the Turks, closely watched developments in Alexandretta in the hope that the separatist movement there would establish a precedent, allowing the Kurdish and Christian communities of the Jazira to pose the question of autonomy in the near future.[44]

The Arab tribes and educated Sunni elites in the towns found common interest with Shihabi, who made it difficult for Christian and Kurdish leaders to acquire access to his office. His various administrative decisions seemed completely impartial to them and only fueled opposition.

[43] Ayme, "La rivalité," pp. 13–18.
[44] FO 371/5371, vol. 20849. MacKereth to Rendel, 8 Sept. 1937; Ayme, "La rivalité," p. 16; 'Adil al-'Azma Papers [Syria], File 17/432. Khalid Mihrat (Director of Police, al-Jazira) to Director-General of Police, 17 March 1937.

The immediate source of the first major disturbance that Shihabi encountered was the struggle for leadership of the Tayy, an Arab tribe. When the Tayy's paramount chief, Talal, died in Beirut in November 1936, Daham al-Hadi of the Shammar opposed Talal's logical successor and cousin, Muhammad ʿAbd al-Rahman, because of his close ties to Daham's enemies, the Shammar of Iraq. Daham, who had captured Shihabi's ear, convinced him to support a little-known chief over Muhammad ʿAbd al-Rahman. This dispute turned into an incident when Kurdish chiefs used it as a pretext for attacking Shihabi's administration.[45]

In late June 1937, in a small village near Qamishli where clan chiefs had gathered to support the nomination of Shaykh Muhammad ʿAbd al-Rahman to head the Tayy, protestors threatened an armed uprising unless Damascus dismissed Shihabi and Qamishli's *qaʾimmaqam* and justice of the peace by the end of July. However, Bahjat Shihabi was not easily intimidated and instead increased the number of police in the towns and arrested the anti-nationalist mayor of Hassaja on July 1. Unable to present himself as anything but a partisan of the nationalist cause, Shihabi turned to the armed Arab tribes under Daham al-Hadi's leadership. But when a Kurdo-Christian rebellion broke out, Shihabi and his senior staff fled Qamishli for Damascus. A few days later, a French officer in the Services Spéciaux managed to reach a temporary truce before the revolt spread.[46]

But now the towns braced themselves for an attack by Daham al-Hadi's forces and on July 14 there were skirmishes between the Arab tribes and the Kurdo-Christian bloc in Hassaja. While Daham called on the National Bloc in Damascus to send more arms and money, Kurdish chiefs recruited their own troops on a village to village basis. In the meantime, the Mardam government tried to restore its authority in the Jazira by sending out a commission to investigate the disturbances. But the terms on which the separatist forces were prepared to enter into discussions with the commission were that the *muhafiz* of Jazira be a local personality and not the nominee of Damascus; that all administrative and judicial officials in the Jazira be locals; that a representative of the High Commission be retained permanently in the province; that the French Army not be withdrawn; and that all rebels be amnestied. In response, nationalist leaders in the Jazira and representatives of the Arab tribes decided in conference to boycott Qamishli and Hassaja on the grounds that their inhabitants were traitors to the Arab cause.[47]

---

[45] Ayme, "La rivalité," pp. 18–20.
[46] FO 371/5371, vol. 20849. MacKereth to Rendel, 8 Sept. 1937; Ayme, "La rivalité," pp. 21–22; MAE, Syrie–Liban 1930–40. "Note", 29 Sept. 1937, vol. 495, pp. 214–15.
[47] FO 371/4076, vol. 20849. Davis (Aleppo), to FO, 16 July 1937; FO 371/4718, vol. 20849. Davis to FO, 5 Aug. 1937.

Daham's emissary to Damascus returned with arms and money on July 25, the same day that he called for holy war and launched attacks against the Christian opposition in Qamishli and Hassaja. After a series of minor incidents in and around ʿAmuda, a large village in the Qamishli region where nationalists had some influence but which also had a significant Christian population, a Kurdish tribe aligned with Daham al-Hadi and under the influence of local nationalist functionaries pillaged ʿAmuda's Christian quarter and set it on fire, on August 9. The Kurds also massacred more than two dozen Christian inhabitants. Although Daham's rival, Mizan, chief of the Shammar of Zur, forced the Kurdish invaders to retreat, the French military chose to intervene by resorting to punishing air raids on surrounding Kurdish settlements, which killed an additional 30 people. At this time, the French reasserted their authority in the towns of the Jazira and increasingly on the side of the Kurdo-Christian separatists.[48] Adding dimension to the separatist versus unionist movements in Jazira, were the overlapping struggles between Kurds and Arabs, Christians and Muslims, merchant-moneylenders and indebted tribes, and town and countryside.

Although the Jazira would not again witness the kind of violence which visited it in the summer of 1937, French military intervention now emboldened the Christians to step up their campaign for regional autonomy. They refused to accept the nationalist government's disavowal of any complicity in the disturbances at ʿAmuda and continued to blame the National Bloc cadres in the province for instigating the incidents. No one less than Count Ostrorog, the French Delegate in Damascus, supported their contention. At the same time, Christian leaders asked: if an ʿAmuda can occur with French troops stationed in the Jazira, what will the fate of the minorities be once the French withdraw at independence?[49]

The Christian separatists adopted a two-pronged strategy after ʿAmuda. On one front, they kept up a steady level of political activity in the towns, especially Hassaja, by agitating for the replacement of unsympathetic officials by locals. Occasionally, they resorted to symbolic acts, most notably the kidnapping just before Christmas of Tawfiq Shamiyya, the new *muhafiz* of the Jazira. Although they released him unharmed a few days later, Damascus was furious and demanded that his assailants, who hailed from Hassaja, either be deported or placed under house arrest; that all weapons in Hassaja be confiscated; and that several French officers of the Services Spéciaux be dismissed because of their acquiescence to acts

[48] Ayme, "La rivalité," pp. 23–26; FO 371/4814, vol. 20849. Davis to Eastern Dept., 12 Aug. 1937; FO 371/5356, vol. 20849. Davis to FO, 16 Aug. 1937. Anon., "La vérité," CHEAM, pp. 22–24.
[49] FO 371/5371, vol. 20849. MacKereth to Rendel, 8 Sept. 1937.

of violence and sabotage.[50] Hardly a National Bloc leader in Syria doubted that the French were masterminding the autonomy movement in the Jazira.

On the other front, the separatists brought their case before the Vatican, the League of Nations, and the French government. Directing their international offensive was none other than Cardinal Tappouni of Aleppo whose primary source of information came from the Syrian Catholic Bishop Hibbi who had, himself, been actively involved in the Kurdo-Christian uprisings in Hassaja in July 1937. Tappouni's interventions, however, registered little more than a whimper from the Quai d'Orsay, which was unprepared to support the extreme demands of the separatists at this time. In Syria, High Commission officials privately warned separatist leaders that the Jazira's remoteness and its largely Muslim population necessitated that the Christian minority seek a *modus vivendi* with the majority if it wished to survive. But, in spite of the rather cool French response at this time, it is likely that the Jaziran incidents inspired, at least partly, the exchanges between Jamil Mardam and M. de Tessan in December 1937 which included additional security guarantees for Syria's Christian minorities. Mardam's compromises were received with a measure of satisfaction in the Jazira and temporarily eased tensions there.[51]

Damascus sent out its third *muhafiz* to the Jazira in a year, in March 1938. Haydar Mardam was the first cousin of the Prime Minister and had a Christian wife. His appointment was at first well received for it was thought that he could convey the wishes of the local population directly and speedily to Jamil Bey. He came bearing an olive branch; but he departed a month later after renewed anti-government disturbances, including an effective 15-day strike and something completely new: the boycott of all government officials, regardless of provenance. Shopkeepers now refused to sell to officials even the most basic necessities.[52]

In fact, the boycott continued through the summer of 1938, virtually paralyzing local government. Recriminations were hurled back and forth between nationalists and separatists. At the end of July, some 200 separatists held a convention in a village near ʿAmuda to restate their demands, including local autonomy and the permanent deployment of French troops in the province, an amnesty for all Jazirans in jail or exile for involvement in separatist activities, and the resumption of government subsidies to tribal shaykhs who refused to support the government. If these terms were unacceptable then the boycott of all Syrian officials

---

[50] MWT, *al-Intidab al-faransi: Qadaya mukhtalifa*, 57/1159–755/185. Jamil Mardam to Count Ostrorog, 15 Feb. 1938.

[51] FO 371/877, vol. 21914. Davis to FO, 8 Feb. 1938.

[52] FO 371/1492, vol. 21914. Davis to FO, 15 March 1938; FO 371/2943, vol. 21914. Davis to FO, 14 May 1938.

would continue and the local populace would refuse to pay any taxes imposed by the government. A British official remarked at the time that the separatists had formed what amounted to their own countergovernment at whose center were local tribunals which issued decisions that the populace accepted voluntarily and that compared "more than favourably with the . . . Syrian courts both for speed and impartiality."[53]

By the beginning of 1939, the situation in the Jazira had deteriorated, as it had throughout Syria. New strikes occurred in Hassaja in January as separatists armed themselves for what appeared to be their final push. A group of Jaziran notables who had previously supported union with Syria now called for the attachment of their province to Turkey. Some of them were former Ottoman army officers who hoped that if the Franco-Syrian Treaty came into force that they would receive plumb posts in the Syrian Army. But, when the French Parliament refused to ratify the treaty at the end of 1938, they fell into despair. Alongside their movement came an increase in Turkish propaganda in the Jazira.[54]

By early 1939, many houses in Hassaja flew the French flag, perhaps in anticipation of a visit by the new High Commissioner. In preparation for the inevitable day, the National Bloc in Aleppo dispatched 1,000 Syrian flags to Qamishli only to see them confiscated by militant separatists. Finally, in early March, M. Puaux made a whirlwind tour of the Jazira in a fashion reminiscent of his recent visits to the Jabal Druze and Latakia. There, as elsewhere, he encountered unionist and separatist demonstrations and he met with representatives of both parties, including Shaykh Daham al-Hadi and Hajo Agha. What Puaux admitted to learning from his visit was an indication of the course the French would follow in the Jazira and the other peripheral provinces. He concluded that all responsible leaders in the Jazira wanted to preserve their friendship with the French; they wanted to maintain the French Army; and they saw the necessity of some form of decentralization or local autonomy.[55] The High Commissioner was not obliged, of course, to provide a definition of what constituted a responsible leader!

Nevertheless, even after the Mardam government's resignation in February 1939, Puaux had hesitated to take a decision on the Jazira's future legal status. But in early June, matters reached a head as fighting between the Syrian Gendarmerie and separatists broke out over the hoisting and tearing down first of Syrian flags and then French flags in Qamishli.

[53] FO 371/4710, vol. 21914. Davis to Halifax, 3 Aug. 1938.
[54] FO 371/1293, vol. 23276. MacKereth to Baxter, 11 Feb. 1939; MWT, al-Dawla: al-ahzab, 220/431, 1 Feb. 1939.
[55] FO 371/1894, vol. 23276. Davis, (Aleppo), to FO, 6 March 1939; MWT, al-Intidab al-faransi: Qadaya mukhtalifa, 67/1168—256/10. Muhafiz (Jazira) to Minister of Interior, 3 March 1939.

Events in the Jazira, when coupled with developments in the Jabal Druze and Latakia, finally brought about a long-awaited French decision. On July 2, the High Commissioner decreed for the Jazira, as he did for the other two governorates, a special regime under direct French control.[56]

THE OVERARCHING FRENCH POLICY of playing minority against majority, countryside against nationalist towns, and elite against elite had by 1939 come full circle. With the three provinces no longer under the authority of Damascus and with the Sanjak of Alexandretta now completely detached from Syria, the propects of Syrian unity and independence seemed as remote as in the early 1920s. On the one hand, internal differences within French policy-making circles on the Syrian question had left deep scars on the Syrian political fabric. On the other, the refusal or inability of the Syrian nationalist leadership to demonstrate sensitivity in its dealings with the various regional minorities impeded the crystallization of a new national identity for Syria. In the short-run, this meant that three more nails had been hammered into the National Bloc's coffin.

[56] MWT, al-Intidab al-faransi: al-Dakhiliyya: islahat, 31/5672–38. Qa'immaqam of Qamishli to Minister of Interior, 29 March 1939; FO 371/4393, vol. 23277. Davis to FO, 10 June 1939; Longrigg, Syria, p. 251.

CHAPTER TWENTY-ONE

REBELLION IN PALESTINE

The new National Bloc government of Syria . . . must provide bread
and services. Palestine is first in Syrian exports; Syrian labourers in
Palestine return money to the country and the Government is interested in Jewish financial and technical aid. The leaders of the National Bloc told the Palestinians even before independence that they
want quiet in Palestine.[1]

No EVENT OF THE 1930s captured the attention of the Arab world as did
the Arab Revolt in Palestine. Its progress was eagerly followed in the
daily press of Cairo, Baghdad, Damascus, and in the capitals of North Africa. It was also carefully monitored by Arab leaders and regimes. On the
one hand, the revolt aroused Arab nationalist sentiments in ways not witnessed in the region since the days of Faysal's Arab Kingdom; on the
other, it alarmed Arab rulers who feared its repercussions on domestic
political life in their respective countries.

The impact of the revolt on the Arab world differed from country to
country. It coincided with and helped to erode Egypt's longstanding political insulation from the Arab nationalist movement (despite Cairo's
own central role in the birth of the nationalist idea and as a political asylum for nationalist activists from Syria, Lebanon, and Palestine) and contributed to her new Arab orientation.[2] It helped an independent Iraq to
establish herself as a vital center of Arab nationalist activity, enhancing
Baghdad's political reputation among the Arabs. In Transjordan, the ambitious Amir ʿAbdullah, while not at all pleased by the use of his territory
as a conduit for arms and fighters, sought to benefit from the revolt by
expanding his influence in Palestinian politics.[3] In Syria, the impact of the
revolt and the reaction of the political leadership was especially mixed.

[1] Statement by Moshe [Shertok] Sharett, cited in Simha Flapan, *Zionism and the Palestinians* (London, 1979), pp. 151–52.
[2] See James P. Jankowski, "The Government of Egypt and the Palestine Question, 1936–
1939," *Middle Eastern Studies*, 17 (Oct. 1981), pp. 427–53; Ralph M. Coury, "Who Invented Egyptian Arab Nationalism?," part 2, *International Journal of Middle East Studies*,
14 (Nov. 1982); Israel Gershoni, *The Emergence of Pan-Arabism in Egypt* (Tel Aviv, 1981),
pp. 37–38.
[3] Wilson, *King Abdullah*, Chapter 7.

The major dilemma facing the National Bloc in 1936 was that as its
prospects for getting control of government grew brighter, it encountered
a number of obstacles which had the potential to ruin these prospects. A
resurgence of pan-Arab sentiment focused on developments in Palestine
was one such obstacle. The Bloc leadership could neither avoid involvement in the Palestine question nor allow Palestine to divert it from its
quest for governmental power. A delicate balance had to be struck between pan-Arab commitment and local self-interest; otherwise the widening gulf between the nationalism of elites and the nationalism of popular sentiment might become unbridgeable. If this happened the Bloc
could lose control of the independence movement.

Syria and Palestine before 1936

A combination of political, socio-economic, and cultural factors had long
been at work in Syria shaping popular opinion about Palestine. This crystallized into massive Syrian support for the revolt of 1936–39. There
were the traditional bonds between Syria and Palestine which fostered
the belief among many Syrian (and Palestinian) nationalists that Palestine was an appendage of Syria. Indeed, before World War I Syria and
Palestine had belonged to a single geographic region united under an Ottoman administration and linked by trade. The inhabitants lived in a relatively homogeneous cultural environment in which language and social
custom were largely similar, despite some ethnic and class variations. Although the Ottoman government, Arabs, and Jews all referred to a *geographic* area called Palestine, in terms of administrative unity Palestine,
as such, did not exist before World War I. In the second half of the nineteenth century, Palestine was part of the *vilayet* of Syria (*Sham*) and was
divided into three *sanjaks* (Jerusalem, Nablus, and Acre). Then, in the
1880s Ottoman administrative reorganization created a more autonomous *mutasarriflik* of Jerusalem which was attached to the new *vilayet* of
Beirut, which the Ottomans had carved out of the *vilayet* of Syria.[4] Between these different units peoples and goods moved back and forth
unencumbered by the bureaucratic processes and taxes associated with
borders.

   Ties between Syria and Palestine were undoubtedly strongest among
the upper classes. In both territories there existed an active urban notability, which derived power and influence from control of local government offices and religious institutions, and wealth from extensive land-

[4] See ʿAbd al-ʿAziz Muhammad ʿAwad, *al-Idara al-ʿuthmaniyya fi wilayat suriyya
1864–1914* (Cairo, 1969); Neville J. Mandel, *The Arabs and Zionism before World War I*
(Berkeley, 1976), pp. 19–20.

ownership and usury in the countryside. In the course of the nineteenth century this class acquired practically undivided control of political life in Palestine and Syria. Its members moved freely between Damascus and Jerusalem, Beirut, and Jaffa; intermarriage was frequent and it was common to find families in Damascus and Beirut owning land in Palestine.[5]

The various ties between the local elites of Palestine and Syria were eventually transformed into political bonds, especially in association with the rapid growth of the idea of Arabism after 1900. Arab elites first formed political bonds in Istanbul, where they acquired an Ottoman professional education. Afterwards these bonds were strengthened through shared experience in provincial administration, in the Ottoman Parliament where Syrians joined Palestinian representatives in lobbying for greater political and administrative automomy in the face of Young Turk centralization and Turkification policies and against Jewish immigration into Palestine, and in a variety of secret nationalist societies before and during World War I. They acquired their greatest strength in Damascus after the war, where Syrians and Palestinians, now joined by Iraqis, worked for the establishment of an independent Arab state under Amir Faysal.[6]

The historical record indicates, however, that after the collapse of Faysal's kingdom and the partition of geographical Syria into separate British and French administered Mandates, the bonds between Syrians and Palestinians loosened perceptibly. Indeed, it took the rebellion of 1936 in Palestine to restore the close ties and cooperation of the early period. Of course, Syrian and Palestinian nationalists had maintained ties and supported each other during the decade and a half preceding the rebellion, but the relationship was not as active as it had been before.

During the 1920s, cooperation took place through the medium of the Syrian–Palestine Congress which defended both Syrian and Palestinian rights before the League of Nations.[7] With so large a fraction of the Syrian nationalist leadership in exile or in prison during much of the decade, moral and material support flowed more regularly from Palestine to Syria than in the other direction. The Arabic press in Palestine printed daily articles critical of the French and exhorting the Syrian people to overthrow the yoke of French imperialism. Demonstrations and protests against French policy and in the name of Syrian independence often assumed a violent character in Palestine. Syrian nationalists, in particular

[5] For example, the Jaza'iri and Yusuf families in Damascus and the Salam family in Beirut.

[6] See Khoury, *Urban Notables* , Chapters 3, 4.

[7] See Chapter 9 and Marie-Renée Mouton, "Le congrès syrio-palestinien de Genève," *Relations Internationales*, 19 (Autumn 1979), pp. 313–28.

members of the radical Istiqlal Party, also found refuge in Palestine where they waged a propaganda campaign against the French Mandate while British authorities looked the other way. The French High Commission accused the British of openly assisting Syrian nationalists in Palestine and Transjordan in order to upset French rule, with the aim of one day replacing the French in Syria. Although the French exaggerated the extent of British complicity, Britain did purposely hinder French efforts to crush the Great Syrian Revolt of the mid-1920s by refusing to extradite Syrian rebels who had taken refuge in Palestine and Transjordan, a breach of diplomatic good manners the French never forgot.

Throughout the 1920s, Syria did not neglect the Palestine question. Whenever the Syrian nationalist press was not under suspension (it often was in this period), it took the opportunity to criticize Zionist activities and British policy. Most active among the newspapers was the leading Arabic daily of Damascus, *Alif ba'* whose editor, Yusuf al-'Issa, was a Palestinian Christian and the relative of 'Issa al-'Issa, the nationalist editor of the Jaffa newspaper, *Filastin.* Syrians also demonstrated against Zionism and British policy usually in response to developments in Palestine or, as in 1925, during the visit of Lord Balfour to Syria.[8] However, Syrian interest in the Palestinian cause was irregular and rather mild in this period.

Palestine was comparatively quiet in the twenties, owing to the slowing of Jewish immigration and a more or less working relationship between the Palestinian-Arab leadership and the British. Syria, by contrast, was alive with regular and violent disturbances against the French and their local allies. Indeed, Syria's political future seemed gloomier in this decade than Palestine's; the most significant political upheaval of the 1920s in the Arab East occurred in Syria, and not in Palestine. The Great Syrian Revolt attracted support far and wide, not just from the Arab territories but from the Muslim world at large and from Syrian émigré communities in the Americas. Palestine did not experience a similar upheaval until ten years later. Simply put, in the 1920s there was more political activity of the kind that aroused pan-Arab sentiments in Syria than in Palestine, a point generally lost on historians of Arab nationalism.

The largest popular manifestation of Syrian support for the Palestinian cause came at the tail end of the decade when the lull in Palestine was finally shattered by Arab riots against Jews, known as the Wailing Wall incident. The importance of these riots on Syrian political life, apart from demonstrating the intensity of popular feeling in Syria for Palestine, was the establishment of a pattern for National Bloc activity which would repeat itself time and again during the Mandate years. This entailed dis-

[8] See Chapter 5.

couraging, whenever possible, all pan-Arab activities which might force the nationalist leadership to stray from its principal course of relaxing French control over Syria. Specifically, it meant avoiding any pro-Palestinian activities that might deny the National Bloc British diplomatic support, or, even more alarmingly, that might get out of control and turn into anti-French manifestations, resulting in a military crackdown and the isolation of the Bloc from the summit of politics in Syria.

The National Bloc was steered by moderates, headed by Jamil Mardam, the chief architect of its strategy of "honorable cooperation." At the level of inter-Arab affairs, this strategy dictated that the national movement should not be sidetracked by any issues—regardless of their merit or appeal—which diverted the Bloc from its major goal. And the Bloc staked its claim to be the paramount political organization in the country on its ability to harness and direct the energies of the urban masses; this included making certain that popular manifestations did not disrupt the delicate diplomatic negotiations between the Bloc and the French.

Contributing to the Bloc's pragmatism was the idea, gradually adopted after the failure of the Great Revolt, that Syria could not hope to participate in any Arab union scheme without first securing her own independence. Furthermore, Palestine was Syria's most valuable export market and any disruptions there damaged Syria's economy as a whole, and, in particular, the financial interests of the Muslim commerical bourgeoisie with whom a number of Bloc leaders were socially and financially linked. In view of such prospects, the reluctance of the Bloc to become deeply involved in Palestine becomes understandable.

This pattern repeated itself in the summer of 1931 when the Bloc leadership purposely avoided the limelight at several large public rallies staged in solidarity with a variety of pan-Arab and pan-Islamic issues, including Palestine and Libya, and again in December 1931 when the Bloc failed to send an official delegation to the Jerusalem Congress organized by the Mufti, Hajj Amin al-Husayni, to drum up worldwide Islamic support for the Palestinian cause. In both instances, the Bloc wanted to avoid annoying the French and possibly jeopardizing the coming national elections.

It was only after Jamil Mardam and other Bloc moderates failed to secure a treaty in 1933 that the National Bloc temporarily scrapped the strategy of honorable cooperation and became more involved in pan-Arab issues. In fact, Mardam and his cronies, their reputations tarnished by collaboration, now looked beyond Syria's frontiers for political support. They needed to rehabilitate their reputations and pan-Arabism provided an ideological tool to do so, especially with the intractable French offering no reasonable opportunities for the resumption of honorable cooperation. Moreover, by turning his attention to the question of Palestine and to strengthening his contacts in Iraq and Saudi Arabia, Jamil Mardam would be in a better position to neutralize the radical wing of the Damascus Bloc headed by Shukri al-Quwwatli and the newly created pan-Arab League of National Action.[9]

One outcome of the National Bloc's re-orientation was the establishment of the first significant propaganda organization in the Arab world devoted to pan-Arab activities, the Bureau for National Propaganda. Founded in 1934 by Fakhri al-Barudi, the Bureau devoted itself to the systematic dissemination of information on critical issues of the times, and in particular on the question of Palestine. The other significant area in which the Bloc joined hands with other Syrian nationalists in support of Palestine was in working to prevent financially-strapped Syrians owning land in Palestine from selling their holdings to the Jewish National Fund at inflated prices.

SYRIAN REACTIONS: 1936

Historians seem to agree that the rebellion in Palestine had several causes.[10] Two related factors were certainly the growing Arab fear that the Zionist movement was rapidly gaining ground in its drive to establish a Jewish national home and eventually an independent state in Palestine, and the Arabs' own growing desire for national independence. By the mid-1930s, the Zionists appeared to be more successful at securing British support for their ambitions than were the Arabs. This widening gap was reflected by a gradual shift in the locus of power in Palestine away from her traditional absentee landowning class, which provided the bulk of the Arab political leadership, toward Jewish commerical classes, including an emerging Jewish industrial bourgeoisie; it was a shift taking place more or less with the complicity of the British Mandate authorities. The transformation of Palestine under the impact of increasing commercialization and Zionist land colonization caused the dispossession and alienation of vital sections of Palestine's Arab peasantry and her urban poor. This in turn produced a reservoir of resentment which "touched the

---

[9] For an example of League of National Action activities on behalf of Palestine at this time, see France: MAE, Syrie–Liban 1930–40. Martel Telegrams, 3 Nov. 1933 and 5 Nov. 1933, vol. 486, pp. 246–54; *ibid.*, pp. 268–79.

[10] On the causes of the revolt, see Porath, *The Palestinian Arab*; A. W. Kayyali, *Palestine: A Modern History* (London, 1978); Ann Mosely Lesch, *Arab Politics in Palestine, 1917–1939* (Ithaca, 1979); Ghassan Kanafani, *The 1936–39 Revolt in Palestine* (Committee for a Democratic Palestine, n.d.); Tom Bowden, "The Politics of Arab Rebellion in Palestine 1936–1939," *Middle Eastern Studies*, 11 (1975), pp. 147–74; ʿAbd al-Qadir Yasin, *Kifah al-shaʿb al-filastini qabl al-ʿamm 1948* (Beirut, 1975); Theodore Swedenburg, "The 1936–39 Revolt in Palestine: Ideology and History," unpublished paper (University of Texas at Austin, Jan. 2, 1983).

fringes of open revolt." By 1936 Palestine found herself in the throes of a popular uprising, the intensity of which had not previously been experienced in the Arab East.

This growing restiveness clearly alarmed the traditional Arab leadership, now faced with new class forces threatening to break out of the established political framework of factionalism.

> The ascendance of young militants . . . combined with the unrest of the peasantry in turn forced the notable leadership to react more vigorously to the deepening crisis caused by massive Zionist immigration, a peasantry threatened with bankruptcy and dispossession in the lowland plains, and the unwillingness of the British government to grant Palestinian Arabs even a modicum of self-rule.[11]

The valiant but unsuccessful effort of a popular Muslim religious shaykh of Syrian provenance, 'Izz al-Din al-Qassam, to spark an armed peasant uprising around Haifa in November 1935 led this Arab leadership to adopt, albeit uncomfortably, a less accommodating approach toward the British.[12] A showdown was inevitable and it took the form of a General Strike starting in April 1936. That the strike drew its inspiration from the one in Syria earlier that year seems certain.

The immediate and spontaneous popular support in Syria for the Palestinian Arabs in 1936 had much to do with a heightened political awareness of the importance of Palestine to the future of the Arab world. By the mid-1930s, Syrians had acquired the same fear that the Palestinian Arabs had about the Zionists being in a much better position than ever before to create their own independent state and, in the process, to erect yet another obstacle to Arab unity. Syrians also feared that a Jewish state, with its expertise and powerful ties to the West, would eventually jeopardize the future of neighboring territories. From an economic standpoint, Zionist enterprises posed a potential danger to the Syrian economy. By this time, the valuable Syrian transit trade faced intense competition from a developing Palestinian transit trade, especially with Iraq, which was associated with the dramatic growth of the port of Haifa as a serious competitor to Beirut.[13] As Syria slowly developed a modern industrial base in the 1930s, she faced the more dynamic industrial movement in the increasingly separate Jewish sector of Palestine's economy. Syrian businessmen, particularly those involved in the cloth-weaving

[11] Swedenburg, "The 1936–39 Revolt," p. 28.

[12] Porath, *Palestinian Arab*, pp. 142–43.

[13] See FO 371/1247, vol. 17946. Havard to Simon, 14 Feb. 1934; FO 371/2883, vol. 19002. Rendel Memorandum, 28 May 1935; FO 371/7527, vol. 19024. Havard to FO, 20 Dec. 1935.

and confectionery industries, all along had supported Arab boycotts of Jewish products both in Palestine and locally. Of course, there were Syrian merchants interested in promoting trade with the Jewish economy and indeed trade went on virtually uninterrupted until the late 1930s. Some even accepted the idea that Zionist economic enterprise could lead to a mutually beneficial relationship through the extension of Jewish expertise and capital. But this was a minority view.

As for radical pan-Arabists in Syria, they welcomed a large-scale revolt at this time. It had the potential to cause a setback to British interests, perhaps leading to Britain's withdrawal and possibly precipitating a French withdrawal from the region as well. As conditions for a new World War ripened with the rise of Nazi Germany, nationalist leaders throughout the Arab East, including Egypt, could not conceal their hopes that both imperial powers might lose their grip on the region. But in 1936, with Syria and Egypt bound by treaties or the promise of treaties, and Iraq already a member of the League of Nations, Palestine held out the only real chance for such a revolt.

Although the Syrian people were only beginning to recover from their own General Strike, they extended support immediately to Palestine. Apart from the natural ties of kinship, culture, and politics between Syria and Palestine, Syrians could not easily forget that the strongest outside support they had received during their strike came from Palestine. There, several large demonstrations and strikes in solidarity with the Syrian masses were sponsored by the pan-Arab Istiqlal Party and different Muslim religious groups. Money and flour were collected for the victims of the Syrian strike and telegrams were sent to Syria expressing the solidarity of the people of "southern Syria," a term still in fashion in radical nationalist circles in Palestine and Syria.[14] The Syrian strike was an event closely followed in Palestine where the Arab leadership had been unable to register any significant concessions from the British mandatory authorities on the question of restricting Jewish immigration (which had been accelerating since 1933) and land sales to Jews. Just as the Syrian nationalists had derived inspiration from the Wafd in Egypt, Palestinian nationalists could not but notice that the use of militant tactics seemed to bring favorable political results.

Syrian aid to the Arab Revolt in Palestine took several forms. To start with, there was considerable media support. The Syrian propaganda machine launched a war of words through pamphlets and anti-British and

[14] George Antonius File, no. 17. Antonius Memorandum (Jerusalem), 8 Feb. 1936, Middle East Centre, St. Antony's College, Oxford; FO 371/1293, vol. 20018. Palestine CID to Colonial Office, 18 Feb. 1936.

anti-Zionist petitions and letters to the British Consulate in Damascus, the High Commission in Palestine, London, and the League of Nations. Most active on this front was Fakhri al-Barudi's Bureau for National Propaganda.

Strikes and demonstrations were another expression of moral solidarity with Palestine and these were frequent in the late 1930s. At the forefront of such activities was the League of National Action and various Islamic benevolent societies (jam'iyyat), which were the prototype for the Syrian Muslim Brotherhood.[15] A Palestine Defense Committee was hurriedly established in Damascus to coordinate all support efforts in Syria. Headed at first by Yusuf al-'Issa, it was taken over in the spring of 1937 by more experienced members of the Syrian Istiqlal Party whom the French, much to the dismay of the British, had recently amnestied.[16]

As for material aid to Palestine, in the first month of the strike the Palestine Defense Committee reportedly sent £S 4,500 and contributions increased significantly in the months ahead. A variety of voluntary associations led by the Islamic societies conducted fund-raising drives in the Syrian towns.[17] Women were noticeably active, contributing jewelry and participating in solidarity demonstrations.[18] Palestine Day activities were especially successful.[19] Meanwhile, arms smuggling to Palestine was on the upswing.

Another way in which Syrians demonstrated their solidarity was by boycotting Jewish products; however, the enforcement of a boycott of British goods was less successful.[20] In the late summer of 1937, the Palestine Defense Committee sponsored a major pan-Arab Congress at Bludan which helped to launch the second and most intense stage of the rebellion. The Syrian government, by that time under National Bloc control, immediately granted (in spite of strong British protestations) political asylum to numerous Palestinian leaders and guerillas who escaped the British dragnet. Meanwhile, Syrians continued to smuggle arms and

[15] On the emergence of jam'iyyat, see Chapter 23. Muslim societies in Egypt, most notably the Muslim Brotherhood, were instrumental in organizing support for the Palestinian Arabs during the revolt. See Gershoni, The Emergence, p. 37.

[16] In 1938 the Defense Committee included Nabih al-'Azma (President), Lutfi al-Haffar, Sabri al-'Asali, Fa'iz al-Khuri, Fakhri al-Barudi, 'Afif Sulh, Bashir Shihabi, Hajj Adib Khayr (Treasurer), Muhammad al-Sarraj, and Fu'ad Mufarrij (Secretary). Nabih al-'Azma Papers [Syria], File 6/383, 1938.

[17] Oriente Moderno, 16 (1936), pp. 399, 565.

[18] FO 684/10/1692/2. Davis to FO, 9 Oct. 1937; R. Tresse, "Manifestations féminines à Damas aux XIXᵉ et XXᵉ siècles," Entretiens sur l'évolution des pays de civilisation arabe, III (Paris, 1939), 115–25.

[19] Oriente Moderno, 18 (1938), p. 293.

[20] Ibid., 18 (1938), p. 292.

guerillas into Palestine, and Syrians were leaders of some of the most effective guerilla bands.

Although Syrian activities on behalf of the Palestinian Arabs escalated as soon as the General Strike began to take hold in Palestine,[21] these revealed contradictory developments. From the rebellion's start, the natural impulse of the Syrian people to assist the Palestinians conflicted with the objective political and economic interests of Syria's intertwined political and commercial elites, in particular those resident in Damascus. This conflict lasted for the duration of the revolt and obstructed the flow of Syrian assistance to Palestine.

During the initial phase of the revolt (the period of the General Strike) two major factors—one economic and the other diplomatic—contributed to the reluctance of nationalist circles in Syria to mobilize fully behind Palestine. From an economic perspective, the Palestine strike, coming as it did at the tail end of a paralyzing Syrian strike that had severely damaged Syria's economy, posed a serious danger. The strike severely impeded trade since Palestine was Syria's (and Lebanon's) most valuable export market, causing heavy losses to local merchants. The inability of Palestinian agents to repay their bills as they fell due aggravated the situation.[22] Indeed, for many Syrian merchants the timing of the strike could not have been worse: the Syrian economy had yet to rebound from the Syrian strike and, to compound matters, as the rebellion spread in Palestine during the summer and fall of 1936, Syria faced an unusually poor grain harvest and a new devaluation of the Syrian pound, after a decade of relative stability. The inaccessibility of the Palestinian market in this period, while not the principal cause of Syria's economic plight, certainly contributed to it. In Damascus, some of the leading merchants and industrialists trading with Palestine were also active supporters of the National Bloc. Almost from the beginning of the strike, they counseled Bloc chiefs to apply pressure on the Palestinian leadership to end it.

The other major factor restraining the National Bloc was the fear that the rebellion might jeopardize Syria's current diplomatic activities in France. This fear assumed two dimensions. Above all, nationalist leaders feared that full and open support for the revolt would ultimately alienate the British, whose backing at this time or at some later date might help to finalize negotiations with the French. Britain was, after all, the most influential imperial power in the Arab East and Syrian leaders did not wish to burn their bridges with London. These same leaders also feared that

---

[21] FO 684/9/1956/2. F.C. Ogden Memorandum (Damascus), 21 Aug. 1936.

[22] FO 371/6898, vol. 20069. Furlonge to Eden, 22 Oct. 1936. The irony, of course, is that during the Syrian strike, the Palestinian market absorbed a considerable amount of Syria's surplus, helping to ease the pressures which that strike caused.

the revolt might spark a revolutionary situation that could spill over into Syria.[23] An upheaval at the moment when Syrian prospects for independence were better than at any other time since the French occupation of Syria was politically unthinkable. Moreover, the National Bloc had staked its future on a peaceful resolution of Franco-Syrian relations through a treaty.

Nevertheless, sympathy for the Palestinian cause was undeniably strong in Syria and it reached up into the highest ranks of the nationalist elite. In 1936, Palestine received much more than lip service from its Arab neighbors, and especially from Syria, but with negotiations going full steam ahead in Paris, the National Bloc regarded any call for pan-Arab solidarity as inconvenient at best, and as calamitous at worst.

The National Bloc immediately recognized that it had to find a way to reduce the potential dangers of the Palestine rebellion to Syria. But to do so required great discretion, for no external issue aroused the passions of the Syrian masses more than the question of Palestine. Furthermore, the Bloc leadership was not in full agreement over how to deal with Palestine. The British Consul in Damascus, whose task it was to discourage Syrian involvement, was perhaps overly optimistic when he reported that at a secret meeting in the capital in late April 1936, the Bloc leadership, while openly expressing its sympathy with Palestine, decided to quietly counsel the curtailment of anti-British activities there so that they might not interfere in any way with the treaty negotiations.[24] Whether this decision was unanimously approved is unknown, but it would seem unlikely, since the acting President of the Bloc at the time was Shukri al-Quwwatli, the leader of the Bloc's radical pan-Arab wing in Damascus.

There is considerable evidence that Quwwatli and his Istiqlali network of pan-Arabists still in exile in Palestine and elsewhere were actively campaigning on behalf of Palestine at this time. Moreover, their activities proved indispensable to Palestinian strikers and rebels. Once the rebellion erupted, Quwwatli used his position in the National Bloc and his growing influence with the young, militant League of National Action, whose leaders he was simultaneously wooing, to collect funds in Damascus and other towns. These contibutions he secretly transferred to Nabih al-ʿAzma, in exile in Jerusalem, who passed them to the Palestinian leadership, the Arab Higher Committee.[25] Meanwhile, ʿAzma's older brother, ʿAdil, in exile in Amman, was a leading arms distributor for the revolt.

---

[23] These same fears were expressed in Egypt: see Coury, "Who Invented," part 2, p. 463; and in Transjordan: see Wilson, *King Abdullah*, Chapter 7.

[24] FO 371/2177, vol. 20065. MacKereth to High Commissioner (Palestine), 21 April 1936.

[25] Nabih al-ʿAzma Papers [Syria], File 4/147. Shukri al-Quwwatli to Nabih al-ʿAzma, 4 June 1936.

He headed a small group of Syrian and Transjordanian Istiqlalis who supplied weapons stored in Irbid and Ma'an to representatives of the Mufti,
and at rock-bottom prices, according to the Jewish Agency.[26] Whether a
source of these arms was Saudi Arabia, where Istiqlali sympathizers were
prominently placed in Meccan religious circles and in Ibn Sa'ud's administration, is not known, but it would not be unlikely given what is known
about the Istiqlali network and, in particular, Quwwatli's ties to the
House of Sa'ud.[27] In any case, the 'Azma brothers and Quwwatli had
long experience in this kind of activity, much of it acquired during the
Great Syrian Revolt of 1925.[28] That Quwwatli was active in solidarity
work, despite the reluctance of Bloc moderates to become too involved in
the Palestine imbroglio, suggests that the Bloc's Palestine policy would
eventually create awkward problems for its leadership. Syrian nationalists were torn between ideological belief and personal ambition, between
the natural attraction of pan-Arabism and the increasingly powerful pull
of Syrian provincialism.

IN THE FIRST STAGE of the rebellion, the British do not appear to have been
particularly alarmed by Syrian aid to Palestine. British Intelligence
sources only began to acknowledge a significant movement between Syria
and Palestine in July 1936, when they reported that Syrian ex-army officers were reorganizing the loose network of rebel bands in Palestine. In
August, one of the heroes of the Great Syrian Revolt, Fawzi al-Qawuqji,
himself an ex-Syrian Legion captain, arrived in Palestine from Iraq where
he immediately declared himself the Commander-in-Chief of "the Arab
Revolution in Southern Syria."[29] The recently established Palestine Defense Committee in Iraq had sent Qawuqji—it appears at the instruction
of 'Adil al-'Azma in Amman and Mu'in al-Madi, a member of the Palestinian Istiqlal party leading efforts to recruit guerillas and collect arms
and money in Syria at the time. Soon after Qawuqji's arrival, 650 armed
recruits, mostly from the lower classes of the Maydan and Kurdish quarters in Damascus, plus another 50 volunteers, many from notable families in Homs—the major stronghold of the League of National Action—
entered Palestine.[30] By early September, a number of Syrians had as-

[26] CZA (Central Zionist Archives, Jerusalem), 525/10/22. Dr. Joseph to Mr. Sasson, 1
July 1937.
[27] MAE, Syrie–Liban 1930–40. "Dossier," 22 Aug. 1936, vol. 493, pp. 201–3.
[28] See Chapter 9.
[29] Kayyali, Palestine, p. 198; Filastin fi mudhakkirat al-Qawuqji 1936–1948, vol. 2, ed.
Khayriyya al-Qasimiyya (Beirut, 1975).
[30] FO 371/5149, vol. 20069. Ogden to FO, 14 Aug. 1936; FO 371/6709, vol. 20069.
MacKereth to FO, 15 Aug. 1936; Alif ba', no. 4696 (15 Aug. 1936); MAE, Syrie–Liban
1930–40, "Dossier," 21 Aug. 1936, vol. 493, pp. 201–3.

sumed the command of rebel bands in Palestine. Some came with prior experience acquired during the Great Syrian Revolt: best known among them was Shaykh Muhammad al-Ashmar, a popular religious figure from the Maydan quarter of Damascus who had close ties to the Hashemites in Transjordan.[31]

Although British representatives admitted that the arrival of Qawuqji and other Syrians in Palestine caused a perceptible improvement in "rebel tactics" and the bands began to show "signs of effective leadership and organization,"[32] their dispatches suggest that, apart from a few demonstrations, reams of printed propaganda, and the requisite rhetoric in the name of Palestine, the Syrian attitude and contribution to the revolt remained rather subdued by the autumn of 1936. That the National Bloc acted rather halfheartedly toward Palestine during the first phase of the revolt seems plausible. Syria, after all, had yet to recover from her own exhausting strike, and negotiations in Paris absorbed her leaders. And it was not long after the nationalist delegation returned to Syria that the Arab Higher Committee finally called off its strike. In any case, faced with preparations for national elections and the problems of forming Syria's first nationalist government, the National Bloc would not be free to turn its attention to Palestine until the beginning of 1937.[33]

Yet, the evidence also suggests that as long as Quwwatli was in charge of Bloc activities in Syria, he and his Istiqlali comrades consistently aided the Palestinian nationalist leadership. For Quwwatli, the disturbances in Palestine could not have been more timely. Although he had devoted much attention in recent years to channeling pan-Arab sentiments in Syria to his political advantage, he nevertheless advocated a Franco-Syrian Treaty, and therefore saw it as his duty to prevent disaffected Syrian radicals from upsetting the negotiations. Events in Palestine conveniently diverted their attention from National Bloc activities in Paris where radicals suspected that the Syrian delegation might strike some unsavory deal. By tooting the Palestinian horn, Quwwatli not only boosted his own image as a dedicated pan-Arabist, but he also took advantage of the absence of his Bloc colleagues to better situate himself for the various factional struggles ahead.

There is no evidence to suggest that the Syrian nationalist leadership actually pressured the Mufti and the Arab Higher Committee to end the strike in 1936. But the British government made concerted efforts in the summer and fall of 1936 to convince Arab leaders, including ʿAbdullah, Ibn Saʿud, Nahhas Pasha of Egypt, and Nuri Saʿid of Iraq, to apply such

[31] Faris, *Man huwa 1949*, p. 27; al-Jundi, *Tarikh*, p. 561.
[32] Kayyali, *Palestine*, p. 199.
[33] FO 371/6716, vol. 20066. Ogden to Eden, 3 Oct. 1936.

pressures on the Palestinian leadership, which they did.[34] Why the British did not consult Syrian leaders as well is not entirely clear; but it may have been because there was not yet a representative government in Syria, with influence among Palestinian leaders, to which the British could turn. This was not the case after the National Bloc took office at the end of the year, but by then the Arab Higher Committee had already called off the strike.

When the Arab Higher Committee called off the General Strike in October 1936 and then finally agreed a few months later to testify before the British Royal [Peel] Commission investigating the causes of the disturbances in Palestine, a lull fell over the country for nearly a year. Fighting continued in parts of Palestine but not with the intensity witnessed in the summer of 1936 or after the Peel Commission released its report a year later. During this respite, Syrian rebel leaders, including Qawuqji and Ashmar, left Palestine along with many of their fighters.[35]

<h2 style="text-align:center">Zionist Pressures</h2>

If the British were not unduly alarmed by Syrian activities on behalf of Palestine in 1936, the Zionists were, and they actively tried to influence individual National Bloc leaders to call for restraint both in Syria and in Palestine. In the course of treaty negotiations, members of the Jewish Agency paid frequent visits to Syrian and other Arab political leaders in Paris and Damascus to explore the problem of Arab-Jewish relations and to learn more about internal developments and forces in the Arab countries. Among the Agency members engaged in such activities were Chaim Weizmann, David Ben Gurion, Moshe Shertok [Sharett], and Eliahu Epstein [Elath]. Some of the leaders they visited included several National Bloc leaders: Jamil Mardam, Shukri al-Quwwatli, Fakhri al-Barudi, Nasib al-Bakri, Fa'iz al-Khuri, and Lutfi al-Haffar. The Jewish Agency also approached influential Syrian political exiles such as Dr. Shahbandar, Shakib Arslan, Ihsan al-Jabiri, and the Druze chieftain, Sultan al-Atrash.[36]

French sources reported that in June 1936, Chaim Weizmann held a secret meeting with Jamil Mardam in Paris—Mardam failed to inform his

---

[34] See Porath, *Palestinian Arab*, pp. 119–216, and Wilson, *King Abdullah*, Chapter 7.

[35] FO 371/697, vol. 20848. MacKereth to Eden, 5 Jan. 1937.

[36] A list of conversations which Jewish Agency representatives had with Arab leaders in 1935–36 on Jewish-Arab relations and internal developments in the Arab countries can be found in CZA, S25/3051. (n.d.). I am indebted to Mary C. Wilson for making available copies of various reports and memoranda by members of the Jewish Agency on the subject of Syria and the revolt in Palestine. For further details on the role of the Jewish Agency, see Porath, *Palestinian Arab*, pp. 271–73.

colleagues on the Syrian delegation beforehand—at which the Zionist leader proposed a Jewish-Arab accord and asked Mardam to use his influence with other Arab leaders to achieve their goal. Mardam, who personally favored Weizmann's proposal, hoped to get Zionist backing in return for his support.[37]

A month later, Jewish Agency representatives were in Damascus trying to reduce Syrian activities in Palestine. The focus of their attention appeared to be Fakhri al-Barudi. In his capacity as a member of the National Bloc Central Committee, patron of its paramilitary youth organization, the Steel Shirts, and director of the Bureau for National Propaganda, Barudi was probably the most respected political leader in Syria at this time. In mid-July, Eliahu Epstein, a young member of the Agency's Arab Affairs Department, and a recent graduate of the American University of Beirut, paid a visit to Barudi who was summering on his estate in Duma.[38] Epstein's account of their meeting (they had met once before in Palestine) is interesting: it reveals Zionist concern with Syrian participation in the Palestine Revolt and the kinds of subtle enticements the Jewish Agency seemed prepared to offer Syrian leaders to bring about its halt.

Barudi initiated the discussion by attributing the disturbances in Palestine to increasing Jewish immigration and economic activity. Epstein politely disagreed with his host and then shifted the subject to concessions the Zionists could grant the Arabs at this stage: Jewish immigration would not exceed Palestine's ability to absorb immigrants; Jews would not force Arab peasants off lands purchased by Jews; and Jews would not attempt to repress the Arab population politically provided the Arabs did not repress the Jews. He added that the Jews were "interested in the material and spiritual development of the Arabs in order to narrow the differences between both peoples and thus to ensure the development of the country [Palestine] as a whole." He said that "Zionism considers the national awakening . . . among the Arabs as a natural phenomenon," but that he expected the Syrians

> who strive for national emancipation, to understand and appreciate the difficulties of establishing national independence because such an establishment requires many material and spiritual resources . . . in the first place it requires good relations with . . . neighbors and internal peace. And on the basis of such mutual understanding the Jews will be ready to help Arab nationalists in a constitutional re-

---

[37] MAE, Syrie–Liban 1930–40. Bargeton Telegram (Paris), 17 June 1936, vol. 492, p. 227. It is not entirely clear who first proposed the Mardam–Weizmann meeting.

[38] American University of Beirut, *Directory of Alumni Affairs 1870–1952* (Beirut, 1953), p. 235.

spect, i.e., to establish their independence and to forward the development of Arab countries.[39]

Epstein then lamented "how the Arabs did not appreciate the importance of the Zionist movement for the development of the Middle East," and suggested that Syrian nationalists should develop such an appreciation since they "are both neighbors and leaders of the Arab nationalist movement."[40]

Barudi responded candidly that in the case of the disturbances in Palestine,

> I did all I could to calm things down. Thousands of people wanted to go from Syria to Palestine to help their brethren but we [nationalist leaders] prevented them from doing so. We sabotaged many attempts to smuggle arms. This smuggling is done by people who profit from it and are not inspired by national motives. We also defended Syrian Jews from attacks by the press and the street mob. As to the clashes themselves, no power in the world can put an end to them without certain preconditions—even the Prophet Muhammad cannot do this . . . The slogans which are raised now and around which the struggle takes place are, 'an end to immigration.' And the Arab leaders cannot stop the clashes unless some gain is made in regard to stopping immigration. You [Zionists] are very enlightened and farsighted people. You must make the first signal and the Arab leaders will reciprocate. If you only promise to accept this condition then together with other Syrian leaders . . . we will intervene with the Palestinian leaders. Otherwise, we will not be able to take upon ourselves such a task.[41]

Obviously unable to reconcile his movement's differences with Barudi's interpretation of events, Epstein shifted the discussion to his forthcoming trip to Paris. Barudi promised to send him a letter of introduction to the Syrian delegation there. Epstein then asked Barudi if he could do anything to assist the delegation. Barudi said that Epstein should tell the French not to repeat their mistakes, because an "unprecedented uprising will breakout if the delegation returns empty-handed." Barudi, in turn, promised to report their meeting to the National Bloc and to discuss Epstein's suggestions on how to improve relations between Arabs and Jews. Barudi then concluded the meeting by suggesting that if the Jewish Agency helped the Syrian delegation in Paris then Arab leaders could use

---

[39] CZA, S25/9783. Minutes of Conversation with Fakhri Bey al-Barudi at Duma (near Damascus) on 17 July 1936.
[40] *Ibid.*
[41] *Ibid.*

this gesture as a proof of Jewish sympathy and good-will, in spite of the latest clashes between Jews and Palestinian Arabs.[42]

Fakhri al-Barudi reported his conversation with Epstein to the National Bloc leadership and there was enough interest to warrant another meeting. It took place in the summer resort of Bludan in the hills west of Damascus on August 1. Representing the Bloc's Central Committee were Barudi, Shukri al-Quwwatli, and Lutfi al-Haffar. Epstein headed a three-man delegation from the Jewish Agency. From the start, Barudi made it clear that the purpose of the meeting was to gather "further information" from the Jewish Agency, on the basis of which the Bloc would decide "whether or not to begin official negotiations." But he also affirmed that with this meeting the question of Jewish-Arab relations "had now left the stage of personal conversations and has entered into its formal phase." The National Bloc considered the meeting "official."[43]

Epstein took the opportunity to elaborate some of the points he had made privately to Barudi about the national aspirations of the Jewish people, their compatibility with Arab national aspirations, the benefits the Arabs could expect by cooperating with the Jews, and the critical role Syria should play in bringing about a Jewish-Arab accord. He added little that was new to his pitch.

Shukri al-Quwwatli, in his capacity as Acting President of the National Bloc, handled the Syrian response. Favorably impressed by the depth of Epstein's understanding of the Arab national movement, he prefaced his remarks by stating that "we sincerely wish that we may come to an understanding with you on our own accord and not by means of cannon and fire."[44] But then he offered some criticisms of Epstein's analysis. He questioned the Jews' claim to Palestine on the ground of historical connections 2,000 years earlier, asking what if "we [the Arabs] claimed Andalusia on similar grounds." He went on to say that "what makes the problem still more complicated and acute is the ignorance in which you leave us as to the exact interpretation and meaning of . . . a National Home." He asked whether the Jewish Agency intends

> to make of Palestine a Jewish National Home or to make a Jewish National Home in Palestine. If the former, then we are categorically opposed to it and there is no way to come to an understanding. But if it means the latter then we are ready . . . to find a solution to the mutual advantage of both parties . . .[45]

[42] *Ibid.*
[43] CZA, S25/10093. Minutes of the Meeting with the Arab National Bloc of Syria (Arab Nationalist Party) at Bludan (near Damascus) on 1 August 1936.
[44] *Ibid.*
[45] *Ibid.*

Quwwatli then concluded by stating that the Syrian independence movement has "always borne high the flag of Arab independence" but that if
Syria were to get her independence first then she could devote her attention to the question of Arab independence and an "Arab-Jewish entente."
He suggested to Epstein and his colleagues that the Jews should therefore
"help us in every way to gain this independence, which would also be of
real advantage to you." Epstein in turn thanked the National Bloc leaders
and announced that "the Executive of the Jewish Agency . . . has appointed an official delegation which will soon proceed to Damascus and
join us in our further deliberations."[46]
      Whether another round of official meetings between the National Bloc
and the Jewish Agency ever took place is not entirely clear. But, for the
Agency to have significantly improved Syrian-Zionist relations, it would
have had to intervene on behalf of the National Bloc with the French government before the conclusion of the treaty negotiations in Paris in early
September. It seems unlikely that this happened. In retrospect, the various conversations between the Jewish Agency and the National Bloc do
not appear to have amounted to much. Barudi and Quwwatli were not
persuaded by the Agency's arguments. The forces that combined to exercise leverage over the Bloc's approach to Palestine were mainly associated with the Syrian economy and, above all, with the treaty. And although it is possible that some National Bloc chiefs believed the Zionists
had direct influence with the French Prime Minister, Léon Blum, because
he was both a Jew and a socialist, this thesis was quickly disproven in
practice.

BRITISH PRESSURES

British pressures to halt Syrian aid to Palestine only began to be felt by
nationalist leaders in the spring of 1937, several months after the formation of the National Bloc government. Throughout the period of the revolt, Britain's relations with the Syrian leadership were maintained almost exclusively by Colonel Gilbert MacKereth, the British Consul in
Damascus. One historian, a severe critic of the behavior and abilities of
many British officials who operated in the Middle East during and after
World War I, has written of MacKereth that "he was one of the shrewdest
and most knowledgeable of British representatives in the Middle East—
perhaps even the most intelligent and the soundest of judgment during
this particular period (1936–1939)."[47] Indeed, MacKereth's dispatches

[46] Ibid.
[47] Elie Kedourie, "The Bludan Congress on Palestine, September 1937," Middle Eastern
Studies, 17 (Jan. 1981), p. 108.

from Damascus were not only perceptive and exacting, reflecting his familiarity with the politics of nationalism and above all with the social and political habits of the Syrian upper class, but they were also scathing and witty, enough so to annoy his seniors at Whitehall.[48]

MacKereth's first opportunity to intervene with the Syrian government came in May 1937, when he met with Prime Minister Jamil Mardam, with whom he was on "very good terms,"[49] and who was one of the few nationalists he sincerely admired on the grounds that he was "popular," "ambitious," "skilful," and had an "agreeable personality."[50] Despite their disagreement over whether Syrian fighters in Palestine were "brigands" (as MacKereth contested) or "patriots" (as Mardam assured him), Mardam promised that the British ". . . could count on the energetic co-operation of his government in repressing, within the boundaries of the [Syrian] republic, any activities or plotting hostile to British administration in Palestine." Mardam also added that his government would not "shirk their international responsibilities. He and his colleagues certainly feared for their Arab brothers south of the border [in Palestine] but they had to think of Syria first, and he for his part was most anxious to live on the best of terms with Great Britain."[51]

The British did not find the need to press the issue of Syrian support to Palestine until the following month, after "rumors regarding the recommendations of the Peel Commission became more persistent." The Mufti had already visited Damascus on June 27, where he discussed the idea of fusing the Palestine Istiqlal Party with the Syrian National Bloc and the "impending scheme for the partition of Palestine." According to MacKereth, Hajj Amin al-Husayni sought National Bloc support against his political rivals in Palestine. Meanwhile, Amir ʿAbdullah, eager to keep a finger in the affairs of Palestine, sent two agents from Amman to Damascus to shadow the Mufti.[52] One outcome of the Mufti's visit was the decision to convene a pan-Arab congress in order to rally Arab forces against the idea of partition, which the British were rumored to have decided upon.

In early July, the Peel Commission published its recommendations: the abandonment of the British Mandate and the partition of the country into a Jewish state and an Arab state which might be merged with Transjordan. A day after the report's release, the Arab Higher Committee re-

---

[48] Perhaps most interesting were MacKereth's brief personality reports completed in 1936 and revised and updated in 1937, in which few Syrian politicians were spared his caustic wit. See FO 371/2142, vol. 20849. "Personalities," 6 May 1937.

[49] FO 371/2579, vol. 20840. MacKereth to Eden, 5 May 1937.

[50] FO 371/2142, vol. 20849. "Personalities," 6 May 1937.

[51] FO 371/2579, vol. 20850. MacKereth to Eden, 5 May 1937.

[52] FO 684/10/58/1. MacKereth to Eden, 1 July 1937.

jected it and the Mufti appealed to the Arab states and to nationalist groups to support this decision. From his perspective, the partition scheme redounded to the benefit of the Zionists and his arch rival, Amir ʿAbdullah, who was the only Arab ruler to endorse the report.[53]

In order to rally Arab public opinion, the Mufti activated the idea of a pan-Arab congress, "to increase the pressure both on the British and Arab government."[54] The congress was held at Bludan in the second week of September. The principal organizer of the congress, which attracted over 400 nationalist leaders from Syria, Lebanon, Iraq, Palestine, Transjordan, Egypt, and Saudi Arabia, was the Palestine Defense Committee in Damascus, now headed by Nabih al-ʿAzma who, along with several other radical nationalist leaders, had been amnestied in April.[55] ʿAzma had been the main go-between for radical pan-Arabists in Palestine, especially the Istiqlalis, many of whom had taken refuge in Damascus from British security forces in Palestine.[56]

On the eve of the Bludan Congress, Consul MacKereth intervened again with the nationalist government in Damascus, this time to ensure that no official Syrian delegate be sent to Bludan. He also took the occasion to remind Jamil Mardam of their previous conversation in May and of his suggestion then that "an unfortunate impression might be made were the Syrian government to take part in discussion concerning the internal affairs of a neighbouring and friendly country." But just to make certain that Mardam got the message, MacKereth "shared his fears with the French Delegate who spoke emphatically to the P.M. [Mardam], explaining that it would be embarrassing to France were a member of the Syrian government to attend the Congress." As a result of MacKereth's démarches, "no official delegate was present."[57] Nevertheless, a number of prominent Syrians were at Bludan and played a leading role in its organization and deliberations, including members of the Central Committee of the National Bloc and its paramilitary Steel Shirts, who handled security.[58]

Although the Bludan Congress was "a landmark in the increasing involvement of the Arab world in the Palestine problem,"[59] its resolutions

[53] Wilson, *King Abdullah*, Chapter 7.

[54] Kedourie, "Bludan," p. 107.

[55] FO 684/10/1692/2. MacKereth Memorandum (to Eden), 14 Sept. 1937; FO 371/2142, vol. 20849, 6 May 1937; al-Jundi, *Tarikh*, p. 541.

[56] FO 684/10/1692/2. MacKereth to Eden, 14 Sept. 1937; Nabih al-ʿAzma Papers [Syria], File 4/146. Quwwatli to ʿAzma, 25 May 1936. Porath, *Palestinian Arab*, pp. 243–44.

[57] FO 684/10/1692/2. MacKereth to Eden, 14 Sept. 1937.

[58] *Al-Ayyam*, (Damascus), no. 1479 (9 Sept. 1937).

[59] Kedourie, "Bludan," p. 107. Additional information on the Bludan Congress can be found in R. Montagne, "Réactions arabes contre le Sionisme," *Entretiens sur l'évolution des pays de civilisation arabe, III* (Paris, 1939), pp. 43–55. *Al-Ayyam*, no. 1479 (9 Sept.

were surprisingly mild in their criticism of Britain, though "vehemently anti-Zionist" and categorically opposed to the Peel Commission recommendations. This moderation can be attributed to the role of certain Arab politicians who were quite well-disposed to the British government.[60] Indeed, the mild tone officially adopted toward the British at Bludan so angered a large number of radical Syrian and Palestinian nationalists that they decided to convene a secret meeting early in the morning on the day after the Bludan Congress ended. It was held at the Damascus home of Hani Jallad, a former National Bloc stalwart and commission agent, where plans were discussed for escalating pan-Arab resistance in Palestine.[61] This meeting and others which followed it truly alarmed the British Consul. They foreshadowed a second stage of rebellion; indeed they served as final preparations for its launching.[62]

MacKereth's alarm increased during the early fall as members of the Arab Higher Committee and Istiqlal Party of Palestine piled into Damascus, where other leaders had already taken refuge. The British had declared martial law in Palestine, closed down the Arab Higher Committee and other nationalist associations, and issued arrest warrants after disturbances broke out again. Granted asylum and protection by the Syrian nationalist government, Palestinian exiles formed the "Central Committee of the Jihad" in Damascus headed by several Istiqlalis, including ʿIzzat Darwaza and Akram Zuʿaytir.[63] This committee took charge of the revolt's organization and had the close cooperation of the Syrian-led Palestine Defense Committee in the areas of fund-raising, arms purchases, the recruitment of Syrian volunteers, and the boycott of Jewish and British products. With the resumption of the rebellion, security on the borders slackened, and the smuggling of Syrian fighters and arms into Palestine increased. The complicity of the Syrian gendarmerie assigned to police the borders in aiding and abetting rebels received the full encouragement of the Syrian Interior Ministry, whose director was none other than ʿAdil al-ʿAzma.[64]

There is no doubt that the unattractive recommendations of the Peel Commission, coupled with the appearance of popular Palestinian leaders in Syria, intensified pro-Palestinian activity. That the radical wing of the National Bloc, led by Shukri al-Quwwatli, turned these pan-Arab senti-

1939) and no. 1477 (7 Sept. 1937); *Alif ba'*, no. 5001 (9 Sept. 1937); *The Palestine Post* (11 Sept. 1937).

[60] FO 371/684/10/1692/2. MacKereth Memorandum, 14 Sept. 1937.

[61] *Ibid.*

[62] Porath, *Palestinian Arab*, p. 232.

[63] *Ibid.*, pp. 242–43; conversation with Akram Zuʿaytir (Beirut, 11 Aug. 1975).

[64] FO 684/10/1692/2. Davis (Aleppo) to FO, 9 Oct. 1937; conversation with Zuʿaytir (Beirut, 11 Aug. 1975.)

ments to its advantage in its internal struggle with Bloc moderates is certain. Palestine was another thorn in the side of the already problem-ridden Mardam government.

Meanwhile, Colonel MacKereth intervened more actively and regularly with both the French authorities and the Syrian government. Immediately after the Bludan Congress, he assembled considerable documentation on the growing traffic in arms from Syria to Palestine and on preparations to enlist Syrians in rebel bands. He discovered that a gang of Palestinians belonging to the ʿIzz al-Din al-Qassam brotherhood was plotting from Damascus a series of assassinations in Palestine. MacKereth also obtained information on the recruitment of bands by two agents of the Mufti, Muʿin al-Madi and Fakhri ʿAbd al-Hadi, both Palestinian Istiqlalis. He presented this information to French authorities in Syria in a bid to have the most "dangerous" Palestinian plotters expelled from Syria to Palestine, a request which MacKereth cynically noted would most probably not "bear much fruit." His numerous meetings in the fall of 1937 with the French Delegate in the Syrian capital, Count Ostrorog, failed to achieve the desired results. Ostrorog told him "there seemed to be insuperable practical difficulties in carrying out the operations of expelling the undesirables."[65] French authorities did, however, order Muʿin al-Madi to leave Syria, but he was deported to Iraq where he received the protection of the Baghdad government.

At the same time, the British Ambassador in Paris also made a *démarche* at the Quai d'Orsay on the subject of Syrian involvement in the Palestine disturbances. In early October, Jamil Mardam, in a surprising public declaration, deplored the "terrorism" going on in Palestine, adding that the Syrian government, in concert with French and British authorities, "was taking all steps to prevent arms smuggling and rebels into Palestine." Although MacKereth acknowledged that Mardam's pronouncement "demanded considerable personal courage in face of violent pan-Arab and anti-Zionist feeling current in Syria," the Syrian Prime Minister was most probably prompted by the intervention of the French High Commissioner and, in any case, his declaration was only reported in the French language papers of Damascus, and was never "reproduced in the Arabic press."[66]

Less than a week after Mardam's announcement, MacKereth had established

> beyond a reasonable doubt that small bands of Syrians had been formed under group-leaders, had received earnest money in amounts varying between two and four Palestinian pounds, a rifle, a

[65] FO 684/10/2207/2. MacKereth to Eden, 19 Oct. 1937.
[66] *Ibid.*

few rounds of amunition, a warm *jalabieh*, and a water-bottle. They were only waiting a signal from Palestine to make their way across the frontier in parties of three or four to a rendez-vous somewhere in the Nablus hills.[67]

This evidence and other information that he had been accumulating since September prompted MacKereth to return to Ostrorog's office on October 12 with a number of proposals for French action to improve the situation. Ostrorog promised to notify the French High Commissioner and to "confront" the Syrian Prime Minister, which he did.[68]

The High Commissioner, also under pressure from Paris, sought to convince the Mardam government to end Syrian assistance to Palestine. But MacKereth was noticeably apprehensive that Syrian rebel leaders like Muhammad al-Ashmar would not obey the Syrian government and that the French would never be willing to accept a British request for direct French military intervention. That the French planned to drag their feet at this time is certain; they had not forgotten that the British "failed in 1925 . . . to show adequate sympathy with the difficulties the French had themselves in Syria at that time." As MacKereth reminded his superiors in London,

it is a noteworthy fact that the British authorities in Palestine and particularly in Trans-Jordan showed a hospitality to Syrian bandits and rebels which now we must ruefully regret. A sharp thorn in our side to-day is Mahomet al-Ashmar. A bandit chief . . . who was directly responsible for the death of two French officers and three French non-commissioned officers in 1925, he had a previous criminal record and was condemned to death by French court martial. He escaped in Palestine where we insisted on treating him as a political refugee. His case, like that of Fawzi Kawokji [al-Qawuqji], a deserter from the French forces, was only one of many. Most of those who then benefited from British asylum are now planning to go, or have already gone, to Palestine, to continue their acts of terrorism, this time directly against the British administration.[69]

"Faced with this dilemma," MacKereth chose the highly irregular course of, in his own words, "endeavouring to frighten the Syrian government into taking steps," to halt Syrian aid to rebel forces in Pales-

---

[67] *Ibid.*

[68] *Ibid.*

[69] *Ibid.* A British official in Lebanon and Syria during the interwar period claims that Amir 'Abdullah harbored Druze and other "agitators" during the Syrian Revolt and the French blamed the British for supporting this policy. Conversation with Sir Geoffrey Furlonge (London, 26 March 1975).

tine.[70] His opportunity came at an informal dinner party on October 17 at the Syrian Prime Minister's residence. He was able to discuss the situation with Mardam and two other members of his cabinet, Dr. 'Abd al-Rahman al-Kayyali and Shukri al-Quwwatli. Never one to mince his words, MacKereth immediately raised the question of Muhammad al-Ashmar and several well-known "political agitators" in Damascus. Mardam responded that he had only the day before "sent for and warned " Ashmar to stop meddling in the affairs of Palestine. But MacKereth already knew that Ashmar, on returning to his followers in the Maydan, a quarter in which the National Bloc had little influence,[71] had replied to Mardam that "he had no intention of being dictated to by the Syrian or any other government."[72]

MacKereth then opened up with his "threat" which he had designed to hit Mardam and his colleagues where it hurt the most, in the area of future British support for the completion of the treaty and the ultimate realization of Syrian independence. MacKereth prefaced his threat with the comment that "he had noticed . . . with growing concern for Syria many outspoken articles which had been recently appearing in the British press stating openly and with some truth . . . that troubles in Palestine were being actively fomented in Damascus." He suggested that "this rising anger in British public opinion was not only harming the Arab cause, of which perhaps England was its only western friend, but might in time strike vitally at Syrian independence itself." He then went on to say that even though "the British and French government had a united policy in the Near East as elsewhere . . . they [the British] would not, out of respect for France dream of opposing French plans for Syrian independence . . ." yet "public opinion in England had before now been lashed into a vehement fury such as had obliged the government radically to change its plans." He mentioned a "notable instance of this" that had occurred two years earlier (most probably the public outcry against the Hoare–Laval agreement over Ethiopia, which compelled Hoare to resign as Foreign Secretary) and added that he ". . . could readily conceive of a similar reaction were public disturbance to continue in Palestine where so much of its inspiration could be laid at the door of Syria." He concluded his démarche by suggesting that "one result of rising public opinion in England might conceivably be an uncompromising refusal to countenance the admission of Syria to the League of Nations."[73]

The British Consul left the party confident that he not only had stirred Mardam, who as always had assured him that notwithstanding the very

[70] Ibid.
[71] See Chapter 11.
[72] FO 684/10/2207/2. MacKereth to Eden, 18 Oct. 1937.
[73] Ibid.

real pressures of pan-Syrian and pan-Arab sentiment in Syria upon his government (which MacKereth naturally believed were exaggerated) that it would "make a very real effort" to end Syrian activities on behalf of Palestine, but that he had also shaken the hardliner Quwwatli out of his "complacency." In his dispatch to London recounting his evening at Mardam's, he remarked, with a touch of arrogance, that he left feeling that "[he] had sown the seeds of real alarm in their minds which would grow and embolden them to face public opinion to take some practical steps to stop the abuses. . . ."[74]

For a brief while his optimism seemed warranted. That very same evening he learned from the head of French Intelligence (Commandant Bonnet) that four emissaries were sent from Damascus to urge the Arabs in Palestine to halt their "terrorist" activities and that four Syrians who had been recruited in Damascus for action in Palestine had been arrested while trying to enter Transjordan from Syria, "a hitherto unheard of proceeding."[75] Not long after his most recent *démarche*, MacKereth could write his Foreign Secretary, Anthony Eden, that Syrian government actions had already produced a marked change in the position of the rebels, and that the situation no longer "presents the dangers it did a month ago."[76]

British intervention did have a lasting impact on the Syrian government. But it was not exactly what they had hoped for. Rather than clamping down on pro-Palestinian activities, the Mardam government tried to distance itself as much as possible from them. The pattern was familiar. Given the narrow area left for the government to maneuver in, this was the best that could be expected. The government responded to British pressure but within the domestic structural constraints imposed upon it.

DIVIDED LOYALTIES?

Other factors contributed to the position taken by the Syrian government vis-à-vis the revolt. To start with, the government was divided over how to treat the events in Palestine. While Jamil Mardam wanted to keep it out of the thick of things, Shukri al-Quwwatli did not. Quwwatli was a committed pan-Arabist and intimately tied to the radicals on the Palestine Defense Committee and the exiled Palestinian leadership. He resigned from the government in 1938, in part because he sensed that his own credibility had suffered by his identification with policies opposed by

---

[74] *Ibid.*
[75] *Ibid.*
[76] FO 684/10/2207/2. MacKereth to Eden, 25 Oct. 1937.

growing numbers of nationalists.[77] Among them was the government's Palestine policy. As long as he was part of the government he protected it against attacks by radicals in his own Istiqlal group and the young militants in the League of National Action. His departure now unleashed these forces against a beleaguered Mardam. No one realized more clearly than Quwwatli that, in order to prevent the traditional political framework in Syria from completely collapsing, the National Bloc government had to accommodate the interests of new, ascendant classes and forces, which by the late 1930s threatened to break out of that framework. He had staked his political future on his unrivalled influence with the young radicals, but if he continued to support the government even he might be swept aside. Mardam, on the other hand, had staked his own career on a policy of "honorable cooperation" with the French and believed that giving in to the radicals' demands would surely upset his delicate negotiations with the French.

Since taking over government, Jamil Mardam had purposely kept the National Bloc loosely organized so that none of his Bloc colleagues could use it to challenge him. But, by 1938, Quwwatli's resignation, a widening split in the Aleppo Bloc over whether to support Mardam, and the defection of several Bloc stalwarts to Dr. Shahbandar's camp virtually incapacitated the Bloc, which now looked like a skeleton of its former self.[78]

Shahbandar's return to politics in Damascus after his release from house arrest at Bludan, his large following among veterans of the Syrian Revolt of 1925, his longstanding pro-Hashemite and anti-Istiqlali stance,[79] his persistent criticisms of Mardam's collaboration with the French, and his known flirtations with the British made him suspect in the eyes of radical pan-Arabists, the Mardam government, and the French. Moreover, on the question of Palestine Shahbandar supported the ambitions of Amir ʿAbdullah, a position which was hardly considered more attractive than the Mardam government's. Yet, no Syrian politician rivalled Shahbandar in terms of his following among veterans of the Syrian Revolt of 1925. His ability and willingness in 1938 to discourage Syrian rebel leaders from continuing the struggle in Palestine[80] was an indication of his personal strength, something he did not hesitate to demonstrate daily before Mardam and his government.

Given the extent of internal opposition to Mardam's domestic policies in 1938, the events in Palestine actually served to divert some of the an-

[77] Quwwatli resigned in early March 1938. See L'Asie Française, no. 358 (March 1938), p. 93.

[78] Al-Mudhik al-mubki (Damascus), no. 400 (31 Dec. 1938), p. 14.

[79] See Chapter 9.

[80] Porath, Palestinian Arab, p. 244; conversation with Akram Zuʿaytir (Beirut, 11 Aug. 1975).

tagonism away from his government. The revolt's escalation at this time also relieved some of the pressures on Mardam. So did French reluctance to force his government to curtail pro-Palestinian activities in Syria. Since the Syrian Revolt of 1925, the French had wanted to even the score with the British and they quite enjoyed British discomfort in Palestine.

Therefore, up until the autumn of 1938 public support in Syria for the Palestine Revolt, even among National Bloc cadres, remained strong. Money flowed into the coffers of the Palestine Defense Committee from Syria and other Arab territories, the rest of the Muslim world, and the Americas as never before; more funds, arms and fighters were smuggled from Syria into Palestine; the wheels of anti-British and anti-Zionist propaganda turned faster; and boycotts of Jewish and British products organized by Muslim benevolent societies in the Syrian towns were never more successful.[81] But as the revolt lost its momentum, owing to divisions within its leadership command, to the attacks of "peace bands" organized by the rival Nashashibi faction (and supported by Amir ʿAbdullah and the British),[82] and, above all, to a massive British counteroffensive toward the end of 1938, pro-Palestinian activities in Syria also waned. By the end of the year solidarity groups, and especially the Palestine Defense Committee, were preoccupied with local Syrian politics. Nabih al-ʿAzma was reported to be diverting funds earmarked for Palestine to his Syrian Istiqlali comrades who, with a number of Muslim religious societies, were actively pressuring the Mardam government to resign.[83]

The French government's refusal to ratify the treaty of 1936, coupled with the French cession of Alexandretta to Turkey, had finally ruptured the National Bloc's policy of "honorable cooperation." With Franco-Syrian relations polarized, the British Army about to reconquer Palestine, and a new World War looming large, French authorities no longer found it advantageous to allow Syria to continue as a base for radical pan-Arab activities, in particular those associated with the revolt in Palestine. They had settled their score with the British and now saw greater advantage in emphasizing their historic alliance rather than their rivalry.[84] The arrest of Nabih al-ʿAzma in Damascus in the second week of March and other efforts to curtail the movement of Palestinian leaders in Damascus spread alarm among members of the Palestine Defense Committee, which

[81] MWT, *Dakhiliyya*, 72/547–1547. Sayf al-Din al-Maʾmun to Ministry of Interior (Damascus), 26 April 1938; *Oriente Moderno*, 18 (1938), p. 293; FO 371/6597, vol. 21914. MacKereth to Baxter, 28 Oct. 1938.
[82] Swedenburg, "The 1936–39 Revolt," pp. 36–38.
[83] FO 371/677, vol. 23276. MacKereth to Baxter, 20 Jan. 1939.
[84] Conversation with Akram Zuʿaytir (Beirut, 11 Aug. 1975).

quickly "lost its cohesion and unity."[85] Already the French authorities in Damascus had suspended publication of two radical nationalist newspapers controlled by the Defense Committee,[86] and encouraged a Syrian and Lebanese press campaign against the Mufti, with the object of discrediting the leaders of the revolt as little more than self-seekers.[87] These attacks and the publication of evidence that ʿAzma pilfered Defense Committee funds[88] sealed the fate of Palestinian activities in Syria. Soon thereafter, the Bureau for National Propaganda reduced its own press campaign[89] and the structure of pro-Palestinian organizations that had played such a decisive role in the prolongation of the revolt in Palestine disintegrated.

By the summer of 1939, with the simultaneous collapse of the revolt in Palestine and the nationalist government in Damascus, and with radical pan-Arab elements in jail or underground, the politics of pan-Arabism in Syria receded into the background.

The struggle within the ranks of Syrian nationalists over participation in the pan-Arab issues that emerged between the wars, especially in the Palestine Revolt, has haunted Syrian politics ever since.[90] All Syrian regimes have legitimized their rule in terms of Arab nationalism (far more than any other Arab states), but all of them sooner or later have come up against an awkward contradiction between pan-Arab ideology and Syrian self-interest, whether of state or regime. This was the kind of awkward situation in which the National Bloc found itself in the late 1930s and it contributed to the nationalist government's demise.

[85] FO 684/12/2746/2/. MacKereth to Halifax, 28 Oct. 1939; FO 371/2996, vol. 23276. MacKereth to Baxter, 13 April 1939.

[86] The newspapers were *Al-Istiqlal al-ʿarabi* and *Al-ʿAmal al-qawmi*. See FO 371/265, vol. 23276. MacKereth to Baxter, 2 Jan. 1939; FO 684/12/2746/2. MacKereth to Halifax, 28 Oct. 1939.

[87] *Ibid*; FO 684/12/542/2. MacKereth to High Commissioner (Palestine), 10 Jan. 1939.

[88] FO 684/12/2746/2. MacKereth to High Commissioner (Palestine), 31 May 1939.

[89] FO 371/2996, vol. 23276. MacKereth to Baxter, 13 April 1939.

[90] The one attempt to pursue a pan-Arab policy regardless of the consequences—that of the Baʿth regime of 1966—led to the disaster of June 1967.

CHAPTER TWENTY-TWO

FACTIONALISM DURING THE LATER MANDATE

DURING ITS TWO YEARS in office, the Mardam government faced acute problems which eventually forced it to resign in February 1939. Some of these have already been discussed in depth—the French failure to ratify the treaty of 1936; separatist movements in the Jabal Druze, the Latakia governorate, and the Jazira; the step-by-step separation of the Sanjak of Alexandretta from Syria and its annexation by Turkey; and the complications caused by the rebellion in Palestine. Underpinning these problems was a Syrian economy hobbled by skyrocketing inflation, poor harvests, and rising unemployment. But a recrudescence of local political factionalism, whose intensity had not been experienced since the collapse of the Great Revolt, was the final nail in the nationalist government's coffin.

OTHER NATIONALIST ORGANIZATIONS

With the rise of new political forces bent on breaking out of the traditional framework of political factionalism in the 1930s, owing to the acceleration of social and economic change in this period, the National Bloc might have faced a serious challenge to its leadership from this direction. But, it did not. Neither the extreme secular Left, represented principally by the Syrian Communist Party, nor an emerging group of radically conservative *jam'iyyat* (Muslim benevolent societies) can be credited with bringing down the National Bloc government. In fact, the Communist Party, at the instruction of the French Communist Party, backed the treaty of 1936 and, while critical of certain Syrian government policies, it supported the Mardam government. In the late 1930s, collaboration damaged the Communist Party's reputation with more than a few sympathetic, up-and-coming radical intellectuals. As for the Islamic *jam'iyyat*, they were still too loosely organized and at odds with one another to cause any serious damage. They and the Communist Party would not truly take their place on the stage of modern Syrian politics until the end of World War II, that is, long after the Communists had ceased to cooperate with the National Bloc and the *jam'iyyat* had metamorphosed into the Muslim Brethren.

Even the better-established pan-Arab League of National Action, though a more effective critic than either the Communists or the *jam'iyyat*, was unusually subdued. It focused on the Mardam government's ineffective handling of the Alexandretta debacle and its lukewarm commitment to the rebels in Palestine, but its assault on the Mardam government and on the National Bloc was ineffective in comparison with the movement associated with Dr. 'Abd al-Rahman Shahbandar.

The League's ineffectiveness can be blamed on the Istiqlal Party's effective muting of its opposition to the Bloc by containing the League within the traditional framework of political factionalism. The League's loss of influence correlated with the growth of Istiqlali strength. Radicalization apparently had built-in limits in Syria before World War II.

As the League's political fortunes dipped owing to its internal divisions, smaller pan-Arab organizations cropped up. The most active of these was the Arab Club (al-Nadi al-'arab) of Damascus. Founded in February 1937, it major principle was

> . . . to revive the history of the Arabs and to establish strong ties between all Arab countries, to spread and unify education, to establish good morals, to work for the individual and the family, to encourage national industries, to emphasize sporting activities, and to work for everything which is in the Arab interest and which helps [the Arabs] socially and economically.[1]

Its vision was not unlike the League's, and, indeed, their memberships partly overlapped.

The Arab Club was a secularist, pan-Arab organization which counted 108 regular members, including 26 educated women, in the late 1930s. It had an elitist orientation and attempted to gather the best-educated elements in Damascus together in pursuit of its aims. It was headquartered on the third floor of a downtown building and in its clubroom hung flags of all Arab countries and the pictures of leading Arab politicians, past and present. Conscious of Arab history, the Club enjoyed commemorating great days and momentous events in the Arab past. At the same time, its members sought to distance themselves from the more immediate past associated with the National Bloc. One familiar manifestation of this was the Arab Club's rejection of the fez, the headgear popularly associated with the Bloc. It relied on small group meetings in the different quarters of Damascus to develop and defend its position, but by World War II it had not established club branches in other towns.[2]

The Arab Club's major differentiating characteristic was its pro-Ger-

---

[1] Nabih al-'Azma Papers [Syria], File 5, no. 212(A). Invitation of *Nadi al-'arabi* to 'Azma, Feb. 1937.

[2] See Anonymous, "Le club arabe de Damas," CHEAM, no. 351, 12 Jan. 1939, 3 pages.

man orientation. This correlated with the growth of German interest and activity in Syria in the late 1930s; French and British Intelligence claimed that the Arab Club was the major vehicle for Nazi penetration of Syria and that the club received considerable financial assistance from Berlin. Although the extent of Nazi involvement remains shrouded in mystery, one of Germany's principal contacts in Damascus was Sa'id al-Fattah Imam, the Arab Club's founder and president and a practicing dentist who had studied briefly in Germany. The first scrap of evidence linking Dr. Imam to Nazi Germany was a trip he made there in 1936 in the company of six Syrian students. French Intelligence reported that the National Bloc encouraged Imam to further nationalist contacts with Hitler at the time.[3] This was the first of several trips to Germany before the war.

German involvement in Syria, while not as pronounced as elsewhere in the Middle East owing in part to Italy's longer and more developed interests there, nonetheless reflected overall German strategy in the region. The Germans wanted to court the Arabs, to expand German trade and Nazi propaganda, and "even to undermine French and British prestige in the Middle East; but at the same time to avoid the danger of too flagrant a provocation, certainly any incitement to violence." The Germans wanted to capitalize on a growing feeling among Arab nationalists in Syria and elsewhere that, while their own activities were gradually loosening the French and British imperial grip on the region, to complete the break they required a stronger concentration of international pressure and assistance. No foreign power was in a better position to provide this than Germany.

Under the watchful eye of Dr. Imam, the Arab Club operated on two levels: it tried delicately to spread anti-French propaganda and German influence in Syria while it actively supported the anti-British and anti-Zionist revolt in Palestine. In September 1937, Syrian nationalists approached the German Consul in Beirut to request that German weapons be shipped to Palestinian rebels while Dr. Imam, on behalf of the Mufti, proceeded to Berlin to secure greater German assistance for the revolt.[4] The Arab Club was closely linked to Nabih al-'Azma's Palestine Defense Committee in Damascus, although personal relations between Imam and 'Azma soured in the last months of the revolt.[5]

A fairly steady stream of ranking German officials visited Damascus in the late 1930s, beginning in early December 1937 with the Hitler Youth

[3] MAE, Syrie–Liban 1930–40. Meyrier (Beirut) to MAE, 31 July 1936, pp. 43–45; Faris, Man huwa 1949, p. 43.

[4] Howard M. Sachar, Europe Leaves the Middle East, 1936–1954 (New York, 1972), pp. 47–49.

[5] FO 684/12/2581/10. MacKereth to Halifax, 29 April 1939; FO 371/6891, vol. 21914. MacKereth to Baxter, 7 Nov. 1938.

leader Baldur von Schirach. Accompanied by a delegation of 15, he visited the Arab Club where he reportedly discussed ways of strengthening Nazi propaganda among Arab youth. His immediate mission was to secure Nazi control over all German institutions in the Middle East and to propagate Nazi ideas by reminding the Arabs that Germany, unlike Britain and France, had no territorial designs on the region.[6] Other German visitors included Walter Beck who in June 1938 followed up on von Schirach's visit by selecting some 70 Syrians for education in Germany at the expense of the German government.[7]

The French observed an increase of pro-German activity in Syria in late 1938 and early 1939, but they were always much more concerned about Italian activities.[8] The Arab Club clearly escalated its own activities, sending delegations to Baghdad, the center of Nazi activity in the Arab East, and maintaining strong ties with a sister organization, the pan-Arab Muthanna Club.[9] Meanwhile, more and more German representatives visited Damascus while Fakhri al-Barudi's Bureau for National Propaganda devoted special issues of its Bulletin to German policies, which were portrayed in a most favorable light.[10]

The Arab Club's fate was similar to that of other radical organizations in Syria. Although it outlived the League of National Action, which the French shut down in March 1939, and even took in Leaguers for a brief period, it was suppressed a few months later after being implicated in a plot against the state. Many of its members fled abroad, mainly to Iraq, where they sat out the early years of the war in anticipation of their return to Damascus.[11]

DIVISION WITHIN THE NATIONAL BLOC

The declared policy of the National Bloc from its assumption of power was to suppress all opposition to itself and to the French until the expira-

---

[6] *Filastin* (5 Dec. 1937), cited in FO 684/10/2735 -10; FO 371/7457, vol. 20850. MacKereth to Eden, 14 Dec. 1937.

[7] FO 371/7806, vol. 21914. MacKereth to Halifax, 9 Dec. 1928.

[8] France's greater concern with Italian activities is reflected in the greater attention devoted to Italian propaganda in the Levant in the French Foreign Ministry and Defense Ministry archives and in the French press in the late 1930s. See MAE, Syrie–Liban 1930–40, vol. 470; MD, 7N 4190, Dossier 3. The British Foreign Office archives support this observation.

[9] F0 371/6597, vol. 21914. MacKereth to Baxter, 21 Oct. 1938. On the Muthanna Club, see Batatu, *The Old Social Classes*, pp. 297–99.

[10] MAE, Gabriel Puaux Papers, Carton 36, Dossier S-3-5. Robert Montagne Note, n.d.; MAE, Syrie–Liban 1930–40. Puaux (Beirut) to MAE, 4 March 1939, vol. 457, pp. 186–88; FO 371/1895, vol. 23276. MacKereth to Baxter, 3 March 1939.

[11] FO 371/2840, vol. 27291. Gardener to FO, 10 April 1941; FO 226/233/31 -236. Table on Syrian Political Parties, 7 Oct. 1942.

tion of the Mandate, and to extend its power into the important sectors of society.[12] It pursued this policy by distributing offices and certain perquisites to loyal Bloc supporters or, more accurately, to the clients and families of individual Bloc chiefs;[13] by getting Bloc members elected to influential positions, such as the presidency of the Damascus Lawyers' Union, through offers of government positions to influential union whips;[14] and by distributing money to newspapers and other media to ensure their sympathy or to neutralize them.[15] Nevertheless, within the broad nationalist camp, opposition to the Mardam government came from four sources: members of the cabinet; the Bloc's Damascus branch; the Bloc's Aleppo branch; and nationalists associated with Dr. Shahbandar. What prevented these forces from quickly toppling Mardam were their own factional squabbles and a shared sentiment that a nationalist government, whatever its complexion, should not be sacrificed on the altar of the French High Commission.

By early 1938, deep cracks in the National Bloc's edifice had appeared. Jamil Mardam had all but rendered the Bloc politically ineffective by reducing it to a bare skeleton of an organization so that it could not be turned against him. Meanwhile, rumors abounded that Mardam was on the take, accused of accepting kickbacks from foreign oil companies in return for concession rights.[16] Although the charges were never proven, Mardam suffered a great loss of prestige. Then, as if to fan the flames, he resumed negotiations with the French without first seeking the Bloc's approval. He even kept his cabinet in the dark about his dealings and about the modifications he agreed to in the treaty of 1936. But neither the Bloc nor Mardam's cabinet dared to stop him, probably because they feared that a serious public rift might encourage the French to unseat the nationalist government.[17]

Jamil Mardam's loudest critic in his government was Shukri al-Quwwatli who was deeply disturbed by Mardam's actions. It appears that he had asked Mardam to resign. Mardam's refusal to do so meant that

---

[12] FO 371/697, vol. 20848. MacKereth to Eden, 5 May 1937.

[13] Among the many examples of family appointments under the Bloc was the Syrian Foreign Ministry's announcement in January 1938 of the appointment of three new consuls to be posted abroad. Hashim al-Atasi's son, 'Adnan, was appointed to Turkey, replacing 'Adil Arslan who became Minister to Paris; Sa'dallah al-Jabiri's nephew, 'Awnallah, became consul in Cairo; and As'ad Harun, son of 'Abd al-Wahid, a Bloc chief in Latakia, became consul in Baghdad. *Oriente Moderno*, 18 (1938), p. 79.

[14] *Al-Mudhik al-mubki*, no. 393 (5 Nov. 1938), p. 13.

[15] Yusuf al-'Issa, the editor of *Alif ba'*, complained bitterly of Bloc efforts to bribe newspaper editors. See FO 684/10/2896/1. J. Teen interview with Y. Issa, 5 April 1937.

[16] Conversation with Farid Zayn al-Din (Damascus, 22 April 1976). The middle-man was the Bloc lawyer, Sa'id al-Ghazzi.

[17] *Ibid*.

perhaps Quwwatli should resign lest he be tainted by charges of corruption and secret dealings. But Quwwatli had to await the right opportunity. This came in February 1938 when he learned of Mardam's compromise on the sensitive issue of renewing the Banque de Syrie concession. Quwwatli's public outcry against Mardam's double-dealing came not a moment too late. He had been privately but severely rebuked by his Istiqlali colleagues for not resigning earlier.[18] With Quwwatli's departure from government, the Bloc became even more fragmented and hence even less capable of checking on Mardam's political innuendos.

The results of Jamil Mardam's last trip to Paris in the fall of 1938 set off another wave of defections. Among those to resign from the Bloc Executive were Faris al-Khuri, Lutfi al-Haffar, and Nasib al-Bakri, its vice-president. Already that summer it was observed that at the *haflat* (parties) arranged by the Bloc in the quarters to rally supporters and to raise money for the Nationalist Youth and other activities, a number of prominent Bloc officials were conspicuously absent, including Sayf al-Din al-Ma'mun of the Steel Shirts and Shafiq Jabri, the popular nationalist poet. Mardam's dealings in Paris and the Bloc's noticeably weak stand on the Franco-Turkish Agreement concerning the Sanjak precipitated further defections.[19] Few Bloc chiefs remained in Mardam's immediate circle and the increasingly isolated Prime Minister was reported to have tried to bribe the financially hardpressed Bakris to return to the Bloc fold.[20] Although Mardam could still count on the support of several prominent merchants such Tawfiq al-Qabbani and Husni Tillu, the men on whom he depended most were lesser and younger political lights such as the Nationalist Youth leaders, Bayruti and Shiliq, his brother-in-law, Najib Armanazi, the newspaper editor Najib al-Rayyis, a Shi'i boss named Mahdi Murtada who was his link to the popular quarters, and his personal secretary, 'Asim al-Na'ili.

By the end of 1938, the Damascus Bloc had fractured into at least three rival camps. Apart from the Mardam faction, there was one associated with Shukri al-Quwwatli and which included the industrialist Khalid al-'Azm, the merchant Adib Khayr, the 'Azma brothers, the journalist, 'Uthman al-Qassim, and the young lawyer, Sabri al-'Asali;[21] another composed of Faris al-Khuri, Ihsan al-Sharif, and Lutfi al-Haffar who turned his nephew Wajih's newspaper, *al-Insha'*, into an anti-Mardam

---

[18] *Ibid*; 'Adil al-'Azma Papers [Syria], File 17/457. Chief of Police of al-Jazira to Director-General of Police, 10 May 1937.

[19] *Al-Mudhik al-mubki*, no. 376 (3 July 1938), p. 9.

[20] A well-informed source gave the figure of £S 12,000. *Ibid.*, no., 422 (8 July 1939), p. 4.

[21] Nabih al-'Azma Papers [Syria], File 6/384. Radio Broadcast by 'Azma, 25 Jan. 1939. Khalid al-'Azm, *Mudhakkirat Khalid al-'Azm*, vol. 1 (Beirut, 1973), pp. 183–85.

instrument;[22] and a third faction led by the Bakri brothers and Fa'iz al-Khuri.

Another source of division within the National Bloc was Aleppo. Almost from its foundation, the Bloc had been split by tensions between its branches in Damascus and Aleppo. The Aleppo branch was always better organized and more cohesive than the Damascus branch but at the same time it suffered from an inferiority complex, derived from living in the shadow of the Syrian capital. Damascus compounded matters by snubbing Aleppo. By the late 1930s, hostilities between the two branches reached a level of intensity not previously experienced, not even in 1933 when the Aleppo branch, under Ibrahim Hananu's direction, forced Jamil Mardam and Mazhar Raslan to oppose the first Franco-Syrian Treaty by resigning their ministries.

Under the Bloc government, two grievances were especially resonant in Aleppo. One was the timeless complaint that Aleppo bore the brunt of taxation. Aleppo's only reward, as the British Consul in the town suggested, was "maladministration, a lack of stability, and increasing subordination to Damascus." The other grievance concerned the Sanjak's fate which affected the welfare of Aleppines much more than it did Damascenes, owing to Alexandretta's role as Aleppo's principal port, its link to the world of the Mediterranean and to Europe. That Aleppine Bloc members were prominent in Mardam's cabinet meant little. Just as in Damascus, nationalists dissatisfied with Mardam's policies began to leave the Bloc.[23]

THE SHAHBANDARIST OPPOSITION

Local political struggles in Syria in the 1930s took place principally within the framework of the national independence movement. On one level, they were restricted to the National Bloc—either within the Damascus or Aleppo branches or between them. But on another level, they took place between the Bloc and what the Syrian press simply called "the opposition" (al-mu'arada), or the movement associated with Dr. Shahbandar.

The origins of the struggle between the National Bloc and "the opposition" date from the mid-twenties when the Syrian independence movement experienced serious divisions in its ranks, reflected most clearly in the Syrian-Palestine Congress, which split down the middle in the wake of the Great Revolt's collapse. At that time, two major factions crystallized, one around the veterans of the revolt led by Dr. Shahbandar and the

---

[22] Al-Mudhik al-mubki, no. 396 (3 Dec. 1938), p. 5.

[23] Ibid., no. 374 (18 June 1938), p. 6; FO 371/5213, vol. 23277. Davis (Aleppo) to FO, 12 July 1939.

other around the Syrian Istiqlal Party headed by Shukri al-Quwwatli.[24]
For a while, both factions fought out their battles in exile, each blaming
the other for the revolt's failure and each playing the pan-Arab card
against the other, the Istiqlalis depending on the House of Saʿud and the
Shahbandarists on the Hashemites, especially Amir ʿAbdullah, Ibn
Saʿud's bitterest rival.[25]

Eventually, the French amnestied Quwwatli and by the early 1930s he
had become a full-fledged member of the National Bloc. Shahbandar, on
the other hand, remained in exile but kept a close watch on political developments and, in particular, on Bloc activities. His eyes were a number
of disaffected Bloc members and youth leaders headed by the populist
lawyer Zaki al-Khatib. Inspired by Shahbandar, Khatib had founded in
1935 the Party of National Unity which adopted a more radical, less compromising platform than the Bloc's and which was one of the few political
organizations to denounce the 1936 treaty on the grounds that its terms
prolonged French hegemony in Syria for 25 more years.[26] But Khatib's
party was not taken very seriously until Dr. Shahbandar's return to Syria
after the general amnesty of April 1937.

Shahbandar was greeted by enormous welcoming demonstrations and
parades.[27] A decade in exile had elevated his reputation to new heights.
He represented the era of revolutionary fervor and heroism when the
Syrian people had sought complete and immediate independence. Since
then they had allowed the National Bloc to experiment with delicate diplomacy; but already by mid-1937 there was much to worry about as
rampant inflation, the growth of local separatist movements, Turkish encroachment on the Sanjak, rebellion in Palestine, and an unsympathetic
government in Paris jeopardized hopes for independence and the Bloc's
wish to be in the driver's seat when independence finally arrived. For disaffected groups, Shahbandar's appearance was a breath of fresh air, even
though he lived more on his past glory than on recent achievements.

Shahbandar's return was not exactly welcomed by the National Bloc.
Its Istiqlali wing applied pressure on newspaper editors to cease referring
to Shahbandar as "the Great Syrian Leader." One observer remarked at
the time that "a new generation was raised in Damascus who heard about
the great leader and who came to believe in him and his leadership."[28]
What alarmed the Bloc was the fear that Shahbandar would direct his

---

[24] Conversation with Hasan al-Hakim (Damascus, 12 March 1976).

[25] MWT, al-Qism al-khass, Nazih Muʿayyad al-ʿAzm Papers, no. 190. ʿAbdullah
ʿAbrid to Muʿayyad al-ʿAzm, 11 June 1939.

[26] See Chapter 17 and FO 684/10/2605/1, 1937.

[27] Conversation with Nasuh Babil (Damascus, 20 Feb. 1976).

[28] Nabih al-ʿAzma Papers [Syria], File 5/206. Muhammad ʿAli Tahir to ʿAzma, 1 Feb.
1937.

criticisms not at the French but rather at the Mardam government. In Bloc circles there was considerable debate in early 1937 about how to handle Shahbandar: should he be welcomed into the Bloc and honored, or should efforts be made to isolate and discredit him? Some Istiqlalis who had observed him in Cairo over the years found Shahbandar honest and committed but politically naive and hence prone to being led astray by more wily companions. They strongly encouraged Shukri al-Quwwatli to reach an agreement with Shahbandar. Because Shahbandar returned openly opposed to the treaty, they thought that Quwwatli might be able to play him against Jamil Mardam, in their rivalry for control of the Bloc.[29] Although Shahbandar loathed Quwwatli, he did ask his trusted friend, Hasan al-Hakim, to act as a mediator between them.[30]

Of course, by the time Shahbandar returned Jamil Mardam was at the helm of government. At first he actually tried to win Shahbandar's support by asking him to represent Syria in international forums in Europe. There was mention in the Syrian press that the National Bloc was prepared to open its doors to Shahbandar and that a Mardam–Shahbandar axis would be formed. Mardam and Shahbandar had no history of personal antagonism, as had Quwwatli and Shahbandar. With Quwwatli making his ascent within the National Bloc, Mardam intended to keep both men apart, and there was no more expedient way than by trying to enlist Shahbandar's support. Although Shahbandar and Quwwatli never reconciled their differences, it was not because of anything Jamil Mardam had done. Quwwatli and Shahbandar so distrusted one another that a *rapprochement* was impossible.

Shahbandar arrived in Damascus with vengeance in his eyes and although he remained in the capital only one month before returning to Cairo, his presence galvanized "the opposition," which focused on the treaty, on the question of the Sanjak, and on Jamil Mardam himself.[31] At this level of politics, the line between issues and personalities was a fine one. The opposition press accused Mardam of one egregious sin after the next. It had no qualms about blowing up the slightest bit of unsubstantiated evidence into a major scandal in an effort to discredit him.[32] In time, "the opposition" focused its assault solely upon Mardam in a bid to drive a wedge between him and his cabinet, and ultimately to force his

[29] *Ibid.*, File 5/249. As'ad Daghir to 'Azma, 1 May 1937.

[30] Conversation with Hasan al-Hakim (Damascus, 12 March 1976); MWT, *al-Qism al-khass*, 'Abd al-Rahman Shahbandar Papers, nos. 24/40, 25/41, 26/42, 27/43. Shahbandar to al-Hakim, 2 May 1937 and 7, 23, 25 July 1937.

[31] Nazih Mu'ayyad al-'Azm Papers, no. 43. Shahbandar to Mu'ayyad al-'Azm, 20 May 1938; FO 371/7010, vol. 2194. MacKereth to Baxter, 19 Nov. 1938.

[32] Conversation with Nasuh Babil (Damascus, 20 Feb. 1976), the pro-Shahbandar editor of *al-Ayyam*.

resignation.[33] But Mardam met Shahbandar blow for blow. He resurrected the familiar accusation that Shahbandar was in fact a British agent who had diverted Syria from her rightful goal of independence.[34] He denounced his unsavory ties with Amir 'Abdullah, especially after 'Abdullah became the only Arab leader to support the British Royal Commission's partition plan for Palestine. Mardam got the High Commission to support his government's decision to deny Shahbandar the right to open a political office in Damascus, compelling him to use his clinic for this purpose.[35] He enforced strict press censorship laws to prevent opposition newspapers from printing unflattering articles about himself.[36] He dismissed government bureaucrats known to be sympathetic to Shahbandar's movement.[37] After facing large demonstrations against his compromises with the French government over the oil and Banque de Syrie concessions in late 1937 and early 1938, Mardam cracked down on the Shahbandar organization, arresting Zaki al-Khatib and other prominent opposition leaders, and closing down anti-government newspapers.[38] And when Shahbandar finally returned to Syria permanently in early 1938, the Mardam government, again backed by the High Commission, placed him in forced residence at Bludan for several months; and then, after his release, he was kept under close police surveillance, gendarmes stationed in front of his Damascus home around the clock.[39]

Tensions between Mardam and Shahbandar reached new heights when an explosive went off in Mardam's car on June 16 as he returned to Damascus from a trip to the countryside. Miraculously, he escaped unharmed but immediately accused elements close to Shahbandar. Six men were tried and found guilty of the assassination attempt, including Shahbandar's brother-in-law, Nazih Mu'ayyad al-'Azm, the reputed ring leader; but not before Mardam had the presiding judge dismissed out of fear that he might refuse to sentence the defendants.[40]

Unlike Mardam and Quwwatli, Shahbandar was not a master of patronage politics. Nor did he come from one of the established families of Damascus. Yet, he could draw on the political machine of Zaki al-Khatib and the financial resources of his wealthy brother-in-law, Nazih Mu'ayyad al-'Azm. Therefore, he had at his disposal an extensive pa-

[33] Nazih Mu'ayyad al-'Azm Papers, no. 45. Shahbandar to Mu'ayyad, 15 Feb. 1938.
[34] Conversation with Hasan al-Hakim (Damascus, 21 March 1976).
[35] Al-Mudhik al-mubki, no. 397 (10 Dec. 1938), p.4.
[36] Ibid., no. 396 (3 Dec. 1938), p. 5.
[37] Nazih Mu'ayyad al-'Azm Papers, no. 112.
[38] Oriente Moderno, 18 (1938), pp. 118–19.
[39] Al-Mudhik al-mubki, no. 420 (24 June 1939), p. 18.
[40] Nabih al-'Azma Papers [Syria], File 6/374. Transcript of Court Trial, 16 Oct. 1938; al-Ayyam, 18 March 1938.

tronage network in the Syrian capital comprising politicians, merchants, journalists, youth leaders, and *qabadayat*. Apart from Khatib and Mu'ayyad al-'Azm, the Shahbandar network included his longtime friend and supporter from the days of Great Revolt, Hasan al-Hakim; wealthy merchants such as Hani Jallad, who had parted ways with the National Bloc during the strike of 1936, and Bashir Lahham whose warehouse in Suq al-Hamidiyya was renowned throughout Damascus; Nasuh Babil, the editor of *al-Ayyam*, which had been anti-Bloc since 1935; the nationalist poet 'Umar Abu-Rishi; and Munir al-'Ajlani, who in 1937 defected from the Steel Shirts taking with him a number of his young followers.

Two vital areas in Damascus where the Shahbandarists were noticeably stronger than the National Bloc were the Upper Maydan and the Kurdish quarter on the town's southern and northern peripheries. The key to the Maydan was Hasan al-Hakim whose family had been prominent in local politics there for several generations, and who attracted the sympathy of its wealthy grain merchants.[41] In the Kurdish quarter, relations between the population and the National Bloc had never been particularly positive, perhaps because the Kurds disliked the Bloc's heavy stress on Arabism. In any case, Shahbandar relied on the support of several Kurdish notables including 'Umar Agha Shamdin and the young nationalist lawyer, 'Ali Buzu.[42] That the Kurds generally aligned with political organizations which de-emphasized pan-Arabism is evident from the fact that the major political rivalry in the Kurdish quarter was not between the Shahbandarists and the Bloc but rather between the Shahbandarists and the Communist Party under the leadership of Khalid Bakdash, himself a Kurd.[43]

Shahbandar's movement capitalized on the bankrupt strategy of Jamil Mardam's government and the fragmentation of the National Bloc, although the mystique of Shahbandar, whom a new generation knew only through the hagiography of the Great Revolt, certainly furthered its aims. The denial of his right to reside in Damascus after his return only contributed to his image as a patriot dedicated to saving Syria from corrupt politicians masking themselves as nationalists.

Shahbandar became a critical focal point around which politicians out of favor with the National Bloc or possessing some grievance with it rallied. When Nasib al-Bakri resigned as vice-president of the Bloc in late 1938, he returned to Shahbandar's camp, after an absence of more than a decade. Shahbandar also attracted followings in Homs, where the League of National Action was stronger than the Bloc, but not in Hama, where

[41] *Al-Mudhik al-mubki*, no. 380 (30 July 1938), p. 5.
[42] Conversation with Nasuh Babil (Damascus, 20 Feb. 1976).
[43] *Oriente Moderno*, 18 (1938), pp. 118–19.

the Bloc prevailed under Tawfiq al-Shishakli's dynamic leadership. In Aleppo, several prominent politicians who opposed the Bloc's grip on that town's politics were linked to his organization, including Ahmad Khalil al-Mudarris, a wealthy landowner whose family were longtime rivals of the Jabiris.[44] Here, Shahbandar exploited the growing divisions in the Aleppo Bloc organization. And for a brief moment after the French finally rejected the treaty at the end of 1938, Shahbandar even formed an alliance with one faction of the League of National Action to organize strikes against the arrival of the new High Commissioner, M. Puaux, and against the Mardam government whose resignation they demanded. But, because Shukri al-Quwwatli opposed the strikes (although not Mardam's resignation), the League quickly backed out of the deal, making any further collaboration impossible.[45]

Shahbandarists operated within the traditional framework of political factionalism in Syria and largely thrived on their opposition to the National Bloc government and Jamil Mardam. But once Mardam resigned as Prime Minister in February 1939, the opposition lost its *raison d'être*. While efforts to reconcile Shahbandar and Mardam failed and their personal relations became even more strained,[46] the Shahbandar network began to disintegrate. A bitter dispute over what strategy the opposition should pursue pitted *al-Ayyam's* editor, Nasuh Babil, and its major financial backer, Hani Jallad, against the more radical Munir al-ʿAjlani and his followers in the Shahbandarist Youth. ʿAjlani established a new organization, the People's Parliamentary Bloc and *al-Nidal*, a rival newspaper to *al-Ayyam*.[47] Meanwhile, a long simmering rivalry between Zaki al-Khatib and the moderate president of the Lawyers' Union, Saʿid al-Mahasini, another Shahbandar supporter, finally boiled over. Khatib emerged as the leader of his own faction within the Shahbandar organization, al-Ahrar (the Liberals). By the summer of 1939, Jallad and Babil had parted ways, Jallad aligning with Mahasini and Babil with Khatib.[48] Shahbandar was powerless to prevent this fragmentation as he desperately tried to improve his relations with the French, who soon rejected his secret offer to negotiate a new treaty on the basis of a very large measure of decentralization in Syria. The French had absolutely no interest in pro-

[44] MAE, Puaux Papers, Carton 34. Puaux Telegram, 19 Feb. 1939; *al-Mudhik al-mubki*, no. 391 (22 Oct. 1938), p. 16.

[45] *Ibid.*, no. 402 (14 Jan 1939), p. 12; no. 403 (22 Jan. 1939), pp. 6–7.

[46] *Ibid.*, no. 409 (18 March 1939), p. 7.

[47] *Ibid.*, no. 419 (17 June 1939), p. 7; no. 407 (4 March 1939), p. 15; no. 404 (11 Feb. 1939), p. 14; no. 425 (29 July 1930), p. 20.

[48] The Khatib and Mahasini families had been rivals since the mid-nineteenth century when they competed for the post of *khatib* (preacher) at the Umayyad Mosque in Damascus. See Khoury, *Urban Notables*, pp. 13–14; *al-Mudhik al-mubki*, no. 415 (6 May 1939), p. 6; no. 425 (29 July 1939), p. 20; conversation with Nasuh Babil (20 Feb. 1976).

moting relations with him, owing to his ties to Amir ʿAbdullah and to the British.[49]

By the end of 1938, the handwriting was on the wall. France's final decision in November not to ratify the treaty meant Jamil Mardam would have to resign as Prime Minister. Despite all the internal criticism he had faced, the separatist movements he had failed to suppress, the loss of the Sanjak, his reluctance to become involved in Palestine, and the stagnant Syrian economy, his political credibility hinged ultimately on the treaty. Lesser politicians would have been forced out of office much earlier. Only a man with his instinct for survival could have held on as long as he did, and then not have to resign in disgrace.

The immediate conditions for his resignation were laid during Gabriel Puaux's first visit to Damascus on 12 January 1939. Puaux's appointment around the time of the treaty's collapse signalled a resurgence of French authority in Syria. The 56-year old Protestant, a career diplomat who had most recently been French Minister to Vienna and who had previous experience in Tunis before World War I, announced his arrival with a radio broadcast from Beirut which Syrian leaders interpreted as a "veiled threat."

I shall always speak to the Syrian people in the language of truth. I come to them as a friend, and by their acts I shall judge them. Let them have no doubts as to the strength and generosity of France.[50]

Massive anti-French demonstrations organized principally by the Shahbandarist opposition and supported by the League of National Action greeted Puaux. In Damascus, the springboard for these protests was the *tajhiz* and in no time students in Homs, Hama, Aleppo, and Latakia organized strikes in solidarity.[51] Matters reached a climax after Puaux returned to Beirut on January 12 and the Mardam government staged counterdemonstrations. Violent clashes, continuing into early February, led to more defections from the National Bloc and for a brief moment two members of the Mardam government tendered their resignations. Vir-

---

[49] MAE, Puaux Papers, Carton 36, Dossier S-3-5. Puaux (Beirut) to Robert Montagne, 1 June 1939.

[50] *L'annuaire diplomatique*, (Paris, 1947), p. 546; FO 371/677, vol. 23276. MacKereth to Baxter, 20 Jan. 1939.

[51] MAE, Puaux Papers, Carton 34. Puaux to MAE, 8 Jan. 1939; ʿAdil al-ʿAzma Papers [Syria], File 16/400, 12 Feb. 1939; FO 371/57, vol. 23276. Davis (Aleppo) to FO, 3 Jan. 1939; *al-Mudhik al-mubki*, no. 403 (22 Jan. 1939), p. 9; MWT, *al-Intidab al-faransi: Qadaya mukhtalifa*, 62/1163/ -319/30h. Muhafiz (Aleppo) to French Delegate (Aleppo), 18 Jan. 1939.

tually every prominent nationalist in the country, with the exception of Jamil Mardam's closest allies, demanded that he step down.[52] When a final bid to reconcile Mardam and Shahbandar failed,[53] Mardam seized the one issue that allowed him to resign honorably and gracefully.

Under mounting pressure from Muslim religious organizations, in particular the Jam'iyyat al-'ulama' led by the influential Shaykh Kamil al-Qassab, the Mardam government refused to apply the recently modified High Commission decree regulating the religious communities.[54] When the original decree was laid down in March 1936, it was not well received in Syria and was never effected. But when the High Commission modified it in mid-December 1938 to allow, among other things, Muslims to change their religion and for Muslim women to marry non-Muslims, religious leaders were outraged.[55] Few issues could have been more "ill-chosen" by the French than the personal status issue, especially since Syrians had still not recovered from "the shock of the recantation of the 1936 Treaty."[56] Muslims believed that "it treated [them] as one sect among many, and thus struck at the root of the traditional Moslem conception of the State."[57]

Mardam instructed the courts to ignore the decree which caused the French Delegate in Damascus to intervene, calling upon the government to withdraw its instructions. As the British Consul in the capital remarked:

for the French authorities to have adopted any other course would have meant the abdication of all mandatory authority over Syria, and for the Syrian government to have adopted any other course would equally have meant the abdication of all Syrian authority.[58]

This new twist to Syrian political affairs showed Mardam's political astuteness. He might have found a way to skirt the personal status issue and temporarily to remove the wind from "the opposition's" sails, but with so many other problems staring him in the face, he could not expect to govern effectively any longer. Since the fall of 1938 he had witnessed his government's popularity rapidly dwindle and the recalcitrant mem-

[52] Al-Mudhik al-mubki, no. 402 (14 Jan. 1939), p. 14; FO 371/677, vol. 23276. MacKereth to Baxter, 20 Jan. 1939; 'Adil al-'Azma Papers [Syria], File 16/404. Muhammad Dandashi to Director-General of Police, 7 Feb. 1939.

[53] MAE, Puaux Papers, Carton 34. Puaux Telegram, 22 Jan. 1939.

[54] Al-Mudhik al-mubki, no. 405 (6 May 1939), p. 6.

[55] MAE, Puaux Papers, Carton 34. "Chronique politique 1939"; Gabriel Puaux, Deux années au Levant; souvenirs de Syrie et du Liban (Paris, 1952), pp. 32–33. Arrêtés, nos. 60LR (13 March 1936) and 146LR (15 Dec. 1938).

[56] FO 371/2144, vol. 23276. MacKereth to Baxter, 24 Feb. 1939.

[57] Hourani, Syria and Lebanon, pp. 225–26.

[58] FO 371/1452, vol. 23276. MacKereth to Baxter, 18 Feb. 1939.

bers of the National Bloc drift over to "the opposition." By refusing to
implement the High Commission's decree, Mardam had little to lose and
his political integrity to regain. Therefore, he cleverly used Syrian public
opinion to cushion his resignation on February 18, and he went out on a
large wave of public enthusiasm.

After considerable jockeying for position within the National Bloc,
Lutfi al-Haffar succeeded Jamil Mardam as Prime Minister. Although he
and President Atasi were not on good terms, Atasi's only option was to
appoint him.[59] The new cabinet was composed almost entirely of Bloc
members. But it lasted barely a month; it was forced to resign on March
16 under heavy pressure from the opposition and from Bloc dissidents.
Haffar was unable to install a nationalist *muhafiz* in the Latakia province
where he faced a growing separatist movement led by the French-backed
Alawite leader, Sulayman al-Murshid; and he was unable to get the personal status decree reversed. Damascus was full of anti-Bloc slogans at
this time, the most popular one being: "although we used to put the *Kutla* [the Bloc] next to God, now we seek our freedom from it."[60]
Precipitating the Haffar cabinet's resignation were demonstrations opposing its seeming willingness to effect a compromise with the French
over the personal status law. These demonstrations spread all over Syria,
were violent, and lasted on and off for several weeks. In Damascus,
ulama' and high school and university students closed the bazaars and
enforced the strike. On March 20, French military authorities withdrew
the local police and occupied the central quarters of the town, removing
the barricades rioters had placed in the streets. When the crowds "tested
the tempers" of a Senegalese post by throwing stones, the Senegalese
fired into the crowd killing two.[61] On March 21, Nabih al-'Azma and several other prominent nationalist leaders were arrested, which gave demonstrators added impetus. In the meantime, Jamil Mardam, who had
gone into hiding, fearing that he too might be arrested, paid a surprise
visit to High Commissioner Puaux at the *Résidence des Pins* in Beirut in
a bid to return to power; but no compromise was possible and the following day Mardam became an opposition leader in Damascus.[62]
In Hama, a recently established party, the Shabab al-hamawi (Hama
Youth) organized large demonstrations against the Haffar government

[59] *Al-Mudhik al-mubki*, no. 408 (11 March 1939), p. 5; FO 371/1535, vol. 23276.
MacKereth to Halifax, 23 Feb. 1939.

[60] *Al-Mudhik al-mubki*, no. 408 (11 March 1939), pp. 5–6; FO 371/2265, vol. 23276.
MacKereth to Baxter, 16 March 1939.

[61] FO 371/2311, vol. 23276. MacKereth to Baxter, 22 March 1939.

[62] MAE, Puaux Papers, Carton 34. Puaux Telegrams (15, 16, 21, 25, 26 March 1939; 1
April 1939); *ibid.*, Carton 33, Dossier S-8. Puaux Note, 31 March 1939.

and French rule. They kept the town on strike for a month after Haffar stepped down; their aim was to replace the National Bloc leadership in the town. Clashes were especially violent.[63]

In Aleppo, the Bloc leadership decided on March 23 that all shops and offices were to be closed until further notice in protest against the arrest of prominent nationalists in Damascus. There, not everyone obeyed the Bloc; Christian merchants and shopkeepers were especially unobservant. This led to widespread violence as Muslim youth gangs stormed the downtown area of Aleppo, overturning tramcars, breaking the windows of any shops found open, and smearing black paint over signs in French on banks, stores, and offices. Bombs in the Christian quarter and at the Banque de Syrie led to a military crackdown, but soon the strike resumed and was not lifted until April 25.[64]

Even as the demonstrations and strikes proceeded, the Syrian Parliament on March 29 unanimously passed a resolution that negotiations between the Syrian government and the French could be resumed only on the basis of the treaty of 1936. President Atasi then appointed on April 5 Nasuhi al-Bukhari to head a neutral government, none of whose members belonged to the Bloc.[65] Because it did not enjoy the support of the Bloc-dominated Parliament, the Bukhari government was continually paralyzed. But equally feeble was the National Bloc; on April 20, Fa'iz al-Khuri, Fakhri al-Barudi, and Najib al-Rayyis in Damascus and Rushdi al-Kikhya, and Nazim al-Qudsi in Aleppo resigned from the organization. Jamil Mardam and Sa'dallah al-Jabiri lost control of the Bloc and in their place a directorate of three—Shukri al-Quwwatli, Lutfi al-Haffar, and Ahmad al-Lahham—took over.[66] Mardam announced his intention of retiring from public life to devote himself to his country estate. The British Consul remarked at the time that

> it is difficult not to attribute [Mardam's] sudden appreciation of the bucolic life to the persistent attacks made recently by the local press accusing the Mardam government of consistent misappropriation of public funds throughout their term of office.

But, he also added that "the public memory being as short, if not shorter, in Arab countries than elsewhere, he will probably pop up again when he feels the time is ripe."[67]

[63] MWT, al-Nadi al-'arabi, 135/346-450. Chief of Police (Hama) to Muhafiz (Hama), 28 Feb. 1939; ibid., al-Intidab al-faransi, 13/619/705. Muhafiz (Hama), 28 March 1939.

[64] FO 371/3199, vol. 23276. Davis to FO, 31 March 1939; MAE, Puaux Papers, Carton 34. Puaux Telegram, 5 April 1939.

[65] FO 371/2896, vol. 23276. MacKereth to Baxter, 13 April 1939.

[66] FO 371/3254, vol. 23276. MacKereth to Baxter, 28 April 1939; MAE, Puaux Papers, Carton 34. Puaux Telegram, 20 April 1939.

[67] FO 371/3254, vol. 23276.

After a visit to Paris, M. Puaux returned on May 10 and two days later delivered a radio broadcast from Beirut in which he outlined the course of French policy. He declared that his government was willing to resume negotiations based on the terms of the 1936 treaty as amended in November 1938, provided that there were satisfactory reassurances for safeguarding the vital interests of both countries and especially the Syrian minorities. His speech caused the immediate resignation of the Bukhari cabinet on the one hand and a storm of protest from the opposition elements around Dr. Shahbandar, who had recently returned from yet another visit to Egypt.[68]

Toward the end of May, Parliament adjourned until October, indicating no interest whatsoever in accepting Puaux's recent invitation.[69] Efforts by Shahbandar and his loyalists—Zaki al-Khatib and Munir al-ʿAjlani—to form a political organization uniting the different parties in Damascus (Shahbandarists, National Bloc, League of National Action, Nationalist Youth, and independents) aborted. Shahbandar opposed the Bloc's effort to reconstitute the Bukhari cabinet with moderate nationalists and instead demanded that Hashim al-Atasi invite Nasib al-Bakri to form a government. A last ditch effort by Shaykh Kamil al-Qassab to reconcile the Bloc and Shahbandar failed when Shahbandar agreed only if Mardam and Saʿdallah al-Jabiri were excluded from the Bloc.[70]

With no movement on the internal front, a familiar thing happened. The political pendulum swung back toward the pan-Arab arena. Nationalist factions turned to their traditional allies in the Arab world for support against one another and against the French. Syrian leaders visited Iraq, Transjordan, and Saudi Arabia frequently in this period, if only in search of "inspiration."[71]

SYRIAN NATIONALISTS REALIZED perfectly well that the promise of independence was now more remote than ever. While they awaited the French to lower the boom, their various factions maneuvered in order to be best placed to pick up the pieces. The boom fell in early July when M. Puaux issued four decrees suspending the Syrian constitution, dissolving Parliament, placing the administration in the hands of a Directorate composed of the permanent heads of the government departments, increasing local autonomy in the Druze and Alawite regions, and instituting direct French control in the Jazira. President Atasi immediately resigned his office when the pro-French but conscientious Bahij al-Khatib

[68] FO 371/3979, vol. 23277. MacKereth to Baxter, 19 May 1939.
[69] FO 371/4400, vol. 23277. MacKereth to Baxter, 12 June 1939.
[70] MAE, Puaux Papers, Carton 34. "Chronique politique," June 1939.
[71] FO 371/4400, vol. 23277. MacKereth to Baxter, 12 June 1939.

took over the new Council of Directors.[72] The National Bloc was back on the political sidelines less than three years after taking office.

The "political cycle" had been one of "complete revolution." French policy had gone back to the point where it was on the eve of the General Strike of 1936. French efforts to establish a new policy orientation had been condemned to remain sterile owing to a number of factors. Syria's compact minorities continued to be nervous and disturbed by the National Bloc's domination. And, with war approching, the Paris government wanted to indicate that France was not preparing to abandon her position in the Levant.[73] The perceptive Colonel MacKereth offered an astute summation of the consequences of Syrian factionalism in the late 1930s:

> The amount of rope that the French authorities allowed the Syrian nationalists in power between December 1936 and December 1938 sufficed for the Nationalist bloc to hang itself in the eyes of most Syrians. The Bloc has disintegrated into emulous political factions, whilst the bulk of the population has had a surfeit of political intrigue and place-hunting. The French political officers have skilfully played on all the chords. It may therefore be guessed that there will be little or no dangerous internal anti-French reaction.[74]

Indeed, Syria was remarkably subdued.

[72] MAE, Puaux Papers, Carton 34. "Chronique politique," July 1939; FO 371/4872, vol. 23277. MacKereth to FO, 9 July 1939; FO 371/4894, vol. 23277. MacKereth to Halifax, 3 July 1939; FO 371/5341, vol. 23277. MacKereth to Baxter, 22 July 1939.

[73] MAE, Syrie–Liban 1930–40. Lagarde Note, 17 Aug. 1939, vol. 496, pp. 201–18; *Le Temps* (11 July 1939). MD, 7N 4190, Dossier 1. Daladier (Paris) to MAE, 5 July 1939.

[74] FO 371/4894, vol. 23277. MacKereth to Halifax, 3 July 1939.

PART VIII

WAR AND INDEPENDENCE, 1939–1945

CHAPTER TWENTY-THREE

PLAYING ONE AGAINST THE OTHER

SYRIA ESCAPED the serious military engagements and damage of World War II. Nevertheless, the war changed the country in two important respects. It paved the way for independence from France and it stimulated economic and societal changes which accelerated the realignment of political forces in the country. The war also accentuated a number of important trends which would define Syria's course in the postwar period.

The catalyst for independence was the establishment of a large British presence in the heart of Syria. Britain's direct wartime involvement in Syrian political and economic life aggravated Anglo-French rivalry and created new opportunities for the Syrian nationalist leadership. In the end, Britain's weight in the overall balance of power enabled veteran nationalists to realize their main objective: national independence with the National Bloc at the helm of government.

ANGLO-FRENCH RELATIONS

Anglo-French relations in the Levant had been civil for long stretches between the wars. But behind the veneer of civility lay mutual suspicion. France never forgave Britain for not halting the flow of men, arms, and money into Syria from Palestine, Transjordan, and Iraq during the Great Revolt. France tried to even the score during the rebellion in Palestine a decade later. But, owing to Britain's comparative strength in the region, the French continued to feel the weaker of the two. In particular, they had always feared that Britain's toleration and even mild encouragement of Arab nationalism might undermine France's position in Syria and Lebanon.

The events in the Levant during the Second World War gave this fear substance. The Fall of France in 1940, the erection of the Vichy regime, and the eventual placement of the pro-Vichy General Dentz as High Commissioner in Syria and Lebanon brought the conflict to the heart of the Middle East, more than a year before the German occupation of France. France's offer of Syrian airbases to German aircraft during the anti-British Rashid 'Ali coup in Iraq in 1941 prompted the British-organized Anglo-Free French invasion of Syria and Lebanon. Successful, the British then transferred the duties of Mandate administration to Charles de Gaulle's Free French forces. However, a massive British military presence in the Levant states supported the Free French, meaning that final authority was in British hands for the war's duration.

Britain's ascendancy in Syria heightened the mutual suspicion and antagonism between the Allies. In fact, the British did not at first recognize the Free French as the sole representatives of the French nation, which contributed to their difficult relationship in Syria and Lebanon.[1] The principal source of Anglo-French friction in the Levant was Britain's insistence that France grant Syria her independence. De Gaulle, intent on resurrecting France as a first-class world power in the postwar era, supported the renewal and strengthening of France's ties to her colonies. He viewed British policy as designed to support British hegemony in the Middle East after the war, at the expense of France's interests. In this atmosphere of mutual suspicion and rivalry, Syrian nationalist leaders discovered new levers to work toward their eventual independence.

NATIONALISTS UNDER SIEGE

The outbreak of World War II found the nationalist leadership exhausted and politically bankrupt. Out of government and out of power, nationalists welcomed the breather offered by the war. They hoped in particular that the exciting events in Europe might allow the Syrian public to forget the Bloc's mistakes of the past two years.[2]

Syrian towns were unusually tranquil after the High Commissioner's decision in early July 1939 to suspend the Syrian constitution, dissolve Parliament, give greater autonomy to the minority regions, and place the government in the hands of a Directorate composed of non-nationalist permanent secretaries of ministries.[3] There were no protests or strikes. There were no signs of the National Bloc or opposition parties attempting to resist a policy which "but a short time ago would have been regarded as reactionary and totally unacceptable to all patriotic Syrians."[4]

The Allied Declaration of War against Germany stiffened French control in Syria and Lebanon. Martial law was proclaimed. The French military got authority to requisition whatever they needed. Most taxis were commandeered. The sale of petrol for private use was temporarily prohibited. Shopkeepers were ordered to supply only small quantities of

---

[1] See François Kersaudy, *Churchill and De Gaulle* (New York, 1983); Charles de Gaulle, *Mémoires de Guerre*, 3 vols. (Paris, 1954–59); Winston Churchill, *The Second World War*, 6 vols. (London, 1948–1954); Issac Lipschits, *La politique de la France au Levant, 1939–41* (Paris, 1941).

[2] *Al-Mudhik al-mubki*, no. 432 (28 Oct. 1939), p. 6.

[3] FO 371/4872, vol. 23277. MacKereth to FO, 9 July 1939; FO 371/4894, vol. 23277. MacKereth to Halifax, 3 July 1939.

[4] FO 371/5213, vol. 23277. Davis to FO, 12 July 1939.

foodstuffs to any one purchaser, and the price scale was fixed.[5] Strict censorship of the press and other communications was imposed. All radios in cafés and other public places were confiscated to prevent crowds from gathering to listen to the German-Arabic broadcasts, a social event which had become "so much a feature of daily life in . . . neighbouring Arabic-speaking countries." Meanwhile, the French cracked down on their list of political "subversives." They closed down the Syrian Communist Party, the Syrian Social Nationalist Party, the Arab Club, and Fakhri al-Barudi's Bureau for National Propaganda, as well as imprisoning Axis sympathizers and the leadership of the League of National Action.[6]

Although the French spared most members of the National Bloc and Dr. Shahbandar's Party, they stepped up their harassment of nationalist leaders. The High Commission encouraged the new Administrator-General Bahij al-Khatib to delve into the Bloc's affairs during its 1936–39 tenure in government. Relying on the old Ottoman adage that "the fish begins to stink at its head," Khatib revealed information implicating Jamil Mardam in illicit financial dealings when he was Prime Minister. These revelations contributed to Mardam's demotion in the nationalist pecking order.[7] Similar accusations were made against other Bloc chiefs.[8]

During the first year of the war, a number of nationalists, including Mardam, proclaimed their absolute loyalty to France (and Britain) and quietly tried to persuade the High Commission to relinquish the reins of government to the Bloc.[9] They were unsuccessful, however.

Shut out of government and unable to advance the movement toward independence, a familiar pattern reappeared. Whenever a political impasse was reached between the nationalists and the French, nationalists looked outside Syria to her Arab neighbors for leverage to break it. They did not have to look far. Several Arab unity plans were already afloat, associated with the Hashemite houses in Transjordan and Iraq, and with Ibn Saʿud.

As always, Syrian nationalists held divergent opinions about Arab unity. Disagreement came out into the open when a large delegation headed by Dr. Shahbandar went to Amman in June 1939 to discuss unity

[5] FO 371/6637, vol. 23277. MacKereth to Baxter, 4 Sept. 1939.

[6] FO 371/7298, vol. 23277. MacKereth to Baxter, 27 Sept. 1939; FO 371/6637, vol. 23277. MacKereth to Baxter, 4 Sept. 1939.

[7] MAE, Gabriel Puaux Papers. Carton 34, 15 Aug. 1939. Several nationalists were sentenced to long prison terms for their role in an assassination attempt on Khatib. See FO 371/1778, vol. 24591. Ogden, 26 April 1940.

[8] Les Echos de Syrie (21 Aug. 1939).

[9] FO 371/6637, vol. 23277. MacKereth to Baxter, 4 Sept. 1939; FO 371/ 7919, vol. 23277, 28 Nov. 1939.

586 WAR AND INDEPENDENCE

plans. Shahbandar's decision to proclaim Amir ʿAbdullah "King of Syria" caused a minor sensation in Damascus and annoyed Ibn Saʿud.[10] ʿAbdullah had long looked to Syria as a window of opportunity. With Shahbandar back in action and with the approach of wartime conditions, that window had not been opened so wide in many years.[11] To counter Shahbandar's declaration, the National Bloc sought Ibn Saʿud's intervention.[12] Riyadh supported the National Bloc to counter Hashemite plans.

While Syrian leaders turned toward the Arab world, the Arab world returned the interest. Iraqi public opinion felt strongly that Syria should have the independence promised her by France. Iraq also feared that if Turkish designs on the Jazira materialized, Iraq's sovereignty would be threatened. Above all, Prime Minister Nuri Saʿid and his colleagues wanted to make Iraq the center of a large pan-Arab federation including Syria.[13]

As for France, High Commissioner Gabriel Puaux had let it be known that he thought a Syrian monarchy would better serve French and Syrian interests. Under a monarchy, he felt, a treaty had a better chance of enduring. For one thing, he argued, "a Druze or Alawite can accept to obey a monarch from a great Islamic dynasty more than a cabinet of Damascus citizens."[14]

French officials preferred to introduce a Saʿudi dynasty, for the Saʿudis would be likely to emphasize Islam rather than Arab nationalism in Syria, an ideology more easily reconciled with French interests at that time. There was even the assumption that the minorities would receive greater protection as "people of the book."[15]

British opinion was divided. British experts agreed with the French assessment and believed that a Syrian throne occupied by a Saʿudi would above all prevent the development of close and friendly relations between Syria and the Hashemite monarchies in Iraq and Transjordan in addition to providing "an element of stability quite lacking in Damascus politics."[16] Others felt that the realization of Hashemite ambitions in Syria would guarantee British hegemony there.

The battle over unity, though a lively and acrimonious one, was in the

---

[10] Puaux Papers, Carton 36, Dossier S-3-5. Puaux to Lagarde, Beirut, 20 May 1939; FO 371/4826, vol. 23280. Kirkbride to MacMichael, 14 June 1939; *La Chronique* (11 June 1939).

[11] Wilson, *King Abdullah,* Chapter 7.

[12] FO 371/5493, vol. 23281. MacKereth to FO, 25 July 1939.

[13] FO 371/22408, vol. 23276. Eastern Department Note, 29 March 1939.

[14] Puaux Papers, Carton 36, Dossier S-3-5. Puaux to Lagarde (Beirut), 20 May 1939.

[15] Puaux floated the idea of a Saʿudi throne in Syria with Foreign Minister Daladier and Ibn Saʿud's foreign minister. Puaux Papers, Carton 36, Dossier S-3-5. R. Montagne to Puaux, 20 June 1939.

[16] FO 371/2803, vol. 23276. Bullard (Jidda) to FO, 15 April 1939.

nature of a rash of hives. It was irritating and recurrent, but each bout was short-lived. This particular outbreak died down when ʿAbdullah, the most active partisan, learned that the French did not approve of his candidature. The resulting hiatus was of immense relief to Ibn Saʿud who let it be known that he never had designs on Syria or any other Arab territory, fearing only a Syrian union with Transjordan or Iraq which might facilitate Hashemite designs in Arabia. What he wanted was a balance of power in the Arab world.[17] The struggle for Syria, however, was just beginning.

ASSASSINATION

With Jamil Mardam relegated to the political sidelines and radical nationalists conspicuously absent from politics, even, in certain cases, from the country entirely, Dr. Shahbandar's political future brightened. Although Shahbandar was still considered Britain's premier agent in Syria, a few important French officials, including Gabriel Puaux, were beginning to see him in a different light. What increased Shahbandar's attractiveness to Puaux and others was his public support of the Allied cause and his unsparing public criticism of the National Bloc and the Istiqlalis. Shahbandar had also been able to attract a following among conservative Syrian notables "who, after having accepted loyally the Mandate experience, found in the party of the Doctor a protection against the Bloc at the moment when France appeared to be transferring power to their adversaries."[18] When Shahbandar was not extolling the virtues of moderate pan-Arabism, he fiercely criticized radical nationalists like Shukri al-Quwwatli and Shakib Arslan, whom he labeled as self-seeking and pro-fascist.[19]

By the time France capitulated to the Axis Powers in June 1940, Shahbandar was the leading political figure in Syria. But he had not turned away from his British friends. On the contrary, he went to great lengths to secure British support for his plan for a loose confederation of Syria, Lebanon, Transjordan, and Palestine under the kingship of Amir ʿAbdullah. Shahbandar's bitter denunciations of his nationalist rivals, his close ties to ʿAbdullah, and his flirtations with the British and with certain French officials engendered much suspicion among his rivals. And, in a rare act (or at least in a rarely successful act) of political violence in Syria, he was assassinated in Damascus at the end of June. Although his assailants were captured, brought to trial, and executed or imprisoned for life,

---

[17] FO 371/6959, vol. 23281. Bullard to FO, 16 Oct. 1939.

[18] Puaux, *Deux années au Levant*, p. 37.

[19] FO 371/599, vol. 24548. Middle East Intelligence Centre to FO, 30 Jan. 1940.

there was much speculation about the actual motives behind his assassination.

Such speculation arose from the way justice was carried out. The trial began more than four months after the assassination and took nearly a month to complete. A special court presided over by a Frenchman was convened and no provisions were made for appeal. One individual was charged with premeditated murder and thirteen others with attempted murder and complicity in premeditated murder. What made the trial so sensational was that among those charged with complicity were Jamil Mardam, Lutfi al-Haffar, and Sa'dallah al-Jabiri, all of whom avoided arrest by fleeing to Iraq before warrants could be issued.[20]

Shahbandar's supporters were certain that French officials had been involved in the plot and had allowed Mardam and the others to escape. Of the seven men actually brought to trial, one was Jamil Mardam's personal secretary, 'Asim al-Na'ili. He was alleged to have been the intermediary between the nationalist leaders and the assassins, the individual, in other words, who made the payoffs. That the Public Prosecutor dropped all charges against Na'ili together with those against Mardam, Haffar, and Jabiri only aroused greater suspicion.[21]

There were various allegations as to the source of the payoffs. It could have been French Intelligence agents sympathetic to Vichy who took advantage of France's capitulation to get rid of Britain's man in Syria. Or Italian agents who wanted to eliminate pro-British activities associated with Shahbandar. Or the Palestinian Mufti, Hajj Amin al-Husayni, who wanted to block Amir 'Abdullah's bid for a Syrian throne, which Shahbandar sponsored. Or Iraqi agents who also wanted to thwart 'Abdullah. Or the Bloc chiefs whom Shahbandar had worked so hard to eliminate as local contenders for power. All were possibilities, although some more likely than others.[22] Shahbandar's supporters were convinced that Jamil Mardam was ultimately responsible. The public too were suspicious of Mardam. There is evidence that National Bloc lieutenants supplied the weapons and the role of 'Asim al-Na'ili seemed pivotal.[23] Mardam's deep distrust and fear of Shahbandar were well known. Even if he did not order the assassination, he may well have wished it. A loyal lieutenant like

[20] FO 371/655, vol. 27330. R. A. Beaumont Memorandum, 11 Jan. 1941.

[21] *Ibid.*; FO 371/2365, vol. 24591. Gardener to FO, 27 July 1940.

[22] Conversations with Hasan al-Hakim (Damascus, 12 March 1976) and with Nasuh Babil (Damascus, 20 Feb. 1976); FO 371/3082, vol. 24595. Gardener to FO, 11 Dec. 1940; MWT, Nazih Mu'ayyad al-'Azm Papers. Mu'ayyad al-'Azm to General H. M. Wilson, 5 Aug. 1941; Puaux Papers, Carton 33, Dossier S-8. Hauteclocque (Damascus) to Puaux, 15 Sept. 1940; *ibid.*, Carton 36. Dentz (Beirut), 13 Jan. 1941; FO 371/172, vol. 27330. Gardener to FO, 11 Jan. 1941; FO 371/2365, vol. 24591. Gardener to FO, 27 July 1940.

[23] Puaux Papers, Carton 34. "Affaire Shahbandar." Puaux Telegram, 13 July 1940.

Na'ili could easily have interpreted that wish to be an order. One witness testified that Mardam had asked him in the past to murder Shahbandar,[24] and there had been an earlier attempt on Shahbandar's life in January 1939, at the height of his efforts to force Mardam's government to resign.[25] And Shahbandar supporters had been accused of trying to assassinate Mardam in 1938.

Whether French officials knew in advance of the assassination plot or were involved in a cover up is unclear. They could have tipped off Mardam and his Bloc colleagues that charges were to be brought against them, allowing them to escape to Iraq. By avoiding the political aspect of the case, the Court was able to drop all charges against them. In any case, the departure of these influential nationalists from Syria weakened nationalist ranks even further, which suited French purposes.

The four men who were found guilty and executed in February 1941 (two others had their sentences commuted to life imprisonment) included a peddler, a furniture maker, and a small shop employee.[26] They claimed that the assassination had been a political and a religious act. They accused Shahbandar of being a spy for Britain and an enemy of Islam. The first accusation was a familiar one, based on the numerous contacts Shahbandar maintained over the years with British officials in Damascus and Cairo and his frequent visits to the British Consulate in the months before his assassination. The second was refuted by a statement from the leading *ulama* of Damascus, although Shahbandar had suggested on numerous occasions that Islam should be removed from politics and relegated to the private realm. But the Court did not allow the political dimensions of the case to be raised. The prosecutor seemed to treat 'Asim al-Na'ili with kid gloves. The judge allowed the witnesses, whose testimony tended to support his complicity and that of Jamil Mardam, to be ridiculed and treated harshly. When the decisions were handed down, the motives of the assailants were explained in terms of *"mistaken* religious zeal."[27]

The assassination crippled Shahbandar's Party. It had never been well organized, depending completely on the charismatic personality of its leader. And although Shahbandar stood head and shoulders above his rivals in terms of intellectual prowess and personal prestige, he had always been a maverick in the world of patronage politics. He had left no institutionalized network to survive his demise.

[24] FO 371/655, vol. 27330. Beaumont Memorandum, 11 Jan. 1941.

[25] Puaux Papers, Carton 34. Telegram, 14 Jan. 1939.

[26] Mu'ayyad al-'Azm Papers. Lieutenant Colonel Couetoux Memorandum on Shahbandar Assassination, July 1940. The profession of the fourth man is not given.

[27] FO 371/655, vol. 27330. Beaumont Memorandum, 11 Jan. 1941; conversation with Nasuh Babil (Damascus, 20 Feb. 1976).

QUWWATLI'S ASCENT

Shahbandar's assassination helped to put the National Bloc back into the limelight, but under a new leader. Mardam, Jabiri, and Haffar were in exile in Baghdad, and Mardam's reputation had been especially scarred by Shahbandar's assassination.[28] Therefore, Shukri al-Quwwatli was able, at long last, to make his bid for the leadership of the national independence movement.[29]

Quwwatli's radical, uncompromising tendencies had long ago alienated France and Britain. He had opposed Mardam's compromises with France over the 1936 treaty, and Britain believed him to be the one member of the Mardam government who opposed British efforts to end Syrian support for the rebellion in Palestine.

Quwwatli's decision to play ball with the Axis added to his unpopularity in French and British circles. However, his decision was opportunistic not ideological. The nationalist objective was to make France's position in Syria untenable. Quwwatli and his closest associates in the Istiqlal wing of the Bloc believed that the Fall of France, the sweep of Germany across North Africa, and the corresponding increase in German propaganda activities in the Levant brought the question of Syrian independence that much closer. Moreover, since Gabriel Puaux had refused the Bloc access to power, nationalists naturally turned to those French officers and officials who disagreed with Puaux. And, since Puaux was unsympathetic to Vichy, those in opposition to him and those sought by the nationalists tended to be pro-Vichy. Although Puaux did not last long as High Commissioner and was replaced by General Henri Dentz, a loyal Vichy follower, by the time of the Allied occupation of Syria in 1941, the Bloc had been colored pro-Axis.[30]

Not all Bloc leaders supported this shift in identity. While Quwwatli cozied up to pro-Axis French officials,[31] Jamil Mardam sought British support in Baghdad, by flaunting his anti-Axis views and his loyalty to Britain.[32]

Despite Quwwatli's cozying, he did not refrain from attacking the French administration, whoever was at its head. His first serious opportunity came at the end of February 1941 when a sudden shortage of bread

---

[28] FO 371/2709, vol. 24594. Crosthwaite Note, 2 Oct. 1940.
[29] MAE, Guerre 1939–1945. Londres (CNF), vol. 39. Report of 15 Oct. 1940, pp. 26–28; Puaux Papers, Carton 36. Dentz, 13 Jan. 1941.
[30] FO 371/2709, vol. 24594. Gardener to FO, 27 Sept. 1940.
[31] In particular, M. Perissé, head of Sûreté in Damascus. FO 371/2365, vol. 24591. Gardener to FO, 21 Sept. 1940; MAE, Guerre 1939–45. Londres (CNF), vol. 39, 14 Oct. 1940.
[32] FO 371/169, vol. 27330. Newton to Halifax, 23 Dec. 1940.

led to a sharp price rise and long bread lines in Damascus. Although Syria was still almost totally self-sufficient in food, there had been scarcities of rice, sugar, paraffin for cooking and light, and petrol. The war had clearly raised the cost of living which in turn aggravated the position of the unemployed, numbering as many as 50,000 in Damascus alone.[33] But nothing could better guarantee an explosion in the towns than bread shortages. The inefficiency of the French military authorities who ran the Département de Ravitaillement and a shortage of petrol for the transport services were behind the crisis.

At Quwwatli's behest, the Bloc used the occasion to launch a strike of shopkeepers in Damascus on February 28. A few days later it spread to Homs, Hama, Aleppo, and Dayr al-Zur. Nationalists employed the familiar methods of intimidation to keep the strike alive in the suqs. Even when the government agreed to reduce the price of bread in the second week of March, the Bloc refused to call off the strike. Marked by violence, French repression, and a number of deaths, it lasted until early April, when the High Commissioner agreed to replace the Council of Directors by one with legislative powers and control over the Département de Ravitaillement.[34]

Khalid al-ʿAzm was appointed to head the new council. He was a prominent landowner and industrialist from the pre-eminent family of Damascus. His appointment launched a political career that came to be of considerable consequence to Syria after independence. Because its complexion was at best mildly nationalist, the Bloc viewed the ʿAzm ministry as only a small step in the right direction. Nevertheless, it was because of a strike mounted by the Bloc that the High Commissioner had been forced to take even this small step. Hence ʿAzm's appointment marked the re-emergence of the Bloc with Quwwatli at its helm.

THE ALLIED OCCUPATION

German propaganda in the winter and spring of 1941 was on the rise in the Levant. The Nazi official, von Hentig, visited Syria and distributed largesse to a number of individuals and organizations, including Shukri al-Quwwatli and the National Bloc, a group of pro-German landlords, and several radical youth groups.[35] Rashid ʿAli al-Gaylani's coup d'état in Iraq in early May further promoted German ambitions and the hope of

[33] FO 371/2365, vol. 24591. Gardener to FO, 19 Aug. 1940.

[34] FO 371/1282, vol. 27290. Gardener to FO, 3 April 1941. The High Commissioner retained the right to approve all laws which affected French interests.

[35] FO 371/348, vol. 27333. Gardener to FO, 1 Feb. 1941; Muʾayyad al-ʿAzm Papers, no. 245. Landlords included Saʿid al-Kaylani, Nuri Ibish, ʿAdnan al-Quwwatli, and Mustafa al-ʿAzm. FO 371/2837, vol. 27291. Gardener to FO, 9 April 1941.

Syrian independence. German sympathizers, Rashid ʿAli and the army officers who surrounded him ousted the pro-British Regent, ʿAbd ul-illah, causing intense excitement among large sections of the Syrian population. Students were particularly stirred; some led demonstrations of support for Rashid ʿAli in the major towns. Meanwhile, others, mainly members of the pan-Arab League of National Action and Arab Club, volunteered to go to Iraq to join the struggle against British imperialism. That the French mandatory administration did little to challenge Axis intrigues graphically demonstrated the demoralization, incompetence, and divisiveness which permeated the High Commission.[36]

Britain, naturally, began to grow alarmed. When the French administration in Syria and Lebanon offered the Axis Powers airbases and other facilities to assist Rashid ʿAli's movement, Britain, in cooperation with the Free French, prepared to do something. A joint military campaign was launched on June 8, a week after the British had extinguished the Iraqi uprising and restored the Regent. The Allies were in control of Syria and Lebanon by July 14. The fear of a German reascendancy in Syria and Lebanon had, for all intents and purposes, been eliminated.

The Allied invasion of the Levant in early June of 1941 shifted the balance of power in Syria. Britain was already in control of Iraq, Palestine, Transjordan, and Eygpt. The massive British military presence in Syria and Lebanon, introduced through the invasion, clinched Britain's predominance. Just as at the end of World War I, Britain's physical presence in the Arab East dwarfed France's, reawakening the fear that Britain intended to ease France out of the region altogether.

The Allied invasion had been accompanied by a Free French proclamation, issued in the name of General de Gaulle by General Georges Catroux, promising independence to Syria and Lebanon.

> Inhabitants of Syria and Lebanon! At the moment when the forces of Free France, united to the forces of the British Empire, her ally, are entering your territory, I declare that I assume the powers, responsibilities and duties of the representative of France in the Levant. I do this in the name of France, which is the traditional and real France, and in the name of her Chief, General de Gaulle. In this capacity I come to put an end to the mandatory régime and to proclaim you free and independent.[37]

De Gaulle's declaration was guaranteed by Britain and came in an exchange of letters between the Free French leader and Oliver Lyttleton,

---

[36] *Ibid.*; FO 371/?, Beirut Appreciation, no. 11/41. 13–24 April 1941.
[37] Hourani, *Syria and Lebanon*, p. 241.

British Minister of State in the Middle East, on August 15. Lyttleton wrote to de Gaulle that

> Great Britain has no interest in Syria and Lebanon, except to win the war. We have no desire to encroach in any way upon the position of France. Both Free France and Great Britain are pledged to the independence of Syria and Lebanon. When this essential step has been taken, and without prejudice to it, we freely admit that France should have the predominant position in Syria and Lebanon over any other European Power. It is in this spirit that we have always acted.[38]

Although Britain was committed to Syrian and Lebanese independence, de Gaulle's declaration was principally intended to sap any internal resistance to the joint occupation. He also realized that a renunciation of France's traditional position in the Levant would give Vichy greater opportunity to discredit his movement back in France, and elsewhere in the French Empire. Moreover, he firmly believed that the revitalization of the French Empire would contribute profoundly to a necessary French national revival. And so, he intended that the promised independence be a long time coming.

In fact, the differing interpretations of the Free French proclamation and the British guarantee colored Anglo-French relations for the duration of the war. The issue of independence became the chief bone of contention between Britain and the Free French in the Middle East. De Gaulle saw Britain perched in the Levant ready to swoop in should France demonstrate, even for a moment, uncertainty about her future role in the region. Britain saw the stubborn tenacity of France's grip on the Levant as an anachronism and a danger to a smooth adjustment to wartime realities.

In addition to greater differences of policy, personality conflicts made the Anglo-French relationship in Syria a most uncomfortable one for the duration of the war. De Gaulle and Winston Churchill were continually at loggerheads. Because de Gaulle was in the weaker position owing to the dependence of his Free French Committee on British support, his paranoia about British intentions directly impinged upon the execution of French policy in Syria. At the next level down, this conflict was even sharper. General Georges Catroux, whom de Gaulle had appointed as his Delegate-General (replacing the position of High Commissioner) for the Levant, and Major-General Edward Spears, Churchill's chief emissary to Syria and Lebanon, locked horns almost daily.[39]

---

[38] *Ibid.*, pp. 244–45.
[39] Kersaudy, *Churchill and De Gaulle*, pp. 192–93. Catroux's distaste for Spears is appar-

The Spears mission was invested with the task of bringing the Levant states more closely into line with Britain's overall strategic interests in the Middle East. This meant guaranteeing British military security in the region. But ultimately it also concerned reinforcing Britain's long-term strategic and commercial interests there.

The British aimed to coordinate their larger Arab policy by incorporating Syria into that policy. Britain recognized that political independence for the Arab countries was both necessary and inevitable. This assessment had as much validity in Syria as in Britain's own spheres of influence. If Arab aspirations in the Levant were ignored any longer, nationalist discontent might jeopardize the Allied military position in the entire region. But given Britain's preponderant strength in the Middle East and the general mood of personal distrust between Britain and the Free French, de Gaulle and his colleagues were unprepared to accept Britain's assessment. To them, any course of action recommended by Britain was suspected of hiding motives prejudicial to France's future in the region. [40]

In spite of the June 1941 proclamation promising independence, Britain had agreed that the Free French should continue to control all the administrative levers in the Levant states, including the Troupes Spéciales, for the time being, while Britain insured the region's overall military security. The Free French, nevertheless, were pathologically afraid of British designs. One issue that particularly irritated the French was the British-funded wheat scheme designed "to make the Levant self-sufficient in cereal production" which they "denounced . . . as a British bid to control the Levant by economic means."[41] In order to assert French control, General Catroux established an administrative regime in Syria that was no more advanced than those of the early 1930s.

To Syrian nationalists it gradually became clear that the Free French did not intend to suspend the Mandate before reaching treaties with Syria (and Lebanon) which satisfied French interests. A second French procla-

---

ent in his memoirs (see Georges Catroux, *Dans la bataille de Méditérranée: Egypte-Levant-Afrique du Nord 1940–44* [Paris, 1949]). For the view of Spears on Catroux, see Major-General Sir Edward Spears, *Assignment to Catastrophe*, 2 vols. (London, 1954) and *Fulfillment of a Mission* (Hamden, Conn., 1977). More information can be found in the Sir Edward Spears Papers, Middle East Centre, St. Antony's College, University of Oxford, Box I, Box II: 3–7. One longtime French official in the Levant argued, however, that regardless of Catroux's distrust of Spears and the British in Syria and Lebanon, he was nevertheless a "connoisseur of Arab affairs" and hence acknowledged the need to compromise with the forces of nationalism; but he was regularly overridden by de Gaulle who when he thought of Arab nationalism and the British always saw red flags. See Pierre Rondot, "Les mouvements nationalistes au Levant durant la Deuxième Guerre Mondiale (1939–1945)," in *La Guerre en Méditerranée (1939–45)* (Paris, 1971), p. 662.

[40] Kersaudy, *Churchill and De Gaulle*, pp. 194–95.

[41] *Ibid.*, p. 196.

mation of independence, by General Catroux, on September 27 was not taken seriously in nationalist circles. How could it have been when it "excluded all Syrian control of the army or police forces, or the public services, or economic affairs, or communications."[42]

Nevertheless, owing to both nationalist and British pressures, the Free French had to pay something more than lip-service to the question of independence. So the Syrian constitution was restored and a cabinet of ministerial rank replaced the Directorate headed by Khalid al-ʿAzm. For the post of President, however, the French turned to the remarkably resilient time-server, Shaykh Taj al-Din al-Hasani.[43] No appointment could have angered veteran nationalists more. Although Hasan al-Hakim, Dr. Shahbandar's old confederate and a longtime opponent of the French, was named Prime Minister, the complexion of the new cabinet was non-nationalist. Some ranking French civilian advisers had opposed Taj's nomination in favor of Jamil Mardam, who by this time appeared to be estranged from the National Bloc. But, higher-ups recognized that Mardam commanded only a small following and was "handicapped by his alleged complicity in the murder of Shahbandar." What influence General de Gaulle may have had over Taj's appointment is difficult to assess. He had visited Syria just before the formation of the new ministry and it was acknowledged in certain French circles that his "overbearing ignorance of local conditions" made it unlikely that a workable government could be formed.[44]

No one inside or outside government could long tolerate Shaykh Taj as President. Prime Minister Hakim accused him of gross interference in his office's affairs, of maintaining an unnecessarily expensive official establishment, and of nepotism.[45] Moderate nationalists stepped up agitation against the government by blaming it for failing to solve the problem of bread shortages and other economic problems. In the towns unrest grew over the frequent inadequacy of bread supplies and other necessities, the rising cost of public transportation, and the failure of government wages to keep up with the rate of inflation. Strikes by students, workers, and other bodies were fairly widespread.[46] About the only positive development from the nationalist perspective was the retransfer of the Latakia

[42] FO 371/6923, vol. 27314. Lampson to FO, 23 Oct. 1941; Longrigg, *Syria*, p. 323.

[43] It appears that de Gaulle and Catroux may have offered to put the National Bloc in power if it agreed to rule without a parliament until the end of the war. FO 371/8097, vol. 27319. Edward Atiyah Report, 31 Oct. 1941.

[44] FO 684/14/30. Gardener Damascus Diary, week ending 16 Aug. 1941 [hereafter cited as Gardener Diary]; MAE, Guerre 1939-45. Londres (CNF). (April 1942), vol. 42, pp. 26–27; FO 226/233/31/24A. Spears to Eden, 28 April 1942.

[45] Gardener Diary, 11 Jan. 1942.

[46] Gardener Diary, 25 and 31 Jan; 8, 15, 22 Feb.; 1 March 1942.

and Druze *muhafazat* to Syrian government control in February 1942. By April it was clear that Hasan al-Hakim could no longer keep his government together. A cabinet crisis broke out and Shaykh Taj forced Hakim to step down. Husni al-Barazi, the wealthy landowner from Hama and a major force in the Syrian hashish market, replaced Hakim. Barazi had lost his nationalist credentials back in the early 1930s by accepting a cabinet post in a government the National Bloc opposed. His government included several moderate nationalists, although no one from the National Bloc.[47]

Barazi's tenure as Prime Minister was shaky. His government was attacked from all sides, owing to the general crisis of the Syrian economy. Big landowners in the Damascus region resented the efforts of the Office des Céréales Panifiables (O.C.P.) to purchase wheat at low fixed prices and did their utmost to subvert its organization by hoarding stocks or selling on the black market locally and in Transjordan and Palestine. The urban masses complained bitterly about irregular supplies of bread and its increasingly poor quality. Accusations were levelled at government officials, including Barazi himself, for taking a percentage of the sum allotted for the purchase of wheat supplies. The urban propertied classes, including absentee landowers, were also enraged by government efforts to enforce the French-instituted income tax. Above all, the cost of living was rapidly becoming a serious economic and political problem. The purchasing power of every section of the Syrian public was falling owing to the reduction in British Army contracts. Unemployment was spreading and even civil servants began to agitate as salaries fell further and further behind the cost of living. In reaction to the lack of initiative from the French to solve the problems, Barazi found himself drawing closer and closer to the position of the nationalists. His relations with Shaykh Taj soured and toward the end of 1942 he resigned.[48]

QUWWATLI AND THE BRITISH

Under Shukri al-Quwwatli's leadership nationalists struggled to close their ranks. On the one hand, they mounted a strong anti-government campaign, levelling charges against Taj of inactivity and nepotism, and demanding that the powers of French advisers be restricted. On the other, they tried to draw out the British in the hope of engineering a split between them and the French over the administration of Syria.

Despite French accusations to the contrary, the historical record indi-

---

[47] Gardener Diary, 19 April 1942; FO 226/233/31/24A. Spears to Eden, 28 April 1942.

[48] Gardener Diary, 14 Nov. 1942, 2 Jan. 1943; FO 226/233/31/296. Simpson (Damascus) to Spears Mission, 17 Dec. 1942.

cates that the British did not at first actively seek out Quwwatli and the National Bloc in an effort to weaken the French position in Syria. Rather, the National Bloc was the active agent and the British, at least at first, were remarkably passive, even suspicious of Quwwatli and his followers.

Quwwatli's major problem was to convince Britain that he was not a stooge of the Axis Powers, that his earlier coziness with the Germans was purely tactical. The injection of direct British influence in Syria broadened the range of options for nationalist leaders, and Shukri al-Quwwatli, in the tradition of Syria's urban notability, moved quickly to take advantage of the new situation.[49]

The record is not entirely clear as to how Quwwatli managed to end up in the good graces of the British. His main advocate outside Syria was Ibn Sa'ud. The monarch interceded with the British on the grounds that whatever Quwwatli had done in the past, his only aim was Syrian independence and that because his influence was unrivalled in Syria, he ought to be the political leader with whom Britain and France dealt. Seconding Ibn Sa'ud was Nuri Sa'id, the Iraqi Prime Minister. Quwwatli's decision to use the occasion of the pilgrimage to Mecca to go into self-imposed exile, eventually in Baghdad, widened his contacts with British officials.

By early 1942, it had become evident that the British had warmed to the idea of dealing with Quwwatli. His excellent relations with Britain's friends in Riyadh and Baghdad, their assurances that he was prepared to cooperate with the Allies, and the reality that as the leader of the National Bloc he was the most highly respected Syrian politician, encouraged the British to cultivate him.

The issue that seemed to seal the political marriage was a dispute over Quwwatli's efforts in the late winter of 1942 to return to Syria, which the French opposed. Under pressure from Ibn Sa'ud and several Iraqi politicians, the British interceded with the French on the matter. But General Catroux balked at the idea, claiming that Quwwatli was a dangerous Axis agitator and that if allowed to return he would most certainly destabilize a government already fractured by internal dissent and outside pressure. The British decision to press for Quwwatli's return was directly connected to their overall Arab policy. If it were known that Britain had unsuccessfully intervened this would only add to British difficulties in Iraq and Saudi Arabia. Moreover, a French refusal would almost certainly lead to widespread public disorders which would inevitably force the British to intervene militarily, something that would not sit well with Britain's Arab friends.

British pressure won the day and in the end Catroux invited Quwwatli to return unconditionally. Conscious, however, that his return might

[49] FO 371/1412, vol. 27330. Gardener to FO, 8 April 1941.

also provoke unrest which France would most certainly blame on British complicity and pressure, the British extracted a promise from Quwwatli that he would caution his supporters from taking any actions that would embarrass Britain.[50]

By the time Quwwatli returned to Syria in September 1942, his relations with Britain had improved considerably, But, Britain had not yet persuaded the French to take serious steps toward independence. In fact, Anglo-French relations had grown more tense in the summer of 1942. The military reversals in Libya and the real threat of an Axis advance on Egypt allowed General de Gaulle to renege on his promise to hold elections in Syria and Lebanon. He also demanded that the British recall General Spears on the grounds that he meddled in French affairs. Churchill refused.[51]

The Anglo-French impasse was only temporary. When Britain stopped German forces at El Alamein, removing the possibility of a German invasion of the Arab East, pressure eased. At the same time, Britain began to show greater willingness to accept French views about the future of North Africa. When Quwwatli returned to Damascus General Catroux agreed to meet him. By that time it had become obvious to the French that not only were President Hasani and the Barazi government at loggerheads but they had no popular appeal either.[52]

NATIONAL ELECTIONS

Quwwatli's return was followed by that of Jamil Mardam. The presence of both men sparked greater nationalist activity, given the opportunity provided by the death of Shaykh Taj on 17 January 1943.[53] A week later, the French announced that constitutional life would be restored. Elections were scheduled for July.

---

[50] FO 371/1995, vol. 27330. Gardener to FO, 4 May 1941; FO 371/4553, vol. 27330. Sir B. Newton (Baghdad) to Halifax, 11 Aug. 1941; FO 371/4553, vol. 27330. Wikely (Jidda) to FO, 9 Aug. 1941; FO 371/414, vol. 31481. Caccia Note, 4 March 1942; FO 371/1432, vol. 31481. Furlonge to FO, 4 March 1942; FO 371/ 1433, vol. 31481. Minister of State to FO, 4 March 1942; FO 371/1466, vol. 31481. FO to Beirut, 6 March 1942; FO 371/1537, vol. 31481. Beirut to FO, 8 March 1942; FO 371/ 1578, vol. 31481. Iraq to FO, 9 March 1942.

[51] Several high-ranking officials at the British Foreign Office also felt that the political intrigues of Spears, especially in Lebanon, were a detriment to the Anglo-French relationship and encouraged Churchill to recall him. But his close personal relationship with Churchill saved him. See Kersaudy, *Churchill and De Gaulle*, pp. 192–210; Ahmed M. Gomaa, *The Foundation of the League of Arab States: Wartime Diplomacy and Inter-Arab Politics 1941–1945* (London, 1977), p. 89.

[52] Gardener Diary, 31 Oct. 1942.

[53] Gardener Diary, 23 Jan. 1943.

The announcement aroused great interest in the towns where it was generally thought that British intervention had brought about the French change of heart. Nothing angered the French more than when public opinion credited Britain for relaxation of French control, even if that opinion was misinformed. Nationalist rumors that Britain had decided to back the National Bloc in the forthcoming elections clearly embarrassed the British who denied any such involvement.[54] Nevertheless, from this time on British involvement in local politics increased significantly.

Once elections were scheduled, the National Bloc moved quickly to put its house in order. Hashim al-Atasi, the elder nationalist statesman, urged Quwwatli and Mardam to resolve their differences. He also used his influence to get Quwwatli to make greater efforts to "compose the differences between the conflicting groups" in Aleppo in order to present a unified front. The result was that a small group of Aleppine moderates, led by Dr. Kayyali, showed their willingness to cooperate, although they made it perfectly clear they would not long tolerate the impulsive Sa'dallah al-Jabiri, whose close ties to Damascus made him suspect in the eyes of his Aleppo colleagues.[55]

A Bloc conference held in the last week of January, however, was marred by the absence of most Aleppine members and all delegates from Dayr al-Zur, the Jazira, and the Hawran. The Alawite and Druze delegations were negligible. Quwwatli and Mardam did manage to effect a reconciliation between themselves, although no one expected that their bitter rivalry had finally been laid to rest. Both leaders also conducted secret negotiations with Catroux's Delegate in Damascus, Colonel Collet, even after Quwwatli had promised the Bloc that he would never meet with him.[56] Meanwhile, other parties and factions also began to position themselves for the elections, some old and some new. In the forefront were the Shahbandarists who sparked a new spate of pro-Hashemite publicity in favor of Amir 'Abdullah as King of Syria.

To remind the French of its importance, the National Bloc threw its support behind a major strike which broke out on February 7 in reaction to a rise in the price (from 8 to 8 1/2 piastres per kilo) of "middle class" bread. The Bloc received the strong backing of local merchants who opposed the current Prime Minister Jamil al-Ulshi's declaration that his government would collect an income tax. The familiar combination of *tajhiz* students and quarter chiefs kept the strike going for five days. The Bloc's principal aim was to discredit the Ulshi government so that it could

---

[54] Gardener Diary, 30 Jan. 1943.

[55] FO 226/241/27/1/47. M.E.I.C. (Syria) to Lascelles, 19 Jan. 1943.

[56] FO 226/241/27/3/132. Gardener to Chancery, 24 Feb. 1943.

not unduly influence the elections.[57] Nationalist expectations that Catroux would respond to the Bloc's demands promptly were not fulfilled. The outbreak of another major strike on March 20 which lasted several days only complicated matters. Again the cause of the disorders was bread: "the reduction in quantity, the bad quality, the malpractices of the bakers, the insufficient surveillance of the Government, the injustices in the lists of the poor, and resentment at the supply of Syrian flour to the Lebanese." This time there was a death toll of seven demonstrators in addition to numerous injuries and extensive damage to tramcars, government buildings, schools, and shops.[58]

Sometime before the second strike, General Catroux, anxious to restore constitutional life in Syria on terms favorable to the French, offered Shukri al-Quwwatli a bargain in order to get around the problem of the elections. He proposed that the 1936 Parliament be reinstated and that Hashim al-Atasi resume the Presidency of the Republic. Atasi would then appoint a moderate interim government to include several members of the National Bloc which Parliament would approve to carry out the elections. Meanwhile, Parliament would dissolve itself. But Atasi, on behalf of the Bloc, would be required to sign a secret agreement that would guarantee Syria's acceptance of a treaty with France as a necessary preliminary to the acquisition of complete Syrian independence.

Realizing that any bargain at this stage might mean a sacrifice of Syria's future independence, Quwwatli rejected Catroux's offer. He had calculated that as long as he was in a position to organize nationalist constituencies, the Bloc would sweep the elections. Hashim al-Atasi, however, showed great willingness to accept Catroux's terms, a fact that would irreparably damage his own political future.[59]

In a move which was reminiscent of 1936, a discouraged and increasingly desperate Catroux appointed the distinguished Damascene notable ʿAta al-Ayyubi as Chief of State. It would be the duty of his government to prepare Syria for elections, just as it had been seven years earlier. Ayyubi's cabinet assumed a moderate nationalist complexion, and he remained on good terms with a number of National Bloc leaders.[60]

While nationalists anxiously awaited a final decision by Ayyubi on the date of the elections, Shukri al-Quwwatli tried to patch up differences between Aleppo's warring political factions. The center of controversy was Saʿdallah al- Jabiri. His close ties to the Damascus Bloc and his refusal to

[57] Gardener Diary, 13 Feb. 1943; FO 226/241/27/2/87. Spears (Beirut) to Cairo, 10 Feb. 1943.
[58] Gardener Diary, 20, 27 March and 3 April 1943.
[59] FO 226/9/2/79/240. Spears to Catroux, 16 March 1943; FO 226/9/2/90/240. Furlonge to Spears, 18 March 1943.
[60] Gardener Diary, 27 March 1943.

support an emerging group of merchant-entrepreneurs and local politicians who believed that Syria should have stronger relations with Turkey
aggravated many Aleppine nationalists. For Aleppines, despite the loss of
Alexandretta, their region's future hinged on the development of wider
commercial links with their northern neighbor. Unlike many Damascene
nationalists who had been anti-Turkish since the days of World War I on
ideological and political grounds, most Aleppine nationalists had never
harbored such ill-feeling toward the Turks. Jabiri was an exception, owing to his early involvement in anti-Turkish activities during the Great
War. His anti-Turkish sentiments were exacerbated by Turkey's annexation of the Sanjak of Alexandretta at a time when he was a member of
the National Bloc government.[61]

Quwwatli led a delegation of his closest political allies, including Hajj
Adib Khayr and Sabri al-'Asali, to Aleppo in May. After days of hard
bargaining he returned with a written agreement signed by Jabiri and his
major rivals, Dr. Kayyali, Dr. Hasan Fu'ad Ibrahim Pasha, and Ahmad
Khalil Mudarris, stipulating that the four leaders swore to be loyal servants of their country and to work together in full harmony in the pursuit
of national aims. Although Quwwatli had not been able to bring the
younger, more radical elements headed by Rushdi al-Kikhya and Nazim
al-Qudsi in on the accord, he got promises from them that they would not
disrupt the elections. Moreover, he could rest assured that with the Jabiri
faction's sway over the 'ulama' in Aleppo and the Kayyali faction's influence with quarter chiefs, Aleppo would vote overwhelmingly for the nationalist ticket. Secure in this knowledge, he felt sufficiently satisfied that
his Nationalist Party (Quwwatli had recently dissolved the National Bloc,
although it was obvious that the new name was merely cosmetic) would
enter the elections on the basis of national unity.[62]

Election primaries were held on July 10 and with only a few incidents
throughout the country, although in Damascus, Aleppo, and Homs
barely a third of the eligible electorate actually voted.[63] The secondary
stage also came off smoothly on July 26. A Parliament was elected which
was about 20 percent larger than the one elected in 1936. Quwwatli
waited to announce his party's list in Damascus until the day before the
second stage in order to deny those colleagues whom he decided should
not stand the opportunity to turn against it. He had to because he included one or two Shabandarists. Although Quwwatli's list was com-

[61] MAE, Guerre 1939–45, vol. 42. Catroux (Beirut), 21 Dec. 1942.
[62] MAE, Guerre 1939–45. Londres (CNF), vol. 42; Gardener Diary, 22 May 1943; FO
226/240/9/4/180. Aleppo to Lascelles, 29 April 1943.
[63] MAE, Guerre 1939–45. Alger, vol. 10024, Report of July–Aug. 1943, pp. 52–66; FO
226/9/9/435/240. Gardener to Chancery, 29 July 1943. Sixty percent of the Hama electorate turned out in the primaries.

posed largely of familiar political personalities from his own generation and from the younger generation of nationalists which he had been cultivating since the early 1930s, there were also some new faces. Most visible was the popular religious leader and merchant from Quwwatli's ancestral quarter of Shaghur, Shaykh ʿAbd al-Hamid Tabbaʿ, who headed the activist Muslim benevolent society, *al-Gharra'*. Meanwhile, in Aleppo Saʿdallah al-Jabiri's list won decisively, having been opposed finally by the Kayyali–Mudarris list. Kayyali, however, won his seat. And in Latakia, Hama, and Homs nationalists swept the board. In Homs, however, Hashim al-Atasi did not stand, wishing to avoid further publicity around his recent willingness to accept a treaty before Syria acquired full independence. Two other Atasis, including Hashim's son ʿAdnan, won handily.[64]

The victory of Quwwatli's list in Damascus was the result of a vastly superior and well-endowed organization, a widespread belief that Quwwatli had the blessing of both the French and the British, and his own great personal prestige.[65] In his victory speech before a large gathering at the Tankiz Mosque on August 2, he clearly expressed the nationalist elite's self-confidence and self-view.

> The country has now passed one of the preparatory stages for its free constitutional life and Parliament is now about to meet. Now are our hearts filled with tranquility, joy and assurance. Now throughout its provinces and towns the nation, as a body, has stood by the men it knows and who know it, by those men it has tried and found most constant and loyal to its trust in them, to its cause and to its aspirations. Now the nation has given proof of the unity of its classes and its aims and now all doubts have been dissipated. We now take up an attitude in keeping with our past and with our present, an attitude that prepares us for the future. . . .[66]

Quwwatli could not bask in the light of his victory long however. The sensitive issue of who was to get which political offices had to be arranged in advance of the first session of Parliament. His home became the scene of endless visitations from one or another politician. Once Quwwatli decided upon his choices, he paid Hashim al-Atasi the courtesy of a visit to Homs for the senior Bloc statesman's blessings.

The new nationalist government resulting from these consultations was full of familiar faces: Saʿdallah al-Jabiri (Prime Minister), Jamil Mardam (Foreign Minister), Lutfi al-Haffar (Interior), ʿAbd al-Rahman

---

[64] *Ibid.*

[65] Gardener Diary, 24, 31 July 1943.

[66] FO 226/240/9/10/469. Damascus to J. Y. MacKenzie (Beirut).

al-Kayyali (Justice), Nasuhi al-Bukhari (Education and Defense), Khalid al-'Azm (Finance), Mazhar Raslan (Public Works and Ravitaillement), and Tawfiq Shamiyya (Agriculture and Commerce). Of these, all had previously held ministerial office and four had been heads of government. The scale of the nationalist movement had not changed since the beginning of the Mandate. The nationalist towns of the interior were represented, except for Hama; the Druze and Alawite communities were completely passed over, arousing protests in Parliament. The new government moved quickly to transfer or demote ranking bureaucrats who had collaborated closely with the French in order to replace them by loyalists. This was especially noticeable in the Ministry of Interior and the police.[67]

As in 1936, the self-confidence of the newly elected deputies was remarkable. Unlike in 1932 or in 1936, however, the proceedings were "very matter-of-fact, simple and businesslike, and the speeches delivered were short." The European-like organization of the Chamber, where the 120 deputies were seated in a half-circle facing the President's desk, the pulpit of the orator, and the government bench, contrasted with the variety of dress worn. Nearly half the deputies were attired in either a snow-white or transparent black 'aba' (a cloak-like, woolen wrap) with close-fitting kufiyya and 'iqal as headdress, including Sulayman al-Murshid, the Alawite divine who claimed to be endowed by God with special powers. An equal number sat interspersed among them in light-colored European suits and fezzes. To sharpen the contrasts, the outgoing "neutral" government of 'Ata al-Ayyubi sat under the Speaker's rostrum, facing the Chamber, in black morning coats, while in the front row sat the President-to-be, Shukri al-Quwwatli, and the men he had designated to form the new government, all sporting white suits.

Presiding over the Chamber that morning was Faris Bey al-Khuri the Protestant deputy who had been Speaker in 1936 and who now supervised his own re-election. An experienced parliamentarian, he carried out his duties with great "efficiency and bonhomie," which included seeing to it that Quwwatli was elected the next President of the Syrian Republic. As the British Consul observed, Faris Bey "would make a good chairman of any assembly."

Whereas the Syrian deputies seemed in a generally good mood, the French observers looked "sombre" and "anxious." For one thing, they were furious that their traditional ten-man box, which had been located on the floor of the House and which reflected France's exalted influence in Syria, had been eliminated. Instead, the French were to have only four

[67] Gardener Diary, 16, 23 Oct. 1943.

places in the diplomat's gallery, flanked by the British with three places and the Americans with two. That evening at the Municipality's banquet in honor of Quwwatli the French were still annoyed, not least by the Syrian band which played only the second half of the *Marseillaise* when they entered and left.[68] Times appeared to be changing!

DOMESTIC PRESSURES

The Syrian leadership was prepared to make certain concessions both in content and in form and "to be flexible in its relations" with the French, in order to persuade them gradually to relinquish their authority. But in its willingness to make concessions it could "not go so far as to arouse the suspicion of the younger generation [of nationalists] that it [had] 'betrayed' the national cause." On this front, the government's refusal to discuss a treaty until it secured control of the Troupes Spéciales helped to guard it against such suspicions.

The new nationalist government formed by Sa'dallah al-Jabiri was not immune to criticism on certain domestic issues, however. The composition of his ministry itself was a bone of contention. None of its members was particularly skilled in dealing with the extremely sensitive issue of the compact minorities—the Druzes, the Alawites, and the inhabitants of Jazira. And none had any conception of social and economic reform. In fact, the government wanted to avoid economic changes in industry and agriculture that would foster the growth of an organized urban proletariat and the emancipation of the peasantry. The members of government were nearly all landowners or members of big landowning families and they were anxious to preserve the dominant position of their class.

Opposition to this elite came naturally from the minorities and from those who had been excluded from power but who could hope to attain power given their class background. This was the "political opposition":

> men who live in the same universe of thought as the present Ministers and have the same fundamental limitation but who differ from them on particular points of greater or less importance. They include candidates who want to be deputies and deputies who want to be Ministers and believe they have a grudge against the Prime Minister: Druze or Alawi autonomists . . . ; and most important of all—a group of young deputies who want the Government to go further and be more intransigent in its policy.[69]

Familiar names cropped up amongst this group. Nazim al-Qudsi and Rushdi al-Kikhya, the Aleppine nationalists who had rejected Shukri al-

---

[68] Gardener Diary, 21 Aug. 1943.

[69] FO 371/4292, vol. 40308. "The Situation in Damascus," by A. H. Hourani, 1944.

Quwwatli's efforts to mend political fences in Aleppo before the July 1943 elections, could be counted here as well as the more moderate chiefs of the League of National Action such as ʿAdnan and Hilmi al-Atasi and Ahmad al-Sharabati.

Only one recently elected deputy dared to reject the entire framework of nationalist politics identified with the veterans. This was Akram Hawrani who, by rallying the peasantry around Hama, managed to break the political hold of the big absentee landowning class in that conservative Syrian town. He came from a landowning family that had squandered its wealth and spent his youth and early manhood engaged in radical politics. After a flirtation with the pan-Syrian Partie Populaire Syrien and the acquisition of a law degree from Damascus, he returned to Hama in 1938. There he joined ranks with his older cousin, ʿUthman, a school teacher, to lead the Hizb al-shabab (Youth Party) against the National Bloc and its Nationalist Youth organization. Akram Hawrani's electoral victory in 1943 raised the "social question" in Parliament for the first time.[70]

Hawrani represented a new type of opposition in Syria. This opposition was incapable of forming a working alliance with any section of the National Bloc "because it [was] thinking on another and in general a deeper level and [had] a wholly different system of political ideas." In addition to Hawrani there were other small but growing movements which were also associated with the new opposition. There were the Baʿthists, the Communists, and the Muslim Brethren. Each group sought "to formulate a doctrine and a detailed programme for the nationalist movement," and, in particular, to address two questions which the veteran nationalist elite had dealt with in the most superficial manner: what should be the attitude of the Arabs to their own past and to Islam? And what social and economic policies should the nationalist movement subscribe to?[71] By the war's end, the current of this new, more socially oriented opposition was a force to be reckoned with. Ultimately, it would sweep away the traditional methods and forms of political expertise associated with the veteran nationalists.

Already by the war, students and young intellectuals were turning to the speeches and writings of Michel ʿAflaq, a former school teacher at the Damascus *tajhiz* who offered the most systematic explanation of Arab nationalism's relationship to Islam. ʿAflaq was the son of a Greek Orthodox grain merchant from the Maydan quarter of Damascus who received his higher education in Paris. Though a Christian, he argued that the Arab movement was inseparably connected with Islam and that Muhammad's life was a perfect picture and symbol of "the nature of the Arab

---

[70] Hanna Batatu, *The Old Social Classes*, pp. 728–29; George Faris, *Man huwa 1949*, p. 139; MWT materials on Hama youth in 1939.

[71] FO 371/4292, vol. 40308. "Damascus," by A.H. Hourani, 1944.

soul and its rich possibilities." Every Arab was able to live the life of the
Prophet by virtue of the high qualities which he possesses as an Arab. Indeed, the revelation of Islam was given to the Arabs and to no other nation because of these qualities. Arabs, according to ʿAflaq, had a universal
duty to create an "Arab humanism" but this could only be properly done
if they were a strong nation. To be strong meant preventing dangerous
European concepts, like that of the separation of nationalism and religion,
from weakening the Arabs. The Arabs had to have faith in their special
character and destiny, as molded and confirmed by Islam.[72]

ʿAflaq's movement was purely intellectual in orientation at this stage
but it did attract a growing number of followers who had organized themselves during the war into a party which after the war became known officially as the Baʿth [Renaissance] Party. A formidable competitor for
some of the same constituency was the Syrian Communist Party. It appealed to high school students, liberal professionals, and a small number
of organized industrial workers, especially in the railway workshops and
in textile factories. The Party, which claimed several thousand members
in 1944, also included large numbers of Armenians, Kurds, and other minorities.[73]

The leader of the Communist Party was Khalid Bakdash, an Arabized
Kurd from Damascus who had been converted to communism by an Armenian while a student at the Damascus Law Faculty in 1930. He spent
the early 1930s in and out of jail for pro-communist and anti-French activities.[74] In 1933 the party ordered him into exile and he spent two years
in Moscow acquiring ideological training at the Communist University of
the Toilers of the East where he came under the wing of an aide of Stalin.
By 1936 Bakdash was back in Damascus as the new head of the Syrian CP.
In the summer of that year he went to Paris to assist the nationalist delegation in its negotiations with the left-wing Popular Front government.
In the eyes of formerly sympathetic intellectuals like Michel ʿAflaq who
espoused an uncomproming radical pan-Arabism, the Communist Party's support of the National Bloc made it suspect. The Party was accused
of taking its directives via the French Communist Party and hence via
Moscow. While Bakdash spent the late 1930s attending one Communist
Party conference after another and gaining more and more personal attention from Moscow, the Party back home was highly unstable in its
rank and file.

The Communist Party enjoyed a new lease on life during World War II
largely because the increasingly astute Bakdash kept it on an almost

[72] Ibid.

[73] See Hanna, al-Haraka al-ʿummaliyya.

[74] MWT, Registre des jugements du Tribunal de 1ère Instance Correctionnelle, 1931 et
1932, pp. 210–11.

purely nationalist footing. He built his and the Party's reputation on its active role in underground resistance to Vichy in 1940–41. He also sought a working relationship with the Syrian political and financial establishment. The Party strengthened its pragmatic orientation during the war, becoming pronouncedly Arab nationalist in character rather than socialist. Bakdash supported friendship with the Soviet Union but on a purely nationalistic basis. The Party's role in the numerous bread strikes during the war enhanced its reputation both as a defender of the poor and as a *bona fide* nationalist organization. Although Bakdash lost his bid for a seat in the 1943 Parliament, his reputation won him more than a respectable number of votes. The Party's new National Charter of January 1944 spoke of the importance of complete national liberation, of close relations between the Arab peoples, and of national education. It also demanded a true democratic regime, the guarantee of individual liberties, and a studiously moderate program of social reform offering something to almost every class. The Syrian Communist Party's later switch to a pro-Soviet posture, its anti-establishment and anti-nationalist character, and its ultra-leftism were clearly developments of the postwar era, owing to the debacle in Palestine and the heightened tensions between East and West produced by the Cold War.[75]

The assortment of Muslim societies, including the Muslim Brethren (Ikhwan al-Muslimin) which was established in 1944, was more troublesome to the National Bloc then either the emerging Ba'th Party or the Communist Party.

The structural changes which Syria had experienced during the interwar period had been especially disruptive in the popular quarters of the towns. Traditional merchants and artisans suffered under the weight of expanding European trade. Casual laborers found it increasingly difficult to feed their families owing to the high inflation rates of the late thirties and war period. Uprooted rural dwellers entered the peripheral quarters of the towns in growing numbers, after having been pushed off the land by drought or more commonly by indebtedness to merchant-moneylenders and big landowners. All sought the support and guidance of local leaders who could help them articulate their grievances and needs. But the nationalist leadership in the towns was increasingly preoccupied with developments in new modern quarters and institutions where a rising radicalized generation of activists challenged their authority by calling for a more revolutionary solution to the Syrian Question. With the widening

[75] Batatu, *The Old Social Classes*, pp. 582–83; Lecture by Hanna Batatu on Syrian Communist Party, American University of Beirut, 23 March 1972. MWT, *al-Intidab al-faransi: al-ahzab*, no. 74/101, 8 March 1939; FO 371/2365, vol. 24591. Gardener to FO, 21 April 1940; FO 684/15/28. Furlonge to FO, 21 Jan. 1944; FO 684/15/28. British Security Mission (Damascus) to FO, 18 Dec. 1944.

gulf between the traditional and modern sectors of society, the popular classes found their main comfort in religious leaders and organizations which spoke in an idiom which they understood.

To address the pressing social and psychological needs of the common people there arose a plethora of independent organizations known as *jam'iyyat* (religious beneficent societies). The earliest of these benevolent organizations to appear in Damascus during the Mandate was Jam'iyyat al-Gharra', founded in 1924. During the 1930s more societies came into existence, the most important being the Jam'iyyat al-Tamaddun al-islami (1932), Jam'iyyat al-Hidaya al-islamiyya (1936), and Jam'iyyat al-'Ulama' (1938). Although these were the most prominent societies of the interwar years, a number of smaller, short-lived groups were also formed, especially toward the end of the 1930s in response to a proliferation of Christian clubs and benevolent societies. Groups often called themselves *jam'iyyat* in order to get government subsidies.

In other towns groups with the names Shabab Muhammad or Shaban al-muslimin (Muslim Youth) sprang up and in Aleppo there existed the Dar al-Arqam, founded in 1935, which in 1944 became the Muslim Brethren. It is generally believed that the Egyptian Muslim Brethren influenced the emergence of the Syrian Brethren. Some Syrian students who had studied at al-Azhar in Cairo became familiar with the ideas of the Egyptian Brethren's founder, Hasan al-Banna. Others were inspired by a tour of Syria made by members of the Egyptian Muslim Brethren in the mid-1930s.

The principal goals of the *jam'iyyat* were education in general and Muslim education in particular, based on the reformism of the *salafiyya*, which had been popular in the towns of Syria since the early part of the century. Their aim was to spread their ideas of Muslim ethics and morals, and to inculcate anti-imperialist feelings in the form of an Arab nationalism which sought to rehabilitate the role of Islam in political life. It was through schools and magazines associated with individual *jam'iyyat* that such ideas were disseminated.[76]

The leaders of these societies were mainly religious shaykhs, school teachers, lawyers, and doctors. At first the *jam'iyyat* attracted students of Islamic law (*shari'a*). But also closely associated with them was the small urban trading and artisanal class which produced for and traded in the local market and which had steadily lost economic position to merchants engaged in the more lucrative trade with Europe during the Mandate. In towns like Aleppo these latter merchants were predominantly

[76] *Al-Gharra'* and *al-Tamaddun al-islami* had their own schools. Unpublished paper by Dr. Johannes Reissner (prepared for author), "Muslim societies during the Mandate in Syria," Beirut, 1975.

Christians. The local traders and artisans were "the most religiously oriented class in Syria [and were] akin to the religious shaikhs in values and
way of life."[77] They were also literally kin to religious shaykhs, many of
whom came from the same social strata and some of whom also owned
their own small business enterprises. Workers (*ummal*) began to join
toward the end of the war.

The societies were fundamentally urban in composition but the rank
and file included a certain number of in-migrants from the countryside
around the towns which gave societies ties to rural areas. Some of the
leaders belonged to more than one *jam'iyya* because most societies were
only locally based. Therefore the leader of the Jam'iyyat Ihya' al-'ulum
wal-adab of Hama might well belong to al-Gharra' in Damascus and the
Dar al-Arqam in Aleppo, or later to the Muslim Brethren.[78]

The *jam'iyyat* led campaigns in the towns against the influx of foreign
goods and culture into Syria. Especially popular targets were cabarets
which served alcohol, permitted gambling, and featured female dancers.
The increasingly liberal dress adopted by women from the bourgeoisie
(including the wives of National Bloc leaders), and their habit of fre-
quenting public places, were also matters of concern to the *jam'iyyat*.[79]

There is no evidence that societies such as al-Gharra', al-Tamaddun al-
islami, al-Hidaya al-islamiyya or al-'Ulama' posed any serious opposition to the National Bloc during its 1936–39 tenure in government. This
may have been because they were not yet organized under an administrative umbrella with an identifiable political program. But they did pressure
the Bloc government to support more actively the Arab rebellion in Palestine to which they contributed arms, men, and moral solidarity. The
jam'iyyat also pressured Jamil Mardam to resign as Prime Minister in
1939 over the Personal Status issue, by which the French tried to reduce
Islam in Syria to the status of one religion among many. He did so, but
not because of *jam'iyyat* pressure. Rather, he used the issue as a means
to step down from office with honor at a time when most of his policies,
including the Franco-Syrian Treaty, had failed and his government no
longer had any moral authority.

During the war, the *jam'iyyat* stepped up their public agitation by fo-

[77] Hanna Batatu, "Syria's Muslim Brethren," *Merip Reports.*, no. 110, 12 (Nov.–Dec.
1982), pp. 15–16.

[78] Johannes Reissner, *Ideologie und Politik der Muslimbrüder Syriens* (Freiburg, 1980),
pp. 86–96; Batatu, "Muslim Brethren," p. 14.

[79] MWT, *al-Intidab al-faransi: dakhiliyya, nizam nadi.* File 33/5431-3098. Shaykh
Hamdi al-Safarjalani to Minister of Interior (Damascus), 5 May 1932; Ibrahim Pasha, *Nidal*, pp. 78–79; *Oriente Moderno*, 14 (1934), p. 438; *ibid.*, 15 (1935), p. 636; *ibid.*, 18
(1938), pp. 532–33; 'Adil al-'Azma Papers [Syria], File 16/398, 7 Feb. 1939 and File 16/
398a, 9 Feb. 1939.

cusing on two controversial issues: the status of women and the Syrian education system. Changing patterns of taste, greater opportunity for travel in the Middle East and to Europe, and, above all, the gradual spread of modern secular education during the Mandate allowed women from the upper and upper-middle classes in the towns to acquire new values, new kinds of fashions, and new aspirations which distinguished them from the rest of female society in general and from the generations of their mothers and grandmothers in particular. Most noticeably, these changes brought them into greater public view. The wives and daughters of nationalist leaders became increasingly active in the political arena as participants in strikes and demonstrations and in philanthropic activities.[80] Slowly the issue of women's rights came to the fore. Religious shaykhs saw this trend not only as a dangerous Western corruption of Islamic customs and values, but as another example of their own loss of influence over society. In the early 1940s, the *jam'iyyat* made a concerted effort to slow or reverse this trend.

For example, in May 1942, shaykhs from al-Gharra' and al-Hidaya al-islamiyya led large protest demonstrations in Damascus denouncing women who exposed their faces in public, promenaded on the arms of their husbands, and went to cinemas. They demanded that the government install special tramcars for women during the rush hour to keep the sexes apart, that casinos and cabarets near religious and cultural places be closed, and that a "moral police squad" be created whose duty it would be to repress public vice. On the question of education, which the shaykhs saw as the fundamental problem, they proposed that a commission of Muslim religious leaders be established to reform the educational system so that all students—boys and girls—would receive a formal Muslim education in which the religion and history of Islam and the Arabs were emphasized, rather than European history and the French language.

The government of Husni al-Barazi paid little attention to these protests, and high school students from the *tajhiz* bitterly opposed the religious leaders' demands. After al-Gharra', al-Hidaya al-islamiyya, and al-Tamaddun al-islami failed to unite owing to opposition from the Jam'iyyat al-'Ulama' led by the influential *salafi* religious leader, Shaykh Kamil al-Qassab, their protests died down.[81]

The next major Muslim outburst, in May 1944, brought the *jam'iyyat* and the nationalist government into a head-on conflict. For some time past, a growing feminist movement in Damascus had been making its presence felt by holding public meetings and agitating openly for women's emancipation. The movement focused on the issue of the veil. Its

[80] See Tresse, "Manifestations féminines à Damas," pp. 115–25.
[81] MAE, Guerre 1939–45. Londres (CNF), vol. 42. G. Catroux (Beirut), pp. 37–42.

leader was the wife of Nasuhi al-Bukhari, the Minister of Education, and it included a number of wives of prominent politicians in government and Parliament. Opposition to the feminist demands was led by al-Gharra' which denounced the growing immodesty of Muslim women, particularly those who no longer wore the veil, "and the detrimental influence of the cinema."

The occasion for further disturbances was a philanthropic ball, organized by Madame Bukhari and others, scheduled to be held on May 20. When it was learned Muslim women planned to attend unveiled, religious shaykhs publicly demanded that the nationalist chief of police, Colonel Ahmad al-Lahham, cancel the ball. Lahham responded that since "the ball was predominantly a Christian affair he could do no more than ask the Committee not to admit Muslim women." This angered the crowd assembled at the mosque where the shaykhs had made their demands. It took to the streets, forcing shops in the bazaars to close. Demonstrations took place in front of the Bukhari home and the French Officers' Club where the ball was to be held. The shaykhs and their followers, carrying revolvers and knives, confronted the police at a downtown cinema; the police fired into the crowd killing two people. Prime Minister Jabiri convinced the Committee to postpone the ball while the police rounded up some of the demonstration leaders, including the popular religious shaykh of the Maydan, Muhammad al-Ashmar. More violence occurred on the following day in the Maydan, a quarter in which the National Bloc had little political influence, when trains to the Hawran were blocked.

At the forefront of this protest was Shaykh 'Abd al-Hamid Tabba', the 46-year-old leader of al-Gharra' and a Member of Parliament. Tabba''s role complicated matters for the nationalist government. At the time of the July 1943 elections, he had lent the full support of al-Gharra' to Shukri al-Quwwatli, including the facility of the Tankiz Mosque which was the principal meeting place of the Gharra'. Quwwatli had used this mosque to encourage voters to support his ticket, and in recognition of al-Gharra''s support he included Tabba' on that victorious ticket.

Al-Gharra' clearly believed that the gratitude of Quwwatli and the Nationalist Party would not end with their return to Parliament. They wanted the new government to adopt al-Gharra''s program of educational and social reform. The women's issue was seen as a test: if the government backed al Gharra''s demands, Tabba' and others believed that al-Gharra''s programs would see the light of day. Tabba''s tactic was to show strength in the streets, but to avoid mob violence until peaceful tactics failed. It appears, however, that Ashmar and his followers resorted to violent action while a deputation of demonstrators was still engaged in discussions with the Minister of the Interior.[82] This enabled Prime Minister Jabiri to ignore the issue of female emancipation and treat the whole matter as though it were a breach of public order.

Even before the religious disturbances Jabiri had told a British official that "we are resolved to treat all religious questions as questions of public order. If the Moslems rise against the Christians, we shall penalise them; if Christians rise against Moslems, equally we shall penalise *them.*"[83] Jabiri played his hand well. He succeeded in enlisting the support of the Damascus populace which had been inconvenienced by the closure of the Maydan shops. He even managed temporarily to discredit al-Gharra' by letting it be known in the Maydan that al-Gharra' had better be able to supply flour to the poor of the quarter, because his government had no intention of doing so "unless and until it was fully understood that the government was the sole responsible authority."[84] The nationalist government obviously wanted to make a point. Government in the past had always been the enemy: "to be obeyed under compulsion and ignored or opposed if it is weak. Now the people must be made to grasp a new idea, that the Government is from them and for them but nevertheless, to be obeyed."[85] The nationalist government had made its point loud and clear. Although local forces of opposition were growing in the towns in rhythm with the structural changes of the times, the veteran nationalists could count on the external issue of foreign occupation to stem the tide of internal opposition, at least for a while. But it was also clear that the National Bloc could not continue to ignore the reality of religio-cultural movements or of radical secular movements associated with the emerging Ba'thists and the communists. The time was rapidly approaching when the veteran nationalists would have to define their views and consolidate their positions on the critical political issues raised by these emerging movements.

Syrian and Lebanese Cooperation

The return of nationalists to government seemed to bring with it a change in the political mood of Syria. There was a new feeling of accomplishment and hope for the future, missing for an entire generation. But this was only on the surface. Beneath, the situation was "very brittle." There was the "unspoken fear" that at any moment the French might "stage a

[82] FO 684/15/1/1. British Security Mission to Political Officer (Damascus), 21 May 1944; *ibid.*, Beaumont Memorandum, 26 May 1944.

[83] FO 371/4292, vol. 40308. "Damascus," by A. H. Hourani, 1944.

[84] FO 684/15/1/1. British Security Mission to Political Officer (Damascus), 21 May 1944; *ibid.*, Beaumont Memorandum, 26 May 1944.

[85] FO 371/4292, vol. 40308. "Damascus," by A.H. Hourani, 1944.

'coup' and overthrow the fragile structure of national government."[86] And with the Troupes Spéciales and the Sûreté Générale still in French hands, they would certainly be able to do so. Alongside this fear lay another: that at the war's end British troops would withdraw to be replaced by French forces, enabling France to impose a treaty on Syria which would compromise her independence.

Even before the 1943 elections the French had demanded the insurance of a treaty before they would relinquish control over the vital institutions and levers of power in Syria, including the Common Interests and the Troupes Spéciales. But Shukri al-Quwwatli and his colleagues in the Nationalist Party refused to accept such terms, preferring instead to negotiate from a position of strength after the elections, which they anticipated carrying.[87]

Indeed, the elections did enable the nationalists to lay claim to represent the popular will in Syria. And, the introduction of a new factor helped to further strengthen the nationalist position. This was diplomatic cooperation with Lebanon, brought about by the election of a nationalist government there shortly after the Syrian elections. So, in October, the Jabiri government felt strong enough to present its own terms in a memorandum to the French. These included the cession of all French powers before the conclusion of a treaty.

The emergence in the Levant states of a united Syrian-Lebanese negotiating front in the fall of 1943 was the product of converging political attitudes in Lebanon and in Syria on the future of Syrian-Lebanese relations. Since the mid-1930s, a growing number of Lebanese Sunni Muslim leaders had begun to reject the notion that Arab unity could be achieved before Lebanese independence. Moreover, the goal or idea of reintegrating the four cazas into Syria was becoming itself increasingly untenable. Lebanese Sunni leaders and their supporters in the Muslim bourgeoisie had come to accept that the divison of Syria and Lebanon was a fait accompli. Politically, this meant that Sunnis began to actively compete for power on the Lebanese stage. Commercially, this meant that Sunnis had begun to recognize that Lebanon's commercial links with the West could benefit them as these links benefited Lebanese Christians. At the same time, a number of Muslim merchants and not a few Christians were involved in the re-export trade of Western manufactured goods from Beirut to the Syrian hinterland and in the importation to Beirut of raw materials for a western market. Both feared the consequences of a complete separation of Lebanon from the Arab world which might occur

[86] FO 371/4292, vol. 40308. "Damascus," by A. H. Hourani, 1944; Hourani, Syria and Lebanon, pp. 290–91.

[87] FO 226/?, Beaumont to Chancery, 16 April 1943; FO 226/?. Gardener to Chancery, 20 and 21 April 1943.

if Lebanon became too much of a client-state of France.[88] In 1943, it was an alliance of the Muslim and Christian commercial bourgeoisie that brought the two major proponents of an independent Arab Lebanon to power: Bishara al-Khuri, generally recognized as Britain's candidate, became President and Riyad Sulh became Prime Minister.

Meanwhile, most veteran nationalists in Syria had moved since the mid-1930s in the direction of the evolving Lebanese nationalist movement on the issue of future relations. The National Bloc had already adopted an evolutionary approach to Arab unity, which blended conveniently with its own strategy of gradually relaxing French control over Syria. As of 1936, Syrian independence had become the Bloc's number one priority. Even the Bloc's long-standing demand that the districts annexed in 1920 be returned to Syria had become muted over time. The Bloc had quietly begun to lend its support to a new movement in Beirut, led by Riyad Sulh, to promote better extragovernmental relations between Lebanese Christians and Muslims.[89] Sulh, of course, had been a founding father of the Bloc, a Bloc fund raiser, and its closest Lebanese ally. He also happened to be a cousin of the Bloc politician ʿAfif Sulh and was related by marriage to Saʿdallah al-Jabiri. By 1943, the two Prime Ministers, Sulh and Jabiri, realized the advantage and the necessity of presenting a united negotiating position on the principle of complete independence for both Lebanon and Syria. Never before had the two countries adopted such a cooperative spirit and compatible political aims; never again would Lebanon be a "pawn to be played off by the French against the Syrians."[90]

Several other factors hardened the Levant's new diplomatic front as well. These included Arab support, especially Egypt's, for both nationalist regimes and unqualified diplomatic recognition of the new Syrian and Lebanese governments by the United States and the Soviet Union. This combination of forces in turn encouraged Britain to stick to her position that full and complete independence should be granted before the conclusion of separate treaties with France.

But, despite the array of forces ranged against the French, General de Gaulle was unwilling to soften his position. The Sulh government in Beirut, rather than the Jabiri government, adopted the more confrontational stance. When the Lebanese Parliament on November 8 approved certain measures that Sulh had proposed the previous month, including the

[88] Atiyah, "The Attitude of the Lebanese Sunnis," pp. 150–51; Michael Johnson," Confessionalism and Individualism in Lebanon: A Critique of Leonard Binder (ed). *Politics in the Lebanon*," in *Review of Middle East Studies* 1 (London, 1975), pp. 85–86.

[89] Conversation with Farid Zayn al-Din (Damascus, 14 April 1976).

[90] Gomaa, *The League*, p. 94.

adoption of Arabic as the sole official language in Lebanon, "the deletion from the constitution of all reference to the prerogatives and powers of the mandatory state," and the end of Lebanon's isolation from the Arab world, this precipitated a crisis in Franco-Lebanese relations.[91]

General Catroux's replacement as Delegate-General in the Levant, M. Helleu, took the unprecedented step of imprisoning President Khuri, Prime Minister Sulh, three Ministers, and one deputy on November 11. Strikes and demonstrations over the next two weeks united the country against the French. Syria led the Arab world in support for the Lebanese. Britain quickly threw her support behind the Lebanese government and forced the divided French National Committee in Algiers to release the interned leaders. Helleu was recalled and soon thereafter various powers, hitherto monopolized by the French, were transferred to the Lebanese and Syrian governments, "whose position was greatly enhanced in as much as French prestige had fallen."[92]

In the process of resisting French efforts to impose a treaty on Syria, the nationalist government had happily resolved two of its more pressing regional problems. It enjoyed the collaboration of the nationalist regime in Lebanon and the cooperation of a number of Arab countries, notably Egypt, with whom it had held fruitful discussions in Cairo in October about future inter-Arab relations—discussions which would contribute to the foundation of the Arab League in 1945. Both promoted greater Syrian political self-confidence and strengthened Syrian resolve against the French.

FREE AT LAST

In retrospect, the Lebanese crisis of November–December 1943 signalled the end of the French Mandate. Syrian and Lebanese steadfastness at this critical juncture emboldened both nationalist governments to resist all pressures to accept the persistent French demand of treaties before independence. Still, the French held one last card—the Troupes Spéciales—with which they hoped to impose their will.

Syrian and Lebanese impatience with French intransigence grew during 1944. In the Syrian towns, public opinion was particularly adamant: it would not tolerate a compromise of any sort, something the nationalist government could not ignore. Unable, however, to confront the French militarily, all the Syrian and Lebanese governments could do was to seek international support while they quietly encouraged public demonstrations in Damascus and Beirut against the continued French presence in

[91] *Ibid.*
[92] *Ibid.*, p. 95.

the Levant. But, this latter activity had to be carefully monitored, indeed contained, so as to prevent widespread violence and French intervention. Meanwhile, negotiations continued, but to no one's satisfaction.

The French bargaining position actually improved after the liberation of France in the summer of 1944 and General de Gaulle's return to Paris from Algiers. Discussions with British officials in Paris in September softened the British position on the issue of treaties before independence. General Spears was instructed to apply pressure on the Syrian and Lebanese governments to accept treaties with France. Spears even hinted that Damascus and Beirut could not count on British support, as they had in November 1943, if a new crisis developed. But this did not have the desired effect. Instead, a supportive American government persuaded Britain to ease off the Levant states, at least temporarily.[93]

General Spears was widely regarded in the Levant as a supporter of Syrian and Lebanese independence and his recall in December 1944 created even greater uncertainty about the reliability of Britain's support. When large anti-French demonstrations in Damascus in the last week of January 1945 were countered by a visible display of French military strength in the Syrian capital and renewed statements from Paris about France's special rights in the Levant, Britain renewed efforts to encourage Syrian flexibility. Prime Minister Winston Churchill, on his way back from Yalta in February, even interceded with President Quwwatli, but this came to naught. Relations between France and the Levant governments deteriorated rapidly.[94]

By May the French were reinforcing their garrisons, mainly with the much dreaded and hated Senegalese troops. As tempers flared in Damascus and Beirut, the French added insult to injury by laying down the specifics of their proposed treaties, which did not include the transfer of the Troupes Spéciales until Syria and Lebanon had signed on the dotted line. On May 19, the Syrian and Lebanese governments announced their refusal to negotiate under the conditions of French military escalation in the Levant.

Demonstrations broke out in Damascus, Beirut, and other towns. Anti-French activities quickly spread all over Syria, including the minority districts. Within ten days, law and order had completely broken down. In an act reminiscent of the Great Revolt, the trigger-happy and paranoid French military command, convinced of a British cabal, shelled and bombed Damascus from the air between the evening of May 29 and noon on May 30. This time, however, the newer, modern quarters received the brunt of French punishment, suggesting how far the locus of

---

[93] *Ibid.*, pp. 94–95.
[94] *Ibid.*, p. 95.

urban political protest had shifted in 20 years. The number of Syrian casualties and the amount of physical destruction were heavy. It included
some 400 dead, countless injured, and the destruction of nearly the entire
Parliament building,[95] a bitter reminder of France's quarter-century of
commitment to educating the people under her Mandate in the values of
Western civilization and democracy.

Britain could no longer stand idly by. French actions had the potential
to upset Britain's overall Arab policy. Therefore, the British government
intervened for the second time in 18 months, by ordering French troops
back to their barracks. The British briefly assumed military control until
the Syrian government could resume its normal functions.[96] Protests
from the Arab League, of which Syria had been a founding member two
months earlier, and from the Syrian delegation meeting at the opening of
the United Nations in San Francisco, reverberated throughout the Levant. International criticism of France was also loud. Anti-French feelings reached the highest level of intensity ever known in Syria. Hatred
raged in the hearts of the Syrian people and there was virtually no contact
between French officials and Syrian leaders for weeks.[97]

By July, France agreed to transfer control of the much-contested
Troupes Spéciales to the Syrians and Lebanese. With Syria all but fully
independent, one last step remained: the withdrawal of all French troops
from the Levant. Renewed anti-French protests in the towns of Syria and
Lebanon, regional and international pressures from the Arab League and
the United Nations, and from Washington and Moscow, and, above all,
patient Anglo-French discussions throughout the summer, autumn, and
winter of 1945–46 brought by spring a complete withdrawal of French
troops and other military personnel from Syrian territory.[98] By the end
of August 1946, Lebanon was also cleared of a French military presence.

The veteran nationalists in Syria had finally achieved their long-
awaited goal: political independence from France with the National Bloc
at the helm of government. And they had done so by the methods with
which they were most comfortable: by applying that delicate mixture of
intermittent popular protest and patient negotiation in just the right
measure. The framework of their movement, stretched as it was by the
forces of change, had nevertheless prevailed. The Bloc had restored the
political status quo by tying the Syrian national independence movement

[95] Longrigg, *Syria*, pp. 346–49.

[96] For details of British policy in Syria in 1945, see the masterly study by Wm. Roger
Louis, *The British Empire in the Middle East 1945–1951. Arab Nationalism, the United
States, and Postwar Imperialism* (Oxford, 1984), pp. 147–72.

[97] Longrigg, *Syria*, pp. 349–50.

[98] From the French point of view, what was important was the simultaneous withdrawal
of British and French troops.

to the emerging Arab state system, including Lebanon, and by latching on to Britain's coattails. In the end, by turning to Britain, the veteran nationalists did not have to make any further concessions to France. For the time being, their political credibility was intact. And that was all they had bargained for.

CONCLUSION

THIS STUDY HAS EMPHASIZED the remarkable degree of continuity in the exercise of local political power in Syria from late Ottoman times through the period of French rule under the Mandate. The landowning, scholarly, and mercantile families in the towns, which blended into a fairly cohesive social class in the second half of the nineteenth century, were able to retain their monopoly over politics during the interwar period despite the the collapse of the Ottoman Empire and the imposition of French rule. This class survived the structural changes of the age—the loosening of family ties, the spread of modern education and new ideologies, the establishment of modern institutions, and the reorientation of the Syrian economy.

The continuity of political life grew out of a certain similiarity of form. Paris, like Istanbul, was a distant overlord. In order to govern, the French, like the Ottomans before them, had to depend on locally influential notables who could act as intermediaries between government and society. By virtue of their traditional status in society, their education, and previous administrative experience, notables normally hailed from upper-class families in the towns. This similarity of form was reinforced by the French failure to develop a consistent imperial policy in Syria, a failure that had to do not only with the internal weaknesses of the interwar French economy and the climate of political thought in France about how to administer overseas possessions, but also with the international restrictions imposed on French rule by that new, peculiar version of colonialism, the Mandate system. That France governed Syria with one eye always fixed on North Africa certainly contributed to this failure. However, despite outward similiarities, the French, unlike the Ottomans, were perceived as illegitimate. Hence, France's position in Syria was from the outset inherently unstable. French illegitimacy, in turn, obliged urban notables to try to shift the balance of power away from the French. Those notables who emerged with the greatest political leverage in Syria were identified most closely with the ascendant idea of nationalism.

Nationalism was at the very center of the changing intellectual and political climate in the Middle East and owed its existence to the widening of the region's links with the outside world. In fact, two types of nationalism emerged—one territorial and the other ethno-cultural—and both co-existed in all nationalist movements in the Arab world. Although nationalism had not shed its religious skin, because no interpretation of Arab history and culture could deny the contribution of Islam, it nevertheless had strong secular inclinations. The class that transformed the idea of nationalism into a political movement in the early twentieth century, although by no means politically united, demonstrated a certain discomfort with the ideas of Islamic modernists and activists who argued that Islam could provide the principles necessary to govern a modern nation state. Nationalist leaders believed Islamic law was outmoded. This attitude reflected their upbringing: they were educated in modern professional schools, they had experience in the new branches of the Ottoman administration, they had little attachment to religious institutions, and they shared similar political experiences mainly secular in nature. These experiences were in the political parties and secret societies of Damascus, Beirut, Cairo, and Paris before the First World War, and afterwards in Faysal's short-lived Arab Kingdom.

The brand of nationalism which the urban political leadership sponsored was tailored to its political style and social class. Nationalism, in its hands, was not a revolutionary ideology aiming to overturn existing social hierarchies. Rather, it was restorative; the nationalist elite aimed to establish a more favorable balance of power between France and Syria with the ultimate goal of gradually relaxing French control. Its method was not revolutionary armed struggle but a mixture of intermittent popular protest, diplomacy, and regional and international activity. The popular uprisings of the early twenties which culminated in the Great Syrian Revolt were, in some ways, an abberation. Although the Great Revolt did have revolutionary implications, its eventual collapse allowed the nationalist elite to consolidate its own position with the formation of the National Bloc and to resume a more comfortable, graded path to independence.

The presence of a foreign ruler enabled the National Bloc to direct popular discontent outward, away from the local structure of power. While this obviously contributed to the prolongation of the Bloc's leadership, so too did the inability of interest groups and classes further down the social scale to pose a serious challenge to its leadership until the end of the Mandate. The chaotic struggles and petty rivalries that characterized political life in Syria during the interwar years were rarely expressions of conflict between classes. Rather, they reflected rivalries within the political elite itself, in single towns, or between leaderships in rival towns, or between the urban nationalist elite and the rural-based leaderships of the compact minorities, in particular the Alawites and Druzes.

THE CHARACTER, STYLE, and organization of nationalist politics during the Mandate revealed several trends which were to color political life in Syria after independence. Perhaps the most important trend was a gradual but perceptible change in the organization of political life which resulted from the consolidation of nationalism as the pre-eminent ideology of the times. Even if nationalist objectives were neither new nor particularly revolutionary, nationalist leaders were obliged to employ more sophisticated methods to achieve them. The disruptive effects of French rule required more highly developed and delicate mechanisms for restoring a more favorable balance of power in Syria. Nationalism had to be carefully modulated; it had to possess enough force to have the desired effect on the French, but without upsetting the local status quo.

Nationalist politics, therefore, required more than the mobilization of the traditional active forces in society associated with the popular classes and religious institutions located in the old town quarters; it also required the mobilization of new, emerging forces associated with modern institutions and youth movements which operated outside the old quarters. New forms of political association were encouraged, especially between the towns and the countryside and between different ethno-religious elites. Nationalist leaders adopted new patterns of political organization linked to new secular systems of ideas, and operated on a much larger territorial scale than ever before. They broadened the appeal of nationalism in order to attract moral and material support from neighboring Arab territories and to be heard in Paris and at the League of Nations in Geneva where Syria's fate was being decided. The resulting movements of protest and resistance were of greater intensity and longer duration.

Other trends emerged during the Mandate, however, which hampered Syria's political evolution. Once the National Bloc was given the opportunity to share power with the French, it showed signs of ineffective leadership. The National Bloc as a force of opposition to French rule was one thing; the Bloc at the helm of government was quite another. The calculated simplicity and prudence of the Bloc's brand of nationalism offered little in the way of concrete solutions to the social and economic problems affecting the Syrian people. The debilitating reorientation forced on the Syrian economy by the post-World War I partitions of geographical Syria, the inept and inadequate French financial and commercial policies, the increased sectarianism aided by French activities, and the devastating impact of the world depression of the early thirties produced tensions and conflicts in society which the National Bloc was unable effectively to address.

Factionalism intensified in the late 1930s and the Bloc's administrative incompetence, coupled with its political insensitivity to the aspirations and needs of the compact and religious minorities, damaged its reputation. Some responsibility for the Bloc's shortcomings lay with the French mandatory administration which neglected to train an efficient and dedicated Syrian administrative elite and which quietly aggravated relations between Syria's Sunni Arab majority and the various minority communities. The numerous divisions and redivisions of Syria over a quarter-century obstructed the development of such a unified administrative elite. In addition, France's refusal to give the recognized nationalist leadership adequate consideration for nearly two decades proved disastrous for Syria's future. Denied the opportunity to acquire and assimilate experience in governing, nationalist leaders carried a certain administrative incompetence with them into the independence era.

Despite the higher forms of political organization which were established during the Mandate, most nationalist leaders had failed to transcend their narrow city bases. They were not national politicians who shared a broad vision of the future. Their horizons had not stretched much beyond the four nationalist towns. And Damascus leaders continued to feel more comfortable in Beirut or Jerusalem than in Aleppo, let alone Latakia, while Aleppo leaders looked to Iraq (and even Turkey) as much as they did to Damascus.

Another trend set in motion during the Mandate which carried over into the independence era was the Syrian nationalist leadership's rejection of Arab unity as its principal political goal. Already by the mid-1930s, the National Bloc faced an awkward contradiction between pan-Arab unity and local self-interest. In 1936, it had dropped Syrian claims to the four *cazas* in Lebanon in order to secure a treaty with Paris which would allow it to form a government. Political and economic ties between Syria and Lebanon remained strong, but Syrian nationalist leaders grudgingly accepted Lebanon's claim to a separate political existence.

This awkward contradiction was also revealed by the way nationalists treated the question of Palestine. During the Arab rebellion of the late 1930s, the National Bloc government lent only cautious support to the Palestinian struggle (a very popular cause in Syria) to avoid upsetting treaty negotiations with France. Later, during the 1948 war in Palestine, the nationalist government failed, owing to political naivety and administrative incompetence, to make proper provisions for the war effort either in terms of pushing for greater pan-Arab coordination or of properly equipping the Syrian Army for battle. Syria's poor military showing in 1948 and the arms and financial scandals associated with Syria's lack of preparedness were blamed on the government. Indeed, the first of Syria's numerous coups d'état occurred in 1949 and can be partly attributed to the army's need to find a scapegoat for the humiliation it suffered in Palestine.[1]

---

[1] See Patrick Seale, *The Struggle for Syria. A Study in Post–War Arab Politics, 1945–1958.* (London, 1965), pp. 33–34, 41–42.

The political rivalry between Aleppo and Damascus during the Mandate was yet another development which proved damaging to Syrian politics after independence. Although Aleppo played a critical role in the struggle for independence, it also played a subordinate role to Damascus in almost every aspect of politics. The Aleppo branch of the National Bloc was in competition with the Damascus branch and, like the Damascus branch, it was internally divided. During the Mandate, Aleppo became a provincial capital cast in the shadow of Damascus and dependent on machinations there for its share of the budgets for education, public works, and the like. It naturally disliked this subordinate position.

Moreover, Aleppo suffered more than Damascus from the arbitrary post-World War I partitions. Its loss of the greater part of its commercial hinterland forced a drastic reorientation and reduction of its economy during the interwar period. It was only during World War II that Aleppo managed to re-adjust and re-emerge as Syria's main economic entrepôt. The difficulties of obtaining manufactured goods from traditional foreign suppliers during the war stimulated local industrial growth. In turn, major new investments by Aleppine entrepreneurs in the Jazira expanded the margins of cultivation and increased the productivity of the region. As a result, Aleppo experienced an economic boom during and after World War II from which its merchant-entrepreneurs derived much benefit. Aleppo wanted to expand its northern and eastern commercial hinterland to take advantage of the agricultural boom in the Jazira. Whereas Turkey remained hostile to this idea, Iraq was encouraging. Indeed, in the early 1940s Iraq sponsored a Fertile Crescent scheme which attracted Aleppine merchants and politicians in ways not appreciated by their counterparts in Damascus.[2]

The economic boom encouraged Aleppo to challenge the political paramountcy of Damascus. The rivalry between the Aleppo and Damascus branches of the National Bloc was heightened and this in turn produced a political schism in Aleppo. Although political lines of division were not hard and fast, the faction that broke away from the Bloc was linked to the emerging entrepreneurial group which was deeply involved in the opening up of the Jazira and in broadening commercial relations with Iraq. By the late 1940s, the rupture in the ranks of the National Bloc produced a new organization based in Aleppo, the People's Party (Hizb al-sha'b), which challenged the old National Bloc guard—reconstituted under Shukri al-Quwwatli's leadership as the Nationalist Party (al-Hizb al-watani)—for control of government.[3]

[2] Conversation with Jubran Shamiyya (Beirut, 29 July 1975). Shamiyya was one of the entrepreneurs involved in the opening up of the Jazira.
[3] One faction in Aleppo was associated with the Jabiri family, and its leader Sa'dallah, who maintained strong ties to the Bloc in Damascus. The other was headed by ex-Bloc chiefs

The intensification of rivalries between Damascus and Aleppo and within Aleppo's urban leadership was itself a reflection of changing power relations and the changing economy in Syria. For a multiplicity of reasons, the Syrian economy had failed to develop either in a balanced or a dynamic way between the wars. World War I had damaged productive forces. The sudden reorientation of the Syrian economy, particularly Aleppo's, reduced Syria's natural commercial hinterland. The European commercial invasion continued unabated, especially in the 1920s, thanks to the Mandate system's open door policy which undermined the remaining handicrafts and industries. The franc-exchange system tied Syria's currency to a shaky French franc. The French occupation produced years of political instability which discouraged both local and foreign capital investment. Although some progress was made in developing Syria's infrastructure—for example, its network of communications improved—industrial growth progressed slowly; it expanded fairly steadily after the Great Revolt but slowed down after 1933 and then grew only modestly until the late 1930s. The world depression of the early 1930s, French taxation, and the slow application of protective measures for infant industries obstructed industrial growth. Moreover, Syrian exports suffered owing to the high etatist barriers in Turkey and Iraq, the growth of Jewish industry in Palestine, and the signficant reduction of the large Palestine market, owing to the rebellion of 1936–39. The renewed instability of the French franc at this time drove the cost of living upwards dramatically, leading to workers' strikes and general political unrest which hurt productive forces.

Capital investment in Syria during the Mandate was much larger than ever before, but the long years of instability meant that most investments were made to insure maximum profit with maximum security. Therefore, the bulk of foreign investment went into infrastructure, primarily transport for the movement of Western manufactured goods into the country and raw materials out of it, and into industries devoted to the extraction of raw materials for export such as petrol, asphalt, and cotton and silk; into low-risk public services such as electricity and tramways in the towns; and into banking and insurance.[4] Apart from these, certain import substitution products such as cement, and other products naturally suited to Syria such as conserves and textiles, were bases for local industrial development. But, because banks charged extremely high interest rates,

including the Ibrahim Pashas, the wealthy Mudarris family, and younger nationalists such as Rushdi al-Kikhya and Nazim al-Qudsi. Seale, *The Struggle for Syria*, pp. 29–31; FO 226/240/9/4/180. Aleppo to Lascelles, 29 April 1943; FO 226/240/9/5/209. Aleppo to Chancery, 13 May 1943; FO 226/241/27/1/47. M.E.I.C. (Syria) to Lascelles, 19 Jan. 1943; MAE, Guerre 1939–45. Catroux (Beirut), 21 Dec. 1942, vol. 42, pp. 232–37.

[4] Al-Nayal, "Industry," , pp. 81–85.

borrowing to invest in these industries on a large scale was very difficult. Moreover, the conservatism of Syria's absentee landowning class hindered local investment in modern industry. It preferred to invest in urban real estate or in agricultural lands, but not to develop them; otherwise it was perfectly content to divert its capital into conspicuous consumption or to hoard gold.

Given the constraints on industrial growth and the economic and political upheavals of the interwar years, the landowning-bureaucratic class found itself in a more secure position than Syria's mercantile and industrial classes. Although the French initially set out to break the back of this class through land reforms and increased taxation, they eventually retreated owing to inadequate financial resources for their implementation and a grudging recognition that there was no suitable substitute for this class in its traditional role as intermediary between government and society. As late as 1936, the landowning-bureaucratic class accounted for 15.5 percent of Syria's total population and 57 percent of her national income.[5]

World War II reversed this process. First, conservative landowners suffered a loss of economic power as a class, owing to the exigencies of the war. Because the Allied Powers took measures to control grain and wheat production and kept prices artifically low, landowners who could not skirt these regulations or quickly diversify their agricultural production suffered big losses.

World War II also created a shortage of foreign imports. Industries based on processing local raw materials and semi-manufactured goods prospered while those that were dependent on imports suffered. Industrialists who were not completely dependent on foreign raw materials, or those who could meet local demand for manufactured goods that had previously been imported from abroad, enriched themselves. Textile industrialists were particularly successful during the war. At the same time, a group of entrepreneurs—many from outside the established class of absentee landowners—made vast profits expanding the amount of Syrian land under cultivation, notably in the Jazira. This enabled them to increase the supply of scarce foodstuffs and the raw materials which fed the new modern industries.[6]

How did these wartime economic developments translate politically? By independence, the merchant and landowning entrepreneurs—two groups which could not easily be differentiated from one another—were the most influential economic force in Syria and had already begun to

[5] Adnan Farra, L'industrialisation, pp. 51, 137, 139, 168, citing Ihsan Jabiri, Le Commerce du Levant, Beirut (18 Jan. 1938).
[6] Al-Nayal, "Industry," pp. 86–88.

pose a political challenge to the traditional urban leadership associated with the landowning-bureaucratic class and the National Bloc. Of this group, those nationalist leaders who emerged on top of the political heap at independence were those who forged links with the emerging class of industrialists, either as industrialists themselves or as politicians representing industrial interests in government. Even before the French left Syria, Shukri al-Quwwatli, a landowner turned industrialist, used the Presidency to support the interests of influential textile industrialists and merchants in return for their support against the challenge of more conservative landowning interests that were less inclined to press for full Syrian independence from France. Another prominent Damascene politician with strong links to industry, Khalid al-ʿAzm, positioned himself in a similar manner. Just after independence, an ascendant group of merchant-entrepreneurs in Aleppo formed the backbone of the new People's Party which supported stronger economic and political ties to Iraq on the one hand, and challenged Quwwatli and his supporters in the Nationalist Party for political leadership in Syria on the other.[7]

DESPITE THE REMARKABLE continuity of Syrian political life from Ottoman times through the French Mandate, the rearrangement of power relations consequent to World War II eventually weakened the established framework of nationalist politics. Equally disruptive were the new forms of political mobilization and the new conduits to political power that had begun to emerge by the end of the Mandate.

During the 1930s, new political movements emerged in Syria in response to the gradual socio-economic and cultural changes occurring beneath the political surface. These movements sought to bridge the widening gap between the nationalism of the upper classes and the nationalism of popular sentiment. More radical than the National Bloc, they expressed and harnessed that popular sentiment in a bid to expand the base of political activity in Syria. While the war years forced them to disband temporarily and sent their leaders underground, into exile, or into prison, the war also accelerated the forces which they embodied.

These radicalized movements left their mark on the politics of nationalism. They betrayed a strong middle-class component. In their front ranks stood men from merchant backgrounds or from the middle levels of the state bureaucracy. They were composed of members of the liberal professions and of a nascent industrial bourgeoisie, and were armed with European educations and new, sophisticated methods of political organi-

---

[7] Conversation with Hani al-Hindi (Beirut, 28 Aug. 1975).

zation acquired abroad. They demanded the right to take a more active part in the political process.

By organizing themselves into political parties based on more systematic and rigorous systems of ideas, radicalized movements posed a challenge to the National Bloc's monopoly on nationalism. They wanted to redefine their relations with the old nationalist elite and with themselves and they wanted a redefinition of nationalism that corresponded to and accommodated the structural changes which had begun to accelerate in Syria during World War II. The language of nationalism itself was refined and altered; these ascendant forces placed more emphasis on social and economic justice for the masses, on pan-Arab unity, and, after independence, on neutralism in international relations than on the old nationalist idioms of constitutionalism, liberal parliamentary forms, and personal freedoms.

In terms of its class and educational background, political style, and ideological orientation, this new generation of nationalists in Syria displayed characteristics that were remarkably similar to those of an emerging second generation of nationalists in Palestine, Iraq, and Eygpt. In fact, the politically-active members of this new generation were able to forge a panoply of ties across the Arab world.

The most important and representative of the radicalized organizations to emerge in Syria in the 1930s was the League of National Action. And although the League did not survive the war—its leadership having already been divided by the National Bloc by the late thirties—it proved to be the ideological parent of the Ba'th Party, the political organization with the most long-lasting influence on Syrian, indeed Arab, political life in the postwar era.

The League helped to lay the intellectual and organizational foundations of radical pan-Arabism which the Ba'th Party (officially established in 1947) was to build upon after independence. Among the Ba'th's founders and early leaders were former members of the League, including Zaki al-Arsuzi, the leader of the Syrian resistance movement to the Turkish takeover of the Sanjak of Alexandretta in the late 1930s, and Jalal al-Sayyid, a landowner from Dayr al-Zur. Similar to the League's leadership, which included a number of European-educated young men, several early Ba'thist leaders were trained in Paris including the Party's moving spirits, Michel 'Aflaq and Salah al-Din al-Bitar, not to mention Arsuzi himself. Apart from lawyers, professors, and other members of the liberal professions, the League—and the Ba'th after it—attracted large numbers of school teachers, the profession of Arsuzi, 'Aflaq, and Bitar. The League and early Ba'th leaderships also belonged to the same generation of young Syrian men born between 1900 and World War I; however, 'Aflaq, Bitar, and the Hama strongman, Akram Hawrani, who,

by linking up with the Ba'th in 1952, provided it with its popular following and its ties to junior army officers, were all nearly a decade younger
than the founders of the League.[8]

Just as the League bitterly opposed the old nationalist elite for its compromises with the French in the late 1930s and its willingness to stress
Syrianism at the expense of pan-Arabism, so too did the Ba'th during and
after World War II. And while both organizations recognized the
strengths of communist organization and borrowed from communism,
each, in its own way, rejected communist ideology for a milder form of
socialism with powerful nationalistic undertones. In fact, 'Aflaq and Bitar had been something akin to fellow travellers in the mid-1930s, until
the infant and underground Syrian Communist Party surfaced (through
its new leader, Khalid Bakdash, himself of the same generation as the future Ba'thist leaders) in order to exploit the victory of the left-wing Popular Front in France. By supporting the National Bloc in its treaty negotiations and after it took over government,[9] Bakdash turned the future
Ba'thist leaders sharply away from the communists, setting the stage for
the bitter struggles for political influence that occurred in the 1950s between the Ba'thists and the communists.

There was little opportunity during the Mandate for these radical
forces to break out of the framework of nationalist politics. World War II,
however, began to shake the edifice of Syrian political life. Just as a small,
untested, but aspiring group of disaffected urban notables and middle-
class intellectuals, armed with the new idea of Arabism, was prepared to
make its debut on the political stage at the end of World War I, so too was
a second generation of Arab nationalists poised to make its bid for power
at the end of World War II.

Crucial to this bid for power was the Syrian Army. Least visible during
the Mandate but ultimately most disruptive to Syrian politics afterwards
was the increasingly politicized military. The most important factor in-
fluencing the army's decision to become directly involved in political life
was the attitude of urban Sunni leaders to the military. Since the early
nineteenth century, notable families in the towns had adopted a hostile
attitude to the military which they regarded as a socially inferior institution. They actively discouraged their sons from pursuing military careers
and used their wealth and government connections to secure exemptions.
This attitude persisted throughout the Mandate and for some time after
independence.

In fact, it was only after the mid-1930s, when the possibility of Syrian

---

[8] See Hanna Batatu, *The Old Social Classes*, pp. 722–30.
[9] *Ibid.*, pp. 582, 726.

independence grew, that nationalist leaders began to think more seriously about Syria's institutional future, including the army. Only then did some nationalists begin to encourage the sons of the urban elites to seek military careers by attending the military academy in Homs. But, although there was an increase in the percentage of urban Sunni Arabs who became commissioned officers between 1936 and 1945 (over the period 1925–1935),[10] relations between the officer corps and the nationalist leadership were poor. For one thing, these officers came from lesser branches of leading urban families or from the rising middle classes and resented the more socially prominent and wealthier civilian leaders. This resentment, moreover, was mutual: Syrian political leaders held the army in contempt, a sentiment which did not disappear with the departure of the French. Apart from the problem of social antagonism, nationalist leaders distrusted the officer corps: they accused it of serving the French outright, or at least of serving French interests by remaining aloof from the nationalist struggle. After the French departed in 1946, one of the very first things the independence government did was to assert its control over the army by bringing it under civilian authority. It actually reduced the size of the army from 7,000 to 2,500 men between 1946 and 1948, ostensibly "because the ruling landed and mercantile families of the day regarded the contingent as too large and too financially burdensome."[11] The army's reduction in size at a time when war in Palestine loomed large on the horizon and the scandals associated with the government's inadequate provisioning of the army during that war exacerbated civilian–military relations and contributed directly to the army's entrance into the Syrian political arena with the first military coup in 1949.

Another factor present during the Mandate which contributed heavily to the radicalization of the military after independence was its changing complexion. By French design, the army developed a strong rural and minority complexion, in which the Alawite community featured prominently. This was especially true of the army's rank and file and its noncommissioned officer corps. By the end of the Mandate, several infantry battalions in the Troupes Spéciales were composed almost entirely of Alawites. None was entirely Sunni Arab in complexion, and even those few cavalry squadrons with a significant Sunni Arab component were filled largely with elements from rural areas and far off towns. The French preferred minority and rural recruits for the obvious reason that they were remote from Syria's dominant political ideology, Arab nationalism. In addition, the "depressed economic condition" of Syria's rural and minority communities made the army a vehicle for their social mobility. In this

[10] See Van Dusen, "Syrian Army," pp. 378–89.
[11] Batatu, "Some Observations," pp. 340–42.

way, the lower ranks of the army, including non-commissioned officers, became the preserve of the Alawites, the Druzes, and Sunnis from rural districts. Because Alawites were the largest and perhaps the poorest minority community in the country, they were most overrepresented in the army. The Alawite impact, however, was not felt for a full generation after independence. Sunni commissioned officers held the levers of power in the army in the years after independence and Alawites only came to dominate the Syrian officer corps in the 1960s, after successive purges had cleared the upper ranks of the army of Sunni officers. The Syrian governments of these years, like the French before them, saw the Alawites as remote from Syrian political struggles and therefore politically neutral.[12]

To express their aims and aspirations, ascendant junior officers from the Alawite and Druze communities and from rural Sunni districts required an ideology. Ba'thism provided a framework of ideas which was sufficiently flexible for their purposes. Its program stressed land reform and other more egalitarian economic measures and it inveighed against religious sectarianism. By the 1950s, these officers began to penetrate the Ba'th Party through its base in the Syrian Army and each institution reinforced the other's radicalism. Together, they broke apart the economic and social foundations of the old regime's power and replaced the political expertise of the veteran nationalists with a new, and ultimately, more effective way of playing politics.

THE PROCESS OF POLITICAL radicalization in Syria which was initiated during the era of the French Mandate finally obliged the veteran nationalists to sort out their alignments and to clarify their interests as a class on crucial political issues. This old guard may have landed in the driver's seat on independence but it proved unable to consolidate its position either smoothly or completely—an indication that its days were numbered. That elements from the old guard still retained influence over Syrian political life as late as the early 1960s suggests, however, just how tenacious and resilient the veteran nationalists were in the face of the much more powerful force of radical pan-Arabism. But then, after nearly four generations of accumulated experience, who better understood the meaning and the ways of political survival in Syria?

[12] *Ibid.,* p. 341.

APPENDIX

Sᴏᴜʀᴄᴇs ғᴏʀ Tᴀʙʟᴇs 10-1, 10-2, 10-3, 15-1, 15-2, 15-3

(For translations of Arabic Titles, see Bibliography)

Almanach Français. Beirut, 1930–1940.

The American University of Beirut, *Directory of Alumni 1870–1952.* Beirut, 1953.

Annuaire commercial industriel touristique. La Syrie, 1935–1936. Ed. Alphonse Ghanem. Beirut, n.d.

Anon. "Le club arabe de Damas." CHEAM, No. 351, 12 Jan. 1939.

——. "Note sur le Scoutisme musulman en Syrie et au Liban." CHEAM, No. 684, Beirut, 4 April 1944.

al-ʿAẓm, ʿAbd al-Qādir. *Al-Usra al-ʿAẓmiyya.* Damascus, 1951.

Baldissera, E. "La comosizione dei governi siriani dal 1918 al 1965 (Note e materiali)," *Oriente Moderno* 52 (1972), 517–30.

al-Bīṭār, ʿAbd al-Razzāq. *Ḥilyat al-bashar fī tārīkh al-qarn al-thālith ʿashar.* Ed. Muḥammad Bahjat al-Bīṭār. Damascus, 1961–1963.

de Boucheman, A. "Les Chemises de Fer." CHEAM, No. 6ᵇⁱˢ, 1936.

Brunton, Captain D. "Who's Who in Damascus in 1919," *Brunton File,* Middle East Centre, St. Antony's College, Oxford.

Bulletin économique de la Chambre du Commerce d'Alep. Aleppo, 1921–1943.

Dalīl al-jumhūriyya al-sūriyya 1939–1940. Damascus, n.d.

al-Dāshwālī, ʿAbd al-Laṭīf. *Marāyā.* Damascus, 1947.

Dawn, C. Ernest. "The Development of Nationalism in Syria," *The Arab World from Nationalism to Revolution.* Eds. Abdeen Jabara and Janice Terry. Wilmette, Il., 1971, 55–61.

——. "The Rise of Arabism in Syria," *From Ottomanism to Arabism. Essays on the Origin of Arab Nationalism.* Urbana, 1973, 122–47.

Fāris, George. *Man hum fī al-ʿālam al-ʿarabī.* I. Damascus, 1957.

——. *Man huwa fī sūriyya 1949.* Damascus, 1950.

Fauquenot, Emile. "Les récents Congrès Arabes qui se sont tenus en Orient." CHEAM, No. 365, 30 November 1938.

FO 371/5598, vol. 20067. "Records of Leading Personalities in Syria and the Lebanon," 26 August 1936.

FO 371/2142, vol. 20849. "Records of Leading Personalities in Syria and the Lebanon," 6 May 1937.

Gaulmier, J. "Congrès Général des Etudiants tenu à Hama, 1932." CHEAM, No. 46, 1936.

——. "Notes sur le mouvement syndicaliste à Hama," *Revue des Etudes Islamiques*, 6 (1932), 95–125.

Ghazzī, Kāmil. *Nahr al-dhahab fī tārīkh ḥalab*, 3 vols. Aleppo, 1923–1926.

al-Ḥakīm, Ḥasan. "Al-duktūr ʿAbd al-Raḥman al-Shahbandar." Unpublished biographical sketch, n.d.

——. *Mudhakkirātī*, 2 vols. Beirut, 1965–1966.

al-Ḥakīm, Yūsuf. *Sūriyya wa al-ʿahd al-Fayṣalī*. Beirut, 1966.

al-Ḥuṣnī, Muḥammad Adīb Taqī al-Dīn. *Kitāb muntakhabāt al-tawārīkh li-dimashq*, 3 vols. Damascus, 1927, 1928, 1934.

L'indicateur libano-syrienne. Eds. E. & G. Gédéon. Beirut, 1923, 1928–1929.

Interviews. Personal interviews conducted between 1974 and 1977 in London, Beirut, Damascus, and Paris. See Bibliography.

al-Jundī, Adham. *Aʿlām al-adab wa al-fann*, 2 vols. Damascus, 1954, 1958.

——. *Shuhadāʾ al-ḥarb al-ʿālamiyya al-kubrā*. Damascus, 1960.

——. *Tārīkh al-thawrāt al-sūriyya fī ʿahd al-intidāb al-faransī*. Damascus, 1960.

MAE, Syrie–Liban 1918–29. L. Massignon, "Rapport," November 1920, vol. 235, pp. 134–135.

MAE, Guerre 1939–45. Alger. "Notice," vol. 1004, 101–28.

al-Muḍhik al-mubkī, 1929–1939. Damascus weekly satirical magazine.

al-Murādī, Muḥammad Khalīl. *Silk al-durar fī aʿyān al-qarn al-thānī ʿashar*, 4 vols. Cairo, 1883.

al-Murshid al-ʿarabī. Dalīl sūriyya, lubnān wa filasṭīn 1936–1937. Beirut, 1937.

al-Musāwwar, 1936. Damascus weekly magazine.

al-Nashra al-shahriyya li-ghurfat al-tijāra—dimashq, 24 vols. Damascus, 1922–1945.

Oriente Moderno, 20 vols. Rome, 1920–1940.

al-Qāsimī, Ẓāfir. *Maktab ʿAnbar*. Beirut, 1967.

——. *Wathāʾiq jadīda min al-thawra al-sūriyya al-kubrā*. Damascus, 1965.

al-Qāsimiyya, Khayriyya. *al-Ḥukūmāt al-ʿarabiyya fī dimashq bayn 1918–1920*. Cairo, n.d.

Qudāma, Aḥmad. *Maʿālim wa aʿlām fī bilād al-ʿarab*. vol. 1. Damascus, 1965.

Saʿīd, Amīn. *al-Thawra al-ʿarabiyya al-kubrā*, 3 vols. Cairo, 1934.

Salname: suriye vilayeti.

Salname: vilayet-i halab.

al-Shaṭṭī, Shaykh Muḥammad Jamīl. *A'yān dimashq fī al-qarn al-thāl-ith 'ashar wa niṣf al-qarn al-rābi' 'ashar*, 2nd ed. Beirut, 1972.

Vacca, Virginia. "Notizie biografiche su uomini politici ministri e depu-tati siriani," *Oriente Moderno* 17 (October 1937), 471–95.

Winder, R. Bayly. "Syrian Deputies and Cabinet Ministers, 1919–1959," *Middle East Journal*, 2 parts. 16 (Autumn 1962), 407–29; 17 (Winter–Spring 1963), 35–54.

al-Ziriklī, Khayr al-Dīn. *al-A'lām*, 10 vols, 2nd ed. Cairo, 1954–1957.

GLOSSARY

āghā (pl. āghāwāt)	Ottoman title meaning chief; in reference to the head of the local janissaries (*yerliyye*); also chief of a town quarter and title given to wealthy grain merchants
ʿālim	see *ʿulamāʾ*
ʿamīd	doyen or dean
amīr	prince or commander
ʿarāḍa	parades, demonstrations
ashrāf (sing. sharīf)	claimants of descent from the Prophet
aṣnāf	artisanal corporations or guilds
awqāf (pl. of waqf)	endowments for charitable purposes or for the benefit of the descendants of the founders
aʿyān	notables
al-baladiyya	municipality
bēgawāt	beys; an Ottoman honory title
defterkhāne	public record office
dīwān	council
dunam	one metric dunam equals .25 acres
ḥafla	assembly, social gathering
ḥajj	pilgrimage
ḥāra	town quarter
ḥawāṣil	granaries
ḥayy	town quarter
imām	leader of congregational prayer
jamʿiyyāt	religious beneficent societies
jihād	holy war
khān	large building for travellers and merchandise; caravanserai
khaṭīb	preacher
ketkhuda	steward in a great man's household
khūwa	protection rackets
liwāʾ	administrative district
madāfa	outer salon of residence for greeting or visitation purposes; *salāmlik*
madrasa	secondary school that teaches the Islamic sciences

majlis	council
majlis al-baladī	municipal council
maktab	elementary school that teaches the Islamic sciences
masjid	small mosque
millet or milla	an officially recognized religious community
mīrī	state-owned property
al-muʿāraḍa	the opposition
muftī	person trained in the religious law or *sharīʿa* (q.v.) who gives a non-binding legal opinion or *fatwā*
muḥāfaẓa	governorate
muḥāfiẓ	provincial governor
muḥtasib	market inspector who enforced public morality
mujāhidīn	freedom fighters
mukhtār	village headman; also chief of a town quarter
mulk	privately-held lands (freehold)
muṣāraʿa	wrestling match
mushāʿ	village-held parcels of land which are periodically redistributed among villagers
mutaṣarrif	governor of a province
nāẓir al-waqf	trustee of a religious endowment
pāshā	Ottoman honorary title of high rank
qabaḍāy (pl. āt)	local gang leader in town quarter
qaḍāʾ (caza)	administrative district
qāḍī	Muslim judge whose decisions are legally binding
qāʾimmaqām	district commissioner or subgovernor of a province
salafī	member of Islamic reform movement, *al-salafiyya*
salname	Ottoman government yearbook
sanjak (sanjaq)	administrative district in a province
sharīʿa	Islamic law
shaykh (tribal)	Arab tribal chief
spāhīs	cavalrymen; during Mandate, recruited by French from North African colonies
ṣūfī	mystic
sūq	market or bazaar
suwayqa	small market in town quarter
tajhīz	government preparatory school

'ulamā' (pl. of 'ālim)   Muslim clergy or those learned in the Islamic
                            sciences
'ummāl   workers
vali or wālī   governor
vilayet or wilāyā   province
wakīl   agent
waqf   see *awqāf*
wazīr   minister
wujahā'   notables
yerliyye   local janissaries
za'īm   strongman, popular political leader
zur'ān   organized hoodlums in popular quarters

BIBLIOGRAPHY

I. ARCHIVAL SOURCES

A. FRANCE

Ministère des Affaires Etrangères (MAE): Paris

Série E—Levant 1918–1940.	Syrie–Liban 1918–29, vols. 1–437
	Syrie–Liban 1930–40, vols. 456–637
Guerre 1939–1945.	Londres: Comité National Français (CNF), vols. 39–65
	Alger (CFLN–GPRF) June 1943–September 1944, Levant: vols. 999–1025

Henry de Jouvenel Papers (No. 92)
Gabriel Puaux Papers (No. 252)

Ministère de la Défense (MD): Vincennes

État-Major de l'Armée de Terre, Service Historique Série N (1920–1940): 7N, 16N, 17N, 20N

Centre de Hautes Etudes Administratives sur l'Afrique et l'Asie Modernes (CHEAM): Paris

Mémoires en stage
Anon. "Le club arabe de Damas." No. 351. 12 Jan. 1939.
——. "Etude sur le fonctionnement du Bureau National Arabe de Recherches et d'Informations de Damas." No. 350. n.d.
——. "La question syrienne. La vérité sur les événements de la Djézireh." No. 212078. 1937.
——. "Note sur le Scoutisme musulman en Syrie et au Liban." No. 684. Beirut, 4 April 1944.
——. "Traité d'Amitié et d'Alliance entre France et la Syrie." No. 730. n.d.
Ayme, Lieutenant. "La rivalité arabo-kurde en Djeziré Syrienne, Feb. 1936–Sept. 1937." No. 223. December 1937.
Berthelot, P. "Notes sur la mise en valeur de la région du 'Caza' de Homs." No. 249. Homs, February 1938.
de Boucheman, A. "Les Bédouins en Syrie." No. 126. 23 April 1937.

de Boucheman, A. "Les Chemises de Fer." No. 6bis. 1936.

Casenave, Capitaine. "Nomadisme et sédentarisation." No. 1559. n.d.

Desloges, Delelee. "Aperçu sur la vie rurale dans la Syrie du Nord." No. 876. 6 June 1946.

Dillemann, L. "Les Français en Haute-Djezireh—Une réussite ignorée en marge de l'échec syrien." No. 50538. n.d.

Fauquenot, Emile. "L'état civil en Syrie en relation avec les questions de nationalité et de statut personnel des communautés religieuses." No. 50. n.d.

——. "Les institutions gouvernementales de la Syrie." No. 201. 17 June 1937.

——. "Les récents Congrès Arabes qui se sont tenus en Orient." No. 365. 30 November 1938.

Gaulmier, J. "Congrès Général des Etudiants tenu à Hama, 1932." No. 46. 1936.

Grandjouan. "L'avenir de nos fils." No. 400. November 1935.

Grellet, J. "Mémoire sur la fiscalité municipale en Syrie." No. 331. n.d.

La Croix, André. "Le contrôle bédouin de Syrie." No. 1147. 9 April 1947.

Montagne, R. "L'évolution de la jeunesse arabe." No. 244. 21 June 1937.

——. "Le pouvoir des chefs et les élites en Orient." No. 17. 12 May 1938.

——. "Organisation militaire de la Syrie dans le cadre du Traité." No. 51. January–March 1936.

Massa, Cdt. "Notables de Syrie." No. 1618. 23 June 1949.

Rondot, Pierre. "Islam moderne et la structure de l'état." No. 115220. n.d.

——. "Du nationalisme des Pashas au nationalisme populaire et unitaire en Orient." No. 3215. 20 January 1959.

Weulersse, Jacques. "La géographie humaine du Proche-Orient." No. 754. 26 October 1945.

B. GREAT BRITAIN.

Public Record Office (PRO): London

Air Ministry: AIR 23 (Air Ministry) Miscellaneous
Colonial Office: CO 733 (Colonial Office) Miscellaneous
Foreign Office: FO 371 (Syria) 1921–1945
                  FO 684 (France–Damascus, Embassy and Consular Archives) 1922–1944
                  FO 226 (Turkey: Beirut, Embassy and Consular Archives) 1942–1945

Private Papers

Oxford: Middle East Centre, St. Antony's College
  George Antonius File
  Captain C.D. Brunton File
  H. St. John Philby Papers. Boxes 12, 14, 17.
  Sir Edward Spears Papers

Durham: Sudan Archives, Middle East Centre, University of Durham
  ʿAbbās Ḥilmī II Papers

C. *ISRAEL*

Central Zionist Archives (CZA): Jerusalem

CZA/ S25 (1936)

D. *LEBANON*

Institute for Palestine Studies (IPS): Beirut

ʿĀdil al-ʿAẓma Papers [Syria]
Nabīh al-ʿAẓma Papers [Syria]

E. *SYRIA*

Majlis al-shaʿb. Records of Syrian Parliamentary Debates, Damascus

Markaz al-wathāʾiq al-tārīkhiyya (MWT): Damascus

al-Dawla: al-Intidāb al-faransī (French Mandate)

dākhiliyya (Interior Ministry)
iḍrabāt (Strikes)
niqābāt (Unions)
al-aḥzāb (Political Parties)
qaḍāyā mukhtalifa (Miscellaneous Problems)
intikhābāt (Elections)

al-Qism al-khāṣṣ (Private Papers)

Nazīh Muʾayyad al-ʿAẓm Papers
Nasīb al-Bakrī Papers
Fakhrī al-Bārūdī Papers
Saʿdallāh al-Jābirī Papers
ʿAbd al-Raḥmān Shahbandar Papers

Uncatalogued Court Registers of the Mandate Period, 1924–1945.

Jugements Correctionnels
Jugements de Cour d'Appel de Damas
Registres d'enregistrement
Registres fondamentals concernant le Service du Tribunal de 1ᵉʳᵉ Instance
  Correctionnelle
Registres des jugements civils
Registres des jugements commercials
Registres des jugements criminels
Registres: Tribunal de Commerce de 1ᵉʳᵉ Instance Mixte de Damas

Uncatalogued Correspondence

M. Demeulenaere (Administrative and Finance Inspector of Aleppo and
  Idlib: Adviser to the Municipality of Aleppo), 6 vols. (1930–1936).
Gennaoui Cousins. *Copie de Lettres*, 4 vols. (1925–1932).
Siouffi et Sabbagh et Cie. *Copie de Lettres*, 3 vols. (1929–1932).

Uncatalogued Reports

"Rapport de la liquidation de la Société Sheikh et Mahayni." Damascus,
  4 July 1937.

F. UNITED STATES

National Archives (USNA): Washington

Records of the Department of State Relating to Internal Affairs of Asia,
  1910–1929. Record Group (R.G.) 59. Syria (890.d 00/01 . . .)

II. MISCELLANEOUS UNPUBLISHED MANUSCRIPTS AND
PRIVATE PAPERS

Damas. Rapport d'enquête monographique sur la ville 1936. Drafted by
  René and Raymond Danger, Paul Danger, M. Ecochard. 85 pages plus
  drawings and pictures. Institut Français d'Etudes Arabes, Damascus.
al-Ḥakīm, Ḥasan. "Mūjaz tarjama ḥayāt al-zaʿīm al-khālid al-maghfūr
  lahu al-duktūr ʿAbd al-Raḥmān al-Shahbandar" (Biographical sketch
  of the life of the late glorious leader, ʿAbd al-Rahman al-Shahbandar),
  5 pp. Manuscript lent to author.
al-Kilāwī, Ḥasan (Abū ʿAlī). "Thawrat ʿāmma 1925. Al-Faransiyyīn fī
  sūriyya" (The Revolt of 1925. The French in Syria). Damascus, n.d.
  Manuscript lent to author.
Rabbath, Edmond. *Courte Histoire du Mandat en Syrie et au Liban*, 3

parts: 1. Untitled (45 pages), 2. "L'expérience Ponsot" (72 pages), 3. "La république libanaise" (27 pages). Manuscript lent to author.

III. OFFICIAL REPORTS AND PUBLICATIONS

A. FRANCE

Les Armées Françaises d'Outre-mer. *Histoires des troupes du Levant.* Paris, 1931.

Débats parlementaires. Chambre des Députés (1920–1939).

Débats parlementaires. Sénat (1920–1939).

Haut-Commissariat de la République Française: Direction du Service des Renseignements du Levant. *Les Tribus nomades et semi-nomades des états du Levant placés sous Mandat Français.* Beirut, 1930.

Haut-Commissariat de la République Française en Syrie et au Liban. *Bulletin Economique Trimestriel (Syrie-Liban).* n. pl., 1922–1939.

Haut-Commissariat de la République Française en Syrie et au Liban. *Bulletin Officiel des Actes.* Beirut, 1930–1933.

Haut-Commissariat de la République Française en Syrie et au Liban, *Statistique générale du Commerce extérieur des Etats du Levant sous Mandat Français, 1931–1933.* Beirut, 1934.

Journal Officiel. Paris, 1920–1939.

Ministère des Affairs Etrangères. *Rapport à la Société des Nations sur la situation de la Syrie et du Liban* (Annual Report presented to the League of Nations), 1922–1923, 1924–1938. Paris, 1923–1939.

Recueil des actes administratifs du Haut-Commissariat de la République Française en Syrie et au Liban. Beirut, 1919–1920, 1921–1939.

Le service géographique des forces françaises du Levant. *Syrie: Répértoire alphabétique des noms des lieux habités.* 3rd ed. Beirut, August, 1945.

B. GREAT BRITAIN

Department of Overseas Trade. *Report on the Trade, Industry and Finances of Syria, May 1925.* By H. E. Satow, London, 1925.

——. *Economic Conditions in Syria, July 1930.* By R. Eldon Ellison, London, 1930.

——. *Report on Economic and Commercial Conditions in Syria and Lebanon (June 1936).* By G. T. Havard, London, 1936.

Documents on British Foreign Policy, 1919–1939. Eds., E. L. Woodward and R. Butler, 1st Series, IV, London, 1952.

Foreign Office. *Handbook: Syria*. London, 1920.
——. *Syria and Palestine* (Handbook). No. 93, London, 1939.
Handbook of the Nomad, Semi-Nomad, Semi-Sedentary and Sedentary Tribes of Syria. London, 1943.
Naval Intelligence Division. *Syria*. B.R. 513. Geographical Handbook Series, London, 1943.

C. *LEAGUE OF NATIONS*

Permanent Mandates Commission (PMC): Geneva
Minutes, 1922–1938.

D. *OTTOMAN EMPIRE*

Salname: suriye vilayeti (Yearbook. Syrian Province). 1288/1871–1872; 1289/1872–1873; 1296/1878–1879; 1302/1884–1885; 1308–1309/1890–1891; 1309–1310/1892–1893; 1312/1894–1895.
Salname: vilayet-i halab (Yearbook. Aleppo Province). 1309/1891–1892; 1310/1892–1893; 1314/1896–1897; 1321/1903–1904; 1324/1906–1907; 1326/1908–1909; 1329/1911.

E. *SYRIA*

Ministry of Education, *Statistical Abstract*. Syria, 1956.
Ministry of National Economy, Department of Statistics. *Statistical Abstract of Syria*. Damascus, 1952.
Charles Pavie, *Etat d'Alep. Renseignements agricoles*. Aleppo, 1924.

F. *UNITED STATES*

American Consulate General at Beirut, "Education in the States of the Levant under French Mandate" (Report for Office of Education, Department of Interior). Beirut, 1 November 1933.

IV. PAMPHLETS, MANIFESTOES, SHORT REPORTS

Association Syrienne Arabe de Paris. "La vérité sur le problème syrien." Paris, 1939.
Bureau National Arabe de Recherches et d'Informations. "La vérité sur la question d'Alexandrette." Damascus, n.d.
Cadastre des Etats de Syrie et du Liban. "Notice sur le démembrement et

l'aménagement des terres 'Mouchaa' possédées dans l'indivision collective." n. pl., 1935.

———. "Notice sur le régime foncier et le cadastre des états de Syrie et du Liban." n.pl., n.d.

———. "Notice sur le rémembrement des propriétés poursuivi en Syrie et au Liban." n.pl., n.d.

Gautherot, Gustave. *Le Général Sarrail. Haut-Commissaire en Syrie. (Janvier 1925)*. Paris, 1925.

Ḥaflat iftitāḥ ḥizb al-shaʿb (The Opening Ceremony of the People's Party). Damascus, 1925

al-Khaṭīb, Zakī. *Bayān al-jabha al-waṭaniyya al-muttaḥida* (Declaration of the United National Front). Damascus, 12 March 1936, 27 December 1937.

———. *Iḥtijāj al-jabha al-waṭaniyya al-muttaḥida* (Protest of the United National Front). Damascus, Manifestos of 29 December 1937, 24 July 1938.

———. *Minhaj al-jabha al-waṭaniyya al-muttaḥida* (Program of the United National Front). Damascus, 22 October 1935.

Maktab al-Bārūdī. "Situation du fait du Sandjak à partir du 30 octobre 1918." Ed. Comité pour la défense d'Alexandrette. No. 11. n. pl., n.d.

Office National Arabe de Recherches et d'Informations. *Syrie 1938. La situation en Syrie après la conclusion de traité franco-syrien. Réponse aux campagnes de MM. Jérome et Jean Tharaud*. Damascus, 1938.

Troupes du Levant. Ecole Militaire de Damas. "Programme des conditions d'admission à l'Ecole en 1928 et Règlement Général." n. pl., n.d.

ʿUṣbat al-ʿamal al-qawmī. *Bayān al-muʾtamar al-taʾsīsī* (The League of National Action. Declaration of the Founding Conference). Damascus, 24 August 1933.

V. NEWSPAPERS AND PERIODICALS

Alif bā' (Damascus daily newspaper)

L'Asie Française (1920–1940)

al-Ayyām (Damascus daily newspaper)

La Chronique (Damascus)

Le Commerce du Levant (Beirut weekly 19 July 1929–16 August 1932; bi-weekly thereafter)

Correspondance d'Orient

Les Echos (Damascus)

L'Humanité (Paris)

al-Jihād (Aleppo daily newspaper)

Le Matin (Paris)
al-Muḍhik al-mubkī (Damascus weekly satirical magazine 1929–1939)
al-Mufīd (Beirut daily newspaper)
al-Muqtabas (Damascus newspaper)
al-Musāwwar (Damascus weekly youth magazine 1936)
Oriente Moderno (Rome, 1921–1940)
al-Qabas (Damascus daily newspaper)
al-Qibla (Mecca newspaper)
Revue des Deux Mondes (Paris)
Revue de L'Histoire des Colonies Françaises (1920–1930)
Revue des Troupes du Levant (1935–1937)
La Syrie (Beirut newspaper)
al-Ṭalīʿa (Damascus monthly journal, 1935–1939)
Le Temps (Paris)
The Times (London)

VI. YEARBOOKS, MONTHLY AND ANNUAL REPORTS, STATISTICAL ABSTRACTS

Almanach Français. Beirut, 1930–1940.
Annuaire Commercial Industriel Touristique. La Syrie, 1935–1936. Ed. Alphonse Ghanem. Beirut, n.d.
Atlas de Géographie Economique de Syrie et du Liban. Eds. Z. Khanzadian and L. de Bertalot. Paris, 1926.
Banque de Syrie et du Grand Liban. *Bulletin Annuel*. Paris, 1927–1938.
———. *15 Ans de Mandat*. Beirut, 1936.
Bulletin du Comité de l'Asie Française.
Bulletin Economique de la Chambre du Commerce d'Alep. Aleppo, 1921–1943.
Crédit Foncier d'Algérie et de Tunisie. *Répértoire économique & financier de la Syrie et du Liban*. Paris, 1932.
Dalīl al-jumhūriyya al-sūriyya 1939–1940 (Handbook of the Syrian Republic). Damascus, n.d.
L'Indicateur Libano-Syrienne. Eds. E. & G. Gédéon. Beirut, 1923, 1928–1929.
Le livre d'or des troupes du Levant, 1918–1936. n. pl., n.d.
Al-Murshid al-ʿarabī. Dalīl sūriyya, lubnān wa filastīn 1936–1937 (The Arab Adviser. Handbook for Syria, Lebanon and Palestine). Beirut, 1937.
Al-Nashra al-shahriyya li-ghurfat al-tijāra—dimashq (The Monthly

Bulletin of the Damascus Chamber of Commerce), vols. 1–24, Damascus, 1922–1945.

Recueil de Statistiques de la Syrie et du Liban, 1942–1943. n. pl., n.d.

Recueil de Statistiques syriennes comparées 1928–1968. Damascus, 1970.

VII. DISSERTATIONS

Atiyah, Najla Wadih. "The Attitude of the Lebanese Sunnis Towards the State of Lebanon," Ph.D. Diss. University of London, 1973.

Joarder, Saffiuddin. "The Early Phase of the French Mandatory Administration in Syria; with special reference to the Uprising, 1925–1927," Ph.D. Diss. Harvard University, 1968.

Kalla, Mohammad Sa'id. "The Role of Foreign Trade in the Economic Development of Syria, 1831–1914," Ph.D. Diss. American University, 1969.

Khoury, Philip S. "The Politics of Nationalism: Syria and the French Mandate, 1920–1936," Ph.D. Diss. Harvard University, 1980.

Longuenesse, Elisabeth. "La classe ouvrière en Syrie. Une classe en formation," 3ème cycle Diss. Ecole des Hautes Etudes en Sciences Sociales, Paris, 1977.

McDowall, David Buchanan. "The Druze Revolt, 1925–27, and its Background in the late Ottoman Period," B. Litt. Diss. University of Oxford, 1972.

Mufarrij, Fuad K. "Syria and Lebanon under the French Mandate," M.A. Diss. American University of Beirut, 1935.

Nashabi, Hisham. "The Political Parties in Syria 1918–1933," M.A. Diss. American University of Beirut, 1952.

al-Nayal, M. Abdul-Kader. "Industry and Dependency with Special Reference to Syria: 1920–1957," M.A. Diss. Institute of Social Studies, The Hague, 1974.

Sanadiki, Chafiq. "Le mouvement syndical en Syrie," Doctorat en Droit Diss. University of Paris, 1949.

Shamiyeh, S. "The Taxation System of Syria," M.A. Diss. American University of Beirut, 1945.

Tomeh, Ramez George. "Landowners and Political Power in Damascus, 1858–1958," M.A. Diss. American University of Beirut, 1977.

Van Dusen, Michael H. "Intra-and Inter-Generational Conflict in the Syrian Army," Ph.D. Diss. The Johns Hopkins University, 1971.

VIII. INTERVIEWS

A. BEIRUT

Munīr al-ʿAjlānī (2 September 1975)*
Hānī al-Hindī (28 August 1975)
Yūsuf Ībīsh (4 July 1975)
Ẓāfir al-Qāsimī (24 July 1975, 26 July 1975)*
Fawzī al-Qāwuqjī (16 July 1975)
Edmond Rabbath (21 August 1975, 27 August 1975, 3 September 1975)*
Ḥusnī Ṣawwāf (25 August 1975)*
Jubrān Shāmiyya (29 July 1975)
Amīr Aḥmad al-Shihābī (21 January 1976)
Wajīha al-Yūsuf [Ibīsh] (15 August 1975, 29 August 1975)*
Akram Zuʿaytir (6 August 1975, 11 August 1975)*
Qusṭanṭīn Zurayq (10 January 1976)

B. CAMBRIDGE, MASSACHUSETTS

Fāḍil al-Jamālī (21 November 1978)

C. DAMASCUS

Shaykh Muṣṭafā Yusr ʿAbdīn (22 July 1977)
Anwar al-Bābā (8 April 1976)
Naṣūḥ Babīl (20 February 1976)
Maḥmūd al-Bayrūtī (10 March 1976)
Ṣabrī Farīd al-Bidaywī (9 July 1977, 12 July 1977, 17 July 1977)
ʿAli ʿAbd al-Karīm al-Dandashī (21 October 1975, 9 March 1976)
Nikita Elisséeff (30 November 1978)
Ḥasan al-Ḥakīm (12 March 1976, 21 March 1976)
Yūsuf al-Ḥakīm (21 February 1976)
Shafiq Imām (9 April 1976)
Samīr Kaḥḥāla (12 February 1976)
Colette al-Khūrī (11 February 1976)
Suhayl al-Khūrī (8 February 1976)
Ḥasan (Abū ʿAlī) al-Kilāwī (14 February 1976, 3 March 1976, 15 May 1976)
Naṣūḥ (Abū Muḥammad) al-Mahayrī (10 March 1976)
Nuzhat Mamlūk (15 July 1977)
Amīn al-Nāfūrī (22 February 1976)
Ẓāfir al-Qāsimī (29 November 1978)

*Interviews conducted with Ramez G. Tomeh.

Aḥmad Shawkat al-Shaṭṭī (5 February 1976)
George Sibāʿ (13 February 1976)
Fuʾād Sidāwī (13 February 1976)
Farīd Zayn al-Dīn (18 October 1975, 14 April 1976, 22 April 1976)

D. LONDON

Sir Richard Beaumont 2 (June 1975)
Nadim Demichkie (25 June 1975)
Sir Geoffrey Furlonge (26 March 1975)
Brigadier Stephen H. Longrigg (17 April 1975)
Salma Mardam (25 November 1974, 7 December 1974)
Elizabeth Monroe (3 April 1975)
Patrick Seale (18 April 1975)

E. PARIS

Jean Gaulmier (23 June 1976, 7 March 1977)

IX. BOOKS AND ARTICLES

Abdel-Nour, A. *Introduction à l'histoire urbaine de la Syrie Ottomane (XVIIᵉ-XVIIIᵉ siècle)*. Beirut, 1982.

Abdulac, Samir. "Damas: les années Ecochard (1932–1982)," *Les cahiers de la recherche architecturale* 10/11 (April 1982), 32–43.

Abī-Rāshid, Hānī. *Jabal al-Durūz*. Beirut, 1961.

Achard, E. "Etudes sur la Syrie et la Cilicie. Le coton en Cilicie et en Syrie," *L'Asie Française* (Documents économiques, politiques, et scientifiques), No. 3 (June 1922) 19–62; No. 4 (July–August 1922), 65–113.

al-ʿAhd al-waṭanī fī sūriyya thalātha sanawāt 1944–1946 (The Nationalist Era in Syria during Three Years 1944–1946). Wizārat al-muwāṣalāt. (Ministry of Communications). Damascus, 1947.

Ajlani, Munir. *La constitution de la Syrie*. Paris, 1932.

Alexandre, A. "Conflits de l'arabisme et des nationalismes voisins. Le conflit syro-turc du Sandjak d'Alexandrette d'octobre 1936 à juin 1937, vu d'Antioche," *Entretiens sur l'évolution des pays de civilisation arabe, II*. Paris, 1938, 105–41.

al-ʿAllāf, Aḥmad Ḥilmī. *Dimashq fī maṭlaʿ al-qarn al-ʿashrīn* (Damascus at the Beginning of the Twentieth Century). Ed. ʿAlī Jamīl Nuʿīysa. Damascus, 1976.

ʿAlūsh, Nājī. "al-Ḥaraka al-ʿarabiyya baʿd al-ḥarb al-ʿālamiyya al-ūlā" ("The Arab Movement after the First World War"), Dirāsāt ʿarabiyya (December, 1965), 44–75.

American University of Beirut. Directory of Alumni, 1870–1952. Beirut, 1953.

Andréa, Général C.J.E. La révolte druze et l'insurrection de Damas, 1925–1926. Paris, 1937.

Andrew, Christopher M. and A. S. Kanya-Forstner. The Climax of French Imperial Expansion 1914–1924. Stanford, 1981.

——. "The French Colonial Party and French Colonial War Aims, 1914–1918," The Historical Journal 17 (1974), 79–106.

Antonius, George. The Arab Awakening. London, 1938.

——. "Syria and the French Mandate," International Affairs 13 (1934), 523–39.

al-Armanāzī, Najīb. Muḥadārāt ʿan sūriyya min al-iḥtilāl ḥattā al-jalāʾ (Lectures on Syria from the Occupation to the Evacuation). Cairo, 1953.

al-ʿĀs, Shākir. "Naḥnu wa al-thawra al-sināʿiyya" ("We and the Industrial Revolution"), al-Ṭalīʿa, 2 parts (April 1936), 118–27 (May 1936), 231–38.

Asfour, E. Y. Syria: Development and Monetary Policy. Cambridge, Mass., 1959.

ʿAwad, ʿAbd al-ʿAzīz Muḥammad. al-Idāra al-ʿuthmāniyya fī wilāyat sūriyya 1864–1914 (Ottoman Administration in the Province of Syria, 1864–1914). Cairo, 1969.

al-ʿAzm, ʿAbd al-Qādir. al-Usra al-ʿAzmiyya (The al-ʿAzm Family). Damascus, 1951.

al-ʿAzm, Khālid. Mudhakkirāt Khālid al-ʿAzm (Memoirs of Khalid al-ʿAzm), 3 vols. Beirut, 1973.

Azmeh, Abdullah F. L'évolution de la banque commerciale dans le cadre économique de la Syrie (1920–1957). Lausanne, 1961.

Baedeker, Karl. Palestine and Syria. Handbook for Travelers. Leipzig, 1906.

Baer, Gabriel. "The Evolution of Private Landownership in Egypt and the Fertile Crescent," The Economic History of the Middle East. Ed. Charles Issawi. Chicago, 1966.

——. "The Office and Functions of the Village Mukhtar," Palestinian Society and Politics. Ed. Joel S. Migdal. Princeton, 1980.

——. Population and Society in the Arab East. London, 1964.

Bagh, A. S. L'industrie à Damas entre 1928 et 1958. Etude de géographie économique. Damascus, 1961.

Bakdāsh, Khālid. "al-Fāshistiyya wa al-shuʿūb al-ʿarabiyya" ("Fascism and the Arab Peoples"), al-Ṭalīʿa (May 1939), 369–81.

Baldissera, E. "La comosizione dei governi siriani dal 1918 al 1965 (Note e materiali)," *Oriente Moderno* 52 (1972), 517–30.

——. "Note di Storia siriana: gli ultimi giorni del regno siriano di Faisal ibn Husein," *Oriente Moderno* 52 (1972), 341–56.

Bankwitz, Philip C. F. *Maxime Weygand and Civil–Military Relations in Modern France.* Cambridge, Mass., 1967.

al-Bārūdī, Fakhrī. *Mudhakkirāt al-Bārūdī* (Memoirs of al-Barudi), 2 vols. Beirut/Damascus, 1951, 1952.

Batatu, Hanna. "The Arab Countries from Crisis to Crisis: Some Basic Trends and Tentative Interpretations," *The Liberal Arts and the Future of Higher Education in the Middle East.* Ed. American University of Beirut. Beirut, 1979.

——. *The Old Social Classes and the Revolutionary Movements of Iraq.* Princeton, 1978.

——. "Some Observations on the Social Roots of Syria's Ruling Military Group and the Causes of its Dominance," *Middle East Journal* 35 (Summer 1981), 331–44.

——. "Syria's Muslim Brethren," *Merip Reports*, no. 110, 12 (November–December 1982), 12–20, 34.

Baurain, Paul. *Alep. Autrefois, aujourd'hui.* Aleppo, 1930.

Bazantay, Pierre. *Enquête sur l'artisinat à Antioche. Les états du Levant sous Mandat Français.* Beirut, 1936.

de Beauplan, Rousseau de. *Où va la Syrie?* Paris, 1929.

Beradi, Roberto. "Espace et ville en pays d'Islam," *L'Espace social de la ville arabe.* Ed. Dominique Chevallier. Paris, 1979.

Bernard, A. "Les populations de la Syrie et de la Palestine d'après les derniers recensements," *Annales de géographie* 33 (1924), 73–79.

Berque, Jacques. *Egypt: Imperialism and Revolution.* New York, 1972.

——. "L'idée de classes dans l'histoire contemporaine des Arabes," *Cahiers Internationaux de Sociologie* 38 (1965), 169–84.

——. "L'univers politique des Arabes," *Encyclopédie française*, vol. 11. Paris, 1957.

Berthé, George-Gaulis. *La question arabe; de l'Arabie du Roi Ibn Sa'oud à l'indépendance syrienne.* Paris, 1930.

Besnard, G. "Damas, son oasis, ses habitants," *L'Asie Française* 31 (1931), no. 292, 239–50.

Betts, Raymond F. *Assimilation and Association in French Colonial Theory, 1890–1914.* New York, 1961.

Bianquis, Anne-Marie. "Damas et la Ghouta," *La Syrie d'aujourd'hui.* Ed. André Raymond. Paris, 1980, 359–84.

Bianquis, P. J. *Eléments d'une bibliographie française de l'après-guerre pour les états sous mandat du Proche-Orient.* Beirut, 1934.

al-Bīṭār, Shaykh ʿAbd al-Razzāq. *Ḥilyat al-bashar fī tārīkh al-qarn al-*

thālith ʿashar (The Decoration of Man in the History of the Thirteenth Century). Ed. Muḥammad Bahjat al-Bīṭār. Damascus, 1961–1963.

Bodman, Herbert L. *Political Factions in Aleppo, 1760–1826.* Chapel Hill, 1963.

Boghossian, Roupen. *La Haute-Djézireh.* Aleppo. 1952.

de Boucheman, A. "Note sur la rivalité de deux tribus moutonnières de Syrie. Les 'Mawali' et les 'Hadidiyin,' " *Revue des Etudes Islamiques* 8 (1934), 9–58.

———. *Une petite cité caravanière: Suhné.* Damascus, 1939.

———. "La sédentarisation des nomades du désert de Syrie," *L'Asie Française* (1934), 140–43.

Le Boulanger, Commandant. "Homs," *L'Asie Française* (Documents économiques, politiques et scientifiques), 6 (November 1922), 135–44.

Bowden, Tom. "The Politics of the Arab Rebellion in Palestine 1936–1939," *Middle Eastern Studies* 11 (1975), 147–74.

Brogan, D. W. *The Development of Modern France (1870–1939).* London, 1940.

Brunschwig, Henri. *French Colonialism, 1871–1914: Myths and Realities.* New York, 1966.

al-Budayrī al-Ḥallāq, Shaykh Aḥmad. *Ḥawādith dimashq al-yawmiyya* 1154–1175/1741–1762 (Daily Events in Damascus 1154–1175/1741–1762), Ed. Aḥmad ʿIzzat ʿAbd al-Karīm. Cairo, 1959.

Buheiry, Marwan R. "Colonial Scholarship and Muslim Revivalism in 1900," *Arab Studies Quarterly* 4 (1982), 1–16.

Burke, III, Edmund. "A Comparative View of French Native Policy in Morocco and Syria, 1912–1925," *Middle Eastern Studies* 9 (May 1973), 175–86.

———. *Prelude to Protectorate in Morocco. Precolonial Protest and Resistance 1860–1912.* Chicago, 1976.

———. "The Sociology of Islam: The French Tradition," *Islamic Studies: A Tradition and Its Problems.* Ed. Malcolm H. Kerr. Malibu, 1980.

Burns, Norman. *The Tariff of Syria, 1919–1932.* Beirut, 1932.

———, and Allen D. Edwards, "Foreign Trade," *Economic Organization of Syria.* Ed. Saʿid B. Himadeh. Beirut, 1936.

Caplan, Neil. *Futile Diplomacy. Early Arab-Zionist Negotiation Attempts 1913–1931,* vol. 1. London, 1983.

Carbillet, [Capitaine]. *Au Djébel Druse, choses vues et vécues.* Paris, 1929.

Catroux, Georges. *Dans la bataille de Méditérranée: Egypte-Levant-Afrique du Nord 1940–44.* Paris, 1949.

Catroux, Général [Georges]. *Deux missions en Moyen-Orient, 1919–1922.* Paris, 1958.

Chatila, K. *Le mariage chez les musulmans en Syrie*. Paris, 1934.

Chevallier, Dominique. "A Damas. Production et société à la fin du 19ᵉ siècle," *Annales* 19 (1964), 966–72.

——. "Un exemple de résistance technique de l'artisinat Syrien aux 19ᵉ et 20ᵉ siècles. Les tissus ikatés d'Alep et de Damas,"*Syria* 39 (1962), 300–24.

——. "Lyon et la Syrie en 1919. Les bases d'une intervention," *Revue Historique* 224 (1960), 275–320.

——. "De la production lente à l'économie dynamique en Syrie," *Annales. Economies, Sociétés, Civilisations* 21 (1966), 59–70.

——. *La société du Mont Liban à l'époque de la révolution industrielle en Europe*. Paris, 1971.

——. "Techniques et Société en Syrie: I. Le filage de la soie et du coton à Alep et à Damas," *Bulletin d'Etudes Orientales* 18 (1963–1964), 85–93.

Churchill, Winston. *The Second World War*, 6 vols. London, 1948–54.

Clément-Grandcourt, Général. *Au Levant. Histoires de brigands, histoires vraies*. Paris, 1936.

Clements, Frank. *The Emergence of Arab Nationalism from the Nineteenth Century to 1921. A Bibliography*. London, 1976.

Cleveland, William L. *Islam against the West: Shakib Arslan and the Campaign for Islamic Nationalism*. Austin, Tex., 1985.

——. *The Making of an Arab Nationalist. Ottomanism and Arabism in the Life and Thought of Sati' al-Husri*. Princeton, 1971.

Cohen, William B. *Rulers of Empire: The French Colonial Service in Africa*. Stanford, 1971.

——. "The Colonial Policy of the Popular Front," *French Historical Studies* 7 (Spring 1972), no. 3, 368–393.

Consul Werry's Report. "Rural Syria in 1845," *Middle East Journal* 16 (1962), 508–14.

Couland, Jacques. *Le mouvement syndical au Liban (1919–1946). Son évolution pendant le mandat français de l'occupation à l'évacuation et au Code du Travail*. Paris, 1970.

Coury, Ralph M. "Who Invented Egyptian Arab Nationalism?," part 2, *International Journal of Middle East Studies* 14 (November 1982), 459–79.

Crolla, G. "La Sirie e la competizione anglo-francese," *Oriente Moderno* 1 (1922), 513–23, 578–91.

Cuinet, Vital. *Syrie, Liban et Palestine. Géographie administrative, Statistique, Descriptive et Raisonnée*. Paris, 1896.

Daghestani, Kazem. *Etude sociologique sur la famille musulmane contemporaine en Syrie*. Paris, 1932.

Dāghir, As'ad. *Mudhakkirātī 'alā hāmish al-qaḍiyya al-'arabiyya* (My Memoirs Concerning the Arab Question). Cairo, 1956.

Dahhān, Sāmī. *Muḥammad Kurd ʿAlī. ḥayāh wa athārahu* (Muhammad Kurd ʿAli, his Life and his Influence). Damascus, 1955.

Danger, René. "L'urbanisme en Syrie: la ville de Damas," *Urbanisme* (revue mensuelle) (1937), 123–64.

Darwaza, Muḥammad ʿIzzat. *Ḥawla al-ḥaraka al-ʿarabiyya al-ḥādītha* (On the Modern Arab Movement), 6 vols. Sidon, 1950.

Dāshwālī, ʿAbd al-Laṭīf. *Marāyā* (Mirrors). Damascus, 1947.

David, Jean-Claude. "Alep," *La Syrie d'aujourd'hui*. Ed. André Raymond. Paris, 1980, 385–406.

———. "Alep, dégradation et tentatives actuelles de réadaptation des structures urbaines traditionelles," *Bulletin d'Etudes Orientales* 28 (1975), 19–50.

——— and Dominique Hubert. "Maisons et immeubles du début du XXᵉ siècle à Alep," *Les cahiers de la recherche architecturale*, 10/11 (April 1982), 102–11.

Davis, Eric. *Challenging Colonialism. Bank Miṣr and Egyptian Industrialization, 1920–1941*. Princeton, 1983.

Dawn, C. Ernest. "The Development of Nationalism in Syria," *The Arab World from Nationalism to Revolution*. Eds. Abdeen Jabara and Janine Terry. Wilmette, Il., 1971, 55–61.

———. *From Ottomanism to Arabism. Essays on the Origins of Arab Nationalism*. Urbana, 1973.

Deeb, Marius. "The 1919 Popular Uprising: A Genesis of Nationalism," *Canadian Review of Studies in Nationalism* 1 (Fall 1973), 105–19.

de Gaulle, Charles. *Mémoires de Guerre*, 3 vols. Paris, 1954–1959.

Depaule, Jean-Charles. "Espaces lieux et mots," *Les cahiers de la recherche architecturale*, 10/11 (April 1982), 94–101.

de Porte, A.W. *De Gaulle's Foreign Policy, 1944–46*. Cambridge, Mass., 1968.

Dettmann, K. *Damaskus. Eine orientalische Stadt zwischen Tradition und Moderne*. Nürnberg, 1967.

Dillemann, L. "Les Français en Haute-Djezireh (1919–1939)," *Revue Française d'Histoire d'Outre-Mer* 66 (1979), 33–58.

Djabry, O. *La Syrie sous le régime du mandat*. Toulouse, 1934.

Ducruet, Jean. *Les capitaux européens au Proche-Orient*. Paris, 1964.

Eickelman, Dale F. "Is there an Islamic City? The Making of a Quarter in a Moroccan Town," *International Journal of Middle East Studies* 5 (1974), 274–94.

Eleftériadès, Eleuthère. *Les chemins de fer en Syrie et au Liban. Etude historique financière et économique*. Beirut, 1944.

Elisséeff, N. "Damas à la lumière des théories de Jean Sauvaget," *The Islamic City: A Colloquium*. Eds. A. H. Hourani and S. M. Stern. Oxford, 1970.

——. "Dimashk," *Encyclopedia of Islam*, new ed., vol. 2.

Entretiens sur l'évolution des pays de civilisation arabe, vols. II, III. Paris, 1938, 1939.

Epstein [Elath], E. "Le Hauran et ses inhabitants," *L'Asie Française* 343 (September–October 1936), 244–51.

——. "Notes from a Paper on the Present Conditions in the Hauran," *Journal of the Royal Central Asian Society* 23 (1936), 594–615.

Essaleh, Salah. *L'état actuel de l'économie syrienne: agriculture, industrie, commerce en comparison avec les pays limitrophes.* Paris, 1944.

al-Farhānī, Muhammad. *Fāris al-Khūrī wa ayyām lil-tunsa* (Faris al-Khuri and the Unforgettable Days). Beirut, 1965.

Fāris, George. *Man hum fī al-ʿālam al-ʿarabī. I* (Who's Who in the Arab World. I). Damascus, 1957.

——. *Man huwa fī sūriyya 1949* (Who's Who in Syria 1949). Damascus, 1950.

Farra, Adnan. *L'industrialisation en Syrie.* Geneva, 1950.

Farzat, Muhammad Harb. *al-Hayāh al-hizbiyya fī sūriyya bayn 1920–1955* (Party Life in Syria, 1920–1955). Damascus, 1955.

Feis, Herbert. *Europe, the World's Banker, 1870–1914.* New Haven, Conn., 1930.

Filastīn fī mudhakkirāt al-Qāwuqjī 1936–1948 (Palestine in the Memoirs of al-Qawuqji). Ed. Khayriyya al-Qāsimiyya. Beirut, 1975.

Firestone, Yaʿakov. "Production and Trade in an Islamic Context: *Sharika* Contracts in the Transitional Economy of Northern Samaria, 1853–1943," *International Journal of Middle East Studies* 6 (1975), part 1, 185–209.

Flapan, Simha. *Zionism and the Palestinians.* London, 1979.

Froidevaux, Henri. "Les élections aux Conseils Représentatifs des états sous Mandat," *L'Asie Française* (January 1924), 9–13.

——. "Quelques causes du malaise syrien," *L'Asie Française* 237 (1929), 6–9.

Gamelin, Général. *Servir.* Paris, 1946.

Gaulmier, J. "Note sur une épisode poétique de la rivalité séculaire entre Homs et Hama," *Bulletin d'Etudes Orientales* 2 (1932), 83–90.

——. "Note sur l'état présent de l'enseignement traditionnel à Alep," *Bulletin d'Etudes Orientales* 9 (1942–1943), 1–33.

——. "Notes sur le mouvement syndicaliste à Hama," *Revue des Etudes Islamiques* 6 (1932), 95–125.

[Gaulmier, J.]. "Note sur la propriété foncière dans la Syrie centrale," *L'Asie Française* 309 (April 1933), 130–37.

Gellner, Ernest and John Waterbury, eds. *Patrons and Clients in Mediterranean Societies.* London, 1977.

Gershoni, Israel. *The Emergence of Pan-Arabism in Egypt.* Tel Aviv, 1981.

Ghazzī, Kāmil. *Nahr al-dhahab fī tārīkh ḥalab* (The River of Gold in the History of Aleppo), 3 vols. Aleppo, 1923–1926.

al-Ghazzī, Najm al-Dīn. *al-Kawākib al-sā'ira bi-a'yān al-mi'a al-'ashira* (Wandering Stars with the Notables of the Tenth Century [A.H.]), 3 vols. Ed. Jibrā'il Jabbūr. Beirut, 1945–1959.

Gibb, Sir Alexander and Partners. *Economic Development of Syria.* London, 1947.

Godard, Charles. *Alep. Essai de géographie urbaine et d'économie politique et sociale.* Aleppo, 1938.

Gomaa, Ahmed M. *The Foundation of the League of Arab States: Wartime Diplomacy and Inter-Arab Politics 1941–1945.* London, 1977.

Gordon, Alec. "The Theory of the 'Progressive' National Bourgeoisie," *Journal of Contemporary Asia* 3 (1973), no. 2, 192–203.

Gouraud, Général H.J.E. *La France en Syrie.* Corbeil, 1922.

Greenshields, T. H. "'Quarters' and Ethnicity," *The Changing Middle Eastern City.* Eds. G. H. Blake and R. I. Lawless. London, 1980.

Grunwald, Dr. Kurt. "The Government Finances of the Mandated Territories in the Near East," *Bulletin of the Palestine Economic Society* 6 (May 1932).

al-Ḥaddād, 'Uthmān, Ḥasan al-Qaṭṭān and 'Abd al-Ḥasīb al-Shaykh Sa'īd. *Thawrat ḥamāt 'alā al-ṭughyān al-faransī* (Hama's Revolt against French Tyranny). Hama, 1945.

al-Ḥaffār, Luṭfī. *Dhikrayāt* (Reminiscenses), 2 vols. Damascus, 1954.

Haim, Sylvia G. *Arab Nationalism: An Anthology.* Los Angeles, 1962.

———. "Islam and the Theory of Arab Nationalism," *The Middle East in Transition.* Ed. W. Z. Laqueur. London, 1958.

Hakim, George. "Fiscal System," *Economic Organization of Syria.* Ed. Sa'id B. Himadeh. Beirut, 1936.

———. "Industry," *Economic Organization of Syria.* Ed. Sa'id B. Himadeh. Beirut, 1936.

al-Ḥakīm, Ḥasan. *Mudhakkirātī. ṣafaḥāt min tārīkh sūriyya al-ḥadītha* (My Memoirs. Pages from Modern Syrian History), 2 vols. Beirut, 1965–1966.

———. *al-Wathā'iq al-tārīkhiyya al-muta'illiqa bi-al-qaḍiyya al-sūriyya fī al-'ahdayn 1915–1946* (Historical Documents Pertaining to the Syrian Question in Two Periods 1915–1946). Beirut, 1974.

al-Ḥakīm, Yūsuf. *Sūriyya wa al-'ahd al-Fayṣalī* (Syria and the Faysal Era). Beirut, 1966.

———. *Sūriyya wa al-'ahd al-'uthmānī* (Syria and the Ottoman Era). Beirut, 1966.

Halstead, John P. *Rebirth of a Nation. The Origins and Rise of Moroccan Nationalism, 1912–1944.* Cambridge, Mass., 1967.

Hamidé, Abdul-Rahman. *La région d'Alep. Etude de géographie rurale.* Paris, 1959.

———. *La ville d'Alep. Etude de géographie urbaine.* Paris, 1959.

Hannā, ʿAbdullāh. *al-Haraka al-ʿummāliyya fī sūriyya wa lubnān 1900–1945* (The Worker's Movement in Syria and Lebanon 1900–1945). Damascus, 1973.

———. *al-Ittijāha al-fikriyya fī sūriyya wa lubnān 1920–1945* (Intellectual Trends in Syria and Lebanon 1920–1945). Damascus, 1973.

———. *al-Qadiyya al-zirāʿiyya wa al-harakāt al-fallāhiyya fī sūriyya wa lubnān (1820–1920)* (The Agrarian Question and the Peasant Movements in Syria and Lebanon [1820–1920]), vol. 1. Beirut, 1975.

———. *al-Qadiyya al-zirāʿiyya wa al-harakāt al-fallāhiyya fī sūriyya wa lubnān (1920–1945)* (The Agrarian Question and the Peasant Movements in Syria and Lebanon [1920–1945]), vol. 2. Beirut, 1978.

Harry, Myriam. *Damas, jardin de l'Islam.* Paris, 1948.

Harvey, John. *With the Foreign Legion in Syria.* London, 1928.

Hassler, Commandant. "Les insurrections druses avant la guerre de 1914–1918," *L'Asie Française*, no. 239 (March 1926), 143–47.

Helbaoui, Y. *La Syrie. Mise en valeur d'un pays sous-développé.* Paris, 1956.

Henry-Haye, J. and Pierre Viénot. *Les relations de la France et de la Syrie.* Paris, 1939.

Hershlag, Z. Y. *Introduction to the Modern Economic History of the Middle East.* Leiden, 1964.

Hilan, Rizkallah. *Culture et développement en Syrie et dans les pays retardés.* Paris, 1969.

Himadeh, Saʿid B. " Monetary and Banking System," *Economic Organization of Syria.* Beirut, 1936.

———. *The Monetary and Banking System in Syria.* Beirut, 1935.

———, (ed.). *Economic Organization of Palestine.* Beirut, 1936.

———, (ed.). *Economic Organization of Syria.* Beirut, 1936.

al-Hindī, Ihsān. *Kifāh al-shaʿb al-ʿarabī al-sūri 1908–1948* (The Struggle of the Syrian Arab People, 1908–1948). Damascus, 1962.

Hirszowicz, Lukasz. *The Third Reich and the Arab East.* London, 1966.

Hobsbawm, E. J. "Peasants and Politics," *Journal of Peasant Studies* 1 (October 1973), 3–22.

———. *Revolutionaries. Contemporary Essays.* London, 1977.

Hodgson, M.G.S. "Duruz," *Encyclopedia of Islam*, new ed., vol. 2, 631–34.

Homet, Marcel. *Syrie, terre irrédente; l'histoire secrète du traité franco-syrien; où va le Proche Orient?* Paris, 1938.

Hourani, Albert. *"The Arab Awakening* Forty Years After," *The Emergence of the Modern Middle East.* London, 1981.

——. *Arabic Thought in the Liberal Age, 1798–1939.* London, 1962.

——. "The Decline of the West in the Middle East," part 1, *International Affairs* 29 (1953), 22–42.

——. *The Emergence of the Modern Middle East.* London, 1981.

——. *Europe and the Middle East.* London, 1980.

——. "The Islamic City in the Light of Recent Research," *The Islamic City.* Eds. A. H. Hourani and S. M. Stern. Oxford, 1970.

——. *Minorities in the Arab World.* London, 1947.

——. "The Ottoman Background of the Modern Middle East," *The Ottoman State and its Place in World History.* Ed. Kemal H. Karpat. Leiden, 1974.

——. "Ottoman Reform and the Politics of Notables," *Beginnings of Modernization in the Middle East: The Nineteenth Century.* Eds. William R. Polk and Richard L. Chambers. Chicago, 1968.

——. "Revolution in the Arab Middle East," *Revolution in the Middle East and Other Case Studies.* Ed. P. J. Vatikiotis. London, 1972.

——. *Syria and Lebanon. A Political Essay.* London, 1946.

——. *A Vision of History.* Beirut, 1961.

——. and S. M. Stern, eds. *The Islamic City.* Oxford, 1970.

Howard, Harry N. *The King–Crane Commission. An American Inquiry in the Middle East.* Beirut, 1963.

Huber, M. *La population de la France pendant la guerre.* Paris, 1931.

al-Ḥukūma al-sūriyya fī thalāth sinīn min 15 shabāṭ 1928 ilā 15 shabāṭ 1931. ʿalā al-ʿahd riʾāsa ṣāhib al-fakhāmat al-sayyīd Muḥammad Tāj al-Dīn al-Ḥasanī (The Syrian Government during three years, from 15 February 1928 until 15 February 1931. In the Period of the Leadership of His Excellency al-Sayyid Muhammad Taj al-Din al-Hasani). Damascus, 1931.

al-Ḥuṣnī, Muḥammad Adīb Taqī al-Dīn. *Kitāb muntakhabāt al-tawārīkh li-dimashq* (Selected Passages from the Histories of Damascus), 3 vols. Damascus, 1927, 1928, 1934.

al-Ḥuṣrī, Saṭiʿ. *Yawm maysalūn* (The Day of Maysalun). Beirut, 1947.

Husry, Khaldun S. "King Faysal I and Arab Unity, 1930–33," *Journal of Contemporary History* 10 (1975), 323–40.

Huvelin, Paul. "Que vaut la Syrie?" *L'Asie Française* (Documents économiques, politiques et scientifiques), No. 1 (December 1921), 1–50.

Ibrāhīm Pāshā, Jamīl. *Niḍāl al-aḥrār fī sabīl al-istiqlāl* (The Freedom Struggle on the Road to Independence). Aleppo, 1959.

"L'importance des intérêts français dans l'empire ottoman," *L'Asie Française* (1920), 179–83.

al-ʿIsh, Anwār. *Fī tārīq al-ḥurriyya min iʿtiqāl al-Bārūdī ilā safar al-*

wafd ilā Pārīs (On the Road to Independence from the Arrest of al-Barudi until the Delegation Travelled to Paris). Damascus, 1936.

Issawi, Charles, ed. *The Economic History of the Middle East, 1800–1914*. Chicago, 1966.

al-Jābirī, Iḥsān. "Masālat ʿummāl al-mudun fī sūriyya." ("The Question of Urban Workers in Syria"), *al-Ṭalīʿa* 5 (June 1939), 280–94.

———. "Min ayn yuʿaysh al-shaʿb al-sūrī?" ("On What do the Syrian People Live?"), *al-Ṭalīʿa* 3 (1937), 846–55.

———. "al-Qaḍiyya al-iqtiṣādiyya al-sūriyya" ("The Syrian Economic Question"), *al-Ṭalīʿa* 4 (January–February 1938), 70–77.

Jacquot, Lieutenant-Colonel Paul. *L'état des Alaouites, Guide*, 2nd ed. Beirut, 1931.

Jāmiʿat Dimashq (University of Damascus). *al-Majmūʿa al-iḥṣāʾiyya* (Statistical Collection), 2 vols. Damascus, 1967.

Jankowski, James P. "The Government of Egypt and the Palestine Question, 1936–1939," *Middle Eastern Studies* 17 (October 1981), 427–53.

al-Jazāʾirī, al-Amīr Muḥammad Saʿīd. *Mudhakkirātī* (My Memoirs), 2nd ed. Algiers, 1968.

Joarder, Safiuddin. "Syria under French Mandate: An Overview," *Journal of the Asiatic Society of Pakistan* 14, no. 1 (1975), 91–104.

———. "The Syrian Nationalist Uprising (1925–1927) and Henri de Jouvenel," *Muslim World* 68 (July 1977), 185–204.

Joffre, A. *Le mandat de la France sur la Syrie et le Grand–Liban*. Lyon, 1924.

Johnson, Michael. "Confessionalism and Individualism in Lebanon: A Critique of Leonard Binder (ed.) *Politics in the Lebanon*" *Review of Middle East Studies* 1 (London 1975), 79–91.

———. "Political Bosses and Their Gangs: Zuʿama and Qabadayat in the Sunni Muslim Quarters of Beirut," *Patrons and Clients in Mediterranean Societies*. Eds. Ernest Gellner and John Waterbury. London, 1977.

Jones, John M. *La fin du Mandat français en Syrie et au Liban*. Paris, 1939.

Jovelet, L. "L'évolution sociale et politique des pays arabes (1930–1933)," *Revue des Etudes Islamiques* (1933), 425–644.

al-Jundī, Adham. *Aʿlām al-adab wa al-fann* (Eminent Personalities in Literature and the Arts), 2 vols. Damascus, 1954, 1958.

———. *Shuhadāʾ al-ḥarb al-ʿālamiyya al-kubrā* (Martyrs of the Great World War). Damascus, 1960.

———. *Tārīkh al-thawrāt al-sūriyya fī ʿahd al-intidāb al-faransī* (The History of the Syrian Revolts in the Era of the French Mandate). Damascus, 1960.

Jung, E. *L'Islam et l'Asie devant l'impérialisme*. Paris, 1927.

Kanafani, Ghassan. *The 1936–39 Rebellion in Palestine*. Committee for a Democratic Palestine, n.d.

Kassimy, Zafer [al-Qasimi, Zafir]. "La participation des classes populaires aux mouvements nationaux d'indépendance aux XIXᵉ et XXᵉ siècles: Syrie," *Mouvements nationaux d'indépendance et classes populaires aux XIXᵉ et XXᵉ siècles en Occident et en Orient*. Ed. Commission Internationale d'Histoire des Mouvements Sociaux et des Structures Sociales. Paris, 1971, 334–56.

al-Kayyālī, ʿAbd al-Raḥmān. *al-Jihād al-siyāsī* (The Political Struggle). Aleppo, 1946.

———. *al-Marāḥil fī al-intidāb al-faransī wa fī niḍālina al-waṭanī* (The Stages of the French Mandate and of our National Struggle), 4 vols. Aleppo, 1958–1960.

———. *Radd al-kutla al-waṭaniyya ʿalā bayānāt al-mufawwad al-sāmī* (The Reply of the National Bloc to the Declarations of the High Commissioner). Aleppo, 1933.

Kayyali, A. W. *Palestine: A Modern History*. London, 1978.

Kedourie, Elie. *In the Anglo-Arab Labyrinth. The McMahon–Husayn Correspondence and its Interpretations, 1914–1939*. Cambridge, 1976.

———. *Arab Political Memoirs and Other Studies*. London, 1974.

———. "The Bludan Congress on Palestine, September 1937," *Middle Eastern Studies* 17 (January 1981), 107–25.

———. *The Chatham House Version and Other Middle-Eastern Studies*. London, 1970.

———. *England and the Middle East*. London, 1956.

———. "Political Parties in the Arab World," *Arabic Political Memoirs and Other Studies*. London, 1974.

Kemp, Tom. *The French Economy 1913–39. The History of a Decline*. London, 1972.

Kersaudy, François. *Churchill and De Gaulle*. New York, 1983.

Khabbāz, Ḥannā and George Ḥaddād. *Fāris al-Khūrī: Ḥayātuhu wa ʿaṣruhu* (Faris al-Khuri: His Life and Times). Beirut, 1952.

Khadduri, Majid. "The Alexandretta Dispute," *American Journal of International Law* 39 (1945), 406–25.

———. "Constitutional Development in Syria with Emphasis on the Constitution of 1950," *Middle East Journal* (1951), 137–60.

Khalidi, Rashid I. *British Policy Towards Syria and Palestine, 1906–1914*. London, 1980.

Khayr, Ṣāfūḥ. *Madīnat dimashq. Dirāsa fi jughrāfiyyā al-mudun* (The City of Damascus. Studies in the Geography of Cities). Damascus, 1969.

Khoury, Philip S. "Divided Loyalties? Syria and the Question of Palestine, 1919–1939," *Middle Eastern Studies* 21 (July 1985), 324–48.

——. "Factionalism among Syrian Nationalists during the French Mandate," *International Journal of Middle East Studies* 13 (November 1981), 441–69.

——. "Islamic Revivalism and the Crisis of the Secular State in the Arab World: an Historical Appraisal," *Arab Resources: The Transformation of a Society.* Ed. I. Ibrahim. Washington, D.C., 1983, 213–36.

——. "Syrian Urban Politics in Transition: The Quarters of Damascus during the French Mandate," *International Journal of Middle East Studies* 16 (November 1984), 507–40.

——. "The Tribal Shaykh, French Tribal Policy, and the Nationalist Movement in Syria between Two World Wars," *Middle Eastern Studies* 18 (April 1982), 180–93.

——. *Urban Notables and Arab Nationalism. The Politics of Damascus 1860–1920.* Cambridge, 1983.

Khoury, Youssef. *Prix et monnaie en Syrie.* Nancy, 1943.

Khuri, Albert. "Agriculture," *Economic Organization of Syria.* Ed. Saʿid B. Himadeh. Beirut, 1936.

Khūrī, Raʾīf. "Naḥnu wa al-fāshistiyya" ("We and Fascism"), *al-Ṭalīʿa* 2 (1936), 838–844.

Klat, Paul J. "Musha Holdings and Land Fragmentation in Syria," *Middle East Economic Papers* (1957), 12–23.

——. "The Origins of Landownership in Syria," *Middle East Economic Papers* (1958), 51–66.

Kurd ʿAlī, Muḥammad. *Khiṭaṭ al-shām* (The Plan of Damascus), 6 vols. Damascus, 1925–1928.

——. *al-Mudhakkirāt* (Memoirs), 4 vols. Damascus, 1948–1951.

Kuzbari, Nadir. *La question de la cessation du mandat français sur la Syrie.* Paris, 1937.

Labeyrie, Irène and Muhammad Roumi. "La grande traversée de Damas," *Les cahiers de la recherche architecturale* 10/11 (April 1982), 44–51.

Laffargue, A., *Général Dentz, Paris–Syrie 1941.* Paris, n.d.

LaMazière, Pierre. *Partant pour la Syrie.* Paris, 1926.

Landes, David S. *The Unbound Prometheus. Technological Change and Industrial Development in Western Europe from 1750 to the Present.* Cambridge, Mass., 1969.

de Lanessan, J. L. *La Tunisie,* 2nd ed. Paris, 1917.

Lapidus, Ira M. *Muslim Cities in the Later Middle Ages.* Cambridge, Mass., 1967.

Lapierre, J. *Le Mandat français en Syrie.* Paris, 1937.

Latron, André. "En Syrie et au Liban: Village communautaire et structure sociale," *Annales d'histoire économique et sociale* 4 (1934), 224–34.

Lecerf, J. and R. Tresse. "Les ʿarada de Damas," *Bulletin d'Etudes Orientales* 7–8 (1937–1938), 237–64.

Lesch, Ann Mosely. *Arab Politics in Palestine, 1917–1939.* Ithaca, 1979.

Lewis, N. M. "The Frontier of Settlement in Syria 1800–1950," *International Affairs* 31 (1955), 48–60.

Lipschits, Issac. *La politique de la France au Levant, 1939–41.* Paris, 1941.

Lloyd, E.M.H. *Food and Inflation in the Middle East 1940–45.* Stanford, 1956.

Longrigg, Stephen H. *Syria and Lebanon under French Mandate.* London, 1958.

Louis, Wm. Roger. *The British Empire in the Middle East 1945–1951. Arab Nationalism, the United States, and Postwar Imperialism.* Oxford, 1984.

Lutskiy, V. B. *Nasional 'no-osvobodityel'naya voyna v Sirii (1925–1927)* (The National Liberation War in Syria, 1925–1927). Moscow, 1964.

MacCallum, Elizabeth P. *The Nationalist Crusade in Syria.* New York, 1928.

Maestracci, Nöel. *La Syrie contemporaine: Tout ce qu'il faut savoir sur les territoires placés sous mandat français.* Paris, 1930.

Maier, Charles S. *Recasting Bourgeois Europe. Stabilization in France, Germany, and Italy in the Decade after World War I.* Princeton, 1975.

Mandel, Neville J. *The Arabs and Zionism before World War I.* Berkeley, 1976.

Mansur, Abed al-Hafiz. "Great Britain and the Birth of Syrian and Lebanese Independence," *International Studies* 16 (1977), 245–73.

Maʾoz, Moshe. "Society and State in Modern Syria," *Society and Political Structure in the Arab World.* Ed. Menahem Milson. New York, 1973.

———. "Syrian Urban Politics in the Tanzimat Period between 1840 and 1861," *Bulletin of the School of Oriental and African Studies* 29 (1966), 277–301.

Mardam-Bek, Khalīl. *Aʿyān al-qarn al-thālith ʿashar fī al-fikr wa al-siyāsa wa al-ijtimāʿ* (Notables of the Thirteenth Century [A.H.] in Ideas, Politics and Society). Beirut, 1971.

Mardin, Şerif. "Power, Civil Society and Culture in the Ottoman Empire," *Comparative Studies in Society and History* 11 (June 1969), 258–81.

Marseille, J. "L'investissement français dans l'Empire colonial: l'enquête du gouvernement de Vichy (1943)," *Revue Historique* 122 (1974), 409–32.

Marston, Ellen. "Fascist Tendencies in Pre-War Arab Politics," *Middle East Forum* 35 (May 1959), 19–22.

Massignon, Louis. "La structure du travail à Damas en 1927," *Cahiers Internationaux de Sociologie* 15 (1953), 34–52.

Mathews, R. D. and Matta Akrawi. *Education in the Arab Countries of the Near East.* Washington, 1949.

Mears, E. G., ed. *Modern Turkey.* New York, 1924.

Mickelsen, Martin L. "Another Fashoda: The Anglo–Free French Conflict over the Levant, May–September, 1941." *Revue Français d'Histoire d'Outre–Mer* 63 (1976), 75–99.

Migdal, Joel S. "Urbanization and Political Change: The Impact of Foreign Rule," *Comparative Studies in Society and History* 19 (July 1977), 328–49.

Miller, Joyce Laverty. "The Syrian Revolt of 1925," *International Journal of Middle East Studies* 8 (1977), 545–63.

Mockler, Anthony. *Our Enemies the French, being an account of the war fought between the French and the British, Syria 1941.* London, 1976.

de Monicault, Jacques. *Le port de Beyrouth et l'économie des pays du Levant sous le mandat français.* Paris, 1936.

Monroe, Elizabeth. *Britain's Moment in the Middle East, 1914–56.* London, 1963.

———. *The Mediterranean in Politics.* London, 1938.

Montagne, R. "French Policy in North Africa and Syria," *International Affairs* 16 (March–April 1937), 263–79.

———. "Réactions arabes contre le Sionisme," *Entretiens sur l'évolution des pays de civilisation arabe, III.* Paris, 1939, 43–55.

———. "Le traité franco-syrien," *Politique Etrangère* 5 (October 1936), 34–54.

Mounayer, Nassib. *Le régime de la terre en Syrie. Etudes historiques, juridiques et économiques.* Paris, 1929.

Mouton, Marie-Renée. "Le congrès syrio-palestinien de Genève," *Relations Internationales* 19 (Autumn 1979), 313–28.

al-Mu'tamar al-dawlī al-thānī li-tārīkh bilād al-shām (The Second International Congress on the History of Greater Syria), 2 vols. Damascus, 1980.

al-Muḥibbī, Muḥammad al-Amīn. *Khulāṣat al-athār fī aʿyān al-qarn al-ḥādī ʿashar* (Excerpt of the Traditions on the Notables of the Eleventh Century [A.H.]), 4 vols. Cairo, 1867.

Müller, Cdt. Victor. *En Syrie avec les bédouins. Les tribus du désert.* Paris, 1931.

al-Murādī, Muḥammad Khalīl. *Silk al-durar fī aʿyān al-qarn al-thānī ʿashar* (The String of Pearls of the Notables of the Twelfth Century [A.H.]), 4 vols. Cairo, 1883.

Musil, Alois. *The Manners and Customs of the Rwala Bedouins.* New York, 1928.

Naaman, A. "Précisions sur la structure agraire dans la région de Homs–Hama (Syrie)," *Bulletin de l'Association de Géographes Français* (March–April 1950), 53–59.

Nevakivi, Jukka. *Britain, France and the Arab Middle East, 1914–1920.* London, 1969.

Niéger, Colonel. "Choix de documents sur le Territoire des Alaouites (Pays des Noseïris)," *Revue du Monde Musulman* 49 (March 1922), 1–69.

"Notizie storiche sulla famiglia el-Atrash," *Oriente Moderno* 5 (September 1925), 465–467.

Owen, Roger. *The Middle East in the World Economy 1800–1914.* London, 1981.

O'Zoux, Raymond. *Les états du Levant sous Mandat français.* Paris, 1931.

——. "Les insignes et saluts de la jeunesse en Syrie et au Liban." *Entretiens sur l'évolution des pays de civilisation arabe*, II. Paris, 1938, 96–104.

Paxton, Robert. *Vichy France.* New York, 1972.

Perry, Elizabeth J. *Rebels and Revolutionaries in North China 1845–1945.* Stanford, 1980.

Picard, Elizabeth. "Retour au Sandjak," *Maghreb-Machrek* (January–February 1983), 47–64.

"La politique du mandat français—Iraq et Syrie," *L'Asie Française*, no. 257 (February 1928), 68–70.

Polk, William R. and Richard L. Chambers, eds. *Beginnings of Modernization in the Middle East. The Nineteenth Century.* Chicago, 1968.

Polleau, Alice. *À Damas sous les bombes. 1924–1926.* Paris, 1926.

Porath, Y. *The Emergence of the Palestinian-Arab National Movement, 1918–1929*, vol. 1. London, 1974.

Porath, Y. *The Palestinian Arab National Movement. From Riots to Rebellion, 1929–1939*, vol. 2. London, 1977.

A Post-War Bibliography of the Near Eastern Mandates. Beirut, 1933.

Priestley, H. I. *France Overseas. A Study of Modern Imperialism.* New York, 1938.

Proust-Tournier, J. M. "La population de Damas," *Hannon. Revue Libanaise de Géographie* 5 (1970), 129–45.

Puaux, Gabriel. *Deux années au Levant. Souvenirs de Syrie et du Liban.* Paris, 1952.

Qarqūṭ, Dhūqān. *Taṭawwur al-ḥaraka al-waṭaniyya fī sūriyya, 1920–1939* (The Development of the Syrian Nationalist Movement, 1920–1939). Beirut, 1975.

al-Qāsimī, Muḥammad Saʿīd. *Qāmūs al-sināʿāt al-shāmiyya* (Dictionary of Damascus Crafts), 2 vols. Ed. Ẓāfir al-Qāsimī. Paris, 1960.

al-Qāsimī, Ẓāfir. *Maktab ʿAnbar* (Anbar School). Beirut, 1967.

——. *Wathāʾiq jadīda min al-thawra al-sūriyya al-kubrā* (New Documents from the Great Syrian Revolt). Damascus, 1965.

al-Qāsimiyya, Khayriyya. *al-Ḥukūmāt al-ʿarabiyya fī dimashq bayn 1918–1920* (The Arab Governments in Damascus, 1918–1920). Cairo, n.d.

al-Qāwuqjī, Fawzī. *Mudhakkirāt Fawzī al-Qāwuqjī 1914–1932* (Memoirs of Fawzi al-Qawuqji 1914–1932). Ed. Khayriyya al-Qāsimiyya. Beirut, 1975.

Qudāma, Aḥmad. *Maʿālim wa aʿlām fī bilād al-ʿarab* (Places and Eminent Personalities in the Arab Countries), vol. 1. Damascus, 1965.

Rabbath, Edmond. "Esquisse sur les populations syriennes," *Revue Internationale de Sociologie* 46 (1938), 443–525.

——. *Les états-unis de Syrie!* Aleppo, 1925.

——. *L'évolution politique de la Syrie sous Mandat.* Paris, 1928.

——. "L'insurrection syrienne de 1925–1927," *Revue Historique* 542 (April–June 1982), 405–47.

——. *Unité syrienne et devenir arabe.* Paris, 1937.

Rabinovich, Itamar. "The Compact Minorities and the Syrian State, 1918–1945," *Journal of Contemporary History* 14 (1979), 693–712.

——. "Germany and the Syrian Political Scene in the late 1930's," *Germany and the Middle East 1835–1939.* Ed. J. L. Wallach. Tel Aviv, 1975.

Rafeq, Abdul-Karim. *The Province of Damascus, 1723–1783.* Beirut, 1966.

Raymond, André. *Artisans et commerçants au Caire au 18ᵉ siècle,* 2 vols. Damascus, 1974 and 1974.

——. *Grandes villes arabes à l'époque ottomane.* Paris, 1985.

——. "Remarques sur la voirie des grandes villes arabes," *Proceedings du 10ᵉᵐᵉ Congrès de l'UEAI.* Ed. R. Hillenbrand. Edinburgh, 1982, 72–85.

——, ed. *La Syrie d'aujourd'hui.* Paris, 1980.

al-Rayyis, Munīr. *al-Kitāb al-dhahabī lil-thawrāt al-waṭaniyya fī al-mashriq al-ʿarabī. al-Thawra al-sūriyya al-kubrā* (The Golden Book on National Revolts in the Arab East. The Great Syrian Revolt). Beirut, 1969.

Reid, Donald M. *Lawyers and Politics in the Arab World, 1880–1960.* Minneapolis, 1981.

Reissner, Johannes. *Ideologie und Politik der Muslimbrüder Syriens.* Freiburg, 1980.

al-Rifāʿī, Shams al-Dīn. *Tārīkh al-siḥāfa al-sūriyya. al-Intidāb al-far-*

ansī ḥattā al-istiqlāl (The History of Syrian Journalism. The French Mandate until Independence), vol. 2. Cairo, 1969.

Rihāwī, ʿAbd al-Qādir. *Madīnat dimashq* (The City of Damascus). Damascus, 1969.

Roberts, S. H. *A History of French Colonial Policy 1870–1925*. London, 1929.

Rondot, Pierre. "L'expérience du Mandat français en Syrie et au Liban (1918–45)," *Revue de Droit International Publique* 3–4 (1948), 387–409.

——. "Les mouvements nationalistes au Levant durant le Deuxième Guerre Mondiale (1939–1945)," in *La Guerre en Méditerranée (1939–1945)*. Paris, 1971.

——. "Tendances particularistes et tendances unitaires en Syrie," *Orient* 5 (1958).

Roumi, Muhammad. "Le hammam domestique: nouvelles pratiques et transformations de l'espace," *Les cahiers de la recherche architecturale* 10/11 (April 1982), 74–79.

Royal Institute of International Affairs. *The French Colonial Empire*. Information Department Papers, no. 25. London, 1940.

Ruppin, Arthur. *Syria: An Economic Survey*. New York, 1918.

Saba, Paul. "The Creation of the Lebanese Economy—Economic Growth in the Nineteenth and Early Twentieth Centuries," *Essays on the Crisis in Lebanon*. Ed. Roger Owen. London, 1976.

Sachar, Howard M. *Europe Leaves the Middle East, 1936–1954*. New York, 1972.

de Sacy, Antoine Issac Silvestre. *Exposé de la religion des Druzes*. Paris, 1838.

al-Safarjalānī, Muhī al-Dīn. *Tārīkh al-thawra al-sūriyya* (History of the Syrian Revolt). Damascus, 1961.

Saʿīd, Amīn. *al-Thawra al-ʿarabiyya al-kubrā* (The Great Arab Revolt), 3 vols. Cairo, 1934.

Salibi, K. S. *The Modern History of Lebanon*. London, 1965.

Salih, Shakeeb. "The British–Druze Connection and the Druze Rising of 1896 in the Hawran," *Middle Eastern Studies* 13 (May 1977), 251–57.

Salzwedel, Klaus. "Typologie des caravansérails dans la vieille ville de Damas," *Les cahiers de la recherche architecturale* 10/11 (April 1982), 52–59.

Samman, Ahmad. *Le régime monetaire de la Syrie*. Paris, 1935.

Samy, E. "I Partiti e le associazioni politiche in Sirie e nel Libano visit da un siriano (1921–1939)," *Oriente Moderno* 21 (1941), 101–23.

Sanjian, Avedis K. "The Sanjak of Alexandretta (Hatay): Its Impact on Turkish-Syrian Relations (1939–1956)," *Middle East Journal* (Autumn 1956), 379–84.

al-Ṣaqqāl, Fatḥallāh. *Dhikrayātī fī al-muhāmā fī miṣr wa sūriyya* (My Reminiscences of Law Practice in Egypt and Syria). Aleppo, 1958.

Sauvaget, Jean. *Alep. Essai sur le développement d'une grande ville syzienne des origines au milieu du XIX siècle*, 2 vols. Paris, 1941.

———. "Esquisse d'une histoire de la ville de Damas," *Revue des Etudes Islamiques* 8 (1934), 421bis–480.

———, and Jacques Weulersse. *Damas et la Syrie sud*. Paris, 1936.

Schatkowski Schilcher, Linda. *Families in Politics. Damascene Factions and Estates of the 18th and 19th Centuries*. Stuttgart, 1985.

Schmidt, H. D. "The Nazi Party in Palestine and the Levant, 1932–9," *International Affairs* 28 (October 1952), 460–69.

Scott, James S. "Patron–Client Politics and Political Change in Southeast Asia," *American Political Science Review* 66 (March 1972), 91–113.

Seale, Patrick. *The Struggle for Syria. A Study of Post-War Arab Politics, 1945–1958*. London, 1965.

Sékaly, A. "Les deux Congrès musulmans de 1926," *Revue du Monde Musulman* 64 (1926), 3–219.

Seurat, Michel. "Le rôle de Lyon dans l'installation du Mandat français en Syrie: intérêts économiques et culturels, luttes d'opinion (1915–1925)," *Bulletin d'Etudes Orientales* 31 (1979), 131–64.

Shahbandar, ʿAbd al-Raḥmān. *Mudhakkirāt ʿAbd al-Raḥmān Shahbandar* (Memoirs of ʿAbd al-Rahman Shahbandar). Beirut, 1967.

———. *al-Qaḍiyya al-ijtimāʿiyya fī al-ʿālam al-ʿarabī* (The Social Question in the Arab World). Cairo, 1937.

———. *al-Thawra al-sūriyya al-waṭaniyya* (The Syrian National Revolt). Damascus, 1933.

al-Sharif, Ihsan. *La condition internationale de la Syrie; analyse juridique du mandat*. Paris, 1922.

al-Shaṭṭī, Shaykh Muḥammad Jamīl. *Aʿyān dimashq fī al-qarn al-thālith ʿashar wa niṣf al-qarn al-rābiʿ ʿashar* (Notables of Damascus in the Thirteenth and the First Half of the Fourteenth Century [A.H.]), 2nd ed. Beirut, 1972.

al-Shihābī, al-Amīr Muṣṭafā. *al-Zirāʿa al-ʿamaliyya al-ḥadītha* (Modern Practical Agriculture). Damascus, 1922.

Shimizu, Hiroshi. "The Mandatory Power and Japan's Trade Expansion into Syria in the Inter-War Period," *Middle Eastern Studies* 21 (April 1985), 152–71.

Shirer, William L. *The Collapse of the Third Republic. An Inquiry into the Fall of France in 1940*. New York, 1971.

Shorrock, W. I. *French Imperialism in the Middle East. The Failure of Policy in Syria and Lebanon 1900–1914*. Madison, 1976.

———. "The Origin of the French Mandate in Syria and Lebanon: The

Railroad Question, 1901–1914," *International Journal of Middle East Studies* 1 (1970), 133–53.

Shoukr, Samir. *The Syrian Cities: Structure and Characteristics Till 1965.* Warsaw, 1974.

al-Sibāʿī, Badr al-Dīn. *Adwāʾ ʿalā al-rasmāl al-ajnabī fī sūriyya 1850–1958* (Spotlights on Foreign Capital in Syria 1850–1958). Damascus, 1968.

Ṣidqī, Nahāl Bahjat. *Fakhrī al-Bārūdī* (Fakhri al-Barudi). Beirut, 1974.

Ṣidqī, Najātī. "al-Ḥaraka al-waṭaniyya al-ʿarabiyya min al-inqilāb al-ittihādī ilā ʿahd al-kutla al-waṭaniyya" ("The Arab Nationalist Movement from the Unionist coup d'état until the Era of the National Bloc"), *al-Ṭalīʿa* 4 (May 1938), part 5, 318–28, part 6, 413–24.

Sluglett, Peter. *Britain in Iraq 1914–1932.* London, 1976.

——, and Marion Farouk-Sluglett, "The Application of the 1858 Land Code in Greater Syria: Some Preliminary Observations," *Land Tenure and Social Transformation in the Middle East.* Ed. Tarif Khalidi. Beirut, 1984.

Smilianskaya, I. M. "The Disintegration of Feudal Relations in Syria and Lebanon in the Middle of the Nineteenth Century," *The Economic History of the Middle East 1800–1914.* Ed. Charles Issawi. Chicago, 1966.

Sourdel, D. "Hamat," *Encyclopedia of Islam,* new ed., vol. 3. 120–121.

Spagnolo, J. P. "French Influence in Syria prior to World War I: The Functional Weakness of Imperialism," *Middle East Journal* 23 (1969), 45–62.

Spears, Major-General Sir Edward. *Assignment to Catastrophe,* 2 vols. London, 1954.

——. *Fulfillment of a Mission.* Hamden, Conn., 1977.

Springett, Bernard H. *Secret Sects of Syria and the Lebanon. A consideration of their origin, creeds and religious ceremonies, and their connection with and influence upon modern freemasonry.* London, 1922.

Stein, Kenneth W. *The Land Question in Palestine, 1917–1939.* Chapel Hill, 1984.

al-Ṭabbākh, Muḥammad Raghīb. *Iʿlām al-nubalāʾ bi-tārīkh ḥalab al-shahbāʾ* (Eminent Personalities in the History of Aleppo), 7 vols. Aleppo, 1923–1926.

Tamari, Salim. "Factionalism and Class Formation in Recent Palestinian History," *Studies in the Economic and Social History of Palestine in the Nineteenth and Twentieth Centuries.* Ed. Roger Owen. Carbondale and Edwardsville, Ill., 1982.

Tannenbaum, Jan Karl. "France and the Arab Middle East, 1914–1920," *Transactions of the American Philosophical Society* 68 (October 1978).

———. *General Maurice Sarrail: The French Army and Left Wing Politics*. Chapel Hill, N.C., 1974.

al-Ṭawīl, Muḥammad Ghālib. *Tārīkh al-ʿalawiyyīn* (History of the Alawites). Beirut, 1966.

Tharaud, Jérôme and Jean. *Alerte en Syrie!* Paris, 1937.

Thobie, Jacques. *Intérêts et impérialisme français dans l'empire ottoman: 1895–1914*. Paris, 1977.

———. "Le nouveau cours des relations franco-turques et l'affaire Sandjak d'Alexandrette, 1929–1939," *Relations Internationales* 19 (Autumn 1979), 355–74.

Thomé, Mohammad. *Le rôle du crédit dans le développement économique de la Syrie. Depuis la Première Guerre Mondiale jusqu' à nos jours*. Madrid, 1953.

Thoumin, R. "Damas. Notes sur la répartition de la population par origine et par religion," *Revue de Géographie Alpine* 25 (1937), 633–97.

———. "Deux quartiers de Damas. Le Quartier Chrétien de Bab Musalla et le Quartier Kurde," *Bulletin d'Etudes Orientales* 1 (1931), 99–135.

———. *Géographie humaine de la Syrie centrale*. Tours, 1936.

———. "Le Ghab," *Revue de Géographie Alpine* 24 (1936), 467–538.

———. *La maison syrienne dans la plaine hauranaise, le bassin du Barada et sur les plateaux du Qalamoun*. Paris, 1932.

———. "Notes sur l'aménagement et la distribution des eaux à Damas et dans sa Ghouta," *Bulletin d'Etudes Orientales* 4 (1934), 1–26.

Thureau, Joseph. "Les chemins de fer en Syrie et en Palestine," *Revue Politique et Parlementaire* 9 (1918).

Tibawi, A.L. *A Modern History of Syria including Lebanon and Palestine*. London, 1969.

Tibi, Bassam. *Arab Nationalism. A Critical Inquiry*. New York, 1981.

Tower, Allen. *The Oasis of Damascus*. Beirut, 1935.

Traboulsi, I. *L'agriculture syrienne entre les deux guerres*. Beirut, 1948.

Tresse, R. "L'évolution du costume syrien depuis un siècle," *Entretiens sur l'évolution des pays de civilisation arabe, II*. Paris, 1938, 87–96.

———. "Irrigation dans la Ghoûta de Damas," *Revue des Etudes Islamiques* 3 (1929), 459–573.

———. "Manifestations féminines à Damas aux XIXᵉ et XXᵉ siècles," *Entretiens sur l'évolution des pays de civilisation arabe, III*. Paris, 1939, 115–25.

ʿUbayd, Salāma. *al-Thawra al-sūriyya al-kubrā 1925–1927* (The Great Syrian Revolt). Beirut, 1971.

Vacca, Virginia. "Notizie biografiche su uomini politici ministri e deputati siriani," *Oriente Moderno* 17 (October 1937), 471–95.

van Dam, Nikolaos. *The Struggle for Power in Syria: Sectarianism, Regionalism and Tribalism in Politics, 1961–1980*, 2nd ed. London, 1981.

Van Dusen, Michael H. "Political Integration and Regionalism in Syria," *Middle East Journal* 26 (Spring 1972), 123–36.

———. "Syria: Downfall of a Traditional Elite," *Political Elites and Political Development in the Middle East*. Ed. Frank Tachau. New York, 1975.

Veccia-Vaglieri, L. "La situazione economica della Siria secondo due recenti pubblicazioni," *Oriente Moderno* 16 (1936), 425–40, 485–96, 541–51.

du Véou, Paul. *Le désastre d'Alexandrette*. Paris, 1938.

Verney, Nöel and Georges Daubmann. *Les puissances étrangères dans le Levant, en Syrie et au Palestine*. Paris, 1900.

Warner, Geoffrey. *Iraq and Syria 1941*. London, 1974.

Warriner, Doreen. *Land and Poverty in the Middle East*. London, 1948.

———. *Land Reform and Development in the Middle East. A Study of Egypt, Syria and Iraq*. London, 1957.

Weakley, E. "Report on the Conditions and Prospects of British Trade in Syria," Great Britain, *Accounts and Papers*, 1911. LXXXVII, in *The Economic History of the Middle East 1800–1914*. Ed. Charles Issawi. Chicago, 1966.

Weingrod, Alex. "Patrons, Patronage, and Political Parties," *Comparative Studies in Society and History* 10 (July 1968), 377–400.

Weisband, Edward. "The Sanjak of Alexandretta, 1920–1939: A Case Study," *Near East Roundtable, 1967–68*. Ed. R. Bayly Winder. New York, 1969.

Wetterlé, Abbé E. *En Syrie avec le Général Gouraud*. Paris, 1924.

Weulersse, Jacques. "Antioch, essai de géographie urbaine," *Bulletin d'Etudes Orientales* 4 (1934), 27–79.

———. "Aspects permanents du problème syrien: La question des minorités," *Politique Etrangère* 1 (February 1936), 29–38.

———. "Damas. Etude de développement urbain," *Bulletin de l'Association de Géographes Français* 93 (January 1936), 5–9.

———. "La nouvelle géographie politique de la Syrie," *Bulletin de l'Association de Géographes Français* 107 (June–October 1937), 102–5.

———. *Le pays des Alaouites*. Tours, 1940.

———. *Paysans de Syrie et du Proche-Orient*. Paris, 1946.

———. "La primauté des cités dans l'économie syrienne. (Etude des relations entre villes et campagnes dans le Nord-Syrie avec exemples choisis à Antioch, Hama et Lattaquié," *Congrès International de Géographie, Amsterdam 1938*. Leiden, 1938, 233–39.

———. "Régime agraire et vie agricole en Syrie," *Bulletin de l'Association de Géographes Français* 113 (April 1938), 58–61.

Weygand, Général. "Le Mandat syrien. Quelques réflections, quelques précisions," *La Revue de France* (May–June 1927), 241–58.

———. *Mémoires: Mirages et réalité*, 3 vols. Paris, 1940–1957.

Widmer, Robert. "Population," *Economic Organization of Syria*. Ed. Saʿid B. Himadeh. Beirut, 1936.

Wilson, Mary Christina. *King Abdullah of Jordan: A Political Biography*. Cambridge, forthcoming.

Winder, R. Bayly. "Syrian Deputies and Cabinet Ministers, 1919–1959," *Middle East Journal*, 2 parts. 16 (Autumn 1962), 407–29. 17 (Winter-Spring 1963), 35–54.

Wirth, Eugen. *Syrien. Eine Geographische Landeskunde*. Darmstadt, 1971.

Wolfers, Arnold. *Britain and France between Two World Wars*. New York, 1940.

Woodward, E.L. *British Foreign Policy in the Second World War*. HMSO, London, 1970.

Woolman, David S. *Rebels in the Rif. Abd el Krim and the Rif Rebellion*. Stanford, 1968.

Wright, Gordon. *France in Modern Times*. London, 1962.

Wright, Quincy, "The Bombardment of Damascus," *American Journal of International Law* 20 (April 1926), 264–79.

———. *Mandates under the League of Nations*. Chicago, 1930.

———. "Syrian Grievances Against French Rule," *Current History* (February 1926), 687–93.

al-Yāfī, Luṭfī. *ʿAwāṭif wa ʿawāṣif al-shabāb* (The Passions and Tempests of Youth), 2 vols. Damascus, 1927–1928.

Yamak, Labib Zuwiyya. *The Syrian Social Nationalist Party: An Ideological Analysis*. Cambridge, Mass., 1966.

Yasīn, ʿAbd al-Qādir. *Kifāḥ al-shaʿb al-filasṭīnī qabl al-ʿamm 1948*. (The Struggle of the Palestinian People before 1948). Beirut, 1975.

Young, George. *Corps de Droit Ottoman*, vol. 6. Oxford, 1906.

al-Yūnis, ʿAbd al-Laṭīf. *Shukrī al-Quwwatlī. tārīkh ʿāmma fī ḥayāt rijāl* (Shukri al-Quwatli. A General History in the Life of Men). Cairo, n.d.

———. *Thawrat al-Shaykh Ṣāliḥ al-ʿAlī* (The Revolt of Shaykh Salih al-ʿAli). Damascus, n.d.

Zakariyyā, Aḥmad Waṣfī. *al-Rīf al-sūrī: muḥāfazat dimashq* (The Syrian Countryside: The Damascus Province), vol. 2. Damascus, 1957.

Zeine, Zeine N. *The Emergence of Arab Nationalism*. Beirut, 1966.

———. *The Struggle for Arab Independence*. Beirut, 1961.

Zeldin, Theodore. *France 1848–1945*. Vol. 1: *Ambition, Love and Politics*. Oxford, 1973.

al-Ziriklī, Khayr al-Dīn. *al-Aʿlām: qāmūs tarājim li-ashhar al-rijāl wa al-nisāʾ min al-ʿarab wa al-mustaʿribīn wa al-mustashriqīn* (Eminent Personalities: A Biographical Dictionary of Noted Men and

Women among the Arabs, the Arabists and the Orientalists), 10 vols. Cairo, 1954–1957.

Zuʿaytir, Akram. "Ittifāq al-ʿarab ʿalā waḍaʿ lubnān al-khāṣṣ" ("Agreements of the Arabs Concerning Lebanon's Special Position"), *al-Ḥawādith* 978 (August 1975), 64–66.

INDEX

'Abbas, Munir, 522–23

'Abdullah ibn al-Husayn, Amir, 130, 227, 230, 380; and Arab revolt in Palestine, 535; endorsement of Peel Commission report, 554; and Hananu revolt, 108; and Shahbandarists, 355, 570, 572, 586; and Syrian nationalism, 115; and Syrian throne question, 220, 586–87, 599

al-'Abid, 'Izzat Pasha, 378

al-'Abid, Muhammad 'Ali, 374; and al-'Azm government, 379–81; background and offices, 258, 377–79; and Btayha Society, 448–49; election as President, 377

al-'Adali, Muhammad Yahya, 389, 470–71

'Aflaq, Michel: and Ba'th Party, 427, 606, 627; and relationship between Arab nationalism and Islam, 605–606

Agha, Hajo: and Jazira autonomy movement, 528; meeting with Puaux, 533; threat of rebellion, 529

agriculture: and Carbillet's policies, 156–57; commercialization of, 61, 216, 398; and economic boom, 625; dependence on urban families, 7–10; harvest failures and droughts, 168–69, 185, 375, 398–99, 446; potential for Alexandretta, 497; and rebel form of taxation, 193. *See also* peasants

Ahali (newspaper), 371

Ahali group, 403–404

al-'Ahd, 195, 353; and Arab Liberation Society, 401; and Istiqlal Party, 220

al-Ahrar (the Liberals), 574

al-'A'idi, 'Abd al-Karim, background, 417

al-'Ajlani, Munir: background and offices, 420, 435–36; and Nationalist Youth, 437; and Shahbandarists, 573, 574; and Steel Shirts, 473–74

Alawites: in Alexandretta, 495, 499, 504; confrontation with Sunnis in Latakia, 385–86, 521; exploitation by Sunnis, 496, 515, 520–23; and the military, 81, 82, 629, 630; political importance of, 59–60; proportion of, in population, 12, 13, 14; refugees after Turkish annexation of Alexandretta, 513; resistance to French, 99–102; similarities to Druzes, 515, 521

Alawite state or territory, 59, 73; and election of 1923, 132, 133; and election of 1926, 188; and Federal Council, 128; insulation from Great Revolt, 205–206; landownership in, 63; and National Bloc, 267; renaming as Latakia, 521; status in Franco-Syrian treaties, 394, 465, 466–67; and Syrian unity, 138, 231, 466. *See also* Latakia (province or state)

Aleppo: and Alexandretta, 17, 111, 134, 505, 512, 569; and Arab nationalism, 102–105, 112; Armenians in, 135, 364; Christians dependent on French patronage, 361–62, 372; call for separation from Damascus, 183, 470; as commercial center, 17, 128; demonstration (1928), 344; economic and political problems in, 123, 185, 381; and election of 1923, 132, 133; and election of 1926, 185–87; and election of 1928, 335; and election of 1931–32, 351, 371–73; and election of 1943, 601; and Federal Council, 128; French establishment of civilian administration in, 112–14; French occupation of, 98, 106; Franco-Syrian relations in, 71, 72; heterogeneous population of, 103; industries in, 282; leadership rivalries, 440–41, 569, 574; and National Bloc, 250, 270–73, 390–91, 428; opposition to French, 135; opposition to League of National Action, 427–28; opposition to Shaykh Taj's government, 443; population of, 10, 11, 12; public works controversy, 90; and Red Hand, 125–26; representation in Mardam's government, 471; Representative Council, 134; resistance to French, 105–110; state of, 58, 59; and Steel Shirts, 468, 474; and Syrian unity, 138; and taxation policies, 569; ties with Qamishli, 527; ties with Turkey, 103–104, 111–12, 185, 601. *See also* Damascus–Aleppo rivalry

Alexandretta (Sanjak of): and Aleppo, 17, 111, 134, 505, 512, 569; Arabic-speaking population, 503–505; arrival of Turkish troops in, 511; ceded by France to Turkey, 21, 59, 512–14; divisions within,

LIBRARY OF CONGRESS CATALOGING-IN-PUBLICATION DATA

Khoury, Philip S. (Philip Shukry), 1949–
Syria and the French mandate.

Bibliography: p.   Includes index.
1. Syria—History—20th century.   2. Nationalism—Syria—
History.   3. Nationalism—Arab countries—History.   I. Title.
DS98.K46   1986   946.08   86–42859
ISBN 0–691–05486–X